The Great Gallivanting

A Journey of Realisation and Discovery Across the World

Jack Rogers

The Great Gallivanting: A Journey of Realisation and Discovery Across the World
Copyright © 2025 Jack Rogers
All rights reserved.

Published by **Jack Rogers**
https://www.jackrogersauthor.com

Library of Congress Control Number: 2025905258
ISBN: 979-8-9929049-0-1 (Paperback)
ISBN: 979-8-9929049-1-8 (eBook)
ISBN: 979-8-9929049-2-5 (Barnes and Noble Press Paperback)

Cover design by **Jack Rogers**

This is a work of nonfiction. The events, locations, and experiences described are based on the author's personal travels and observations. Some names and identifying details may have been changed to respect privacy.

Printed in the United States of America
First Edition

Published by Jack Rogers
Hallsville, Texas, USA

To the women in my life. Be you family or friends, exes or bosses, it was because of you that I took off on this grand adventure.

Table of Contents

Part Two: Reflections

Preface

Some journeys change you forever. This is one of those stories.

On 27 June 2023, I set off on a year-long journey around the world with my friend, Jo Jordan. Over the next twelve months, I saw six of the Seven Wonders of the Modern and Ancient Worlds, followed a matador through Spain, dived three sides of the Mediterranean Sea, spoke with convicted terrorists, and came face-to-face with extreme poverty. It was a journey I would never forget—nor ever fully explain to my friends and family back home. I had quit my six-figure job, left everything behind in my thirties, and embarked on an adventure that would change my life forever.

I never intended to write this book. Jo and I had planned for an adventure of a lifetime before returning to our careers in the United States. This trip was meant to be a temporary sojourn from normal life—not a permanent break from reality. But somewhere along the way, something shifted. The shift wasn't sudden, but it was irreversible. One day, I was planning my return; the next, I was deep in the Cambodian jungle, realising I had no home to return to, only a past life I no longer fit into.

It was my granddaddy who insisted I write this book. A farmer in East Texas, he still rode horses, tended his fields, and split firewood at eighty-four years old. He had no interest in seeing the mountains of New Zealand; he was perfectly content in his East Texas home. Still, he wanted to hear about his grandchild's exploits, crazy as he may have found them. On his eighty-third birthday, when I called him from a jailhouse in New Zealand, he asked me to write a book. And so, The Great Gallivanting was born.

Before this journey, I scoured travel vlogs, adventure books, and online blogs. The experiences were extraordinary, but they were highlight reels, snapshots of the best moments. But what was long-term travel really like? Jo and I boarded our one-way flight with wide eyes and open minds, but we had no idea how much of our trip would be spent on the mundane details. Travel is not just breathtaking sunsets and spontaneous adventures. It's also missed flights, long waits, and unexpected loneliness. I want to show it all—because the magic isn't just in the grand moments, but in the ordinary ones too. Struggling through bus ticket websites in foreign languages, losing entire days to torrential downpours, scheduling laundry days, and figuring out how to stretch every last dollar were daily trials. No one told us how exhausting it was to move constantly, how difficult it was to spend every waking moment with the same person, or how anxious it could feel to walk through a city whose language you didn't speak.

And beyond the logistics, how does travel change you? I had strong opinions on Islamic culture, Spanish bullfighting, and global poverty, but I had never seen them up close, let alone lived in the places where they were a part of daily life. Traveling through five continents challenged my assumptions in ways I never expected. I became more grounded in my faith, critical of some cultural practices and accepting of others, and wrestled with dormant emotions I had been avoiding for almost a decade. I saw beauty in places I never expected and confronted harsh realities that forced me to cowboy up or go home.

I started my journey weary of everyday life and looking for a way out. I was with Jo, my friend, ideological sparring partner in graduate school, and, for five months, constant companion. As we jetted around Europe, seeing Roman ruins in Italy, drinking in Munich during Oktoberfest, and cramming in every possible sight, we each underwent our own personal transformations. Eventually, those personal transformations sent us on separate journeys.

You'll notice that my tone changes as the journey marches on. By the end of my year of travel, I was a fundamentally different person. I had gone from a casual sightseer to a reflective observer. As I steadily made my way East from Europe to Mexico, my thoughts changed from observing the whats and the whens to contemplating the hows and whys. Travel forces you to shift perspectives, and as I ventured deeper into the unknown, my storytelling transformed with me.

This book isn't just a collection of stories; it's my raw, unfiltered account of what it was like to leave everything behind and step into the unknown. It's about the highs and the lows, the awe of discovery and the exhaustion of life in perpetual motion. If you've ever dreamed of taking a journey like this or simply wondered what long-term travel is really like, then I invite you to join me on this adventure. Through these pages, you'll experience the world as I did: one step, one train ride, and one unexpected moment at a time.

— **Jack Rogers**

Part One

Travelogue

Chapter One

Beginning The Great Gallivanting: Plans, Conversations, and Decisions

June 27th, 2023, felt like a typical day. I was visiting home in Texas from Colorado for a couple of weeks, which meant catching up with friends and seeing different parts of my family. I ate breakfast with my dad and stepmom this morning at a local hotspot. We'd eaten breakfast here many times before, with us heading off to our various jobs afterward. I worked in Colorado, so after many of these breakfasts before I had headed off to the airport to fly home. This time, I drove to my mom's house, and we, along with my aunt just for fun, headed off to the airport in Dallas.

But this wasn't just another airport trip to head home. This time was different. In the back seat, I had a backpack packed just like it had been for many trips over the last few years, from Hawaii to Barcelona to Cancun. What made this time different was that I only had a one-way ticket. I wouldn't be coming back any time soon. This wasn't going to be a week-long adventure vacation.

We were on our way to meet my friend Jo. Jo and I had met in grad school a few years before, and in a past life, we were both in the military. We had gone our separate ways after grad school but kept in regular contact, and, through a series of random events and conversations, we were now setting off on a year of travel around the world together.

That's right. At the ages of thirty and thirty-one, she and I were leaving everything behind to go on The Great Gallivanting, our term for our twelve-month jaunt around the globe. We had dedicated the last ten years of our lives to the security of the United States in some form or another, but now we had our eyes set on the horizon, far-off places, and unforeseeable adventures. We didn't have much in the way of a plan. In fact, we didn't have much outside of the packs we carried, one-way tickets to Paris, and a couple of bullfight tickets awaiting us in Spain in a week. The next year of our life was almost wholly unscripted, a blank canvas ready to be filled in with whatever escapades and shenanigans we could get ourselves into.

And what escapades and shenanigans they would be! Over the next year, we would get stranded at 02h00 without a hotel in Spain, take camels across the Sahara, see underwater wonders in Jordan, and even find ourselves readying for a bar fight in Australia! We would fall in love with certain cultures and out of love with others, have our notions of morality and normalcy challenged repeatedly, and learn more about ourselves and the world than we could have imagined.

But let me not get ahead of myself.

The Decision to Go

I had been fascinated with travel for nearly ten years before taking off on The Great Gallivanting. I went through some hard times right after graduating from university and joining the military, and one of the ways I coped with it all was by watching travel vlogs. From the Vagabrothers to Hey, Nadine! to Bryce Conway, I immersed myself in the world of long-term travel. The only trouble was I was in the military, and they didn't exactly just let you go off on a wild, open-ended adventure on a whim. Something about needing to fight and win our nation's wars, and me having signed a contract to that effect.

But that didn't stop me from traveling. While in the military, I became an artisan in the art of short-term travel, enjoying long weekends and periods of paid leave in locations across the United States and Europe. By the time I left the military five and a half years later, my designs on long-term travel had fallen to the background as life got in the way. I started (and left) a new career in law enforcement, graduated with a master's degree in one year, and eventually found myself working in risk analysis for a security company in Colorado.

Of course, in 2020, COVID-19 hit and ended nearly all recreational travel. Luckily, I was in grad school during the bulk of the pandemic, so I didn't miss out much on the travel experiences as I was spending nearly every waking hour during the week studying. At one point, though, as I was about to graduate, my mom asked me, "Do you miss traveling?" My response was an immediate and pointed, "Yes."

Fast-forward to 2022. I had been at my company for over a year, started short-term traveling again, and had a boss who supported my jaunts across the world. I took one or two trips every month, from diving in Mexico to camping in Hawaii to watching hockey in Boston. It was a lot of fun and, unbeknownst to me at the time, propelling me towards a brand-new life.

One night in September of 2022, Jo and I were on the phone talking about our jobs. We had both hit a glass ceiling (in our eyes) and were starting to look for options. We decided that July 2023 was our target to be somewhere else. At some point in the conversation, I joked, "If we don't get any of these jobs we're looking for, we should just quit our jobs and travel the world."

Jumping ahead one month, I had just completed the second of many interviews over lunch for a new company when I called Jo. "What if we just did this anyways?" I wasn't sure what had clicked with me, but something about that interview (which went really well) made me realise that long-term travel was imminently within my grasp. All I had to do was take the leap of faith.

Her exact response was: "I mean, I'm not going to try to talk you out of it." And with that three-minute conversation, the decision was made. Come July, we would be unemployed, long-term travellers. We had no clue what that would entail and no plans at that moment. All we knew was that we would be taking off on a year-long adventure around the world in eight months.

Getting the Plan Together

After that conversation, Jo and I started making preparations in our own way. She got a second job as a bartender to pull in extra money, and I called my financial advisor to recalibrate my financial goals. One of the first planning calls we made about the trip was to decide our budget. We arbitrarily agreed to 2,500 USD per month, about 80 USD per day. No serious math went into that number; we pulled it out of thin air as our best guess. In that conversation, we agreed that we didn't want to adjust the budget for every country we visited. We knew 80 USD per day would be extremely tight in some countries and beyond luxurious in others, so it seemed like a good middle ground. We were only planning for twelve to thirteen months on the road before heading home to return to our old careers, so having a decent but sustainable budget was a no-brainer to us.

We remained committed to the July 2023 timeline for two reasons. First, it gave us time to save money and wrap things up nicely in our careers. Second, it was a trip I had already planned. I was going to go to La Fiesta de San Fermín in Pamplona, Spain, in July anyway, so we decided to make that our target start date. San Fermín was a massive party, making it the perfect way to kick off our year of living dangerously.

In preparation for the journey ahead, I got every ailment and medical issue checked out. My time in the military had wrecked certain parts of my body, and I had some mental health issues that I, thus far, refused to deal with. If I was going to be going around the world for a year, I needed to be medically ready. I didn't want to find myself with a blown knee in a foreign country just because I didn't go to the doctor out of stubbornness. I also started therapy for the mental health issues I had developed during my time in the military. I was more than a little concerned about having night terrors in shared rooms with people who wouldn't understand some of what my past life entailed. Ultimately, I ended up on antidepressants as a result of therapy. From a preparation standpoint, this added some complexity. I had to convince my care team at the Department of Veterans Affairs to give me a year's worth of medication instead of ninety days. Luckily, my provider was terrific, talked through my plans, goals, and treatment plan, and agreed to make the prescription. She assured me that antidepressants weren't considered controlled in any part of the world, but I decided to do some of my own research. It turned out that was not the case, so Jo and I struck a few countries from the list in the Middle East. While I wanted to visit every country in the Middle East, I wanted to get my mental health issues addressed more, so it was an easy sacrifice.

A year around the world sounded like a long time, but Jo and I quickly realised it wasn't much time at all when we started digging into the details. There were 193 countries in the world. To visit them all meant spending less than two days in each one. Clearly, that wasn't attainable, so we would have to prioritise our travels. Out of stubbornness, though, we didn't want to have too much of a plan. We had spent our entire adult lives with a plan and were tired of it. The plan we devised was to spend three months, each, in Europe, the Middle East/North Africa (MENA), Southeast Asia/Oceania, and South America. I only had two requirements for the plan: 1) we go nowhere cold in the winter, and 2) we only cross the Pacific Ocean once. Seemed simple enough.

Conversations

Jo and I were great friends from grad school, but that was all we were. Friends. That said, we were about to spend every waking moment together for the next year. Regardless of how good of friends we were, we had never spent even a whole day together in our everyday lives, and we had lived across the country from each other for the last year. Having both been leaders in the military, we knew we needed to discuss a few things before taking off to ensure this was the experience of a lifetime instead of a trip from Hell. After all, we still wanted to be friends when we returned home.

The first topic up was our friendship. If either of us had feelings for the other, we needed to sort that out before leaving, because that was a recipe for disaster, especially if one of us met someone along the way. We didn't. At the time, we couldn't imagine us being anything more than friends (after our two months on the road together, we definitely couldn't imagine it!). This left us free to meet anyone we wanted without lingering feelings of jealousy. As odd as it sounds to be a primary concern to some, I had friends who had gone on trips with people they had feelings for, and it had not gone well for them a single time.

The second topic was what we would do if we got tired of each other. How many married couples did anyone know that spent every second of every day with their spouse? Zero, but that was about to be us as friends. We agreed that before we got to hating each other, we would split up and go our separate ways. We could always link back up again after we enjoyed some time solo.

The third topic was the budget and experiences. We had already decided on 80 USD per day, but that was just an arbitrary mark on the wall. We learned from travel vlogs that having different budgets on the same trip could make for some serious consternation. We agreed we would stick to the same budget together. We didn't want one of us to be able to afford an experience and the other not, or for one of us to pay for both of us to do something simply because it wasn't in the budget for the other. Being on the same financial page would save a lot of heartache.

These conversations happened over time, not all at once. We had a few calls where we specifically talked about details, which helped to keep the stress levels down as we worked for the next eight months to save money. It also served to get us excited for the trip! With each planning call, more and more fell into place, and by the time came to leave the country, the stress had faded, and we were heading into the wild blue yonder, bright-eyed and bushy-tailed!

Telling People

When people do something exciting, they want to tell anyone and everyone. We were no exception. With one catch: I didn't want to tell anyone on my side of things until Christmas.

I lived in Colorado, and my family and university friends were in Texas. As supportive as they were, I knew questions and concerns would be thrown at me once I made the announcement. The last thing I wanted was to have these conversations over the phone or to say, "We haven't thought that far ahead", when asked perfectly logical questions. Waiting until Christmas gave us time to set wheels in motion and allowed me to sit down and answer questions face to face.

I also didn't want to tell my boss until after the New Year. While my boss had been highly supportive of my travels thus far, I didn't want to find myself pigeon-holed simply because I would be leaving in eight months. He knew that I was look-ing at other opportunities, both inside the company and out, and had kept it between us, but I knew he would have to say something once he knew for sure I was leaving.

Jo, for her part, had no such concerns. When she got hired as a bartender, she told them in the interview that she would be leaving sooner than later. She was ex-tremely close with her family, so they knew almost immediately. It irritated her a little that I wanted to keep things quiet until Christmas, but she respected my desires.

Christmas seemed to take forever to arrive. In the intervening months, I had been to Cancun, Aruba, a friend's wedding in Dallas, and made plans to visit Maui, Washington DC, Los Barriles, Mexico, the Dominican Republic, and Tulum, Mex-ico. I had even told my team at work that I was returning to Pamplona, Spain, to run with the bulls.

When Christmas finally arrived, I was nervous. My parents were divorced, and my dad lived down the road from my mom's family, so timing the announcement to have as little time as possible between them was key. I told my mom's side first. We had a large, joint Christmas gathering with her and my stepdad's sides of the family, so it was an easy, one-shot event. I would see my dad and stepmom for lunch the next day and tell them then.

Once dinner was over and presents opened at my mom's, I stood up to make the announcement. My heart started beating hard, and I couldn't remember the last time I was this nervous. I said, "So, I have some big news." My mom, not one for sur-prises, said, "Are you about to say something I don't know about?!" Yes, yes, I was! I cut to the chase: "You all know I've been working at my company for a year and a half now. I will be leaving my job in July, and my friend Jo and I are going to travel the world for a year." The response, for the most part, was underwhelming. Everyone chalked it up to just another crazy thing I would do (welcome to having a reputation). My mom's response was the best, though. Her first words were, "Does your dad know?!" I immediately said, "No, I'm telling him tomorrow, and no one had better say anything before I get to!"

At my dad's, it was a different story. It was just my dad, my stepmom, and me, and there was no good time to tell them gently. I decided to rip the band-aid off, leaned over the back of a chair, and said, "So I have something to tell you. You know I've been looking at other jobs. Well, I'm leaving my company in July, but I don't have another job. My friend Jo and I are going to travel the world for a year." My dad was stunned, as I knew he would be. He initially started with, "are you sure?" and that quickly gave way to the logical questions dads ask, like money, career im-plications, and safety.

Whereas my mom's side of the family quickly accepted (and moved on) from my decision, I knew my dad would take some time to process it. I figured he would take about six months to be okay with the decision, transitioning from apprehension to acceptance to excitement. To my surprise, he went through all those stages in about thirty minutes! (He said it took him all night, but he put on a good face). And with that, I told my entire family. The only people left to tell back home were my buddies from university and other friends. I sent out a video on Snapchat announcing it to everyone, which was met with everything from excitement to disapproval to jealousy to encouragement.

I told my boss after the new year. He took it well. He started with, "I'm kinda mad, because I wish I could do something like that!" He quickly moved from me telling him to asking about where we would be going and telling me places he had seen that I should visit. He also agreed to keep it quiet. Over the next few months, whenever someone talked about the future or where we would be the next year, he would shoot me a sideways glance and a smirk. He jokingly asked me once, "So where do you see yourself in a year?" and I replied, "This time of year? Somewhere in Asia!"

We eventually came clean to the entire team, and I used an official trip to our company's main office in Washington, DC, to tell our higher-ups. They were equally excited and even told the CEO, who expressed his support publicly in a company meeting. As frustrated as I had been at certain things in my job, I had to say I really did like our senior leaders as people. They wanted the best for us and were incredibly encouraging regarding life and career decisions, which made me feel great about leaving.

Wrapping Up and Heading Off

Eight months came and went rather slowly. A lot of things happened in those eight months, both professionally and personally, and not all of them were good. My therapist would tell me, "You just have to make it to June, then everything will change." While this was true, it seemed like I was postponing dealing with things, hoping that traveling would fix them. Nonetheless, time marched by at an agonisingly slow pace until the day came when Jo and I would board our flight with a one-way ticket to Paris.

I prepared as much as possible for the trip, including practising travelling with my bag. Except for my company trip, I packed my bag for every travel experience like I was leaving for the year. The same clothes, shoes, bags, everything. Even if I would only be gone for four days, I packed like I would be gone for the year. This allowed me to adjust my packing list as I encountered new issues. For example, in Tulum, I realised I needed to have two towels, a thick one for the hostel and a thin one for the beach, and in Maui, I realised I needed proper hiking shoes, not just trainers.

I visited Jo one weekend with just what I would be taking with us to show her my pack job and give her an idea of what she might need. She had never travelled earnestly and was lost on what to/not to pack. On this trip, we searched for and bought her travel pack. She committed to the Osprey Fairview 55, which was a bit bigger than my bag (I was using the Erblestock Halftrack from my military days), but she liked it. It was a fantastic decision and would serve her well in our adventures.

When June 4th rolled around, I started packing up my apartment. Two weeks later, I walked into the office for my last day of work. This was a surreal experience. My last morning meeting, my last set of meeting minutes, my final lunch with the team, and, finally, turning in my company access badges. My boss was on a trip, so we had said goodbye a week before. As I drove away from my work, I got a call from the moving company telling me they were on the way to my apartment. A few hours later, all my worldly possessions were in a storage room, sans the things I needed to leave at my parents' houses. I spent the night in a hotel and, the next day, drove thirteen hours back to Texas.

Life as I knew it was over.

It felt odd to be driving away from the job I'd committed so much to for the last two years. It wasn't just the job, but everything. My medical team, my motorcycle, my therapist, my bed, my PlayStation, my books, everything in my life seemed to be in the rearview while a busy two weeks lay ahead. Over the next two weeks, I would see family, visit friends, celebrate birthdays, play with my parents' dogs, go shooting with my dad, and pack and re-pack my bags. The final nail was when I pulled my car behind my mom's shed and put the cover over it the night before I left. So long, old friend! I got queasy at thinking of the future after that. It got real real, real quick.

The next thing I knew, I was meeting Jo at the airport. She met my mom, we took a few pictures, said "I love yous," and then Jo and I headed inside. A few hours later, we were on an American Airlines flight to Paris.

Reflecting on Beginning The Great Gallivanting

Mitigating risk. Jo and I were both concerned about unforeseen circumstances on this trip around the world. We had discussed traveling to some places with tenuous political situations and minimal Western medical capabilities, which meant we would need travel insurance while abroad. While we couldn't agree on the same one, we both ended up with a company we trusted. In all likelihood, we wouldn't need it, but life is unpredictable, especially in remote parts of the world. Of course, the best way to mitigate risk is with sound finances, and we both had emergency funds, so that was a relief on its own. Some people argued we needed other things, like personal locator beacons and registering with the State Department, but we thought these were overkill. If we encountered a riskier situation than we had planned, we would deal with it in the moment.

We also agreed that, should we go somewhere worrisome or risky, we wouldn't tell our families until afterwards, both for their safety and ours, but we would keep one person up to date just in case. Our original person bailed on us about two months before leaving, but luckily, I was close with a guy I used to work with in the military. He was deployed for most of our travels, but he had good contact with people who could help us in a bind should the need arise.

Setting travel goals. Jo and I didn't discuss our travel goals outside of countries we thought we might want to visit. We hadn't thought about them much, at least not that we disclosed to each other. Predicting how we would react or think about certain things wasn't exactly something we were great at, but I did have a few goals for myself.

First, I wanted to get better acquainted with religion. I was (and am) a proud Southern Baptist (the dancing and drinking kind), but over the years, I had fallen out with the church over doctrine that, to me, wasn't well grounded in the Bible. At the same time, I realised that I knew next to nothing about the Church's early history. I wanted to educate myself and become more intimate with the religion I was so proud of.

I also wanted to get acquainted with other religions. Religion was one of the most powerful forces in society, both for peace and conflict. In the modern world, it played both roles. I once heard it said that a true atheist explored all religions and came to the well-informed conclusion that there was no supreme being, whereas morons do no research whatsoever to make such a declaration. I was no moron, and I thought that such a sentiment should ring true for anyone who professes such an important conclusion. This knowledge was also crucial in shaping my understanding of the world and the role I could play in it.

Second, I wanted to see a bullfight. I regretted not attending one on my trip to Pamplona in 2022, as it was an integral part of the fiesta. Jo agreed. We wanted to be able to have an informed opinion on the performance. We were sure we wouldn't like it, but we didn't know why. The bullfight symbolised a more significant part of our travels: experiencing things we were sure we wouldn't like so we could be informed rather than judgmental.

Third, I wanted to write. Jo wanted to make social media generate income for us, which turned out to be much harder than it sounded, but I wanted to keep a blog to document and communicate our experiences. At my security firm in Colorado, I did a lot of writing to communicate analysis and conclusions to stakeholders so they could make informed risk management decisions. I wanted to do a version of the same for family and friends and maybe even develop a revenue stream as a travel writer. I even had a contract travel writing job lined up, but it fell through just before we left.

The hardest part about leaving. The question I received most often on my travels was, "What do you miss about home?" The answer was always, "Tex-Mex." Some people would expect family, friends, normalcy, hobbies, or something along those lines, which was why this was the hardest part about leaving for The Great Gallivanting: I didn't feel like I was leaving anything behind.

Several very close friends had walked away from me over the year prior, and I had lived away from family for so long between university, the military, grad school, and my job in Colorado, that I was used to not seeing them for months on end or having them involved in my everyday life. I wasn't really leaving anything behind; this was just another adventure without everyone else from my life. That realisation saddened me, especially when I was traveling with someone who was extremely close with her family, had a cat, and was already calculating decisions about when we came home, which only made my feelings more pointed.

The good news was that I had the whole world in front of me. On more than one occasion, my mom told me she hoped I would find somewhere to settle down and be happy, even if that didn't mean a lot of money. While I didn't set out on such a quest, it was something that I would think about anytime I found myself enjoying a country. The bright side of feeling like I wasn't leaving anything behind was that I had everything to look forward to, and life could take me in any direction I wanted to go.

Someday. I have never been a "country collector," one of those people that said, "Thirty countries by thirty!" or "How many countries have you been to?" I chased experiences. I always wanted to travel long-term someday, and all of my short trips in the past were a means of steadily marching towards that goal.

I watched many travel vlogs in the years since graduating from university. I read every book by Levison Wood and had learned about the great explorers of old, like Ernest Shakleton and T.E. Lawrence. I loved Hemingway's books and played the *Uncharted* games over and over again. Adventure, travel, and the horizon constantly called out to me, but I never answered. I promised that I would "someday." For too many people, "someday" was a word they used to postpone their dreams until it was too late to achieve them. The Great Gallivanting provided the opportunity to turn "someday" into "today."

Chapter Two

The First Week: Learning to Travel at a Whirlwind Pace

We were a week early for San Fermín in Pamplona. When booking tickets, Jo and I decided we would either fly into Barcelona a few days early or Paris a week early, depending on which flight was cheaper. The flight to Paris won out, so we spent a week in France and northern Spain's Basque Country before heading off to the rager that would commemorate the start of our adventures.

I had been to France several times before Jo and I set off on The Great Gallivanting, and Paris was one of my favourite cities in the world. Jo had never been, but she didn't care about Paris or France. She didn't know why; it just wasn't a place that appealed to her. But that was where the flights were cheapest to fly to kick off our journey, so that was where we decided to start.

Paris

At about 17h00, Jo and I boarded the American Airlines flight to Paris. In about nine hours, we would begin our year-long, non-stop adventure in one of Europe's most famous capitals. I was in the aisle seat, and she was by the window. We hoped this would dissuade anyone from booking the seat between us. This worked right up until the day we left. At the last second, a man reserved the seat. C'est la vie. When we asked him why he booked at the last second, he told us that he had a relative die suddenly and was flying back for the funeral. Valid reason.

In playing around with the video screen, Jo figured out we could message each other (and anyone else on the plane) using the controller. It was a full keyboard, button controller, just like the first smartphones when we were growing up (it reminded me of using my Blackjack II in high school). Did we turn into high schoolers with this newfound technology? Absolutely. We messaged each other for no reason at all, and all anyone around us could hear was the click-click-click of us dusting off our texting skills. If one didn't know any better, they'd think we were overly excited for this trip.

Once we were wheels down in Paris, we boarded public transport for the nearest train station. We had the paper first-class Eurail passes and had to have them activated so we could buy reservations. This took a long time at the train station, hours, as the queue was long and only a few people were working in the office. Once we got to the counter, we found the attendant didn't speak much English. This wasn't a big deal, as I spoke a decent amount of French, and we had Google Translate, so we got it all sorted without issue.

Because we couldn't check in to the hostel until mid-afternoon, we stashed our bags at the train station and hit the ground running. Well, walking, but it would feel like running by the end of the day. We only had a half day, one full day, and another half a day in Paris. I loved Paris, but I managed to find the one woman to travel with that had no interest in it. She wanted to say she'd seen the Eiffel Tower, had a croissant and baguette, and that was it, so we did all of those in one fell swoop. We put it in two-foot drive, grabbed lunch, then set off to see all the major sites. From the L'École Militaire to the Eiffel Tower to the gardens of the Louvre and everything in between, we saw every major site that day except for Notre Dame, which we would see later. By the time we checked into the hostel, Jo's watch logged us at over seventeen kilometres of walking!

Over the next two days, we would rack up more than forty kilometres of walking. We explored parks, neighbourhoods, and French cuisine. Funnily enough, our two favourite parts of our short time in Paris were two things we had never heard of. The first was a game called Boules, or Balls in English. We had never seen such a game, but the entire community was out to watch old men enjoying the afternoon. They took turns throwing a metal ball as close to a smaller ball (called the Jack) as possible, and whoever was closest won the round. It was a simple concept, but we sat and watched these men play for over an hour. We were mesmerised by the combination of simplicity and strategy involved.

The second thing was the Memorial to the Martyrs of the Deportation. This was a Holocaust memorial located behind Notre Dame. We stumbled upon it just by walking around the cathedral (which was still under renovation from the fire of 2019). It was free, our favourite price, so we decided to go. We were wholly unprepared for the intensity of the relatively simple memorial. Inside were maps of deportation routes, stories of deported individuals, and eerie red writing in serial killer fonts on the walls. We spent a full hour there despite its small size. It was by far the most imposing, moving Holocaust memorial I had ever seen, including Dachau.

Unfortunately, on our last night in Paris, riots broke out over a police shooting. We had planned to see the Eiffel Tower lit up at night, but it didn't get dark until after 23h00, and the Prefecture of Police had ordered all public transport closed after that time, so we'd have no way of getting back to the hostel except for an expensive taxi. When we awoke the following day, we learned the Deportation Memorial had been vandalised in the riots. Dumb kids directing their anger at the wrong target, defiling a memorial to the worst genocide of our time.

Bordeaux

After Paris, we headed to Bordeaux. We had the same itinerary: half day, full day, half day. When we arrived in Bordeaux, I quickly learned that Jo expected me to know much more about public transport options than I did. I was a walker, even with a pack, unless it was an unreasonably far distance. When I couldn't figure out the transport options in less than a few minutes, Jo became noticeably irritated (although, looking back, this was probably more of a function of being tired after walking more than fifty kilometres in Paris than anything else at this point in the trip), so I decided to say screw it and walk. It was about a thirty-minute walk with our packs on to get to the Airbnb, which was, admittedly, a bit brutal.

Our Airbnb was in a good location, just off the beaten path to avoid late-night partiers wandering the streets but close enough to easily walk into the city centre. We thought we had it to ourselves, but it was a shared one where the host may or may not be there. The hosts would show up from time to time, specifically at night when they got off work, which I discovered when I woke up to someone walking through the living room while I was asleep on the couch (Jo was in the bedroom). Outside of that, it was a cool Airbnb with a terrace room, incredible views of French town homes, and, much to Jo's happiness, a cat that would hang out with us in the evenings.

It rained most of the first day in Bordeaux. This was not a surprise for anyone that has been to Bordeaux, including me. Bordeaux was near the west coast of France, so it frequently received ocean rains. We spent most of the morning in a café reading and drinking coffee. When the rain finally turned into a drizzle, we set off to see the town.

We started at the Bordeaux Cathedral. I had seen it a few years before, but this was Jo's first time in France. The cathedral was massive and clearly the central focus of the town. Jo's first reaction when she walked in was: "Woah." That was mine, too, a few years before. We didn't spend too much time there, just enough to take pictures and take in the scenes in the paintings and stained glass, before walking aimlessly around town. I loved Cathedrals, and one of my travel goals was to get more acquainted with religion, but Jo was not as enthralled with them as me. It was one of those compromises we would have to make in our time as a travelling duo.

The afternoon was much more exciting, especially for Jo. She was a wine aficionado, and Bordeaux was home to some of the best wines in the world. Jo managed to find a wine museum called Cite du Vin, which we bought tickets to in the afternoon. I have never liked wine, but even I had to admit that this museum was cool. It had exhibits covering every aspect of wine, from ancient history to religion, technology to television, my favourite of which was the panoramic videos showcasing the terroirs and vineyards. I could have sat there for hours watching those beautiful scenes.

We spent hours and hours there. I told Jo I should have dropped her off when it opened at 09h00 that morning and picked her up when it closed at 17h00 that evening, because she would have easily spent all day there enjoying the exhibits and drinking wine at the upstairs bar. Our tickets came with a complimentary glass of wine, so she got two different ones out of this visit (I didn't want mine). Consequently, we may have had to stop for a bottle or two of wine on the way back to the Airbnb that night. Sipping wine and petting cats in France was a bucket list item for Jo.

On our last morning, we toured the National Customs Museum. This small museum was nestled in the corner of the old trading outpost where imports and exports were once processed. We discovered it entirely by accident on Google, but it was a happy accident. This museum commemorated the French customs service, which, like most Western customs services, started as a paramilitary organisation dedicated to protecting the frontier. Over time, and especially with the introduction of the European Economic Community and European Union, it transitioned to more of a law enforcement and revenue role, similar to U.S. Customs and Border Protection's role in the United States.

The museum was the highlight of Bordeaux for me. It covered the custom service from its inception to modern times, depicting the hard life of patrolling the frontier with just what they could carry on their backs. When I was in the military, I was really enthralled with expeditionary nature of operations, so seeing that depicted as a law enforcement function fascinated me. I daydreamed about what it must have been like to patrol the border with Spain with my partner, sleep under the stars with my horse, and survey the ocean while watching for smugglers and spies. As a former cavalryman, it was undoubtedly a good dream.

San Sebastian

Fortunately, we figured out the public transport situation in Bordeaux when we went to Cite du Vin, so getting to the bus exchange was easy. We only had to walk a few minutes to get there. The rest of the trip was on the tram.

Our next stop was San Sebastian. We couldn't take the train, because domestic train tickets in Spain had to be booked in person at a Eurail office located in Spain. We technically could have taken a train to the border, gotten off, booked a train, and then continued, but, in the words of the grandfather whose first name was my own, that was just too much trouble. Instead, we took a long bus ride through the French and Basque countryside.

We had an extra day in San Sebastian, which meant two full days to enjoy the seaside city. That was an eternity for us, given the breakneck pace we'd been traveling at so far. We had an Airbnb just outside of town that, luckily for us, was directly on the bus line that led straight into the city centre. Not so lucky for us was that the San Sebastian bus and rail stations were under serious renovation, so we had to walk quite a ways up and down stairs to get to the local train that would take us to the bus that would take us to the Airbnb. As in Bordeaux, which would become a norm over the next many months, irritations ran high on this travel day. I inevitably wouldn't know enough about public transport and we'd walk too far with our bags for Jo's liking which would translate into her being frustrated at me for it all and me be frustrated at her for being frustrated at me over something she knew no more about than I and I no more than her. Travel days were never our friend

Nevertheless, we made it to the Airbnb. We noted on the local train that many people were decked out in the same hats and sports jerseys. Jo did some research and learned the Tour de France had come through San Sebastian that very day. We just missed it! If we could see the Tour de France, that would be a major highlight, so we agreed that if the starting point for the next day was an hour or less away by public transport, we would go watch. Alas, it wasn't. It was two hours away, which wasn't worth it for us. It would have been cool to see, but, again, c'est la vie.

San Sebastian was a beach town, and the bus near the Airbnb could take us straight to the shore. Unbeknownst to us, however, the bus route to the beach had changed. We were supposed to be dropped off right on the beach. Instead, the bus cut out the entire beachfront segment of its trip, and we got off about a thirty-minute walk away. We were both confused, and Jo was convinced I had misread the bus schedule. Fortunately for both of us, that was not the case. The bus had been diverted because the road was blocked so the Tour de France could come through the middle of town! Talk about a fantastic surprise. I even confirmed with a local worker that the race would come through town at around 13h00 that afternoon.

Excited about this new opportunity, we decided to hang out on or near the beach all day so we wouldn't miss the cyclists coming by. Now, I had been to Spain before, but I had forgotten something about beaches in Spain: They were topless beaches. Not only that, but young toddlers ran naked everywhere. This was a moderate culture shock for us, but it quickly became normal because it was normal there. There was no ogling, no half-hearted attempts at modesty, and no one was excluded. It was just normal. What Jo and I found more interesting were the surfers in the water. The water was much too cold for us to swim, but the surfers looked like they were living it up with their wetsuits at a beach that seemed especially made for them with the waves and tide. Talk about living the life!

Well, 13h00 came and went, and nothing. About thirty minutes to an hour later, all of the support vehicles for the different teams came through like a giant parade, playing music and tossing goodies out to the crowd. I might have gotten Jo on video taking a bag of jelly beans to the face (and I might have put it in slow motion on social media). We thought, surely, that the riders would be next, but no. They didn't come by for two hours, which we spent roasting in the sun in anticipation. Apparently, I should have been more straightforward with the race worker in what I was asking.

Finally, two hours later, they came. The first-place cyclist flew by us, followed by a support car and television crew. Then came the second-place racer. Then came everyone else, all at once. They flew by us in a vast, long pack. It took twenty-seven seconds for them to pass us (we know because we got it on video), and the last guy waved to the crowd while cycling one-handed. We were right on the fence, up close with the action, and it felt like watching NASCAR cars go by.

Just as suddenly as they appeared, they were gone on the next leg of the race. To celebrate our excitement at seeing the Tour de France, we went to the Whiskey Museum, a bar Jo found on Goggle Maps. Unfortunately, it was closed. The sign specifically said it was closed for that day, but it didn't open the next day either, much to our annoyance. So, instead, we wandered about the historic city centre. We visited shops and cathedrals and even wandered towards the other beach (where the swimmers were). I decided to buy a local SIM card with more data allowance than I could possibly use for 20 Euros (EUR), which proved to be a lifesaver on more than one occasion during our ninety days travelling the Schengen Area.

Our second day in San Sebastian, we decided to go for a hike up Motako Gaztelua, a Medieval castle which once served as both a prison and coastal defence for the bays on either side. But, first, we had some administrative tasks to address. Fortunately, it was raining, so we wouldn't be missing much by not doing the hike in the morning. The first thing we had to do was book accommodations for Barcelona and Madrid. That was simple enough. The second thing we had to do was book our tickets to and from Pamplona. Like I said before, we had to be physically in Spain to book our Eurail reservations, so we couldn't buy them before getting to San Sebastian. Unfortunately, this was more problematic than we anticipated.

La Fiesta de San Fermín was one of the biggest tourism draws in Spain. For eight days every year, millions of people flooded Pamplona, Spain, to enjoy the festivities, which meant that for the days prior and after, millions of people saturated public transport getting to and from the festival, especially on the days we were traveling on for the opening ceremonies. For us, that meant there were no trains available for Eurail pass holders going to Pamplona on July 5th, and there were no trains available for Eurail pass holders leaving Pamplona on July 9th. The Renfe agent (the official rail company of Spain) was polite but direct and spoke little English. All he would say was "No hay" when there wasn't a train, meaning "not possible." We got the other trains we needed sorted (from Barcelona to Madrid to Porto, Portugal), but Pamplona was a problem. We had already paid for our hostel and bullfight tickets, so we had to figure out how to get there.

We sat at a nearby café and found a bus to Pamplona with seats available. Crisis number one averted. Unfortunately, there was nothing going from Pamplona to Barcelona. We even headed to the bus company offices to talk to them in person, but all we heard was "Se completo" ("They're full"). We put our hike on hold and returned to the Airbnb to figure out how to avert the nearing transportation crisis. We somehow discovered an app called BlaBlaCar, which was like Uber, except that it was just to fill up space in a car already making a trip. After several attempts at registering for it (because they flagged us as fraudulent accounts), we finally managed to book two seats in a small car with a guy and his friend who were traveling from Pamplona to the outskirts of Barcelona. Thoroughly frustrated, annoyed, and mentally exhausted, we finally set off to hike up Motako Gaztelua.

And what a great rest of the day we had! The hike wasn't challenging, but it gave us some beautiful views of the surrounding countryside. We had a lot of laughs and fun taking photos and shooting videos, and the frustrations of that morning seemed to have never happened. The castle itself wasn't even that impressive, but it felt good to be outside and free from the administrative nightmare that was the morning. The only downer was that it was overcast, but neither of us was going to complain.

After lunch at a tapas bar, we visited the San Telmo Museum, a museum dedicated to Basque culture, history, and lifestyle. The Basque people were an ethnic group which had inhabited the northeast of Spain and southwest of France since before Spain was kingdom. Their culture and history were on full display in what were now the autonomous communities of Basque Country and Navarre.

We spent the entire afternoon at this museum learning about Basque culture and life. Between San Sebastian and, later, Pamplona, we fell in love with the Basque country (the region, not the autonomous community) during our time in San Sebastian. We felt the national pride everywhere we went, from the Basque flags to the food to the architecture. We saw a solid, unified Basque identity, which was refreshing for us two Americans. Our country was as disunified as it has been in a long time (if ever, including the Civil War), and every discussion about American history seemed to turn into an argument back home, especially in grad school. Seeing the opposite in San Sebastian made us smile as we were reminded that domestic American politics stopped at the water's edge.

After the museum, we had dinner and drinks in Constitution Plaza, just a few blocks away. We talked about our time in San Sebastian and agreed that having two full days here was a fantastic decision. Neither of us really wanted to leave, but San Fermín lay ahead, and we were both excited (and nervous) to run with the bulls not once but three times. So were the Australians sitting behind us. They were, as Aussies are when they drink, loud and obnoxious, but they were fun to listen to. They were all in their early twenties, talking about how cool and brave they were for running with the bulls in Pamplona. Jo had never been to San Fermín, but I had, and I had to say that running with the bulls was not what I expected. It was impossible to explain, except that there was no way to know how one would react until they were in the moment and saw the bulls running at them. Jo laughed at them and joked that they would opt out at the last second. She also said, "Watch them be in our hostel when we get there."

After getting me more than a little tipsy on 18/70 beer (I was a lightweight), we headed back to the Airbnb. The next morning, we packed up, ate breakfast and lunch, and boarded the bus for Pamplona.

Reflecting on the First Week

We went way too hard. Long-term travel was a sprint, not a marathon. Well, Jo and I sprinted the marathon our first week. We wore ourselves out by walking over seventy kilometres in one week's time. We certainly acted like we were only in Europe for a week rather than gallivanting around the world for a year. I had a bad knee from the military, and it was throbbing by the time we left San Sebastian. During our dinner at Constitution Plaza, we acknowledged we needed to slow down after San Fermín. Generally speaking, we would have a travel day, spend three full days in a city, and then have another travel day. That seemed like a good schedule that wouldn't wear us out for us to try in Barcelona and Madrid.

Aisles, windows, and bunk beds. When you travelled as a group, it wasn't the big things that caused fights; it was the little ones. Fortunately, Jo and I learned early on that there were two areas we would never fight over: bus seats and bunk beds. Jo was a window person, and I liked the aisle. Whenever we got on public transport, we instinctively sat in our "assigned" seats. The same was true of bunk beds in hostels. She liked bottom, and I didn't mind the top. Any time we were given a bunk, we traded keys to make sure that was how we were situated. In a world where anything and everything could become a massive argument, being in sync about these two things most definitely kept us from getting into too many fights.

Two-foot drive. As Americans, we were used to driving everywhere. In Europe, where cities were highly accessible, we learned to put it in two-foot drive to save money and see the cities. What did that mean? Walk! We went a little too hard in our first week, but walking short to moderate distances saved a lot of money, and we got plenty of exercise. We also encountered some of our most memorable

17

experiences in Paris, like the game of Boules and the Deportation Memorial, simply because we were walking around.

Antifa, ACAB, and Communists. Starting in Paris, but continuing in every city except Prague and Budapest, Jo and I saw the hammer and sickle, anarchist "A," and/or "ACAB" spray-painted all over (ACAB stood for "All Cops are Bastards"). In only two cities (Bordeaux and Rome) did we see swastikas, and, even then, they had been rubbed away. This annoyed us both, mainly because the youth participating in this graffiti probably had no idea what true anarchy or communism was (or how incompatible they were). I had family in law enforcement, so I knew for sure that not all cops were bastards. This would be an eternal frustration for me, especially in Western countries which had defeated both anarchism in the early 1900s and Communism in the 1990s. Despite the graffiti, I never saw a pro-communism, pro-anarchy rally or protest. I did, however, see anti-communist rallies. I also found the notion that someone would label themselves as "antifascist" amusing. I figured that was the default setting.

Chapter Three

Spain: La Fiesta de San Fermín

La Fiesta de San Fermín was my favourite celebration in the entire world. It was an eight-day party that celebrated the Catholic Saint Fermín, one of the patron saints of Navarre. I attended the year before to run with the bulls for my thirtieth birthday, but the fiesta was so much more than that. I made great friends and developed a new hobby of running with the 600-kilogram Spanish fighting bulls every year. Before Jo and I decided to take off on our year of travel, I had already planned to attend San Fermín again, and I was adamant that we incorporate it into our travels. Like Hemingway's Jake Barnes, this was a fiesta I wanted to attend every year.

The Night Before

The bus from San Sebastian passed through the northern stretch of the Pyrenees Mountains, some of the most beautiful scenery I had ever seen. I took a different route from Pamplona to Bilbao the year before, and it was equally stunning. I leaned over Jo several times to snap photos. She had taken some Dramamine before we took off, so she was dead to the world.

The bus stop was close to the hostel, much closer than the train station, so we could walk our way in. I told Jo back in San Sebastian that we'd have to walk once we got to the city centre because it was compact and buses and taxis couldn't get through. Luckily, it wasn't too much of a walk with our bags on our backs. It was hot, but that was about it.

We had booked our hostel in November, a full eight months before leaving the United States, which was fortunate, because it filled up quick. We were in the same room I was in the year before. I loved this hostel; it was close to the fiesta, had a fairly large common area to hang out in, and had amazing owners. It also prohibited outside alcohol. The way they put it, "The party is outside. The inside is for rest." This was somewhat annoying, because we couldn't buy sangria, wine, and beer from the supermarket and stow it, but it was nice not to have drunken parties going all night long.

Our first order of business was to buy the right clothes. The traditional garb for San Fermín was a white shirt, white pants, a red sash around the waist, and a red pañuelo around the neck. I brought a few white t-shirts, my pañuelo, and a sash from last year, but I needed white pants, and Jo needed everything except the shirts. I went ahead and bought an extra pañuelo and sash, too; I knew the ones I had brought were going to be covered in alcohol before noon the next day, and I didn't want to go the entire time smelling stale alcohol around my neck. I had plenty of that my first time around.

After getting our clothes situated, we hit the Estafeta, the main road that would be the central drinking point of the fiesta. After last year, I was hyped for the craziness that would ensue. Unfortunately, such craziness didn't materialise. It was a calm night, a stark contrast from the same night the year before. The 2022 fiesta was the first one in three years because of the COVID-19 pandemic, so it was more than a little overboard compared to other years. This year, it was much calmer. Well, at least as far as the night before was concerned.

La Fiesta Comienza

The fiesta itself dated to at least the 1500s, although bull runs had occurred for a few hundred years before. The fiesta was originally two different festivals: a local Basque festival centred around the cattle trade and a religious festival celebrating Saint Fermín, one of Navarre's patron saints. They were eventually combined into one festival but remained relatively local until Ernest Hemmingway published his book *The Sun Also Rises* in the 1920s. Ever since, it has exploded in international popularity with millions of foreign tourists flooding the provincial city every year to prove themselves in the true test of masculine bravery by running with the bulls.

The running of the bulls, called the *encierro*, was rooted in both the Basque festival and the religious one. To get their bulls to sale, farmers would guide them through town, and local men would run alongside them. This was the way of the business in towns all over Spain, which was why many outside of Navarre included encierros in their patron saint festivities. Specific to Saint Fermín, he was killed in the 300s, and it was a local legend that he was executed by being dragged through town with bulls running after him. Thus, when the two festivals combined, the bull herding merged with the religious legend, and the encierro dedicated to San Fermín was born.

But before the official first encierro, on July 7th, came the Chupinazo, the opening ceremonies, on July 6th. The opening ceremony was the polar opposite of the night before, full of people, flying sangria, and inflated beach balls sailing through the air. We would have to get there early if we wanted to see the opening ceremonies. Real early. Earlier than 10h00 in the morning. We showed up around 09h30 to have a good spot. That was a mistake, because at 10h00 sharp, the police cleared out the entire plaza in front of the town hall. We had seen lots of Basque separatist posters, flags, and slogans around town, and we were initially concerned that some security risk or threat was causing them to clear the area. There wasn't. This was just a part of the standard security sweep before the Chupinazo. Before too long, we were back in the town square, sangria in hand, ready for whatever might happen.

We ended up around a group of locals who loved the party more than life itself. They were singing songs, flinging sangria everywhere, lighting off smoke bombs, and generally having a grand ol' time. If they saw that you had a fresh bottle of sangria, they splashed it all over you. No white allowed! Everyone was pink, purple, and red, soaked in alcohol, laughing, cheering, and celebrating the annual festival. The people in the balconies above showered us with wine and champagne, and other balconies tossed inflated beach balls into the crowd to bat them around.

All of a sudden, the craziness died down, and it felt like the crowd multiplied by ten. Everyone turned to face the town hall, held up their pañuelos, and awaited the first rocket to be fired into the air and commence the week-long party. When the first rocket exploded overhead, the crowd exploded in our ears. In his book *The Sun Also Rises*, Hemingway described the town as exploding during the opening ceremonies. I had never heard a more apt description. Pañuelos, sangria, beach balls, and even shoes flew into the air. The crowd surged back and forth, to the great annoyance of everyone. It soon became wholly uncomfortable and even a bit scary that someone should fall and end up trampled. Jo lost her shoe in the sway, which was terrible given that we were running with the bulls the next day. Miraculously, she somehow found it as we swayed around and managed to get it back on her foot without looking or trying.

As the rockets continued to explode overhead, we decided to go out and explore the rest of the festivities. We found cookouts, drinking contests, street game scams, and a jump roping competition. This was the fiesta I loved so much. Over the next few days, we would follow street bands around the city, watch rural sports (the women's wood chopping competition was intense!), and march along with parades of giant heads of kingdoms passed. Of course, we also had plenty of drinks, tapas, and fun with new friends!

Running with the Bulls

The main reason we were there, though, was to run with the bulls, to display what Hemingway called "grace under pressure," and experience one of the most famous and dangerous traditions in the Western world. We were up early on July 7th, the first day of the bull runs, to get into the main plaza. This was the only authorised starting point, and we wanted to ensure we wouldn't be pushed off the route. We got there around 07h00, and the plaza was already packed. We managed to squeeze ourselves in before the police established their cordon to clear everyone off the rest of the route. At about 07h45, we moved to our starting point. This was Jo's first time, so we started about 100 metres from La Curva de Estafeta, colloquial called Dead Man's Curve (even though no one has ever died there). Starting here would give us a decent chance of running side-by-side with the bulls and plenty of outs should one of us decide to bail. I figured I wouldn't, but I had done this before. Jo was unsure of how she would react, which was entirely fair. With six bulls and six steers running at you for the first time, it was impossible to predict how you would respond.

At 08h00, we heard the first rocket. The gates were open. Seconds later, we heard the second rocket. The bulls were out of the pen. Not too long after, we saw people running towards us. I yelled to Jo to wait. These people were running far out in front of the bulls. More people passed, and we waited. Then we heard the "boom." A bull had slammed into the wooden barrier at La Curva, tripping on the cobblestone streets as it tried and failed to make the ninety-degree turn. I looked at Jo and yelled, "Now!" And off we went. We got separated immediately. There was no time to look back. Either I'd see her in the bullring, or I'd see her on the news at the Café Iruña, our designated meeting place. As the bulls got close, I jumped to the side to let them pass, my heart pounding.

Once they passed, I ran to the bullring. The stands were full of spectators cheering on the runners who braved the bulls. I stopped near the entrance to wait for Jo. Hopefully she would come here instead of the café. After a few minutes, she showed up, excited almost as much as I was. We had just done something none of our friends would ever do (me, for the second time!). After all of the festivities in the bullring, we headed for celebratory churros y chocolate at the Café Iruña. Jo wasn't a fan of the churros, but it was a tradition I wanted to continue after last year. Plus, we got to have our morning espresso.

I asked Jo if she wanted to do the next two bull runs with me. She, quite wisely, said she wanted to wait until she had calmed down from the adrenaline rush before saying 'yes.' After dinner that night, she said she definitely wanted to do it. She was hooked! She wanted to start a little farther forward next time, closer to the front, which sounded great to me.

After another day of drinking, parades, tapas, bands, and a rained-out fireworks show, we again found ourselves in front of City Hall at 07h00. Jo and I figured we were the only two tourists there that had run the day before. We made friends with several people: Jeff "The Best" from Texas, and Summer, Caitlin, and Rick from New Zealand. We met because we saw Jeff wearing his sash through his belt loops, a recipe for disaster should a bull's horns get hooked in there. Being true professionals by this point, we knew the slip knot was the only way to go. That's when we talked to the Kiwis, because they saw that we had done it before. We gave them our best tips before parting ways around 07h45. They were headed to the Estafeta, and we were headed to the Calle de Santo Domingo, the opening sprint of the run.

Along the Calle de Santo Domingo, adjacent to the miniature statue of San Fermín set into the wall, the crowd chanted three times in Spanish and Basque, imploring San Fermín to protect them during the run. The first time was at 07h55. Then, several people ran to their spots on the route. The second was at 07h57, and several more people ran off. The last was at 07h59. A few people ran off, but with only a few seconds until the 08h00 rocket, those who remained were committed.

The first rocket went off, and we immediately heard the hooves pounding the cobblestone streets, the echoes reverberating off the high stone walls. The second rocket went off, and seconds later, we saw the bulls and steers headed our way. Jo and I wanted to get closer to the bulls this time, so we waited it out and let people run past. We finally started running right as they were upon us. Jo ran right in front of the news camera, and she was broadcast live on Spanish TV! Fortunately, the camera didn't capture the three guys just stopping in front of her and preventing her from completing the run. I didn't fare much better. I was directly in front of the bulls, but just as they were getting close, a guy tripped, fell, and grabbed my shirt on the way down. Right in front of the bulls! To put it extremely mildly, I was miffed as he held on and laid there as the bulls ran by. I said some choice words before ripping myself from him.

Jo and I were both irritated as we headed to the Café Iruña. We had already resolved to try the same place again the next day. We watched the run over and over on YouTube, and every time it showed us, we swore at the mozos that got in our way. But, all in all, we were still at the fiesta, and there was plenty of fun to be had, so, after churros, chocolate, and espresso, we went on with our day.

Most of the crowd that was there for the opening ceremonies left that day. Most hostels and hotels required a stay of July 5th through the 8th for the festival, so new crews of tourists would be showing up. We were booked through the next day, a lesson learned for me from the year prior. Plus, we wanted to run three times and see the bullfight that night.

Our First Bullfight

One of my travel goals was to see a bullfight. Jo agreed; we wanted our opinions of them to be informed by experience instead of ignorant emotion. After watching several travel vlogs and videos about them, we were sure we would hate them. Neither of us would enjoy inducing any level of animal suffering just for spectator entertainment. We couldn't see any honour in the performance.

Nevertheless, we had tickets for la corrida (as they were called in Spanish) on July 8th. We picked them up at the hotel I had bought them through months before, but only I was allowed back to the office. Bullfight tickets in Pamplona were highly-prized and sought-after items, and there was plenty of thievery and scams during the fiesta as tourists competed for the few tickets season pass holders didn't have.

Neither Jo nor I knew anything about bullfights. Somewhere along the way, we learned that they were bring-your-own-alcohol events. As long as you didn't bring glass containers in, you could bring whatever you wanted, and it was customary to bring enough to share with those around you. Well, when in Rome, as they say, so we hit up a market for some beer, wine, and Coca Cola (for kalimotxos) before setting off for the bullring.

Our seats were in the andanadas, the very highest section. Fortunately, they were in the shaded section (bullrings had three sections: sun, sun and shade, and shade), so we weren't roasting in the Navarrese sun for the first half of the performance. Coincidentally, Summer, Caitlin, and Rick sat in the same row as us, and we were seated next to some Americans who had been to bullfights before. With their help, we slowly came to understand the performance taking place before us.

And by performance, I do mean performance. As a colloquialism, bullfighting was called a sport, but in aficionado community, it was no such thing. It was an artistic performance, a test of one's honour, an intimate dance between man and bull in which each member of the cuadrilla (a bullfighting team) played an important role. Known in cultures around was the matador, the bull killer, the one with the red cape (called the muleta) that faced down the bull with intricate passes. Additionally, there were the *picadores*, horse-mounted bullfighters who tested the bull's courage and showcased its aggressive qualities for the president and the crowd. And then there were the *peones*, the matador's assistants who, depending on which part of the bullfight you were watching, played a number of roles. They placed the banderillas (barbed flags) in the bull's back, distracted the bulls in between the tercios (literally,

23

thirds, like the thirds of a hockey match or the quarters of an American football game), and often kept the matador safe should something not go as planned. They were all known as toreros, bullfighters, because that's what they all were in their own way.

Jo and I knew none of this walking in.

The bullfight started with the paseíllo, where everyone involved in the performance, from the matadors to the teams that cleaned the ring between bulls, entered in a procession and saluted the president of the bullfight. Then the performance started. Over the course of the night, we watched three matadors take on six bulls. We could not have asked for a better first bullfight, as we witnessed four events that would be forever seared into our memories and, eventually, fuel our love for the performance that was la corrida.

The first one came with the first bull. This was the senior matador's first bull of the night. We watched the spectacle before us with sheer bewilderment, taking in as much as possible in this all-too-real environment. All went well...until it didn't. The matador mistimed one of the passes, and the bull drove a horn into his leg and tossed him into the air. It looked bad, even way up where we were sitting. The peones from all three cuadrillas quickly rushed in to distract the bull and carry the torero off to the infirmary. We later learned he received a sixteen-centimetre gash in his leg that put him out of commission for several weeks. The seriousness of what we were watching sunk in at that moment. The bull could beat the matador, and the matador could die. We knew that, but seeing it at our first corrida washed away the romantic view pop culture lore bestowed upon the matador. Bullfighting was serious, deadly business.

By the rules of bullfighting, when a matador was carried out of the ring, the senior-most matador remaining stepped in to finish the bull. That would be the intermediate matador, the term Jo and I used to refer to the second-most experienced matador in the ring. This would lead to the second event that stayed with us.

The intermediate matador continued the performance with the muleta. We could tell he wasn't as comfortable with the bull as the senior matador, but he still did well, as best as we could tell. Eventually, the dreaded moment (for us) came: the estocada, the final killing blow. The matador lined up his strike, charged in, and slipped his sword effortlessly between the bull's shoulder blades. Based on the reaction of the crowd, it was a clean blow. However, rather than dying in short order, the bull stayed in the fight. Jo and I watched as this bull refused to die and reared its horns towards any of the toreros that came near it. At one point it laid down, but when one of the peones (the puntillero, in this case) approached to administer the coup de grace, it stood up and continued to fight on. It took almost five minutes for it to finally succumb to its wounds. One of the men next to us told us that he had never seen one take that long to die. It was hard to watch for sure, but something about watching this bull refuse to let the matador send him into the next life really impressed us.

The third event came during the second bull with the junior matador, the term we used to describe the matadors who were the least experienced (in terms of time in the profession). He started this faena (the name given to each individual bullfight in a night) on his knees in front of the corrals. He was directly in the bull's path as it entered the ring. As the bull charged out, he whipped his capote (a fuchsia and

24

yellow cape all the toreros used) in front of his face, over his head, and around his back. The bull followed the capote, leaving the matador wholly intact. Throughout this faena, this torero stayed close to the bull. Really close. He wore a white suit, and even from the cheap seats, we could see the red blood stains smeared all over him. He demonstrated a level of respect for the bull that could only be felt in the moment as he enticed the bull to charge in a series of excellent passes. While he struggled to get the estocada (he took more than one try), he clearly had a natural talent and passion for the art of bullfighting. His name was Borja Jiménez. That wasn't important at the moment, but it would be later, as he would become both Jo's and my favourite matador.

The fourth event that endeared to my memory was one Jo missed because she was in the bathroom. During the third faena, the intermediate matador performed exceptionally well. He had bolstered his confidence after dispatching the first bull of the night. His estocada was aggressive, clean, and an impressive act to watch. It was so impressive that the crowd demanded that he be rewarded. In bullfighting, the way the awards went was the matador could receive one of the ears from the dead bull, both ears, or both ears and the tail, depending on the performance. The crowd demanded the first ear by a simple majority vote, indicated by waiving white handkerchiefs (or, unique to Pamplona, red handkerchiefs). The President awarded the ear, and the matador walked a celebratory lap around the ring to a standing ovation from the crowd.

Jo and I left the bullfight excited. We had made new friends and experienced something we could never have imagined. We also left with our minds racing as we processed the night's events. What we witnessed did not conform to our preconceived notions. We later captured some initial thoughts on camera, but even those were still developing.

At 23h00 that night, Jo and I made our way to the Ciudadela de Pamplona for the fireworks show. The one the night before had been rained out, but this one was still on as far as we knew. We found a nice round spot to watch them on one of the roads that was packed full of people. We knew that these fireworks would be impressive, because the display was a part of an international fireworks competition that took place every year during San Fermín. What we didn't know was just how impressive they would be. They were the most astounding fireworks I had ever seen. Jo recorded them with the timelapse on her phone. Watching them later, it was like there was a laser show on her phone, because it was just one series of lights after another.

After the fireworks, we went straight to bed. We were running our third encierro the next day, and we had to be there at 07h00, just like every other morning.

Our Last Day

After the prior day's issues with other runners, we decided to try the front of the pack again. We met up with Summer, Caitlin, and Rick in the town square wholly by accident. It turned out that Summer hadn't been allowed to run the day before. At the last minute, a police officer decided she wasn't wearing suitable enough shoes and told her to leave the route, so she was wearing Caitlin's shoes for the third day.

Rick, her boyfriend, had run the day before, so he was doing it for a second time. Like all good boyfriends at an event like this, he promptly left her to her own devices to make his own daring memories.

Jo and I pushed as far as possible to the front of the route, joined with the chants, and waited for the rockets. The first rocket went off, and people started running. We waited. Jo even yelled, "You can't even see the bulls yet!" at the tourists trying to get us to run. We didn't have to wait much longer. The bulls were upon us before the second rocket exploded over us. When I saw those eyes and horns before I expected to, I felt a surge of pure fear. I ran, while Jo waited another few seconds. I didn't get dragged to the ground this time. I was running with the bulls when I crested the hill at the top of the Calle de Santo Domingo, where it met the plaza in front of the town hall. And I stopped. Not because I wanted to, but because three mozos stopped right at the corner as the road opened up and took a sweeping curve to the left. I literally ran into them.

Jo caught up with me shortly after, and she had the same issue further back. We were both miffed but excited that we had completed every encierro while in Pamplona. We headed to Café Iruña for churros, chocolate, and coffee, and sat back to enjoy the scene. We had nothing to do but pack, so we took our time enjoying the morning.

While the party itself hadn't lived up to the year before, the overall experience was 1,000 times better. I had already resolved to return the next year, so long as our travels didn't interfere. I wasn't sure how Jo felt about the entire fiesta; I just knew that she really enjoyed the opening ceremonies and the encierros. I also knew that she was more than a little tired. We had been going hard for a week and a half now, and I knew how it felt to be beginning one's travel journey. I had worn myself out on many of my travels before, and it took stamina to keep up the pace we were going. I was tired, too, but I also partook in that greatest of Spanish traditions, the siesta, every day, which helped a lot.

Our final act before heading to meet our ride to Barcelona was to throw away all our San Fermín clothes. Our stained purple t-shirts, formerly white pants, and even shoes all went into the dumpster outside of the hostel. We had been wearing them for three days now, and there was no way we were sticking those clothes back in our bags. I still had my pants from the last year back home; they were still stained from the party.

Reflecting on La Fiesta de San Fermín

Why I ran with the bulls in the first place. The first time I ran with the bulls, I was two weeks from turning thirty years old. I had a reputation for being more than a bit crazy. I voluntarily deployed with the military, rode a motorcycle, and was an avid skydiver. All of this was a result of a deep emotional pain from a long-lost relationship. I heard the song "A Feelin' Like That" by Gary Allan many years before, and the second verse stuck with me as he described running with the bulls as he chased the feeling of the love he once had across the world.

As my thirtieth birthday approached the year before The Great Gallivanting, I went to Spain to run with the bulls. Thirty was pushing back, and nothing followed the feeling I had lost from that relationship. Was it the best reason to do something so dangerous? Absolutely not. But, at the time, it made sense. The pain of that loss had driven me so hard for so long that it became an intricate part of my decision-making paradigm. Luckily, I had such a fantastic experience, and the fiesta endeared to me so much, that after my second time there with Jo, I was there for the experience, tradition, and history, not some long-lost relationship that would never return.

The Aussies from San Sebastian. The Australians we overheard in San Sebastian made an appearance at the fiesta. Jo must have been psychic, because they were in our hostel! The night before the first encierro, they were all hyped up for their direct confrontation with fear, honour, and courage the next morning. After the encierro, they were singing a different tune. I talked with one of them, and he swore he would never do it again. It was the scariest, stupidest thing he had ever done, and he simply couldn't understand why anyone enjoyed doing that. I merely commented, "Yeah, I didn't get it when I first ran, either," and that was the end of that. It wasn't for anyone, and it was sobering to actually experience a dangerous event rather than simply talking about it with your buddies over tapas and cervezas.

The underbelly of the party. I loved San Fermín and resolved to return to run with the bulls as often as possible. That said, it wasn't all sunshine and rainbows. There was a dark underbelly to it all. Despite the ample supply of portable bathrooms, people would pee wherever they thought was "private enough." Behind dumpsters, under trees, down side streets, between cars, everywhere. Men and women both could be found relieving themselves in certain areas. Pamplona had posted signs everywhere imploring people not to relieve themselves outside of bathrooms, but no one paid attention to these. As far as Jo and I were concerned, we had a centrally-located hostel, so we could easily go back to use the bathroom. Unfortunately, there were three dumpsters out front, which were also centrally located and, thus, prime public urination real estate.

Alcohol was another issue. Granted, it was a defining feature of the fiesta, but, like all festivals with alcohol, it caused more than a few problems. People would drink themselves into unconsciousness in the streets, and it was not uncommon to see people passed out on curbs or leaning against buildings. People would get drunk to the point of being dangerous. I even found myself border-lining on a hospital stay one night the year before from drinking so much. Some people went straight from drinking into the encierro. The police did as much as they could to stop this, but drunk tourists still slipped through cracks and put themselves (and others) in serious danger.

Finally, almost all the alcohol served during the festival was in plastic cups. People discarded them on the street when they were done. Fortunately for the residents, Pamplona had a sizeable public sanitation apparatus at work during the festival, so it was all cleaned up before the encierro, but it was still annoying and disheartening to see people have such disregard for the city.

Basque Separatism and Spanish revisionist history. The Basque people have long sought independence from Spain and, to a lesser extent, France. The Basque kingdoms existed before the Kingdom of Spain, and there were arguments that the Spanish identity had eroded the Basque identity for centuries. As a result, not long ago, Basque terrorist groups were responsible for some of the deadliest terrorist attacks in the West.

In the autonomous community of Navarre, the Basque separatist movement was a fringe minority. About ten percent of Navarrese people agreed with such a movement. The separatist movement became outspoken during San Fermín, because the fiesta had *some* of its roots in Basque history, and there was a lot of anonymity afforded to those pasting posters and holding signs when there were thousands upon thousands of people around them.

That said, part of the reason the Basque separatists were so fervent in their beliefs was because there was an active, concerted effort to suppress Navarre's Basque heritage at the governmental level. I experienced this on social media by referring to Navarre as "Basque Country" on YouTube after the fiesta. To be sure, Navarre was not a part of the autonomous community called Basque Country; however, those railing against me were adamant I open a history book, because Navarre was not and never had been Basque Country. I took them up on that suggestion.

I learned that the Kingdom of Navarre was one of the original Basque kingdoms long before the Kingdom of Spain was established! Furthermore, the Kingdom of Navarre included the region, which was now the autonomous community of Basque Country! Moreover, it had been conquered by Spain in the 1500s! So, not only was Navarre a part of the historical "Basque Country," it was *the* original Basque country.

As someone who used to work on terrorism issues in the military and my security firm, I was well-acquainted with the root causes of terrorism. One of these was the destruction of a communal identity. The Spanish had indeed done this and were actively still doing so by denying the factual, historical past to the faces of those directly connected to it. While I didn't support terrorism or illegal separatist movements, after my experiences with history-denying social media warriors, I could understand why the Basque separatists took such strong positions on the subject.

Chapter Four

Spain: Madrid, Barcelona, Disappointments, and Las Ventas

We had all but decided to skip Spain when planning The Great Gallivanting. It wasn't that we didn't want to see the country; we absolutely did. We just didn't think we would have the time to explore it as thoroughly as we would like. At the same time, we both wanted to go to Barcelona, and it only seemed natural to head to Madrid on our way to Portugal. As part of my trip through Spain the year before, I spent a few days in Barcelona and loved it, so I had high hopes for our return trip. My excitement fuelled Jo's, and we were excited to see what this world-famous city had to offer to a couple of budget travellers.

Barcelona

I would never again take a BlaBlaCar from Pamplona to Barcelona.

Jo and I had never experienced using BlaBlaCar before. BlaBlaCar was a ride-sharing service where ordinary people already making a trip offered empty seats in their vehicle. It was just a way to make money doing things they would already be doing. That was fair enough and, in concept, a great idea.

However.

Our first (and only) experience with BlaBlaCar was far from a great idea. We met our driver on one of the main roads in Pamplona. The BlaBlaCar app indicated to us that he had three empty seats, with one of them already full. We thought this was fantastic. We wouldn't be crammed into someone's backseat, and it would be easy on Jo's carsickness (in fairness, I got carsick on occasion, too, but not often). How wrong we were.

When our car pulled up, the driver had a friend in the front seat of a very small hatchback. That meant the three of us passengers would all be crammed into the back seat. Worse, even though the app clearly stated what we could bring our baggage, his hatchback couldn't hold our bags plus the other traveller's plus the luggage cover, so we ended up with our day bags between our legs and the luggage cover laying across all three of us for the four-hour drive to Barcelona. Worse, Spain loved its traffic circles, and this guy loved taking them too fast, so there was no way we were getting any sleep along the way. Even worse, Jo and I both were on the verge of puking at several points. Still worse, in typical European fashion, our driver didn't believe in running the air conditioning, so it was hot and stale, even with the windows down. Neither of us were in a good mood by the time we got to Barcelona, and all we wanted to do was drink water and take a nap.

After about an hour on Barcelonan public transport, we finally arrived at our Airbnb just outside the city on the northeast side. It was close to the beach, and the host, Sergei, was terrific. He ensured we had all the necessary access and was always available to answer questions. We had a one-bedroom, which was fine by this point, but unfortunately, it had an east-facing window and no air conditioning. That meant it would get really hot during the day. Sergei warned us about this, but he may have understated how hot it could get.

We spent part of the first day in Barcelona at the nearby beach. Even in July, the Mediterranean waters were cold, but the water was incredibly clear. I hopped in for a bit before taking off to find a coffee shop while Jo lounged in the Spanish sun. We didn't have anywhere to be until the afternoon, and it was nice to have a slow morning after the last two weeks. Plus, a slow morning meant not spending money, which was crucial.

That afternoon, we headed to La Sagrada Familia, a cathedral designed by the architect Gaudi which had been under construction for over 140 years. I had seen it the year prior from the outside but didn't go in. It wasn't the cheapest place to see, but I soon learned that it was worth every Euro we paid and more.

Gaudi's basic concept was to tell the story of Jesus Christ through his architecture. Each façade told a different part of His life story, from the birth to life to death to resurrection, in intricately carved, stoney detail that overwhelmed the senses. Twelve towers stood for the Twelve Disciples, four even taller towers would stand for the Four Evangelists (only two were complete when we visited), and one central tower standing above the rest would symbolise the Virgin Mary. Inside, the stained-glass windows reflected the mood of the day, with red, orange, and yellow glass on the east projecting the sun's warmth and brightness and the blue, green, and purple glass on the west soothing the cathedral's interior as the day turned into night.

Jo and I knew next to nothing about architecture and structural engineering, but we learned that the flying buttresses common amongst Catholic cathedrals were totally absent at La Sagrada Familia. Instead, the massive cathedral was supported by towering tree-like columns, which opened up the sanctuary and gave the outer silhouette a distinctive look. Apparently, Gaudi hated flying buttresses. He saw them as an architectural and engineering crutch. We laughed at that, and from then on, we became architectural critics. Every time we saw flying buttresses, we would joke, "Psh. They needed a better engineer. This guy was using a crutch!"

One of my travel goals during this world tour was to learn more about religion. La Sagrada Familia's audio guide provided an invaluable introductory course for Christian history, lore, and symbolism. I learned about the symbols common to each of the Four Evangelists, how to decipher painted scenes depicting the annunciation, betrayal, and crucifixion, and some of the fates of the Evangelists and Disciples that I didn't know. While I had learned the story of Jesus's life growing up, I was never taught the subsequent symbolism and historical narrative attached to those who followed Him. While I wanted to learn more about the Old Testament and travels of the Evangelists and Apostles in AD times, I still stood in wonder and amazement as I learned things I should probably have learned long ago.

We stayed there from 13h00 until closing and could easily have stayed longer. I was glad Jo enjoyed La Sagrada Familia, because it allowed me to reflect on what the religious part of our journey would mean for me. She wasn't as committed to faith as I was, but being raised a Christian, she appreciated the story and emotion Gaudi's architecture tried to convey.

The next day started with a frustrating morning. We wanted to buy the Barcelona City Pass, which provided free public transport and access to museums and cathedrals across the city. We struck out at the first three tourism information points, which were not close to one another. They were all closed. We were walking a lot just to strike out, and Jo grew increasingly frustrated both at the situation and at me. I was irritated, too, but these things didn't bother me too much. We finally found an open vendor, and our moods changed instantly. We were so relieved that we couldn't stop laughing as we recorded our success with the GoPro.

After such a frustrating morning, the one thing we wanted was air conditioning. Barcelona was hot in the summer, so we found a nearby museum, the Frederic Mares Museum, to escape the July sun. This museum was full of Christian-themed artifacts, from sculptures to paintings to crucifixes. While it became repetitive at times, we both commented that this was a must-see for anyone who was an aficionado of Christian (specifically, Catholic) art and archaeology.

The rest of the morning, we toured around the Gothic Quarter, bouncing from museum to museum and cathedral to cathedral. Our Airbnb was an hour away via public transport, so we had no intention of going back once we were out and about. We would stop for tapas, cañas, and wine every so often, and even visited the Olympic Museum in the afternoon. Due to navigator error (i.e., my error), we actually ended up standing on top of the museum at one point without knowing it.

Dinner was the highlight of the day. Jo's mom paid for us to eat at the Michelin Star restaurant Con Gracia. It was expensive, almost 100 EUR per person once we factored in drinks, but when would we ever eat at a Michelin Star restaurant again? And on someone else's dime? We had a nine-course, specially-designed meal over several hours, with paired wines, pallet cleansers, and dessert. It was delicious.

While the expensive dinner and La Sagrada Familia were amazing experiences, I was most looking forward to seeing Tibidabo, the cathedral on the hill with the arms of Christ outstretched towards Barcelona. I opted not to see it on my visit the year before, but after watching *Uncharted*, where Christ's outstretched arms created a stunning cut-scene, I wanted to see it up close. Jo was on the fence, mainly because she didn't feel great, but she ultimately decided to go with me in the morning.

It was a total letdown. Getting there required three trams/buses in town, a cable car up the hill, and another minibus from the cable car to the cathedral. We expected grand views from the hilltop but were rewarded with no such thing. Instead, the amusement park at the top of the hill obstructed the surrounding scenery. On top of that, the air quality was terrible, and you could barely see through the haze and dust. Jo's phone indicated the air quality was considered "unhealthy" during our visit, which was one reason she wasn't feeling well. What we hoped would be a breathtaking scene worthy of travel magazines was just a polluted city skyline.

Worse, the cathedral itself was tiny. It looked far larger in pictures and films, and the chapels were unimpressive in their depictions of Biblical scenes, canonised saints, and Catholic lore. Even if they had been impressive, a school field trip was happening at the same time as our visit, so we had to contend with local schoolchildren everywhere. It was not the best time. C'est la vie. Rather than let it dampen our trip, we returned to the Airbnb to pack our bags, took a nap, and enjoyed our last meal in Barcelona at an oceanside restaurant.

Next stop: Madrid.

Madrid

Our time in Madrid kicked off in a most unusual fashion: walking past the heads of babies. I don't mean decapitated babies; we probably would have turned around and headed out of town if that was the case. These were stone sculptures which, apparently, were intended to represent the day and night. We wouldn't learn this until our next time in Madrid a month later. Instead, all I knew about them was Jo calling out "giant baby heads!" I was confused until I saw them, then I was more confused. It was certainly an intriguing, albeit concerning, way to welcome travellers to the city.

Our hostel, Mola, was located right in the heart of Madrid. It was a few minutes' walk from Plaza Mayor, had ample restaurants and cafés nearby, and provided a great base to explore the city. That said, it was moderately expensive at 30 EUR, each, per night. That was pretty standard for Madrid's peak season in July.

Jo and I, again, opted for the City Pass. This one was less helpful, as it didn't include as much as the pass in Barcelona. We also didn't use the free public transport in Madrid as much as in Barcelona courtesy of our centrally-located hostel. Nonetheless, we visited some free museums, including the History Museum of Madrid and a museum dedicated to San Isidro, Madrid's patron saint. These were alright, but I could tell Jo was getting tired of museums (she would later tell me that she was "museum-ed out" after Porto, Portugal).

During our aimless wanderings around the city, we discovered a couple of great food options that stuck with us for the rest of the trip. The first was the plato del día, a set lunch menu for a low price. Our introduction to this concept was a pumpkin bisque. It had never occurred to either of us to eat pumpkin bisque, but we quickly changed our minds because it was fantastic! We would still talk about how great it was even a year later.

The second food option was a place called 100 Montaditos. There was one thirty seconds from our hostel. I wouldn't call 100 Montaditos the best food in the world. It was fast, tapas-style food. But it had the cheapest drinks we had ever experienced. A full pint glass of beer, wine, sangria, tinto de verano, you name it, was only 2 EUR! They filled the glass to the top, to the point where I had to walk slowly to avoid spilling the drinks. We would spend several afternoons across Spain at a 100 Montaditos enjoying the most mediocre food at the most amazing prices.

During one of these stints at 100 Montaditos, I decided to look up the bullring in Madrid, La Plaza de Las Ventas. It turned out there was a bullfight going on the next evening, and I considered going. I didn't want to admit it, but I kind of enjoyed the first one. It would cost 15 EUR for the cheap seats, and I was willing to spend it. I brought it up to Jo, and she wasn't a fan of going to another one. She wasn't morally opposed or anything; her standpoint was we had already been to one and were set to leave Spain in a few days, so why go again? A little dejected, I let it go. At least for then. Later that evening, she could tell I wanted to go, and said to go ahead and get two tickets. We both had come around to the same idea; now that we weren't totally shocked at what we were seeing, we could really evaluate the performance, both as individual faenas and as a cultural whole, and settle how we felt about the performance once and for all.

The morning of the bullfight, we hopped a bus out to the royal residence outside of Madrid proper. While we had done a lot of walking the past two weeks, Jo wanted to go on a proper hike, and there were allegedly hiking trails out at the residence. Neither of us would describe the area around the royal residence as a hiking area. It was more of a large city park, like Central Park in New York City, that surrounded the residence. Still, it was forty-five minutes outside the city in nature, which was a nice change of pace. We took it easy and strolled through the trails, unwinding as we went. Some of them passed by military barracks for the soldiers who guarded the residence, and several times, we saw soldiers and officers going for runs through the trails.

And dogs. Plenty of dogs. Jo and I loved dogs, so seeing them having fun on the trails and in the creek was smile-inducing. At one point, we detoured out of the trails and into the military housing area because Jo heard dogs barking in the distance. Naturally, we had to go find them. Apparently, we were near the training area for the Spanish military's K-9 programme, and the dogs we heard were at the kennels there. We found ourselves wandering towards the back side of the kennels, where we saw one very hyper Belgian Malinois sprinting back and forth up and down the cages. It would have been cool to see them training, but it was a Sunday morning in Spain, so we had no such luck.

Once we had our fill of the trails, we headed back to the city. We hoped we could see the residence's gardens, which looked beautiful online, but they were closed to visitors while we were there. Forty-five minutes later, we were back at 100 Montaditos enjoying a mediocre lunch and 2 EUR beers and wine. After a siesta, we were headed to Las Ventas.

Las Ventas

With alcohol packed into my messenger bag, we boarded the metro for Las Ventas. The station was plastered with sculpted bullfighting scenes, but they were nothing compared to what we would see at the surface. As we emerged above ground on the escalator, we were treated to one of the most beautiful buildings we had ever seen: La Plaza de Toros de Las Ventas. The bullring in Pamplona was grey, concrete, and dull (and a bit of an eyesore). Las Ventas was majestic, historic, and exuded the aura of a Spanish bullring with its neo-Mudejar façade. Outside were sculptures dedicated to bullfighters of old, and there was a crowd around the ticket office, exactly as Hemingway would have described it. Along one of the walls was a mural of vaqueros guiding bulls to the sale, just as it would have happened long ago.

We were early enough to see the stands empty once inside. It was a breathtaking sight, even from the cheap seats. To our left, we could see the president's box and the ornate box where the royal family presided over fairs, events, and individual performances. A special seat for the royal family; this was the bullfighting arena we had dreamed of.

This bullfight followed the same pattern as the one in Pamplona, with one exception. There was a *confirmación* happening that night. A confirmación was when a matador performed for the first time at one of three bullrings in the world: Las Ventas in Madrid, El Monumental in Mexico City, or Arènes de Nîmes in Nîmes, France. During a confirmación, the junior matador, who usually performed during the third and sixth bulls, performed first (and sixth). This was to celebrate his (or her, in rare cases) entrance to the world of professional bullfighting on the grand stage.

The confirmación went well but uneventfully. The matador got thrown at one point but stood up, dusted himself off, and went straight back into his performance, much to the crowd's approval. The second faena, performed by the senior matador, seemed eerily familiar. His passes, mannerisms and closeness to the bull reminded me of the junior matador from Pamplona, and I commented as much to Jo. Then we heard a man behind us comment that his name was Borja Jiménez, and he had just performed in Pamplona. We didn't know that was his name back then, but we had to know now, so we looked up the poster from Pamplona. It was him! We had inadvertently seen this torero twice in a row, and both times, we were impressed. He was the junior matador the week before, but this time, he was the senior matador, and he acted like it.

During the fifth faena, the intermediate matador was thrown and injured badly on his second bull of the night. Like the week before, the peones rushed in to distract the bull. Not just the peones but also the senior matador. Borja was one of the first to reach him and helped carry him off to the infirmary. Bullfighting, we learned over these two corridas, was a team event. It wasn't three teams in the ring when something went awry; it was one. They were all in it together. Their honour depended on it.

The peones distracted the bull until Borja returned. As the senior matador, he was responsible for the bull now. We had watched him struggle with the estocada on more than one bull (of the four we had seen him face), but there was something different this time. His mannerisms, his movements, they were serious. He was no longer performing but stepping in to perform a solemn duty. He nailed it. His *estoque* (the killing sword) sunk between the bull's shoulder blades, and it died swiftly thereafter. This time, there was no celebration. Borja simply folded his muleta into his arm and walked out of the ring. It was something to see, vastly different from the performances that were the norm at these events.

Once the bullfight was over, Jo and I, tipsy from the alcohol, recorded our thoughts on bullfighting from the terrace of Las Ventas with the city as a backdrop. It would seem ridiculous later as I was editing videos, but we were doing everything we could not to admit that we liked bullfighting. We worried it would make us out to be terrible people, but it wasn't what we were led to believe before we left home. It was a performance, a team event, and there was a level of seriousness, respect, and high expectations that we could never have imagined. Causing undue suffering to the bull was met with widespread protest and condemnation from the crowd. For the first half of his one-on-one with the bull, the matador had only a plastic sword in his hand, and it was truly a performance where the matador and the bull shared the spotlight.

Outside, as we walked to the metro, a Spanish man in his mid-to-late twenties stopped us to ask where we were from. He was astounded to hear we were Americans and thanked us profusely for giving his culture a chance, as not many Americans would. He was eager to listen to our thoughts and delighted to hear we had changed our minds on the performance.

Jo and I were glad we had attended the second corrida in Madrid, and we were both a bummed that we wouldn't be seeing another one. But life and the adventure moved on, and the next day, we had first-class tickets to Porto, Portugal.

Well, halfway to Porto, anyways.

Reflecting on Madrid and Barcelona

Time vs. distance. Jo and I were budget travellers. While we had a substantial budget in Europe compared to other backpackers, it still wasn't much, especially as the dollar plummeted against the Euro while we were in Madrid. In Barcelona, we stayed in an Airbnb because it made logical sense to us on the budget. What we didn't account for, though, was the time it would take to get to the central part of the city. There was no direct route to get there, so we spent a lot of time on public transport. Compared to Madrid, where we were centrally located, this annoyed us. Minding the budget and balancing accommodations against other expenses was important, but so was having an enjoyable experience. As we left Spain, we decided to be more conscious of balancing the cost of accommodations against the ease (and time) of getting to the main parts of a city.

Morning and night people. If there was one thing we were not aligned on, it was what time to get up or get back from an evening out. I was a morning person. I have been since my military days, when I had to be at work at 05h30. Even at my security company, I had to be at work at 05h45. Jo, on the other hand, was a night owl. She had no problem staying up until 03h30. This became a friction point, especially in Barcelona, that we would have to deal with for months to come. I had no problem getting up and heading out for coffee or to explore on my own in the morning. Jo, on the other hand, was apprehensive about staying out late on her own. Part of this stemmed from her being a woman in a foreign land (which certainly would be founded in certain parts of the world where males dominate society (read: Morocco)), but most of her apprehension stemmed from her being uncomfortable as a traveller. She admitted on several occasions that she just wasn't comfortable as a traveller being on her own yet.

That was fair enough. We all had to start somewhere. I will never forget walking the streets of Venice alone at 01h00 on my first solo trip to Europe. It took me a long time to get to the point of being okay with wandering around foreign places alone at any time of day. Unfortunately for Jo, I was still a morning person, so by 22h00, I was ready for bed, which meant she stayed in the hostel. She got a lot of reading done on her Kindle, but this was something we would never overcome in our travels together.

Sickness. On top of being tired, Jo was not feeling well in Barcelona. She wasn't sick with a virus or anything, but four days of having to yell to be heard in Pamplona, combined with the unhealthy air quality in Barcelona, really took its toll. I wasn't feeling the best, either, because of the air quality. She did her best to power through, but I could tell she was miserable. I had loved Barcelona the year before, but her first experience there wasn't the best. To her credit, she will be the first to say that she would love to give it a second chance when she wasn't feeling bad, but, until then, it wouldn't rank on her list of top destinations.

Kids at the bullfight. Jo noticed before I did: many children were at the Madrid bullfight. Not just locals, either, but tourists. It hadn't occurred to us that this would be a place to bring children as a tourist. While there was something to be said about exposing your kids to other cultures, bullfighting seemed to us to be something that we would save for teenage children at least.

The life of a *toro de lidia*. Jo and I would do our research about bullfighting in the weeks after Madrid, and we learned that the life of the Spanish Fighting Bull (the toro de lidia) was a great life, and we could no longer morally afford to condemn the practice of bullfighting on humanitarian grounds so long as we ate meat.

The average cattle raised to provide meat was slaughtered at eighteen months old, and it spent most of that time in a cattle farm eating processed food designed to bolster the meat's quality, flavour, texture, and bulk. The toro de lidia, on the other hand, lived to be between four and six years old before being led to the bullring. It lived as a free-range bull, nearly completely free from human interaction. Because of Spanish bullfighting regulations, the toro de lidia could never encounter a man on the ground before entering the ring, so any interaction it would have would be with horse-mounted ranch hands.

I won't go into the manner of death that cattle raised for meat undergo, but it certainly wasn't pleasant, quick, nor humane. However, the toro de lidia in the ring was granted two things not afforded in the cattle farms: the opportunity to face its killer (and to take him/her out or even win its freedom) and a quick death. The toro de lidia was also celebrated by the crowd. After all, it gave its life for us, and it deserved our respect and admiration for displaying courage and bravery in the face of certain death.

Jo and I both will be the first to say bullfighting was not for everyone, but understanding it at a deeper level helped us to gain an appreciation not just for the performance, but for how our senses of morality came (and didn't come) into play when judging such practices in relation to others in which we were active, if unknowing, participants.

Chapter Five

Portugal: Not Our Scene

A constant refrain from my prior travels was, "You need to check out Portugal!" That was the extent of the refrain, so I had no idea what to see or do once we were there, but I had saved some reels on Instagram from micro-influencers, so hopefully those would help. This was our last (planned) stop on the Iberian side of Europe, as we wwere flying to Italy in about two weeks, and we planned on staying on that side of Europe until we had to leave the Schengen Area.

Porto

Getting to Portugal was a trick. There were no direct trains from Madrid to Porto, and the Renfe agent was less than helpful. When we told him that was what we wanted, he said, "No hay" ("there are none") without even looking at his screen. We moved on with the other tickets we wanted to book until he eventually told us we could go to Vigo, change stations, and then travel to Porto. Why not say that in the first place? We were clearly travellers, and we weren't the only ones going from Madrid to Porto during his entire time working at Renfe.

When we arrive in Vigo, we decided to grab lunch on the way to the other station. We had three hours between trains, so we weren't exactly in a hurry. Fortunately for us, it was all downhill to the other side. Downhill with bags on was always the better way to go. Unfortunately for us, Portugal was notorious for impromptu rail strikes, and one of them struck us. Our train was cancelled. The ticket agents at the station were extremely helpful, and told us to get a bus to Porto as the bus company was laying on extra buses that afternoon to help offset the impact of the strike. Even though the rail operator wouldn't pay for the bus, it was still cheaper than staying in Vigo unexpectedly, especially considering we had already paid for the hostel in Porto.

Where was the bus station? Easy, it was just outside the other train station, the one we had just walked from, the one at the top of the hill. Our morale fell through the floor. We had just walked fifteen minutes downhill, which meant it would be twenty to thirty minutes going back up with our packs on. Talk about brutal. Downtrodden, we slowly slogged back up the hill from whence we came.

By the time we got to the hostel in Porto, we were smoked, tired, exhausted, and irritable from a longer-than-expected day of traveling. But the hits just kept on coming. Our hostel room didn't have air conditioning in the Portuguese summer; it only had a single fan to cool the large room. In retrospect, this wasn't too big of a deal (Europeans didn't believe in air conditioning for some unholy reason), but in the moment it sucked big time. With the hits of the day, Jo had no problem convincing me to head downstairs to the bar for a caña (what she would that night start calling "Jack-sized" beers because I wasn't a big drinker).

We had no idea what we wanted to see or do in Porto. One of the pitfalls we had fallen into in our intense desire not to have a plan was that we didn't have one. We didn't even have research. We were shooting from the hip in a country where neither of us spoke the language (it turned out Portuguese and Spanish weren't as closely related as we had hoped).

Luckily, we found a great bakery nearby to enjoy breakfast, espresso, and some research. This bakery had a nice, shaded outdoor seating area across the street from a cathedral, creating a beautiful, Instagram-worthy breakfast scene. We ate breakfast here several times during our stay in Porto, mainly because it was on the way to the city centre. It also had what was, apparently, our favourite breakfast item: croissant mixto. It was just a ham and cheese croissant, but it was substantially better quality than the processed foods we had in the United States. We would have a croissant mixto for breakfast many times during our travels. Simple, cheap, and delicious, an excellent combination for budget-conscious travellers.

The bakery also had this thing called the chocolate rat. It sounded unappealing, but we were morbidly interested and had to try it one day. Basically, the chocolate rat was a chocolate cake in the shape of a rat. Unlike most cakes, though, it was different every time because they used the leftovers from other cakes to make the chocolate rat. As a guy on Bumble told Jo, it was the sausage of the bakery world. Well, we both loved sausage, and the chocolate rat was no exception.

We had four full days in Porto, which was longer than anywhere else so far. This really came down to where we wanted to spend an extra day, because our flight from Lisbon to Rome was cheaper if we extended our plan in Portugal. It also was a function of where I wanted to spend my birthday. I could have spent it on a travel day from Porto to Lisbon or enjoying a single city. I opted for the latter.

Our first stop was to buy the Porto City Pass. It didn't come with free public transport, but it came with a lot of museum access and discounts. The tourism office was also outside a beautiful cathedral, and we could see out across the rooftops of Porto for miles. As much as I wanted to visit the cathedral, I knew Jo wasn't really into them, so I didn't push it.

Passes in hand, we headed down towards the river that flowed through Porto to the Atlantic. And it was down. We learned the hard way that Porto was built on a steep hill in Roman times as a way to defend the city and provide a lookout from the high ground. Modern Porto expanded around the Roman outpost. We wound through the narrow alleys that headed down to the river, and it seemed like that quintessential old European town. At least, it would have had we not known that a bustling, sprawling city was just outside the neighbourhoods.

We kicked off exploring the city with a museum dedicated to Henry the Navigator, who was known locally as "Infante." Infante was related both to the Portuguese royal family (by direct blood) and the King of England (through his mother).

It reminded me of how all of the major leaders during World War I were cousins, despite being on opposite sides of the war. Infante played crucial roles in combatting the Barbary Pirates from North Africa, exploring the African coasts and gold trades, and developing sailing technology that freed sailors from the limits of sailing into the wind. He was a significant and revered part of Portugal's history.

Unfortunately, I learned none of that from the museum. Jo and I had a habit of doing extra research and reading online after seeing something, which was a great habit because the museum was utterly lacklustre. It was built on the site of an old Roman house and was dedicated more to that purpose than anything else. After our so-so experience with the city pass in Madrid, things were not looking up in Porto.

Undeterred, we set off for lunch at a local spot (the plato del día was alive and well in Portugal) before searching for the Romantic Museum. We had no idea what we would find there, but it was included in the pass. There was no direct route there, and it was mostly uphill, which was wholly unpleasant despite walking through narrow alleyways. Google Maps took us to the wrong door, so we had to walk further than anticipated. I said on my GoPro that if the entrance wasn't around the next corner, I would have to run for it because Jo would kill me (which she thought was funny).

We finally got there, and it was not what we expected. It was a museum set in a Romantic-period house and dedicated to showcasing what a Romantic-period home may have looked like. It probably would have been awesome for purveyors of that kind of history. We found it intriguing, but it wasn't what we were looking forward to (which, to be fair, we didn't know what that was, either). There were two cool things inside, however. The first was a beautiful, if abstract, painting of Moses on Mount Sinai, where he received the ten commandments from God. The second was a room full of mirrors and glass shelves with various artifacts and replicas of things that may have populated homes in the Romantic period. This was an art display more than it was a historical presentation, but to Jo and me it was a disaster waiting to happen. We talked and joked about how bad it would be if someone accidentally fell into one of the shelves. The entire room would have come crashing down!

With a full day of moderately disappointing museums behind us, we grabbed drinks at a bar near the hostel. Alcohol was pretty cheap in Portugal (just as in Spain), and we enjoyed just sitting around talking, joking, and sharing funny Instagram reels. The *sobremesa* had become one of our favourite Spanish dining traditions, and we would carry it forward.

After the day before, we knew there was a sure-fire way to cheer us both up: the beach! Porto was on the ocean, and the beach was pretty accessible, so after breakfast, we headed out. Little did we know what awaited us.

Porto was on the west side of the Iberian Peninsula, but, more importantly, it was on the east side of the Gulf Stream. That meant the North Atlantic waters had cooled the warm Caribbean waters from the Gulf Stream, and the water was freezing cold. Unbearably cold for us Texans. As much as we wanted to swim (and I wanted to go diving), there was no way we could stand the water. Additionally, the beach was extremely windy. Locals had wind screens surrounding their spots, and those who didn't were camped behind large rocks along the shore. As much as we wanted to lay out in the sun, we couldn't take it, so we moved to a small café to enjoy a beer, wine, and our Kindles. While there, we may have even had chips, salsa, croissant mixtos, and tacos. Despite the frigid water and high winds, this day at the beach did wonders for our attitudes about Porto. After all, a bad day at the beach was better than a good day at work.

We split up the following day. Jo was getting a tattoo on a whim, and we agreed to meet for lunch. I headed for the cathedral we saw on our first day in Porto, the Sé do Porto. Built in the 12th Century, there wasn't anything spectacular or unique about this cathedral compared to others I had seen, but it was important to local history. The queue was long, and I texted Jo that it was a good thing she wasn't there. There was no way she would stand in that queue to see another cathedral.

I took my time inside to study the chapels, paintings, and sculptures. I wanted to see just how much I could interpret and understand without having to be told. As I stood in various parts of the cathedral studying the scenes, I noticed tourists giving me sideways glances of annoyance. In this 900-year-old cathedral, most tourists were more interested in Instagram pictures than they were the history and religious significance of the site. As someone who was interested in exploring religion in my travels, this started off as a bit of an annoyance and rose over time to being almost offensive. Holy places were holy places, and deserved respect as such, even if you, personally, didn't believe in the religion. Taking photos of interesting things wasn't what bothered me; it was the obsession with making them perfect for the vanity of social media that perturbed me so much. It flew directly in the face of what these places stood for.

After we reunited, Jo and I headed to the Porto military museum. Fingers crossed, it would be better than two days before. Before we went inside, though, we detoured through the cemetery next door. It was oddly beautiful and relaxing and full of mausoleums and religious symbols. We wondered aloud if enjoying a stroll through a graveyard made us morbid, terrible people. We also found it funny that this was the most relaxing of all the places we had been in Porto.

Fortunately for us, the military museum was excellent. It had arms, equipment, and stories from centuries of conflicts. On the first floor (second floor for American readers), the museum had a massive display of military figurines, which was my favourite part. Unit upon miniature unit from Portugal's long military history stood in formation as though on grand parade. From infantrymen in wool uniforms to horse-mounted cavalry to modern tanks, this display paid homage and respect to Portugal's veterans, both present and past.

That afternoon, I had a surprise for Jo. She had been to museum after museum with me, so it was her turn. Porto, she had told me, was home to one of her favourite kinds of wine, Port wine. The only government-chartered winery was located in Porto, and they offered both tours and tastings for reasonable prices. I asked her if she wanted to go the next day, but she was apprehensive because it was my birthday. There would be more birthdays, but who knew if she'd ever be in Porto for a wine tasting again? So, we booked it.

I had to admit, it was cool. The winery was called Real Companhia Velha. I didn't like wine, but the whole operation was quite impressive. We were the only ones there for an English-speaking tour, so we had our own guide, a sort of personal

tour of the facility. Our guide walked us through the fermenting and casking processes, and we got to see massive barrels of wine that had been special ordered by
some rich person or government or another that was awaiting its final delivery...in a
few years when it was ready. The winery also had a metal silo that held 1,000,000
litres of wine! The silo was in a specially-designed room, sunk into a large, concrete
hole in the ground which, our guide told us, was designed specifically to save as
much of the wine as possible in the event of a rupture in the tank. Oh, and to prevent
the rest of the winery from being flooded with wine, but mostly to save the wine. It
was a matter of priorities, after all.

As part of the booking, we ordered a tasting, which Jo knew more about than I
did. Wine was wine to me, with white and red being the only differences, but she
convinced me to try them all. She was sophisticated about it. She checked the aroma,
looked at the sediment, and gave each glass a proper tasting. I might as well have
been at a college frat party, because I downed each [small] glass in one gulp. She
took videos of me doing so, sent them to our mutual friends, and posted them on
Instagram. Apparently, you weren't supposed to "shoot" Port wine, and I quickly
learned why. It was like doing shots of white rum as far as alcohol content went, and
I had done five of them in less than ten minutes. Being a lightweight, I quickly felt
tipsy, much to Jo's entertainment.

The final leg of the tour was a trip to the wine cellar. It was behind an old iron
door locked by big metal keys, just like old prison doors. This was where the winery
kept its wine collection. None of this wine was for sale or consumption; it was a
proper collection. There was hardly any light, and it was damp and dusty, like some
Hollywood film. Some of the bottles had been down there for over 100 years. Now,
I didn't see the point in collecting full bottles of alcohol, but I knew people who did,
so I could understand the importance. It was too bad the lighting wasn't very good,
because there would have been some great photos. But, as I had learned the year
before, "algunas cosas son solo par mi." Not every experience needed to be digitally
immortalised on our phones.

We decided to explore a bit since we were already on the opposite side of the
river from the hostel. Somehow, we ended up at yet another wine tasting. I didn't
partake this time, and Jo was a little apprehensive about how terrible the wine might
be, given that it was five glasses for 5 EUR. But, then again, it was five glasses for
5 EUR, so how much complaining could we really do? She enjoyed this tasting and
was somewhat confused as to how they could sell good tasting wine for 1 EUR per
glass. But, hey, no complaints from the budget travellers.

We left for Lisbon the next day, but not before being thoroughly annoyed with
a group of five Australians that had moved into our room. Our hostel was located
near a social district, and the noise from even hushed conversations outside rever-
berated off the walls so much that it felt like they were in the room with you or,
worse, yelling. As I said, though, we only had the one fan for the entire room, so we
had a choice: close the windows to stop the noise and be unbearably hot all night,
or leave the windows open for air flow and endure the noise. Every night so far,
everyone had been in agreement to leave the windows open. This night, though, the
Australians closed them on their own in the middle of the night. Jo and I woke up
sweating profusely. Once we figured out why, we were beyond irritated, and

couldn't leave the room fast enough. To make things worse, this was a travel day, which was already exhausting enough, even on a short train ride to Lisbon. This was the final nail in the coffin. We were ready to leave Porto.

Lisbon

The train to Lisbon was uneventful, and our hostel was not far off the metro line. It was a little far from the main part of the city, but the close metro made going places easy, and, as much as we had heard the opposite, Lisbon was nowhere near as bad of a hill as Porto. Everything seemed to us to be a straight, flat walk from the hostel.

The first thing I did when we arrived was get a massage. In addition to the knee, I had back and shoulder problems, and after flying through three countries, I desperately needed one. Jo headed out for a walk and to read a bit while I was gone. She was on the lookout for food and managed to find a vegetarian place to eat. Neither of us was vegetarian, but why not try something new? Wasn't that what traveling was all about?

I planned on diving on our first full day in Lisbon, so Jo was going to sleep in, read her book, and drink coffee and/or wine while I was gone. Lisbon's public transport options, however, had other plans. None of the buses to the dive shop showed up. I watched them drive in the opposite direction, but then they disappeared into the ether somewhere. This phenomenon was common amongst public transport in Lisbon and would eventually leave Jo and me stranded outside of town. So, instead of diving, I went back to sleep before Jo and I walked the city.

We didn't know much about Lisbon, but we knew the general direction we needed to go, so we made a beeline for the harbour. The Elevador de Santa Justa was on the way, and was one of the must-see things in Lisbon, according to all of the influencers we had followed in the lead-up to The Great Gallivanting. Apparently, it cost a lot of money to go up, but there was a nearby shop that had an elevator you could use to get to the observation deck. It was once a secret travel hack that had become popular amongst tourists. Well, that elevator was out of commission, and we weren't going to pay a ridiculous amount of money just to go somewhere we could walk, so we headed up a road that made its way to the buildings, and tower, above. We were able to walk straight out to the tower's observation deck completely free of charge, and, boy, was it a letdown. It barely crested the surrounding rooftops. Sure, we could see the castle in the distance, but it was by no means the best city view we could imagine. We were incredibly thankful we didn't stand in the queue or pay a lot of money to take the tower elevator.

After some fresh orange juice and wine in a nearby plaza, we headed to see the rest of the city, starting with the Praça do Comércio, the old trading square now populated with tourist-trap restaurants and shops. We wound our way around to the Castle of Saint George, which overlooked the entire city. Unfortunately, it cost too much for our liking to go in, so we just explored the local alleyways.

Much to my disappointment, we didn't get to visit many cathedrals in Lisbon. Almost all of them required a fee to enter. While I understood the need to offset the costs of wear and tear thousands of tourists a year brought, charging to visit a consecrated religious site did not sit well with me. Even if they weren't currently consecrated, the impact their interiors, scenes, and auras could have on people should have been the goal of their conservators, at least in my mind.

In our aimless wanderings, we discovered the Aljube Museum of Resistance and Liberty. This museum was dedicated to remembering the fascist Salazar regime that ruled Portugal for forty-eight years. It was built in a former secret police prison and torture centre and did an excellent job at conveying the horrors the regime perpetrated on its people. What amazed me was that Portugal was under a monarchy at the time of the regime, similar to how Italy was under a monarchy during the Mussolini regime. Yet, the civil servants, military, and national police went along with the oppressive state rather than stand up for their national identity. The monarchy was near-powerless to affect or inspire changes in a government that constitutionally required royal assent. It was also not lost on me that, over the past three weeks, I had seen a lot of anarchist and communist graffiti, including in Portugal, yet no one seemed to be raising the alarm about their harms.

The museum's top floor was dedicated to the fall of the fascist regime and the subsequent end of the Portuguese colonial empire. In these celebratory pictures from the time, the communist hammer and sickle were on proud display, yet there was no acknowledgement of the role the Soviet Union's communist revolutionaries played in bringing down the regime. Seeing as Portugal transitioned to a democracy after the regime, it may have seemed an irrelevant (or inconvenient) part of history to remember, because it had no long-term effect. I noticed, however, than the colonial displays failed to mention the ensuing civil war in Angola which was instigated by Cuba's Soviet Union-backed communist revolutionaries that it exported across the world. As far as the museum was concerned, the colonial empire was over, and everything was grand after that. I wondered if anyone there knew or cared that the abrupt end to colonial rule directly caused the Angolan Civil War which would last off and on until the early 2000s. Not likely. I left with a bad taste in my mouth with the selective history this museum portrayed.

Having had our fill of aimless wanderings in Lisbon, we made for the beach the next day. The beach in Lisbon was about an hour away by local train, but that didn't stop us from going the next day. It took us a while to figure out how to buy train tickets because all the physical offices were closed, but by mid-morning, we were lying out under the Portuguese sun. The water was still frigid, but at least it wasn't obscenely windy. We brought a box of cookies to snack on because we didn't know when/if we would have lunch near the beach. I may or may not have eaten the entire box on my own.

Getting back to Lisbon was problematic. We arrived at the station to board a train according to the timetable and waited. And waited. And continued waiting. We watched outbound train after outbound train go past, but none of them returned. They must have been going to the same place the buses were going the morning before. We were there for over an hour when we decided to grab the bus, which only came every thirty to forty minutes. Just as we were stepping away, the train pulled up. We ran to the train only to find it packed full of people. We couldn't even force ourselves on. There was no room. Apparently, every station up the line had people like us trying to get into Lisbon on the non-existent trains. The bus left during this time, so we waited for the next train. Luckily, it wasn't far behind and was mostly empty.

We didn't do much that night. Neither of us were party people, but the hostel had given us a discount on pizzas from their pizza oven, so we opted to partake. It was some of the best pizza I would have during the entire adventure across the world. Typically, hostel food wasn't the best, but this was amazing. Combined with 1 EUR beers and 2 EUR wines, we went to bed fat, dumb, and happy.

On our final day in Porto, we wandered around the city some more. There wasn't much that was overly noteworthy, and Jo and I talked about how we didn't understand the hype behind Lisbon. Granted, we were in our thirties, and most of the people we had met who loved Lisbon were in their early twenties, which probably had something to do with it. I had heard Lisbon had great nightlife, but I preferred a good morning café to a late-night bar.

At some point between our wanderings, we ended up at a rooftop café for lunch. The only reason we were there was because it was the only place open around where we were exploring. It was a decently cheap place, and had a set menu of a choice of mains, a side, a drink, and an optional desert. One of their mains was an absolutely delicious-looking lasagna. It was one of the best-looking lasagnas we had seen before (and I would argue since). The catch? It was a seafood lasagna; the meat was a locally-sourced fish. Even though neither Jo nor I liked fish, she gave it a try. I couldn't blame her; it looked really good. I have always been a picky eater, and wasn't willing to take a chance on fish lasagna. That turned out to be a good choice. Jo took one bite, and I could have sworn she was going to puke. She immediately came out with, "Nope! That is *very* fishy!" I couldn't smell it, but I would take her word for it. I actually felt really bad for her, because we were both quite hungry, but I would never admit that to her. This effectively ruined her next few hours in Lisbon, as it would have mine had I been subjected to that terrible lasagna.

For my part, I had my first ever McDonald's McFlurry while in Lisbon. When Jo discovered I had never had one, she was flabbergasted. She started messaging our friends, and the next thing I knew, I was under fire and having to defend myself. It was just McDonald's soft-serve ice cream, right? No! I had to try one, and we just happened to have a McDonald's on the walk back to the hostel. I don't remember which one I got, but I was vindicated. It was just soft-serve ice cream with a little bit of a candy bar sprinkled on top. Jo was adamant that they weren't "real" McFlurries, and I would have to try one again. Uh huh, sure, I said. (To be fair to Jo, I had a McFlurry in the Bangkok airport eight months later, and it was much better. They actually mixed the toppings in with the ice cream, so I conceded that they were good in a pinch).

Our First Budget Airline Flight

We had an early morning flight to Rome. We were leaving westernmost Europe behind. We had travelled exclusively by ground transportation by this point, and neither of us had ever flown on Ryanair, EasyJet, or WizzAir before, so we didn't know what to expect. Of course, people told horror story after horror story on social media and YouTube, so we were mentally prepared for the worst.

44

It never materialised. We understood that Ryanair was a budget airline, so we weren't expecting much in terms of amenities or comfort. We had to check our bags, but we knew we would have to do that on intra-Europe budget flights, so it wasn't a big deal. The seats were comfortable enough, and every interaction with the process and airline staff was easy. The horror stories were definitely overblown.

What irritated us the most were the customers on the flight. This may sound a bit elitist, but the people who flew on Ryanair were certainly not those I was used to flying with as a status-holding member with American Airlines. No one seemed to respect anyone else's personal space. By the time I boarded, the man in the seat next to me (I was in the aisle) was asleep with his leg under the seat in front of me and his arm hanging into my seat. I had learned not to be a pushover on airplanes long ago, so I simply kicked his leg aside and sat down abruptly (and roughly) to get him to move his arm.

I also wasn't a subscriber to the idea that one should stand up as soon as the plane landed, but, apparently, that was the norm on Ryanair. I was in the back of the aircraft, so I kept my seat when the fasten seatbelt sign went off. The man stood up, hunched beneath the luggage compartment, and stared at me. He told me to get up, and I just stared back at him and said, "No." Why would I stand up just to be hunched under the luggage compartment (like he was) when I could stay seated in a much more comfortable position? Talk about annoying.

But at least we were wheels down in Italy. This was the part of the trip Jo was looking forward to the most.

Reflecting on Portugal

The first law of travel. Anyone who learned science in grade school heard of Newton's third law of motion: What goes up must come down. After Porto, Jo and I coined the First Law of Travel: What goes down must come up! Walking downhill meant later walking uphill, and going down stairs meant later going up stairs. When we added our packs to that, we became intimate with the reality of this first law of ours. From then on, whenever we encountered a serious descent, we looked at each other before starting and reminded each other, "What goes down must come up." It was our way of saying, "Are we sure we want to go down right now?" Inevitably, we did ninety-nine percent of the time, but there were times when we made sure there was an elevator or escalator around before committing.

Instagram vs. reality. As our parents, teachers, and authority figures always said, you couldn't believe everything you saw online. In the world of micro-influencers and Instagram models, travel content was everywhere. Jo and I learned that not everything was worth seeing, and not all the "must-sees" lived up to their moniker. A lot of editing went into those videos, even the ones that seemed unedited, to make everything look as picturesque as possible. One of my favourite examples of this was the Liberty Bell in Philadelphia. It was a significant part of American history, and the centre which ran the museum really played it up. Ultimately, it was a major letdown. It was a bell with a crack in it in a room. It was wholly underwhelming. The same was true of the Mona Lisa in the Louvre; it was a small painting behind glass in a room full of bigger, more impressive paintings. After the Elevador de Santo Justo in Lisbon, Jo and I agreed that if we weren't interested in seeing a so-called "must-see" thing, we would skip it. We'd save time, money, energy, and shoe leather and go elsewhere.

Our last Eurail reservations. France, Spain, and Portugal required Eurail pass holders to make reservations in person at a local train office. This meant we couldn't make any intra-country reservations until we actually got there. As I described when trying to get to and from San Fermín, this could be highly problematic when changing cities every few days. When we arrived in Porto, one of the first orders of business was to book our train to Lisbon, because we didn't want to be caught without reservations again.

This was the last reservation we had to make at a train office, and thankfully so. Every other country we planned on visiting (in order: Italy, Austria, the Czech Republic, Denmark, Germany, Poland, Hungary, Ireland, and the UK) either allowed us to book them online or didn't require them in the first place. We didn't realise the untold amount of stress this relieved until we were booking our trains around Italy. We were no longer looking at trains that may or may not be full by the time we arrived at the train office. The trains we looked at and made reservations for provided us real-time information. After almost a month in Europe, we finally felt we were in control of our train-traveling journey.

Chapter Six

Italy: Budgets and Trade-offs in Europe's Boot

Italy was a significant point of discussion when Jo and I were planning The Great Gallivanting. We knew we only had ninety days in the entire Schengen Area, so we had to pick and choose what we wanted to see on this once-in-a-lifetime trip and what we would see on a subsequent vacation. For my part, I wanted to visit southern France, but I figured I could come back to Europe and explore that region at almost any time in my life. Jo wanted the same for Italy, and we seriously discussed skipping it altogether. We decided otherwise when a friend from grad school, Layne, said she wanted to meet up with us sometime in our travels. Italy was as good a place as any to add another woman into the mix, so that settled that.

By the time we were wheels down in Rome, we were only a few days away from meeting up with Layne, but that didn't mean we would sit around idle. We had an ambitious plan to see Rome, Naples, and two days in Florence before meeting up with her. If we thought we had walked a lot before, we were in for a surprise.

Rome

We landed in Rome around midday, and getting to our hotel was a long process. We had to take an express bus from the Ciampino airport outside the city into town, then walk for twenty minutes to our hotel. It was a straight shot but still a long way to go in the Italian summer. This was our first time staying in a proper hotel on the trip. Hostels in Rome were 50+ EUR per night, per bed, which was obscene, so we widened our search. We settled on a hotel on the outskirts of the heavy tourism circuit because it was cheaper when split two ways.

The hotel itself wasn't a brick-and-mortar hotel. It was instead a hotel concept. Individual people owned multiple-bedroom flats with large common areas and entered into an agreement with the hotel management company to offer up their rooms. We had all of the amenities of a European hotel, like private showers, dining area, coffee on demand, and daily room servicing, with the feel of an Airbnb. Sure, there was only one bed, but it was fairly large, so we had no issue sharing it. The hotel was also located in a nice area that had a supermarket and plenty of restaurants nearby, so it was definitely worth it.

After such an early morning and a long day of travel, we didn't do anything that afternoon. I took a nap, and Jo worked on making an Instagram reel about everything that she had brought with her. After dinner at a nearby restaurant, we turned in early. We had a long day the next day.

Our budget was seriously constrained in Rome. The American dollar was weaker than the Euro, and we were in an expensive city, even by European standards, so by the time we paid for our hotel, we only had 24 EUR left in our daily budget. Those 24 EUR were for everything: food, transport, coffee, entry fees, and anything else we wanted to enjoy. It wasn't much, but it would soon become a lot less because we were heading to the Colosseum. It was one of the modern Seven Wonders of the World, and, after talking it over, we agreed that we couldn't pass it up. And by "we agreed," I mean Jo convinced me. Even though we weren't too strapped for cash on this trip and could afford to go over here and there, I didn't want to make a habit of it this early on. But she had a point. We were in Rome and knew it was an expensive city when we went there. But who knew when we would come back, if ever? So, 19 EUR later, we only had 5 EUR left in the daily budget. Oh boy.

We set off early the following morning to explore the streets of Rome. So far in our travels, I had been the navigator and researcher, but Jo took over in Rome. She had a list of places she wanted to see, and who was I to question her judgment? Over our entire time together (both before Rome and after), I don't think she ever struck out when it came to seeing something. She was in her black dress and Mules (which I learned were a type of shoe), and I was in shorts, a polo, and a baseball cap. How the roles had reversed! I was usually the one in khaki pants, a polo, and brown fedora, and she was usually in shorts or jeans and a t-shirt.

While we didn't see all of Rome on this day, we certainly came close. We saw the Pantheon, the Trevi Fountain, Piazza Novanna, and the Neptune Fountain, all before lunch. The Pantheon we only saw from the outside, because just days before the policy had changed, so you now had to buy tickets. There were two long queues out front, one for cash and one for cards, and we wondered if the people queuing to enter knew that was what they were for or if they simply saw a queue outside and figured it was for the entrance. The Trevi Fountain was socked full of people, too, many of them trying to get that perfect Instagram photo or video with no one else in the background. While the fountain itself was impressive, all the people around really took away from the ambience. Even so, we got the requisite photos and videos to show the folks back home.

Our tickets to the Colosseum were timed-entry for 13h00, and thank God we bought them in advance. There were massive queues out front of people trying to get tickets in the moment, not to mention all of the tour groups that had arrived after lunch. There were so many people there, more than any crowd we would encounter ever again on our travels. It took us a while to get through the entry point, but we were free to roam around once we did.

Having walked the halls of Las Ventas in Madrid, we couldn't help but feel a level of familiarity in the Colosseum. The Spanish bullfighting tradition was likened to the gladiatorial games of Ancient Rome, after all. At the same time, it was wholly different. The Colosseum was massive, much bigger than any stone stadium we could have imagined. It also had an extensive subfloor network, where men, animals, and props once staged for the above spectacles. It was more like the film *Gladiator* than we could have imagined. And all built with hand tools!

On one side of the arena, there was an iron cross. Mussolini had erected this cross when he was dictator in direct defiance of the Church (there had once been an effort to erect a Catholic church on one end of the arena, but that had been put to a halt; the Catholic Church didn't like the image of being intertwined with blood sport). It amazed us both that the cross was still standing, not because of its relationship with the Church but because of its relationship with Mussolini. Then again, we were Americans, and in our country at the time, there was a widespread effort to remove statues and memorials to people and events that didn't reflect well in our modern, popular, revised version of history, so maybe that was why we were so surprised.

The Colosseum's hallways were a museum of various archaeological finds related to it and the surrounding area. Unfortunately, it was hard to enjoy, because there were so many people. It wasn't the number of people that made it unenjoyable; it was the tour groups. They would plow through the crowds following their tour guides, utterly oblivious to people like Jo and me who were also trying to enjoy the site. Several times, we would be studying a display to have members of guided tours shuffle in front of us to listen to their guide talk about the same display. This behaviour was regardless of the tour's language. Regular travellers knew that certain demographics behaved certain ways while traveling (if you know, you know), but we encountered this behaviour across the European continent. Wanting to stay with the guide was understandable, but not at the expense of others visiting the site.

The Colosseum was well worth the trip, guided tours notwithstanding, and our Colosseum tickets came with entry into Palatine Hill and the Roman Forum, a nearby archaeological site. We had no idea what a Roman Forum was. We assumed it was a specific place or type of building, but we learned a few days later in Naples that it was the name for the town square around which Roman cities were built. After a long time wandering around Palatine Hill, we finally realised that the whole site must have been the forum. Had we been archaeologists, we probably would have enjoyed it more, but we weren't, so we didn't. It wasn't that the site wasn't impressive; it was that it was just a site. There were very few information boards, and we weren't well-read in Roman social history (read: we weren't at all read in such things), so it was cool but not the coolest.

Our train to Naples was the next day, but not until the evening, so we packed our bags, left them in the common area, and headed to the Vatican Museum. Tickets were available in advance if we had planned that far, but we didn't, so we had to wait in a long queue. We waited, waited, and waited but eventually gave up. We didn't want to waste the day waiting in one place. However, it wasn't a total loss because we got a lot of trip-planning done. We made hostel, hotel, and Eurail reservations, and I got the final details on Layne's train to meet us sorted. By the time we abandoned the queue, we were in a solid travel position for Prague and Vienna when we left Italy.

After a quick coffee and croissant at a café next to the Vatican (the owner there was unashamedly preying on susceptible tourists like us who abandoned the queue), we headed into Vatican City. We were technically leaving Italy, but we weren't technically entering another official country, as the Holy See was only an observer state, not a member, of the United Nations (with UN membership being the widely-accepted manner of determining who was an official, internationally-recognised country and who was not). It didn't matter because it wasn't like they were checking passports. We wandered about the grounds, as the queue to get in to St. Peter's Basilica was insanely long. Even so, we enjoyed taking pictures and people watching.

There was still more to see and do before our evening train, so we departed the Vatican after a while and headed towards the Spanish Steps. They were impressive, especially with the cathedral at the top, but, at the same time, they were just a bunch of steps with a fountain down below. Jo got some cool pictures (she was much better at framing than I was, and, to be begrudgingly honest, the camera on the iPhone 15 could not be beaten). More importantly, however, before heading up the steps, we sat on the curb, and I dialled up Spain.

Why? Well, we had both followed Borja Jiménez (the bullfighter from Pamplona and Madrid) on Instagram, and he had advertised a special bullfight called an *único espada*. It was so special that we couldn't figure out what it was. We scoured the internet with little success. With what little information we had, we figured it was a fight where he would be the only (*único*) matador (*espada*, which literally meant *sword*, but was synonymous with *matador* in the bullfighting world) that night, meaning he would fight six bulls back-to-back. Jo really wanted to go back to Spain to see it, but I wasn't sold. I really wasn't sold. What about the rest of Europe? We had a notion to see Denmark and northern Germany, and going back to Spain would require us to totally rethink our path to Poland to see Auschwitz.

When traveling as a duo, you had to compromise, so I told her that if we could get tickets, we could go, which was how I ended up sitting on a curb in Rome talking in broken Spanish with a man in Cazalla de la Sierra trying to reserve tickets to the bullfight. This was the first day tickets became available, and we called as soon as the bullring office opened (because it didn't have a website). By the time I hung up, I was eighty percent sure we had tickets, and that was good enough for us to change course after Vienna.

What a turn life had taken in the last two months. I went from working in an office making six figures at a security company to booking bullfight tickets in Spain while sitting in Rome making no money whatsoever. Livin' la vida loca.

After a bit more exploring, lunch, and the best haircut I had ever received, we headed for the train station. Next stop: Naples.

Naples

Napoli was supposedly home to some of the world's most incredible pizza, which was why we went there in the first place. Italian songs in the United States glorified Napoli, which was why it was on Jo's list of places to go. Neither of us realised it was also home to Pompeii until we passed an enormous mountain with its top blown off. As we passed it on the train, I looked at Jo and said, "That's a volcano. Wait. Is that Mount Vesuvius?" A Google Maps check confirmed that it was. Score! We added that to the list of things to see.

We were wholly unprepared for what awaited us outside of the train station. As we exited, we weren't met with the stereotypical Italian city we had expected. It looked more like downtown Los Angeles or the old manufacturing district of

Boston. It was a modern, almost dirty-looking city. But maybe that was just the first impression. We headed for the bus stop out front to get to our hotel. It was a solid thirty-to-forty-five-minute walk, and neither of us wanted to do that after our earlier day in Rome.

But, as we learned in the military, we could want in one hand and poop in the other and see which one filled up faster, because the buses never showed. Not the first on the timetable, not the second, and not the third. I knew it was bad when Jo said, "if the next one doesn't show, let's just walk." It didn't, so we did. As we walked what seemed like the entire length of Naples with our packs on, we looked around and were shocked at what we saw. It was a congested, dingy, unsafe-feeling city. It wasn't at all what we expected. We didn't see many tourists headed in our direction, either. It felt off when compared to the rest of our time in Europe.

We settled into the hotel and began our internet research on what to see and do in Naples. We knew we wanted to go to Pompeii, which Jo promptly reserved for us the next day. I also wanted to go diving, but there was no availability, so we decided to head to a nature preserve instead. We would have to reserve tickets when they came available the next day because it was under strict erosion management, but that was fine with us. Anything for a beach day.

Pompeii was one of the top highlights of our time in Europe. Getting there was a mild pain, as it was outside of the city, but it was a piece of history we had learned as kids but never thought we would see in person. A long day awaited us ahead, but it would be worth it.

We didn't have a guide, which, we learned, was crucial, as most of the Pompeii archaeological site didn't have information boards. We had no idea what we were looking at. Somehow, we found a Rick Steves audio tour for download. Rick Steves was a world-renowned traveller and travel documentarian, and his company led tours all over Europe. This audio tour turned out to be one of the best things we would come across in all of Europe.

Rick guided us through almost the entire site, from the front gate through the Roman forum to the theatres and brothel. While some areas were closed that day (the site rotated which areas were open for preservation), we explored most of what was open. We had no idea that Pompeii was so big! Over 20,000 people lived there when the infamous eruption happened, and it was a bustling and vital port and trade centre for the Roman Empire. We could see Mount Vesuvius far off in the distance as we walked the site, which drove home just how huge of an eruption it had to have been. To cover the entire city from that far away with ash and lava to the point where it was essentially erased from history for centuries to come was almost too much to imagine. Fortunately for the inhabitants, they had several days' warning that an eruption was at hand, and around 18,000 of them left the city and survived. The 2,000 that remained were not so lucky.

And neither were we when it came to seeing the museum. Jo had always wanted to see the ashen figures of the long-dead Romans who were buried in the rubble. It was a picture we had seen in history classes in primary school, and there we were witnessing it all. Unfortunately, the COVID-19 pandemic adversely affected that. The museum was originally open-air and located on one side of the Roman Forum where visitors could see the artifacts on display against the backdrop of the ruined city. During the pandemic, the Italian Ministry of Culture moved the displays into the newly-constructed antiquarium, which was a climate-controlled, indoor museum. While a nice retreat from the summer heat, it was small, so there were fewer artifacts on display than we had anticipated. We still saw the ashen figures, but they just didn't have the same impact as they would have had we seen them outside on the site.

Despite our disappointment with the antiquarium, we had a fantastic day in Pompeii. We learned more than we could have imagined about Roman history and culture, and Jo made friends with a lot of cats (and I had the pictures to prove it). Even my hair-brained idea of walking to the harbour afterwards, which was much, much, much farther away than I thought it was, couldn't put a damper on our day after Pompeii. I even stripped down to my underpants and jumped into the harbour with the locals! (Jo was very jealous because she wasn't wearing swim-appropriate clothing under her shirt and shorts). We had a long walk back to the hostel afterwards, but we had just spent an hour or so watching the sun set over the Mediterranean, so we were in good spirits. We joked and laughed most of the way back to the hotel. By the time we arrived, though, we were done and ready to rest.

We spent the next day exploring the city. There weren't many noteworthy things to see, at least not to us. Sure, there were cathedrals, old monuments, and buildings, but the modern city had grown around them, which took away from the ambience. We did, however, walk through a local weekend market where we bought a 6 EUR collapsible cooler. Jo saw it and had the idea to buy it. If we were going to be spending time at the beach, we might as well have a cooler, and if it was garbage, at least it was only 6 EUR. It was highly sound, extremely useful logic. Plus, we could take the cooler to the bullfight in Cazalla de la Sierra. It folded up and fit perfectly into the laptop section of my day pack, which meant it would be no problem to travel with around Europe.

For lunch, we landed in off some random alleyway at a small pizza place. While waiting for our food, an old man smoking a cigar came out and started talking to us. He was seventy years old, had been in the navy, and spent time as a machinist in the United States. He was now retired and spent his days talking with tourists in the alley while smoking his cigar. Talk about a way to live! When he discovered we were traveling long-term, he asked if we were working while traveling. When we told him we weren't, he gave us the single best line of the trip: "You're G** d**** right! F*** work!" We raised a glass to that sentiment, which went a long way towards raising our spirits whenever we became down on ourselves.

Even though we were looking forward to the beach the next day, we couldn't go to the nature preserve. To make a reservation, we needed an Italian tax identification number, which we didn't have because we weren't Italian. Some websites would generate fake ones for us, but we didn't see an upside to committing a version of tax fraud in Italy, so we decided to just go to Mappatella Beach, the local beach next to the harbour. It wasn't too far from where I jumped in with the locals, and it was a straight shot (albeit a long one) from the hotel.

Mappatella Beach itself wasn't the most impressive we had ever seen. It wasn't dirty, but it wasn't white sands with coconut drinks, either. But it was local. There weren't many tourists there, and locals camped out in their lawn chairs and umbrellas watching the kids play in the water. The water was warm, too, which made for a delightful day. Jo and I took turns sunbathing and swimming (we didn't want to leave our phones, wallets, and Kindles unattended). We had brought our masks and snorkels with us, and there were plenty of small fish to follow around. We stayed there for several hours. After the cold waters and high winds in Porto, this was a dream come true for us. Swimming in the Mediterranean on our Italian vacation; it didn't get much better than that.

We had a moderately early train the next day to Florence. We wanted to get there and do laundry before meeting Layne. There was just one problem: We didn't have a place to stay that night. This seemed too much of an oversight for us to have simply forgotten to book a night, but it turned out that was what we had done. We knew we had an extra day before Layne arrived, and we had agreed in Lisbon that we would make a call on whether to spend that day in Naples or Florence once we were in Italy. The only problem was we forgot to make that call. No problem, though. We jumped on Hostelworld and booked the cheapest hostel with a seven-star rating we could find in Florence. All was well that ended well.

Florence

To say our first hostel in Florence wasn't the best was an understatement. No air conditioning, mute staff, and tiny showers combined with the toilets were not on our list of things that made for a good European hostel. Thankfully, it was only for one night.

What it lacked in amenities, staff, and facilities, it made up for with a view. Up a short flight of stairs was a small balcony that looked over the surrounding rooftops and into the mountains in the distance. We popped a bottle of wine and a couple of beers and enjoyed the sunset as it sank behind the town. This was the Italian city scene we had seen only in films. To still find this view in a city as large as Florence was a serene moment in a travel life of constant change and controlled chaos. I even video called my parents as the sun went down so they could enjoy the views from across the ocean. It was one of those small moments that could make or break a trip, and we were very happy to have had it to ourselves.

Through a series of miscues and not reading her tickets correctly, Layne got into Florence late the next evening, so Jo and I had the whole day to explore town. First things first, we moved to our new hostel, which was situated in a former Catholic convent connected to a cathedral. The convent had long since closed down, but the long corridors still had the same feel and ambience as it would have when it was full of nuns. Or maybe it felt like an old hospital. It was hard to tell. In any case, we dropped our bags at the luggage storage and headed off into the city centre.

It was a long walk to the historical part of the city from the hostel, but such was life when it came to visiting Italy during peak tourism season. We didn't have a tour guide or know anything about Florence, so we needed a tour option. We enjoyed Rick Steve's audio tour of Pompeii, so we tried his Florence city walk. I downloaded his app, and Jo had a pair of earbuds, so between the two of us, we had the full setup to enjoy our tour.

The tour started at the Duomo, the giant cathedral in the middle of the city. It consumed the cityscape around it, and we could see the large, domed cathedral anywhere we went. For this reason, the tour told us that if we got lost, "Dome is home." That would turn into a joke of ours for months to come, even though there were no more domes!

Rick walked us all over this historical city centre. We often paused the tour because we saw something that interested us. That worked to our advantage because it made the time go by as we awaited Layne's eventual arrival. We saw the baptistry where Dante Alighieri, the author of Dante's *Inferno*, was baptised, the site of the original *David* by Michaelangelo, the Loggia dei Lanzi with its statues immortalising historical and mythical scenes alike, and eventually the Ponte Vecchio, a large bridge and marketplace selling shiny jewellery which connected the main city centre with the neighbourhoods across the Arno River. It felt as though we had gone through the entire Renaissance history of Florence in a matter of hours, and all within a short stretch of road. And it was with a free app!

After lunch at a streetside pizza and sandwich place (ok, two places, because we couldn't agree on one), we headed back to the hostel to check in. Because of room availability and prices, Jo and Layne were in one room, and I was in another (this would happen again in Venice, only Jo would be the odd one out then). After a short nap, we went to pick up Layne from the train station. It was right beside our last hostel, so we knew the way.

Layne looked exhausted and exasperated when she walked through the ticket checkpoint. She clearly had been traveling overnight and all day. She had a large suitcase and a duffle bag, along with her carry on, which I wish I could have made fun of, but I couldn't. The duffle bag was full of stuff Jo and I had asked her to bring for us to change out. Little things like a pair of pants and a phone for me, and extra Tevas and some changes in clothes for Jo. I had the bus tickets on my phone, so after a short reunion we went straight to the bus and the hostel.

Jo and I played tour guide for Layne. We were experts, after all, after the day before. Layne wanted to see a few specific things, like the Ponte Vecchio and the Duomo, which made our jobs as makeshift tour guides even easier. After the touring, we settled into a rooftop bar overlooking the Duomo and drank a few cocktails. I had seen this place on Instagram, and it was pretty nice. Granted, I knew it was all over Instagram, and the prices reflected that, but it was worth it for the experience. At least, that's what Jo and I told ourselves.

They also wanted to go to something called a wine window. I had no idea what that was, but I also didn't know anything about wine, so that wasn't a surprise to anyone. Apparently, back in the olden days, people would serve wine out of these tiny windows in buildings. I didn't know why, nor did it matter. It was a wine experience that they were going to have. So, we (they) walked up to one, rang the bell, and ordered with the man who came to the tiny opening. When their wine was ready, the man rang the bell, and the glass appeared in the window. It was a bit gimmicky, but we were traveling, and Layne was on vacation, so gimmicky had a bit of a draw to it.

Rather than go out that night, we bought a few bottles of wine (for them) and beer (for me) and caught up in the courtyard at the hostel. We had all gone our separate ways over the past two years after grad school, so it was nice to catch up. Plus, Jo and I had been together non-stop for a month and a half. It was nice for her to have girl time (and for me to have alone time; I was a solo traveller at heart).

I turned in early, as was my custom as an early riser, but they stayed up talking for several hours. They stayed up late enough to enjoy the sound of the winds blowing through the trees and the screams of a girl getting her personal needs met somewhere in the hostel. Apparently, the latter went on for hours. Welcome to hostel life. Even in a former convent connected to an active cathedral, young travellers were going to do young traveller things in the shared room.

Our last full day in Florence was a special one for me, because we took a side trip to Pisa. Jo and I had talked about going out there to see the Leaning Tower of Pisa, but ultimately decided it was too far out of the way. However, my dad really wanted me to go get a picture there, because my granddaddy had taken a picture of it when he was stationed in Italy during World War II. Seeing as Layne had joined us, and we needed something to do anyways, we decided to take a day trip. I didn't tell my dad we were going, and had for several weeks told him how bummed we were that we weren't going to make it. I wanted him to wake up to a surprise picture of me in front of the Leaning Tower.

It was about a two-hour train ride one way to get to Pisa. Jo and I didn't need reservations for our Eurail passes; we were only limited by the tickets Layne could get (and what time she would wake up in the morning). By 10h00, we were standing beneath the Leaning Tower. Unbeknownst to us, the Leaning Tower was a part of a larger church complex, including a cathedral, large baptistry, museums, and high walls protecting the site. Also unbeknownst to us, because we had failed yet again to do any research, we needed to buy tickets to enter the cathedral, so while Jo and Layne took some cliche photos with the tower, I went in search of the ticket office. I followed the signs around the complex only to end up right next to where I started. It seemed to me that they could have just pointed the arrows in that direction instead of sending unsuspecting tourists on a long walk, but, at the end of the day, no harm done, although I was sweatier than I intended.

The Leaning Tower was, well, leaning, but it looked like it was standing straight if you got the wrong angle. We didn't come all that way to get the wrong angle, so we leisurely strolled the grounds to find the best shot. We finally found the best angle in the far corner of the grounds. Fortunately for us, most tourists didn't take the long walk around, so we didn't have much trouble getting photos. Jo wanted one that looked like she was taking a bite of the Leaning Tower, but with the camera angle, it looked like she was doing something much more... phallic. Not the picture she wanted, but a picture we immortalised in our shared photo album.

I, of course, wanted to see the cathedral. Layne was all in, but Jo's face said, "Really? Another cathedral..." Even so, she got some great photos from the inside. I wanted to examine the chapels, sculptures, and paintings to learn more about Christian lore and test my understanding of the symbols. While the inside was beautiful and impressive in its own right, the most remarkable piece, to me, was the old stand-alone pulpit. It was intricately carved on all sides to portray scenes from Christ's life. This pulpit was carved between 1302 and 1310, but looked like it had been made yesterday. As impressive as that timeline was, it was carved a full 200 years after the cathedral was built. As an American, I often forgot that timescales were measured differently in certain parts of the world. When it came to European history, time was measured in centuries, not decades.

As would be expected, shops and carts peddling tourist trinkets lined the streets outside the complex walls, as did restaurants waiting for weary tourists to sit down for an over-priced lunch. We took part in both. I bought a straw hat for 12 EUR. My brown fedora was great and had served me well, but it was too hot and humid to wear it everywhere. I wouldn't abandon it, but I it wasn't a bad idea to have the straw one around. We also settled for some pizza at one of the restaurants just outside the walls, mainly so we could have pizza in Pisa. Jo was all about the puns, and I would more than once roll my eyes when she posted them on Instagram. Somehow, I ordered the best Quatro Formaggi pizza of the entire trip. It was cheesy, salty, and delicious. Jo, on the other hand, ordered one of her least favourite culinary experiences of the trip, because, while I had many cheeses on mine, the one she ordered had none. It was all vegetables and sauce, and Layne and I had several good laughs at Jo's expense.

We headed back to Florence in the afternoon, as Jo and Layne had a whole night planned for us. We would watch the sunset at Sunset Point and then find a karaoke bar several people had told us to check out called the Red Garter. The weather was against us, though, and right as we unloaded the bus at Sunset Point, it started raining. It rained long and hard, and we spent the entire evening at a nearby restaurant, spending way too much money on food, drink, and dessert, waiting for the rain to pass. Actually, Jo and Layne were feeding off each other in ordering drinks, and I was trying to catch up with dessert, but then they decided to get dessert, too, and I eventually realised it was a lost cause trying to even out the bill. I was more than a little perturbed at the amount of money we were spending on a dinner that we hadn't planned on having, but, as Jo said, it wasn't often we would get to do so, and Layne was there for vacation, so there wasn't much harm done. That didn't help my mood in the moment, but she had a point.

Eventually, it stopped raining. Finally! It was a long walk to the Red Gater, but that didn't mean we didn't have a good time on the way. Layne had to pee really badly the entire way, and Jo did everything she could to make her laugh. It didn't help that we walked by two stories of a waterfall fountain. Layne had to stop several times from laughing so much on a full bladder, which only gave Jo more time to prod her on. I didn't think Layne would make it, but luckily, they were both tipsy, so she wasn't mad about it. She did make a beeline for the bathroom as soon as we got to the bar, though!

The bar was full of people, mostly young kids, and it took a minute to find a seat in the upstairs balcony. Jo and I had been trying to get each other to sing karaoke at some point on this trip. This would have been a great place for me to sing "Bat Outta Hell," but Jo swore I'd never get her drunk enough to sing karaoke. Despite seeing that as an obtainable goal, there was no way we were heading down into the madness. There was a wedding party, several hostels, and regulars there, each trying to get their turn on the mic, so, instead, we sang along in the balcony and drank the night away. It was a fun environment, and it had everything we could have asked for in a young person's karaoke bar: off-key singing, people getting kicked out by security for tomfoolery, guys and girls pairing off to wake up in a strange bed the next morning, and too-drunk patrons passing out at the tables. Who knows what trouble Jo and I would have gotten into ten years ago!

However, all good things must end, and the walk back to the hostel quickly became a bad time for all three of us. Jo and Layne let the alcohol and their dynamic get the better of them, and I ended up on the receiving end of ill-advised jokes and criticisms of the male species. At first, I tried to explain the male perspective, but it quickly became apparent that they were more interested in womansplaining what it was like to be a man than actually learning what it was like. I became increasingly irritated to the point of not wanting to be around them. They would stop periodically, and I just kept walking. Eventually, and admittedly with some intentional effort, I lost them and made my way back to the hostel. I was fuming mad by this point. Both of them knew my troubles with women over the prior nine years, both from friends and relationships, and I did not appreciate two people who knew better targeting me over those troubles simply because they had alcohol flowing through them. They were mad that I had left them behind, but I, quite frankly, didn't care. If they wanted to treat me like they were, they could find their own way back.

Hopefully, their antics and my reaction wouldn't be an issue on the stop ahead.

Venice

Jo and I laughed at Layne's expense on the train from Florence to Venice. Layne had a second-class ticket, whereas Jo and I had first-class Eurail reservations. We had a meal, an attendant, charging ports, and comfortable seats. Layne had none of that. We kept sending her photos of our experience in the first-class cabin and asking her what it was like sitting with the peasants (a joke Jo and I had between us knowing full well that the only reason we weren't in the second-class cabin was because Jo found our tickets on sale at just the right time). Layne got increasingly irritated with us. After their behaviour the night before, I didn't care.

Our hostel was in Venezia Mestre, which was across the bridge from Venice proper. It was significantly cheaper to stay in Mestre and take the train into Venice than it was to stay in Venice. It was only a ten minute or so train into Venice, the tickets were included with the Eurail pass, and it was less than 2 EUR each way for Layne to buy a ticket. I had learned this during my first trip to Venice in 2017, and Jo was all for it for the amount of money we saved. Just like in Florence, there was an availability and cost difference to the rooms, so Jo ended up in one and Layne and I in another just down the hall.

We got into town just before dinner, so we dropped our bags and headed straight into the city, where we planned to stroll the canals, have dinner, and enjoy a drink and gelato while watching the sunset over the city. Luckily, we could do all of these more or less in a straight shot, and we weren't in a hurry, so Layne and Jo took their time looking at jewellery shops. We also perused the Venetian mask shops, because Layne wanted to take one home. Neither Jo nor I had the room to haul one around the world, but we had to admit that these masks were intricate works of art that would look fabulous hanging on our walls. The locals regarded them as significant works of art as well, and they wouldn't let us take pictures of them. I got yelled at (twice) by a shop owner because I tried to take a picture of one. The first time, I had the GoPro out as we entered the shop and was putting it away when she yelled at me. The second time, I forgot about the rule and tried to take a picture of a fantastic mask in the shape of the Spanish Fighting Bull. Jo was annoyed on my behalf because, as she put it, these were undeniably fantastic works of art, but they weren't actual artworks like paintings that would end up in museums and hold substantial value one day. What were we or anyone else going to do, go home, create a forgery of these masks, and then pass them off as the real thing?

After dinner along the canal, we steadily made our way towards the southeast of Venice. This was pretty far from where all the tourists would be for sunset and was the perfect place to enjoy an evening to ourselves. Of course, I had been to Venice before, so I knew how far the walk would be. About twenty minutes in, I started to get questions from behind, but luckily, we were almost there. We only had seven more bridges to cross! It was a good thing I kept this information to myself, because we might not have made it had I been forthcoming from the beginning. Of course, just as what goes down must come up, what goes out must come back, which I may not have considered when I was entrusted to find a place to enjoy the sunset.

And what a sunset it was! It was just cloudy enough that we weren't blinded by the sun, but not so cloudy that we didn't get to see magnificent red, orange, and purple colours painting the sky over the cathedrals and city on the horizon. It was the kind of scene everyone imagined for their Venetian vacation. There we were, a couple of budget travellers who didn't even intend to go to Italy in the first place, and we had the scene almost entirely to ourselves. No people were walking by, no tourists were taking pictures and interrupting our view, and there was plenty of alcohol and gelato on demand from our waiter. Alas, all good things must come to an end, so we headed back to the hostel after the sun went down and the streets went dark. Travel days always took it out of us.

As fate would have it, we were in Venice on the first Sunday of the month when many museums were free. We weren't entirely sold on going to several of the free ones, but we kept an open mind and gave them a shot. Venice was an expensive city, even for a vacationer like Layne, so we added anything we could do to keep costs down to our itinerary.

Before the free museums, however, I had a surprise in store for Layne. She and her dad were both fans of *Indiana Jones*, and I knew she would be interested in seeing some of the sites in the film. The Library of Saint Barnaba from the third film was, in reality, the Church of Saint Barnaba. Well, the façade was, anyway. Inside the church was the Leonardo DaVinci Museum, which, while cool, wasn't exactly what she was looking forward to seeing. Regardless, we still got to see it and get her picture in front of it. Little things like this could make entire trips.

The first free museum we visited was our favourite: Gallerie dell'Accademia. This was an art museum full of pieces primarily focused on Biblical and religious scenes and themes by Venetian painters, although there were other historical scenes on display as well. The ceiling of the opening hall was fascinating to Jo and me. I was interested because of the four Old Testament figures on display. Jo was interested, because the centres of the ceiling tiles were dotted with circles. Ordinarily, this wouldn't be noteworthy, but those circles were actually faces. Individually painted faces. These creeped me out once I realised what they were, and I could not get out of the hall fast enough. Jo, on the other hand, loved them so much that she made them the background on her iPhone (although, I think she partially did that so I would have to look at them any time I looked at her phone).

This museum was fantastic for bolstering my knowledge of Christian lore. I learned about the travels of Saint Mark, one of the Four Evangelists and patron saint of Venice, the crucifixion of Saint Peter, and the execution of Saint Sebastian. I also learned much about the Annunciation, Archangel Gabriel, War in Heaven, and Archangel Michael. Interestingly enough, only Michael was actually mentioned in the Bible with the rank of archangel. The Catholic Church enshrined both Gabriel and Raphael (who appeared in the Catholic Bible in the book of Tobit, which I was unfamiliar with as a Protestant) as archangels; however, neither were mentioned as archangels specifically. One thing that was becoming increasingly clear to me in my travels was just how much Biblical history, doctrine, and lore were influenced by various administrations of the Catholic Church and not the Scriptures themselves. While this would have disillusioned many people I knew (who were already weak in faith and not committed to their beliefs), this really only drove me to understand the Bible more deliberately. Discerning what was written in Scripture and what was written in religious doctrine was a key point of contention for me with the modern Church, and one of the reasons I had decided to learn more in the first place.

After a quick lunch, we explored the rather disappointing National Archaeological Museum of Venice. The free section of this museum was limited to the Greek and Roman displays, which were both small and, to us, unimpressive. We moved through the museum in a single file queue with every other tourist enjoying the free museum just off San Marco Square. We left disappointed, but c'est la vie.

During our time in the museum, the infamous Venetian high tide took over the square. It had started before we walked into the museum, but it was in full swing when we exited, and San Marco Square and the surrounding walkways were covered in water from the canal. The café waiters around the square wore knee-high rubber boots, gondolas in the canal hovered just over the concrete walkways, kids played in the water, and tourists took photos and videos of something they had only read about. Of course, so did we, but as we walked around, we discussed how much of a concern this must be for locals living in the sinking city. When it was founded many centuries before, mass tourism, modern technology, and climate change weren't exactly a concern for a city that was a metre or less above sea level.

High tide notwithstanding, it was afternoon in Venice, which meant it was time for a drink. We opted for Ombra del Leone, a canal-side bar just down from Harry's Bar. We originally wanted to go to Harry's because it was a famous old haunt from Hemingway, but I knew from my last trip that Harry's was expensive, prohibitively so. Ombra del Leone was a great second choice, and it was just the three of us sitting under an umbrella, sipping our drinks, and enjoying the fantastic views of the Grand Canal as the water seeped up from the wooden planks and lapped at our feet. We were even visited by a few seagulls, with which Layne had quite the fascination (along with pigeons, for reasons totally foreign and unknown to Jo and me).

Surprising to those who knew me, I was a gambler, so we split up that evening, and I headed for the Venice Casino. I had been here before, so I knew the drill: pants, collared shirt, and passport were required. I quickly established myself at the rou-lette table, my favourite table game. I loved roulette, because it was the only table game where the odds would never be in your favour; they were established as 36-to-1, based on the numbers on the wheel, but they were actually 37-to-1 or 38-to-1 once the 0 and 00 were factored in (depending on whether the wheel had one or both). I also liked it because James Bond played it in painstaking detail in the first James Bond novel, *Casino Royale*. I had once adopted the so-called "James Bond Strategy" mentioned in the book but never found it lucrative enough to sustain long-term play at the table, so I had developed my own system which, more often than not, saw me walk away with more than I brought in.

This was not one of those more often than not times. The table beat me and beat me quick. Before I knew it, I found myself enjoying my "free" drink (it was "in-cluded" with the entry fee) at the casino bar. This was my second time in this casino, with my last having been six years before. Just like then, the Venice Casino bested me. Like any roulette player, I held superstitions about the game and the house; this house was not on my side. It had taken me twice, and I decided there would not be a third. I headed back to the hostel and straight to bed. Jo and Layne were still up and on their second (maybe third) bottle of wine of the night.

Despite Layne waking me up when she came in from downstairs, I was up early the following day. I found a lovely café to enjoy breakfast and a book on the history of the Catholic Church that I was reading. It was directly on one of the canals, and there wasn't much foot traffic, so it made for a peaceful morning. I texted Jo the location so they could meet me when they woke up, which, apparently, would be some time around noon for Layne. I was starting to wonder if I should start sight-seeing on my own as lunchtime quickly approached (maybe it was a holdover from my military days, but my mealtimes were on a biological clock), but they finally made their way into town.

After a short coffee break for them, we set off for what we would call our "In-stagram day". Layne had compiled some places she had seen on social media that were some cool places in Venice. We didn't have much of a plan, so Jo and I didn't mind checking out some of the niche places. But, first, Jo and I dropped Layne off at the Doge's palace, a large palace and adjacent prison that used to house royalty (and prisoners) in Venice. I had been once before, and it was too expensive for us to go again, but Layne was all in. We dropped her off like parents dropping their kid off for school (Jo and I were a few years older than Layne) and headed for the Café Florian, another of Hemingway's old haunts.

The Florian was situated on San Marco Square, and Rick Steves had an audio tour specifically for the square, so we combined these two into one lovely afternoon of sipping beer and wine at an Italian café while learning about Venetian history. Even though we were just sitting at a café with an ear bud in one ear, we had a great time. We spent most of our days walking, so getting to sit down for several hours while still enjoying a tour was fine with us. We also watched unsuspecting tourists get their first interaction with high tide. Jo and I were seated on an elevated walkway at the café, but most of the seating area was located on the actual square. As the tide rose, water seeped up from the underground system and started to puddle up around the square. One man got angry about it, and demanded an answer from the waiter.

The waiter simply shrugged his shoulders and casually said, "It's high tide," before moving on. The man was still angry about it, but what were the waiters going to do about this substantial architectural and engineering problem which had plagued the city for decades?

Once Layne was done at the palace, we set off for some photo ops. We found the narrowest road in Venice, which was only wide enough for one person to pass through at a time, which led straight into the canal. The narrowest road led to nowhere (unless, I thought, you were a criminal on the run, then this would have been a great getaway boat location). From there, we headed to the Ponte Chiodo, the only bridge in Venice without a railing. This bridge was technically a private bridge that led to Italian residences. A sign stated it was private property, but that didn't stop anyone from standing on it and taking pictures. As with all photogenic places, we struggled to get some of our photos as there was a semi-professional photo shoot going on with a group of girls. Welcome to travel in the age of Instagram and Tik-Tok.

Without much of a plan, we wound our way back to the train station through the side streets of Venice. We passed some beautiful cathedrals we didn't go in along the way, and I resolved to see several in the morning before leaving. Near one of these cathedrals, the Chiesa Parrocchiale, we watched the stunning sunset from a boat dock. We were in the northernmost part of the city, away from most tourist areas, and it was like we were the only ones in the world enjoying the fading sun, warm colours, and sparkling sea.

I awoke early the next morning to go on a church walk. I had two hours to see a list of cathedrals. I had mapped them out on my phone the night before to be efficient with my wanderings, but I was still pressed for time. I had ten, maybe fifteen, minutes in each Cathedral if all went according to plan, which it didn't. Some of the cathedrals were closed, and some opened at different hours than posted, so I called a lot of audibles in the plan along the way. I moved quickly, and I was sweaty and tired when I met up with Jo and Layne back at the hostel. All in all, though, it was worth it. I visited six cathedrals that morning, saw magnificent interiors, frescoes, and scenes, donated to the upkeep of the Church, and learned a bit more about Christian lore. Nonetheless, I decided to pay for the Chorus Pass, a 12 EUR pass to enter a collection of cathedrals, if I were ever in Venice again and enjoy a day or two delving into it all.

Trieste

Our next stop was Trieste, which none of us had heard of two weeks before. Layne was flying back to the United States from Venice, so we needed a nearby city with a train she could hop on with plenty of time to get to the airport (which, given her mishaps and miscues in meeting us in Florence, was a bit risky in its own right). We'd wanted to go to Dubrovnik, Croatia, but there were issues with the tracks which would have forced us to divert around the country. I found Trieste with a Google search, so we decided we might as well give it a try. It was a direct train to Venice that took right around two hours, had beaches, and was apparently a port of call for several cruise liners.

As I was up long before the others, I took a nap when we got to Trieste, as did Layne. Jo went on a date with a guy who questioned why we would visit Trieste of all places. She also explored the local area for us so we would know some things around when Layne and I woke up. That didn't matter much, because an action film was being filmed along the nearby canal, so we couldn't explore the local area very much anyway. Just drinks and a leisurely stroll until the nighttime rolled around.

We hit the beach on our first full day in Trieste, which sounds easier than it was. We planned to go to a beach called Dog Beach. Dogs plus a beach; what more was there to want? Sure, it was an hour away by public transport, but it would be worth it. It wasn't. Instead, the so-called "beach" was just where the land met the sea, and there was a sign that said no swimming except for dogs. On the one hand, we admired the sentiment. On the other hand, it was annoying, especially since we had travelled an hour to get there.

Much later in the day, we headed to Barcola, a Trieste neighbourhood with a long oceanside promenade serving as the local "beach." Instead of sand and waves rolling in, the stone promenade stretched for several kilometres and had metal stairs leading into the water. Beachgoers laid out on towels spread atop the seawall, and picnics dotted the park that ran the length of the promenade. It may not sound ideal, but the casual ambience made for a wonderful day in the warm Aegean water. It wasn't oppressively hot, the water was stunningly clear, and sand didn't get into every bag and crevice. Jo and I had our masks and snorkels with us, which meant we could have fun watching the fish living in the rocks. It reminded me of Naples, where the locals jumped into the water from the seawall, and I loved the carefree nature of it all.

Unknown to us then, Trieste was more than just a port town with a lovely beach (ish) scene. It was also home to substantial Italian history, including the only World War II Nazi concentration camp with a crematorium in Italy. The Risiera was a rice mill turned concentration camp located in the middle of a neighbourhood. It wasn't expansive, but that didn't keep it from committing abhorrent atrocities. The Risiera was first and foremost a transit and labour camp, but, being small and in Italy, it took on the role of an extermination camp when the need arose. Over 3,000 people were killed at The Risiera by the Nazi regime and its sympathisers.

The site had since been converted to a memorial to those who were imprisoned and killed there. It was free to enter, reliant upon donations and audio guide fees (which, at 5 EUR each, was more than worth it) for operations. Rather than restore the site to its Nazi-era looks, the memorial's architect decided to amplify the horrors there by removing certain things. The floors from the barracks, for example, were removed, leaving only the cross and support beams. It was an eerie sight to see this building both gutted and full, and we got a sense of how many people would have been forced to live in this one building.

The same was true of the crematorium. Like most of the crematoriums across Europe, the Nazis destroyed it when they withdrew. They didn't need the Allies finding evidence of their crimes against humanity and genocide as the Nazi regime fell. Nonetheless, the modern memorial conveyed the dread of the crematorium with a shiny metal plate inlaid into the ground where the crematorium once was. The metal led across the courtyard to a spire, symbolising the pipes and smokestack which led from the crematorium. It was a sobering sight, and, just as with the Deportation Memorial in Paris, it was difficult to describe the scene and aura of the place to others. It forced us to pause and reflect on what the phrase "Never Again" meant, especially in a world where "Never Again" was happening all over, from the Uyghurs in China to the Yazidis in Iraq.

We spent the rest of our time in Trieste enjoying the city, from the Roman theatre (which was still in use for theatrical performances and concerts) to dress shopping (for the girls) to visiting churches and cathedrals (for me) to enjoying a good beer, wine, and meal at one of the many cafés. I read somewhere that Trieste had been termed "Little Paris," and I found that an apt description for this hidden gem of a city. It was a fantastic place to relax for every sort of traveller, from the casual city-goer to history buffs to those who enjoyed water sports. It had something for everyone, and I would recommend it to people visiting Italy many times during my year across the world.

Before we knew it, it was time to put Layne on a plane back to the United States. Well, Jo and I put her on a train back to Venice at too-early-o'clock in the morning, but the sentiment was the same. Our ten-day stint with a friend was over, and it was time to return to being our dynamic duo. It was just Jo and me once that train pulled away, and we had a long road ahead of us, both that day and for the months to come.

The two of us returned to the hostel for breakfast before embarking on our fourteen-hour, three-train journey to Prague.

Reflecting on Italy

Rick Steves Audio Europe. To get this out of the way, neither Rick Steves nor his company didn't sponsor us, so our thoughts on his "Audio Europe" application were formed solely from our experiences.

Those experiences were beyond amazing. We discovered his application in Pompeii, and it became a staple of our European travels from that point forward. From Prague to Madrid and Berlin to Dublin, we always took advantage of these free tours. We looked forward to them because they were a fun mix of history, culture, and jokes. We would play them on my phone through Jo's EarPods, each of us using one. This allowed us to enjoy the same tour, pause and start as we saw fit (many times we stopped for food and/or drink along the way), and learn and see things that a regular walking tour guide may not even know. Whenever we met a new solo traveller in Europe, we always recommended the Rick Steves application to them.

Researching ahead of time. Jo and I were militantly against having a plan for our travels. Unfortunately, this bit us several times in Europe when we needed advanced tickets, especially in Italy. We committed several times to do more research ahead of time, but as our travels went on, the less research we actually did. We missed out on things, like the Vatican Museum, or found ourselves in places with not much going on, like Hammamet, Tunisia, later on, simply because we didn't do research ahead of time.

I would fall into the same trap many months later in Southeast Asia. Luckily, by then, I learned how to tour the region from a time-management perspective. I learned to theme-out my visits, so putting together a travel itinerary on the fly wasn't exactly difficult. Still, it induced more stress than doing a minimal amount of research in advance would have.

Introducing a third. By the time Layne joined us, it had been just Jo and me for over a month. We had become accustomed to our dynamic as a duo, but, at the same time, we were looking forward to having a friend join us to shake things up. And shake things up we did. The saying "three's a crowd" came to mind multiple times as I found myself on the wrong end of jokes and criticisms as Jo and Layne fed each other's energy. This was one reason I was glad to get out in the mornings in Venice and enjoy time to myself; it was time to both recharge and mentally prepare for the day ahead.

Jo, to her credit, recognised this in Venice, even though she was in a different room than Layne and I. Layne once asked her if I was tired of her being there, to which Jo replied, "No, he's tired of us together." Which was absolutely true. We all stayed friends long after that trip, but I told Jo after Layne left that I would not be traveling with the two of them together again. I just took way too much abuse as the only guy in the group (and as the one doing the vast majority of the planning). They meant it all in good fun, but, eventually, good fun turned into not fun, and we crossed that threshold for me really early in our ten days together.

Chapter Seven

Prague and Vienna: Hapsburg History, Soviet Influence, and Hyping Ourselves Up

Because Jo had talked me into flying back to Spain to see Borja Jiménez's único espada, we had a bit of trickery to get through when booking flights and scheduling our time in Spain. The único espada was on August 20th outside of Sevilla, but the best flights we could find were on the 15th into Madrid from Vienna, which meant figuring out the best way to spend our time before then. We eventually settled on visiting Prague and then Vienna, even though the series of trains to Prague changed in Vienna. That path entailed fourteen hours on trains when we left Trieste, but only a short hop from Prague to Vienna on the back end. We figured we would rather have one long travel day now to make things easier later than a series of short ones; even the shortest travel days took it out of us.

Prague

After a couple of hours in the Vienna first-class lounge during a stopover, Jo and I finally pulled into Prague at about 23h00. We knew Prague was a major party scene for young backpackers because it was a cheap destination for drinks, and that was confirmed the instant we stepped out of the train station. Our first scene in Prague was a guy carrying a girl who was passed out drunk over his shoulder to a park bench for her to recover (we figured he wasn't kidnapping her seeing as he was in a mixed group of guys and girls, but the thought did occur to us at first). Jo and I looked at each other and said, "Welcome to Prague!"

Our hostel was very close to the train station, much to our celebration. It had been a long day on trains and in a couple of non-air-conditioned train stations, and we were ready for bed. But just because it was close, didn't mean we weren't initially concerned when we finally found it. The hostel was at the end of a long, dark alleyway off one of the main roads, and the only sign was a giant, orange "HOSTEL" over the locked door. When we turned down the alleyway and saw this, I looked at Jo and said, "Welp, today's the day," meaning "today's the day we get kidnapped." This was a running joke of ours, and we weren't actually concerned about it. It did, however, make for a funny story later on.

While Prague was a cheap destination for food, drinks, and activities, it was extraordinarily expensive when it came to accommodations. Rick Steves even addressed this with a local guide in one of his podcasts. Being budget-conscious travellers, we had to take the cheapest room in a decent hostel we could find. In Prague, that meant a twenty-four-bed room. Twenty-four beds! Eight bunks of three beds each. At least it would be a story. We settled into our beds at the very back of the room next to the showers, with Jo on the bottom, me on the top, and another traveller between us. There was hardly any room for bags, so we kept ours locked next to our bunks.

Our first order of business was laundry. After five cities in Italy during August, we desperately needed clean clothes. We thought about pushing to Viena to do laundry, but all the laundromats there were ridiculously expensive (at least in our research). Besides, this would set us up to do laundry at the perfect time in Spain, so it worked out just fine to lose our first morning in Prague to laundry and coffee at a nearby café.

Once we had fresh clothes in hand, we headed off for our now-customary Rick Steves audio tour. We started at the statue of Saint Wenceslas, wound our way around to the Powder Gate Tower, saw the 600-year-old astronomical clock in the historic city centre, and eventually finished at the Charles Bridge, which led to the Prague Castle, the former seat of the Hapsburg Empire (even though his app is free I don't want to steal Rick's thunder by detailing out stops on the tour).

What stuck out to us during our tour was that the city, which was once under Soviet rule, didn't look very Soviet. A few places here and there had the authoritarian look of the Soviet utilitarian style, but not many. This would starkly contrast with Warsaw and Budapest in a month, where the Soviet influence was clear. How did all of the centuries-old architecture in Prague survive the Soviet age? Simple: luck. Prague somehow escaped most of the widespread strategic bombing campaigns during World War II, so there was no need for the Soviets to rebuild. To hear the locals tell it, there were only two bombs that hit the city; one didn't hit anything of importance, and the other hit a building that everyone hated anyways, so no harm done. Some even considered it a public service on the part of the Nazis.

Of course, just because Prague managed to escape Soviet architecture didn't mean it escaped Soviet oppression. Not far from the statue of Saint Wenceslas was a memorial to young men who lost their lives protesting the Soviet regime. Not much further away, we saw wall art arguing against a particular political candidate because of his communist sympathies. It wasn't lost on us that in a city where communist oppression once ruled, we didn't find any pro-communism propaganda. It may well have existed, but despite looking, we didn't see it anywhere. We not-so-silently wondered what pro-communism Westerners who didn't know any better would think about the opinions of those who actually lived under Soviet rule.

On the walk back towards the hostel from the Charles Bridge, we passed stand after stand selling funnel-cake-looking things filled with ice cream. This was the chimney cake for which Prague was known (even though it wasn't native to the Czech Republic; it originally came from Transylvania). Not one to pass up ice cream, I gave in at Jo's first suggestion to try the chimney cake. It tasted like it looked: like ice cream in a funnel cake. It was good, but neither of us was overly impressed. Not one to give up on ice cream at first try, Jo already knew I would get it again, so she found some places that supposedly sold the best chimney cakes in Prague for us to try a few days later.

As luck would have it, we found ourselves talking to a solo American traveller in the hostel that night. He was sitting alone at a table beside us, so we brought him into the conversation. The world was a small place, and we learned he had just graduated from the same university Jo and I attended for grad school! I wasn't wearing my school ring on this trip, but it never failed that we would find each other anywhere in the world. He was traveling Europe after graduating from university as he awaited a start date for his job. He was an engineer, which made him far more employable than me with a history degree. When he and others would ask, "What can you do with a history degree and international policy masters?" my answer was always, "Have an opinion!" Meanwhile, he would go on to solve society's infrastructure problems, maybe even put a man on Mars.

We explored Prague Castle on our second day. It was a long walk, but it was the same path the Hapsburg monarchs had taken to the castle to assume the throne. Centuries later, throngs of tourists followed in their footsteps.

We also knew that the entrance queues would fill up quickly, so we got an early start. Not early enough, we learned. Tour groups and families alike filled the castle walls at the various ticket offices. Not being ones for long queues or large crowds, we opted to simply enjoy the exterior and courtyards. It wasn't like we were being spoiled brats because of one queue. In fact, we found a ticket office around a corner that we could have walked straight up to the counter and gotten tickets in less than a minute. The problem was there were queues for everything. Once you got your ticket, you then had to stand in the queue for the church, and then the museums, and then the whatever else there was, because by that point we had given up. Even looking at the outside façades of the buildings was difficult, because, in addition to the long queues everywhere, young girls were trying to get the perfect Instagram photo.

We did, however, get to see the changing of the guard at the castle. We happened upon it, just like the Tour de France. It seemed like every castle in Europe had a changing of the guard ceremony at some point, and they were all equally cool to watch. They each had their own protocol, music, security, and rules, which we enjoyed seeing as former military types. The changing of the guard was a ceremony that temporarily compromised security while simultaneously drawing large crowds, so in addition to traditional uniforms and inspections, we also witnessed up-armoured tactical officers sporting the best equipment, firearms, and training. In today's world, a terrorist attack could be just around the corner, and a country wouldn't risk their monarch or heritage solely for the entertainment of tourists. To our amusement, we also got to see the guys whose job it was to keep the tourists from interfering on accident. "Stand behind the line," "Step back, please," "Excuse me, sir, coming through." It was worth a laugh; these guys wouldn't have anything to do if tourists behaved themselves.

After lunch and some exploring in Prague 6, a neighbourhood near Prague Castle, we headed to see something that piqued our interest the day before. During our audio tour, we passed something purporting to be the Museum of Torture. Gimmicky? Yes. Touristy? Yes. Cheap? Also, yes. Did we go? Absolutely. This museum was, in a word, concerning. It was designed in such a way as to be entertaining, not a major history lesson, but it was still quite informative. We learned about torture methods we couldn't even dream of, despite our direct confrontations with terrorists overseas in the military. Humans had come up with some astounding, sadistic ways to inflict pain and suffering on others since the beginning of civilisation, and some of the worst (or best, depending on your point of view) were on full display at this museum. Being the dark-humoured types we were, we compared and contrasted the pros and cons of each method, wondering which ones would work best and which ones would only lead to quick deaths or minor suffering. We may have left the military, but the acquired dark humour would last a lifetime.

Naturally, after an afternoon of pain, suffering, and torture, we grabbed coffee, desert, and read at a nearby café. Life was all about balance, after all.

We split up in the morning on our last day in Prague. Jo got a tattoo while I went to explore a cathedral I had seen and a nearby public garden. The cathedral was under renovation, so I only got to see so much of it. The garden, on the other hand, was an interesting experience. I hadn't realised just how much public green space Prague had until we started our Rick Steves tour. These gardens dotted the city, and in some of them you didn't even feel like you were in Prague. With every step you took inside the gates, you left the city farther and farther behind. There were cafés, vineyards, and even a law consortium in this garden, and friends and couples laid out on the grass enjoying the morning sun. I even saw one girl sunbathing topless in a bikini. One this was for sure: This certainly wasn't Central Park!

Now, we couldn't very well have gone to Prague without seeing the famed Infinite Book Tower. This was an artistic display that was all over social media. It was an optical illusion that made a stack of books look like it continued on forever. It was free to see at the public library, so we headed on over after Jo got her tattoo.

Like the Liberty Bell, Mona Lisa, and Santa Justa tower, it was a letdown in many of the same ways. There was a long queue that the security guys for the library strictly enforced. It was single file, and only one person or group at a time was allowed up to the tower so as not to block the walkway. The tower was also substantially shorter than it looked online. The term "tower" was generous; we would have called it a large stack. And the illusion was one as old as time. We thought it may have been something special, given the social media popularity, but it was the basic mirror trick: build the cylindrical stack, put a flat mirror on both ends, and watch as they reflect themselves for infinity. We stood in the queue for about an hour just to see this art display for about a minute and a half. Talk about a letdown.

What better way to overcome a letdown than ice cream? The answer: none, so we headed off to the Jewish Quarter to a place Jo had found to have one of the best chimney cakes in Prague. It certainly was! We were able to get a more diverse array of toppings and ice creams, which really made these so much better than the pop-up carts around the city. Jo got a fruit combination with hers, while I went for the chocolate version. I had to live up to my sweet-tooth reputation, after all.

Neither of us wanted to admit it, but we were worn out at this point. We tried to go explore some of the allegedly best gardens in Prague, but once we got there, we took one look at the hill the gardens were on and decided against it. We had walked a lot in Prague already, just spent two weeks in two-foot drive in Italy, and neither of us wanted to go up the hill at this point in our travels. Instead, we turned back, stopped for beers and wine, and spent the rest of the night at the hostel.

And what a night it was.

A couple of girls in our room went out that night. One of them (from Asia) didn't want to drink, while another (from Germany) wanted to drink a lot. Their compromise: They wouldn't go party; they would go to nearby bars, hang out, and the German would drink for the both of them. Drink she did. A lot. She was so drunk, that she threw up in the shower at the back of the room, the same shower that was right next to our bunk. Jo and I had long fallen asleep, but it was hard to sleep through someone heaving their guts out right next to our beds. We texted each other, making fun of her, because we had been there before. What thirty-year-old former warfighter hadn't?

When we woke up, however, the joking about having been there before turned into a horror story. The German girl had clogged the shower with her puking the night before, tried to wash it down the drain, and flooded the shower. Apparently, there was a depression under our bunk, so the puke water from the flooded shower pooled under our bunk...right where Jo was keeping her bag of freshly-washed laundry.

I was up first, saw the flooded area, was annoyed, and moved my bags to the common area to pack up for the day ahead. I had no idea there was a pool of puke water under the bunk, but I soon learned. When she got up, Jo found her bag soaked through in this girl's puke water, and stormed into the common area. She appeared in the doorway in her pyjamas holding her bag of formerly-clean laundry and yelled, "Are you f****** serious?!" Now, normally I would have made a joke, but her eyes were daggers out to kill, and I was not going to be on the receiving end of that. All I could say was, "Yep..." She was rightfully furious, and we went back and forth over whether to do laundry now or when we got to Vienna (not because we were arguing; we were just discussing timing and cost through her rage and me trying to stay on the right side of it).

Our hostel offered laundry, but it was a twenty-four-hour turnaround. I talked to the front desk, and they allowed us to do our own laundry in their machines. Granted, they charged us full price for it, but that was better than packing puke-water-covered clothes into Jo's bag. The guy that worked the night shift was a high-strung guy, so it shocked us when he didn't do anything about the entire situation. The girl that replaced him for the day shift, however, had me re-explain it all to her, and made sure the cleaners took care of it. She probably would have let us do our laundry for free had she been on the night shift or, better yet, made the German girl pay for it.

Ultimately, though, we had clean clothes (again), packed our bags in the common area, and boarded the train to Vienna where we could take a break at the first-class lounge.

Vienna

But not before Jo would lose her water bottle by leaving it on the train. While losing a water bottle while traveling was a truly annoying thing, it bordered on infuriating after her morning of puke-water laundry.

And that was how we kicked off our time in Vienna.

Our hostel was in an Arab quarter of Vienna, which was really lucky for us, because we rolled into town on August 10th. This meant nothing to us, neither of us being Catholic, but this was the Assumption of Mary. Everything was closed. Restaurants, supermarkets, even pharmacies. After a long day of travel and frustrations, we were ready to eat and having trouble doing so. Thankfully, this was the Arab quarter, so Turkish restaurants were still open. Not exactly how we planned on kicking off our culinary experience in Austria (but, we discovered, better than eating Austrian food).

Naturally, we kicked off our time in Vienna with the Rick Steves tour of the historical city centre, which was located inside what was called the Ringstraße, the circular road which formed one of the city walls during the days of the Hapsburg Empire. This guided tour was one of the least impressive we had taken, though not because of any fault of Rick Steves or his team. Vienna was just too modern when compared to other places in Europe. There were historic areas and a few interesting historical places, but, by and large, the city had been swallowed by modernity. What hadn't been swallowed by modernity had become tourist central.

Unimpressed, Jo and I headed off for the American Embassy. We had a professor in graduate school that had been posted there during the Cold War, and we just had to see it for ourselves. We knew we probably wouldn't be allowed in, and we certainly wouldn't get a guided tour of the areas where Americas diplomats and spies were hard at work, but we just wanted to get a sense of what the embassy was like.

The embassy looked bigger than it really was, which was basically a large building, but the standoff from the fences gave it an impressive feel. As Jo and I stood there talking about what it must have been like to work there during the Cold War (because it was essentially the embassy that handled affairs in the entire Soviet bloc), the local guard took exception to our prolonged presence and confronted us. We told him we were two Americans and were just admiring our embassy. He didn't tell us to move along, but we figured that was his implication, so we headed to lunch.

At lunch, I agreed with Jo that priority number one at the moment was finding her a new water bottle. We didn't think that would be a difficult task, but we were what some people call wrong (we would say "mistaken"). Despite being a large European city, outdoor stores seemed to be in short supply. We struck out several times before making our way back inside the Ringstraße to have a look. Jo wanted a HydroFlask, like the one she had lost, but those apparently weren't overly popular, so, eventually and begrudgingly, she settled on a Nalgene until she could find a HydroFlask to replace it with. Good thing, too, as I would eventually end up with that Nalgene myself after leaving my water bottle outside of a bullring in Spain.

We heard the night before from a guy in our room that there was a *Harry Potter*-themed bar not far from the city centre. Being a couple of *Harry Potter* nerds ourselves, we made reservations immediately, so after getting Jo's Nalgene, we headed back to the hostel to freshen up and change clothes after our day of walking. We figured it had to be a somewhat nice place if they required reservations. We weren't too far off. It wasn't swanky, but it wasn't a shorts and t-shirt place, either.

The bar was dark. Really dark. The walls were painted a deep green, and the candle-like lamps didn't give off much light. To get to the back, we walked through a wall of fog, reminiscent of the wall to access Diagon Alley in the book and film.

The drinks were *Harry Potter*-themed, and they called their menu a "book of potions." Being in Austria, their drinks were also expensive. Really expensive. We about had a heart attack when we saw the prices. But this was a place we'd likely never be again, so why not enjoy one? I ordered some rum-based drink that tasted a bit like perfume. I loved rum, but the taste wasn't exactly what I would have expected from a rum-based drink. Jo was equally unimpressed by her drink. Alright. We came, we saw, we conquered, we left.

To alleviate our disappointment, we headed back to the Arab quarter. Jo spoke a bit of Farci after her time in Afghanistan, and she had noticed an Afghan restaurant while we were waiting for the bus earlier that day. We knew the best food in the world could be found in the Middle East, so we decided to try that place for dinner. We were excited for the flavour explosion that awaited our mouths, only to find that the man had sold out of food early in the evening. Talk about a bummer! So, we settled for some döner kebabs not far away, but resolved to have dinner early-ish the next day to ensure we ate some of this delicious food.

Jo convinced me to go out and meet a girl that night. She had a date the next day, and I hadn't met anyone despite my efforts. I wouldn't exactly call it a night to repeat, but, hey, at least it was a start, right? I wasn't the only one going out that night. A couple in our room came in at the same time as me. It was their last night in the room, and it was clear from their body language that they were going to make it one to remember. At least they were quiet about it... more or less.

We were honestly at a bit of a loss of what to do the next day. Vienna had been, thus far, rather unimpressive to us, despite the enthusiastic audio tour the day before. There was another one focused on the Ringstraße itself, so we decided to give it a go. It would involve us taking seats on the tram as it went around the city centre and enjoying the views as Rick and his travel companion talked us through the sites. Easy and simple enough. We couldn't get seats next to each other on the tram, so we sat facing each other on one side, which meant any time we heard something interesting, we would make funny faces at each other. Was it dumb? Yes, but it was entertaining.

We took it easy after that tour. We had a 02h00 wake-up the next morning for our flight to Madrid and then had a follow-on train from Madrid to Sevilla, where we would spend a few days before the único espada. I chilled in a hammock at the hostel, reading *The Sun Also Rises* by Ernest Hemingway to psyche myself up for our return to Spain while Jo went on her date. Before leaving, she made me promise to pick her up some tandoori and pilaf from the Afghan place if she wasn't back in time. Well, she wasn't, so I did, and it was one of the best meals we had had so far on The Great Gallivanting. Was part of it our nostalgia about being in the Middle East in the military? Sure, but it was also excellent food. The man cooked it right in front of me. It was hard to beat fresh Middle Eastern cuisine.

When taking a vacation from home, a 07h00 flight wasn't exactly fun, but at least it was a sign of an escape from reality for a week. A 07h00 flight as long-term travellers, however, hit different. Sure, it was cheaper, but when we lived in a state of constant movement and exhaustion (whether we noticed or admitted it or not), dragging ourselves out of bed wasn't the easiest thing in the world. We arrived at the airport before the security queue even opened. Why we had to be there three hours ahead of time for our flight even though the security queue wasn't open, we didn't understand, but that was not my first experience with such a ridiculous thing, so it didn't bother us too much. As long as we could get coffee and breakfast, life would be good, Ryanair passengers notwithstanding.

In a few hours, we would be wheels down in Spain. We didn't know it then, but these next three weeks would be our favourites of all of our travels.

Reflecting on Prague and Vienna

Czech and Viennese food. One of the most common questions we would get on our travels was, "Which country had the best food?" Well, by this point in our travels, the answer was a resounding, "Prague!" The food in Prague was foreign to us, as we didn't have anything like the common dishes back home. For our first meal, Jo ordered svíčková, which was meat with potato dumplings in a brown vegetable sauce. It sounded as appetising as it looked, i.e., not at all, but it was by far one of the most delicious things we had ever tasted. We had it several times in Prague and on Czech trains later on, and it never failed to please. The same was true of the sundried tomato chicken, barbeque pork ribs, and many other dishes we had. Jo and I were shocked that Czech people could remain so skinny having food that tasted that good (indeed, we met a Czech man later who said, "Yeah, we are pretty lucky in that regard").

Compare that with Viennese food, and we were utterly disappointed. The various wursts and schnitzels we ate in Vienna did not taste good. In fact, the best schnitzel I would have would be several months later in London. Hence, we ate döner kebabs and tandoori for dinner instead of local food. It just was not appetising.

Karma. Jo and I loved to make fun of each other. If one of us tripped, the other would inevitably say, "Watch out for that contour line!" (a military joke). If one of us had a mishap with food, like Jo's fish lasagna in Lisbon, the other would make fun of them for it until the next mishap occurred. That next mishap, as it would turn out, was instant karma. No sooner would one of us make fun of the other would something happen to them. It became a hilarious joke because it ranged from tripping on cobblestones to falling down stairs. Eventually, as we became more hazard-prone as the trip went on, we agreed to cool it on the jokes. Not because we were getting mad, but because we didn't want to tempt fate too much!

And that was why I didn't make fun of Jo for the puke-water laundry or losing her water bottle. That was a lot of serious karma to rack up all in one day, and I did not want to see what sick joke life would have had in store for me had I made fun of her. She even dared me to make fun of her at one point just so she could get the laugh when life came back to bite me!

Social media models and our annoyance therewith. Jo and I often used social media during our travels to keep our family up to date with where we were and to share pictures of what we saw. Even though we were making a half-hearted effort to build an online following, we never let this effort drive our decision-making. If we got the cool shot, great. If not, that was fine, too. There were few things that we absolutely wanted the perfect shot for to show the folks back home. That was not the case for the vast majority of people we saw. From the Colosseum to Prague Castle, Pompeii to Santa Justa Tower, boyfriends were on Instagram duty everywhere we went. Girls were trying to get the perfect shot to share online of them in some dream location. While amusing to Jo and me, it was also annoying because in places like the Prague Castle, which was full of people trying to enjoy the space, these wannabe Instagram models were selfishly keeping the frames of their pictures clear of people. More than once in highly-crowded areas, we watched a girl or woman (it was always a female) ask someone to move out of their way so they could get the perfect picture.

Jo was great at framing pictures and even bought a camera later in our travels to try her hand at photography, but we didn't understand the obsession with getting the perfect shot. We wanted to remember what we had seen as we had seen it. That was part of the experience! Sure, we wanted the perfect picture in some places, but those were a rarity. We were annoyed and irritated at these chronically-online people who cared more about people-they-didn't-know's opinions than actually living in the moment on their European vacation.

Frustrations come out. One night in Prague, we finally had our first real fight. It took seven weeks to get there, but it finally happened. I was irritated that it happened, not because we were on each other's nerves, but because Jo had let it build up inside her instead of talking about it in the moment. We had agreed before we left to be honest with each other when we were having issues. We were in our thirties, not teens, and we could handle some criticism. At least, so we thought.

I could tell when Jo was irritated. I often asked if she was ok, only to be brushed off. As a thirty-one-year-old former military officer, I wasn't going to persist with someone who insisted on not talking to me when asked if everything was alright. If she said yes, I would take that at face value even when it clearly wasn't.

So, as we sat around drinking beer and wine at the hostel that night in Prague, I finally confronted her. I told her she couldn't keep shutting down and walking away when she was frustrated, irritated, or mad at me, especially when it was clear that I had no idea I had done something. She had to communicate because she was starting to make the trip miserable for me, and we were not even two months in. And communicate she did. The last seven weeks of frustrations came at me all at once. Some of them were valid, some of them weren't, and some of them were several weeks old. Even though we both felt much better at the end of the conversation (which was much more heated than I make it sound), it was in that moment that I knew we wouldn't make it the whole year. As much as we wanted to, and as much as we would try, it just wasn't going to happen. Sooner or later, we were going to go our separate ways.

Chapter Eight

Torero: Falling in Love with the Art of Bullfighting

Before leaving Vienna, Jo found another bullfight where Borja was performing after the único espada just outside Madrid, in a town called Colmenar Viejo. It was about a week later and part of the town's patron saint festival and associated bull fair. We went back and forth on whether to go for Borja's one night or buy season tickets and attend all five nights of bullfights, but we ultimately settled on being season ticket holders. More than anything, this made booking flights out of Spain easier. Ultimately, we decided to go to Sevilla with a day trip to Cazalla de la Sierra for the único espada, four days in Valencia, a week in Madrid/Colmenar Viejo, and then a flight to Copenhagen to continue on our trip into Germany and Eastern Europe.

That wasn't what happened, but that was the plan.

Sevilla and La Maestranza

After several hours of trains and buses after our flight, we finally made it to our hostel in Sevilla. We knew it was close to the city centre when we booked it, but we had no idea how close. We were across the street from the Catedral de Sevilla, the third-largest cathedral in the world by volume, and our hostel was connected to a coffee shop and café with outside seating. I would spend most of my mornings at that café; there was no better way to kick off the day in Spain.

Our first order of business was to find a place to eat dinner. As Americans (and someone whose meals seemed to be on a biological clock), we were used to eating dinner around 18h00, but in Spain dinner was typically around 22h00 or later, so really what we were looking for was an open tapas bar. I found a rank-ordered list online, and the supposed third-best tapas place in Sevilla was a five-minute walk away. It turned out to be a toro bar, which were bars in Spain dedicated to the art of bullfighting. All around, there were pictures of bullfights and the heads of bulls which had performed at the bullring in Sevilla. Seeing as we were in Spain specifically for bullfights, this really excited Jo and me.

We met an Australian named Luka in our room, and we all hit it off. We told him we were there to go to a bullfight, and he got super excited. He said he really wanted to go to one but didn't know anything about buying tickets or where they were scheduled. We told him about the different websites we had found, and he started his search for tickets. He couldn't find any that were both within a reasonable distance of his travels and at an affordable cost, but Jo and I had a solution: We offered to try to get him a ticket to the único espada with us. Luka was ecstatic and told us that he would definitely go if we could get him a ticket.

And that was how I ended up, yet again, on the phone with the guy in Cazalla de la Sierra trying to book bullfight tickets in broken Spanish. He told me they had plenty of tickets, but not in the same section as our original two. He offered us a ticket in the same row, but in a different section, and we took it. Jo and I agreed that since I spoke the most Spanish, I would sit by myself with the crowd, and she and Luka would sit together in our original two seats. Even though the único espada wasn't for another three days, we were extremely excited.

After our customary Rick Steves audio tour of the city the next day, Jo and I decided to see the bullring in Sevilla, called "La Maestranza" in the bullfighting world. We thought we would see it from the outside, but for 10 EUR we could do a tour with an included audio guide. That was a no-brainer for us. The next thing we knew, we were looking through a bullfighting museum, an art gallery, and learning about the history of the world that two months before we would have found offensive. We heard personal stories from centuries before about greatness and loss in the ring, were introduced to the safety changes that had occurred over the years (like protecting the picador's horse with a large, thick padding), and eventually found our way to where the toreros, be they matadors, peones, or picadors, staged for the night ahead.

The capilla, or chapel, was a staple of bullrings across the world. Once upon a time, bullfighting was inextricably linked with the Catholic Church in countries which practised the art, but the Catholic Church had long since prohibited conflating bullfighting with the Church. Even so, just as there were no atheists in foxholes, there were no atheists in the ring. The last stop for every bullfighter before the paseíllo was the capilla, and the room bore the weight of all of the prayers that had passed through it in decades past. Jo and I could feel the heavy burden of the bullfighters' thoughts and prayers as we stood in the small room before the Virgin Mary. For such a simple room, this chapel was one of the few places I had ever found where you could feel that people had been praying in the room. On the wall were three prayers etched in tile. These were here for the bullfighters to recite if they couldn't find the words themselves.

Like all of the bullfighters that came before us, our next stop was the ring itself. In our research about Cazalla de la Sierra, we learned that the ring there could hold 3,000 people. This was a far cry from Pamplona and Las Ventas, which held around 20,000 spectators. As we entered the ring from the ground in Sevilla, it was not lost on us that it was significantly smaller than both of those first-class bullrings (despite Sevilla itself being a first-class bullring). Even so, it was hard to imagine what it must have been like to walk through the gates into the arena surrounded by thousands of spectators. Like the bulls charging us in Pamplona, the ring was much larger in person. It was impossible to imagine how the bullfighters must have felt, especially when walking into La Maestranza for the first time.

As these thoughts crossed our minds, the audio guide dropped a bombshell on us: La Maestranza held 12,000 spectators. Jo and I whipped around to face the other with our jaws on the ground. We thought it would have been 5,000 at most. If 12,000 people could fit into this ring, then the 3,000-person experience in Cazalla de la Sierra was going to be, in a word, intimate. If we weren't excited for the único espada before, we certainly were now!

The tour of La Maestranza didn't have a time limit, and we were allowed to enter and sit in the stands for as long as we wanted. We took a seat in the shaded section next to the President's box and watched people explore the ring. We could hardly contain our excitement, but, at the same time, there was a peaceful feeling about being in those empty stands. La Maestranza was a beautiful building in its own right, and the golden-brown sand reflected the sun against the blue sky. Had we brought our Kindles, we could have sat there and read all day.

Before we knew it, the day we had awaited with high anticipation finally arrived. Luka, Jo, and I headed to the rental company around 10h00 (we needed to collect our tickets at the bullring office before 14h00), loaded up in a tiny manual-transmission car, and drove north to Cazalla de La Sierra.

Cazalla de la Sierra and the Único Espada

We couldn't have anticipated the day ahead. It would be the single most incredible day of randomness ever.

I drove us to Cazalla de la Sierra for two reasons: 1) my name was on the rental and 2) I drove a manual car back home. Jo was also more confident in my ability to talk with any authorities should we get pulled over or at a checkpoint of any kind. Our little car struggled to get up the foothills of the Andalucian mountains, but we didn't care. We had our eyes set on that evening's events.

As we pulled up to the bullring, we all stared in amazement. It was tiny. It was really, really tiny. Jo and I figured it would be after seeing La Maestranza, but we were wholly unprepared for how small it was. Luka summed it up perfectly from the back seat: "This is going to be intimate." Those were the exact words Jo and I used in La Maestranza.

We parked our car next to the bullring in an open field that doubled as the parking lot, just like open fields did back in my small Texas hometown for football games. The posters advertising the único espada were plastered everywhere. This was the event of the season for this town. When I approached the ticket office and told them my name, my poor Spanish accent must have given it away, because they had our tickets specially labelled and set to the side. I handed over 120 EUR for the three of us, and the lady handed me the tickets, a bit shocked that three English-speakers drove two hours from Sevilla for their tiny venue.

We couldn't help but open them up immediately, and we were glad we did because that was when we learned why we were paying 40 EUR each for a seat: we had front-row tickets! Our seats were directly behind the barrier that separated the crowd from the performance. We didn't know if I had unknowingly asked for these tickets or if they had taken advantage of us gringos who didn't know any better, but we didn't care. We were in for the night of a lifetime.

We picked up our tickets right around noon on a Sunday in a small town in Spain, which meant nothing was open. This was a day for church and family.

Unfortunately, we had neither as visitors, and Luka had to use the bathroom, so we searched for the only open place we could find, a bar called Círculo Recreativo Casino de Cazalla. I ordered some drinks, Jo grabbed us a table, and Luka went to the bathroom.

While Luka was in the bathroom, the bar started filling up. More and more people showed up in their Sunday best. At first, Jo and I thought this was just the post-mass place to be, but it soon became clear that something was up. And that was the moment that solidified our love for bullfighting.

Borja Jiménez walked through the door.

We knew he was doing a meet-and-greet somewhere but had no idea it was there! Luka saw him, too, and when he returned, he exclaimed, "You have to get a picture with him!" We certainly did! Jo wore the dress she bought in Trieste with Layne in case this opportunity arose, and she was turning several shades of red!

After his roundtable discussion in the back room was over (we didn't attend because 1) we didn't know if we were allowed and 2) we wouldn't have been able to understand what they were saying), I found my way to Borja and told him we were Americans (sorry, Luka!) who had flown from Vienna to see this event. He was surprised to hear that, said "gracias" a thousand times, and asked if we wanted a photo with him. Absolutely! I waved Jo and Luka over, and we took several of the three of us and even a few of just him and Jo. We wished him good luck, and then he headed out. As did we. We saw a restaurant we wanted to try for lunch on the walk in, and we were way too excited to keep sitting there after he was gone. I joked that we might as well start calling Jo "Lady Brett Ashley" (from *The Sun Also Rises*) because she fell in love with a bullfighter!

We walked past the restaurant La Agustina on our way to the bar and saw a sign on the door that indicated it earned a Michelin Star that year. A bit sceptical, I looked on the Michelin website, and it did, so we decided to try it. Was this day quickly getting outside of our budget? Sure, but it had been worth it so far. Luka and I both got the special, pork ribs, which cost us about 25 EUR each, and they were some of the best ribs I had ever eaten, even when compared to those in Texas or Prague. Luka worked in a butcher shop in Australia and said he had never eaten meat that tasted that good. He also couldn't believe the price. The Australian dollar was a weak currency compared to the Euro, but Australian inflation kept up with the West, so everything there was expensive. He could have easily spent 25 EUR in Australia and gotten a terrible meal.

With several hours to kill before heading to the bullring, we wandered the town before settling at the local fairgrounds to drink with the locals. When Luka's round came up, I went with him to translate our order of two beers and a tinto de verano. The total cost? Less than 7 EUR. Luka looked offended and asked me, "Seven Euros? For what?!" I thought he was upset that it cost so much, so I told him it was for our three drinks. That's when I learned his shock was for the opposite reason. "Seven Euros? For all of this?!" I said, "Yes...," a bit sceptical of where this was going, and he blurted out, "I'm moving here!" Apparently, a single beer in Australia could cost 8 EUR!

At about 17h30, the town steadily made its way south towards the bullring. We joined in (granted, we were a bit early) and settled into our seats. It was lucky we got there early, too, because my seat was a point of contention with the men around me. That seat was usually given to someone else. I didn't care and showed them my ticket, indicating it was my seat. I understood they were locals and had their way of doing things, but we had flown halfway across Europe to see this, and I wasn't going to miss being in the front row.

I did, however, give in somewhat. An old man had trouble getting up the stairs, and he asked if he could squeeze in next to me. Sure. I figured, why not? If all else failed, it wasn't like heading up to the top row would impact the view; there were only about twenty rows in total. This old man had clearly seen decades' worth of bullfights in his time. He watched with an intensity in his eyes that told just how well-versed he was in the performance. As he watched throughout the night, he would reach for his cigarettes in his breast pocket and light them up without ever taking his eyes off the performance before him. This was an integral part of his culture and life in Andalusia, regardless of what some protestors or politicians might believe.

At 18h30, the moment finally arrived. The paseíllo entered directly to my left, marched to the centre of the ring, turned right and saluted the president. It was a short procession, given the size of the ring, but it was one of the most important ceremonial aspects of any bullfight. At the head were the Alguacilillos, the President's representatives and enforcers, one man and one woman dressed in a traditional Spanish riding suit instead of the long black robes we had seen in Pamplona and Las Ventas. The woman was stunningly beautiful, a local business owner and creative, and was every bit of the stereotypical Spanish beauty. I lost a part of my heart seeing her riding side-saddle with her flat-brimmed hat cocked slightly to the side. Jo could see from her seats in another section that she was just my type, and she made fun of me with a few texts.

But we were there to see Borja Jiménez, el único espada de la noche. And what a performance this night was! We had seen Borja do well and not so well during our last two bullfights, but those were prime-time performances where he only fought two bulls in a night. He could rest in between, evaluate, critique, and improve his performance, and observe the other bulls from the ranch to glean some insight into their temperament. That was not the case in Cazalla de la Sierra. He was taking on six in a row with little break in between. Any critique or observations would be made and applied on the fly and in the moment. If he did well, he didn't have time to rest on his laurels; if he did poorly, he didn't have time to beat himself up. The next bull would already be on its way.

The corrals were directly to my left; my seat was the last in the row, so the bulls charged into the arena right next to me. Much of the opening work with the capote happened directly in front of me, with the bulls being within arm's reach on several occasions. One of the four barriers behind which the toreros sought safety was just to my right, and I got an up-close glimpse of what happened in the ring. Jo and Luka, while also in the front row, were directly across from the President's box, so they didn't get to see as much of the up-close action as I did.

Borja's performance that night ranged from excellent to poor, depending on which tercio of which bull he was facing. This was an incredibly eye-opening and knowledge-building event for us. We watched this matador test himself and his skills over three hours of non-stop action. We quickly learned what would constitute a good pass with the capote and what would frustrate the bullfighter in the ring. Sometimes, he misstepped, and we could see the frustration with himself written on his face. Sometimes, he excelled, and we could see the triumph radiating from his traje de luces. It was a roller coaster of a night for three foreigners new to the performance, and we loved every second.

Being so close to the action, we could hear every word the toreros said to each other in the ring. Even though Borja was the only matador performing that night, two others were in reserve, along with their teams, to support Borja over the night. And it was a team event. Jo and I didn't realise just how integral the teams were to the performance until that night, and Borja had to control three different ones throughout his performance, two of which were not his own. We got to see the older subalternos, several of which were former matadors themselves, offering their advice and observations, Borja controlling the bull in concert with the picadors, and how the three different teams ultimately worked together towards ensuring the safety and success of the matador in the ring. Over the following months, as Jo and I delved deeper and deeper into the world of Spanish bullfighting, we would learn that what made the difference between a great and an excellent matador wasn't his ability to perform with the bull but his ability to perform with his team. Many great matadors could work the bull, but we would only ever witness a few that could work with their team as well as Borja did.

On his last bull of the night, Borja was exhausted. He had been pouring sweat all evening and quickly approached his last estocada of the night. He had cut several ears, and this last bull was especially challenging for him compared to the others. He performed excellently, demonstrating finesse with each pass and excellent control over the bull. We were sure he would cut at least one ear from this bull, if not two.

We didn't expect to see him get thrown into the air. On his last bull of the evening, as he charged forward for the estocada, the bull hooked under him and tossed him through the air as the estoque sunk between the bull's shoulder blades. One of his shoes went flying as he hit the ground and rolled away from the bull, and the peones jumped into action to distract the bull from the fallen matador. We were sure he was about to be carried off to the infirmary, a pointed reminder of the deadliness of the performance as a punctuation mark at the end of the night.

Fortunately, Borja was unharmed. The horn had hooked under his arm, so while he was caught and thrown, he wasn't gored. He hopped to his feet, kicked off his remaining shoe, and stood victorious over the bull as it quickly faded away. The crowd roared with applause, both for Borja and the bull, as both had put on a spectacular performance. The ovation lasted several minutes. After the first ear was awarded, the ovation became even louder as the crowd demanded a second. The second was entirely up to the President's discretion, and, after a bit of consideration, he awarded it, much to the crowd's pleasure. But the crowd grew even louder! It demanded that the tail be awarded as the team of mules prepared to enter the ring to drag the bull away. One of the peones, a man named Daniel Duarte, was grabbing the tail and gesturing to the crowd and the President, indicating that he thought it should be awarded. As the crowd's protests continued, the President finally flipped the third white handkerchief over the side of his box. The tail had been awarded! The crowd went insane.

The tail was less of an acknowledgement of his performance in that last faena than a celebration of his accomplishment as a matador. Borja had completed his first ever único espada, a testament to his skill and dedication as a bullfighter. This was a milestone in every celebrity-level bullfighter's career, and Borja had joined their ranks with a final estocada and flight through the air.

But it wasn't just Borja's doing. As the final bull was dragged out of the ring, the crowd applauded its bravery and courage in the face of certain death. This would become one of my favourite parts of the art of bullfighting; the crowd respected and celebrated the bull just as much as the matador.

As Borja took his celebratory lap around the ring, he passed directly in front of me. I tossed my hat into the ring in celebration, something common at bullfights even if it was technically illegal. One of the peones picked it up and handed it to him, and he threw it back to me, leaving a bloody handprint on the white straw in the process. I never wiped the handprint away, and its rust-stained impression would be cause for storytelling across the world.

With the bullfight over and the crowd thinning out, I reunited with Jo and Luka. Luka was ecstatic, and Jo and I were excited that he got to witness such a fantastic night as his first bullfight. Before we left, I asked one of the attendants if we could see the capilla, to which he eagerly agreed. The capilla was small and simple, just like the one we had seen at La Maestranza, but we could still feel the weight of the prayers from bullfighters past in the air. God Almighty had indeed smiled upon Borja Jiménez that night.

After the amazing performance in Cazalla de la Sierra and all of my jokes about her being Lady Brett Ashley, Jo wanted to watch *The Sun Also Rises* to see what the joke was all about. Our hostel had a film room downstairs, so we loaded up on snacks and drinks, turned on YouTube, and settled in for one of the greatest commentaries on the Lost Generation in the context of bullfighting ever committed to film. It only made us even more excited to see yet another performance and to delve deeper into this Spanish cultural art.

We spent one more day in Sevilla after the único espada, visiting the Plaza España and watching a flamenco performance, but after the único espada, we had stars in our eyes and our sights set on the next set of performances in Colmenar Viejo in a few days.

But first, we were headed to Valencia.

Valencia and a Change of Plan

Jo and I deliberately skipped southern Spain the last time we were there. We had too much to see in Europe, so we were on a highlight tour. Since we were going to watch more bullfights and had the time anyway, I told her I wanted to spend the few days between them in Valencia. She took no convincing. Even though there weren't any bullfights in Valencia at the time, it was still a historic Spanish town with a rich history of corridas de toros. Plus, it was by the ocean, so I could spend some time in the water.

We got into town late, and there was a SNAFU (military jargon for a screw up) with the room at the hostel, so we ended up in a bigger room than we wanted, but we also were given complimentary breakfast as a part of our stay, so it all evened out. We also got to meet some awesome people from all over the world. During our stay, we formed a large, diverse group of friends from around the world that hung out together. We took paella cooking lessons and walking tours and drank Agua de Valencia (a local alcoholic drink) underneath the stairs at a local bar.

I, of course, went diving for two days, which was a good time even though there was a language barrier. My Spanish was apparently good enough because the owner told his partner, "El entiende" ("he understands") when she was concerned I didn't know what she was saying. I didn't know exactly what she was saying, but I got the gist of all of their instructions. I really got the gist when someone did something they weren't supposed to (like the new divers who didn't take the basic safety precautions inherent in every dive).

At some point along the way, we discovered OneToro TV. This was a subscription streaming service dedicated exclusively to bullfighting. From documentaries to films to live events, if you were an aficionado, you could certainly get your fill with OneToro TV. Jo and I decided to give it a try for thirty days, because you could watch a live event for up to a week after it aired, and they often played reruns of individual faenas and entire events. So, every day when I returned from diving, we headed to the 100 Montaditos for cheap drinks and food, turned on OneToro TV on my phone, and watched whichever bullfights were on demand. We were able to watch both of the ones we had seen originally in Pamplona and Madrid, which, now that we understood what we were seeing, we were able to appreciate with the new perspective gained from the único espada a few days before.

Valencia had a large bullring a good walk away from our hostel. After touring La Maestranza in Madrid, we developed a fascination with the architecture and history of the rings as a component of bullfighting. Each had a unique story to tell, and we were eager to listen. Unfortunately, the bullring was under renovation, so we couldn't visit. Not even the museum was open. As we would later learn, August was the best time for such things, as it was the traditional vacation month in Spain. Shops literally locked their doors and posted signs that said the equivalent of "Back in One Month." A bit bummed that we couldn't tour the ring, we did the next best thing and headed off to 100 Montaditos and OneToro TV.

Were we obsessed at this point? Maybe. Did we care? Not at all.

One day, while I was away, Borja announced two more bullfights shortly after the ones we would see in Colmenar Viejo. One was in Illescas, a town about forty-five minutes outside of Madrid in the province of Toledo, and the other was in Utrera, about thirty minutes outside of Sevilla. Both of these were after our flights from Madrid to Copenhagen. Jo wanted to go, but I put my foot down. We had tickets, and I didn't want to spend all of our short time in Europe in Spain, but she countered and told me I could still go, and we could meet up again later. That wasn't precisely true, seeing as we had booked our tickets together. If one of us changed our flights, we both had to change. Otherwise, she would have to eat the cost of her ticket and get a new one.

We went to bed that night at an impasse. I was adamant about going to Copenhagen, but she really wanted to continue going to the bullfights as long as they were all right next to each other. Unable to sleep, I spent hours that night searching for the best flight options and shaping our post-Spain itinerary should I agree to change the tickets. I found a flight from Málaga to Nuremburg for which we would only have to pay the change fee. From there, we could train to Berlin and continue our trip through Eastern Europe.

I brought it up to her the next day, and she jumped on it. I really put my foot down that time, though. Come Hell or high water, we were getting on that plane in Málaga. She consented, and that was that. I had to admit, I was looking forward to Illescas and Utrera now that we had them on the itinerary. We hopped online, bought our tickets, booked our hostels, and were all set for an extra week in what had become our favourite European country.

All because of one bullfighter!

Colmenar Viejo and Season Tickets

We had a fast-paced first day of the fair in Colmenar Viejo. Our train arrived in Madrid a little before lunch on the first day of the fair, and we had a lot to do in a short time. Our first stop was to drop our bags at the hostel. It wasn't check-in time yet, but we had places to be. We headed to the tourism office to purchase the province-wide travel pass for Madrid, which would give us five days of unlimited travel on public transport around the province. This was essential in getting to and from Colmenar Viejo. It was about an hour outside of town by public bus, and it left every day at 16h30, which would put us at the bullring in Colmenar Viejo about thirty minutes before the doors opened.

Well, it turned out that the tourism office didn't sell those passes; we had to obtain them at one of the ticket machines at a metro stop. We made a beeline for the nearest metro line and bought the passes. We had a quick lunch outside Plaza Mayor (where the tourism office was located), returned to the hostel, and moved into our room. We changed clothes, me out of shorts and into khaki pants and Jo out of shorts and into one of the 10 EUR dresses she bought in Valencia, and headed to the nearest convenience store. Thanks to Jo's foresight, we had purchased a cooler in Italy, so now all we needed was alcohol. Our provisions secured, we loaded up the cooler, sweaters (we always took them to night events because even in the summer it could get chilly outside), and external battery packs, and made for the bus station (via the metro). Before we knew it, we stood outside the Plaza de Toros de Colmenar Viejo.

There were five nights of bullfights planned for the patron saint festivities in Colmenar Viejo. The first night was a *novillada con picadores*. A novillada con picadores was the junior varsity of bullfighting. These young matadors (called novilleros) faced novillos, bulls that were between two and four years old. All of the elements of the bullfight were the same except for the age of the bulls. The novilleros hoped to become full-fledged matadors someday, and their performance reflected that drive. Even though the bulls were younger and smaller, Jo and I both thought they were more aggressive, probably owing to their age. The same could be said of the novilleros. While they hadn't perfected the art of working the capote and muleta, we could tell they were leaving everything they had in the ring. They had coaches and managers behind the barrera (the barrier that encircled the performance part of the ring) who constantly coached them on their performance. These coaches and managers had been involved in the world of bullfighting for decades, and they knew their stuff. Most of the novilleros listened, desperate to improve their skill and achieve their dream of one day performing at Las Ventas in Madrid. All in all, the novillada con picadores was a fantastic night. Even though the bulls were smaller and the novilleros less experienced, it was a part of bullfighting that we had never seen before. There were no disasters or visits to the infirmary, and we could tell that one of these novilleros was going to be a star someday.

On the bus back to Madrid, we met an Australian couple on their honeymoon. They were traveling Europe and decided to go to a bullfight while in Spain. We asked them what they thought, and they said it differed from what they expected. They, like us months before, expected some grotesque horror-scape of torture and bloodshed, but that was not at all what they experienced. Even though parts of the night were hard to watch, they walked away with a greater appreciation for the Spanish artform. This was when Jo and I told them they hadn't seen a proper bullfight. They were shocked to learn that there were different kinds, and we brought them into the fold. We were quickly becoming card-carrying aficionados!

The rest of the fair's schedule was as follows:

- Second night: traditional bullfight
- Third night: *Rejoneo* (horse-mounted bullfight) and traditional bullfight
- Fourth night: Traditional bullfight
- Fifth night: *Novillada sin picadores* (which I will explain)

Borja performed on the second night of the fair. Jo wore her favourite of the four dresses she bought in Valencia, and we tried to shake his hand and get a picture with him as he walked into the bullring. When he finally arrived, he walked right in front of us, but Jo got stage fright. She couldn't bring herself to walk up to him and ask for a picture. Oh well, there would be two more opportunities over the next week.

Borja performed as well as could have been expected that night. The bulls were not at all aggressive, and they challenged the matadors when it came to showing off the bulls' qualities and demonstrating their knowledge of bullfighting performance. MundoToro, the primary bullfighting news site, would refer to the night as a "cattle disaster," and Jo and I commented both in the moment and after reading the news that the ranch owners must have been incredibly embarrassed. Nonetheless, Borja kept his cool. Jo and I both keyed on his tendency never to let his frustrations cloud his judgment or performance. Even when he was frustrated, either with himself or with the bull, he kept himself in check.

Angel Sánchez, however, did not. He was twenty-seven years old but acted like he was about twelve. Like all the other matadors that night, he was frustrated with the bulls. They simply were not aggressive. Unlike the other matadors, he threw temper tantrums. After both of his faenas, he angrily threw his estoque behind the barrier. After the first, he stormed out of the ring, his team in tow, trying to calm him down and convince him to return. This left Miguel de Pablo, the senior matador of the night, three peones down should something happen and he require additional assistance. After both of his faenas, Angel Sánchez stormed out of the ring without saluting the President. This was the single most inviolable rule in being a bullfighter; whether you did well or poorly, you saluted the President of the ring once you concluded your performance. Making it doubly worse was the fact that the President that night was Eutimio Carracedo Pastor, who usually served as the President at Las Ventas in Madrid. After the second violation, I saw his assistant on the phone, and I had a distinct feeling I knew what was happening. The President was calling the alguacilillos. One of them handed the phone to Angel Sánchez, who promptly whipped around and looked up in terror to the President's box. He nodded, hung up, stepped out into the ring, and saluted. The news was not kind to him the next day, and they rightfully ripped him for his behaviour. Jo and I hoped Borja and Miguel de Pablo would pull him aside later that night and give him a stern talking-to, as he did not reflect well upon their profession.

The rejoneo the next night was not our favourite. Diego Ventura, one of Spain's best rejoneadors, performed alongside two traditional matadors (well, modern traditional, seeing as bullfighting was originally conducted on horseback). While the horsemanship involved was phenomenal, it was a starkly uneven match. The bulls' horns were shaved down, which was par for the course for rejoneos, and the horse's movements kept the bulls at a full gallop most of the time, exhausting them rapidly. To us, part of the allure of bullfighting was the match of bull and man, where man, while usually victorious, was not guaranteed victory. There were plenty of other options if we wanted to see a display of excellent horsemanship.

On the fourth night, we saw yet another traditional bullfight. While we thoroughly enjoyed the night, nothing was overly outstanding.

The fifth night, there was hardly anyone in attendance. The roadblocks had been removed, and the venue had even packed away the ticket scanners. This was because this night was a novillada sin picadores. These were the wannabe matadors trying to break onto the scene. Like the first night, they were taking on novillos, but these were the youngest of the young. Also, unlike the first night, there were no picadors to assist the novilleros. It was them, a team of peones, and the bull. The high profile of having the President of Las Ventas judge the performance was replaced with a local leader, and the crowds simply did not turn out for these young novilleros.

Jo and I did, partly because we held season tickets, partly because we didn't know any better, and partly to support these young men in pursuing their dream. Like their fellow novilleros a few days before, their coaches, managers, and parents were on the sidelines guiding them in their journey to stardom. These young novilleros struggled more than their counterparts did at the beginning of the fair, which was to be expected, as they were new to the ring. The crowd, however, was extremely supportive. Passes and estocadas which usually would have drawn condemnation from the crowd were met with a gasp or initial protest, but when the novillero stepped back up to the bull, they applauded and cheered encouragingly.

That encouragement was one of the reasons Jo and I fell in love with the bullfighting community in the first place. The people welcomed and supported newcomers, be they up-and-coming novilleros or two Texans taking it all in on their adventure across the world. Just as with our experience at Las Ventas a month before, we were stopped on our way out of the ring on the final night. Not by a young man this time, but by an older woman. She spoke very little English but wanted to know if we liked what we had seen. We told her we had, and we had seen several before. She thanked us for giving the art a try and handed us her programme as a memento. We had our own, but it was the gesture that counted.

Jo and I talked about the week as we ate tacos for dinner near our hostel that night. We didn't know that we would fall absolutely in love with bullfighting, but after five nights of triumph and failure, cool heads and emotional outbursts, and almost every style of bullfighting Spain had to offer, we had. We were true aficionados, quick to judge poor performances, slow to reward successes with a wave of our white pañuelos, and followers of bullfighting news.

We eagerly awaited the next bullfight on September 1st in Illescas. It would be our first *nocturna*, a bullfight conducted entirely at night.

Illescas and the Nocturna

The nocturna in Illescas didn't start until 22h00 on September 1st, so we spent the day touring Las Ventas, exploring its museum, and having drinks at La Torre de Oro, a toro bar on Plaza Mayor. We finally managed to get on our way at around 20h00 or so. Even though we had rented a car in Sevilla a week before, we couldn't do so in Madrid, so we took a forty-five-minute Uber ride to the bullfight. No big deal, we thought. We could easily catch an Uber or taxi back to Madrid once the nocturna was over.

We arrived early in the hopes of being able to catch Borja before he entered the ring. Jo had bought a stuffed red bull and a fabric pen and wanted him to sign it for her. Of course, I knew she wouldn't approach him herself, so I would ask for his autograph on a stuffed bull, but that was no big deal. Even though I planned to be in Copenhagen by the time the nocturna started, I was happy to be there. Again, we had front-row seats and were excited after the fair in Colmenar Viejo.

The nocturna didn't take place at a traditional bullring. Instead, it was an event centre which hosted concerts, events, and, yes, bullfights. It had a roof and fluorescent lighting, which we weren't excited about. We wanted to see a bullfight out under the moon and the stars of a traditional bullring, not an event venue. It was what it was, and we would still have a great experience.

Borja, well, he did not have such a great experience. His first faena did not go well. He struggled a lot with the estocada, which Jo and I had observed as his major weakness over his past four performances. It was admittedly difficult, as Borja was short, had to reach over the bulls' horns, and sink his estoque in a very narrow space between the bulls' shoulder blades, but the crowd did not care about the difficulty. He was a matador and shouldn't take multiple charges, inducing additional pain on the bull in the process, to finally succeed with the killing blow. As he stood on the side of the ring during the next faena supporting his fellow matador (unlike Angel Sánchez at Borja's last corrida), we saw on his face and in his body language that he was incredibly frustrated, not with the bull, not with the art, but with himself and his performance. That was one of the things we admired about him as a professional; he never took his frustrations out on anyone else.

After the bullfight concluded, Borja dragged himself out of the ring. He was upset with himself and his performance during the night. He only had eighteen performances during the 2023 season, and this one had been mediocre at best. We were sure he would use this as motivation to be better as the season charged to an end on October 12th.

As if by some sort of providence, Jo's and my night was just as unfortunate. Our assumption that we could get an Uber or taxi back to Madrid after the bullfight at 02h00 was entirely invalid. It wasn't that there weren't any Ubers around, there just weren't any on the app. We watched as Ubers pulled up and pulled away, dropping people off at the festival going on at the fairgrounds outside of the event centre, but for some reason none of them were appearing for us. We managed to catch an Uber driver sitting at a red light with his window down and light on (meaning he was open for hire). I asked him if he was working, and he said he was. I asked him if he could take us to Madrid, and he said no. So, I called all three cab companies I could find on my phone (which was a struggle, because the cell service was abysmal with all of the people at the fairgrounds). I asked them all if they could take us to Madrid, and they all said no.

We were stranded in Illescas. All we had on us was an empty cooler of alcohol, our sweaters, and our phone chargers. I wore khaki pants and a polo shirt, and Jo wore a dress. There was rain on the horizon (although we didn't know it at the time). We were living one of the travel horror stories of not having a place to stay. We got really serious (and irritable) really quick.

We stepped away from the festival hoping for better cell service, which helped. I called all the hotels and hostels in town, all two of them, to see if they had room. They didn't. By this time, Jo had resigned to sleeping in a park and catching the first available bus back to Madrid in the morning. That was the other problem: We had a train to Sevilla the next day that we had already paid for. Not only were we stranded, we were against the clock. That first bus was the last possible option for us to get back to Madrid and make our train.

Before agreeing to sleep in a park, I said we should walk to the nearest hotel and ask the concierge to help us. It was only an eight-minute walk away. If all else failed, maybe they would let us sleep in their lobby. We walked up to the counter, and I told the man manning the desk that I was the one who had just called. I knew they didn't have any rooms, but I wondered if they could help us. He told us, "You are in luck. After you called, someone cancelled their reservation. We have one room for the night. Do you want it?" Yes! Yes, we did! It cost us 80 EUR, only had one bed, and we would only be there for about seven hours, but it was better than a park in the rain. We didn't have our passports to give him, but I had my passport card in my wallet, which was good enough. A few minutes later, we were in our private hotel room.

The next morning, we slept straight through the alarm to catch the bus. If we hurried, we still had time to grab a taxi. The concierge ordered the cab, and we enjoyed the most relaxing breakfast of the entire trip. We were already laughing about the story we would have once we made it to Sevilla!

The taxi was late, but it eventually showed up. We trash-packed our bags, all sorts of stuff hanging off them, held on by bungee cords and carabiners, and immediately headed to the train station. We arrived just in time to see the platform number appear on the screen.

All was well that ended well. We were headed back to Sevilla to cap off our bullfighting experience.

Utrera and Our Final Corrida

The bullfight in Utrera was the exact opposite experience of Illescas, and we couldn't have asked for a better way to cap off our three-week adventure of following a bullfighter around like a couple of groupies.

We had no trouble renting a car in Sevilla. We paid 1 EUR for parking outside of the bullring, had dinner and drinks at the fairgrounds outside, and made our way to the driveway where the bullfighters would arrive (but not before leaving my water bottle behind at the fairgrounds). This bullfight was our last opportunity to get Borja to sign the stuffed bull, and we were determined (I say "we" were determined because Jo really wanted it, and I knew it would linger over the rest of the trip if we didn't manage to make it happen).

Unfortunately, we didn't get to see the bullfighters enter the arena. It had a driveway, and they drove straight into the dirt parking area, unloaded, and headed inside. We weren't allowed into that area, which made sense. It just made getting the bull signed that much harder. Even more unfortunately, we couldn't sit in our ticketed seats along the front row of the second tendido (called the *tendido alto*). There had been a hard rain in Utrera all day, and our seats were flooded. We ended up sitting in the empty rows at the top of tendido alto. There was hardly anyone in our section, which meant we could spread out, stand, pace, and enjoy the corrida without fear of interrupting those around us.

At this bullfight, we watched Esaú Fernández as the senior matador, Borja as the intermediate, and Francisco de Manuel as the junior. We hadn't seen Fernández and knew nothing about him, but we had seen de Manuel in Colmenar Viejo. Fernández looked older than us, while de Manuel looked substantially younger. On de Manuel's team was the peón Daniel Duarte. We had seen him perform several times before, including at the único espada, and he rapidly became my favourite peón. He was excellent with the capote, fantastic in placing the banderillas, and seemed to have a sixth sense about what the bulls were thinking and could act accordingly. It was a pleasure to watch him perform in his own right.

As good as the lineup seemed, there was no way we could have prepared ourselves for what would happen during the first faena of the night. Fernández performed well, very well, ear-worthy well, and the bull did the same. We well knew by now that behind every excellent performance by a matador was an equally fantastic performance by the bull. It was a dance, a tango of sorts, where bull and matador were simultaneously performing as one and at odds, and the first faena of the night demonstrated that sentiment in a way that we wouldn't often see, either in person or on OneToro TV. As Fernández lined up the estocada, the crowd bust into an uproar, whistling, clapping, and waving their pañuelos. Fernández backed off, and continued his work with the muleta, much to the crowd's delight. When he lined up the estocada the second time, the crowd again erupted in protest. Fernández looked up into the President's box, hoping to see some sort of direction, but he was met with silence.

By this time, Jo and I had figured out what was happening: The crowd was demanding the bull be pardoned and allowed to live. Pardoning a bull was the highest honour a bull and a matador could receive. A pardon meant that the bull had performed with the utmost bravery, courage, and ferociousness, while the matador had done his part to showcase these qualities to the crowd and the president. The President must have hoped that not pardoning the bull after the second protest would calm them down, but it had the opposite effect. When Fernández lined up the estocada again, the crowd protested even louder. As he backed off, he gestured to the crowd with his hands while looking at the President as if to say, "If you make me kill this bull, they are going to crucify me here and now!"

Then it happened; the President pulled out the orange pañuelo. The bull was pardoned! The crowd erupted with applause and cheering. Fernández tossed away his sword and applauded the bull. Then he lined up as though he was going to do the estocada, but without the estoque, charged in, and tapped the bull on the back with his bare hand. He gestured for the crowd to continue the applause while the corrals prepared the steers to guide the bull out of the arena and back to the pens. From there, it would be rehabilitated under the supervision of a veterinarian and, eventually, released back onto the ranch to live its best life as a free-range bull free from human interaction that would mate with a herd of up to seventy-five cows every year. The way we could tell people, it was a life of eating, sleeping, and breeding.

To see a bull pardoned was extremely rare. It had only ever happened once at Las Ventas, and that was in the 1970s. Granted, Las Ventas was a first-class bullring, and Utrera certainly was not, but it was still a rare event. As for the matador, he was symbolically awarded both ears and the tail for his performance. Fernández took his celebratory lap around the ring with flowers in his hand as the crowd roared with approval. Talk about a way to kick off our last in-person bullfight of the year!

Borja performed excellently that night as well. It was a far cry from his so-so performance in Illescas two days before. He was awarded two ears, one from each bull. Francisco de Manuel, a bullfighter we had not paid attention to before but would start following closely, also performed well and was awarded two ears that night, the same as Borja. That meant that all three matadors could be carried out on the shoulders of their fans through the puerta grande (literally, the "Great Door"). This was a first for us, and it was a thing to see, except for one small detail: the stuffed bull.

After Borja's first performance, Jo had gone down to the barrier to throw the bull and pen into the ring for him to sign and return, but she got stage fright again. The same happened after he was awarded his second ear. It appeared she had missed her chance, so I took matters into my own hands.

I took the bull, went down to the barrier while the President was setting up to give out some awards from the night, and called out, "Borja!" He turned around and lit up when he saw me. We had been following him for three weeks, tagging him in Instagram posts and stories along the way. He had responded to almost every single one with at least a like, if not a comment. I asked, "Puedes firmarlo?" and he replied, "Sí! Sí!" I tossed down the bull and the pen, and he signed it. Then he offered to sign my hat. I told him thanks but no thanks and showed him his bloody handprint, which stained the straw.

After the awards were handed out and the matadors carried through the puerta grande, we met him by his van with his other fans. I asked him if we could get a picture of Jo with him and the bull, and he readily agreed. We couldn't have asked for a better way to end our bullfighting trip around Spain!

The Aftermath of Utrera

As a joke in a conversation, Jo referred to the bull with Borja's signature as "Little Borja." It was just an easy way for us to call it something rather than just "the bull." But the bull was Spanish, I said, so "Little Borja" was actually "Borjito." And, so, the name stuck. From then on, Borjito accompanied us across the world.

Before heading to the train station the next morning, I wrote an Instagram story about the night before. I commented in it that while we were leaving Spain, we would be keeping up with Borja's career with OneToro TV, and we couldn't wait to see him perform the following year. We had seen every one of his bullfights in person since we entered the Schengen Area, and we were not going to give up on him now.

As a testament to how great of a guy Borja was, he replied to my story immediately. He told us how thankful he was to have fans like us and appreciated our support over the past several weeks. He also told us to tell him when we returned to Spain the following year. He would take us out to a tentadero, one of his practice sessions, so that we could get an appreciation for the temptation of bullfighting. I assured him we would be taking him up on that offer!

We spent the next several days on the beach in Málaga. We needed a bit of a rest after three weeks of jetting around Spain supporting our favourite bullfighter before heading to Germany. Like all good budget travellers, we had a 02h00 pickup for the airport. We were leaving Spain behind again.

For good this time.

Reflecting on Following the Torero

The rest of our experiences in Spain. The three weeks we spent in Spain following Borja Jiménez from bullfight to bullfight were primarily focused on bullfighting, but that wasn't all we did. Bullfights were only three hours on any given evening, so we had plenty of time to explore the rest of the cities.

We loved Sevilla. It tied with San Sebastian as our favourite city in all of Europe. We visited the Cathedral of Sevilla, the gardens in the Alcazar, and the Jewish quarter and ate more than our fair share of tapas. We watched impromptu flamenco shows, Jo got a tattoo, and I got the best sports massage of my life.

Our second time in Madrid was even more fulfilling than the first, as we had already been on the tourist circuit. We did the Rick Steves audio tour, which was far more enjoyable and informative than the free walking tour we did with the hostel last time we were there (although that first tour was quite enjoyable). We also toured Las Ventas, which had an extensive bullfighting museum and a bullfight simulator that we both tried our hands with (with one of us doing better than the other). Of course, I spent my mornings at a coffee shop, and eventually, the waiter didn't even bring me the menu and would simply bring my croissant, double espresso, and orange juice when I sat down.

In Málaga, we attempted to tour the bullring, which doubled as a cultural centre in the off-season, but it was closed to the public. So, we settled for exploring the Moorish castle on the hill, the Revello de Toro Museum dedicated to a local painter (although with Toro in the name, we thought it would be a museum to bullfighting...), the Málaga Museum dedicated to local archaeology and fine arts, and enjoyed a lovely evening with an Irish woman named Patricia who was backpacking through Spain in search of a place to buy a house her grandchildren would love to visit.

While our entire time in Spain this time around was framed by the art of bullfighting, we couldn't help but fall in love with Spain as a whole. Our experience in Barcelona weeks before notwithstanding, the culture in Spain was right up our alley. It was laid back, cherished its culture and history, warm, and welcoming. For me, I loved that Christianity was still alive and prominent in Spain. While I was not Catholic, I was of the opinion that a nation unified in religion (when done so by choice, not force) was stronger than those who were divided in their views. Christianity was a force for good and unity, not evil and divisiveness, no matter what modern American media was saying at the time, and Spain was a clear example of that, at least in my eyes.

A resurgence of bullfighting? Bullfighting was on the decline. The Catalan regional government had attempted to ban it outright several years before, but the Spanish Supreme Court overturned the ban. Nonetheless, there has never been a bullfight in the Catalan region since. The Canary Islands had done the same. Bullfighting was on its way to the history books.

In 2023, however, interest in and support of bullfighting was on the rise in Spain. The younger generation rejuvenated its interest in the art not because they had a sudden change of heart but because they opposed how the Spanish government handled the COVID-19 pandemic. Many festivals and traditions that had occurred for centuries, such as La Fiesta de San Fermín, had been quashed by the government in the name of public health. As a result, there was a resurgence of Spanish national pride and identity in the young Millennial population, and the bullfighting industry received a much-needed economic and cultural bump.

While I wish that resurgence would continue, the signs were not indicative that would happen. While Jo and I would see special events that would pack Las Ventas to standing room only (such as the retirement of El Juli after twenty-five years as a bullfighter), it was rare to see bullrings that were even half full. Even in Cazalla de la Sierra; the 3,000-person ring in a 5,000-person town was half full. While I was certain bullfighting would continue long into the future, I was equally certain it would never return to its former place in Spanish culture. The times had moved on.

Leaving my old life behind. When Jo and I started The Great Gallivanting, we intended it as a resume builder. Yes, we would enjoy our adventures across the world. Yes, we would take every chance to experience things no one we knew would ever see or do. At the end of the day, though, we were focused on the future. We both had aspirations in the security field, and being well-travelled would set us up for those aspirations.

After our three weeks following a bullfighter around Spain, however, those aspirations, for me, were gone. I had relaxed more than I ever had, finally accepted that the relationship of ten years before was gone forever, and found myself happier than I had been in a long time by disconnecting from the news. In my old career, I was intimately familiar with every terrible thing going on in the world. I had seen some of the most unspeakable horrors perpetrated by man, and it was all just a day in the office. After coming face to face with life and death in the ring, having a lot of time to reflect on my inner thoughts and who I wanted to be, I ultimately concluded that I would not go back to my old life.

This was a scary prospect. I didn't have a plan. The only life I had ever known was the security field, whether in the military or the private sector. Even my master's degree was focused almost exclusively on security issues. Security, risk, terrorism, they were all I knew, and I had decided to walk away from it all. Would I miss it? Absolutely. How could I not? It shaped who I was as an adult. But I couldn't deny all of the benefits walking away for those past two months had done for me, my mental and emotional health, and, ultimately, my happiness. I resolved to myself that, no matter how alluring it may be one day or how much of a plan I didn't have, I would not go back to that life.

I didn't share this with Jo, although, looking back, she could tell something was up. I would turn the conversation away from potential careers and plans for our return. You can't play a player, though, and she was just as versed in conversational techniques as I was, so there was no way she didn't pick up on it. I wanted to keep the status quo as long as we were together. As long as we had the same plan while traveling together, that would alleviate a lot of friction and stress. However, as I said in the last chapter, I already recognised that we wouldn't travel together forever. Eventually, we would split up. That's when I would share my career decision and lack of a plan with her. Until then, it was business as usual.

Chapter Nine

Push to the End: Germany, Poland, and Hungary

In planning The Great Gallivanting, Jo and I had few "must-do" items on our itinerary, but some of the things we wanted to see were in Germany and Poland. The Berlin Wall, Oktoberfest (if we could make it), and Auschwitz were three places we built our travels around. We weren't entirely committed to touring Germany, Poland, or Hungary in their entirety like some people liked to do. We just wanted to check off a few more capitals and experiences we had only read about in the history books.

Berlin

By the time we lifted off from Málaga, Jo and I had spent forty-eight of our ninety days in the Schengen Area in Spain. We didn't intend to spend over half our time in one country. We deliberately intended not to do that. We planned to zip through the whole continent and agreed to forego certain places, like the French Riviera, because we wanted to enjoy them more than this trip would allow.

Even so, we were both bummed to be leaving Spain behind, especially because we were throwing ourselves into culture shock. We only had a few cities left on our itinerary: Berlin, Warsaw, Krakow (to see Auschwitz), Budapest, and Munich (just to go to Oktoberfest). We would hit all these, including travel days, in just two and a half weeks. After our relaxing few days in Málaga, we were in a mad push to the end of our time on the European continent.

We couldn't not go to Berlin on our way through Germany. Even though we had planned to see more cities before our Spanish detour, we knew we still wanted to at least see the German capital. It was full of history that was becoming increasingly relevant in modern times. From the largest remaining stretch of the Berlin wall to being at the centre of the genocidal Nazi war machine to the German and Prussian people's own storied past, this city was rich with things to see and learn.

Of course, we couldn't see it all. We could not see all of Berlin in three days, so we decided to put a theme on our time there. We would focus on the Cold War and World War II, with a couple of exceptions here and there. We made this decision after our Rick Steves audio tour the first day when we passed by the first-ever government-sponsored Holocaust memorial, the former site of Hitler's bunker, the cold-war era television spire, and the statues to Karl Marx and Friedrich Engels while also passing by opera houses, beautiful cathedrals, and Museum Island. We simply could not see and do everything.

Of course, after making that decision, we immediately headed for the Neues Museum, an archaeology museum with exhibits on all sorts of ancient civilisations. Why? Because Jo wanted to see Nefertiti's bust. This wasn't a spur-of-the-moment decision. When making the list of things we wanted to see and do on The Great Gallivanting, Nefertiti's bust in Berlin was on her list, just as Tibidabo was on mine in Barcelona.

We had no idea what was in store for us at the Neues Museum. It was huge. We had a full day planned, so we got there as soon as it opened, which was fortunate as we were there until lunch. There were exhibits on Alexander the Great's conquests, Egyptian, Greek, and Roman empires, mythology, and large rooms full of original religious documents. I knew it was interesting because Jo said, "It's a good thing we didn't get the audio guide. We could have been here all day!" She was right. We were there for hours before we realised we hadn't seen the entire reason we were there in the first place.

Nefertiti's bust itself was a magnificently-preserved item of Egyptian history. It had minimal damage, and the colours were bright and defined. We amused ourselves that Nefertiti's bust was in such good condition when nothing related to her husband, the actual ruler of Egypt at the time, was so well preserved. Annoyingly, we weren't allowed to take pictures. Signs and cameras were everywhere, and multiple minders enforced the rules. They even had staff in the adjacent rooms making sure you didn't take a picture from afar with the new iPhone's fantastic camera. We understood the concern about using flash on ancient objects, but this was extreme. Clearly, this was more about money and merchandise than preserving the artifact, because plenty of photos and postcards were available at the museum gift shop.

With Nefertiti behind us, we headed towards the Topography of Terror, a free exhibit hosted by the public library system dedicated to the Reich Main Security Office (RSHA) and its role in the Holocaust. It was actually built on the site of the RSHA. The building itself wasn't huge, but the exhibit was enormous. Neither of us were prepared for the amount of information we would absorb over the next few hours. The photos and information boards walked visitors all the way through the Holocaust from the perspective of the RSHA, from the pre-war decisions and influences through the end of the Nuremburg Trials. We got an in-depth look at the life, personality, and ideology of Reinhard Heydrich, the first and longest-serving chief of the RSHA until his assassination. We had both heard of Heydrich as a prominent Nazi figure, but I, as someone who had intensely studied the Holocaust in grade school, never really understood his or the RSHA's role in the genocide. They were, after all, just another organisation in the massive, over-blown bureaucracy of the Nazi war machine (which, historically, was common in countries run by a dictator such as Hitler). When we left the exhibit several hours later, we had a much greater appreciation for the vile beliefs behind the RSHA, the intense bureaucratic paranoia which somehow didn't paralyse the Nazi party, and a bit of anger at the nonchalance with which the world let Nazis who were senior officials off the hook for their crimes. Sure, it wasn't exactly feasible to execute tens of thousands of Germans who followed Hitler, but bringing them back into the fold as West German government officials seemed too lenient. Not even during the de-Baathification of Iraq did the world make exceptions for the lower ranks of party members to continue in their posts.

Such was the way of the world in the post-World War II era. The Iron Curtain had quickly fallen, dividing the communist east from the democratic west, and no more starkly was that portrayed than in Berlin with the longest remaining stretch of the Berlin Wall. We opted to visit the Wall and the associated museum (called "The Wall Museum") in the evening, as it was across the street from our hostel.

The Wall Museum's small size (it was only the top floor of a building which housed a bar on the ground floor) was no testament to its story; instead, the museum expertly used every space available to tell vital parts of the Berlin Wall's bleak history. It showed videos of the wall being constructed literally through the living rooms of houses, testimonials from both sides of the walls of those who tried, succeeded, and failed to cross from east to west, and explained the story of the wall's gradual fall across Eastern Europe (while the physical wall was eventually overcome in one swift motion, the other divisions across Europe, such as concertina wire and train checkpoints, were slow to disappear).

Outside the museum, the remaining Berlin Wall started and ran a full 1,300 metres down the street. It was covered in beautiful artwork and murals, with some grey, blank spaces at random intervals. These murals were all restoration works of the original art, which was sanctioned as a project of the East German government. Artists from across the world painted scenes of hope, politics, critique, and division on the bleak, blank canvas the wall provided. It was an effort to distance east Germany from their former Soviet oppressors and oppressive ways by embracing democracy and the freedom of speech, which was not held in high regard by the Stasi, the East German security service, before the Wall's fall. Unfortunately, the artwork was allowed to deteriorate as the years passed. Germany unified, the European Union was formed, and international focus shifted away from rival oppressive states to terrorist actors. It was not until 2008 that a serious effort to restore the murals was implemented. Of the original 106 artists to originally participate in the murals, 99 returned to restore their work. Far from being simple graffiti, their messages held historical value and provided relevant social and political commentary still applicable in the 2020s. The seven artists who didn't participate in the restoration had their murals removed, painted over to resemble the bleak, blank canvas on which their powerful messages once stood. If their work wasn't important enough for them to restore, then it wasn't important enough to keep.

While we thoroughly enjoyed our rather dark-themed visit of espionage and terror in Berlin, we were also eager to give German food another try. Vienna was a bust, but maybe it was a one-off. It wasn't. We were wholly unimpressed with German food yet again; however, we enjoyed two other culinary experiences worth mentioning. The first was a Tex-Mex restaurant located not far from the Neues Museum. We passed it on our walk from the S-Bahn station and agreed to try it. It was by far not the best Tex-Mex food we had ever had (we were both from Texas, after all), but it was what I would have expected the Germans' best guess as to what Tex-Mex was like. I ordered chicken enchiladas, which came with rice stuffed inside the tortilla. They looked a lot more like burritos than enchiladas. As Jo was laughing at it, she said, "Well, I mean, enchiladas usually come with rice on the side, so they got the spirit of it right, right?" Indeed, they did. I gave Berlin Tex-Mex a six out of ten. In Texas, it would have been one of those places that was packed at noon with construction workers, tradespeople, and police officers who needed a quick lunch, tasted good for the low price, and was fast on delivery, but wouldn't be a place that had many customers for dinner simply because there were better places to go.

The second place was Mundo Berlin, a tapas bar not far from the Topography of Terror. I surprised Jo with this place for lunch. It had great reviews online, but so had the Tex-Mex place, and we had just come from Spain days before, so we would judge the food for ourselves. It was delicious. While expensive by Spanish standards, the taste was spot on, the portions exactly what we expected, and they even had the pedron peppers that Jo liked so much. We couldn't even make it a week out of Spain without seeking out Spanish food! We partook in the sobremesa with our beer and wine in Berlin, and Jo summed it up perfectly with one of her may catchphrases, "I miss Spain!"

We certainly did. We missed it so much that we bought dinner at the supermarket in the train station next to our hostel and watched a bullfight we were looking forward to in the lobby on OneToro TV. You could take the aficionados out of Spain, but you couldn't take Spain out of the aficionados!

Warsaw

Warsaw was as foreign as Prague, if not more so. Neither of us spoke the language, the currency differed from the Eurozone, and its history varied substantially from centuries-old cities like Paris, Madrid, and Rome. English was also not as widespread outside of the historic city centre.

Our first encounter with the language barrier came as soon as we arrived at the Warsaw train station. We needed to make reservations to get to Krakow, which could only be done at the ticket counter. The attendant there spoke no English. She was polite (by Eastern European standards), but it was clear we had to figure something else out.

Years before, I had taken my dad to France, where we faced a language barrier in museums. Back then, Google Translate only worked so well. The camera feature was iffy at best, and we couldn't download whole languages in advance to use on our trip. All that had changed by the time The Great Gallivanting came around. By the end of my year of travel, I had downloaded more than twenty languages to my phone, including Polish, which was how I overcame the language barrier at the ticket counter. I typed what I wanted in English in Google Translate, turned the phone around to show her the translation, and she said, "Ah! Ok!" and promptly printed our reservations. It was the smoothest in-person Eurail interaction I had on the entire trip.

Our hostel was not close to the train station, and I knew how Jo could be if we walked more than we needed to with our bags on, so I offered to her to drop our bags in once place, her stay with them, and I go in search of the metro stop and figure out how to use it. She readily agreed. Much of her apprehension about being alone in a foreign country where she didn't speak the language had faded as she became increasingly familiar with being out of her comfort zone. After about twenty minutes of wandering outside trying to figure it out, I returned for Jo and my bag, and we headed to the hostel. Naturally, a large set of stairs at the end of the metro stop dampened the mood, but luckily, our hostel was close to those stairs. We settled in, grabbed dinner, and turned in for the night.

We didn't have a plan for Warsaw. In fact, we didn't have a plan for the rest of our time in Europe except for our one day in Krakow to visit Auschwitz. In some ways, this was annoying because that meant we were trying to balance what the other would want to see and do against our time clock. In others, it was great because we weren't obligated to squeeze anything in. While we didn't want to admit it, we were slamming against the energy plateau that all long-term travellers hit at some point. We were tired, physically and mentally; physically, because we had been walking and changing cities constantly, and mentally, because we were constantly changing our environment and making decisions at every turn. Our brains weren't designed to be in continually changing environments, so they stayed on alert as we moved, which meant ours never really switched off. It had started to reflect heavily in our moods in Berlin, and we needed a bit of a slowdown. We planned one in the United Kingdom, but we needed it sooner than expected.

So, rather than hit the ground running, we took it easy getting started each day. I grabbed coffee and a croissant while reading a book at a nearby coffee shop while Jo slept in, and on two of our mornings, she joined, and we sat there until around lunch. This was enjoyable in its own way. We were in Europe reading our books at a local café! This was the European vacation dream that many people posted on Instagram. We had taken opportunities to enjoy the leisurely, quiet mornings for granted, and hitting that plateau forced us to appreciate what had been right in front of us the entire time. I was working through Hemingway's *To Have and Have Not* while Jo read *The Sun Also Rises*. At the equivalent of 5 EUR a breakfast, these mornings in Warsaw's old town were well spent.

Warsaw's old town was in remarkable shape. It was hard to believe that this was the same place that saw so much death, destruction, and carnage during World War II. Our visit to the Warsaw Uprising Museum turned that notion on its head. The museum was dedicated to the Warsaw Uprising against the Nazi regime in 1944. The Uprising was doomed to fail from the beginning, but it had been accepted that failing to act was substantially worse than acting and failing. The Germans handily stopped the uprising, and, as retribution, Hitler personally ordered Warsaw razed to the ground. Everything from churches to the historic city centre to the Warsaw Castle were set ablaze and/or bombed with dynamite, but not before being looted of their treasures. The museum had an exhibit dedicated to the Allied forces that delivered aid to Warsaw during its razing. The Allied aircrews said they knew they had reached Warsaw because the glow of the entire city on fire lit up the horizon.

This was difficult for us to imagine, as by the time we went to the Uprising Museum, we had already toured the Warsaw Royal Castle (for free, because we happened to be there on a Wednesday). We knew the Castle had been intentionally bombed by the Nazis, but not to that degree. As we learned the story of the uprising, I couldn't help but think of the beautiful, golden interior, irreplaceable paintings, and grandiose nature of Warsaw's Royal Castle. Given Hitler's obsession with historical artifacts, it shocked me that he would order the castle, which had stood since 1619, destroyed, but such was the nature of psychologically unstable dictator; nothing took precedence over complete obedience and subservience to the Nazi regime.

In the aftermath of World War II, the Polish people rebuilt the historic city centre brick by brick, just like before. Every shop, townhouse, church, and, yes, even the castle was restored as the Polish nation recovered from the trauma inflicted on them by the Nazis. That was why the city centre looked to be in such good shape when compared to the city centres of other cities which, while taken care of, still betrayed their age.

The city centre also stood in stark contrast to the sprawling, modern city around it. As the Polish nation rebuilt and healed, the world continued, technology progressed, and the Iron Curtain rose and fell shortly after the castle's restoration finished. The city centre was full of tourist-centric restaurants, entirely walkable, and was home to many governmental offices, including the President's office with its high-tech security measures expertly integrated into the surrounding architecture. Walk just ten minutes in any direction, however, and we were in a totally new environment of motorways, metro stops, and high-rise buildings.

One of the tourist attractions in the city centre was the Vodka Museum. It was a museum dedicated to, well, vodka. Jo had found it, and I agreed to give it a try. It was unexpectedly closed on our first visit, but we had success the following afternoon. While tiny, with only a few rooms, the museum was full of Polish vodka memorabilia, from advertising posters to ceremonial bottles to travel spirit sets; it had it all. Thankfully, our entrance ticket came with an audio guide to help us understand what we saw. It also came with a tasting of three different vodkas, which the curator expertly timed with the pace of our visit. He handed the drinks to us far enough apart so that we wouldn't get drunk, but kept them close enough together that we had a buzz going the entire time once the first shot hit (which, for me, was almost immediately, because I was the most lightweight of lightweights when it came to alcohol). The novelty of the museum wore off quickly, though, as it was a massive collection of items which, frankly, we didn't care about. But, hey, we got free alcohol out of it.

And what paired well with free alcohol? More alcohol. It was September in Warsaw, which meant the evenings were chilly when the sun dropped below the horizon. Being the wine connoisseur she was, Jo quickly identified a place that sold mulled wine on our initial walk into town. Before turning in for the night, we stopped by for some warm, liquid fortification. In a funny turn of events, Warsaw's version of mulled wine was about the same as Berlin's version of Tex-Mex: a best guess. Rather than serve properly mulled wine, the shop we went to simply frothed the wine with an espresso machine's milk frother. Initially in shock, Jo quickly found it amusing. What could we expect, honestly? At least it was warm.

An outside observer may have deemed our time in Warsaw boring. We didn't see all the must-see sites, wander too far from the city centre, or immerse ourselves in the nightlife. To an extent, they may have had a point. Our bodies and brains were forcing us to slow down, whether we liked it or not. But that didn't mean it was boring for us. Those mornings in the coffee shop worked wonders for our moods, as we relaxed in a way we hadn't taken advantage of for weeks. With just under ten months of long-term travel remaining, we needed to take these breaks, even if only in the mornings, for our health, our mood, and the sake of our friendship. If we were going to travel together long-term, we had to take the time to decompress.

Auschwitz

Nothing could prepare you for your first visit to a Nazi concentration camp. I had visited Dachau with my dad a few years before, but Jo's only experience with one of these visits was La Risiera in Trieste. While La Risiera was highly impactful, the concentration camps in Germany and Poland were on a whole different level. As we travelled across Europe, we unintentionally built ourselves up to Auschwitz. We started with the excellent Deportation Memorial in Paris, visited La Risiera in Trieste, delved into the retributions in Warsaw, and now we were headed to the most notorious extermination complex of the Nazi regime.

Our hostel in Krakow was an hour or so away from Oświęcim, the nearby city and namesake of Auschwitz, via train. As we rode through the Polish countryside, we couldn't help but notice how normal things were. As we pulled in Oświęcim, it was eerily so. Businesses, restaurants, parks, people running, mothers out for a walk with their babies in prams, nothing betrayed the horrors that occurred there seventy years before. We wondered aloud what it must be like to live in a town whose claim to fame was the horror inflicted upon the world at the Nazi death camp. On the one hand, we thought it must have been a rather depressing thing for those who lived there; on the other, it must also have been a great responsibility to be an ambassador of history and human rights.

Our tour was scheduled for 12h45. Because we hadn't planned out our time, none of the English tours were available, so we registered for an Italian tour. We decided that, even if we didn't understand the guide, we would at least be able to enter the site and take it all in. The language of the tour wasn't that important to us; we wanted to lay eyes on the place where it all happened. I knew from my time in Dachau that, while a tour guide was helpful, it wasn't necessary to get the immersive experience we desired.

Luckily, Jo managed to get us in with an English-language tour. She asked if we could join the tour, and, much to our delight, the guide said yes. We weren't the only ones, either. Others who had signed up for a French tour were in the same situation as us.

The tour was divided into two parts: Auschwitz I and Auschwitz II-Birkenau. We started at Auschwitz I, where the welcome centre was located. Auschwitz I looked like a standard military base, complete with a perimeter fence, guard shacks, and barracks that looked like the dorms I lived in while at university. Had we not known any better, we could easily have believed we were in the garrison area at Fort Knox, Kentucky. It was all rather normal for a place where such unimaginable horrors took place. Even the infamous and mendacious "Arbeit Macht Frei" sign above the main entrance was unassuming. The only thing that betrayed the camp's true nature from the outside was the concertina wire atop the fence; it angled inwards, not outwards, meaning it was designed to keep people in, not out. At the same time, it struck me as extreme hubris that the Nazis were so arrogant and unconcerned that they didn't make even the most basic attempt to preventing saboteurs from entering the camp.

The barracks buildings at Auschwitz I housed the museum. It was impossible to describe the emotions behind what we saw in a succinct paragraph. Prosthetic limbs of victims were piled high, confiscated children's suitcases struck home with parents, and hundreds and hundreds of eyeglasses laid before us, cracked, shattered, and broken, demonstrating just how little regard the Nazis had for Jews, gypsies, homosexuals, ethnic minorities, and even Catholics. Photos of prisoners lined the walls, and the Death Wall, where thousands of people were executed, served as a memorial to those who would never leave the camp for reasons as mundane as contracting the common cold.

The one crematorium at Auschwitz I was dynamited as the Nazis withdrew from the camp, just as it was at La Risiera. To me, this betrayed just how hollow they were in their beliefs. If they truly believed they were doing the best by the German people and humanity by ridding the world of "undesirables," then they should have stood by the evidence of their crimes and proudly proclaimed their propaganda at their trials. Destroying the evidence as they withdrew was proof that they didn't truly believe in what they were doing. As I looked at the crematorium's ruins, I couldn't help but think back to Governor Richard Coke of Texas when he said, "Stand by the right, even to the sacrifice of life itself, and learn that death is preferable to dishonour." Clearly, they knew what they were doing wasn't right, but they did it anyways.

Auschwitz I was not what most people thought of when they thought of Auschwitz. They thought of Auschwitz II-Birkenau, which was a site outside of town where tens of thousands of prisoners could be held at any given time. This was where Josef Mengele, the infamous Nazi doctor who experimented on prisoners, would so casually stand outside arriving trains and decide who lived a bit longer for the sake of his experiments and who died immediately in the gas chambers with a flick of his wrist.

Auschwitz II-Birkenau was bigger than we could have imagined. The walk from the front gate to the crematoriums in the back was a long trek along the train tracks. The tracks came to a dead end at the back of the camp, next to the now-destroyed crematoriums. It was a horribly efficient apparatus with a palpable disdain for human life. There were four crematoriums at Auschwitz II-Birkenau, with two of them in the camp and two further into the forest behind. All were destroyed during the Nazis' withdraw; their ruins stood undisturbed as they fell seventy years before.

Jo and I were struck by the beautiful scenery as we walked around the site in mid-September. There were blue skies that met mountains off in the distance. In any other context, this large, open field would have been a pleasant place for a family outing on an autumn afternoon. I asked Jo, "Can you imagine being a prisoner here and having that view?" It was an emotionally disturbing juxtaposition. Jo agreed; it was a fantastic view, and it was hard to imagine seeing something so beautiful while being subjected to such a horrible life. Then she snapped us both to reality. "Can you imagine being here in the summer? Or when it rains? Or snows?" She was right. Auschwitz II-Birkenau was one giant field that was once filled with either brick or wooden buildings crowded with people in the days long before air conditioning and modern insulation. The summer heat would have been oppressive at best, torrential rains would have flooded the field, and snowy days were on record as having frozen prisoners to death. It was the perfect location to perpetrate the evils of the Nazi regime, simultaneously wondrously beautiful and terrifyingly brutal.

On our way back to Krakow, Jo and I reflected on the importance of such a place as Auschwitz in modern times. The world had declared "Never Again!" after the Holocaust. Never again would the world stand by and allow entire peoples be subjected to such horrors and affronts to humanity. But, we knew, the world was actively standing by as just such things happened all over the world. The Uyghurs were in "re-education camps" in China. Unlike the Nazi camps of the Holocaust, the world was acutely aware of these camps thanks to the worldwide news system. The Russian Army was perpetrating war crimes by attacking children's hospitals in Ukraine on camera, yet neither NATO nor the European Union stepped in. For such a virtuous declaration of "Never Again," "Again" was happening in front of our very eyes all over the world. It was a sad prospect to end our day and our time at Auschwitz.

Budapest

Our time in Krakow was limited to our one day at Auschwitz by design. We had our sights set on Oktoberfest in Munich in our last days in the Schengen Area, so we had to be deliberate with our time, both in cities and with our travel days. It was better for us to head to Budapest before Munich than to stay longer in Poland, despite all the great things we had heard about Krakow.

Unlike our long ride from Trieste to Prague, we only had to take one train from Krakow to Budapest. We spent nine long hours traveling through Poland, the Czech Republic, and Slovakia before finally arriving in Budapest. It was a long day, and we arrived after the ticket office had closed, so our train from Budapest was still up in the air when we arrived. Ordinarily, this would have been no big deal, but we were a week away from being legally required to leave the Schengen Area, and we were not keen on being fined or arrested for overstaying our visas.

Unlike Warsaw, which had been substantially rebuilt after the war, Budapest still had ruins across the old city. Much of the inner workings of the buildings were restored to be functioning businesses, but the Hungarians felt it important to keep the aesthetic as a reminder of the war's impacts, especially in the Jewish quarter. Unfortunately for Hungary, the horrors of war continued under Soviet influence.

We spent our first day at the House of Terror, a museum dedicated to the oppressive political organisations that ruled Hungary from the 1940s through the 1990s under both fascist and communist regimes. It was interesting to me that the fascists and communists hated each other so much yet behaved in the same manner. Political persecutions, extreme institutional paranoia, and strict adherence to the almighty party were common themes under the Arrow Cross Party (fascist), the State Protection Authority (communist), and the Ministry of Internal Affairs III (communist). There was also a seamless transition from one to the next, often with the same members simply changing the patches on their uniforms to serve in the next state secret police service. Like the men who served the Nazis and the Soviets, it was all about power; ideology hardly factored into it at the individual level.

We lost our entire second day to rain. Hard rain. It rained non-stop from dawn until dusk. Eventually, though, we had to venture out to secure our Eurail reservations to Munich. We did what we could to keep from getting absolutely soaked through, but getting wet was inevitable considering the train station was under renovation and the ticket office was temporarily moved to a separate portable building. Lucky for us, Jo had long since solved the problem of getting our tickets wet, because she suggested in Spain that we buy a waterproof document holder for our tickets, postcards, and other mementos we wanted to take home. It came in handy more times than I would be able to count over the course of our travels.

All told, Budapest wasn't as fascinating as everyone made it out to be. Sure, there was the nightlife and the so-called "ruin bars" (bars built into the old ruins), but they were expensive. We had one drink at one, almost had a heart attack at the price, and decided that we came, we saw, we could not afford to conquer. Given that the main draw for budget travellers to visit Budapest was their budget, it was shocking to see all the young people spending that much money on a night of drinking.

The historical locations, too, were not that impressive to us. The Buda Castle was beautiful, but we could only marvel so much at architecture. Granted, part of it was closed for a film set, but that didn't affect the museum portions, which, again, were not overly impressive. Despite the fantastic view from the hilltop cafés outside the castle, it was a long way to travel for a lacklustre experience. Not even the view of the magnificent parliament building across the river entirely made up for the lack of "wow factor." I noticed a travel couple I followed on Instagram posted about their prior experience in Budapest while Jo and I were there. The reel and locations they shared were the same ones we visited. This told me that we hadn't missed anything in terms of the city's aura; it just didn't have much that appealed to us.

We did, however, check out one of the bathhouses that Budapest was famous for. A girl in our hostel told us about one where the locals went, which didn't have many tourists and was free after a specific time. Free? Few tourists? Done. We didn't quite know what to expect, but we figured we couldn't have a bad day at a spa, so we gave it a shot.

Was it a mind-blowing experience? No. Was it a pleasant evening? Totally. The bathhouse had several pools of varying temperatures, ranging from an ice bath to more than forty degrees Celsius. We only had a few hours, so we pool-hopped to find which one we liked best. Even though there were a lot of people at the bathhouse relaxing after work, we managed to sample every pool. The hottest pool was my favourite (and the most crowded), while Jo preferred the second-hottest. We also gave the steam rooms a try. I had never tried a steam room before, and, I had to say, it was a pleasant experience. I could see the relaxation benefits of coming to a place like this after a hard day of physical labour or a sports competition.

One thing about me is that I have never tolerated the cold well. I don't like cold showers, I don't like cold weather, and I became a different person when the weather changed in Texas. Even so, Jo declared we should take a cold plunge after our time in the steam rooms. I was not about that life, but she was insistent (in a joking manner). She jumped straight on in with no problem. I stuck one toe in and decided it was too cold for me. Unfortunately, that wasn't a good enough excuse, so I slowly made my way in. We stayed there for a few minutes when Jo finally said, "You can get out if you want to." I couldn't get out of it fast enough!

After a disappointing day of exploring Budapest, the evening at the bathhouse did wonders for our mood. It left us hopeful for the following day before we boarded our train for Munich. Unfortunately, it was another letdown. We had been told to explore the Jewish Quarter but found it just another part of the old city. Maybe it was because we had fallen in love with Spain, perhaps it was because we were mentally tired, or maybe it was because the city wasn't our scene, but we didn't understand the hype surrounding it in travel circles.

Oktoberfest

That same sentiment held for Oktoberfest in Munich.

We arrived in Munich after dark and still had two S-Bahn trains and a bus to get to our "hostel." "Hostel" was a generous term. It was a pop-up tent hostel in Campingplatz, a giant camping area outside of the city centre, called the Hangover Hospital. Walking through the campground, we passed single-person tents that covered the green camping areas. I was confident we had booked a hostel with beds, but the longer we walked, the less confident I became. Jo told me that if we were in one of these tents, we would eat the cost and get a hotel room. I certainly was not going to argue the point.

Luckily, we had beds. The Hangover Hospital was constructed using army-style pole tents, each divided in half with five bunk beds on each side. We would be subjected to the Munich cold at night, but at least we would be sheltered from the rain and morning dew. Plus, we didn't figure we would spend much time there anyway. After a cold night and late morning, we made our way towards Oktoberfest.

We wore our standard travel clothes, not the traditional Oktoberfest dress of lederhosen and dirndls. We were only going to be there for two days, and we weren't looking to spend over 100 EUR on clothes that we would only wear twice, nor did we have the room to take anything extra with us on our remaining nine months of travel. We weren't the only ones with this sentiment. Despite what we read online, tourists everywhere wore whatever they wanted. Budgets were budgets everywhere.

Oktoberfest in Munich was a night-and-day difference from San Fermín in Pamplona. For starters, it was a long way from the main part of town. We had to trek in with everyone else to get to the fairgrounds where the festivities occurred. Secondly, and most importantly, alcohol was not permitted outside the "tents" (which were really large, permanent, hard-stand buildings). Third, to drink in a tent, you had to have a seat, which was notoriously difficult to come by after about 11h30, so the idea of bar-hopping Oktoberfest was almost entirely out of the picture for us. Finally, there were no associated activities: no parades, no shows, no cultural displays, nothing. The entire festival was built around sitting in tents and drinking beer.

Unsurprisingly, our first visit to the fairgrounds was an utter disappointment. We tried to get into several tents, but they were all full. Instead, we wandered the fairgrounds, which were host to a travelling carnival similar to the county fairs we had back in Texas. Eventually, we looked at each other and decided we would much rather be elsewhere. We found our way to an Irish pub where an important regional football match was being streamed, and we had several pints and some snacks. This was a more interesting scene than standing around waiting for a seat in a tent while not drinking alcohol. And neither of us was even into non-American football.

Undeterred by our experience on the first day, we decided to go to the tents at around 10h00 on the second. At least this way, we stood a chance of securing seats. Besides, can't drink all day if you don't start in the morning.

Well, we did get a seat and steins of beer, but we missed the ambience. There was hardly anyone there so early in the morning, and it was just the two of us that we knew. At least it was a pleasant day to sit outside and enjoy our drinks. By the time we had our fill of sitting around enjoying the morning, the place had filled up, and people were asking if they could sit at our table.

We moved on at that point. I had read about a tent focused on wine, and I knew Jo would want to check it out, so we scoured the fairgrounds in search of it. It was challenging to find. We walked around the fairgrounds, but we couldn't find it. Not even a Google search helped. We eventually agreed that if we made it back to the tent we started in, we would give up and head out.

That turned out to be a bad plan, because the wine tent was directly across from the tent we started in. We hadn't even bothered to look up when we walked out. In all of the expansive fairgrounds, we didn't consider that we could be right next to the one place we wanted to check out.

This tent was pretty empty compared to the others. There were large groups of people taking up the central tables, but upstairs, where we were seated, there was hardly anyone. I grabbed a beer and Jo grabbed a wine-based drink, and we enjoyed a relaxing rest of the morning reading our Kindles. Several times, we wondered if we should get up and leave seeing as we weren't drinking a lot while taking up a table, but there was no one waiting and there were plenty of empty tables, so we put it out of our minds.

As with all things, though, we got bored after a while. Oktoberfest in Munich, the most famous of the world's Oktoberfest festivals, had been an absolute letdown. It wasn't that we were against drinking, but we had long since passed the age where drinking in and of itself was the event. Maybe we would have felt differently if we were there with a large group of people, but with just us, it was quite simply not worth our time. We headed back to the hostel in the mid-afternoon to pack our things for our early train to the airport the next morning.

That night, we paid 4 EUR to access the wireless internet at the main campground office to watch a bullfight on OneToro TV. We needed something to salvage our utterly disappointing few days in Munich. We were always careful to position the computer screen away from the public's general view because we knew some people would take offense, and we didn't want to deal with some commenter who had never seen a bullfight or even knew what they were talking about. Even so, people still walked by, but we were surprised when one man stood behind us, watching. He was a Basque man who worked at the campground, and he was as into it as we were. I offered him a seat, but he said no. He was working after all.

On September 25th, we boarded a train for Frankfurt to catch a flight to Dublin. We were on our ninetieth day in the Schengen Area, so we had to leave. Even though we had seen so much across the European continent, there were so many places we missed. The Amalfi Coast, the French Riviera, Amsterdam, Copenhagen, the Alps, we just couldn't fit it all in. Even though we were leaving the continent for the duration of The Great Gallivanting, we both knew we would return before too long. There was just too much to see to leave it be.

Reflecting on Our Final Days in the Schengen Area

Making decisions. Every traveller added to a group exponentially increased the stress of making decisions. Jo and I travelled as a pair, only adding a third for about ten days in Italy, and making decisions as a duo proved to be more stressful than we anticipated. Even though we had been friends for a long time, we had never spent so long in close proximity nor gotten to know each other on a seriously deep level. We actually joked about this leading up to The Great Gallivanting. What this meant, though, was every decision had to be a joint decision to prevent minor irritations from blowing up into something bigger. In the early days of our travels, this was a no-brainer, as we were both eager to see and do everything. On the days when we got tired, however, decision-making became a serious chore. Often times, we were going from a city we had only just become comfortable in to a new city in a new country with a new language and a new way of handling mundane things like public transportation. This was hard enough to figure out as a solo traveller, and balancing two personalities, sets of travel goals, and notions of what was acceptable when moving from one place to another only compounded The Troubles of the day.

A solo traveller at heart. The decision-making paradigm led me to a conclusion when we left Berlin: I was a solo traveller at heart. It wasn't that I didn't like being with people. I liked the ease of making decisions, the freedom to see and do what I wanted, and the ability to say something without worrying about offending someone over the next few days. As much as Jo and I got along as friends, I longed for the days of travelling on my own. I knew these days would come sooner than later, even if I didn't know when, so I just stuck it out until then. Before too long, I would be back in my element.

Next time. We made the same mistake every first-time Europe backpacker made: We tried to see the whole continent in one go. This was simply not possible. As much as we knew that in our heads, it didn't translate into our actions. We zipped around the continent, checked off nine countries and twenty-six cities in ninety days, and barely scratched the surface. We averaged between three and four days per city, including travel days, which wasn't enough time to get the authentic feel of where we were.

We also used all our time in the Schengen Area, which would come back to haunt us financially regarding flights. We closed off any possibility of doing a self-transfer for a cheap flight because doing so meant we had to officially enter the Schengen Area, which we weren't allowed to do. We would have to buy direct flights on national airlines to travel around North Africa. While this wouldn't be a deal- or bank-breaker, it was an added complexity we induced on ourselves.

The next time I visited Europe, I decided, I would do two things. First, I would slow down. If that meant spending all available ninety days in the same country, so be it. If that meant taking a short trip to a nearby country that was outside of the Schengen Area so I could attend a festival, I would do that. As a long-term traveller, it had become worth it to me to spend longer in one place to both really experience the local culture and to reduce the stress on both my body and mind.

Second, I wouldn't use all of my ninety days. I would only spend eighty-five or so in the Schengen Area before heading out. This would give me flight flexibility when traveling elsewhere, especially in Africa. Many African countries didn't have long-haul flights across the continent, which meant going to Madrid, Paris, or Rome first before continuing on. Those extra few days would considerably help to not break the bank on expensive, continuous tickets that avoided officially entering the Schengen Area.

Chapter Ten

The Emerald Isle and Great Britain

Jo and I originally hadn't planned to visit Ireland or the United Kingdom. We had too much to see to spend time in English-speaking countries that were easily accessible from the United States. Our plans changed when her cousin invited us to visit her in England, which was perfectly fine with me. We had talked about taking time between England and Morocco to slow down anyway, so this invitation fit naturally into what little we had in the way of plans. If we were going to visit England, we figured we might as well visit Ireland, too.

Dublin

We lifted off for Dublin late in the evening, which meant landing even later. Neither of us had been to Dublin before, so we didn't know the airport was a forty-five-minute bus ride from the city centre nor how that bus worked. For starters, they drove on the wrong side, i.e., the left side, of the road in Ireland and the United Kingdom, which was a bit of a trip for us to figure out, but the bus loaded from the right side of the road, which confused us even more. As we tried to figure it all out, we had our bags on our backs after a full day of traveling through Germany to Ireland, so we weren't in the cheeriest of moods. In any case, we finally figured it out, paid our 45 EUR for the bus into town, and made our way to the hostel, which was still another twenty-minute walk away from the bus stop.

Consequently, we got a late start on our first day in Dublin. I, of course, went out for coffee and breakfast at a nearby café while Jo slept in. Once she awoke, we went for our customary audio tour with Rick Steves Audio Europe. It started at St. Stephen's Green, a large, storied park in Dublin's city centre about thirty minutes away from the hostel, so we leisurely made our way there, stopping for photos and food along the way. Dublin was the first city we had visited where English was the official language, and, as we walked, we joked about how we had become so accustomed to English signs being tourist traps that we were probably walking by fantastic food and drink places as we judged them for catering to English-speaking tourists, or, you know, locals. We didn't realise how much of a mental transition it was to go from non-English-speaking countries to an English-speaking one, but we managed.

St. Stephen's Green was famous for its role in the Easter Rising of 1916, where the Irish rebels dug in against the British security forces in pursuit of Irish independence from the British Crown. The grand arch marking the main entrance to the park still had bullet holes where the British opened fire on the entrenched Irish nationalists. As a former military man, I couldn't help but notice the tactical blunder the rebels made by seeking refuge in the park. It was wholly indefensible, especially when facing the comparatively unlimited resources of the British Army. Of course, the tactical missteps were minor prices to pay when seeking the strategic goal of an independent Irish Republic, which, ultimately, the Easter Rising succeeded in obtaining as the impetus for the Irish War of Independence.

From the St. Stephen's Green, we made our way down winding alleyways to churches and government houses, explored expensive shops along Grafton Street, took in the beauty of Trinity College, and ultimately found ourselves seeking refuge from the rain in an Irish pub (or was it just a pub, seeing as we were in Ireland?). One thing led to another, and we wandered into another Irish pub not long later where a local duo was performing Blues music and selling CDs. Being the lightweight I am, a few pints of Guinness in and I was feeling them. We abandoned our tour when we stumbled into The Whiskey Reserve, much to Jo's delight.

I hadn't drunk whiskey for years, thanks to an unfortunate incident at university ten years before, but Jo loved the stuff. The barman was a local Irish guy who talked to us about whiskey, Ireland, and traveling and gave us a pub recommendation for the next night. A pub called "disndat" served 5 EUR pints with live music on Wednesday nights. We were sold instantly.

Unfortunately (or fortunately, depending on how we looked at it), it rained all day the next day, so our first stop of the day was the pub at six in the evening. We had intended to settle in for a night of 5 EUR pints and live music, but we ended up getting much, much more. Jo somehow got us in with a group of seven friends that all meet up at the same pub on Wednesdays for drinks. Six of these guys were gay, one was bisexual, and all of them were a hell of a lot of fun at the pub. In between drinks, we talked American politics (one of them did a lot of business in the United States), travels, Ireland, and about ourselves. Jo pulled out her dating apps to get some "professional" input from the group at one point. Speaking from her experience, it was a toss-up when it came to who they swiped left and right on. People were people everywhere. Go figure.

One of the guys taught me how to drink Guinness like a true Irishman. "It goes in t'rees", he said. In the first "sup," you drank it down to the "G" on the glass, which they called "splitting the G." Then, a few minutes later, you drank another third of the way. Then, a few minutes after that, you finished it off. In a perfect world, there would still be plenty of head left on the Guinness to cover the glass. According to him, drinking it that way would cause us to be less hungover than drinking beer slowly, which was my usual practice. I didn't buy it then, but after many trials across the world, I eventually concluded that he was right. Sure, I got hammered faster than usual, but I was never hungover.

In what I would consider one of my life's most outstanding cultural achievements, we were eventually forced to leave the pub. When I ordered another round after several hours of drinking, the bartender told me we were all cut off. Cut off! In

Dublin, Ireland! Our newfound friends were just as shocked as we were. One of them tried to argue the point, as he was friends with the manager, but was ultimately unsuccessful, so seven drunken Irishmen and two Americans headed into the streets of Dublin to find our next pub. Personally, I thought we should have received honorary Irish citizenship for our achievement.

I ended up heading back to the hostel early after our next pub. I was an early bird, not a night owl like Jo. She made her way back somewhere around five in the morning with a bundle of stories and memories that I was honestly sad to have missed. From drunken heart-to-heart conversations to one of the guys calling her mom, it was indeed a night for the travel books.

We took it easy the next couple of days. It rained intermittently, and we were exhausted from zipping around Europe for three months and staying out all night drinking with our Irish friends. We split up for a few hours to enjoy some attractions we wanted to see. I went to some museums while Jo went to the old Jameson distillery, and we took plenty of time to read and write at cafés in rainy Dublin.

Naturally, we finished our time in Dublin at the Guinness brewery at Saint James Gate, where we learned all about the history and development of the godly nectar that was Guinness. I won't spoil the experience here. You'll have to check it out for yourself if you are ever in Dublin!

After the brewery and a couple more pints, we boarded the train for Galway.

Galway

Galway was as incredible as all traditional Irish songs made it sound. It was also as rainy as all the Irishmen we met over the months told us it would be. Although we only had two full days there, we were determined to experience it to the fullest.

First, though, was to find a pub for a couple pints of Guinness. Our hostel was off the beaten path, which meant heading into the city after dropping our bags. We found ourselves back at the train station at Darcy's Bar. It was full of locals; we were the only tourists there. In a conversation with the barman, I learned most of the drinking crowd (mostly younger university students) were in the Latin Quarter, so we would have a relaxed, traditional pub experience. There was a local man going solo with the guitar for music, the soft rumbling of conversations and laughter between friends, and a football match on the large projector screen. At 6 EUR a pint, it was an evening well spent singing and relaxing after a long day. I especially enjoyed the intermixing of traditional Irish songs from the singer. I was a lover of traditional Irish music and the stories they told. Maybe that was the romantic traveling historian in me, or maybe it was because my dad listened to Celtic Thunder while I was growing up.

Our first full day in Galway was wet. Wet wet. The wettest I had ever been. It rained and rained and rained and rained and rained. I had intended to get out to a coffee shop to write a bit before Jo got up, but that was an ill-fated journey, and I had to settle for a quick double espresso at Starbucks instead. I preferred to avoid chain coffee shops if I could, but the only place open with a chance of having Wi-Fi access was Starbucks. It didn't matter; I high-tailed it back to the hostel to stash my computer in my bag before the rain came.

And came it did.

Jo was tired of museums by this point, and she told me as much, but with the torrential downpour, we wanted to spend more time inside than outside, so museums became the plan. To her credit, she had done more than her fair share of research for things to do inside while I was out that morning, so we had a generally easy day of going about. I intended to record for our travel vlog and posterity, but the rain was coming so hard that all I managed to record was us saying how hard it was raining.

We visited two main venues: the Galway City Museum and Claddagh Jewellers. While the Galway City Museum was interesting, especially its exhibit on the Easter Rising and Proclamation of the Irish Republic, it was a pretty standard city museum. It was an enjoyable place to get out of the rain, for sure, but it wasn't incredibly large, and we weren't exactly aligned with our views on museums after three months of seeing them across Europe. That said, the museum gave a view of the Long Walk, famous from the song "Galway Girl." While I was sure that it was a pleasant place to meet a Galway girl when the weather was nice, with the storm outside it show-cased just how dangerous nature could be. The Long Walk ran adjacent to the meeting of the River Corrib and the sea, and with the storm the waves along the quayside were violent and unpredictable as the two opposing forces of nature collided. It was an interesting juxtaposition of the picturesque view everyone portrayed to us on our way there.

The other venue, Claddagh Jewellers, was, well, a jewellery shop, albeit a famous one. Claddagh Jewellers was just a chain jewellery shop, but adjacent to it was a small exhibit on the Legend of the Claddagh Ring. The Claddagh ring was a national symbol of love in Ireland, with men and women from all across the country wearing it as a sign of both their Irish heritage and their dedication to their lovers. The ring got its name from the nearby Claddagh village, where its creator, Richard Joyce, lived out his life with his sweetheart for whom he fashioned the ring. As the legend went, as a boy, Joyce was taken prisoner by Corsairs on a journey to the West Indies and enslaved for fourteen years. While in captivity, he served as an apprentice to a goldsmith, where he learned the art of making jewellery. In this captivity, Joyce dedicated himself to making the finest ring Ireland had ever seen. Following his release as a part of demands from the King of England to the Moors, Joyce returned to his home in the Claddagh with the ring where he hoped to find his sweetheart of old waiting for him. When they reunited, he presented her with the ring, which she accepted, thus cementing the ring's place in Irish legend and society.

Being a sucker for cultural symbols and mythology, I highly considered buying a Claddagh ring while in Galway. I ultimately decided against it for three reasons. Firstly, to me, it was too feminine of a design to wear as a single man. I had no problem wearing one if I was in a serious relationship; I welcomed such a symbolic representation of love, but I couldn't bring myself to wear it as a single guy. Secondly, and more practically, Jo and I were headed to MENA soon, and I didn't want to look anything remotely like a flashy Westerner with money in a land where I was obviously the foreign tourist. The goal was to minimise our standing out in the crowds, not amplify ourselves. Thirdly, and probably most importantly to me, my family didn't have an Irish heritage. We hailed (generations upon generations ago) from England and France, and I didn't feel I should claim this cultural symbol as my own when I had no personal connection with it. I wasn't afraid of so-called "cultural appropriation." Quite the opposite, as I was sure the Irish would welcome a traveller partaking in their traditions. It just didn't sit right with me.

What did sit well with me was the rain going away overnight, so Jo and I were able to see the Cliffs of Moher the next day in the beautiful sunshine. This was the one place in Ireland Jo told me she wanted to see, so we hopped on the first bus out of Galway, took the two-hour drive around the bay, and found ourselves standing 200 metres above the ocean admiring some of the most beautiful views in all of Ireland, if not Europe or the world. These cliffs were just that: cliffs, the edge of the Emerald Isle rising out of the ocean, eroded for millennia upon millennia by ocean waves and wind. Despite their simple topographic description, they were stunning. As we walked along the hiking path, we were treated to landscapes worthy of paintings and Pulitzer Prizes. The long, beautiful, green grass, swept over by the constant winds, fluttered in the breeze. The golden rays of sunlight reflected off the grounds still wet from the rain. Inquisitive cows grazed in the adjacent pastures just a few metres away from certain death on the rocks hundreds of metres below.

We started at the visitor's centre at the halfway point, where the bus dropped us, and hiked south along the path. We walked for hours and stopped more times than a man should admit to take pictures, although we were sure they wouldn't do the views justice. The southernmost point of the walking path ended at the Moher Tower at Hag's Head, a point overlooking the sea. We debated doubling back on the trail and heading for the northernmost point, which ended near Doolin, but that was several hours of walking away, and we wouldn't arrive until after the last evening bus had departed Doolin for Galway.

Not that that solved our bus problem. Because of how the bus tickets worked, no one was guaranteed a seat on the bus; it was a first-come, first-serve system. Despite being in the front of the queue, an entire tour group of nearly fifty people was allowed to board ahead of us. Apparently, the driver had previously made a special deal with their guide, leaving us and too many others out to dry. A girl next to us, Jenny, was just as dumbfounded as we were, especially considering that the queue commanded the utmost social respect in the United Kingdom and Ireland. Fortunately, we made friends with one of the visitor centre attendants who helped us all get on a special reserve bus a couple of hours later.

Recharged from our several hours off of walking, Jo talked Jenny into going out for a pint with us that evening. Jenny said she could do "just one," but that one turned into two turned into a few turned into a few more. We wound up going to a few different music venues that night. The first was a local band playing a sort of acoustic, speakeasy-style rendition of some modern popular songs. They were excellent, and the lead singer had that sort of raspy voice that I could only compare to The Dead South in the United States. When that place closed down (rather early, in my opinion), Jo, Jenny, and everyone else headed over to the Roisin Dubh, a famous music venue in Galway. I had had enough for the night, so I headed back to the hostel for the night. (More on Jenny in the "Reflecting on the Emerald Isle and Great Britain" section of this chapter).

With our two days in Galway over, I woke up early enough to pack. I wasn't sure what time Jo returned that night, but I figured she knew when our train to Dublin was and let her sleep in. We had a long, boring day of train travel ahead of us to get to Belfast.

Belfast

The only train to Northern Ireland from the Republic of Ireland left from Dublin Connolly station in Dublin. This train was the only way to cross the border by rail, which, for us, meant taking the train from Galway station to Dublin Heuston station, taking the Red Line tram from Dublin Heuston to Dublin Connolly, the train from Dublin Connolly to Belfast Central station, and another train from Belfast Central to Botanic station before walking a few minutes to the hostel. It was a boring day of travel that somehow managed to take it out of us.

We weren't sure what we wanted to see or do in Belfast. We knew it was central to The Troubles, but even then, we didn't have a concept of what that meant outside of the domestic conflict that plagued Northern Ireland for thirty years. Fortunately, we didn't have to make any decisions about touring Belfast on our first day. Jo had seen the Giant's Causeway on Instagram and added it to her list of things she wanted to see, so we headed off to the windiest place in Ireland early our first morning. It was a few hours away by train and bus, so we hoped it would be worth it.

It was.

The Giant's Causeway was, essentially, a national park overlooking the causeway between Northern Ireland and Scotland, complete with scenic outlooks, rock beaches, hiking paths, and an optional, pay-to-enter tourist centre at the top of the hill, which led down to the rest of the causeway. It was raining when we arrived, but it cleared up after a few minutes of wandering around the visitor's centre, so we gathered our audio guides and started walking.

The audio guide was less of a description of the fauna and geology and more of a folklore story of how the beautiful rock formations, hills, and the causeway itself were formed. According to Irish lore, Finn McCool, a giant, lived in the giant's causeway, and several of the rock formations get their name from his residence, including his boots and chimney. The causeway, again according to lore, was originally a land bridge connecting Ireland and Scotland, where a rival giant lived. The rival giant challenged Finn McCool to a battle to see who was the bigger giant, but when the rival arrived in Ireland, Finn pretended to be a baby in his living room. The Scottish giant decided that if Finn could produce a baby that size, he wanted nothing of the fight, so he ran off back to Scotland, tearing up the causeway and filling it with water in the process.

Of course, this was all lore, and there were perfectly sound geological explanations for how the rocks, beaches, and cliffs were formed, but it was still fun partaking in the Irish legends that I had relished in since I was a kid. On top of the lore, Jo and I were treated to some astonishingly beautiful landscape sights. The sun reflecting off the moistened grass, roads, and rocks made for stunning photos worthy of being showcased on the Google Chromecast home screen. Energised by the desire to get better photos and keep exploring the area, Jo set off along a hiking path on the west side of the causeway and visitor centre. This path was a part of the national park system but was substantially less travelled than the main tourist area down the hill. It wound around the cliffs that overlooked the sea, through gates that crossed in and out of farmland with signs imploring you to close them after passing so the sheep didn't get out, and down the coast farther than we could walk. It was just the two of us out in nature enjoying breathtaking scenery, which did wonders for our moods after the long journey here from Galway the day before. The cows that ambled up to the fence line probably also helped; I didn't think I would get Jo away from petting them. Like the Cliffs of Moher, though, we had a long journey back to our hostel, so we reluctantly made our way back towards the visitor centre in the mid-afternoon.

Back at the hostel, we met two older Canadian women visiting Northern Ireland on a two-week vacation. They told us about the tours they had discovered, including a free (minus tip) walking tour of Belfast and a political tour specifically about The Troubles in West Belfast. Jo wasn't interested in the political tour, so we agreed to do the walking tour that morning and then split up that afternoon. The walking tour was good but standard in our experience over the last several months, as we learned about the city's history in and out of The Troubles. The best part, for me, was meeting a girl named Annie who was solo-traveling Europe for a few months (like Jenny, I'll talk more about her in the "Reflecting on the Emerald Isle and Great Britain" section of this chapter). The three of us became fast friends before the tour ended and agreed to grab drinks later that evening.

After lunch, I headed off for the political tour. (Truth in lending, I had to agree not to describe the path of the tour for commercial purposes, as this has caused tour guide licensing issues for the tour company in the past, but I can describe it in general terms). I wasn't sure what to expect, as I didn't know anything about The Troubles to any substantial degree. All I knew was I would be spending about an hour and a half with a Protestant militant and an hour and a half with a Catholic militant, each presenting their side of the story on their side of the peace walls which still divided the two communities in Belfast, Derry, and other areas of Northern Ireland to this day.

The tour started on the Catholic side of the wall with a guide who was a convicted terrorist, former member of the Irish Republican Army (IRA), and current member of Sinn Fein, the socialist and nationalist political party in Northern Ireland (nationalist meaning Irish nationalist seeking reunification of Northern Ireland with the Republic of Ireland). I was shocked by his honesty with us. At sixty years old, he openly admitted he had partaken in political violence, that looking back he sees that such violence wasn't the answer to political problems, and religion was just an excuse for what each side did to the other. That didn't mean he regretted his actions or beliefs; far from it. He still believed in the nationalist cause, and he understood why violence was common in pursuit of those beliefs during The Troubles. As an older man, however, he simply wanted a peaceful world for his grandchildren and to use the political process to achieve reunification instead of violence.

Notably, as an outside observer and storyteller, I noticed he shied away from describing the infamous Catholic-on-Catholic violence perpetrated by the IRA, the no-notice bombs that killed innocent people, including children and babies, and the fault Sinn Fein still bore for the gridlocked, non-functioning government of

Northern Ireland. He focused on the politics of reunification and internment, the history which spanned 1,000 years of English and Norman intervention, and the symbolic struggle against the English monarch's suppression of Irish Catholics (all of which, I would learn in further reading, were perfectly valid commentaries when put into full context). He also talked of the personal toll the conflict took on him, as he pointed to the very spot where his best friend was killed, the place where he met his wife during The Troubles, and his brother's name on the IRA memorial wall. Before handing across the peace wall to the Protestant guide ("checkpoint Charlie" he jokingly called it), he succeeded in making the personal impression he was aiming to make, at least on me.

Crossing to the Protestant side of the wall was like stepping into another city altogether. The streets looked different, the neighbourhoods less orderly, and the peace wall towered over the street beside it. On the Catholic side, the wall was obscured behind houses, painted with murals, and had memorial gardens arranged beneath it, which took away from its towering, authoritarian role in the community. On the Protestant side, the peace wall stood as a sort of Soviet-style reminder of the violence that could come at any minute from the other side, no matter how unrealistic or far in the past the violence may or may not have been.

The Protestant guide was a convicted member of the Ulster Volunteer Force (UVF), the Protestant answer to the Catholic IRA. Unlike the Catholic guide, the Protestant guide never once talked about why he was convicted, his role in The Troubles, or how he came to join the UVF. Nor did he discuss the UVF's political goals or objectives in any detail; he only stated that they would react to IRA violence should it ever occur again. Instead, he focused on the no-notice bombs and ambushes which the IRA perpetrated on the Protestant community in West Belfast. Such acts were plentiful. Walking down Shankill Road, we passed memorial after memorial of innocents who were killed in no-notice car explosions, drive-by shootings, and bombs thrown from the windows of IRA cars as they drove by. Neither supermarkets nor libraries nor bars were safe from the IRA violence, and our guide impressed upon us that "Sinn Fein-IRA" (as he called them) never once took responsibility for these innocent deaths and simply cited them as "casualties of war." The still-lingering anger towards the Catholics for these deaths was evident both in the memorials and our guide's demeanour. To the Protestants, there would be no peace nor acceptance of the Catholics or Sinn Fein in Northern Ireland until they publicly acknowledged these illegal acts as such and imprisoned those responsible.

While the Catholic guide focused on the political process, the Protestant guide impressed upon us that this conflict was far from over. He took us to a mural dedicated to the UVF painted on the large side of a shop along Shankill Road. The mural celebrated the creation of a new UVF company in 2022. He asked us why a new UVF company needed to be formed if this conflict was genuinely headed in the right direction with the peace process. That was when he let us in on the dark secret that the government on both sides wanted to keep quiet: the IRA and UVF weapons caches had been cleaned out. No one knew where the weapons had gone, and it was the UVF belief that Sinn Fein-IRA violence was an imminent threat to which the UVF and other loyalist paramilitaries would have to respond.

By the end of the tour, I had learned more than I thought possible about The Troubles and the world of political violence in Northern Ireland. While I had by now resolved to stay away from the world of terrorism and political violence by not returning to my old career, I couldn't help but feel the allure of learning about and advocating for a solution to a simmering conflict that could explode at any moment. As I walked the forty-five minutes back to the hostel, I took in the streets of Belfast in a whole new light. Around every corner, there once was and could be again a car bomb, IRA or UVF hit squad, or secret meeting taking place. I had to admit, I loved Belfast for that feeling and history.

Of course, that feeling dissipated when I arrived back at the hostel and found Jo wearing an entirely new wardrobe. She had apparently gone shopping while I was on the political tour. On a personal level, I didn't really care. I knew that she had been wanting some cuter clothes ever since Layne came to visit in Italy, and if she was happy with her new wardrobe that would be a lot of stress off of me. As a travel partner, I wondered how on Earth was she going to pack all that into her bag and how much that was going to make her bag weigh on travel days. While ultimately a problem for her, it was something I would have to deal with once it came time to pack for a flight or to walk a long distance, which we had to do the next day for our flight to England.

Newcastle Upon Tyne

Jo had family in Newcastle Upon Tyne, in England, who offered us a place to stay, so we jetted from Belfast to Newcastle to enjoy a week of relaxation and family. It wasn't until we got there that we realised how much of a break we needed. While we both wanted to go out and explore Newcastle, after one afternoon of visiting the mall and getting lunch, we quickly agreed we would stay in, watch films and bullfights on TV, and, most importantly, play with Jo's cousin's dogs. After several months on the road, it was odd to be in a proper family home, telling stories, catching up on life, and watching the TV screen on the couch. It was a little slice of what normal used to be. Jo was close with her family back in Texas, so having a touch of that in England brightened her travel experience. On the other hand, I was terrified of going back home because I had no idea what that held for me, and I struggled with the family home atmosphere. Nonetheless, it was a much-needed break from the constant moving and exploring we had been doing at a breakneck pace across Europe, and we both took several long naps to recoup our energy.

Jo's cousin introduced us to several English traditions, such as Sunday roast and traditional fish and chips. We ate more in a few days than we had eaten in a long while, and we begrudgingly had to admit that we enjoyed the fish and chips. We both hated seafood, but when it came to fish and chips, you really only tasted the seasoned batter it was fried in.

As a part of the family reunion, we spent one morning with Jo's aunt near Alnwick, home to the Alnwick Castle of *Harry Potter* fame. After a morning of playing with her aunt's dog on the beach, she dropped us off at the castle. Apparently, the Duke of Northumberland was a prominent businessman and really enjoyed his peerage, so he actually lived in the castle and was making large-scale land purchases for development purposes that angered the local population. The on-going legal battles between land-owners, the town council, and the Duke were the subject of much local controversy. I found it all humorous as someone from small-town Texas where there were four dominant families who collectively held influence over just about every business and political decision which occurred. Small towns were small towns everywhere.

After lunch, we ignored the local controversy and visited the castle. Only the grounds and the fortification walls were open to tourists, but as the castle was featured in one of the most extraordinary cultural phenomena of the 21st Century, that's all they needed. The grounds were perfectly manicured, the castle's façade immaculate against the rural backdrop of meadows leading to forests, and the *Harry Potter* connection was on full display. From paid tours focused explicitly on the castle's role in the film to broom "flying" lessons that seemed straight out of the film, the Duke capitalised on the franchise's twenty-year-old fame, even though the castle had only been featured in the first two films, having lost the bid for subsequent films due to disputes over royalties and film rights.

As much as we enjoyed the break in Newcastle, we had flights from London to Marrakech in a week, so it was time to pack our bags and head back out on the road. After a lazy week of sleeping whenever we wanted, not having to pack our bags, and not walking 20,000 steps a day, the 05h00 alarm to catch an early-morning train to Scotland was a jolting return to the realities of long-term budget traveling.

Edinburgh

Jo and I initially didn't intend to go to Scotland. It had been a deliberate discussion the year before when we were planning The Great Gallivanting. She had lived in New England, so getting to the United Kingdom was an easy flight she could get whenever she wanted. As such, we opted against touring too much of Great Britain. At the same time, we were budget travellers, and we always checked multiple itineraries to get the cheapest deal on travel. It turned out that it was cheaper to travel to Edinburgh from Newcastle Upon Tyne via train, spend two days in Edinburgh, and then take the train from Edinburgh through Newcastle on the way to London than to take the train directly from Newcastle to London. So that was exactly what we did.

By 08h30, we were settled into coffee and breakfast in Edinburgh after dropping our bags at the hostel. It was one of those funny moments of travel where we woke up in one city and had breakfast in another to save money. We had no idea what we would see or do in Edinburgh, as this was a spur-of-the-moment detour, so we spent the morning reading and drinking coffee in the warmth of a local coffee shop not too far from the hostel. It was mid-October by this point, so Edinburgh was chilly and windy as the winter weather started rolling in.

As we couldn't check into our hostel until the afternoon, we unsurprisingly pulled out the Rick Steves Audio Europe app and took a tour down the Royal Mile, the road that connected Edinburgh Castle and the Scottish royal residence. The views from the castle were fantastic, even though we didn't go in during the walking tour. We could see out over most of the city and far off into the distance from "The

Rock," as the Edinburgh Castle was colloquially known because of its position on top of a large rock formation which provided an excellent defence against invading forces. Out front, in an obscure corner of the parking area, was a fountain dedicated to all of the women in Edinburgh who were falsely accused of being witches and executed for their practice of witchcraft. As Americans, we knew of the Salem Witch Trials, but those were on a much smaller scale than the films and television would have you believe. The Scottish Witch Trials, however, were a severe epidemic of irrational fear, and estimates for the number of women executed for witchcraft in the 1500s and 1600s ran into the several hundreds. There were only twenty-five in Salem.

Along the Royal Mile, we passed several beautiful churches; however, Jo was tired of visiting churches and cathedrals, especially if we had to pay to see them, so we admired them from the outside. Even so, the St. Giles Cathedral was an imposing structure that seemed to be crammed onto the road, sandwiched between the Royal Mile and the Scottish Supreme Court building. It was also Presbyterian, which was different from our usual encounter with Catholic cathedrals (the last cathedral I had seen that wasn't Catholic was in Trieste when I visited the Greek Orthodox cathedral).

As the tour went on, we wore out quickly. We loved the Rick Steves walking tours, but after such an early wake-up, we were ready to partake in that greatest of Spanish traditions. It didn't help that the royal residence was closed to visitors outside of organised tours, which cost far more than we were willing to pay. That was one thing about the Rick Steves tours: sometimes they looped you back around to where you started, and sometimes they left you at the far end of town. In Edinburgh, it was the latter. Fortunately, it was check-in time, the hostel rooms were cool, and we turned in for a few hours before joining a group for traditional Scottish dancing that evening. As per usual, Jo stayed out later than me, she being the night owl and me being the early bird.

On our second and final day in Edinburgh, we decided to be what we had never been: stereotypical tourists. We had been budget travellers and adventurers for three months, so we treated ourselves. We started by paying to visit the Edinburgh Castle. The castle was nice, and the museums inside were an excellent display of arms, art, and history. The included audio guide helped as well, especially with it being on our phones. Really, though, we were just turning our brains off and milling about with the other tourists before heading to the most touristy thing we had done before: a *Harry Potter* tour of Edinburgh.

The author of the *Harry Potter* books, J.K. Rowling, wrote them predominantly in Edinburgh, and she took many of the inspirations for her characters and locations from scenes and names around the city. Specifically, she took a lot of names from tombstones in Greyfriars Kirkyard, a cemetery which sat in the shadow of the castle. Of course, these were just names, not the actual lives of the deceased, but that hadn't stopped *Harry Potter* fans from flocking to the cemetery to live out their fantasies of what the real-world inspiration for their favourite characters must have been. In fact, during the tour, we learned the kirkyard had a problem with vandalism against the gravesites because of revelations in the book. Jo and I both loved *Harry Potter*, but that didn't seem a reason to desecrate the graves of those whose lives came and went long before the books were conceived. Just another gentle reminder to remain grounded in reality and not get sucked into the lives of others, especially fictional characters.

Unfortunately, most of the other hotspots for *Harry Potter* lovers were either closed or burned down. It was fifteen years after the last book was finished, after all. So, instead of visiting the café where J.K. Rowling wrote the books, we stopped at scenic spots in town to learn more about Edinburgh's influence on the *Harry Potter* universe. Luckily for us, however, the tour ended on Victoria Street, the top contender for the street that inspired Diagon Alley (J.K. Rowling never confirmed which street was the inspiration). Victoria Street was colourful, with different shops painted to contrast with those around it, and many played into the *Harry Potter* tourism by tailoring their products to sound like they came from the Magical World of Witchcraft and Wizardry. According to the guide, if we searched for "Diagon Alley" on Google Maps, the pin would drop on Victoria Street, which was enough for her to say that this street was the "real-world Diagon Alley" (we tried it out ourselves and found that the pin would drop either in Orlando or London, so we remained sceptical of this justification).

With the tour complete, we set about exploring a bit more. Seeing as we had nothing planned for Edinburgh, we searched for a camera shop. Jo had talked for about a month of trying to get into landscape photography, and we had seen enough beautiful sights over the last two weeks in Ireland and Scotland to solidify her desire to give it a try. After a lot of walking and about 200 British Pounds (GBP) later, she was the proud and eager owner of a used DSLR camera. I had to admit, it took great photos at a pretty good distance. Naturally, she tested it out, taking photos of every dog we saw on the long walk back to the hostel.

This being mid-October, it had been a solid month and change since we left Spain. While we had watched a couple of bullfights online since leaving, we missed the food. I surprised Jo by walking us to an Andalusian restaurant on the way back to the hostel for dinner. It was just what we needed. Croquettas, albondigas, pedron peppers, it was a small taste of our favourite country in cold, windy Scotland. The food wasn't quite as good as the tapas place in Berlin, but it was certainly better than no tapas at all, and the meal prepared me for my favourite Spanish tradition before we joined in the pub crawl that night. I didn't stay out too late, because we had another 06h00 train ahead of us, but Jo wandered in with just a couple of hours to spare (and pack...) after what was surely a fun night out, based on the pictures she had taken.

By 10h00 the next morning, we would be in London, our last city in Europe.

London

Jo and I arrived just before lunch at Battersea, a neighbourhood on the south side of the River Thames. We could have taken a later train that left and arrived later, but the early morning departure was the cheapest by a substantial margin (over 100 GBP each!), so we resolved to enjoy the morning before calling it an early night.

I also was (and still am) a lover of all things James Bond, so I looked forward to seeing Vauxhall Cross and the home of the British Secret Intelligence Service,

MI6. The bus into the city centre from our hostel drove us right by it! This was exciting for me. I had seen Bond race a boat from its walls, jump from its highest stories, chase assassins through its halls, and have countless meetings with M and Q as he prepared for his missions to save the world in its offices. Call me a kid in a candy store, but just seeing the building brightened my early morning. Jo was facing away from the building as we passed, so I told her to look behind her. She said, "What? It's just a building." "No," I replied, "that's MI6!" She whipped around to look and was dumbfounded we could drive so close to the headquarters of one of the world's most well-known secret intelligence services.

As our bus turned right onto the street across the Thames, we got a great look at Vauxhall's iconic façade, but as we drove, something else struck me. I knew the building on our left, too, from one of my favourite spy TV shows, *Spooks*. I got Jo's attention and nodded behind me, "And that's Thames House." She didn't know that one offhand, so I clarified, "MI5!" In the span of thirty seconds, we had driven by two of the four pillars of British intelligence all while riding a public transport bus. That would never happen in the United States. The CIA building was protected by large grounds, fences, and hedges, and the FBI building was an ugly, obtrusive, decrepit structure in the middle of Washington, DC, in an area where you didn't walk unless you have a reason to (not because it is forbidden or dangerous, but because there is nothing of non-government interest on that block). You would never find tourists, businessmen on lunchbreak, or people going about their daily business walking by the United States' intelligence headquarters, but in the middle of London, they were a part of the cityscape to which no one paid any mind.

Rick Steves offered two different city walks in London, so we started with his City of London tour, which focused on the central City of London. As most people knew it, London was a metropolitan area called "Greater London," comprising thirty-two boroughs, including the City of London, the heart of London's financial business, and the City of Westminster, the heart of its government business. While London had a city-wide mayor and police service over the City of Westminster and other thirty boroughs, the City of London had its own mayor, elections, police service, city council, and more. It still served a function as part of Greater London and was physically indistinguishable to the untrained eye, but the technical jurisdictional separation was something that intrigued me from my days in the military police, where I dealt with such technicalities on a regular basis.

The City of London had some beautiful architectural sites. St. Clement Danes Church was an Anglican church that served as a main church for the Royal Air Force. Inside, the church displayed the rolls of those Royal Airmen who had been killed in service to their country, and the tiles on the floor were each dedicated to a different Royal Air Force unit. The Royal Courts of Justice, while we couldn't visit the interior, was one of the most impressive buildings in all of London with its grandiosity and neo-Gothic architecture that pictures couldn't do justice. Of course, St. Paul's Cathedral, one of Europe's top ten largest churches, towered over the City of London. For 1,500 years, there had been a church on the site of St. Paul's Cathedral, although the last incarnation had been destroyed in the Great Fire of 1666. For us modern tourists, that fire was a blessing, as it gave us the monstrosity that awaited us as we walked down Fleet Street. I found it ironic that investment firms surrounded such a massive and imposing house of God. Vice and Virtue were two sides of the same coin.

Just after we passed St. Paul's, it started to rain, so we dipped into a coffee shop to wait it out not far from London Bridge. Jo had her camera with her, and understandably didn't want to get her new purchase and hobby wet before we headed off to Africa later in the week. We were both tired, too, after her late night, our early morning, and our hours-long walking tour. We took the rain delay as a chance to upload pictures, schedule Instagram posts, and, importantly, use the toilet. Something we learned during our time in Europe was to never pass up the chance to use a toilet free of charge. We never knew when the next opportunity would come.

The City of Westminster was on the agenda for the next day. While the City of London had its fair share of tourists, it was nothing compared to Westminster. Huge tour groups and buses filled every corner of every square as traffic filled the streets, and government bureaucrats pushed through the crowds to get to meetings, lunch, and coffee. This was the first time since leaving the United States that I was genuinely concerned about pickpockets. Most of the historic city centres in Europe were primarily pedestrian areas with traffic diverted around the government houses and tour groups spreading out to leave room for everyone else. Hence, the situation in Westminster took some getting used to. Getting Instagram-worthy photos without tourists wandering into the shots was nearly impossible. Jo fared much better than I did with her camera zooming in to capture architectural shots from interesting angles.

Parliament Street/Whitehall (the same road that changed names at a certain point) housed most important government buildings, from the British Parliament to the Ministry of Defence to the Ministry of Energy to Number 10 Downing Street (the home of the British prime minister). As such, security was heavy, with barricades protruding far into the pedestrian sidewalks. Most of the tourists probably only saw the armed guards out front with their automatic rifles and tactical kit, but Jo and I noticed there was plenty of non-overt security in place, including strategically, but inconspicuously, parked vans which contained heavily armed emergency response teams. We talked aloud about how Americans who decried the so-called militarisation of the police and pointed to the British model of policing had no clue of what the reality in London was. We figured if someone tried to commit political violence on the street or jump one of the barriers, they would be dead within five to seven seconds.

Which was why things like the horse-mounted soldiers we watched at Horse Guard Parade and concepts like the King's Guard in general confused me. Officially, the King's Guard (at Buckingham Palace at St. James Palace) and the King's Life Guard (at Horse Guard Parade) patrolled and protected the grounds of the Royal buildings. They were formally charged with protecting them, in conjunction with the Metropolitan Police Service (aka "The Met"). Unofficially, however, Jo and I noted that these guards, while probably highly-trained, wouldn't be able to handle much on their own. During the changing of the guard at Horse Guard Parade, the King's Life Guard "secured" the change with sentries wielding swords. I doubted these swords were rated for lethal use in the first place, but if they were, I seriously doubted if these nineteen-year-old kids were actually capable of running one through an attacker if need be. Luckily, that need would never arise, because the Met provided heavily-armed officers to manage the crowd and provide security. I had always been for military ceremony, but only when it served a military purpose, and, to me, the horse-mounted soldiers at Horse Guard Parade were little more than tourist attractions which the real security personnel had to protect.

However, none of that changed the fact that we took the touristy pictures with the horses. By "we," I mean I took photos of Jo with the horses. Unlike most other tourists, she kept the requested respectful distance and didn't try to touch the horses or their reins. The same could not be said of others, and the horsemen were constantly pulling the reins out of people's hands and moving their horses' heads out of the way of tourists who tried to pet them for clicks and likes. Jo and I joked that these tourists clearly didn't know anything about horses because we were sure that, given the opportunity, they would bite the tourists after becoming sufficiently annoyed. It was good that the horses were backed into the guard houses because some unknowing tourist would have found themselves on the wrong side of a mule kick if the horses were standing out in the open.

Our walking tour ended at Trafalgar Square, outside of the British Museum. Trafalgar Square celebrated the Battle of Trafalgar and the ensuing British naval victory over the French and Spanish. Unfortunately, we were unable to enjoy the square and its military glory because of all of the Palestinian flags and related graffiti. The week before, while Jo and I were in Newcastle Upon Tyne, Hamas had launched over 5,000 rockets from Gaza into Israel, and Israel was in the middle of its initial retaliatory actions as we stood in Trafalgar Square (more on our encounter with the October 7th attack in the "Reflecting on the Emerald Isle and Great Britain" section of this chapter). Just a couple of days before, this square had been full of protestors demanding to "Free Palestine" "From the River to the Sea," and they left their mark. As disappointing as it was to have such a magnificent square marred by protests as a tourist, this was real life, and that's what we wanted to experience as travellers.

But that didn't stop us from visiting the British Museum after lunch. It was free (our favourite price as budget travellers), housed extensive archaeological exhibits, and was home to the Rosetta Stone, so it seemed a great use of our time.

Unfortunately, the outside protests from days before put a damper on our experience. We wanted to see the Middle East exhibits, as we had both deployed there while in the military. Every Middle East exhibit on every floor was closed. The signs said "for cleaning," but we found it a thinly-veiled cover story for the real reason which had plagued other nations: to prevent protestors from destroying precious artifacts in the name of a modern political movement. We didn't want to be so cynical about it, but the Middle East exhibits were in different places on each floor of the very large museum. We were sorely disappointed in the museum, protestors, and, quite frankly, the police that the problem had become this big in such a short amount of time. Jo looked at me and said, "Do we really want to see this whole thing if these exhibits are closed?" She didn't need me to answer before we were heading for the front door.

Before departing the museum, we made it a point to see the Rosetta Stone. We couldn't pass up seeing the rock discovered by French explorers displayed in a

British museum that unlocked the secrets of ancient Egypt by allowing us to translate from Greek. As incalculable as the Rosetta Stone's importance in understanding history and societies going back thousands upon thousands of years was, it was unimpressively small. Like, really small. I could wrap my arms around it if I wanted to. Given its prominence, we had imagined it to be a massive work, but it was just a small, pretty rock with writing on it. Sure, an important rock with important writing, but still not as grandiose as the historical documentaries made it seem to the unlearned mind. Luckily, it was close to the entrance/exit.

In all our time in London, one thing we hadn't yet seen were the soldiers in the tall, fuzzy hats. I didn't care much about them, but it was something Jo wanted to see. Unfortunately, we had a flight the next day, so the likelihood of us seeing them was slim to none. Undeterred, we headed to Buckingham Palace to try to glimpse them. We were moderately successful. The King's Guard in the famous fuzzy hats still patrolled the grounds and manned their posts, but all of their operations had moved inside the gates years before. We could no longer get the up-close pictures and videos that had become so famous (or infamous, depending on the video) on travel blogs, YouTube videos, and Facebook pages. Worse, the unit on duty that day didn't wear the fuzzy hats; they wore service covers similar to what she and I had worn in the military. I was unbothered, but Jo was bummed. Like, really, really bummed. I hadn't seen her that disappointed in something since we started our travels. Even the picturesque palace with the sunset backdrop didn't make up for it.

Well, call me a sucker for severe disappointments, but we resolved to go in search of the fuzzy hats the next morning. We packed our bags early, stashed them in the luggage room at the hostel, and dedicated our final half-day in Europe to finding the famous red-coated soldiers. And find them we did.

We, somehow, accidentally wandered into the changing of the guard at Buckingham Palace. We split up, because I needed to find a bathroom, but we both got a great view of the ceremonies. She found a spot right on the gates of the palace, able to watch the parade of men, horses, and bands pass in review and officially change the guard while I was at the far end of the street where all the units entered and exited the ceremony. The blue-uniformed, service-cover-wearing soldiers changed out for the famous red coats and fuzzy hats with all of the pomp and circumstance we could expect. We both took great photos as they passed by, and the change in her demeanour was night and day from the evening before.

However, we both noted the same situation we observed at Horse Guard Parade the day before. Vans loaded with heavily armed men ready to lay waste to any threat were located on the outskirts of the ceremony and as part of the parade through the street itself. Unlike the vans we had seen before, these windows weren't blacked out, and we could clearly see the security officers inside. We agreed: We weren't sure how much use the King's Guard would have been in the face of a threat to the ceremony, but those vans would have crushed an armed assault before most people realised what was happening.

With our time in London coming to an end, we grabbed our bags and headed to London Stanstead International Airport, one of the three "London" airports (although none were actually in London). After an hour on public transport, we breezed through security and waited to board our Ryanair flight to Morocco. We were leaving Europe and Western society behind and heading to North Africa and my beloved Sahara. Even though we had travelled to eleven countries so far, this was our first time to change continents. We were both excited to be in Morocco and apprehensive about how the significant culture shift would affect us.

I couldn't wait.

Reflecting on the Emerald Isle and Great Britain

Jenny. Jenny, the girl we met at the Cliffs of Moher, was an astonishingly beautiful woman from Belfast. She had her doctorate in business management and worked for a pharmaceutical company in London. She had long, brown hair, a beautiful Northern Irish accent, and was sharp, really sharp, in our conversations while waiting for the bus. I was smitten almost immediately, and Jo knew it. We hit it off right from the start, and after dinner and a couple of pints, we were headed in the right direction. I'm not sure if I would have moved to London after only a few hours of knowing this girl, but man, was I interested.

Unfortunately, life had other plans, and not in the usual travel way of going our separate ways. I was not the only guy who fell for her in seconds. Several guys at the pubs we went to for live music found themselves wrapped around her finger (although, I'm quite confident that I was the only one that didn't have the sole intention of getting her into bed that same night). Jenny had mentioned that she was trying to quit smoking, and told both Jo and me not to let her smoke while drinking. Well, I tried and failed in that endeavour, and at one point she disappeared for a long time outside for a smoke. I still had her jacket and wallet (it was cold outside, but warm in the pub), and when I went to get her as the bar was closing down, I found her deep in conversation with one of the band members, who was also from Belfast. She invited him along to the next pub with us, and walked the whole way lost in conversation with him about Belfast and the Catholic-Protestant conflict there.

Needless to say, I found myself outside her orbit by the time we made it to the Roisin Dubh (the pub we were heading to, and the most famous in Galway). I had severe issues with sudden rejection stemming from past relationships and friendships, and I could feel myself heading into a downward spiral in my head. I didn't even finish my Guinness before deciding to leave. Jo could tell what was up and, as usual, stayed out to have her own adventure (which culminated with her watching some Australian guys railing lines of cocaine back at the original bar). Before I left, I found Jenny, gave her a hug, and fired off one of the best lines I had ever used:

"I meant what I said before. You are the most beautiful girl in this bar."

"That's because you haven't looked at the other girls."

"I didn't have to. I had already looked at you."

The line didn't work, nor did I expect it to. It was my way of helping myself walk out of the bar with my head held high. I took a sleeping pill when I got back to the room. I didn't want to stay awake too long with the thoughts I knew would be heading my way by the time I got back to the hostel.

Did I really think that this astonishingly beautiful Belfast girl and I would live happily ever after? Probably not. But the way the night ended and the ensuing downward spiral told me that I still had a long way to go to recover from the cascading effects of the last several years that led to me leaving everything behind and heading off on some grand adventure. As much as I told myself I was ready for a relationship, I hadn't quite gotten to that point.

Annie. Of course, that ill-fated day with Jenny didn't stop me from trying. Enter Annie, the North Carolina girl Jo and I met in Belfast (Belfast was a common theme with women I met on the road). She, too, worked in the medical field, except she was a legitimate scientist. She had left her company to travel for six months but had an open-ended offer to return. Annie, Jo, and I met up for drinks one night in Belfast, and it went great. We talked travel, Jo and Annie swooned over her pictures of matador butts, and, again, we hit it off straight away.

We tried to link up in Edinburgh, but the timeline didn't quite work out, so I decided to pull the trigger and ask her out on a date when we were all in London. To my surprise and glee, she ecstatically agreed. While Jo and I were waiting out the rain in a coffee shop in the City of London, I planned the date. I got us reservations at a nice Spanish restaurant, mapped a walk through a park for us afterwards, and found an upscale cocktail bar to end the night. I would pick her up at her hostel, we would take the tube (the London underground metro) into town, and then see where things went from there.

Storm clouds were present from the beginning. She wasn't there when I arrived at her hostel. She was on her way back from touring the Tower of London. Now, she was a traveller and had more things to do than go on a date with me, but I sort of expected her to be more date-ready than showing up fresh from walking all over London. But I just chalked that up to travel dating, and off we went. The dinner at the Spanish restaurant went great, and we talked about our past lives, what we wanted to do in the future, our travels, and *some* of our beliefs. We were heading in a great direction by the time I paid our 100 GBP bill, and we headed for the walk in the park.

The scene at the cocktail bar was another story. The conversation naturally turned towards certain political issues, and it all collapsed instantly, despite my efforts to keep things light-hearted and easy-going. I was a moderate conservative from Texas with a military background, two deployments, and time in the security world, where I worked on international issues for my firm. She described herself as: "I'm pretty far left. Like, I'm a lefty." As much as I tried to put on the air of mutual respect for differing opinions, she was not interested. I was wrong, she was right, and if she couldn't convert me, then she wasn't interested. After we finished our first drinks, we headed to the tube and went our separate ways, my offer to escort her back to her hostel notwithstanding.

When Jo asked me how it went, I told her, "The 'tolerant left' strikes again." She knew exactly what I meant; those who preached tolerance in our country tended to be the least tolerant of different ideas. I tried to keep up with Annie, me being able to put differing political beliefs aside in a relationship (at least on most issues), but to no avail. She had no use for someone with my views in her life. I wasn't upset at this like I was with how things went with Jenny. I was, however, sorely disappointed that someone of such high calibre and with such a sharp mind as Annie could fall into such a mind trap.

A not-so open relationship. I didn't fall for every girl I met, as the stories of the Emerald Isle might indicate. In fact, Jo and I met a lot of people who intentionally didn't display any interest in us, because they thought we were in a relationship. We dealt with this misconception constantly. Usually, it was a simple dismissal of the idea based on an offhand comment in a conversation. Sometimes, however, we didn't know someone thought we were dating until it was too late.

We hoped to quell such misconceptions by talking about our (though, mostly Jo's) Tinder and Bumble dates. Some funny stories made for excellent hostel conversation, so it wasn't like we were overplaying them to make a point. On our last morning in Galway, I was eating breakfast downstairs when one of the travel friends we had met came down, saw me by myself, and asked, "Where's your better half?" This was after we had told some of the aforementioned Tinder and Bumble stories. I replied, "Contrary to popular belief, we're not dating, but she's in the shower upstairs." Our friend replied, "That makes so much more sense! You guys were talking about your Tinder and Bumble dates, and I was thinking, 'Man, they are in a *really* open relationship!'"

Well, I quelled those thoughts as we laughed hard over her confusion, but we would have to deal with that in the coming months. Spoiler alert: Jo and I went our separate ways at one point in our travels, but we still had our Instagram posts and stories that we would tag each other in, especially regarding the bullfighting schedule and inside jokes. Luckily, we were both in the "Not no, but hell no" category when it came to dating each other, so as we spent more time apart, quelling the notion became much easier.

El Juli's retirement. One of the most impactful travel experiences for both of us was our three weeks following a matador around Spain in September. Even though we had left Spain a month before, we still kept up with the bullfighting season and the Feria de Otoño, the final bull fair of the European season. This year, El Juli, the child prodigy and a world-famous matador, had announced his retirement, and his last performance would be in Madrid at the Feria de Otoño. We decided to watch it live from Galway.

El Juli was a master torero, and he put on an emotional final performance. Every single seat at the Plaza de Toros de Las Ventas in Madrid was filled, and thousands gathered outside and in bars to watch him close out a life dedicated to bullfighting. When a bullfighter retired, it was customary to have someone cut off the fake ponytail they wore on the back of their heads (which helped to stabilise the montera, the bullfighter's hat). When El Juli retired, as fans were pouring over the barriers into the ring to carry him out of the puerta grande on their shoulders, his brother came out with a knife to cut off his ponytail.

Had we been at Las Ventas, Jo and I wouldn't have seen the emotion involved, but watching it on live television, we had a closeup view. When El Juli finished with his last bull, we watched the realisation hit him that he would never again be walking away to the deafening cheers of the crowd in one of the world's oldest, most controversial, and intense cultural phenomena. He could barely make it through the puerta grande, as the sea of aficionados swarmed around him. We didn't see him shed a tear, but we were sure that once he was safe in his van with the door closed, he broke down as his entire life moved on to its next chapter.

As Jo and I watched all of this from Galway, it only endeared bullfighting to our hearts even more. This wasn't some torturous spectacle put on purely for the sake of bloodlust or entertainment of the masses. It was a performance, a cultural virtue, which unified people who would otherwise never have come together. The aficionados who gathered for El Juli's final performance weren't the same sort of fans that follow the likes of Taylor Swift or the Jonas Brothers. They were aficionados who had followed his career for decades, watched him perform at his best and worst, and been faithful devotees through it all. Matadors didn't sell albums, most of them didn't sell any merchandise whatsoever, and massive security teams didn't escort them to separate them from the community. They eagerly took photos, signed autographs, served as role models for children, and waded through throngs of people while shaking hands with those wishing them luck night after night. Even in his final performance, El Juli personified the values and character that Jo and I had come to expect from matadors. While we never got to see him in person, after watching his final performance on OneToro TV, we were solidly indoctrinated into the ranks of aficionados and in love with the performance that was bullfighting.

October 7th. Not every television experience was so happy and emotional as El Juli's retirement. On 7 October 2023, Hamas, a terrorist group and the governing body of the Gaza Strip, launched over 5,000 rockets indiscriminately into Israel, executed cross-border raids, and assaulted a youth music festival. While such unprovoked and indiscriminate attacks were not uncommon out of Gaza, the scale was unprecedented. Over 1,100 people were killed, 254 people were taken hostage, and the stories of Hamas' rape of women in the assault horrified the world. Those killed included teenagers, babies, old women, and people with no affiliation with the Israeli government whatsoever. Citizens of more than thirty countries perished brutally and unceremoniously at the hands of a brutal, in my opinion evil, terrorist organisation. As Israel mourned the dead, they feared for the kidnapped, as did the rest of the world, as the names of the disappeared were slowly revealed. Citizens from twenty-five countries, including the United States, were missing.

As Jo and I watched the live footage from her cousin's house, we were instantly thrust back into the world of terrorism, war, and conflict, a world which we had both left behind when we began our travels, and a world which I had, by now, decided I had no intention of returning to, regardless of my emotions or professional ties to the fight against terror. We had planned to spend Christmas in Israel and to visit Iraq, including Baghdad, and we wondered how this attack would change things. We both felt the same sentiment: This conflict flared up every so often. In all likelihood, it would fizzle out in some half-hearted ceasefire in a few weeks, and we would be free to visit Israel without issue.

The kidnapped nagged at us, though. A terrorist organisation in Gaza had taken American citizens hostage. Jo and I were sure that the United States *should* be taking direct action against Hamas and Gaza to get our citizens back, which may have impacted our plans to travel to Israel. As much as we wanted to visit Israel for Christmas, we didn't want to be there if a ground war broke out, especially if it involved direct American involvement. We were also sure, although we didn't acknowledge it until much later, that the kidnappings would prolong the conflict. Whether we wanted to admit it or not, our plans for traveling to Israel were quickly deteriorating. We resolved to monitor the situation and make a final decision as the time drew closer.

"One eighteen-year-old d***head away." I heard this phrase from a man from Dublin whom I met in Mexico towards the end of my year traveling around the world. In April of 2023, a full six months before Jo and I visited Belfast, a protestant police inspector was brutally murdered. While the perpetrator was never found, the protestants blamed Sinn Fein and the remnants of the IRA for the attack. The protestant guide on my political tour told us that the UVF, the protestant para-military, confronted Sinn Fein over the killing. The UVF stance was to treat this murder of a protestant police inspector as a one-off, isolated incident; however, if it were to happen again, the UVF would shred the ceasefire established in the Good Friday Agreement (which the Protestants disapproved of anyway) and sectarian vi-olence would begin anew.

The Dublin man I met told me the underlying conflict on the Emerald Isle was simmering and the temperature was increasing. The rest of the world didn't see it, because it was focused on the conflict between Israel and Hamas, Iraq, the Afghan-istan withdrawal, and the war in Ukraine. I certainly felt his sentiment as I walked away from the political tour in October. The man told me that it was his and many others' belief that there would again be a united Ireland, but that it shouldn't happen until several generations had passed since The Troubles. Unfortunately, he said, "We are one eighteen-year-old dickhead away from all of that s*** popping off again." All it would take was one troubled youth, one self-radicalised extremist, one errant or ill-advised bullet landing in the wrong house, one protest crossing the wrong street, and sectarian violence would return to Ireland.

Chapter Eleven

Morocco: Slowing Down in my Beloved Sahara

Jo and I were excited to visit Morocco in planning The Great Gallivanting. Neither of us really knew why, but it was a place we both wanted to see. After mapping out our general route around the world, we agreed to plan some time to slow down and recharge. We figured Morocco would be a great place, as we would have just zipped around Europe for three months and be preparing to embark in a new region amongst new, foreign cultures. We elected to spend a week in each city we visited. That way, we could take it all in while moving at a slower pace.

I couldn't wait to get to Morocco and North Africa. I deployed to the Sahara for the military, and in the years since, I always referred to the Sahara Desert as "my beloved Sahara." I had gone through some extremely hard personal times back then, and serving alongside our African partners was one of the happiest and proudest moments of my life. When my unit redeployed to the United States, I felt like a piece of my heart and soul had been left behind, and I longed to return to the harsh beauty of the world's largest desert.

I could hardly contain my excitement as we boarded our Ryanair flight from London to Marrakech.

Marrakech

My face was glued to the window as our plane crossed from the Mediterranean to North Africa. My smile could have lit up a room. I was back in Africa. Off in the distance, I could see the vast expanse of the Sahara, both the dirt, rocky parts at the outskirts and the golden-tan sand of its interior. Beneath us were the irregular-patterned villages of square, mud-rock buildings common in the region. A flood of memories and feelings came back to me from my last time in the Sahara. I knew things would be different this time around, both because I was a tourist and we weren't going anywhere near where I served, but as our plane touched down in Marrakech, I felt like a part of me was being welcomed home to a place where I left a piece of myself too many years before.

Clearing customs was simple enough. Jo and I were apprehensive about what the impression might have been with the customs officer with her being a solo female traveller, but no one made an issue of it. Around us at the baggage claim were European tourists coming for their African adventure. We listened as they talked about the beautiful hotels they had booked and the intricately planned excursions and itineraries their travel agents had arranged. Jo and I would have a completely different experience living the hostel life in Morocco's most stereotypical North African city.

Before heading out of the airport, we stopped to withdraw Moroccan Dirhams (MAD) at the cash point. We had no idea what the money exchange situation would be in town, but we were confident that paying with card, which was the norm in Europe, would be a luxury on the Continent. I booked us a taxi, both because I was the man and spoke enough French, to get us near the hostel, and before we knew it, we were zipping in and out of traffic. The loud horns, non-existent rules of the road, constant yelling and waiving from the drivers, and entire families on mopeds were sights and sounds that infected my soul.

Our hostel was located in the old city, the "Medina," as such areas were known. We had to walk to our hostel from the taxi drop-off because once the paved road ended, there was no way the car could squeeze between the pedestrians, street vendors, and motorbikes. Along the way, every street vendor and wayward teenager offered to "help" us get to our hostel, but we knew better than to accept. We knew the MENA region all too well, and any offered help came with the expectation of a tip for services rendered. This bothered some people I knew who travelled there before. To them, it was a way for the locals to rip off tourists. In some way, I supposed that might be true, but, in reality, that was just how things were done. Hardly anything was expensive, but everything came with a price, especially for white foreigners like us who were spending our strong dollars in weak dirhams.

I haven't gone to great lengths thus far in describing our hostels, because hostels in Europe were, well, hostels in Europe. The demand was high, they were hardly ever empty, and they provided a basic service of a bed to sleep in. Some of them offered breakfasts, but more often than not it was better and cheaper to find your own at a café or cook it yourself in the kitchen. That was not the case in Marrakech. The hostel was of basic, mud-walled construction, just like every other building in the Medina, but that simplicity betrayed its true essence. These mud walls insulated the hostel against the heat, so even with the sun high in the sky, the hostel remained cool. The receptionist served as a sort of travel agent, with special deals arranged with excursions and tours which were booked directly through the hostel. Most importantly, on the rooftop terrace every morning, they served a traditional Moroccan breakfast. For less than 5 USD, we had fried eggs, khobz (Moroccan bread), baghrir (a sort of spongy pancake) and msemen (another type of Moroccan shortbread) with honey, individual pots of tea, and coffee, all with a view over the Medina with the rising sun. Needless to say, as hostels went, it was a nice place, even without the massive common area, air conditioning, or self-catering facilities.

Jo and I intentionally booked a week in each Moroccan city we visited to force us to slow down and relax before kicking our travels back into high gear (and to give us some time to acclimatise to the sudden culture shift). That was the extent of our plan for Marrakech, so when morning came, we set out to experience the city. We decided to start with the Bahia Palace. Built in the mid-1800s, it expanded through the early 1900s and was eventually occupied by the French Army as a garrison headquarters; now it served as a tourist attraction. To get there, we had to traverse nearly the entire length of the Medina on foot. The "on foot" part didn't bother us. We loved taking in the hustle and bustle of the Medina and souks, the large market areas filled with vendors selling trinkets and supplies.

What did bother us, however, were the men leering at Jo. In European crowds and narrow areas, I walked in front and guided us to our next destination. This was just how our travel relationship developed. For some reason, Jo was in front of me that morning, and we both noticed the leers and stares. I leaned forward and whispered to her, "I think while we're here, you should walk in front of me, and I just tell you where to turn." To my honest surprise, she had already had the same thought. Jo could easily handle herself in a fight, but we didn't want to put ourselves in that situation in the first place. As the man, it also allowed me to identify other men who may want to do something they shouldn't and pre-empt them. Jo could handle herself, but men were in charge in Morocco, and we decided to use that to our discreet advantage.

The Bahia palace, when compared to royal palaces of Europe, was basic, with only a ground floor and little-to-no ornamentation in the form of paintings, artifacts, or displays. What it lacked in grandeur, it made up for in its simplistic elegance. Grand architecture in MENA was not ornate in the Western sense. Instead, beautiful buildings relied on simple mosaic patterns interwoven with Islamic arches in Euclidian fashion to convey their beauty. The Bahia palace was no different, and while the visit was decently quick, this was a wonderful place for beautiful photos. The riads (inner courtyards) filled with fauna and fountains served as the perfect backdrop for tourists seeking Instagram-worthy pictures. The arched doorways and large, bay-style windows weren't simply functional, but were themselves works of art intertwined with the mosaic floors. This palace was proof that elegance and simplicity were not mutually exclusive.

Being at the far end of the Medina from our hostel with midday rapidly approaching, we left the palace in search of food. We intended to visit the Badi Palace along the way, but it was closed for renovation. Ultimately, we settled on a Tuareg restaurant called Dar Touareg. I had worked with a Tuareg years before and knew their food was excellent. We were the only ones on the covered rooftop terrace as we enjoyed a three-course meal of some of the best food we had ever eaten. Harira, pastille, and tangine were just some of the dishes we enjoyed with our Moroccan tea before heading to the Saadian tombs, which were mostly closed due to earthquake damage, and back to the hostel for a siesta while the African sun was high in the sky.

We wandered back out at night to the main square. During the day, there were plenty of vendors and animal "trainers" (a very loose term), but it turned into the centrepiece of nighttime entertainment once the sky faded to black. Food stands, trinket peddlers, musical groups, and simple carnival-style games filled the entirety of the outdoor space. There was something for everyone, with young boys competing in football shootouts in makeshift goals, old ladies playing music around a fire, and snake charmers putting on shows for the European tourists. Jo quickly found herself the proud owner of henna tattoos on both hands, which made me laugh because she couldn't touch anything for almost an hour, including her water bottle. Of course, this being North Africa, everything had a price, and in each group of performers, there was one man whose job was to keep a watchful eye for anyone taking photos or videos. His job was to identify you and reach his hat out for a tip for the photo. There wasn't a standard price, but he would demand more if you tried to be too cheap. I fell for it once, but, as the saying went, c'est l'Afrique.

We got a late start the following day. I got up early for breakfast and wrote some for my travel blog. I could have asked for worse places than a rooftop overlooking Marrakech! When Jo got up, we grabbed some coffee from a lady who owned a small breakfast café nearby in the souk before making our way to the culinary museum. We read great things online about it, and it was something Jo wanted to see. Unfortunately, like the Badi Palace, the museum was closed for renovation. This was a letdown because as part of the museum tour, they offered a cooking class that we were looking forward to. The kitchen was still open, however, so we could enjoy a Moroccan lunch in the museum's large atrium constructed in the simple yet elegant Islamic style.

A man we had met the day before told us we should explore the Jewish quarter of Marrakech. It was one of the oldest parts of the Medina, and the Moroccan king was actively making it a point to restore and preserve Morocco's Jewish history. To be sure, unless you knew what you were looking for, which we didn't, there wasn't a good way to distinguish which parts of the Medina were a part of the Jewish quarter and which parts weren't, but one of the synagogues was open to visitors, so we figured that was a good place to start. The Slat Al Azama Synagogue was located just south of the Bahia palace, cost 30 MAD (about 3 USD) to enter, and served as a small museum to Marrakech's long-gone Jewish population. At one point in history, after the 1492 Alhambra Decree expelling practising Jews from the Kingdoms of Castille and Aragon, Marrakech was home to over 50,000 Jews. As Islam became more dominant, French colonisation expanded and collapsed, and Israel became home to the world's Jewish diaspora, that population shrunk to just eighty in 2023, with the majority of those being elderly. A city which once served as a refuge for Jews persecuted in Europe would soon have none at all. It was not lost on me that I, with degrees in history and international policy, had never learned of the Spanish expulsion. I figured that was because, in American history, 1492 was studied from the perspective of the Kingdom of Castille's arrival in the New World in the form of Cristopher Colombus. With the on-going anti-Israel protests after October 7th, I wondered how many of the protestors in Europe had studied or even knew of this expulsion as they protested the very existence of the Jewish state.

The deep musings, beautiful architecture, and lively atmosphere aside, I had to admit that there wasn't much *to do* in Marrakech as a traveller. It was a place you went to learn history and enjoy the local atmosphere, not stay busy with excursions and walking tours, although these did exist. As such, Jo and I looked at each other several times and asked, "Now what?" after visiting the synagogue. I was content to wander the streets with no goal or destination in mind, but Jo was more objective-minded. That was understandable. When else would we be free to visit these countries and do anything, and why waste time just existing?

Nonetheless, reality was reality, so we wandered into the House of Photography, a museum dedicated to Morocco's earliest photography and videography. Admittedly, we didn't have high hopes for a photography museum in Marrakech, and we figured it would be just a bunch of photos of Marrakech and Morocco. Thankfully, we were sorely disappointed in that assumption because we discovered so much more. It was at the same time a photography, art, and history museum, and it used still images ranging from 1870 through 1960 (and even some more recent) to tell the story of Morocco, the Atlas Mountains, and the native tribes (collectively referred to as the Berber people). For 50 MAD (about 5 USD), it was worth spending an hour or so exploring this unique perspective on the region.

On the museum's rooftop was a terrace coffee bar. Both of us were tired at this point, probably due to walking so much and the heat, so we sat down to give it a go. We were lucky we did because we saw a sandstorm coming when we took our seats. It was moving slowly, but I had been caught in enough sandstorms during my deployment to the Sahara several years before to know they could range from a mildly unpleasant inconvenience to a total brown-out. After a quick rest and a coffee, we decided to head back to the hostel, mostly at my behest. In hindsight, I was probably being a little over-cautious as we were in a city, and the buildings would tamp down most of the effects from the storm. Still, I didn't want to be caught out in a sandstorm trying to make our way back to the hostel while we were both tired, hot, and able to get on each other's nerves when something unexpected caused us to walk a long way.

Along the way, however, we became geographically mislocated within the winding streets as the GPS on our phones struggled to keep up amongst the earthen buildings. Fortunately so, because we stumbled upon a beautiful street of artisan shops, including one specialising in headscarves. Jo and I had already decided to take our hostel up on a three-day Saharan excursion, and she was in the market for a "Sahara passport," the headscarf worn by the nomadic tribes to protect against the sun and sand. I had my shemagh that I had gotten my last time in the Sahara (in fact, I was wearing it at that moment), so I didn't need one, but we stepped into the shop to look. Most of the scarves were made onsite, and they had several different lengths and a range of beautiful colours, dyed using a number of traditional methods. I told her she should go with a deep blue one, as it was the traditional colour worn by the Tuaregs, and the shop owner agreed, both because of my knowledge and because the blue one was more expensive. It was a beautiful, deep blue that contrasted wonderfully with the bright orange and yellow pants she would buy that night for the excursion.

We had our hostel rooms through the end of the week, and we had only been there a few days, so we had a decision to make: ask for a refund and take all of our belongings with us on the excursion or keep our beds and pack our day bags for the trip. Given that the excursion was all-inclusive for only 990 MAD (about 33 USD per day), we kept the beds. That way, we could lock our bags and computers in the lockers rather than risk anything getting lost in a van or off a camel.

With bags packed and alarm clocks set, we settled in for an early morning pick-up for a trip into the Atlas Mountains and the dunes of the Sahara.

Sahara Excursion

We had no idea what to expect for the Sahara excursion. There was an itinerary outline at the hostel, but that was only worth so much, especially when it came to Western tourism in this part of the world. As if to reinforce the point, breakfast wasn't actually included that morning like we were told, which for Jo wasn't a big deal, but I needed to eat in the mornings to take my medicine. Further, we hadn't even made it a few minutes out of the city in the van when we pulled over and were told to get out. We weren't sure why, as my traveller's French only got us so far, but we went with the flow. It turned out we were just one of a large number of people from all over the city going on some version of this excursion, and this first stop was the meeting and organisation point. After a short time, we were headed off in a van with a trio of Spanish women, a Colombian couple, and five Australian girls.

The morning was chilly and foggy as we set off for the Atlas Mountains. Behind the sandstorm the day before came rain, and fog sat heavy in the valleys on either side of the road. The first overlook we stopped at was disappointing, to say the least, but we took that first stop to mean at least we would be stopping relatively frequently rather than being cooped up in the van all day. Not long after that, we stopped at a roadside café (clearly meant for tourists), which served coffee and snacks. Our driver announced it as "Café! Café!" using the French word for coffee. Having learned the lesson early, Jo had the idea to stock up on some snacks in case food options were few and far between. There was also a free-to-use toilet downstairs, which we knew we should take advantage of from our military days. Jo had the foresight to bring toilet paper as well, something other members of our group would come to regret not doing.

By the time we arrived to Aït Benhaddou, we had clear blue skies, the bright North African sun reflecting off the golden-brown rocks and buildings, and a dry, hot wind making its way across the vast, open spaces. Aït Benhaddou was a village built on a towering rock which overlooked the surrounding landscapes and the adjacent river. Once upon a time, it was only accessible during the dry season when the river was low or dried up. In recent years, the Moroccan government had built a large bridge to allow year-round passage for inhabitants and tourists. Aït Benhaddou once served as an outpost and guard for major trans-Saharan trade routes, but modern technologies made such outposts obsolete, so most of the families that once lived there moved across the river to take advantage of the tourism economy. Those who remained in the village still lived traditional lifestyles, but they, too, thrived on the tourism dollars.

The village itself was beautiful in that unique, desert style. Simple construction with views to kill for and colours that made for amazing photo and video backdrops. In fact, several blockbuster films had used the location to film desert scenes, including the Bond film *The Living Daylights*, *Gladiator*, and *The Mummy*. I had to admit, I was a little jealous of Jo's new camera and her iPhone, because she was capturing some amazing shots that my GoPro just couldn't do justice.

Standing on one of the lookout points as we waited for the rest of our group (something that would be a frequent occurrence on this excursion), I became lost in my thoughts and emotions as I stared out over the never-ending desert. I had longed to return to the Sahara for many years and many reasons, and there I was. Sure, I was a tourist and not an adventurer or warfighter, but I was near where I had left a piece of my soul several years before. While I wouldn't make it to that part of the desert this time, I was sure I would be there again someday.

With the group finally assembled, we descended the village and crossed the bridge to a shop selling headscarves. The guide made it seem as though we were required to have one to continue the tour the next day, but Jo and I were sure that this wasn't the case. Not that it affected either of us. She had hers from Marrakech, and I had my shemagh, so we watched as the others shopped and attempted to negotiate prices. After they made their purchases, the guide informed us his services weren't included in the excursion, and we each needed to pay 50 MAD. Jo had been adamant that we should take plenty of extra cash in small bills in case we found ourselves in this exact scenario. As she well knew, there was always a catch in MENA.

After a late lunch at La Kasbah café and Restaurant in Ouarzazate, we headed toward our hotel for the night. The restaurant had terrible reviews on Google, but we thought it was fine, if a little expensive for Morocco (it was the main tourist stop in the area, so that was to be expected). It was about a three-hour drive to our hotel, so we stopped at the Taferdout viewpoint to take in the breathtaking view of the Atlas Mountains along the way.

Once we arrived in Ait Oudinar, we learned that we had booked a "lower-tier" version of the tour, so the driver dropped us at a hotel with the Spanish women before taking the other two groups to the "nice" hotel. We later learned that we saved a lot of money by booking the "cheap" tour, even though it didn't feel cheap. The hotel booked Jo and me in separate rooms because we weren't married. I had a four-bed shared room to myself, while she had a single room with a large bed. We thought it was a funny difference, and it didn't bother me in the least. We knew we could stand some time apart anyways, even if it were just for the evenings and mornings, after spending every waking and sleeping moment together for more than three months.

It was at this hotel we realised how much of an issue the Spanish trio would be. As soon as we arrived, one of them lit up a cigarette in the lobby. To be sure, smoking was allowed most everywhere in Morocco, but there were clear "no smoking" signs up, and she argued with the receptionist when he told her to put it out or go outside. Later, as the hotel was providing dinner, the trio was late, so late that the kitchen staff told us to eat without them, and that they would simply have whatever food was leftover. Being the amiable types, we didn't eat more than our share, but by this point we knew we were in for two more days of annoyance with them. The same story played on repeat for breakfast the next morning, any time we had a stop, and at every meal. We were always waiting on them to take pictures, enjoy a smoke, finish their drinks, or finish a conversation. At one point on the trip, while I was outside the van on a stop, one of them started smoking inside the van while Jo was in the back seat. When asked to move outside of the van, she only moved to the door while remaining in the van and out of the sun. Apparently, according to our driver during an off-hand conversation while everyone was waiting for them at one of the stops, this was a common occurrence with Spanish tour groups in Morocco. While annoying, it was nice to hear that it wasn't just Americans that had stereotypical behaviours abroad.

Luckily, we had most of the day out of the van, so we didn't have to deal with them much. After stopping at a popular outlook, we went to another village. This one wasn't a UNESCO World Heritage Site like Aït Benhaddou; instead, it was a typical Berber village that made money sourcing the tourism trade. They had shops in homes, local guides, dinners, and carpet makers who provided handmade carpets to shops in the bigger cities, all while tending to fields and livestock to live. Electrical wires were strung haphazardly across walkways as the Moroccan government worked to bring consistent electricity to rural areas.

In this village, Jo and I learned a few things. Firstly, to pay close attention to "authentic" experiences. Under the façade of traditional clothing, many men in the village wore denim jeans and flannel shirts. There was something to be said for the value of traditionalism, but where people could afford cheap, Western-style clothing, they often chose it out of both practicality and fashion. Second, despite the clothing façade, living in impoverished areas was arduous work. The women laboured for hours on end making carpets, sometimes spending months on a single item, while children who should have been in primary school worked the fields. In areas like this, there was no welfare or social safety net. Finally, do not underestimate the intelligence of people who lived outside of what Westerners like us would call normal lives. Most people we met, from guides to drivers to restaurateurs, spoke multiple languages fluently. They constantly apologised for their English before breaking into flawless explanations in English, Spanish, and French. They knew their history, both local and international, and they knew their religion better than most European Catholics.

After leaving our guide, whose fee was also not included in the all-inclusive tour, we headed further east into the desert for the night. Outside of Merzouga, near the Algerian border, several Berber companies had erected permanent accommodations of varying quality. At the high end was what Americans would call glamping, with beautifully adorned tents made up in the styles of hotel rooms, complete with carpeted outside walkways and pools. At the low end, like where Jo and I stayed, were basic tents with ok beds, no power outlets, and ensuite toilets without doors. But to get there, we had to split back into our groups, link up with other tours, and mount our camels near the main road. It was about an hour and a half winding ride to the camps, about half of which we did in the dark of night beneath a beautiful blanket of stars. It was a surreal feeling. The dunes turned into dark shadows against the moonlit sky, and the only sounds were the camel's grunts as they sailed across the sand.

Our evening consisted of a communal meal of chicken tangine, harira, and bread, followed by Berber music and dancing around the fire. I wasn't much into the dancing, but I took a video of Jo joining in the conga line before I headed off to bed. We had an early morning before a long, ten-hour drive back to Marrakech. While I would take the camel back to Merzouga, Jo opted for an add-on where she would take a jeep to the tallest nearby dune to see the sunrise and go sandboarding. She busted her butt a time or two, but refused to share the video.

By the time we got back to Marrakech, we were exhausted. The driver made one stop for lunch in the ten-hour drive, and we were both on the verge of getting carsick. Luckily, the five Australian girls didn't return with us as they headed to Fez, so we could spread out in the van. With no rest for the weary, once at the hostel, we pulled some cash out of a nearby cashpoint, packed our bags for our bus to Agadir the following morning, and made our way to the main square for a last meal.

At the square, we ate at the same place every meal. It was one of the food stalls owned by a man named Aziz, stall number fifty-two. He had talked us into eating with him our first night, and he kept an eye out to make sure none of his competition tried to wrangle us to them before we settled at his place. Aziz was a fun guy, as were his wait staff and cooks. They sang, clapped, and made a standard Moroccan meal a fun event all to itself. When we went to pay, our bill was 400 MAD fort the two of us, about 20 USD each. We absolutely ate that much food, and we did not feel at all as though we were being overcharged. Aziz, however, disagreed, and re-funded us half of our money. He told us that he made plenty of money from us for just 200 MAD, and he didn't want word to get out that he was an expensive place to eat. We tried to insist on paying the full amount, but he was hearing none of it. All he asked of us was to return to eat at his food stall the next night. So, we did. When we walked up, the entire wait staff recognised us, welcomed us in, shook our hands, gave us hugs, and sat us right next to the kitchen staff. The food was just as good as the night before, and, again, Aziz refused to let us pay full price, despite our efforts to do so. All he asked of us was to tell people of his food stall, which we did time and again across the world. It was at Aziz's we ate our last meal after the Sahara excursion. By this point, it was a no-brainer for us, as it gave us the experience of wandering the souks on our way there, the entertainment of the music and games at the square, and an amazing meal.

While I enjoyed Marrakech's stereotypical MENA feel, Jo and I were ready to head to Tamraght, north of Agadir on the Moroccan coast, for a beach vacation. It had been a while since we last saw the sea, and this was a city we had looked forward to for months before leaving. So, with bags packed, we boarded the bus and left the Sahara behind.

Tamraght

Two hours later, our bus pulled into Agadir. We had to take a taxi about fifteen miles to our hostel in Tamraght. Public transport in Morocco wasn't as popular as in Europe, and being a taxi driver for tourists was considered a good way to make a living. In Morocco, the taxis were well organised amongst themselves, and it was an easy discussion to determine whose taxi we would take and what the price would be. We were apprehensive at first, but, as they say, c'est l'Afrique.

Our hostel was the Sunset Surf Hostel, just off the main road. It was adjacent to its associated surf shop and a short walk to the beach. This hostel was by far one of the best hostels I stayed in during all my travels. Every morning, the owner's wife and their lone employee made everyone a traditional Moroccan breakfast, which was included with our stay. During the day, for 45 EUR, the hostel offered all-day surf lessons and practice with their surf shop, all necessary equipment, transport to the surf site, and lunch. To finish the night, they offered a homemade family-style dinner for just 10 EUR. Once we added in the rooftop hangout area, the hostel cats, and the daily group walks to the beach to watch the sunset, this was the best place for us to enjoy a beach getaway far from the chaos of the city life we had been living the past many months.

We had a week in Tamraght with no specific plans. We just wanted to chillax. I spent time writing for the travel blog we were keeping, reading, and enjoying drinks by the beach. I only went surfing once. Not that it wasn't a great time, I just had other things on my mind. Jo went surfing a couple of times and read just as much as I did. One day, we decided to grab a drink at a bar set on top of a cliff overlooking the sea. We sat right on the edge of the cliff, and we drank and read for hours. Every so often, one of us looked up to ask if the other was doing alright, and then we kept on reading in the ocean breeze. That evening, we laughed about how we had all of that magnificent beach, and all we did was read and drink all day.

While we planned to see and do much more in Agadir, Tamraght was a much-needed break. Jo and I were able to spend time apart while hanging out with new friends and doing things we individually enjoyed, which did us a lot of good. Our personalities were wearing on each other after so much time together. It helped that the hostel crowd was like one giant family, a fortunate consequence of two communal meals per day. Everyone got to know everyone, and laughter over Moroccan cuisine and tea kept everyone in good spirits.

A week in Tamraght flew by, and, before we knew it, we were back in a taxi heading for the Agadir bus station. We were bound for Casablanca, our last stop in Morocco before heading to Tunisia. While neither of us wanted to stop traveling, both of us were bummed to be leaving the Sunset Surf Hostel. We had a great time there and met so many great people. We knew moving on to Casablanca and Tunisia entailed staying in hotel rooms and Airbnbs with just the two of us and our personalities steadily grating on each other. Plus, we were starting to disagree over what came next, and that was causing tension. The conflict in Gaza showed no signs of letting up, throwing a wrench in our travel plans. The Department of State, Canadian government, and United Kingdom's Foreign Office all warned against unnecessary travel to specific areas in the Middle East. While I knew how those advisories were made from my time in the security field and wasn't overly concerned, Jo had valid concerns about going to places governments publicly told travellers to avoid. We had decisions to make sooner than later, and we weren't anywhere close to agreeing on a course of action.

Casablanca

Jo and I were surprised to learn Morocco had a burgeoning train system. It was still under construction, but major cities in the north were already connected. Our bus took us to Marrakech, and it was a short taxi ride to the train station. It was surprisingly modern, complete with fast-food restaurants of both local and Western flavour. The train was basic, with no internet, moveable seats, or meal car, but it was inexpensive, generally clean, and got us from Marrakech to Casablanca on time, so there wasn't much for us to complain about.

We stayed in a hotel in Casablanca that was just inside the city centre. It was the cheapest option on Hostelworld, we each would have our own bed, and we had our own bathroom. After almost four months on the road, it was funny the things that we now considered a luxury. Jo even found a gym to go to since we would be there a week. She had been talking about trying to find gyms in different cities, and it was a great way to spend time doing something she liked and away from me (not that she didn't like me, but I would probably have ended up with a weight thrown at my head if I went with her... and I undoubtedly would have deserved it).

Unlike Marrakech, Casablanca was a very modern city. It wasn't quite New York City, but only the Medina had that "traditional" MENA feel. I had worked with a woman who lived in Morocco years ago, and she described Casablanca as "the tourist city." I wasn't ready to go quite that far, especially after the heavy tourist feel of Europe's major cities, but Casablanca certainly wasn't as off-putting to Westerners as Marrakech.

Our first stop was to do laundry. We had a flight coming up, and it had been two weeks since our last wash. Fortunately, there was a laundromat not far from our hotel. Unfortunately, there were no self-service laundromats, so we had to pay an average of 10 MAD per item to have it laundered. Ten Moroccan Dirhams was the equivalent of 1 USD, which wouldn't have been so bad had we not washed all our clothing. We paid something like 300 MAD for one load of laundry. Two months before, we did laundry in Prague because it was cheaper than in Vienna by about five to ten EUR. How little that now seemed! It was good we did laundry that day, as I had a major migraine that came out of nowhere (a multiple-time-a-year gift that kept on giving from my military days).

On our first day out and about, we explored aimlessly on foot. We walked most of the main part of the city centre. Nearby to the hotel was the Mohammed V Square, officially named after the former King of Morocco, but it was better known as the Pidgeon Fountain because of the large fountain and obscene number of pigeons which lived there. Our friend Layne had a strange obsession with pigeons, so we walked through it to see what it was all about. There were pigeons everywhere, and a few men had figured out how to make a living selling bird feed to tourists and kids, which only helped to keep the pigeons living at the square. Unknown to me, there was a military compound at the corner of the square, and a guard yelled at me for pointing my camera in the wrong direction, much to Jo's entertainment.

We went to two museums in Casablanca, both on the first day. The Ville d'Art showcased local Moroccan art, some of which was political and some of which was artistic. The Abderrahman Slaoui Foundation Museum showcased contemporary Moroccan art, from jewellery to paintings to glassware. These were cool, but they didn't particularly interest us. Neither of us were art gurus, nor were we knowledgeable of nor interested in the Moroccan modern art scene.

What did interest us that day was Arab League Park. Originally constructed in 1913, this park provided a large, public space for kids to play sports, adults to read, and soldiers and police officers to exercise. It was immaculately kept, with perfectly manicured lawns, beautifully arranged palm trees and fountains, and walkways leading to every corner of the park in symmetric fashion. And cats, which Jo took plenty of time to play with and take pictures. At the far end from where we entered stood the Sacred Heart Cathedral, a tall, white structure which towered over the northeast corner. The cathedral was deconsecrated and under renovations stemming from its conversion to a cultural centre. Even so, it made for beautiful views both from the park and while eating at a café across the street.

The highlight of our time in Casablanca was the Hassan II Mosque. It was about an hour's walk from our hotel, but it was beyond worth it. The Hassan II Mosque was constructed between 1986 and 1993, was the second-largest mosque in Africa, and had the tallest minaret in the world at 220 metres tall from base to spire (although the Djamaa el Djazair Mosque in Algeria disputed this on a technicality). The Hassan II Mosque was designed as a "throne of God on the water," and it was exactly that. Over 100,000 people could attend Islamic services at once between the prayer hall and the grounds outside. The grounds were beautifully designed in the Islamic style, with arched windows, mosaic patterns in the tile floors and the stone walls, and rectangular gardens. Jo and I could have stayed outside for hours, taking pictures from different angles and staring out over the ocean under the minaret's shadow.

We arrived at the top of the hour, which meant we could attend a free (i.e., included) guided tour in English. We were grateful for this opportunity, as neither of us had been invited into a mosque on a tour before seeing as neither of us were Muslims, and the last time either of us were in the Middle East was on official business. Seeing that one of my goals on this trip around the world was to become more knowledgeable in religious beliefs, even if they weren't my own, I was excited to hear about such a monumental place where so many people could come to practise their faith.

Stepping into the main prayer hall, we were astounded to see a giant, open space as we removed our shoes (which, to Muslims, were considered unclean, but, more practically from the tourism perspective, would also track dirt and debris from outside into the large, carpeted area). In hindsight, we shouldn't have been shocked. Even the worship areas of Europe's cathedrals were wide, open spaces. Maybe it was because, in mosques, there were no pews, no ornate paintings or carvings (as any images of the prophet Mohommed were strictly forbidden), and no grand pulpit for the imam (the spiritual leader) to preach. As intricate and elegant as the architecture and design were, the layout was simple and designed to welcome as many worshipers as possible into a place where they could focus not on the lore or legends of the Islamic faith in specifically designed chapels but on their prayers, the Qur'an, and the Hadiths.

The irony of my own professional life was not lost on me as our guide taught us of some of the Islamic traditions, such as the segregating of the men and women in the mosque, the direction of prayers, and the positioning of imams. Early in my military career, I had spent a substantial amount of time working to identify and prevent Islamist terrorist attacks. I read extremist groups' magazines in detail to discern how to best design or update protection programmes. I could speak in detail about the histories, operations, and core beliefs of Islamist terrorist groups. As much as I knew about Islam from a professional standpoint, everything I knew was an extremist version of the faith. I knew nothing of what a "standard" or "normal" Muslim believed or practised. While I had dealt with the issue of mosques within the legal framework of extremism, I had never seen one from the inside from the perspective of a Muslim believer. I didn't know when or even if I would be able to do so again, so I took it all in as much as I could while the other tourists busied themselves with getting the perfect photos (and there was no shortage of those, either).

Downstairs, we visited the ablution chamber, a vast space containing many large fountains to facilitate thousands of worshipers' ritual cleaning before entering the prayer hall. Such cleaning, called ablution, involved systematically washing one's feet, hands, forearms, head, face, ears, nostrils, and even mouth so that worshipers would be clean before Allah. As I later learned, ablution areas varied in size and sophistication, with some mosques simply having sinks available outside, others having fountains, and others having extraordinary chambers like this one. The cleansing lasted only a few minutes, and our guide used this time to communicate the importance of conserving water during the ritual. "We conserve water because, to Muslims, water is life. Here in the desert, if there is no water, there is no life." As profoundly philosophical as that statement was, it reminded me of the Old Testament laws and traditions, which were given Holy reverence but were probably only set down as a matter of practicality and survivability in the times they were written.

We couldn't go into the minaret, which surprised neither of us, as it was reserved for the muezzin to conduct the call to prayer and, on occasion, for the imam to issue sermons. We were, however, free to remain on the grounds to take more pictures before we were told we needed to leave as the mosque would be closing to visitors for midday prayers. I appreciated that the mosque closed for these. It always irritated me in Europe that tourists would wander around cathedrals while priests conducted mass upwards of four times a day. Even though I was a Christian, I maintained a steadfast belief that religious sites should be treated with reverence and respect, even by those not of that specific faith.

After a late lunch nearby, we took a stroll down the Casablanca Corniche, a seawall with a paved walkway that led towards the Port of Casablanca. There was nothing fancy about this stroll; it was just a paved foot and bicycle path that passed by the sea. On the land side, the retaining wall was covered in graffiti; on the sea side, large, stone caltrops broke the square-shaped waves (which, being a diver, I knew to be among the most dangerous, as they were generally a sign of strong undercurrents due to conflicting wave pave patterns). The retaining wall was high, so we spent most of the walk in the shade enjoying being outside with no stress or street hustlers.

After the long walk back to the hotel, we decided to check out a nearby Spanish restaurant for dinner. Were we obsessed with Spain? Absolutely, but given that Western Sahara, which Morocco claimed as its own, was once called "Spanish Sahara," and there was still substantial Spanish influence given the proximity to Spain across the Strait of Gibraltar (not to mention Spain still held sovereignty over the North African enclaves of Ceuta and Melilla), we thought we should give Moroccan Spanish cuisine a try. Would we end up calling it a letdown? Not necessarily, but it certainly didn't live up to expectations. The croquettas were good, but most of the menu consisted of Moroccan dishes, pizza, and a few Moroccan twists on Western food. While the decor consisted of matador paintings and bull heads, the food was just dressed-up Moroccan cuisine.

We agreed to have an easy day on our last full day in Casablanca and Morocco. We spent it at the beach and the Morocco Mall. While we were prepared for a beach day with our day bags, we knew we needed to dress conservatively for the mall. This worked in our favour because our lazy day reading by the ocean turned into a long walk down the beach. The beaches on Morocco's western coast tended to stretch far into the sea with long, shallow slopes, and their undercurrents were notoriously strong. We noticed next to no one swimming, probably for good reason, and as we walked, the surf would take the water far away from us before bringing it so far in that we were soaked up to our knees. We acted like two kids as we tried to get the perfect videos of the incoming waves and got soaked in the process.

After a four kilometre walk along the beach, we arrived at the Morocco Mall. We weren't sure what to expect, but it certainly wasn't what we found. The Morocco Mall was three-story monstrosity of a modern mall. It was air conditioned, had sports and outdoor stores, name-brand jewellery shops, a food court, and even a 1,000,000-litre fish tank complete with sharks, rays, and a spiral viewing platform. Jo spied a desert stand serving ice cream and waffles, and as we enjoyed our unexpected desert, we couldn't believe we were in a place like that. We explored the entirety of the mall, both a little relieved to be in a place that resembled some sense of Western normalcy after three weeks in Morocco. We weren't necessarily missing home nor did we dislike Morocco; it was just nice to take a short reprieve from North African life before continuing our life on the road, especially considering we had no idea what that life would entail once we landed in Tunisia.

Something we didn't particularly enjoy in Casablanca were the souks in the Medina. They were small, which was fine in and of itself, but they weren't particularly wow-ing. Souks were usually large markets where people could get anything and everything they could want or need, from tourist trinkets to school supplies to weekly groceries. With Casablanca being a large, modern city with supermarkets and chain stores, the role of the souks in the Medina had fallen to solely providing for the needs of the inhabitants of the Medina. In a city like Casablanca, the souk's decline represented the shift away from traditional ways of life to the "modern" (i.e., Western) ways.

With our week in Casablanca drawing to a close, we began making plans for Tunisia and beyond. We finally agreed to go to Egypt after Tunisia on an organised tour Jo's mom had found. We would see all of the major sites with a reputable tour company while staying away from the Sinai Peninsula and the effects of the conflict in Gaza. That gave us a plan for about three weeks into the future, but beyond that was still an open question. We still didn't agree about where we should go or what we should see. Actually, we both had a similar list of things we wanted to see, but we weren't in agreement about whether or not we should go to the places where those things were. For example, Petra in Jordan, Erbil in Iraq, and Turkey in general were open questions as the post-October 7th conflict continued far longer than we expected. Every conversation thus far had ended in a stalemate with no decision, but I knew that we would have to hash it all out sooner than later. I didn't know where Jo stood on that, but, knowing her, she probably knew the same.

So, with Egyptian visas in hand and an unknown future rapidly approaching, we hailed a taxi at 02h00 in the morning and headed to the Casablanca airport bound for Tunis.

Reflecting on Morocco

Earthquake. The September before Jo and I went to Morocco, the Atlas Mountains were rocked by an earthquake which registered a 6.8 on the Richter scale. A few minutes later, they were rocked again by a 4.9 aftershock. Thousands died, thousands more were injured, millions either displaced or lives seriously disrupted, and the infrastructure damage was nearly incalculable. From homes in small villages to historic sites in Marrakech, structural collapses occurred across the country. Whenever we wanted to go somewhere in Marrakech that turned out to be closed for renovation, it was because of damage from the earthquake. Even in the main square, there was a large, long crack running through the road which connected to its centre showcasing just how far reaching the damage was.

What struck Jo and me both was the rapidity of the recovery effort. Morocco's economy was heavily dependent on Western tourism dollars. As airlines cancelled flights and refunded travellers whose vacation plans had been affected, the Moroccan government rushed to address the damage. Within a month, most of the rubble had been cleared from roads and tourism destinations, security personnel posted at sites which still posed a danger, and the Moroccan government was imploring airlines and travellers to return to the country.

While the recovery wasn't totally complete by the time of our arrival, had we not known about the earthquake in advance, we never would have guessed there had been one in the first place. We were amazed at how resilient the Moroccan people were in the face of such a tragedy. This was also the first in a long line of instances that reinforced the realities of living in places where the only help you would get is the help you give yourself. We said it many times in Morocco, and I would say it many times in the future: It was amazing what you could do when you didn't have a choice.

Ramifications of October 7th. As protests and riots rocked the Western world and parts of the Middle East, mainly against Israel for retaliating against Hamas (but, notably, not against Hamas for launching an attack which killed the most Jews in a single incident since the Holocaust), Jo and I kept our heads and news feeds focused on detecting the slightest sign of trouble or unrest as we entered North Africa. Governments across the globe were scrambling to issue travel advisories and warnings, but most of them lacked real-world, real-time updates, which only made these advisories and warnings more alarmist than they needed to be.

For its part, Morocco was proud of its Jewish heritage, and the King of Morocco was taking great pains to preserve this heritage stemming from the Castilian, Aragonese, and Portuguese expulsion in 1492. Morocco also wanted to stay in the United States' good graces. President Trump had recognised Morocco's long-disputed sovereignty over Western Sahara (formerly "Spanish Sahara") in exchange for Morocco's signing of the Abraham Accords, which normalised relations between Arab nations and Israel. Neither Jo nor I were under any illusion that Morocco's ambivalence toward its Jewish population and heritage didn't include a practical, political component.

While we didn't see or hear protests related to the conflict in Gaza, we did witness the government reaction in another way. Outside of the synagogue we visited were two armed police officers. They were basic patrol officers, so Jo and I figured we had simply showed up on the back end of some police response, as they paid us no attention. While we were visiting the synagogue, however, an Arab woman dressed in Western clothing with a black Hijab entered carrying a purse. One of the police officers, clearly apologetic and reluctant, told her she needed to leave her purse at the front desk. She was confused and, understandably, more than a little upset at the insinuation that she might be a terrorist, and she gestured to the Westerners (including Jo and me) who had bags. That was when we realised what was going on: security theatre, Africa-style. Because she was Arab, she couldn't have a bag. She eventually left her bag, and even offered to the police officer to strip down so he could fully search her. He, of course, declined, as it was unnecessary, and it was clearly a sarcastic offer.

As Jo and I left, I turned to her and said, "I'm fairly confident we just witnessed racial profiling in the extreme." "Oh, yeah, most definitely," she replied, "but that's how things work in places like this." She was right. As shocking as it may have been to Westerners, in most of the world, racial and ethnic stereotypes, especially when it came to security, were not just accepted, they were the norm. As we walked away, we talked about how, had the roles of the entire conflict been reversed, we would see security at a Mosque treat Jews the same way. As we crossed onto the main road from the alley leading from the synagogue, the point was driven home. There was a General Directorate for National Security, the Moroccan national police and security force, vehicle filled with officers in full tactical gear and fully-automatic rifles. They were there to respond to any attack on the synagogue and the Jewish quarter. To any passer-by, the message was clear: Don't bring the conflict between the Palestinians and Israelis to Morocco.

Women, culture, respect, and the patriarchy. Jo and I were warned several times that traveling to Morocco as a woman was "different," as the Moroccans had different ideas of gender roles and equality than the West. We knew this, but we didn't pay it any mind as we were traveling as a man and woman pair. While not married or even in a relationship, we figured that would be enough to do away with some of the gender differences.

We were partially correct. As I said before, Morocco was highly dependent on Western tourism dollars, so Western women were generally given a free pass on social norms. Jo, being the respectful person she was, still made it a point to dress modestly by wearing long dresses or pants and t-shirts, and I always wore pants anyways. While that didn't necessarily stop the stares, it at least reduced them. My mean-mugging men from behind whose gaze lingered too long did the rest.

That said, we had some polite interactions with the patriarchal cultural difference. Jo tried some of artisan solid perfume blends at one man's spice shop in the souks, which required him to touch her. He had been nothing but respectful to us and spoke pretty good English, so when he asked me if he could touch Jo, both Jo and I took that not as him so much asking my actual permission as him showing us respect in his own way and culture. The same was true of Aziz in the square. He always shook my hand first, but then he would do the same for her. They understood, as did we, that we were from different cultures, and there was a way for us to meet in the middle out of mutual respect.

That was not always the case, however, especially in Casablanca. When we went out to eat at night, waiters bombarded us with their menus to get us to eat at their restaurants. They always came to me, totally ignoring Jo. At first, this was annoying to me and funny to her, because we always needed to agree on where to eat. She was happy not to have to deal with these hustlers. However, oftentimes they took it to the extreme, and the local restauranteurs would literally push her out of the way to get to my side. There was no sense of mutual respect for cultures there; this was trying to bring in Western tourism dollars without regard for the cultural differences. I would have to order for both of us in some places because men did the ordering. While we weren't on a civilising crusade or attempting to change cultures, we were both properly annoyed or even mad about these occurrences. She never said it directly to me, but I could tell it was starting to wear on Jo (understandably so).

Forced collective identities. Jo and I had our master's degrees in international affairs, deployed with the military, and had a pretty good handle on the nuances of ethnic differences and identities. Even if we didn't know the details, we knew where and how to research them to come up to speed quickly. While neither of us subscribed to the intersectional obsession that consumed the United States, respecting others was still an imperative, both as travellers and decent human beings.

So, we were shocked to learn that two terms which we had always known and used in relation to North Africa turned out to be totally meaningless. "Berber," which referred to the nomadic and Bedouin tribes across North Africa, was simply an overarching label for all of said tribes, despite their lack of a cohesive identity. While there were political movements to advance the causes of the "Berber" peoples, those peoples were hardly united under a single banner, let alone political ideology. We learned that the term stemmed from an Arabic word which translated roughly as "barbarian," and the label was both a holdover from Muslim imperial rule in the region and French colonial times. While some of the nomadic tribes wanted to use the overarching term for the greater good of all of the Bedouins, some of them were wholly opposed to being included, both because of the offensive and meaningless label and because they didn't have the same political or social aspirations as the other tribes.

In a similar vein, the word "Moor" and its demonym "Moorish" were almost entirely meaningless beneath the surface. While the origin of these terms was uncertain, the European Christians adopted it to refer to the collective North African and Iberian Muslims, and it was even exported to other Muslim-majority countries to refer to Muslims writ large, regardless of their nationality, ethnicity, or origin. In Western architecture and art, the word "Moorish" really meant "Islamic," but, as I would soon learn, in Muslim countries, they used the word "Islamic." After traveling to Morocco and other parts of North Africa, I resolved to erase this word from my vocabulary. I had worked with various Saharan tribesmen before, and they certainly did not identify with each other, let alone the people in the major cities, in their

145

religious beliefs, cuisine, or daily lives. The same was true in Morocco. The so-called "Moors" accepted their identities as African, North African, and Saharan based on where they lived, Moroccan, Tunisian, or other nationalities by nature of being citizens of those countries, and their local tribes, as that was their ethnic belonging, but to be lumped together with people who shared none of these characteristics was not pleasing, if not offensive.

Chapter Twelve

Tunisia: What Were We Thinking?

Tunisia was a country which neither Jo nor I knew much about. One of our former professors insisted we go, which was how we settled on heading there after Morocco. Like Morocco, it was in North Africa, and we assumed we would have a similar experience. But as anyone versed in the ways of the Continent would tell you, if you visited one African country, you had visited one African country. There were fifty-two, fifty-three, or fifty-four countries (depending on which United States government agency you asked), each with their own cultures, ethnic subdivisions, and national histories. As we touched down in Tunis after an early-morning flight from Casablanca, we entered our second African country of the trip (my third over-all). We were in for one heck of an eye-opening experience.

Sousse

Sousse was a beach town about a two-hour drive south of Tunis. We had booked a taxi in advance to take us from the airport to Sousse at a reasonable price, but we never received a final confirmation of the pickup time. After waiting a few hours at the arrival hall, we checked out the taxi stand to broaden our options. We never made it. "We" fell for the most obvious tourist trap there was and ended up riding with a guy who offered "taxi" services to arriving passengers in the arrival hall. By "we" I mean my travel companion and over my objections. These guys were unauthorised, unregulated drivers who took you in their personal vehicle masquerading as a taxi for an exorbitant price, something we both knew all too well. However, by this time in the travel day and the overall trip, it was simply not a fight I was willing to have. So, for 400 Tunisian Dinar (TND) (about 130 USD), we got into this random guy's "taxi" and drove south to Sousse.

I wasn't worried about safety. We knew how to handle ourselves; we were both keenly aware of our surroundings in such situations, and neither of us opposed roll-ing out of a moving vehicle if our lives depended on it. Besides, for 130 USD, this guy would get us where we needed to go. I was, however, irritated at the price we were paying simply for the convenience of the first guy who asked despite knowing it was a tourist trap. Travel days were becoming more and more days when Jo and I didn't like to talk to each other. Her to me, because I rarely had more information than her when trying to figure things out, and I would sarcastically remind her of it every single time. Me to her, because any extra or unnecessary step I took with our bags trying to figure things out was met with annoyance, frustration, and anger.

In any case, we arrived at our Airbnb without any substantial interruptions. We were staying at Airbnbs our entire time in Tunisia because there weren't hostels. Fortunately, they weren't unreasonably priced, especially for what we got. Jo and I each would have our own rooms, which was a godsend of much needed time apart during the day. I had already made up my mind that I would let her have the master bedrooms at each place. That way, she could spread out and have her own bathroom, and I wouldn't disturb her when I awoke for coffee in the mornings.

Sousse was a so-called resort destination. There were major hotels along the beaches with tourists, mainly from Canada and Italy, but by and large, the city was formerly a major port that had fallen from glory. That said, it still held historical and cultural importance. Sousse was once the main outpost for Muslim empires to attack and defend against mainland Europe, and the rabat (military garrison), which was constructed for that purpose, still stood watch over the sea and was in excellent condition. Additionally, according to Christian lore, Saint Peter, the disciple who denied Jesus three times, spread the Gospel in Sousse, and recent archaeological finds were suggested to confirm the lore as historically accurate. For those interested in the religious wars waged in the region, Sousse was a fantastic source of primary material.

We only had a few days, so we planned a beach day, a day in the medina, and a day visiting museums. Although, as we said in the military, plans rarely survived first contact with the enemy. In this case, the "enemy" was a polite Tunisian man offering to take us to a festival. It was in town for just one day, and we were lucky to have arrived to see it. It was close to the beach, where we were headed, so we sceptically followed.

Add that to the list of scams. There was no festival; he led us to his and his friend's shops on the beach road. They sold faux-authentic bags, souvenirs, and jewellery, and they were very pushy. They insisted Jo and I be a couple, and even tried to pull the "you're the man" card on me to get her to buy something when she didn't want it. I knew better than to pull that with Jo except for as a joke, and, even then, only as a well-timed one. She ultimately bought something small from them to get them off our backs. While I rolled my eyes at it, she had a good point: she felt she could only say "no" so many times, and she had the money to buy our peace. While this was the exact mindset that these sorts of men preyed on, she was right, and I would have that same attitude later on in Jordan. Even so, I offered, half-jokingly, to be "the man" and put my foot down with people if she wanted me to do so. The expected disapproving glare told me that was out of the cards.

Like many before, our beach day was ill-fated, as had become the running joke on our travels. It was windy outside, unpleasantly so, and the beaches near our Airbnb weren't tourist beaches, so Jo had to remain covered to respect the culture. We also noticed none of the locals were in the water with the large waves, which we took as an indicator that we should probably not go in anyway. Jo made the point, which I wholeheartedly agreed with, that if we weren't going to be able to enjoy the beach fully, then we should find a beachside café to read. That was what we did at the beach when we weren't in the water, so it was a natural course of action. A lazy, wholly unproductive day? Maybe, but one we both wanted and needed after the travel day before.

We spent the next day in the Medina, which was shockingly well-preserved given the state of the section of the city where our Airbnb was located. On the walk over, we encountered a second popular scam. This one was pretty transparent. It entailed a man walking past us and saying, "Hey! Do you recognise me? I work security at your hotel!" (although sometimes he was a cook, driver, receptionist, you name it). The man would then offer, out of the goodness of his heart, to show you around his city on his day off, and you would only pay him something "from your heart." The only problem was Jo and I weren't at a hotel. We shared a sarcastic laugh at this and had a good time with those who claimed to be cooks on the breakfast shift by telling them that we wanted to lodge a complaint because breakfast was never ready and waiting when we woke up. Some of these scammers made earnest attempts to win us over; others weren't even half-hearted.

The Medina was surrounded by mud-brick walls, as was the norm when such coastal cities were built within the Muslim empires of the Middle East, North Africa, and Europe. Within the Medina were two main thoroughfares, one cutting across the centre north and south and the other from east to west, along with a winding route which passed by the major sites, such as the Rabat, Grand Mosque, museums, and main gate. We walked all of these at some point or another, either because we were on a dedicated archaeological walk or because we wanted to wander through the souks.

As far as the souks were concerned, they were concentrated mainly on the central thoroughfares. On the east-west route were the shops selling sports jerseys, jewellery, and [allegedly] artisan goods, while the north-south route contained everyday needs, like shoes, kitchen tools, and school supplies. While wandering the souks was fun, Jo and I became increasingly annoyed with the shop owners. In Morocco, while they wanted you to come into their shop, they left you alone after telling them no or sufficiently ignoring them. Not so in Sousse (or Tunisia writ-large). When the shop owners couldn't get our attention, they would wave their hands at (or even in front of) us and yell "Hello?!" in a sarcastic tone. Needless to say, we ignored these guys.

The Rabat, the military garrison and coastal defensive position, was at the modern main entrance to the Medina at the northeast corner. It cost 8 TND each (about 2.50 USD) to visit, an excellent price for an entire morning. The Rabat was built sometime during the Islamic conquests of the region, with the oldest inscription reading the year 821. It was remarkably well-preserved, some due to restoration and some due to the original engineering. As with most military garrisons, at its centre was a rectangular parade ground with rooms along the walls which served as barracks, storerooms, and offices. The internal garrison was two stories tall, with the south side including a prayer hall on the second floor. The threshold into this prayer hall had a deep impression in the stone, which had been made by over 1,000 years of feet stepping onto it. While Europe was still in its Dark Ages, long before the Castilians carried Christianity to the New World, Muslim soldiers were praying in this exact spot. While this prayer hall was no longer a consecrated mosque, people, including Jo and me, treated it with the reverence and respect due to such an important religious site.

The Rabat's roof had access to the minaret, which gave great views over the city and the sea. From the top, any guard could easily have spotted an invading European navy on the horizon and alerted the garrison. On each wall was a defensive position from which the garrison could defend itself against a land force. (Interestingly, when the Rabat was constructed, the cannon hadn't yet been used in war, so men with small arms such as swords, bows, and spears manned these positions.) The exception was along the south wall, where the prayer hall was located. Instead of a defensive position above the hall, there was another room with a mihrab, which indicated the direction of prayer, suggesting it belonged to the imam.

From the roof of the Rabat, the stereotypical golden-brown view of MENA cities was spectacular, especially when combined with the smattering of white buildings that were popular along the Tunisian coast. Add in the deep blue sea to the east and the towering Kasbah to the west, and I couldn't feel more like I was in an ancient part of the world where the sea provided life and the towering buildings provided protection.

It was no surprise that the Great Mosque, constructed in 851, stood just outside the Rabat's main gate. As a soldier standing between the empire and invaders from the sea, I would have wanted any level of divine intervention I could get. Unfortunately, we couldn't visit the mosque as we were not Muslims. The exclusionary nature of the self-proclaimed "religion of peace" was not lost on us. While we understood that Muslims and governments alike didn't want their places of worship turned into tourist sites where their practices and rules may not be respected, we couldn't help but notice the glaring difference from cathedrals and synagogues, which welcomed visitors of all faiths. In a modern world where Muslims, justly or not, had become ostracised due to the acts of theocratic governments and extremists within their ranks, it seemed to us that welcoming visitors would have done more for their relationship with the world than forbidding them.

On our last full day in Sousse, we visited the Sousse Archaeological Museum, housed within the Kasbah, the old military fort on the west side of the Medina. The museum cost 7 TND, a shocking value for what was inside. We expected an adequate-at-best museum which housed an accumulation of artifacts discovered in the region. What we found was, allegedly, the second-largest collection of Carthaginian, Roman, and Byzantine mosaics in the world. Some were only half-preserved after excavation, such as one elaborate meadow scene adorned with animals on its edges, but others were in fantastic shape. One large floor mosaic, which must have been six or seven metres across, depicted the head of Medusa with snakes shooting out at odd angles, while another, which we presumed to be a wall hanging, portrayed the god Neptune in his chariot pulled by seahorses. There was even a beautiful Byzantine baptistry. It turned out that Tunisia was one of the most archaeologically important areas in North Africa for understanding Byzantine, Phoenician, and Roman incursions, settlements, and campaigns on the Continent. Even Jo, who had become tired of "looking at old things" in MENA, commented on how impressive of a museum it was. Was it impressive enough for a dedicated visit to Sousse? No, but if someone were to take a resort vacation there, I would undoubtedly insist they give it a visit.

After three days passed faster than we anticipated, it was time to head to Hammamet, about an hour up the coast. We opted for the train from Sousse to Hammamet. After all, we were budget travellers, the train was public transport, and we didn't want the 400 TND experience of an unregulated taxi again. The train station was, however, quite a distance to the south from our Airbnb when we factored in our bags, so we grabbed a cheap taxi for the ten-minute drive through the city before being deposited at a run-down outpost of a train station. We got there a little too early, because we couldn't buy tickets online, and the small departure hall was already full of people. Jo picked us out a spot on the floor in the corner while I paid the 14 TND for our two tickets. Then, we played the waiting game.

And thus began the adventure.

The train was delayed. Really delayed. Hours delayed. We didn't know why, and my French wasn't good enough to get anything from the ticket desk. We planned to arrive in Hammamet for lunch but ultimately wouldn't arrive until late enough for dinner, so I stepped outside to order us one of the most mediocre, if not absolutely horrible, pizzas we had ever eaten while sitting on the train station floor. When the train finally did arrive, everyone quickly made their way towards the tracks, which were surprisingly unguarded by rails, chains, or guards. We decided not to rush with the crowd. We had our seats on our tickets, and we didn't want to inconvenience everyone by crowding in with our bags.

That was a mistake. People were jumping onto the train before it came to a stop and long before anyone disembarked. It was a total madhouse of pushing and shoving while those on the train tried to get off and those off the train tried to get on. Jo and I looked at each other in total confusion at the chaos. After all, everyone had a ticket with a coach and seat number, and hardly anyone had luggage. There was no reason for literally throwing elbows to get on the train, let alone jumping onto it while it was moving.

We soon learned that there was a reason for all this: the tickets meant nothing. If someone asked for a ticket on the train, they were given one, and the train was sold to, we guessed, about 200 percent capacity. It was standing-room-only in the carriages, the wells where the bathrooms were located, and even the engine compartment. We should have thrown elbows with everyone else. Maybe, then, we would have gotten a seat. Instead, we stacked our bags against the wall next to the bathroom and sat on top of them. At first, we were annoyed, but after the absurdity of it all settled in, we started laughing near-hysterically. Not six months before, we were working in the security field, and now we were riding our bags on some rickety train through the desert as men smoked around us, the train doors were forced open by men wanting to smoke in the open air, and people used the toilet as just another seat (probably because it didn't work in the first place) as they charged their phones in the bathroom USB port (which, unlike the toilet, did work). Life took a hard left somewhere along the way, and we were along for the ride!

Hammamet

The train didn't drop us exactly in Hammamet. We were dropped at a station outside of Hammamet and took a taxi into town. To take the train to Hammamet, we would have had to connect at a city farther north and head back south. While that would have been cheaper, it had already been a day, and we were worn out from what should have been an easy travel day. Fortunately, our Airbnb was just around the corner from the main taxi stand in Hammamet.

Once again, we had an entire apartment to ourselves, and we shared the rooftop with a French woman who lived in an adjacent apartment. This was her retirement home, and she didn't like being bothered by Airbnb guests; luckily, we didn't see her a single time. On the ground floor was an elementary school of sorts for local children. It seemed to Jo and me that there were children in that classroom from dawn until long after dark, which was incredibly different from the United States, which was charging hard and fast towards a four-day school (and work) week. It wasn't lost on us, either, that we hadn't met many uneducated people in MENA. They may not have had master's degrees and formal education credentials, but they had local schools like this one where parents prioritised their children's learning about the world.

So, what were we going to do in Hammamet? That was the question. Jo had mapped our route through Tunisia, and I was happy to be along for the ride, at least as far as planning was concerned. Hammamet was a beach town. It was divided into two parts: Hammamet and Hammamet Sud. The former was the older part of the city. It contained the primary government services, the Medina, the local university, the original fort, and local beaches. The latter was the newer part of the city. It contained the cultural centre, a local amusement park, and tourist resorts which lined (and prevented direct access to) the beaches that looked out into the Gulf of Hammamet. So, while we didn't have much of an idea of what we would do, the beach and the Medina were our main ideas.

The beach was just a ten-minute walk from our Airbnb, so we spent a fair amount of time over there. If we weren't on the beach, we were at beachside café or wandering the sidewalk that wrapped around the coastline. The beach itself was a welcome reprieve from Morocco and Souse. The surf and waves were calm, the water was crystal clear, and the temperature was perfect. I took my mask and snorkel out our first day out there, and was welcomed into one of the magical sites of the marine world: a long seafloor plateau which extended as far as the eye could see until it dropped off the continental shelf. Consequently, there wasn't a lot of marine life, seeing as the water was only about chest deep, but it was still beautiful swimming. Because of the water's clarity and the flatness of the seafloor, I found it difficult to navigate by sight as I swam, and as I looked around, the realisation hit me that anything could come from any direction and would see me long before I saw it. Was I concerned about shark attacks or anything like that? Not really, given the lack of marine life, but it was a humbling and eerie feeling for a new diver.

The nearby Medina, which served as the business and restaurant hub, especially for tourists, was quite different from the Medinas in Morocco and Sousse. Hammamet's Medina was small, very small, and situated directly on the water. The kasbah (military fort) wasn't an adjacent structure but a reinforcing one whose high walls protected the city's inhabitants from attack. When we entered the Medina from the main road, it was like entering a different town. There were some shops, but not the expansive souks we were used to, and the streets twisted and turned in a labyrinth through a residential space that had stood since long before the Europeans discovered my country. We had planned to spend a long time wandering the streets, souks, and museums within the old city walls, but there wasn't much to spend our time on between its size and the lack of tourists. The bustling souks we had read about had packed up for the off-season, the museums were on limited hours, and we could only spend so much time wandering the small space. After a while, we looked at each other and asked, "Now what?" That was the question, a question which became a fixture of the rest of our time in Tunisia.

One thing I enjoyed about Hammamet was that it gave me time to write for the blog and work on Instagram posts. I awoke before Jo every morning and headed to the beachside café for breakfast with my computer. I sat on the shaded rooftop terrace, eating crepes or croissants, sipping my espresso, getting experiences, thoughts, and feelings onto paper, and basking in the salty ocean breeze. It wasn't hard to see why Canadians, Frenchmen, and Italians retired to places like this. It was quiet, peaceful, and away from the world's chaos, at least on the surface.

Beneath the surface, there was always the undercurrent of government and politics, which I experienced on our second day in the city. Our Airbnb owner took me to the police station to register as a tourist. While this wasn't a widely-publicised requirement, he was an official tour guide, and he made sure to do everything by the book. He told me that it wasn't a big deal if we didn't register so long as nothing happened. If something did happen, Jo and I could have found ourselves in a real bind with the local police as unregistered foreign tourists, even though we entered the country legally. I had to go in person with both of our passports and visas. Luckily, Jo didn't have to go with me. It was an unspoken understanding between us that we didn't want to both be in a foreign police station at the same time. Not that we thought anything would go wrong, but better one of us be outside and able to get with the State Department if it became necessary. Fortunately, it was a simple bureaucratic necessity, and I was in and out within minutes (although, the Airbnb owner told me this was because I was with him and he was a personal friend of the head of the tourism department; had I come on my own, it would have taken hours).

On the way back from the police station, we drove along the road that led to the coast and passed an abandoned, run-down, former cultural and activities centre. He told me it was once a hotel that the government planned to convert to an amusement park to serve the northern part of the city. When I asked him why it hadn't happened, he replied it was because of the revolution during the Arab Spring. He lamented the revolution. He told me he had supported its ideals, but it only served to replace one ineffective government with another. The high hopes for post-revolution prosperity were dashed in places like Hammamet. The politicians and activists, he said, only cared about themselves. He tried to say it like the professional tour guide he was, but he couldn't mask the deflated air of disappointment which surrounded the subject. I felt his sentiment. In the United States, the Arab Spring was touted as the end of authoritarian-esque religious rule in MENA and the ushering in of democratic values and governing systems. That may have been the case on paper, but those ideals and promises of prosperity hadn't made it too far or changed things outside of capital cities and diplomatic circles.

At our Airbnb owner's recommendation, Jo and I headed to Hammamet Sud on our last day in town. We were told it was worth a visit, so we decided to start at the archaeological park, wander the streets, and make our way to the beach. After a twenty-minute taxi ride, that plan was shattered. The beaches in Hammamet Sud were not easily accessible, unlike those in Hammamet proper. Resorts and hotels lined the beaches, and their thick walls and fences lined the road separating them from the city. The only way to access the beach was to access the resorts, and the resorts all had front gate security verifying you were staying with them. We walked and walked and walked to no avail. After a long while, we finally found a public access path. Had we not found it, we would have gotten a taxi back to our Airbnb and called it a day. Given how far we had walked, we called off our other plans anyway. In the immortal words of my grandfather, it was just too much trouble.

We ended up at a small beach restaurant with no one around. We had a lovely meal in looking out into the Gulf of Hammamet as the breeze blew gently around us. There was hardly anyone else in eyesight up and down the beach, as the tourism season was only about a week away from being over. We didn't have our books or anything, so we enjoyed sitting, talking, and staring out into far off horizon. I wondered what the next week would hold. The end of our planned-out journey was quickly approaching, and we were at a crossroads that we were actively avoiding discussing. Fortunately, these wonderings were interrupted by a street merchant peddling his cheap tourist trinkets on us, and we played the usual games of gifts not being gifts and trinkets being priced "from the heart." Such was life as a tourist in these resort towns.

Leaving Hammamet for Tunis was an ordeal that was no less frustrating than leaving Sousse. Our Airbnb owner was insistent that we not take the train. When he learned we had taken the train from Sousse to Hammamet, he exclaimed, "Why would you do that?!" His son had the same sentiment, as did every Tunisian I met from that point forward. Instead, he recommended the bus, which left every hour from the taxi stand. That seemed simple enough, so after breakfast on our travel day, I went to ask for bus tickets. This was about ten minutes before the bus in front of the station left at 11h00, and we wanted tickets for the noon bus. The bus attendant was having none of it. He gave me a ticket for the bus in front of us, and when I told him we wanted to get on the next bus at noon, he refused and told us we could get on the current bus. He even printed out the tickets and tried to give them to me. No matter how many times I told him, "No, we want the next bus," he wouldn't budge, so Jo and I just walked away.

That caused a problem. He yelled at me while pointing at the tickets on the counter. I just waved him off and turned, but he stood up and continued yelling at me that I had to pay for the tickets. That was when I understood what was happening. The tickets were charged when printed, so if I didn't pay for them, he would be short money and, in all likelihood, out of a job unless he paid for them himself. While this wasn't our problem, nor were we particularly in a caring mood towards his problems after him not being in a caring mood about ours, we faced a traveller's dilemma: do we stick to our guns and let this spiral out of control, or do we pay for the tickets and move on in life. We opted for the latter. It was only 12 TND (about 4 USD) for the two of us, and if that meant avoiding problems with the locals and, likely, the police, so be it.

This experience made us not to want to take the bus. We would have to buy the ticket from the same guy, and neither of us wanted any more interaction with him. We decided we would just grab a taxi and take the train to Tunis. After all, we knew how it worked this time, and it really had not been that bad of an experience before. Our host, however, was insistent, so he drove us to the shared taxi, which I knew as a colectivo from my time in Mexico earlier that year. The way these van taxis worked was they drove a set route between cities, and people got on and off as necessary. They were much cheaper than the bus or the train, but they didn't run on a set schedule. They departed their embarkation point when the van was full. Fortunately, there was a van with two vacant seats that was ready to depart when we arrived. About five minutes and 3 TND later, we were barrelling towards Tunis with Jo in the front seat and me in the back. Our last city in Tunisia and an uncertain future awaited us.

Tunis

We decided to visit Tunisia's capital city at the end of our time in Tunisia so we could be closer to the airport. After our experiences with taxis, trains, and colectivos, that was a practical idea. With our disagreements over travel plans, it turned out to be a great call because we had a massive Airbnb apartment in the middle of town where we each had our own bedroom and bathroom at opposite ends of the apartment. I could get up and leave in the mornings without waking up Jo, and we could have some time apart in the evenings. By this point, we had been together non-stop for five months, so any time apart was becoming a necessity rather than a luxury.

On our first night in Tunisia, we ran some errands. We needed groceries, and Jo was looking for a planner and notebook for an online class she had decided to take. While we were out and about, we got detailed insight into the aftermath of October 7th. There was pro-Palestine, anti-Israel graffiti everywhere, especially on the walls surrounding embassies. The French embassy was especially tagged with accusations of supporting genocide, probably because the embassy was in the middle of the city and because of the French's colonial history and subsequent feelings of resentment. Architecturally beautiful synagogues were guarded by Tunisian security services with metal barricades erected around them to prevent cars from getting too close and closed to visitors for the foreseeable future. It was an ugly mark from a centuries-long ethno-religious conflict on a different continent.

When the morning came, I got a text from Jo at the other end of the apartment asking what we planned on doing that day. This became an every-morning occurrence. She had planned our route through Tunisia, but I was apparently planning the day-to-day. I had been doing this the entire trip, and it hadn't bothered me until we got to Tunisia. She was losing interest in North Africa, but I wasn't, and putting those two together was frustrating, at best. I could have walked the entire city, wandering from site to site up and down modern streets as they gave way to old ones, but that was not something she was interested in doing. Maybe it was because she was tired or something had happened that I wasn't aware of, but for whatever reason, she wouldn't tell me what was up. So, I did my best and planned half-days where we could do our separate things in the mornings, go out and about midday, and then relax at the Airbnb in the evening.

Fortunately for us, someone Jo matched with on a dating app recommended a beach on the northeast side of town, so we spent a day out there. As was tradition by this point, the wind picked up during our visit, and with winter approaching it was chilly laying out on the sand. Even so, we got in the water a bit (mainly because there were no bathrooms in the area...) and enjoyed reading in the sun. I eventually put my long pants and sweatshirt on. I had zero tolerance for even slightly cold weather, and I was always the first to admit I was whiny about the cold. Even though we were on the African side of the Mediterranean coast, we were solidly in November by this point, and winter weather was winter weather.

The next day, unbeknownst to us, non-essential government and private sector services shut down. Sundays were a legally mandated day off for most industries in Tunisia, at least according to our Airbnb host and some others we met. Not even regulated taxis were providing service. So, Jo and I stayed in and around the Airbnb all day. We finally took this opportunity to have the uncomfortable conversation we had been avoiding: What did the future look like? We had the tour booked in Egypt, but that was it, and we needed to know if we needed to get visas, flights, special permissions, etc. for wherever we went in the Middle East.

The last half of that sentence was the rub. I wanted to stay in the Middle East. She wanted to leave for Australia or Southeast Asia. She wouldn't tell me why; she was just "burned" on the region, but she was adamant that she wanted to leave. I was equally adamant about staying. I had been looking forward to this part of the world for a year, and I had no intention of skipping it when I was so close. I wanted to see Alexandria, Petra, Erbil, and Istanbul at the very least. She did not, at least not at this point. She pointed to the Department of State travel advisories and the civil unrest on the news and social media, while I put little stock in what she saw. In my mind, these countries needed Western tourism dollars more than they needed to support Hamas in Gaza, and, as Americans, I was confident we would be fine.

I put my foot down on Petra. I told her I wasn't going to be this close to Petra and skip it. That's when she said the fateful phrase: "Well, you can go." That was that for me. We discussed the possibility of splitting up for a bit when planning our travels, but it hadn't come up since we started in June. I took advantage of the opening, took out my phone, and booked a flight from Cairo to Aqaba, Jordan, for December 8th right then. Truthfully, I had already looked at flights and knew exactly which one I wanted. Jo was taken aback, although I didn't think she was offended. We had arrived to the point where we quite literally wanted to go different ways and see different things, and me booking that flight was the act that turned those feelings into a concrete reality. Jo didn't make any decisions right there, but she was distracted over the next few days as she thought through what she did and didn't want to do.

That said, putting that mark on the wall and getting the idea that we might actually split up out into the open really helped reduce the tension in the air. We were both relieved that we finally had the talk, even though we wouldn't admit it to each other. Our days now went from trying to keep the other one happy for the long haul to enjoying the last couple of weeks we had together. As far as our moods went, it was like we travelled back in time to when we first started traveling. We were laughing more and exploring with wide-eyed wonder like we had during our first fifty kilometres in Paris.

With the tension finally cut, we excitedly headed for the Medina once Monday rolled around. At its east end, the modern city centre gave way to a large square that led into the Medina and the souks inside. This Medina was much more like the Medina in Marrakech. It was large and expansive, and alleys jutted out seemingly in every direction. It was also packed with people shopping. Not just tourists, but locals, especially those who lived within the Medina's walls, and we were constantly squeezing between women negotiating prices with shop owners. After Hammamet, this was a welcome scene for us. This was the MENA we knew and I loved, albeit with the modern twist of nice restaurants disguised behind centuries-old walls.

The Medina wasn't the only old city in Tunis. In the northeast of the city's metropolis was Sidi Bou Said, a white and blue historic area that felt more like Greece than Tunisia. Sid Bou Said was, essentially, where Tunis' wealthy resided in the 1700s. Who could blame them? It sat on a hill overlooking the Gulf of Tunis and was close to the historic ruins of Carthage and, eventually, the Presidential Palace. Sidi Bou Said had a reputation for producing artists, film producers, and government officials, and it was immaculately kept as a result, much to the chagrin of many of the Tunisian middle class. While tourism in the beautiful white and blue neighbourhood was a significant source of income, Jo and I didn't understand the hype. It was just a neighbourhood on a hill with inauthentic-feeling merchants and mediocre food. Amazing views notwithstanding, we were not that impressed.

Seeing as we were close to the ruins of Carthage, which was my only must-see in Tunisia, we decided to walk them. Well, "we" decided to walk them. I started walking with Jo in tow to the nearest site. It was a good thing we were in better spirits by this point, thanks to our discussion the day before, because we definitely would have had it out over the amount of walking we did without talking about it in advance.

The Carthaginian ruins themselves were unimpressive. It was unfortunate, but they were not well-kept, to put it mildly. Some of the sites had little security protecting them, and had clearly become a hangout spot for teenagers and the city's underclass when the sun went down. Trash was everywhere, and there were no walking paths, so the ruins were trampled and damaged from people climbing on them. Even though each individual archaeological site was separate from the others, sometimes not even within walking distance, they all told the same story: the legacy of one of the world's most prolific ancient empires tarnished by a modern society that didn't see its value. As we walked the different sites, Jo and I discussed how strange we felt to be walking on such historic ruins. We felt like we were being disrespectful not just to the site but to Tunisia and its people. These ruins were their history that we, as foreigners, were literally trampling. Ultimately, though, we cared more than they did, so we, a bit begrudgingly, put it out of our minds.

The ruins cost 12 TND per person, with eight sites included in the ticket, including the Bardo Museum, the Roman theatre and amphitheatre, and the residential quarter. We didn't get to see all of them, as some were closed, but with the help of a taxi driver named Ali, we visited several we wouldn't have otherwise been able to walk to. He offered his taxi to us for 40 TND (about 13 USD) to drive us to all the sites we hadn't yet seen. He was a lovely old man who spoke very little English, but between his lack of English and my lack of French, we could communicate well enough. He even took us to one of his favourite scenic spots in a lagoon where the old men fished in the evening. Like every other old man we met in MENA, he was adamant that Jo and I get together and have "beautiful babies," and he kept us laughing the entire afternoon. He even helped us return to the city centre on the public train. Ali was exactly what you thought of when you heard stories of the locals doing things for you out of the goodness of their hearts. He wasn't a pushy taxi driver trying to rip off the tourists. He was just a man trying to make a living while making his customers happy by welcoming them into his world for a short time.

By the time we returned to the city centre, the sun was down. It was time to pack it in and prepare for our flight the next day. After stopping for some wine (and after Jo accidentally broke a bottle all over the supermarket floor, prompting an angry response from the manager despite telling him we would pay for it) and some local pizza, we returned to the Airbnb. Jo had had a couple of days to think over her plan by this point, and she came to the conclusion that she wanted to see Petra as well, but she didn't want to see Alexandria, Egypt, with me, so she booked a flight to leave Egypt for Jordan the day after our tour ended. It was official: We would go our separate ways in ten days.

That was when she asked me to help her do something I never thought she would ask me to help her do: thin out her backpack. She had too much stuff, specifically clothing. She knew she needed to get rid of some of it, but she couldn't decide which. Now, I didn't begrudge her for having more clothes than me. I was a guy that could wear the same thing over and over again, whereas women have more trouble with that, especially considering the different cultures we had been traveling through. So, we dumped all of her clothes on her bed, and I started going through them. This may sound odd to a lot of people considering we weren't a couple, but we had been doing laundry together for more than five months by this point, so it wasn't like we were hiding anything from each other. To both of our surprise, she readily got rid of things I suggested she abandon, and to my surprise I actually wanted her to hold onto some things "just in case," such as the dress she bought when Layne visited us in Trieste (it was also expensive, she really liked it, and it looked really good on her). After about thirty minutes, she had a pile on the floor of things to get rid of, and she was far less anxious about packing than she had been an hour before.

At noon the next day, we loaded our bags into a taxi and headed to the Tunis Airport. Our flight didn't leave until 22h00, but we had to leave the Airbnb, so we camped at the airport all afternoon. There was a small food court and a couple of suitable spaces to tuck ourselves away from everyone coming and going, so it wasn't that bad of a day. Before we knew it, we were leaving Tunisia behind, hopping across the Gulf of Tunis, Libya, and most of Egypt, and descending into our nine-day mostly-inclusive tour of Ancient Egypt, this time with an air of certainty about what the future would hold.

Reflecting on Tunisia

What were we thinking? We knew nothing of Tunisia. We only went there because one of our professors from graduate school insisted we go. While that professor had visited Tunisia several times, all of them were for work, not pleasure. While he had his fair share of pleasure, it was a different experience for Jo and me, who were there for travel. With only a limited time and needing to consider two personalities, Tunisia was not somewhere we should have gone at this point in The Great Gallivanting. On top of that, had we done our research, we would have known that most of the archaeological sites in Tunisia were, while important, not well-maintained and barely worth a visit (except for the Rabat and the archaeological museum in Sousse). Would I go back in the future? Maybe if the reasons were just right, but Jo and I agreed, both at the time and in later retellings of our adventures, that Tunisia was our overall least favourite destination.

"Yes, Palestine!" The post-October 7th attitudes in Tunisia stood in stark contrast to Morocco. Whereas Morocco wanted to preserve its Jewish heritage, keep the peace, and keep the United States happy with the Abraham Accords, Tunisia had no such aspirations. I, personally, felt the ramifications of this daily. Every day, I wore my desert yellow and black shemagh from my last experience in Africa. I wore it for practical purposes: keep the sand out of my face, the sun off my neck, and to trap sweat to keep me cool. Admittedly, I also liked the overall look (I may have been going for the Nathan Drake in *Uncharted 3* look...).

The colour choice was strategic; the shemagh was called the keffiyeh in Palestine and Jordan, and Palestinians traditionally wore the black and white checkered keffiyeh as a symbol of Palestinian nationalism. Jordanian Bedouins and Palestinians living in Jordan wore the red and white checkered keffiyeh. Mine was desert yellow and black, which I knew not to be affiliated with any side of the Palestine conflict. I also wore it as a shemagh around my neck, not a keffiyeh around my shoulders, to further distance myself from making a political statement.

Unfortunately, none of that seemed to make a difference. Everywhere we went, but especially at restaurants, I would be met with people gesturing to my shemagh and saying, "Yes, Palestine!" I would smile, nod, and keep walking; I wasn't looking to get into a shouting match over a political situation in which neither side acknowledged the facts of the other. I found it disheartening, however, that I, as a traveller and tourist, was being dragged into the pro-Palestine protest by locals, despite my deliberate efforts to do just the opposite.

My new normal. When Jo and I landed in Tunis, we were clearly in different headspaces. One night, Jo finally admitted to me that she missed having something to look forward to and to work towards. While she loved the long-term travel experience day-to-day, the uncertain, post-travel future was bothering her in the back of her mind. That was completely understandable. We had both been in the military, which was an "up or out" system where you were constantly angling for your next job, followed by a cutthroat graduate school experience, which in turn was followed by the steep competition of getting a job working somewhere in the security field.

The Great Gallivanting

The Great Gallivanting was the first time either of us had been left wholly to our own devices and desires in a decade, and it was an adjustment.

I, however, had hit the opposite point in life. Like Jo, I had originally wanted to travel for a year, the use the experience to try to land a nice job in the security sphere. I had spent a long time in anti- and counter-terrorism, and I would surely land back there again. By the time we were halfway through our time in North Africa, though, my entire outlook had changed. I wasn't sure I wanted to go back to that life. For one, I was, for the first time in a long time, in a positive headspace and escaping the depression that had settled in partly from being deeply tied to all of the negative and horrible things going on in the world. For two, I had finally escaped my professional habits. I was no longer worrying about rooftops, kidnappings, surveillance, or anything else I had once actively concerned myself while walking around in foreign countries. I was wandering the souks, enjoying the cafés, and taking taxi rides without a worry. I even laughed to myself about it in the Tunis Medina. Not six months before, my stress levels would have been through the roof as my mind constantly evaluated the environment and calculated the infinite possibilities of bad things that could happen. None of that was even registering by the time we left Tunisia.

When we left Spain in September, I decided I wasn't going to return to my old life as I had planned. After over a month in North Africa, I was positive that, while I didn't know what the future held, I was in the travel life for the long haul. I wanted to figure out a way to make a career transition where wandering the souks brought me happiness, not fear, watching bullfights was a part of everyday life, not an offhand cultural experience, and learning about and communicating cultures was something I did to help make the world a better place. I had found a "new normal" in life and preferred it to the "cool-guy" experiences of the life I had left behind.

Chapter Thirteen

Egypt: Long Days and Fast Friends

Egypt had been a toss-up over the last few weeks. We both wanted to go, but Jo was burned out on "seeing old things" in MENA, and we were starting to get on each other's nerves, partly because I never tired of seeing old things. But we couldn't be this close and not see the only remaining Wonder of the Ancient World and the source of so much ancient mythology. I was generally opposed to organised tours, but Jo's mom found one at a reasonable price, and I knew it was about the only chance I had at getting her to Egypt before we decided to go our separate ways. So, with Tunisia and five months of travel together behind us, we set our sights on one final adventure as a travelling duo.

Kicking Off

Our late flight from Tunis made for an early landing in Cairo, landing around 02h00 on the first of our nine-day tour. Jo had been in contact with our tour company, Timeless Tours, to figure out what we needed to do to meet up with the tour later in the day, but they took care of everything. When we stepped off the jet bridge, a member of the tour company was standing there with our names on a sign, just like out of a film. He escorted us through immigration and customs with little fuss, took us to a cashpoint to withdraw some Egyptian Pounds (EGP), and rode the almost two hours with us to the hotel where he handed us off to one of the coordinators. It was too early for an early check-in, so we thought, and we figured we would sleep on the couches in lobby until the official check-in time in the afternoon. Neither of us had been so happy to be wrong. For 18 USD, we checked into our room early. After confirming some tour details for the next day, we were relaxing in our own beds in a very nice hotel room. If this was the treatment we could expect for the next nine days, we would feel like royalty.

We met with our tour guide, Meena, and the rest of our group late the following evening. Meena was a little awkward at first, especially for a tour guide, but he was one of the coolest people we would meet in our travels. He was a government-certified tour guide and Egyptologist. He had spent more than two years in training programmes, learning everything there was to know about Egyptian history, archaeology, and culture. He was a deacon in the Orthodox Christian church, but he could easily discuss the details and influences of other religions on Egypt and MENA as a whole. He was also down to earth, a practical jokester, and easily handled different personalities and groups. Without Meena, our tour wouldn't have been half as fun and engaging as it was.

Jo and I were two people in a group of ten. The others were a mother-daughter duo from Canada and six friends from Trinidad and Tobago. The Canadian duo was pretty cool, but the Caribbean crew would end up being a pain, which Jo and I expected. When one group made up the majority of a guided tour, they tended to think the tour was theirs rather than everyone's, and things like timelines became optional even with everyone else waiting. That would be a constant truth over the following nine days. On just the first night, Meena, Jo, and I noticed this when they asked a lot of questions that Meena already said he would answer as the tour unfolded. Meena told Jo and me that we could leave the meeting if we wanted, but we opted to stick around to avoid leaving him to suffer alone. Being the professional tour guide he was, Meena was a quick study when it came to people, and afterwards, he thanked us for staying behind.

People and shaky timelines notwithstanding, we headed out on the second day of the tour to see the Giza Pyramids, the last remaining of the Seven Wonders of the Ancient World. Despite what one might see in films, the pyramids were not lost out in the desert. They towered over Cairo and butted up against the city. You could eat at a Pizza Hut with a window view of the pyramids if you wanted. Well, it was too early for pizza, and we had already eaten breakfast at the hotel, so our group charged straight for the entry gate. Once we were all through, Meena gathered us in the shadow of the Great Pyramid to tell us about their construction, history, and mythology. Most of the group was too enamoured with the colossal structures before us to pay too much attention, but Meena was a smart tour guide. He wanted to give us all the information up front so he could release us to our own devices to explore until the next hit time; he knew full well that once we moved closer to the pyramids, he would lose our attention.

The pyramids were huge, but up close they sort of lost their appeal. Despite their pyramidal shape, they were constructed of large, square stones, something I probably knew but didn't realise until I saw them up close. When I stood facing one of the large sides, it really looked more like a large wall than an imposing pyramid or tomb. It wasn't until we stepped back that we could appreciate their true beauty and magnificence.

The best pictures of the pyramids were at the corners. From that angle, their up-close impressiveness returned as the block wall gave way to sharp angles against the blue, cloudless sky. From some corners, one side would be darkened by the pyramid's shadow while the other shone in the sun. Of course, the "official" photographers knew this as well, and they staked out the corners as "theirs" to take photos of tourists (for a fee, of course). These photographers were, in fact, not official. They were authorised, meaning they had a badge showing they were allowed to be there. To an unknowing tourist, that badge might as well have meant that these photographers were employees with authority over the site and them. Fortunately, Meena had warned us of this, so we didn't fall for such antics, but several people who were visiting on their own did, and their wallets paid the price.

The back side of the Great Pyramid was more impressive than the front closest to the entry gate. The front side was where most everyone stopped to take pictures, merchants peddled water and snacks, and the entrance to the tomb (which required an optional, additional ticket) was located. It was also completely shaded as the rising sun cast long shadows from the east. In contrast, the back side stood golden in the morning sun, had far fewer people, and merchants were noticeably absent. We could also see the other two pyramids (and walk to them, if we so desired). As Jo and I walked in the warm, morning sun along the back side, we wondered aloud how many people wouldn't come back here for the better views simply because it was a long walk, including the rest of our group (whom we hadn't seen). We also talked about the relative emptiness of the site. Sure, there were plenty of people, but it was also December, which Jo and I thought was the low season. It must have been packed in the high season, and we were glad to be able to see it away from vast throngs of people.

We asked Meena about the high season when we met back up with him after exploring the site. He gave a disheartened response that temporarily dampened his mood: "This is the high season..." In a normal year, we would be fighting huge crowds in December, as the temperature was considerably more bearable than in the summer. After October 7th, though, 2024 was anything but a normal year in MENA, and the tourism sector in Egypt took a massive hit as Western tourists avoided the region as a result of the conflict in Gaza just next door (but hundreds of miles away). At the same time, Meena told us, Egypt and Canada were in an unrelated diplomatic spat over visas and immigration policy, and Egypt recently ceased offering e-visas or visas on arrival to Canadians, which had caused Timeless Tours to outright cancel ten tours since the summer, because Canadians had opted to cancel their vacations rather than bother with applying for a visa through the Egyptian embassy in Ottawa. Jo and I couldn't help but shake our heads at the far-reaching, unintended consequences of diplomacy and war. The vendors, tour guides, shops, hotels, and restaurants which relied on peak-season vacationers were paying the price for Canada's immigration policy and Hamas's unprecedented militant actions two months before.

After the pyramids, we naturally moved to the Sphinx. It was smaller than I had pictured, and we couldn't get close because the security fencing kept tourists at a respectable distance (and, I was sure, from climbing on the thousands-of-years-old masterpiece). Despite the diminished number of visitors in peak season, the Sphinx was crowded, mainly due to the security fencing, the one-way movement through the site, and the fact that the ancient Egyptians didn't think to install a viewing platform for wild-eyed Westerners thousands of years in the future. While I would have loved to take it in in a more relaxed or studious manner, I resigned myself to finding it underwhelming in the moment but worthy of a return visit and more perceptive observation.

Our final stop on this day was the Pyramid of Djoser, more popularly known as the Step Pyramid. The Step Pyramid was the first known Egyptian pyramid ever built. Conspiracy theorists often compared this pyramid to step pyramids found in Central and South America and commented that there was no way for such architectural similarities to span multiple continents without the help of aliens. Jo and I took a more straightforward approach: this was the most effective and efficient way of stacking rocks for those without the engineering know-how or technical capability to create other types of pyramids. Even the Giza pyramids, upon closer inspection, were just tightly stacked layers of stones until you reached the capstones.

The Djoser Pyramid complex was massive and not sacked with people like the Sphinx. There was a large open area at the front of the pyramid, several smaller tombs in the surrounding area, and a substantial archaeological dig outside the complex's protective walls. I would have loved to explore the complex thoroughly, but our tour only had so much time before we had to head back to the hotel to catch our buses, flights, and trains bound for Aswan. I was to learn on this excursion that you cannot "do Egypt" in a week or even a month. There were too many sites with too much historical and archaeological relevance to see in one go, especially if you were with a tour group. Nonetheless, Jo and I snapped some fantastic photos, enjoyed a peaceful stroll around the grounds, and got some great people watching in of the others in our group.

As the day came to an end, our group headed our separate ways for our transportation to Aswan, which was in the southern part of Egypt. The tour included an overnight bus (which was a standard bus that drove overnight, not a sleeper), but you could pay to upgrade (in advance) to a sleeper train or flight. One person in our group opted for the flight, while Jo and I opted for the sleeper train. It was only about 70 USD more, which was more than worth it to me. I had a bad lower back and knee from my days in the military, Jo would surely get carsick on a bus for fourteen hours, and we both wanted to arrive in Aswan refreshed and ready to go.

It occurred to us earlier in the day that it was Thanksgiving in the United States. Our families and friends were curious about our plans and what international cuisine we would eat for our Thanksgiving dinner abroad. The answer: a packaged train dinner. It was good, though not quite delicious, and it was more than enough food, so we had no complaints. We just laughed in the moment and wished each other a Happy Thanksgiving as we sat on the bottom bunk and careened down the tracks.

Aswan and The Nile

We arrived in Aswan early the next morning, shortly before the bus. Taking the train was a good idea because everyone who took the bus looked exhausted. Fortunately, we were with a fantastic tour company that factored this into the itinerary, so we had a few hours of downtime before leaving for the Philae Temple. Jo and I took the time to enjoy the views from the pool and terraces. By now, we had budget-travelled for five months and had only stayed in a handful of hotels when it made financial sense for us to do so instead of staying in a hostel. For a nine-day tour of Egypt for less than 700 USD, we didn't have high expectations for our accommodations, but we continued to be blown away, as this place was nicer than almost any hotel I had ever stayed in. Some in our group complained about the accommodations, but we were amazed by the value we got for the price. Plus, we had our own beds again, a five-star luxury for the two of us who were used to sharing a hotel double bed.

The Philae Temple was our only stop for the day, and we stayed there most of the afternoon. This temple was built somewhere in the 500 BC timeframe, and was abandoned just 1,000 years later. In fact, the current Philae Temple was not at the original site. After the Aswan High Dam was built at the south end of the Nile in the 1970s, the temple complex would have been completely submerged by the surrounding river, so teams of archaeologists, tradesmen, and government officials led by UNESCO disassembled the entire complex brick-by-brick and reconstructed it on a nearby island in the river. All in all, it took about two years to move and reconstruct 40,000 bricks on the Agilkia Island. It was a massive undertaking to preserve one of the most important depictions of the religious transition from Egyptian deities to Christianity during Roman rule.

To access the island, we took a short boat ride along the Nile. Jo and I got some great pictures and thoroughly enjoyed the crazy life we were living. After Meena's brief introduction to the site, we had time to explore on our own. Seeing as October 7th had recently re-ignited armed conflict between Israel and Gaza, Jo and I were acutely attuned to the role different religions played in transforming societies and rewriting histories. The Philae Temple was a perfect example from 2,000 years before. Despite being built by the Egyptians to worship deities such as Hathor, Horus, and Isis, the outer chamber of the main temple had Christian emblems and Latin inscriptions carved into the stone. The Romans brought Christianity to the region after its decisive victory in 30 AD (with the death and resurrection of Jesus Christ); however, and interestingly to a hobbyist Christian historian like me, there was no clear record of when or how Christianity arrived in Egypt. Nonetheless, it did, and the Christians quickly took to defacing the faces of the pagan gods in temples which they converted for their use. As a Christian, I understood the sentiment given "thou shalt have no other gods before me," but as a history major, traveller, and former warfighter who served in the region, I couldn't help but feel ashamed of my brethren and disappointed in their utter disregard for what would plainly be historical artifacts someday. This was the behaviour groups like Islamic State engaged in in Iraq and Syria, and it was disappointing to be reminded that all religions were guilty at some point or another of such actions.

Fortunately, such damage was seemingly limited to the inside of the main temple, and the surrounding temples were left alone to withstand the winds and rains of time. It appeared to Jo and me that one of the temples was still used for worship, as we observed a guard instructing people to take their hats off upon entering.

As we waited for the rest of the group to finish taking their Instagram photos (a common theme during our tour through Egypt), we were privileged to observe something neither of us had ever seen in person: the call to prayer. Sure, we heard it many times over the past several weeks and during our service in the Middle East, but those were always over loud speakers from muezzins inside mosques. Here, at the Philae Temple, a man stood at the riverside, cupped his hands to his mouth, and directed the call to prayer down the river to those who lived within earshot. Jo and I felt honoured to witness this in person, and this was the exact sort of experience we sought during our gallivanting across the world. We stood and observed, silently, without taking photos or videos. To some, this was a something they would want to document and take home, a foreign piece of culture to show off to their friends from their Egyptian vacation. To us, this was an important practice of a major religion that deserved our respect.

Back at the hotel, Jo and I took it easy. We had a wonderful dinner of chicken fatteh at the hotel restaurant, enjoyed the cool breeze on the terrace, and turned in for the night. The rest of our group went out for the optional Nubian dinner. We didn't go, primarily because it cost extra, and we knew they would be out late. We also didn't go on the optional excursion to Abu Simbel for the same reason (and the 02h00 wake-up call). We had discussed it beforehand and agreed we could always come back to experience those things. For now, we would enjoy our five-star week of luxury and relax.

Our last afternoon in Aswan was the advertised felucca ride on the Nile. The felucca was a type of sailboat used by merchants to move goods and people up and down the river, and it would be our home for the next day or so. Our group ate, slept, and swam the Nile using the felucca as our base. It was an easy, relaxing day in the cold waters of the Nile, and we fell asleep to the sound of the waves lapping against the hull.

Luxor and Hurghada

We awoke on the opposite side of the river from where we went to sleep. Our felucca had to be towed in the middle of the night because the wind was non-existent. Jo and I laughed at the others in the group as they complained about how badly certain people snored or how they could hear when people went to the bathroom in the middle of the night. Neither Jo nor I had noticed. After five months of hostel living, we were accustomed to donning our eye masks and plugging our ears to drown out the nightly comings and goings. We didn't consider ourselves professional-level travellers, but sometimes, we were reminded just how far we had come.

Our first stop on the road to Luxor was Kom Ombo, a unique temple in Egypt as it was dedicated equally to two different deities. The temple was perfectly symmetrical, giving equal weight and deference to Sobek, the crocodile god of fertility and part of the trinity of world creators, on one side and Horus the Elder, the god of the sky and fertile lands of Lower Egypt, on the other. On each side were silos where priests could call to worshipers and provide sermons, and reliefs depicted the role each god and their respective trinity played in Egypt's history and mythology. Some reliefs crossed between the two sides and symbolised, as did so many across Egypt, the unification of Lower and Upper Egypt into one kingdom. Kom Ombo even went as far as to have a "list" of faceless individuals along one of its walls. These were the enemies of Egypt. Their names were left intact, but their faces were defaced to denigrate their place in Egyptian history. It was the 2,000-year-old version of the modern "murder board" used by militaries targeting terrorists. Some practices transcend time.

By now, Meena had a feel for how our group operated. Jo and I were along for the ride and respected that this was a group tour, not a personal one. The two Canadians generally did the same, but the group of six were always behind, never on time, and preferred taking selfies and social media photos to enjoying ancient history. At Kom Ombo, Meena changed how he managed the tour. Rather than providing a relaxed, slow exploration of the site, he delivered a fast-paced, straight-to-the-point oratory of what we were seeing. He kept us on the move and paying attention, telling the group of six they would have time for pictures in a moment. Jo and I keyed in on this and laughed at the change. We knew why he made the mental switch. We joked with him after we had gone around exploring, and he told us, "You have to know when to be a tour guide and when to be a tour manager." That was a wise piece of advice, and we told him we appreciated his switch for the sake of the group. Of course, he was still willing to give the relaxed version of the tour to those interested (i.e., Jo and me).

One thing that impressed us about Meena was his thorough knowledge of Egypt's general history. To be an Egyptologist guide in Egypt, he underwent a two-year training programme that included mock tours and intensive study to accurately convey Egyptian mythology, archaeology, and history in a manner that would be well-received by vacationers while maintaining the logistics of the tour. In this, he performed excellently, but he also knew parts of Egypt's history that we didn't expect. When Jo and I saw something of random interest, we could ask him, and he always knew the answer. For example, we noticed at Kom Ombo that the temple wasn't naturally eroded; the walls and roof were cut cleanly across the bricks. Meena, naturally, knew why: in the early 1900s, the local government needed to build a sugar mill, and they didn't see a need for these ancient mythological temples anymore, so they cut off the pieces they needed and built the mill. It wasn't until later that the government decided to preserve these sites and took limited steps to restore some of what was cut away.

We spent the rest of the day and evening at the Karnack and Luxor temple complexes. While two separate temples dedicated to different deities and rulers of Egypt, they were connected by the Avenue of Sphinxes, an almost three-kilometre-long walkway lined with sphinxes, chapels, and statues of kings that was used for processions, coronations, and other special celebrations. Unfortunately, walking the entire avenue between the two was impossible, as security guards were posted to prevent such access. We figured this was for two reasons: to maintain the integrity of ongoing archaeological studies and, more importantly, ensure tourists paid the entry fees at both temples.

The Luxor Temple had an active mosque on site, the Abu Haggag Mosque, which was established in 640, just thirty years after the establishment of Islam in Saudi Arabia. However, that was not the whole story, something we didn't learn until researching for the blog. The Abu Haggag Mosque was a converted Christian church established by the Romans in the 300s. As such, this mosque was one of the world's oldest sites of continuous religious worship, with 3,400 years of different religions passing through its door.

The Luxor Temple was also the site of one of the world's oldest conspiracy theories, one which many religions held in some form or another. One of the reliefs depicted a fertile man and the making of a child. Some of the engravings leading from the man's reproductive organs to the child below appeared to be sperm cells. Indeed, they had a similar shape, but the ancient Egyptians had no way of knowing what sperm cells looked like, given the scientific tools of their time. Conspiracy theorists and religious zealots claimed that such depictions were proof of their religion's superior knowledge, that such knowledge was passed on to ancient peoples via aliens or their respective deities, or even that there was a gap in the scientific record and ancient societies were far more advanced than our own. The truth, however, was much simpler. These were not depictions of sperm cells but a symbolic portrayal of the man watering the woman's seed to make it grow and cause her to bear a child. I would later read a similar religious proclamation in a pamphlet about Islam in Istanbul.

Our final day of the historical part of our tour was spent between the Temple of Hatshepsut and the Valley of the Kings. We spent the entire day exploring tombs. To recall it sounds macabre, but it was an interesting, fun-filled day of exploring the funerary rites of the ancient Egyptians.

The Hatshepsut temple was dedicated to Hatshepsut, the Great Royal Wife to Thutmose II and, eventually, the Egyptian pharaoh. Her temple contained chapels to three gods: Anubis, Hathor, and Amun. Although constantly exposed to the sun, the chapels still had vibrantly-coloured reliefs depicting landscapes and animals, which were important to the ancient Egyptians. Unfortunately for us, the main part of the temple and Hatshepsut's actual tomb were closed for archaeological exploration. While some "guides" hovered outside the tomb to "allow" you inside to see the intensely coloured scenes unaffected by the sun's rays, we opted not to pay for their services. We weren't entirely sure their presence or activities were legal, and we didn't want to be like the guy who carved his name into the Colosseum in Rome and go somewhere we weren't supposed to be.

The Hatshepsut temple was just over a ridge from the Valley of the Kings, a large valley with, at the time, sixty-three known tombs. There were tombs on both sides of the ridge, not just in the Valley, and the excavations were continued by a Polish-Egyptian partnership to excavate, study, and preserve their finds. Even a year after our visit to the Hatshepsut temple, more tombs were discovered in the surrounding hillsides.

Unfortunately, but for good reason, it was not possible to visit all of the tombs at the Valley of the Kings. The entry ticket only included three tombs, so we had to be judicious about which ones we wanted to see. We took Meena's suggestion and visited the most popular three, which did not include King Tut's tomb. Because of its popularity, we would have had to pay an additional fee to visit his tomb, and some of our group did. Meena recommended against it, as nearly all the artifacts and significant reliefs had been relocated to a museum in Cairo.

Because the tombs at the Valley of the Kings were mostly protected from sunlight (by nature of being underground), the reliefs and paintings inside were remarkably well-preserved. There was some natural erosion and fading, both of which largely stemmed from excavations, but they were still clear for all to see; however, tour guides were not allowed inside the tombs, so we couldn't ask questions about what story the walls were telling. That did not mean, however, that Meena didn't know, and he readily answered all our questions about pictures we showed him. As a part of his government training, he had to give guided tours of all sixty-three tombs, including the ones that weren't open to the public, to demonstrate his knowledge and proficiency in Egyptology. The more we learned about his tour guide training, the more it sounded like an accelerated PhD programme. If only we spoke Arabic, because it sounded like it would be an intense, rewarding programme to undertake.

Three tombs didn't take long to get through, so we lounged at the visitor centre's coffee shop and waited for the rest of the group to finish perusing the site. Several of them paid for extra tombs, so we had plenty of time. Meena was glad to have the downtime away from us all.

Before too long, we headed to Hurghada, a resort town on the Red Sea just before it split into the Gulf of Suez and the Gulf of Aqaba. We spent two nights in Hurghada at an all-inclusive hotel. Timeless Tours sure knew their clientele to have built this into the itinerary. While a fun and relaxing stay filled with free food, free alcohol, pools, volleyball, and the sea breeze, it was really just downtime before we headed back to Cairo. Some of our group decided to party in town; Jo and I opted to join Meena at a local "Irish" pub for a quiet meal (but, unfortunately, no Guinness, stew, or bangers and mash) and peaceful time on the beach. We didn't discuss it then, but the reality that we would be splitting up soon was sinking in. We only had a couple more days before we broke out on our own. We weren't regretting our decision (and we never have since), but it was about to be a significant adjustment for us both after being together non-stop for more than five months.

Back in Cairo, we explored the Egyptian Museum. It was the oldest archaeological museum in the Middle East, but that didn't mean it looked it. It was beautifully organised and well-kept, telling the story of Ancient Egypt through logically organised exhibitions. Meena gave us the tour manager walkthrough before turning us loose to our own devices. Of course, everyone wanted to see the artifacts from King Tut's tomb, housed in a special exhibit behind a guarded door. The guard wasn't there to check tickets but to remind you not to take photos or videos, which confused us. Virtually none of the artifacts in the museum were encased, and many times, tourists took pictures of their kids sitting on them, but in arguably the most important and distinct exhibit, where everything was encased behind glass and protected by minders, photos were prohibited. And that prohibition was enforced. Every few seconds, the cry of "No photos!" came as an unsuspecting tourist did what every tourist wanted to do when visiting the famous King Tut. Even so, it was a fantastic display, and it was hard to believe the golden relics in front of us were over 3,000 years old.

Another defining feature of the Egyptian Museum was the number of mummies. Some were on prominent display because of who they belonged to and their condition, while others were enclosed in large, glass cases more-or-less stacked on top of each other in atriums. Jo and I were surprised they were allowed to be in rooms exposed to sunlight, given their age and predisposition to decay, but the cases were probably climate-controlled to a degree we couldn't fathom. At the same time, that same thought occurred to us about other artifacts in the museum. Given that many were thousands of years old, we assumed they would be susceptible to the destructive nature of the sun's ultraviolet rays, but that didn't appear to be a concern. Of course, we figured some of the displays allowed people to touch them, so maybe we were overestimating the museum environment's impact on them.

After an hour's stop at the el-Khalili market, which was a typical souk/bazaar of which Jo and I had seen many by this point in MENA, we were back at our original hotel, to full-service breakfasts, and preparing to return to the budget travel life. The following day, the various vans and busses departed for the airport, taking Western vacationers back home and welcoming in the next batch. In Meena's words, "It's

'Goodbye! I'm glad you enjoyed your tour!' and then 'Welcome to Egypt!'" Long, hard work during the peak season, but at least he enjoyed it and it helped his family to have a good life back in Aswan.

As for Jo and me, we packed up around noon and headed off to our next hostel for our last night as a traveling duo.

Our Last Night

It was hard to believe we had travelled five and a half months together and were now going our separate ways. Part of us reconsidered splitting up, but we knew that we were starting to get on each other's nerves and our travel priorities had begun to diverge in a major way. As we later described it, we literally wanted to go in different directions. She was bound for Australia, and I was destined for more time in the Middle East, including another week in Egypt.

So, we made the most of our last night. Jo did laundry, which was our custom before boarding a flight, we hung out at the hostel, met some incredible people, and went out for dinner. Leading the way to dinner were Tahli and her mom, Peta, from Queensland, Australia. They were traveling the region from archaeological site to archaeological site on a budget. Tahli had been in Turkey on a dig as an archaeology student, so they decided to make an adventure of it once she was finished. Tahli was quite the character in her overalls, bucket hat, and characteristic lack of shoes (not that she didn't have any; she just preferred not to wear them). She and I became friends in the coming weeks and months, bonding over archaeology, history, and travel stories.

As we all sat around wondering where to go for dinner, all of our phones stopped working. Some of us had local SIM cards, I had an eSIM, and some were using their SIM cards from back home, but none of them worked, despite the LTE service indicator showing on all of our phones. Not even the Wi-Fi at the hostel was working. We thought this was weird, but Jo and I were no strangers to the internet being shut down at the whim of a government, so we just rolled with it. We later learned there was a presidential election coming up, and the internet outages were related to police operations targeted at ensuring its security. Tahli managed to get enough service to find a restaurant about a ten-minute walk away, so we set off as one giant gaggle of tourists.

Tahli led the way, and I can best describe her navigation as a police dog on the scent of a criminal. She was locked into her location on her phone, and we were just along for the ride, which included crossing busy Cairo streets at night. Crossing the street in Cairo was like playing the old game *Frogger*, just with the added element of the children's game *Chicken*. You made a calculated step into traffic and took it one step at a time. Sometimes, those steps were slower and sometimes backward, but it was still one step at a time. As long as you kept your eye on traffic, an unspoken understanding between drivers and pedestrians allowed this real-life game of *Frogger* to be played out generally without injuries. Unless, of course, your map and navigator charged headlong into traffic without you, at which point you just made it work.

The food at the restaurant was good, mostly a standard combination of dishes based on chicken and koshary, but what drew our attention the most was a guy in the group named Alexander (who I would become friends with as well) who ordered pigeon for the experience. There was certainly no shortage of pigeons in Cairo, but we weren't eating them off the street (although it wouldn't have surprised anyone). Instead, they came from breeders who sold them in the market. It was funny to think that New York City and London would do many legal and probably some illegal things to get rid of their pigeons, but they were bred for food in Egypt. Unfortunately, they weren't good eating. There wasn't a lot of meat on an individual pigeon, and their fried legs looked like they skipped leg day their entire lives. Alexander let us all try a bit of it. It wasn't bad, but it wasn't exactly something I would seek out in the future, either.

After dinner, we made our way back to the hostel. Jo's laundry wouldn't be ready until the morning, so we all hung out in the common room until it was time to turn in.

We said our goodbyes the next morning as Jo headed to the Cairo airport. Sort of. The taxi she was taking to the airport broke down right outside the hostel, so she had to come back inside as she waited for another one to take its place. C'est l'Afrique, as they say. I could see on her face that she was pretty nervous about heading off on her own. She had never seriously travelled solo before, and she was jumping in with both feet, with her first serious experience being flying out of Cairo International Airport to Aqaba, Jordan, while the conflict in Gaza raged next door between Hamas and Israel. She made it just fine, but I could sense the stress coming through her texts. I had to give credit where credit was due: she ripped the Band-Aid right off when it came to solo traveling in the Middle East. Cairo International Airport was not for the faint of heart! In a week, she would be in Australia, having had her fill of MENA, lounging on beautiful beaches, diving the reefs, and making new friends up and down the east coast.

I was headed for Alexandria, the heart of Greek and Roman Egypt. Not long after she left for the airport, I donned my bags and walked to the bus station.

I was back to being a solo traveller in the land where I had longed to return for many years.

Alexandria

Alexandria was about two hours northwest of Cairo by bus. From what I read online, the busses were hit or miss. Some of them were in great shape with bathrooms and air conditioning while others were beat up pieces of junk with non-functioning toilets that lacked signage to that effect and consequently smelled terrible. In any case, all of the reviews said to be sure to leave the baggage handler a tip lest he "accidentally" damage your bag. I offered him 10 EGP after he asked for a tip, but he looked at me and said (in probably the only English he knew), "Only ten?" I laughed and said, "Ok, twenty!" which made him happy. Did he just hustle me out of double what I was offering? Yes, but it was a difference between 0.33 USD and 0.66 USD, so it wasn't exactly a hill worth dying on, especially if it kept my bag intact. I repeated the same song and dance at the bus station in Alexandria, although

I noticed that Egyptians weren't hassled for tips. Welcome to being a "rich" Westerner.

I stayed at the only hostel in Alexandria, which was on the main road along the bay, not far from the new Library of Alexandria. I didn't know any better, so I grabbed a local taxi to get me there. It cost 20 USD, which wasn't a bad price for the distance back home, but it was a substantial sum for this part of the world. Something I started to pay acute attention to was overpaying for things simply because I could afford it. This would ultimately cause inflation and drive up the price of goods and services for the locals. Indeed, during my visit, the Egyptian government was cracking down on black market exchanges to combat this very issue.

As if by fate, one by one, the entire group from the hostel in Cairo rolled in that night. We had all said our goodbyes that morning but hadn't discussed our travel plans. Apparently, we all had the same plan. Tahli and Peta only stayed the night, Alexander was there for a couple of days, and all the rest left the next day (one of them had been unexpectedly called into the office for work in Bangladesh!). We all went out for koshary and enjoyed one more night of familiar company before again going our separate ways. Even though none of us spoke Arabic, it was easy enough to order food with the magic of Google Translate.

Alexander and I hit up the Library of Alexandria on my first day there. He wanted a picture of Alexander reading a book about Alexander the Great in the Library of Alexandria in Alexandria. Of course, we had to pay the tourist price of 100 EGP compared to the Egyptian price of 10 EGP, but that was something we were used to by now, although there was a very angry Brit railing against the extortion of tourists outside the entrance, not that such proclamations would do him any good. In no time, Alexander found his book, got his picture, and busied himself reading at one of the tables. I elected to visit the several museums the library contained, which were focused on the Greek and Roman influence over Alexandria and Egypt writ-large. I may have learned somewhere along the line that the Greeks and Romans conquered Egypt, but it wasn't something that stuck with me, and it never once occurred to me that Alexander himself was Greek. The museums were really more displays of artifacts than places of learning. While the artifact tags were in English, there weren't explanations as to why these artifacts were important, which was a letdown, but at least I got a baseline understanding for my next couple of days exploring Alexandria.

After a short siesta (that greatest of Spanish traditions), I made my way to the Qaitbay Citadel, a fortress which once defended the harbour from seaborne invaders. It was built in the 1400s, long after the fall of the Greek and Roman empires that conquered Egypt, by the Sultan Qaitbay of the Mamluk Sultanate after the overthrow of the Abbasid Caliphate (known in some circles as the Third Caliphate of Islam) in Egypt. The citadel primarily defended against the threat from the Ottoman Empire, which ultimately overtook the Mulmak Sultanate in the early 1500s. The Ottoman takeover notwithstanding, the citadel continued to serve as an essential military garrison, defending the bay until the French expedition into Egypt during Napoleon's war against the Ottomans.

The citadel building was small, just large enough for a small garrison stocked mostly with coastal artillery. While the grounds were more extensive than the building might suggest, and the fortress walls were, in many places, layered into two defensive layers, it clearly wouldn't withstand a substantive assault, even by the standards of the time. At best, in my estimation, it could provide just long enough of a delay for a main force to arrive. None of that, however, took away from its beauty, and seeing it under the setting sun was a beautiful sight. It reminded me of the Rabat in Sousse and how North African outposts like these were the first, and sometimes final, line of defence against European invaders.

At Tahli's recommendation, I spent the following day exploring ruins across Alexandria, which meant I spent a lot of time walking. By now, I had learned to be smart with my walking. Start far and work your way back to the hostel (so long as opening hours allowed it). The Catacombs of Kom el Shoqafa were my first stop, forty-five minutes from the hostel. I could have gotten a taxi, but I enjoyed wandering the streets in MENA. Maybe it was because it made me feel a bit like Indiana Jones, but more realistically, it was because it connected me to my first experience in the Sahara several years before.

The catacombs could best be described as "meh." The site wasn't well organised, and artifacts from excavating the catacombs below littered the site's surface. They looked like they had been removed, placed, and left where they lay. It was a disappointing sight, which Tahli warned me about in advance. The catacombs were not much better in terms of wow factor. They were an underground complex of tombs, which were mostly cleared out. To be sure, the archaeological importance of these tombs and their contents could not be overstated, but to witness them as a tourist with most of the contents removed and shipped off for study was underwhelming. By now, the catacombs were just an empty underground mausoleum.

The Serapeum of Alexandria and co-located Pompey's Pillar were equally underwhelming. They were probably impressive structures in their time, and the Serapeum (a temple) even held a portion of the original Library of Alexandria's collection. In modern times, the grounds were ruins. There were some architectural elements left, but the vast majority of the historical aspects had long since passed. Interestingly, though, Pompey's Pillar, which was originally dedicated to the Roman emperor Diocletian, was the only ancient monument still standing in Alexandria. While others may still exist, they had been moved for study or exhibition.

Undeterred by my lacklustre experience thus far, I decided to heed the advice of both Meena and Tahli and visit the Roman theatre. It was a fair walk away, situated next to a market, the train station, and a large roundabout. I was ravenously hungry by lunch, given I had walked for several hours non-stop at this point, and finding somewhere to eat proved to be more difficult than I envisioned as I was still not quite used to finding restaurants and food stands in the land of little signage. I ultimately settled on fried chicken at the food court just outside the theatre complex. Fried chicken in the Middle East might seem like a gamble for some, but I figured it was easy and hard to mess up, and boy was I right! I learned during my deployment to Iraq that fast food places tended not to keep a lot of pre-made stock on hand like they did back home, both as a function of less throughput and not having the facilities to keep food warm, cold, and healthy. This fried chicken was no exception. It took some time to make, as they prepared it from scratch, but it was worth it. It was some of the best fried chicken I had ever eaten. Hot, fresh, crispy, seasoned, and plenty of it. I might regret the decision at the hostel later in the night, but at least in the moment, I left a wholly satisfied customer who would absolutely return.

As I moved from lunch to the theatre complex, I was concerned what I would find there. The ruins in Carthage were in total disrepair, and the ruins so far in Alexandria were not much better, so I braced myself for disappointment. Fortunately, that was not the case, and I found the Roman theatre and surrounding forum to be well-preserved, all things considered, and more substantial than I anticipated. The theatre was smaller than I expected given that two people had told me to visit, but that was the case of most ancient theatres. Not everything was the Colosseum in Rome, after all. What the theatre lacked in size, the forum made up for in variety and, thankfully, English information boards. Down the walkway from the theatre were classrooms believed to have been used for training in the arts. By today's classroom standards, they were small and cramped, but there was probably something to that in terms of intimacy and community in education that we lacked today. Of course, there were plots for affluent homes and a large Roman bath building, both of which were closed for excavation and study, but that didn't diminish the overall experience given that the Habitation Quarter was open for visitors. These homes and rooms were much smaller, a testament to both the simplicity of an earlier time and getting by with what you had and could afford. It occurred to me that the current generations could probably not survive in such "cramped" quarters, although soldiers and ranch hands could make due with little fuss.

The Roman Villa of the Birds on the back side of the theatre was, I thought, a misnomer. I was anticipating, well, birds, which, technically, I got. Inside this large villa, which obviously belonged to someone of substantial means, were mosaics containing depictions of birds. And by mosaics, I mean large, floor-sized tiles of birds, religious symbols, and decorative designs. According to the information board, the villa was destroyed in a fire, but the excavations revealed that the villa's owners had redecorated and re-tiled several times over. I guess the Romans did the same thing as our grandparents and put the new floor on top of the old one when it was time to change the scenery.

After perusing the outdoor museum of artifacts, I returned to the hostel for a new beginning the next day. I planned to visit several museums, and after walking so much to these different sites, I knew I needed to take a break and let my feet air out. Plus, I needed to do some laundry before heading back to Cairo. I had pushed my shirts, underpants, and especially socks to their limit over the last two weeks, and I didn't plan on doing laundry in full until my last day in Egypt. Naturally, my hostel didn't have laundry facilities, so I had to wash my socks and shirts in the shower and hang them to dry. I could have paid to clean them overnight, but I was already going to pay to do laundry in Cairo, so I didn't see the point.

My museum day turned out to be mostly a bust. While the Alexandria National Museum, an archaeology museum dedicated to the history of Alexandria, was neat and had English explanations, it was small and took no time to get through. It was also hard to find, and I walked around the block a few times trying to find the entrance. The Greco-Roman Museum, which was fairly substantial, probably would have been a great visit, but I managed to go on the day that every elementary school class in the city was there. The queue extended far down the street, and the noise of chattering school children echoed against the brick walls in an annoying roar. I opted not to visit the museum. Between the crowd and the children, I was sure I wouldn't have the enjoyable experience I was desired, so I opted to seek out a coffee shop to relax, read, and edit some Instagram posts. It might have been a wasted day in Alexandria, but by now I had come to the determination that this part of the world was highly and easily accessible to Americans, so if it meant that much to me, I could always return. Besides, rest days were necessary, and as I was to soon head deeper into the Middle East, I could use one so I didn't burn myself out.

So, that was it for Alexandria. I learned my lesson to get back to the bus station and booked an Uber. It cost me about 3 USD, including tip, for the ride, which was substantially less than the taxi cost on the way in, and the tip for the baggage handler was another 0.66 USD on both ends of the ride. I watched and rolled my eyes as an Austrian couple tried to argue the point of tips with the baggage handlers. I guess the fact that they didn't hassle the locals and were extorting the Westerners didn't sit well with them, either.

Cairo

Fortunately, I had a nice bus with a working toilet, and I arrived back at the same hostel in Cairo shortly before dinner. Rather than go and blow after a day of traveling, I took the time to get my next series of flights and visas sorted. I was headed to Jordan, Iraq, and Turkey next, and they all required visas in advance. Flights were another sticking point, and it took a while to figure out the best way to handle the next leg of the trip. Flights weren't cheap after October 7th, and the only airlines operating anywhere near Gaza were those based in the Middle East. Ryanair, EasyJet, WizzAir, and others had all cancelled their flights, which meant flying on Royal Jordanian and Turkish Airlines. These were excellent airlines, but they were expensive for short-haul flights. I ultimately gave in, booked the cheapest one I could find, and put all that to rest for the time being.

Egypt's presidential election was nearing, and security was noticeably tightening. Photography and recording in Tahrir Square wasn't prohibited, but the police would confiscate your camera "for security." Temporary barriers appeared outside government buildings and vulnerable targets, such as synagogues, and roving police patrols were abundant. To the untrained eye, it seemed like they were preparing for massive unrest, but President el-Sisi was decently popular, and conversations with locals indicated that these were standard precautions for any election season. With that knowledge in mind and a nearby Costa Coffee in hand, I ventured into the bustling, crazy city known as Cairo.

I wasn't sure what I wanted to see in Cairo; I just knew I wanted to see the city, which wasn't a winning travel strategy. I opted first to visit the Abdeen Palace Museum, a military arms museum in, as the name suggested, the Abdeen Palace. I wasn't sure what to expect, especially considering part of the palace was still used as a military training garrison, but I was pleasantly surprised. The museum contained one of the most comprehensive collections of military arms through the ages I had ever seen. It was arranged in chronological order, starting with crude swords and ending with sophisticated automatic weapons. At the time, I described it as the

Musée de l'Armée in Paris on steroids. I had a few friends in mind as I browsed the collection, and I sent pictures of some especially good pieces to those who were in to such things (a gold-plated Walther PPK was of special interest for a James Bond lover like me!). Any concern I had about this museum taking little time out of my day quickly dissipated.

The palace grounds were also beautiful and well-manicured, and you would never have known you were in the middle of a massive Middle Eastern city. Some friends were doing a photo shoot on the grounds, and it occurred to me that, for the price, this was an excellent location for making photo memories (as long as you steered clear of the active military sections). If I had a book with me, I could have sat in the courtyard and read for hours in this small slice of serenity in crazy Cairo.

I wasn't exactly on the beaten path by this point, so after a truly mediocre pizza from a streetside vendor (apparently a margarita pizza in Egypt came with peppers and olives...), I headed to the Museum of Islamic Art. This was not an art museum in the traditional sense that you would find in Europe. Instead, it was an art museum which showcased the workmanship of sculptors, carpenters, and the like when it came to building mosques and Islamic schools. In Islam, there were no pictorial depictions of events in the Quran to adorn mosques like were found in Catholic churches as such depictions were expressly forbidden and blasphemous. Instead, Islamic artisans used geometric shapes and calligraphy to decorate their creations and bring beauty to their religious sites. Some of these creations were paintings of which Euclid would be proud, while others were intricately designed pulpits used by imams to give their sermons, ablution fountains, sun dials, and even doors and windows. For Islamic artists, the natural world was their canvas and religion their muse.

Carpets, too, had long served as a canvass for Islamic artists, and the museum had a special exhibit dedicated solely to carpetmaking. While I was not one to fully understand the use of decorative carpets as tapestries or floor art, I could appreciate the painstaking skill it took to weave decorative carpets by hand. Back in the West, these sorts of things had been made by machines since the technology to do so came about, and that was indeed the case to an extent in Egypt, but in much of the region, carpets were still made by hand (something Jo and I had witnessed in Morocco).

That was it for my time in Cairo. I had laundry to do and bags to pack for a flight the next day. I intentionally didn't leave a lot of time for Cairo on the back end of this jaunt through Egypt. Jo and I had already seen the major sights, and I was on a timeline staring down the barrel of the new year and still half of the world to go. Over the last several weeks, I had been in contact with a dive shop in Mexico about training and working as a divemaster. That had recently fallen into place, so I now had a timeline to concern myself with as I needed to be in Mexico on May 1st. My free-spirited, leisurely vagabonding around the world suddenly had backstop.

But just because I didn't have another full day in Cairo didn't mean I couldn't enjoy one final night. I met an Irish guy from Dublin named Gav, and we became fast friends. We talked about Ireland, travels, hobbies, you name it, as we hit it off straight away. We even took a chance on a bar to grab a drink. Easier said than done in Egypt. The bars were all behind closed doors, so you had to know where to look, and we had to knock on the doors to try to gain entry. We were utterly unsuccessful.

Every door that opened revealed a bar filled to capacity with locals and tourists alike, and we were refused entry at every attempt. We eventually gave up on the idea and headed to a nearby liquor store (which was out in the open on the street, an odd juxtaposition against the bars) and bought a couple of beers to enjoy at the hostel. Gav was on a short vacation from work, but he had taken long stints to bicycle around Europe here and there. He was well-travelled and experienced in life, and we bonded over stories of how unique hobbies had changed our lives and travelling long-term shaped our views. Gav was planning a long charity trip the following year where he would ride his bicycle from Ireland to Vietnam, and he was working through the sponsorships, funding, and planning to make the trip happen. This was all self-started; no charity had approached him for it. He had seen an opportunity to use his passion and skill to help a good cause and seized upon it. Talk about a first-class guy!

After a night of beers with a new friend, it was time to leave the pyramids behind and make for the airport. Another country and a new adventure awaited. But not before an Egyptian police officer confiscated the pen light Jo had given me before getting on the plane. At least it wasn't my GoPro.

Reflecting on Egypt

Breaking out on her own. Jo and I went our separate ways after Egypt. She and I remained close friends and have travelled together since our first long-term travel experience. We both said the same thing: we literally wanted to go different directions by the time we got to Egypt.

Of course, that meant Jo had to get used to planning her travel details, which I had been handling for the two of us. This wasn't out of some misogynistic view or "airport dad" mentality; it was simply a matter of convenience. I had travelled more extensively and knew the ins and outs of how to make things happen quickly. In hindsight, we both said that we should have taken turns so that she could have the practice before the inevitable split. Instead, she took a crash course in hotels across Egypt as I watched her anxiety and stress skyrocket from the adjacent bed.

She went to Jordan for a week to finish her dive certification in the Red Sea and see Petra, but from there, things got tricky. Her path to Australia took her on a flight from Amman to Abu Dhabi, a self-transfer to Dubai, a flight from Dubai to China, and a flight from China to Australia. It took her around fifty-one hours to make the trip over the course of three days, but she made it. She was slightly delirious but none the worse for wear. While I toured around the historic sites in the Middle East, she soaked up the Pacific sun.

Chilled out with each other. In Tunis, we had decided to go our separate ways. All of a sudden, all of our frustrations and irritations with each other melted away. In Egypt, we got along swimmingly. We knew we only had so much time left as travel companions and wanted to enjoy it. Of course, being in luxury hotels (to us, anyways) helped. Ultimately, Egypt would become one of the most talked-about memories from our time together. Not even when Jo got drunk and became an amateur fire jumper (burning her leg in the process) or when we got wholly and utterly lost in the el-Khalili market did we get irritated with each other. In our subsequent adventures together, we would have the same experience. Knowing that we were only together for a short time and wanting to make the most of it helped assuage any irritations we may have developed.

After all, how many married couples spent every waking and sleeping moment attached at the hip? Given that we weren't even a couple, we did pretty well making it as long as we did.

Fast friends. Egypt was the country where I made the most friends in one place. I would visit Tahli and Peta in Australia for a few days, and Tahli and I would have deep, respectful discussions about history and politics before sitting down to watch *Australian Survivor*. Gav and I talked more about Guinness than any other topic in subsequent months, and we would have a chance meeting in Spain during his charity run from Ireland to Vietnam. Alexander had intended to go to Iraq with me, but some legitimate family concerns about the relationship between Iraq and Russia kept him from tagging along. Even so, he introduced me to the beauty of the mosques in Turkey. "Mosques are my happy place," he would say.

These weren't the only friends I made during The Great Gallivanting, but they were excellent examples of how shared experiences, even short ones, could bring us together with bonds that transcended time and distance. Even after months of not talking to each other, an Instagram reel followed by "hey, man, this made me think of you!" inevitably led to long conversations about how things were going. We may have come from different walks of life, but we were all brought together by our deep passion for exploring the world. It didn't get much better than that.

Chapter Fourteen

Jordan: Highs and Lows

Jordan was the breaking point for Jo and me back in Tunisia. I wanted to visit Petra, and I wasn't going to be so close not to go. Ultimately, we both travelled through Jordan separately, her a week ahead of me. Jordan was a country with which I wasn't familiar. I knew little about the country's culture or history. All I knew was there was supposedly great diving in Aqaba, magnificent sights at Petra, and lots of cigarette smoking in Amman. I was looking forward to exploring an entire new country as a solo traveller. It was sure to be an interesting experience.

Aqaba

The flight into Aqaba was short, uneventful, and roundabout. I had a port-side view of our flight path as the pilot avoided flying over Israeli territory. This could only have been for two reasons; first, because the Israeli airport in Eilat, the town immediately adjacent to Aqaba, was, in aviation terms, right on top of the Aqaba airport, and the Taba International Airport in South Sinai, Egypt, wasn't much further away, so there had to be airspace deconfliction considerations. Second, and the more likely in my estimation, Jordan was at odds with Israel over the conflict in Gaza, and the authorities didn't want Israel having any control over flights into and out of Jordan's sovereign territory. I later learned there were also issues with satellite navigation in this tri-border-ish area, as Israel was manipulating satellite signals to support the ongoing war effort.

All of this notwithstanding, I arrived safe and on time to Aqaba, Jordan, just as Jo was boarding her flights for Australia in the United Arab Emirates. The ambience at the airport was eerie. Even though it wasn't a large airport, it was a ghost town. The border guards seemed more annoyed that they had to be there than anything else, and they didn't even ask for my visa when they stamped me in. The taxi rank out front was full. Full full. There weren't any tourists after the major European carriers suspended their flights in and out of Aqaba because they couldn't avoid flying over the conflict area. It was another one of those wide-reaching, indiscriminate consequences of war.

My hostel was in an undeveloped part of town, so undeveloped that the GPS couldn't find the address, nor could the taxi driver, even with help from local passersby. Despite my insistence, he refused to drop me on the side of the road to find it on my own. Instead, he drove the neighbourhood in circles until we found it. Naturally, he received a nice tip for his trouble.

The Al Amer hostel was a converted house. This wasn't the first time I had stayed in such a place, and it was spacious for being the only person there. The owner had two hostels. Jo stayed with him at the other location closer to the Gulf of Aqaba. Further inland, mine was run by his son, a young man in his early twenties taking online college classes in his spare time. He was an excellent host. When I told him I was in Aqaba for a dive trip, he set me up with Aqaba Shark Dive Centre, a newer dive shop with whom he had a working relationship. He negotiated a reasonable dive rate for me that included pickup at the hostel every day. He didn't have to do that, but I was grateful he did, if only for the price alone.

Price was a constant concern in Jordan. Outside of Amman, Jordanian businesses weren't out to rip off tourists. Their prices were fair in terms of the Jordanian Dinar (JOD) on everything from dates to coffee to restaurants to taxis. The problem was that the Jordanian Dinar was substantially stronger than the American Dollar, at a rate of almost 2-to-1. A 7 JOD taxi ride was 12 USD, and my budget of 80 USD per day, including accommodations and transportation, felt more like 45 to 50 USD per day. That wasn't unobtainable by any means, but considering the cost per day for diving was 50 JOD, the budget was tight, and I did a lot of walking.

Aqaba was just as much of a ghost town as its airport. Shops were closed or at least had their lights off to save electricity, and I could count on one hand the number of tourists I saw during my week's stay. I intended to go out, explore, and enjoy the region during my first couple of days, but that simply wasn't an option. The tours had all but shut down for lack of business. It was better to bring in no money than to open with false hopes and lose money at the end of the day. The hostel owner told me they usually had daily trips to Wadi Rum with upwards of thirty people every trip, but keeping the trips going with such few travellers wasn't feasible. Jo managed to head out the week before simply by the quirk of fate that put her at the same time as others, but I was not so lucky. Oh, well. Such was the way of the world sometimes. I eventually parked myself at various coffee shops and cafés on the beach (the ones that were open) to catch up on some reading as I awaited my upcoming five days of diving.

When those days finally came, I was treated to a first-class dive experience by Aqaba Shark Diving Centre. Aqaba Shark was a newer dive shop operated by Rafat, a Palestinian divemaster, and Karyna, a woman of South American descent who had lived a colourful life in many different countries. They hadn't been open long, but I would never have guessed from their operation. It was small but efficient, and Rafat and Karyna really knew their stuff. Rafat was part fish and could do two consecutive hour-long, thirty-metre dives on a single tank of air. He was quiet in the car but became energetic and engaging when the dive gear came out. Karyna was lively and engaging all the time, and as we drove from the hostel to dive sites, she was eager to have conversations about our different lives, travel experiences, and diving. When I told them I was going to Mexico for the divemaster programme, they offered to help improve my dive skills in the gulf and walked me through what to expect as a divemaster in training. Even though I had a standing personal policy of diving with

PADI five-star dive centres or resorts, Rafat and Karyna provided me no less of a service than a five-star shop would have.

We agreed to do two dives per day over five days, with the option to do a third if it looked like the weather would become a problem. We started at Cedar Pride, a ship that had caught fire and beached in Aqaba. Rather than let it be an eyesore for tourists, the King of Jordan ordered it dragged into the gulf, sunk, and turned into an artificial reef and dive site. The fact that the King himself was an avid diver probably had something to do with the decision. While we were out there, Rafat took me to part of the wreck where there was an air pocket we could "surface" in for a photo. What kind of air was anyone's guess after so many years beneath the surface, so I figured I should keep my regulator in my mouth and breathe the good stuff. The first question Karyna asked when we surfaced was, "Did he take his regulator out in the air pocket?" I guess I passed that test.

Our second dive site was the collection of undersea cables that brought electricity and fibre-optic connectivity to Jordan from Egypt. I knew these existed, but I had no idea they were as big as they were. I figured they were insulated cables lying along the sea floor. No. They were large, metal-encased cables suspended mid-water metres apart from each other. At thirty metres below the surface, they created an excellent artificial reef for corals and fish attracted to the hum of electricity coursing through the cables (we couldn't hear it, but Rafat and Karyna assured me it was there).

As we packed up to leave for the day, another group of divers arrived at the beach. That's when I asked Karyna what this area was like in peak season. Like Meena, she solemnly commented, "This is peak season." Karyna said pickup in December was usually early, sometimes as early as 07h00, so they could secure a parking spot at the beach before the crowds arrived. The beach was usually full of dive gear, umbrellas, lawn chairs, and people from all over the world enjoying the Arabian sun in the depths of winter. Looking across the empty, pristine beach, complete with bored Jordanian naval officers and bathroom attendants, the consequences of the nearby conflict were impossible to ignore. As a traveller on a dive trip, it was fantastic, as we didn't have to share the sites and no other groups interfered with the marine environment. As a human, though, I couldn't help but feel a profound sorrow for the lives impacted. Aqaba's inhabitants surely had an opinion on Hamas, Israel, and the decades-old conflict (or centuries-old, depending on your perspective), but they didn't sign up for Hamas's unprovoked attack on October 7th or Israel's intense retaliation. Nonetheless, they suffered the consequences.

That's when the conversation turned to the conflict in Gaza. Rafat, being the quiet man he was, didn't talk much, but Karyna was interested in my perspective as an American and a traveller. "To us," she said, "Hamas are just a bunch of guys with guns hiding in the woods." Before giving my thoughts, I told her of my professional background, so my opinions were skewed in the way that those who combat terrorism tended to see the world, a stipulation she readily accepted. From there, the conversation continued not as a debate but as a respectful exchange of views on the conflict. We found common ground on some topics and agreed to disagree on others, but mostly, we talked about it in terms of how it was affecting the world. It was the type of conversation you could never have in the United States or Europe because everyone there was so committed to their ideals that they would think of their next point while the other person was making theirs. People where I was from talked, but no one listened; but in the van with two people from wildly different backgrounds than me, we talked, listened, and engaged in a manner that added serious value to our time together.

Over the next several days, we dove at eight more sites, leisurely making our way there, taking long surface intervals to drink tea and talk about the world, and generally staying thirty metres below the surface whenever we were in the water. From the King's favourite dive site (which everyone called "King Abdullah" for that reason) to the beautiful corals of the Japanese Garden to two underwater military museums, it was the most pristine, relaxing set of dives I had ever had. The water, too, was a deep blue, and the gulf dropped off quickly from the shore down to 1,800 metres at its deepest point. Like the crystal-clear water in Hammamet, Tunisia, you could see long distances in every direction. In future months, and especially as a divemaster, when asked where the best place I had ever dived at was, I would always caveat it with the fact that I was in Jordan in the aftermath of October 7th, so experiences may vary.

I learned an essential lesson about diving on my last dive in Aqaba, courtesy of Rafat. When I told him about an experience with a feeding shark in the Dominican Republic earlier that year, he had the idea to find the lone whale shark that lived in the Gulf of Aqaba. She somehow came to the Gulf, probably because of the hum of the undersea cables, and decided to stay despite the high salinity levels. Rafat figured she was probably near the power station but decided we would look for her out in the gulf. After all, there were no ships to be concerned about, courtesy of the Houthis in Yemen firing rockets at commercial shipping coming into the Red Sea via the Gulf of Aden. We left Karyna on the shore, and Rafat took me straight into the gulf. We quickly arrived at twenty-seven metres beneath the surface and maintained that depth while searching for the whale shark. About thirty minutes into the dive, I had a sudden realisation: *all* I could see in any direction was the deep blue sea. No bottom, no shore, not even the surface (outside of the direction of my bubbles). It was just Rafat and me out in the gulf, surrounded by a seemingly infinite expanse of water from which something seeking to make a meal out of me would see me long before I saw it. At the same time, I rolled onto my back to take in the serenity of being surrounded by nothing but water. Apparently, I also started breathing heavier, a sign of panic beginning to set in. I didn't notice, but Rafat told me he saw it as soon as I looked around and had the realisation. He slowly took us to the surface as we continued our search. By the time we surfaced, we were dead centre in what was usually a major shipping lane. Without a ship in sight, we swam fifteen minutes on our backs back to the shore, with Rafat talking to me about what he saw from me and why he ended the dive. It was an important lesson to remember when training as a divemaster.

With my dive trip drawing to a close, I was eternally grateful to Rafat and Karyna for taking me on during the economic downturn. Even though diving wasn't what immediately came to mind when thinking about Jordan, it was a great start to my trek up into the deeper Middle East. After another day of relaxing in town, I was ready to board the bus for my next stop, Petra.

Petra

To get to Petra, I could take a bus, colectivo (shared taxi), or taxi. I opted for a bus service out of the main bus station in Aqaba, although there were ample options out of a parking lot near my hostel where drivers shouted, "Wadi Rum! Petra!" to passersby. It was a two-hour drive straight up the highway with about thirty minutes at a rest stop for coffee, restrooms, and shopping at the gift shop. I opted for the panoramic views of the wadi (a deep ravine created by centuries of flowing water) below at what the rest stop called "The Second Best View in the World." I could only assume the best view in the world was Petra itself.

The road into Wadi Musa, the town outside the Petra archaeological site, was downhill, its winding roads cutting back on themselves as they led to the bus station at the bottom of the hill. The only thing I knew about Petra was that it featured prominently in *Indiana Jones and the Last Crusade*. I had no clue it was located at the bottom of one of the wadis or that a substantial town was carved into the steep hills on its outskirts. I didn't know it, but we drove by my hostel on the way to the bus station. I was quickly re-introduced to the first law of travel: what goes down must come up. I had a twenty-minute walk up a ninety-four-metre hill to get to my hostel from the bus station. Laden with all of my travel possessions, I balked at the notion and paid the 5 JOD for a few minutes' taxi ride. I would walk up and down the hill a lot over the next three days; there was no need to kill myself with a ruck march on day one.

The Nomads Hotel was a combination hotel and hostel. It boasted nice facilities, an upstairs bar with a terrace overlooking the wadi that led to Petra, and a common area which played *Indiana Jones and the Last Crusade* like clockwork every night. As an *Indiana Jones* fan, I couldn't complain. The staff said they were usually booked solid during this time, but the conflict in Gaza meant they were mostly empty. Consequently, they couldn't offer the breakfast or dinner that was usually part of the stay because they couldn't afford to pay the chef or buy the ingredients with tourism being so low and unpredictable. Completely understandable, especially because I was only paying a few Jordanian Dinar per night.

My friend Gav from Cairo had given me some tips for visiting Petra. He told me to get there as soon as they opened, which was 06h00, and beat feet to the far end of the site so I could have the iconic monastery to myself for a few minutes before the tour groups arrived. The groups would take their time introducing sites along the way, so if I put the blinders on, I could enjoy them on my walk back as I crossed in the opposite direction. This was fantastic advice when tourism was at its peak. Just two months into the conflict in Gaza, when tourism in Jordan had cratered, I could afford not to heed his sage guidance. Instead, I ate a leisurely breakfast in town and entered the site around 09h00. This wasn't just me being snooty, either. A few people at the hostel told the same story: the site was empty, and there was no need to arrive ridiculously early. By the time I arrived, a couple of groups were present, but I wouldn't describe the site as crowded. More sparsely populated.

The main road from the visitor's centre to the monastery was over eight kilometres round trip, with the last stretch to the monastery taking visitors up 850 steps. No wonder every description of visiting Petra described it as a hike. Fortunately, the main trail led past all of the iconic sights. Fans of *Indiana Jones* like myself knew of the Treasury from its role as the façade for temple where the Holy Grail was hidden, and we knew the Siq as the winding canyon where Indy and his companions make their triumphant final ride after saving the Grail from Nazi hands. For visitors like me, the Siq came first, and it was as beautiful going towards the monastery as the film made it seem leading away. The Siq was created from water eroding the canyon for thousands and thousands of years, and its imposing, rust-red walls were magnificent in the rising sunlight. I rapidly filled my phone with landscape photos, and I had to force myself to put it away and take in the walk. I had another day to take as many pictures as I wanted.

As I approached the Treasury, all I could see was a thin sliver of carved columns through the canyon. It genuinely felt like a hidden city tucked away for weary adventurers to discover. The rock gave way to a large canyon, making the impressive carved Treasury look distinctively out of place. It looked like a rectangular hole had been cut into the wall and a Greek or Roman building slid into the space. That would have been impressive in its own right, but the building was carved from the space itself. The sculptors of Florence had nothing on this place.

Unlike in the films, where the façade stood alone in the canyon, the opposite side of the canyon had a large trinket and coffee shop where tour guides stood with their groups as they explained the Treasury's historical and archaeological importance. They were only slightly in the way of good photos. The Jordanian police standing around for security were the real eyesore. It wasn't quite one of those "Instagram vs. Reality" moments, but had it been a true peak season, I knew I wouldn't be getting the great experience I was fortunate enough to have.

Further down the path were the Nabatean Theatre, Royal Tombs, and Great Temple. I opted to forego these this go around and continue on to the famed Monastery which lay at the far end of the site. I had plenty of time the following day to really explore the other sites.

Where the path gave way to the 850 steps, men who lived in the wadi offered donkey rides to the top. The price you paid was "from the heart," but at least 10 JOD was preferred, and they let you know that if you tried to hand them a 5 JOD note. Personally, I wanted the hiking experience. It wasn't often I got to go for a proper hike on The Great Gallivanting, despite all of the walking I had done over the last almost six months. And hike I did. In hindsight, the trek up the steps wasn't too bad, but I have never been one to enjoy stairs, so I was winded by the time I arrived at the top and was greeted with "You made it!" from the guide with the donkeys. Made it I had, along with everyone else. All ten of them, max.

The Monastery was beautiful, bigger than the Treasury, and the sandstone shown golden in the now-risen sun. With so few people visiting, I had no problem waiting to grab amazing photos free of gawking tourists trying to become Instafamous. The few of us there were took turns with our cameras before settling in at the small café for a quick lunch in front of the façade. It was one of those surreal experiences that made you wonder how you were so fortunate to be where you were. There I was eating a kebab in front of one of the Seven Wonders of the World with so few spectators that it felt like I had the place all to myself. Well, me and the dog that stared longingly at the lettuce hanging out of my kebab.

Technically, the Monastery was the farthest part of Petra; however, signs in English indicated there were more magnificent views further along. One of them was up a rock formation that provided a birds-eye view of the Monastery and surrounding landscape. I figured I would have to pay something like 5 JOD for the experience, but I also figured I wouldn't be back in this part of the world anytime soon, so it was worth the money. Fortunately for me, but unfortunately for the shop owner, the government had mandated that he vacate his overlook a few weeks before (every "unauthorised" shop owner had been ordered off the site, because there were too few tourists for the government to justify the cost of upkeep). From that overlook, I appreciated the Monastery's magnificence even more. The façade remained prominent, but the handful of people taking pictures were tiny from that distance. I sat up there for a long time taking it in and reflecting on how the conflict on the other side of Israel had negatively impacted so many lives while providing me this once-in-a-lifetime opportunity.

Even further down a game trail (created by humans) was yet another viewpoint which promised even more fantastic views. The man who operated this one was still on site, as he was of the tribe that lived in these ravines, and the viewpoint was his home. This view didn't overlook the Monastery or any other part of Petra; it gazed west towards Israel. If I thought the canyons and ravines of Petra were huge, they had nothing on these mountains. This was a true wadi with mountains that towered over the shadowed, empty riverbed below. The man told me, along with a British couple, that during heavy rains the wadi fills with water, and long-lost coins and artifacts from Byzantine times frequently resurfaced as the water rushed over and eroded the mountains' surfaces. He was a collector, of sorts, and always went out after a heavy rain to see what he could find. He had a few examples to show us, too, of 1,500-year-old coins which he found in the mountains and valleys. Fifteen hundred years ago, these coins travelled here from as far as Istanbul and Rome, got lost to the sands of time, and were reborn again the floods of today. Talk about an amazing journey.

They were for sale, too, if we were interested. Go figure.

After saying my goodbyes to the shop owner and the British couple, I made my way back to the visitor's centre. I had been walking for several hours already and still had about another hour's worth of walking to go before I could settle in at my hostel at the top of the hill for a night of takeout Jordanian food, a beer, and *Indiana Jones* before discovering the rest of Petra the next day.

My agenda for my second and final day at Petra was simple: hit the Temple, the Royal Tombs, and hike the trails which jutted off to the south side of the main trail. Jo texted me that morning, "Happy Hiking!" She had finally recovered from her fifty-something-hour, three-country trek to Australia and was living it up in the warm Australian sun while I was in the Middle Eastern desert hiking for hours just to look at old things from times long gone by. If that didn't sum up our differences, I don't know what does!

I opted to do the hiking first. The Byzantine Church and the Royal Tombs were all along the main trail, and I knew I could handle them if I was worn out from climbing the surrounding hillsides. Naturally, I started by taking a lot of photos in the Siq and of the Treasury; they were just too beautiful to pass up. Then it was down to the Great Temple to start working my way back up the trails.

The first half of the trails from the Great Temple were fairly uneventful, just a lot of walking along narrow, rocky paths. More than once, I thought I had gotten lost, but there was a guide leading a man and his son on a tour with donkeys up ahead who I kept an eye on to keep my bearings. Despite the uneventful tour, I still enjoyed hiking through the beautiful sandstone landscape. Every so often, I came across a cave that had once been someone's home. Small, sure, but architecturally amazing. There were never any support beams to hold up the immense weight of the rock above, even in the larger caves. Some of them were cut to be perfectly rectangular with flat, even floors and ceilings meetings flat, even walls at right angles. It was amazing what experienced tradesmen without the credential of a college degree could do when life demanded it of them.

I eventually reached the Garden Temple, so named because of the beautiful garden it once hosted outside its front doors. The temple was carved into the rock just like the Treasury and the Monastery; however, unlike the Treasury and Monastery, whose inner workings were closed to the public, I could enter the Garden Temple and see just how skilled its builders were. Despite the large façade with its stand-alone columns, the temple's inner sanctum was only a tiny room used by the local tribe as a place of refuge during storms or harsh nights, as evidenced by the home-made bedroll and miscellaneous debris inside. Even so, the outside was beautiful in the now-risen sun that cast long shadows over the canyon walls.

Continuing on, I climbed the carved, sandstone staircase that wound its way up the canyon walls until I reached the High Place of Sacrifice, which, as its name suggested, once served as a sacrificial altar on the highest point in Petra. It was no wonder this was the site preferred for sacrifices. From this point, you were as close to God or the gods (depending on your religious standing) as you could be in Petra, and spectators from the surrounding area could witness the ceremony. I wasn't sure if there were spectators for such things, but it wouldn't have surprised me if there were, based on my cursory knowledge of Mayan, ancient Jewish, and Islamic practices. As with all highly trafficked spots in Petra, a woman had set up a coffee stand for visitors to sit and enjoy the scenery.

It was windy up there amongst the gods, so I returned to the land of the dead to explore the Byzantine Church and the Royal Tombs. The church was, well, a church, eroded by time and rain. It was a small outpost, even by standards of the time. Although, it was one of three Christian churches operating in Petra, so maybe they preferred three smaller ones to one, large, community-wide facility. This one of the three was founded around the year 450 and was destroyed by a fire just 250 years later. Shortly after, Petra's regional cultural, economic, and religious importance waned, and it all but disappeared from the historical record except for occasional references from foreign rulers, so it was understandable that this church was left by the wayside in the aftermath of the fire.

The Royal Tombs, like the Garden Temple, were accessible to visitors, and their architectural and engineering feats were even more impressive. These tombs were multi-story structures, all carved directly into the rock. While their façades were far more eroded than the Treasury or the Monastery, they maintained the same distinct style with inlaid columns before the entrances and windowless towers overlooking the main road as it led towards the Monastery. Inside, the rooms were perfectly flat, rectangular, devoid of support beams, and bore the same distinct right angles where the walls met the floors and ceilings. It was as though a mausoleum befitting for kings was created and the surrounding hillside dropped on top of it. It was truly something to behold.

With closing time fast approaching and too many hours passed by all too quickly, I started back towards the entrance, exhausted. On the other side of the Siq, I decided to be a tourist and ride a horse back. It only cost me "from the heart," i.e., 10 JOD, and it was worth it not to have to walk that last kilometre before taking the twenty-minute walk uphill to the hostel. Too bad they wouldn't let us ride horses from the Treasury down the Siq. That would have been a true *Indiana Jones* experience!

Just like that, my days in Petra had flown by, and it was time to move on to the next city. The days, cities, and experiences were flying by now, and they would only gain momentum as I barrelled towards my Mexican backstop. Before that backstop, though, I had to walk down the ninety-four-metre-high hill with my travel bag on my back and daypack on my front. They say if you want to make an hour feel like a lifetime, put on a rucksack and start walking. Well, then, twenty minutes easily turned into thirty as I tried not to fall or roll my ankle as gravity threatened to get the best of me.

One thing was for sure: I was ready to be on that bus by the time I reached the bottom!

Amman

The bus rolled into Amman just under four hours after leaving Wadi Musa. It was dark, I was worn out from Petra, and I didn't want to deal with the transportation situation in Amman. I didn't know if there was public transport or Uber, and I really didn't care. I was ready to take a shower and get to bed, so I did what I had been so irritated at Jo for doing when we landed in Tunis and hailed a taxi from a group crowding the bus stop, targeting unwitting travellers. Admittedly, it was a solid forty to sixty minutes to my hostel through Amman at that time of day, but I still rolled my eyes when they told me (yes, there were two drivers in the front seats) it would be 50 JOD for the ride. Utterly ridiculous, as that ride in New York City or Paris wouldn't have cost that much, but it was something I knew to likely happen when I got in the car, so I couldn't complain.

Before coming to Jordan, I purchased the Jordan Pass, a tourism initiative by the Jordanian Government which allowed you to visit nearly all of the archaeological sites, museums, and Petra on a single ticket. It also included the visa (which was never checked). If I hadn't got my money's worth at Petra (which I did), I was sure to get every last dollar out of it in Amman.

Amman was a geographically important city long before the Muslims invaded 1,400 years ago. The Amman Citadel, situated on a plateau that had once provided views far beyond the city before the city grew around it, had been continuously occupied by humans since 1800 BC. Architecture and artifacts at the sites bore the hallmarks of the Umayyads, Byzantines, and Romans, each adding to the site rather than destroying and rebuilding it. I found it intriguing that the initial Muslim conquest didn't destroy these hallmarks, especially those dedicated to Roman mythology/theology; those conquests weren't exactly known for tolerating blasphemous practices or symbols as decided by Islam.

As I was traipsing around the citadel's centuries-old ruins, I had the same thought Jo and I had discussed in Carthage and Egypt: Should I be walking here? Clearly, it was allowed, based on the on-site tour guides taking groups around, families taking pictures on the ruins, and the total absence of guardrails, but it didn't sit right with me that we were in this preserved archaeological site steadily eroding it with every step. I thought back to the threshold at the Rabat in Sousse that had a singular footprint eroded deep into the brick as, century after century, one person after the next crossed through it. How long would it be until we irreparably damaged this vital piece of Middle Eastern history that withstood the rise and fall of kingdom after kingdom over the course of nearly 4,000 years? I did my best to keep this at the front of my mind as I moved around the site, but sometimes, clambering over a stone wall or through a well-worn courtyard was unavoidable.

After lunch at the on-site café, I waved off the taxi drivers shouting to take me all around Amman and started the downhill trek to the Roman Theatre. I could only hope this one was more impressive than the one in Alexandria. My hope was to be rewarded. Like the theatres in Trieste and Carthage, the theatre in Amman was still in active use for concerts and performances. Considerable effort to renovate and preserve the rock structure meant people could enjoy it for generations to come. Children played football in the plaza outside the entry gates (but behind the ticket counter), and teenagers gathered in the way teenagers did on the theatre steps as police officers looked on. My Jordan Pass was checked twice before I climbed up for the views; I wondered if these kids had to show a pass or ticket or if that was just something for us Western tourists. This hadn't bothered me in Egypt, but the notion irked me in Amman for some reason. Maybe it was foreshadowing for the happenings of the next few days.

I spent a considerable amount of time at the theatre. It was easy for me to picture watching a performance from the top rows from the time I'd spent watching bullfights in similar arenas in Spain. While this theatre wasn't designed for a battle royale, the effect was the same with the crowds looking down upon the small ring where the night's entertainment performed to the cheers and jeers of those who paid good money for a memorable night.

Next door, but in the same complex, sat the Odeon, a small amphitheatre from the 100s AD. Like the main theatre, the Odeon had undergone preservation work that enabled its use for concerts and other performances. The gates which once led the performers in and out were now locked and protected scaffolding and lighting equipment.

The Odeon was the last of my pleasant experiences in Amman.

I wasn't a Casanova or player by any means. I had never been a proponent of dating apps, nor had I ever had much success with them, but I figured what the hell in Amman and started swiping through both Tinder and Bumble. To my surprise, I matched with a number of women. Some of them were bots, as was the norm on those apps, but many of them were actual people. After talking with one of them over the app for a bit, we decided to meet up for a drink that night. I didn't know the city well, so she suggested the Abdoun area. While I had left the stress and cynical side of my old life behind, some old habits die hard, mainly as a Westerner in a foreign land, so I seriously scoped out the area online before agreeing. Admittedly, it was a really nice area. The main roundabout sported ice cream shops, beauty salons, full-service banks, and even a McDonald's. All in all, it seemed like a legitimate place. We agreed to meet on the east side of the traffic circle, described what we would wear, and would go from there. It seemed like a good plan.

But old habits die hard.

I took a number of security precautions, which would ultimately cause me a lot of headache. I carried two phones in my travels. One I used for local SIM cards and Wi-Fi, which generally meant it was a cybersecurity nightmare. I didn't put any information on it that was connected to my old professional life, my bank or credit cards accounts, or digital ID cards. If that phone was stolen, it would mean losing pictures and contacts, but nothing major. My home phone, on the other hand, would have been disastrous to lose. It was connected to everything. I didn't want to put myself in a position to deal with the consequences of that phone being compromised by a thief or hacker, so I left it at the hostel, locked in my bag.

I also carried multiple wallets. This was mainly contingency planning. I kept a government identification card in each one along with a credit card, insurance card, and cash. If one of my wallets was stolen, it wouldn't be ideal, but it wouldn't be catastrophic, either. For this date, I elected to leave my debit card locked in my bag and take a different credit card with me. I also left my passport, instead opting to take my passport card. It was still issued by the Department of State, so it was an official United States Government identification; it just wouldn't get me onto any airplanes. If that was stolen, outside of having to report it, it had absolutely no effect on my travels.

Finally, I used what I knew as an "OIT;" an old Indian trick. If you were worried about a meeting, show up early. I got to Abdoun early via Uber, waited across the traffic circle at a café, and waited for the girl to show. If she didn't, or if she showed with a posse that quickly dispersed, I knew it was a scam or that I was likely to be robbed. I wasn't sure what I was worried about, but this was the Middle East, and drinking, dating apps, and Western values weren't exactly things that were especially common, especially in conservative areas, so I had the instinct to be especially careful.

She arrived right on time via Uber. If she had a posse, I didn't see them, and I watched as she messaged me saying she was there. She wore a blue top and jeans, just as she had described. So far, so good. I approached her, introduced myself, and we set out to find a place for our date. She had found a spot on Google Maps just a few metres down from the roundabout called Prestige. It was a hookah lounge that served alcohol. It looked like a proper lounge, and it was buzzing with people at the tables in the large room. On our way in, we saw a man being escorted to a cashpoint across the street. I shook my head; this wasn't the first time I had seen someone unable to pay their bar tab, and the scene was always the same. I turned my attention back to the room, settled into one of the booths, and picked up the drink menu.

My heart stopped for a second when I saw the prices. It cost 15 JOD for a bottle of beer. That was 25 USD for one bottle of beer! Cocktails started at 30 JOD. This was going to be an expensive night, one which I figured would ultimately be chalked up to what Dave Ramsey called stupid tax.

After placing our order with a waiter, the manager stopped by the table to inform me that a cover charge for the booths would be added to my bill. Of course, it would. I was already committed, though, so I agreed and resolved to limit the financial damage as best I could by ordering only one beer and nursing it for as long as possible. My date, on the other hand, knocked back vodka tonics as my mind quickly switched from doing the horizontal Mamba to watching my bank account steadily and rapidly dwindle. I felt like I was watching dollar signs disappear with every drink she downed. I started to become legitimately concerned for her health; at this rate, she would be blowing a .400 on the breathalyser within the hour, thus leaving me to deal with a drunk Jordanian girl as a non-Arab-speaking tourist.

But she never got drunk.

I asked if she needed to be drinking that much, but she told me the drinks weren't strong. "Just enough to take the edge off," she said. She occasionally said something to the wait staff, which I assumed was her ordering her next drink, but when she said that the drinks weren't strong, the real picture started to come into focus. The drinks were expensive, she was nowhere near drunk enough for the number of drinks she had (even if they weren't strong), and she was talking in Arabic to the wait staff that had demonstrated they had command of the English language.

My suspicions were confirmed when I got the bill.

The 630 JOD bill.

The 1,000 USD bill.

This whole setup was a scam, and she was in on it. Every girl I matched with on Tinder and Bumble was in on it. They had all suggested we meet in the Abdoun area, and those who hadn't committed already would message me later suggesting it. They all wanted to come to this bar, rack up a substantial, over-inflated tab, have the unsuspecting Westerner pay for it, and then take their cut of the loot once we were gone. It all had the smokescreen of legitimacy, too, as the drink prices, the cover charge, everything, was communicated by the wait staff and menus, so if I wanted to go to the tourism police about it, there was nothing they could do.

So, I resolved to pay the bill. I could afford the tab without substantial inconvenience, chalk it up to a lesson learned, and move on with my life with a story that I could tell over 2 EUR cañas and 5 EUR Guinness. I pulled my credit card out of my wallet and waved the manager over to pay.

The night took yet another turn.

He asked if I had cash to pay for the drinks; it was their preferred form of payment. I was sure it was, given the nature of the scam, but I didn't have cash on me, and I wanted a record of the transaction with my credit card company. I could call the dispute desk later to plead my case to have the charge removed, which had a good chance of success. So, I told the manager that I wanted to pay with card because I knew it would work, and it was *my* preferred method. He stood there and asked if I had the cash on me in case my card was declined. I knew my card worked in Jordan, and I told him so. I didn't tell him I didn't have that much cash on me. The manager rolled his eyes, gave my date a stern, passing look, and headed to the back of the house to retrieve the card machine.

I watched him from afar. The card machine wasn't even turned on. He had to boot it up. When he brought it out to me, I noted it wasn't connected to the internet. It probably had never connected to the internet and was simply for show for the suckers like me who insisted on paying with card. Unsurprisingly, my card declined. I told him to check the connection and rerun it because I could see it wasn't connected. He played along, but the card again declined. When he told me I would have to pay in cash, I told him I didn't have it on me and that we would have to figure something out.

I offered a solution. I would leave my "passport" (i.e., my passport card) with him as collateral while I went back to my hostel to get his money. He looked at me sceptically. "You have 1,000 US dollars at your hotel?" I told him I did, which was true, and I would be willing to retrieve it for him. I pulled out my passport card to hand him, and he said, "I will not take anything from you." I was sure he wouldn't. He didn't want to be implicated in anything should it go sideways.

That's when I became the guy I shook my head at earlier. He escorted me across the street to the cashpoint to take out the cash to pay the tab. He didn't know I couldn't access anything without my home phone or that I intentionally hadn't set up the cash advance PIN on my credit card, but I played along. I put my card in the machine, and it promptly rejected it. He told me I could use my phone to fix it; he clearly had no idea what two-factor authentication was and that texts don't come through with eSIM cards (not that that would have mattered anyways, but it made for a good front).

I again offered him my passport card; he again declined, "I will not take anything from you." Then he escorted me to another cashpoint, more irritable and becoming increasingly so. This attempt, too, failed, and I told him we were at an impasse. He could either accept my offer to hold my passport card while I retrieved the money, or he could call the police.

He, naturally, had a third solution. As it happened, he had a friend with a car right out front. He would send one of his employees with me in his friend's car to my hostel to retrieve the money. Getting into a strange man's car at the direction of a guy who was running a scam wasn't exactly at the top of my to-do list, but it wasn't the first time I had mentally resolved to roll out of a moving vehicle if I needed to, so I obliged. In fairness to the driver and the minder, they were pretty cool guys with some fantastic stories of life in Jordan. They even stopped to buy me coffee and offered me cigarettes because that's what they did in Jordan. Even when they were working to scam Westerners like me, they did it politely. The minder didn't even go with me into the hostel, although I was confident he would come get me if I decided not to return. Besides, he knew where the hostel was, so it wasn't like I could melt into the background. In any case, with money in hand, we headed back to the scam bar known as Prestige.

My "date" was still there when I arrived, dozing off in the booth. I called the manager over to pay, and he had completely forgotten about me. When I handed him the money, he asked me how much change I wanted! All of this rigamarole just for him to not remember how much he wanted from me. I decided to settle the score on what the bill had said and call it good, much to his surprise. He was so incredibly thankful that he offered me a free beer, all of the rest of my visits to the bar cover-free ("you only pay what you drink!"), and a ride home with the same driver as before. I took him up on two of those three offers, but I had already committed never to return so long as I may live. My date tried to make light of the whole ordeal as though she wasn't involved in it all, and she politely declined to go back with me for the rest of the evening. "Not this time," she said. Not ever, then. Talk about insult to injury.

On the way home, the driver regaled me with his adventures as a driver in Amman. He told me of his time driving American generals around Jordan and some of the meetings he was subsequently privy to attending, working for private contractors and the police, and complained loudly about the surge in coffee shops which had opened all across Amman. Personally, I wished we had more places like those coffee shops in the United States, where the men gathered to play cards or dominos while solving the world's problems over cigarettes and coffee without a waiter trying to flip the table to garner more tips. But this was his country; he was entitled to his opinion, and I was entitled to disregard it, given his role in the night's events. Annoyed, but amused now that it was all over, I turned in for the night and looked forward to a day of visiting museums.

That was an ill-fated plan. I discovered, or rather remembered, that it was Friday in Amman after I had my morning coffee. Everything related to the government was closed, including museums, in observance of Yawm al-Jumu'ah, the rough Muslim equivalent to the Sabbath in Judaism and Christianity. I was no stranger to Yam al-Jumu'ah, and I should have planned better so I wouldn't have committed half of my time in Amman to just hanging around. As I started back from the closed Jordan Museum, police filled the streets. This was some procession or event, not a threat, but they still cleared everyone away. Several times, I was directed off the road down alleyways and side streets. I had no idea where I was going; I just knew it wasn't where I had originally planned.

Finally, I settled in for breakfast. I ordered 5 JOD's worth of food but was charged 13 JOD. I couldn't argue the point because I didn't know Arabic, and after the previous night's events, the expensive taxi when I arrived, and my observation of the children at the Roman Theatre who came and went while I had to show my pass, I was over Amman. To me, the city was scam central. No, not scams. Scams imply being suckered into paying for something not real or a service you didn't get. This was legal thievery and extortion targeting Westerners. I was over it, and I resolved to wait out the rest of my time at the hostel.

After, that is, I went to Starbucks. Starbucks was a so-called "Zionist" company, and across the Middle East, efforts to boycott, isolate, and shut down Starbucks for their alleged support of Israel were underway. Well, I didn't like Turkish coffee, and at least Starbucks was an American company that would address franchisee issues should I complain enough. I wasn't one that made political points with my coffee, but after the scams and extortion I experienced, I made an exception. This one time, my Starbucks was a political middle finger to Amman. I stayed there for hours, reading and writing reflections on the blog for my family. It was air conditioned and had Wi-Fi, and the political boycott meant I was the only one there besides the staff.

Perfect. When I left for the hostel, I stopped at a market for cereal that I would eat for lunch, dinner, and breakfast, and I stayed true to my word. I didn't leave.

In a fresh breath of sanity, my Uber to the airport cost me 12 JOD, which I split with a Canadian woman. At the airport, I breathed a sigh of relief. I was leaving Amman forever, never to return, looking forward to the next adventure in northern Iraq. Not even the security screeners tearing apart my bags got me down. I had elected to get to the airport extremely early so I didn't have to stay in the city any longer, so I had plenty of time to repack. With ticket to Iraq in hand, I dropped my bag and headed to the food court.

Never before had I been so happy to get to Iraq.

Reflecting on Jordan

"From the heart." I came to detest this phrase. In the Middle East, it was the culture to perform acts of service and not charge or request tips, instead receiving whatever gratuity the recipient deemed appropriate. In most circumstances, when you tipped someone, regardless of the amount, they expressed gratitude and wished you well. There was an unspoken cultural rule that, as a Westerner, you tipped well if you could afford it.

The irritating thing about this phrase was that it was only said when you asked someone how much something cost and they wanted a large gratuity. I developed a personal practice in Jordan that served me well. If I asked how much something cost and the response was, "from the heart," I handed over a 5 JOD note. It wasn't much as a payment, but it was generous for a tip and always elicited the true price. That note would be met with, "Only five? Not ten for me?" (or whatever price they wanted or were willing to accept). I learned that those who truly wanted something "from the heart" would tell you "no charge," "free," or wave you off as you tried to ask. Those who didn't ask for something "from the heart" truly wanted what you deemed appropriate. Oftentimes, I paid these men more than I would have had they quoted me a price because they were genuine and simply trying to make a living in hard times over which they had no control.

Amman. My opinion of Amman is harsh. I did not enjoy my time there, and I never want to go back. However, I would also love to return to Jordan to explore its beautiful scenery, history, and culture. Until I arrived in Amman, I had pleasant experiences all the way around. Sure, there were the typical tourist traps you had to watch out for in every country, but the people seemed genuinely pleasant and eager to share their culture with Western travellers like me. It wasn't until I reached Amman that I began to dislike things, and I certainly didn't judge the entire country by this one city. That would be like judging Texas because you didn't like Austin politics or the United States because you got robbed in the Bronx. While I never wanted to return to Amman except to transit the airport, I would love to return to Jordan, hike the Jordan Trail, see Wadi Rum, and experience the customary hospitality of the small towns and cities.

Palestinians in Jordan. Part of my intention with this book is to communicate my travel experiences more than my personal opinions, and sometimes, those experiences collided head-on with hot-button political and social issues. Palestinian sovereignty was one of those issues, especially in Jordan. On the whole, I had two types of encounters with the Palestinian people while in Jordan. The first was disheartening and infuriating and deserves mentioning in this chapter, while the second I will address in a later chapter (*Reflection #3 – Narratives from the Middle East: My Experience with the Never-Ending Conflict*).

I discovered just how little regard the Jordanian government had for Palestinians within their borders. Rafat, my part-fish divemaster, was a stateless person. He had a Palestinian passport, which served to a degree as an identity document but was not recognised the world over as a citizenship document. His people didn't have a government advocating for them at the United Nations, and the countries where many of them lived (including Jordan, which was, by some measures, ninety percent Palestinian) refused to offer them citizenship and the rights and privileges that citizenship provided. On multiple occasions, Rafat, Karyna, and I were targeted by the Jordanian security services as we rolled down the road simply because they knew Rafat was Palestinian. They cited him multiple times, and Karyna told me this was a regular occurrence. The two of them had gone to painstaking lengths to comply with the laws regarding diving, including having about thirty sets of unused diving gear sitting in their shop just to meet the regulatory standards to operate. Still, they were constantly hassled simply because there was nothing Rafat could do about it. Knowing Jordan's history with the Palestinian people, including the pre-emptive 1947 occupation of the West Bank and its refusal to accept Palestinian refugees and asylum seekers while simultaneously protesting Israel's treatment of the Palestinian people, this disappointed and infuriated me. I hated government virtue-signalling, and the Palestinians who were born and raised in Jordan, integrated into Jordanian society, and complied with Jordanian law deserved respect and dignity from their government, not incessant hassling at the prejudicial hands of the security services.

Those who live in glass houses shouldn't throw stones, and Jordanians lost the right to lecture me and the West in general about the treatment of the Palestinian people, as far as I was concerned.

Boycott. The conflict in Israel affected every country in the region, an unavoidable circumstance given the politics of Palestinian statehood, Israel's right to exist, and the Abraham Accords seeking to normalise relations between Arab nations and Israel, sometimes at the expense of the Palestinian people. One effect of the renewed conflict in Gaza was a widely held, racist sentiment that Jews and Zionists controlled international businesses and that those businesses should be boycotted. This notion was not new in the United States, but it was a fringe political movement at best.

Not so in Jordan. Boycott was the name of the game when it came to these businesses. McDonald's, Burger King, Starbucks, L'Oreal, Carrefour, and even Nokia were taking hits in the region over the local population's refusal to buy their products or services. Starbucks was forced to close locations and lay off more than 2,000 workers in the Middle East due to profit losses. I was warned in Aqaba that while those places were still open, no Jordanian would go in there, and I would be judged should I choose to eat at a so-called "Zionist" fast-food chain. In Amman, my hostel had a list of prohibited businesses that were not allowed on the premises.

It was nonsensical to me. First off, as a practical matter, my choice of lunch or coffee wasn't a conscious political action. I didn't like Turkish coffee, and Starbucks was one of the few places around that made espresso. It wasn't a political statement on the rightness or wrongness of Israel's retaliation against Hamas in Gaza, and even pretending that international travellers who have come to experience the rich history and culture of their country wanted to be drawn into local political and social issues was ridiculous. Second off, these boycotts ultimately did nothing. McDonald's and Kentucky Fried Chicken weren't exactly going to crumble because the Jordanian people wanted to make a political statement. Sure, it might mean closing a few locations or withdrawing from the region as a whole, but that would only mean the local loss of jobs, not the defeat or destruction of multi-billion-dollar international conglomerates. If anything, these boycotts and trying to drag me into them only turned me off from the point of view these people were trying to make.

My experience at the Amman airport solidified my hard views of these boycotts. The food court had a McDonald's and a Starbucks, and they were in full swing. Travellers awaiting flights all over the world sipped their expensive, Zionist lattes while eating their fatty, Zionist hamburgers and French fries. No one batted an eye as the queues for these restaurants formed, and Jordanians ordered their Zionist meals in Arabic even though there were plenty of other less tasty options. Politics was all well and good until it became an inconvenience. Then, everyone was a Zionist.

Chapter Fifteen

Iraq: A Kurdish Christmas

Iraq was a country I had long wanted to visit. It was one of the most historically significant countries in the world, but its tendency to be war-torn over the last century meant visiting as a tourist was difficult and risky on a good day. Even so, I wanted to give Iraqi Kurdistan a go. I knew it to be a safer region both from personal experience in the military and from videos and stories I had watched and read since the end of the COVID-19 pandemic. Being in Jordan and able to apply for a tourist visa online made the journey so easy that I couldn't help but jump from Amman to Erbil. It would be one of the most memorable weeks in my entire trip around the globe.

Erbil

At the Amman airport, I met someone I would describe as a kid who was an American Army infantry soldier. His unit was on security duty on the Coalition side of the Erbil International Airport. He was returning from emergency leave via commercial air instead of military transport. This had to be a good sign that the security situation was stable enough; otherwise, the military wouldn't fly junior soldiers via commercial air.

The flight was uneventful, and it was nighttime when we landed. At the bottom of the steps leading from the plane, Kurdish and Coalition security forces waited with a van for senior Coalition officers who would be given VIP treatment and a trip through the express lane for customs. The soldier I met was not so fortunate, and he tagged along with me through baggage claim, customs, and the security checkpoints. Someone was supposed to pick him up, and he would be fine at the airport, so I wished him well, hit up a cashpoint for some Iraqi Dinar (IQD), and grabbed a taxi into town.

I was on edge as we made our way to my hotel in the city centre (literally called MyHotel), but that edginess rapidly shifted to cognitive dissonance and confusion. The airport grounds were beautifully kept, roads were well-maintained, and there were towering structures with bright marquees advertising hotels, apartment buildings, and businesses. We passed large malls with Western businesses, two-story Hardees, and all manner of modern-looking buildings and company headquarters. I didn't feel like I was in Iraq; I felt like I was in Las Vegas. After two months of experiencing stereotypical MENA, I was in the most Western place I could imagine. And this was a war zone, according to the United States!

MyHotel was essentially in the city centre, and as we got closer, modernity gave way to the old city. My taxi driver charged me a legitimate rate, unlike the drivers in Amman, carried my bags into the hotel, and wished me well on my vacation. He didn't speak much English, but he spoke enough to know I was a traveller. The manager of the hotel, on the other hand, did speak English, and he welcomed me with a handshake and a big smile. My room arrangements were ready, and all I needed to do was pay. Of course, being in Iraq, my credit card company thought it was a fraudulent charge and wanted me to verify it, which I couldn't do until I connected to Wi-Fi and was able to get into my email (I didn't have a local SIM card, nor would I my entire time in Iraq). It was no bother, the manager told me. I could sort things with my bank and pay the next day. This man, whose name I didn't get, was the perfect example of Middle Eastern hospitality, where mutual trust was still the main currency and what truly mattered was enjoying each other's company and experiences.

My room was on the upper floors, a two-bed room with Wi-Fi and air conditioning. I originally had a single queen bed, but changed to two beds when Sasha (a guy from my time in Egypt) agreed to come with me. After he pulled out, I never bothered to change it back. I was used to a twin bed, so I was unbothered. Sitting on my bed for the first time, the reality of where I was settled in.

I was in Iraq, the Iraqi Kurdish Region to be exact (also called Iraqi Kurdistan), a country I had only been to with the military and whose languages I did not speak. I attempted to download Kurdish to my phone, but the main dialect in this particular region wasn't available for download. I had Arabic, but that would only get me so far. I knew nothing of Kurdish cuisine, security, nothing. The only people from my home life that knew where I was were Jo and one of my old warfighters. This was the first time I felt truly isolated in my years of travelling, and my old habits and security senses came rushing back to me.

There was no time like the present, and I was hungry, so I headed out for food. The concierge recommended a pizza place for takeaway. Typical American, ordering pizza in a foreign land instead of trying something local. I was sold. It would allow me a short jaunt out into the city to get the feel of things. If I wasn't feeling it, I could always buy an expensive flight out of there ahead of schedule. I left my hat behind, not wanting to broadcast myself as a foreigner (not that my white skin didn't give me away), and tried to make myself look as much like a "grey man" as possible. No hat, no sunglasses (it was nighttime, anyways), no shemagh, no messenger bag that was always thrown over my soldier. My five senses were magnified a thousand times as I walked twenty-five minutes to the pizza place. It was mostly down main roads, and even when Google Maps recommended taking a side street, I took the longer main streets until I couldn't anymore.

When I arrived at UK Pizza & More, the juxtaposition of Middle East meets West came forth once again. It was on a typical, residential street, with the same brown bricks, oil-top roads, and occasional run-down buildings that could be found in Amman, Egypt, everywhere in MENA, until you walked up on the restaurant. It was busy, with delivery drivers on motorbikes coming and going, a busy kitchen with uniformed staff, and electronic self-service kiosks that accepted credit cards. It was literally a bright light on a dark street. Fortunately, "pizza pepperoni" translated the same in almost every country, and before too long, I paid with my Iraqi Dinar and walked back to MyHotel with my pizza. It was pretty good, too, unlike the pizza in Egypt, and it was hard to wrap my head around the city's simultaneous old and modern feel.

Then, the electricity went out. I snorted a laugh because the Wi-Fi still worked. The electricity going out didn't bother me. Rolling blackouts in the Middle East weren't uncommon; they were routine in the summer months as the power grids became overloaded. I figured it would come on sooner or later, and after a few hours, I heard the air conditioning click back on.

The hotel offered complimentary breakfast, which I took advantage of every morning. It was simple, consisting primarily of fruit, various breads, dates, orange juice, and... French fries. Beggars can't be choosers, and a complimentary breakfast in an 80 USD per night hotel wasn't something I was going to complain about. The dining room provided some great views of Erbil, too. It was a sprawling city with everything from run-down buildings to skyscrapers. The city's literal centrepiece, the Citadel, stood prominently over the skyline. That was the one place I wanted to visit, and I started making my rough plan for Erbil while eating fresh fruits and enjoying the sunrise over the city. I probably should have made the plan sooner, but I didn't know what to expect, so I waited until I felt more comfortable with my surroundings.

I opted not to venture out too much on my first day. I was still getting the feel of things and wasn't confident about the area yet. I made a short walk into the city centre to see the Citadel after breakfast and stopped at a camera shop to buy a microphone for my GoPro (it had fallen out of my bag in the taxi), but then I headed back to the hotel. There was a supermarket nearby where I bought food for lunch, dinner, and snacks each day, and I loaded up for plenty of meals in my room while I edited some videos for social media and wrote blog posts. I also needed to hand-wash laundry, seeing as there weren't any laundromats for me to use in Amman, which meant hang drying most of my clothes on bungee cords across the room. In hindsight, I could have asked the concierge to point me in the right direction, but I was so amped up and edgy that I didn't think about that. In any case, this allowed me to organise my guided tour through Iraqi Kurdistan. There weren't many tour companies, and the most-recommended one online had three days availability after Christmas, which was perfect. That would give me a full day after the tour to prepare my stuff to head to Turkey.

My second full day in Iraqi Kurdistan was Christmas day. I originally planned to be in Israel, but October 7th changed that plan. I didn't know what to expect from a Kurdish Christmas, but I ventured out for a day of exploring to find out. My plan was to visit the Citadel and its museums, wander around the main parts of the old city, and visit the Sami Abdulrahman Park on the northwest side of town. I would walk the entire time, and the weather went from cool in the mornings to warm in the afternoons, so I brought my messenger bag along this time to stash my Henley when I needed to. After a late breakfast, I left to explore Erbil.

The walk to the Citadel from MyHotel was an easy, straight shot, as the city's streets radiated away from it as though it were the hub of a wheel. The Citadel was so old that many historical documents referred to it as though it had always been there. The city of Erbil was thought to have been first occupied somewhere in the timeframe of 6000 BC, based on artifacts found at the Citadel and commentary in the records of various empires in the region. As such, the Citadel was believed to be the oldest continuously-occupied city in the world. Indeed, one family still called the Citadel its home. It was an impressive, imposing structure on a plateau that would have provided an unobstructed view in every direction to defend against invading armies. I later learned that this was a common feature of major Kurdish cities of old, and I would visit a few in the coming week.

Unfortunately, the Citadel was closed for renovation and excavation. It was classified as "partially ruined" and declared a World Heritage Site by UNESCO in 2014. While there was still one family living in the Citadel, this was only to maintain its status as the oldest continuously-occupied city in the world. The other families, just under 500 of them, were evicted so excavations and renovations could commence. While this was disappointing, that was the way of travel sometimes, and I could still admire the Citadel's beauty from the outside. Hopefully, I would someday see inside of one of the world's most significant, oldest, and lesser-known historical sites.

I walked counterclockwise around the Citadel to explore the old city. It was still organised according to the old method I learned about in Europe: by profession. Along one particular road were all medical services, along another were all electronics shops, down yet another were all carpenters. While location today is determined by competition and strategic placement, old communities like Erbil were focused on ease of access and logic. There wasn't much to *see*, per se, but it was a cultural experience, which, after all, was why I was there in the first place.

Continuing around the Citadel, I approached Shar Park and the surrounding bazaars. Shar Park was a public square with beautiful fountains, neatly-trimmed hedges, and old men drinking tea and solving the world's problems on its benches. The park was also decorated for Christmas. Net lights were draped over the hedges, and a Christmas tree was erected in the middle of the park. When I came to Erbil for Christmas, I certainly didn't expect that! I would have to return at night to see it lit up and send pictures home. My mom loved Christmas lights, so she would really enjoy these.

I wandered around the bazaars for a bit, but they were nothing new for me, so I continued into a local pop-up market on the far side of Shar Park. I could only describe this market as the Kurdish version of a souk. Blue tarps stretched across the street to provide shade and protection from the rain, and it was crowded with people shopping for anything and everything. From school supplies to cell phones to fish to fruit, you could buy it there. Old women went about their shopping for the week's ingredients while children crowded around the toy stalls and marvelled at the newest thing. The market stretched for what seemed like forever down the road (which the police had blocked off). I felt oddly at home in this market. No one was looking at the Westerner or trying to hustle me. Hell, probably no one there knew English, unlike the souks in Marrakech, Souse, and Cairo. This was just another shopping day for them, wide-eyed, out-of-place Westerner notwithstanding.

Outside of the market, jutting off down an adjacent street from Shar Park, were money carts. Lots of them. At these carts, you could exchange almost any currency in the world. Despite the hotel and certain restaurants accepting credit cards, Iraq was a cash-based society, and Kurdistan specifically did business with countries across the globe. I estimated there had to be millions of dollars' worth of money between the carts. I looked around wondering where the armed security was, but it was non-existent, at least as far as I could tell. I didn't know if this was because the city was just that safe or because the Asayish (the internal security and intelligence service) had once made an example of a thief, but it was clear that the carts' operators weren't at all concerned with theft. They even left them on the street and secured them with nothing but a padlock when they went for lunch! They could never get away with that in the United States.

Speaking of millions of dollars, which I certainly did not have, I needed to find a cashpoint to withdraw about 1,400,000 IQD (about 1,000 USD) to pay for my next several days. This would pay for the tour (which cost me 600 USD, or about 790,000 IQD), meals, and any other expenses I would incur. I was sure I had taken out too much, but I didn't want to make too many more withdrawals considering I only got reimbursed 15 USD in cashpoint fees every month from my bank. Fortunately, there was a bank about a ten-minute walk from MyHotel. While the inside was closed, I could still use the cashpoints out front. After a few withdrawals (because the withdrawal limit was 600,000 IQD per transaction), I returned to my room with over a million in currency in my pocket. Sure, it wasn't a million dollars, but I still had never carried a million of anything in my pockets. I couldn't wait to get it somewhere safe; it was just too much cash to carry around.

After lunch, I decided to stay at the hotel for the afternoon. I wasn't comfortable enough wandering around in Iraq too much just yet.

The next day, though, I resolved to overcome my apprehensions and headed off for Sami Abdulrahman Park. The park was named after Sami Abdulrahman, one of the leaders of the Iraqi Kurdish Revolution and one of the founders of the Kurdish Democratic Party, the largest modern political party in Iraqi Kurdistan. He was killed in an al-Qa'ida terrorist attack in Erbil in February of 2004. It was fitting that the park bearing his name was located across the eight-lane highway (which I crossed on foot!) from the Kurdish Parliament and Kurdish Regional Government (KRG) ministerial offices. Like the Parliament, the entrances to the park were heavily guarded by Kurdish security forces. I figured them for Asayish, but I wasn't sure and didn't particularly want to find out by loitering too long or checking them out too much. They were already giving me funny looks as a solo Westerner walking around Iraq by myself.

The park was Erbil's answer to New York City's Central Park. It was large and sported two lakes, horseback riding, playgrounds, monuments, you name it. Police officers and soldiers exercised on its streets, families picnicked at tables, and young couples enjoyed each other's company in the serenity of the park's trees and meadows. When I had decided to travel to Iraq, I never thought I would end up in a place like this. It was so...normal. One could be forgiven for thinking they were back in the United States if they didn't know any better. My mind couldn't reconcile that just a few kilometres away, Coalition forces were working with the Iraqi Security Forces

(ISF) on fighting Islamic State and bringing the non-compliant Iranian-aligned militia groups under control. I had walked to the park, through a warzone, past the Iranian consulate and KRG offices, across a major highway, and I was completely safe, much safer than had I been in New York City. It was a bizarre feeling I reflected on while I sipped tea outside the horse-riding corral, watching children having the time of their lives.

I took an alternate route back to MyHotel. I was becoming more comfortable in Erbil, especially after visiting the park, and I had to get out of my comfort zone some time. I even ventured into a local shop to buy an ice cream bar to get used to interacting with people whose language I didn't speak. Plus, at less than 1 USD, I could justify an ice cream after walking around all day.

After an afternoon at the hotel, I ventured out when the sun went down. I shocked myself with this decision, but I had about decided it was safe to go out. YouTubers, travel bloggers, and independent travellers wouldn't travel the region if it weren't safe; I wasn't a novice when it came to unsafe situations, and it was high time I started acting like it. So, when it was finally dark out, I asked the hotel manager for recommendations for food in the city. He directed me to a shawarma place near the Gulan Mall. I needed a taxi to get there, but I didn't speak a single word of Kurdish, so he helped me order one using the Careem app on my phone (this was the local version of Uber and Uber Eats). He even translated where I needed to go for the driver. The taxi cost 3,000 IQD, about 2 USD, and the driver was floored when I gave him a 5,000 IQD note and indicated that he could keep the change. A 2,000 IQD tip may not have been much to me, but it was almost an entire extra fare for him, and I got the impression that he wasn't accustomed to receiving tips.

After a delicious meal of beef shawarma mixed with macaroni and cheese, I visited the Gulan Mall next door. I didn't know what I would find there, but after the Morocco Mall, I knew I had to at least have a look. Besides, I read online that visiting the malls was something Kurdish families did as a day out in Erbil. It was the same when I was young back home, and I felt a bit nostalgic on Christmas day while my family was preparing to have lunch at my granddad's house.

Whatever I could have expected from the Gulan Mall, I would not have expected what I found. It was like the Morocco Mall times a thousand! From Calvin Klein to Puma to large atriums and a sprawling food court, not to mention the surrounding specialty shops and fine dining restaurants, this was certainly worthy of a day with the family. And it was decorated for Christmas! There were Christmas trees, lights hanging in the atriums, snowmen, and Santa Claus displays – everything we had at the mall back in my hometown. I took plenty of pictures and planned to send them to my mom when I returned to the hotel. She would be more shocked than I was to find all of these Christmas decorations in Iraq.

After exploring the Gulan Mall, I felt far more confident in Erbil and decided to walk back to MyHotel. It was a thirty-minute walk, but it was straight down the main road that led from the airport, so I determined it was safe enough for a nighttime trek. About halfway there, I committed to continuing to the Citadel to see the lights in Shar Park lit up at night. I was glad I did! The blue net lights over the hedges and trees, the white lights lining the adjacent buildings, the fountains, and the large, shining Christmas tree made for a wonderful evening out. The entire city seemed to think so, as families, teenagers, and, yes, the old men solving the world's problems, all filled the park to take photos and enjoy a pleasant Christmas evening with loved ones. It felt like a Christmas celebration in Texas, except that the Christmas tree was lit with green, white, and orange lights in the form of the Kurdistan flag instead of the intricate ornaments cities would have used back home. Up on the Citadel, a bright "2024" sign beckoned in the new year. It was a surreal and wonderful Christmas experience. If I couldn't be in Israel for Christmas, this was a great runner-up.

I video called my family when I returned to MyHotel. I had done this every week since leaving, and I always called in for holiday get-togethers. As fortune would have it, the power went out while I was on the phone with my mom. She was initially concerned that my screen had gone black, but she laughed when I told her it was a rolling blackout, and they had the Wi-Fi connected to the generator to keep it going. It was all about priorities. She knew where I was, now, having guessed it when she felt I was being evasive. Why it was her first assumption that I was in Iraq, I didn't know, but that must have said something about me that my mother automatically assumed I had flown into a war zone for Christmas. My dad, on the other hand, didn't know, and I finally told him I was in Erbil, in Kurdistan, figuring he would chalk it up to just another one of the -stans, which he did... for a bit. But I was already there, so there wasn't much to do about it. He just wanted me to be safe and to send lots of pictures.

With those first days behind me, it was time to embark on an adventure outside of the city. My guide, Govand, messaged me a general itinerary that night, which included staying one night away from MyHotel, so I packed my day bag and went to bed. It was going to be an early morning followed by three days holding God only knew what as I travelled around Iraqi Kurdistan.

The Tour

After breakfast, I waited in the hotel lobby for Govand to arrive. He lived in Erbil with his family and was right on time. We shook hands, loaded my bag into his car, and headed to the frontier.

Govand was a few years older than me, and through our initial conversations about Iraq, I told him that I had deployed there several years before. I was generally familiar with the political and social situation, which he enjoyed, because we could get into deeper conversations as we drove from place to place.

Our first stop was the border between Iraqi Kurdistan and Nineveh province in Federal Iraq. This was the border where the semi-autonomous Kurdish government's authority ended and Iraq's federal authority began. There were actually two checkpoints along this road, an Asayish checkpoint and an ISF checkpoint, separated by a few kilometres. These checkpoints lined the major roads that crossed the KRG border, and the two checkpoints betrayed how much the two sides distrusted each other. I remembered from my time with the military in Baghdad how much the two sides of the border didn't want to work together, not even on simple security issues. In fact, part of these checkpoints' job was to check visitor visas. If I had a visa from Federal Iraq, I could travel anywhere in the country. A KRG visa, which I had, allowed only travel in Iraqi Kurdistan; I could not cross into Federal Iraq without an Iraqi visa, which I could only obtain either in advance at the embassy in Washington, DC, or on arrival at Baghdad International Airport.

The Kurdish side of the line was also symbolic in the fight against Islamic State. Back in 2014, just weeks after I joined the military, Islamic State overran Mosul as the ISF dropped their weapons and literally ran away. The Asayish and Peshmerga (the Kurdish regional armed forces) stopped Islamic State from invading Iraqi Kurdistan at the border, with fighting only extending a few hundred metres in each direction during Islamic State's three-year reign of terror (three years by official accounts, but more like five to seven in reality). Granted, some blamed the Peshmerga for withdrawing from the Nineveh plains for Islamic State's successful, rapid invasion of Iraq, but that wasn't something I was going to mention to Govand.

We then backtracked a bit and made our way to the Mar Mattai Monastery, the oldest Syriac Orthodox (aka Jacobite) monastery in the world. It was founded in 363 by a Christian priest who fled Roman persecution in Assyria. The monastery lived in relative peace in the secluded hills of Kurdistan until the 1100s, when Kurdish forces besieged the monastery on multiple occasions only to be beaten back by the monks and Christians who lived in the area. Unfortunately, the sheer number difference between the Kurdish forces and the monks led to the monks abandoning the monastery or facing death at the hands of their invaders, thus kicking off a series of retaliative attacks between Kurds and the Assyrians who lived in the surrounding hills. Over the next 800 years, the Kurds looted the monastery time and again, each time damaging the structure, its artifacts, and religious texts. While the doctrines of the Syriac Orthodox Church survived through the surviving monks and other churches, the loss of the manuscripts was a priceless consequence of war and conflict.

It was no wonder the original priest had chosen this location for his monastery. It was at the top of a deep draw, which provided unobstructed views to the west, and was built against (and even into) a tall cliff, which provided it protection from the east. During the Islamic State invasion, all but one priest evacuated, and he had told Govand that he watched down the draw as the fighting took place on the hills below. The priest stayed because someone had to stand between the terrorists and their destructive ways, but, ultimately, the Kurdish forces halted the advance and saved the monastery before beating Islamic State back to Kurdistan's front lines. How the times had changed since the 1100s.

Most of the monastery was closed to visitors; it was an active religious site, after all. Even so, it was a marvel to look at as it glowed a golden brown in the rising sun, and it certainly gave the aura of a serene place to contemplate and study one's religious beliefs. However, we were allowed to visit the tomb of Mar Mattai, known in English as Saint Matthew the Hermit, the monastery's founder. It was situated in a small room, fitting for a pious man fleeing religious persecution into the hills of Kurdistan. How many people had visited this venerated saint's tomb over the last 1,400 years?

After I had taken ample pictures and we finished exploring the Mar Mattai Monastery, Govand took me to Lalish, the mountain temple of the Yazidi people. The Yazidis were a sect of Kurds who believed in Yazidism, a monotheistic religion which I could best describe as a combination of local beliefs, Judaism, Christianity, and Islam (although this was only a best estimation as a non-scholar outsider). The Yazidis mostly lived in Iraq, although there was a substantial diaspora in Germany and smaller ones across Europe, North America, and the Caucasus. Despite the diasporas, nearly all of the Yazidi temples were located in Iraq, and I was honoured to be permitted a visit to the holiest one, Lalish.

Unlike mosques and cathedrals, the entirety of Lalish was considered a holy site, not just the inner chambers or sanctuaries, so Govand and I had to remove our shoes before crossing the threshold onto the temple grounds. It was December in northern Iraq, and going barefoot on stone pathways was not something I had anticipated. My feet would hurt from the cold by the time we left, despite Govand doing his best to explain things on sunny ground. Govand guided tours year-round, so he was used to going without shoes in everything from knee-deep snow to the oppressive August summer; he had learned to wear good socks to help deal with walking on the hot and cold stones.

It is difficult, as an outsider, to describe the many tenants of the Yazidi faith based on my singular visit to Lalish, but I would be doing the faith, Govand, and readers a disservice if I didn't make an attempt to explain the basics.

The Yazidis believed in the Seven Angels, emanations of God charged with overseeing the world. These angels, according to the faith, rested on the thresholds of doorways, and, as such, to step on a threshold as you crossed it was considered incalculably disrespectful to Yazidis. While I had demonstrated to Govand that I respected religious practices and sites of other faiths, I noticed he made sure that I stepped over a threshold and not on it. He carefully watched every time we crossed from one room to another and in and out of buildings. I got the distinct impression he had to smooth things over with the inhabitants more than once due to unwitting travellers who weren't paying attention.

In the courtyards and adorning the top of tombs, baptistries, and other important sites were pyramidal shrines, some of which towered above the entire temple. The bases were heptagonal, each representing one of the Seven Angels. Reaching above the base were triangular prism-like structures which converged at a single point, symbolising the sun's rays giving life to those of us on Earth. Each was adorned with a globe as well, but I would be lying if I said I knew what those symbolised in the faith.

Some entrances to buildings had a black snake carved onto the door frame. In contrast to Judaism, Christianity, and Islam, who believe the serpent to be an incarnation of the devil and whose religious texts indicated that the serpent's head will be (or had been, depending on the faith) crushed by the the Son of God, Yazidis believed the snake symbolised Mother Nature and our connection with her. According to Yazidi tradition, there were two stories in which the black snake served for good, which rose above all other instances of evil. One dictated that when Noah's Ark sprang a leak, a black snake took action and used its body to plug the hole, thus saving all on board and, consequently, all life on Earth. The other was similar, except that during a flood which only affected the Yazidi people, a boat filled with survivors sprung a leak, and a black snake curled into a ball and plugged the hole, thus saving the Yazidi people from extinction.

As a non-Yazidi, I was not permitted to enter the baptistries, and I cannot describe them as I do not know what they look like. These were some of the holiest places for Yazidis at Lalish, where believers were baptised and sins washed away, and they could not be tainted by the viewing eyes of non-believers. Govand told me that violating these baptistries would be the one thing that would never be forgiven of him, and if we watched closely, we could see community leaders watching us anytime we got close to one. Stepping on a threshold might have gotten us tossed out this time, but violating the sanctity of the baptistry would be cause for a lifetime ban for Govand. As someone who respected other faiths, although I took great pains not to actively participate in them, it was beyond me how travellers could be so insensitive to a simple request to respect such a holy religious place, but, given Govand's stern caution, I was sure it had happened.

In the Yazidi faith, all Yazidis must make at least one pilgrimage to Lalish in their lifetime, similar to the Hajj in Islam. Part of this pilgrimage included visiting the tomb of Sheikh Adi ibn Musafir, who was considered an incarnation or emanation of the Peacock Angel, the leader of the Seven Angels. Ordinarily, I would not have been permitted to view the tomb as a non-Yazidi, but I must have impressed Govand with my respectful stance towards these things, and Govand had a relationship with the Yazidi people who trusted him to make such determinations, so I was permitted in the room to see the tomb. I was allowed just over the threshold and made to stand in the corner; approaching the actual tomb was forbidden for non-Yazidis, as was taking pictures. I understood and was appreciative just to witness such a holy site in the Yazidi faith. Some residents had come to pay their respects to the Sheikh, and I noticed they walked backwards away from it out of the room, which Govand instructed me to do when we left. It was considered disrespectful, if not blasphemous, to turn your back on the Sheikh's tomb. Some might have found this ridiculous, even Christians, but when you remembered that Peter denied Jesus three times and Jesus called out to God on the cross asking why He had forsaken Him, it was not so demanding of a religious tenet to understand.

Visiting Lalish was an intensely spiritual moment for me. While I wasn't Yazidi (and could never be, according to Yazidi tradition), to see such devout people living at their holiest of places and strictly adhering to their beliefs had a reassuring effect on me that, despite all going on in the world, religions were forces for good. There were still people out there who practised what they preached, despite the recent history of Islamic State, who professed to practise Islam, conducted a genocide against the Yazidis, sold their women and children into slavery (including sex slavery), and displaced more than two-thirds of the global Yazidi population, all in the name of a bastardised interpretation of the Muslim faith. After all of that, prior genocides, and conversion attempts, the Yazidis at Lalish still held firm to their beliefs. That was something to respect and admire.

Despite the intensely spiritual experience, I was glad to have my socks and shoes back on as we headed to our next destination, the Rabban Hormizd Monastery, outside of Alqosh. Like the Mar Mattai Monastery, the Rabban Hormizd Monastery was built into a tall, narrow draw which provided commanding views to the front and protective mountains all around. The modern road leading to it was a series of seven switchbacks, and the Asayish provided security guards at the entrance. While the location of the monastery made strategic sense, it must have been rough going to visit or take up residence there. Walking up the modern, paved road was not something I wanted to do, let alone climbing the draw on foot via dirt paths. One of the guards, however, told us he walked the road several times a day. It was how he got his exercise in being on guard duty all day. Fair enough.

The Rabban Hormizd Monastery was an Assyrian Church of the East and Chaldean Catholic Church monastery founded in the mid-600s by Rabban Hormizd at the urging of the local people outside of Alqosh. Like the Mar Mattai Monastery, the Rabban Hormizd Monastery had been occasionally attacked by the Kurds, and there were many caves in the surrounding hillside where the monks and priests sought refuge from their attackers. Like the manuscripts at the Mar Mattai Monastery, the manuscripts here were looted or destroyed over time by Kurdish attackers, with only some being recovered, copied, and formed into a monastic library.

Unfortunately, such looting did not stop with the Kurds in the 1800s. In the original section of the monastery, a mausoleum containing several tombs, each with a different version of the cross, sat in darkness, the only light being the sun filtering in through the high ceiling and windows. Some of the tombstones were missing, lost in the confusion and chaos from the many wars in Iraq over the last thirty years. While there were many theories about where these tombstones were, the most popular was that a group of United States Marines pillaged them during the 2003 invasion of Iraq. While many would balk at such a notion, it would not have surprised me to learn these stones were encased in some unit display or museum back in the United States. The invasion of Iraq was the Wild West as far as the rules of engagement and standards of behaviour went, and military units of all types and countries liked to keep mementos of their campaigns.

The new sanctuary sat at the monastery's entrance. Like the Mar Mattai Monastery, the original section was built into the rock while later additions protruded outward as large, stone buildings. The new sanctuary was built sometime between 100 and 200 years before, a testament to the difference in how Govand and I measured time. This was around the Civil War in the United States, and we had historians dedicated to studying this part of our distant history. In Kurdistan, this meant the sanctuary was new. In this part of the world, time was measured in centuries, not decades, and "ancient history" had a wholly different meaning.

As it was late in the day, the sun had started its downward journey, making the south-facing monastery glow in the setting sunlight. The grey-ish-brown stones, the green hillside, and the clear blue sky made for some of the most magnificent views of such a building I could have ever imagined, and, again, it was easy to see why this was a serene location to study and reflect on one's religious beliefs.

We stayed in Dohuk for the night, an originally-Christian city in north Iraq and a waypoint for travel to and from Turkey. From a viewpoint high on the ridge, we could see the original part of the city tucked away in an enclave at some foothills while the rest of it sprawled down the valley. Govand told me that most of the expansion I could see had happened in the last twenty years, since the American invasion in 2003. Since the invasion, the city's population had more than doubled. Not exactly the effect one would think twenty years of continuous war would have.

Turning to look in the opposite direction from the city, we could see Mosul Dam Lake in the Nineveh Province of Federal Iraq. This lake had been a point of extreme concern during Islamic State's occupation of the region, as Mosul Dam controlled the flow of substantial swaths of Iraq's water supply, and, if destroyed or completely opened, could result in a wave of flooding that would destroy cities, towns, and countless lives downstream, including Mosul itself, a city of 2,000,000 residents at the time. The battle for the dam lasted three days, after which Kurdish and Iraqi forces secured it for the remainder of the conflict. Despite the dam and the lake being in Federal Iraq, it was the Kurds who played the decisive role in saving it, a fact not forgotten by the Kurdish people, politicians, and armed forces.

One thing about Govand was he was extremely conscious of guest comfort, and Dohuk was no different. He asked where I would rather stay: a tourist hotel with all the amenities or a cheap, local place. After hostel life for so many months, I told him if the cheap place was good enough for him, then it was good enough for me. Good enough was not how I would describe it. It was luxurious! I had the largest bed I had slept in in a long time, a view of the mountains over the city, Wi-Fi, a beautiful bathroom, and a large TV. It cost me 53 USD for two rooms like this, which was unbelievable. It made me wonder what the "nice" place looked like.

Govand's consciousness also extended to food, and I told him whatever was good enough for him was good enough for me. I wasn't too concerned about what we would eat, except that I didn't like seafood. He took me to a local restaurant where we got more than enough food for the two of us for just 10,000 IQD (about 7 USD). The manager was so delighted to have a foreign traveller that he kept bringing us food, and Govand had to tell him we had plenty and I didn't want any to go to waste. Something I had come to be conscious of in my travels through MENA was how much food Americans tended to waste, and I didn't want any food going to waste just to keep me happy. Of course, we left a generous tip for the impeccable service and delicious food.

From there, we walked to a Christmas market in a local square. It was just like a Christmas market back home, just scaled down, with homemade candies and breads, artisan goods, and companies selling promotional adventure packages. I asked Govand about Christmas in Kurdistan, seeing as the vast majority of Kurds were not Christian, Dohuk's Christian roots notwithstanding. He told me they cele-brated Christmas in the same secular manner many in the United States did. Christ-mas was an occasion to spend time with family and the community, reflect on the year gone by, and look forward to the new year. Some families exchanged gifts, Christians celebrated Christ, and Jewish areas observed Hanukah, and some Christ-mas traditions, such as Santa Claus, which started as a religious tenant, were ob-served in their secular manner by all. There wasn't an argument over "Merry Christ-mas" vs "Happy Holidays;" this was a time for celebration, not division. It was a refreshing change from the social conflict back home.

After a fantastic night's sleep and a warm shower, Govand took me to Shahed Café, which he referred to as the Martyr's Tea Shop. Here, we enjoyed a traditional Kurdish breakfast, including flatbreads, fried eggs, cheeses, and dates, served on a communal platter for the two of us. Of course, we also had tea, a staple in the Middle East that I had become accustomed to having every day. Jo even commented once that she could see both of us making traditional Middle Eastern tea once we returned home.

The Shahed Café was a martyr's tea shop for a reason. The walls were adorned with the faces and names of the Kurds who fought and died for Kurdistan in the many conflicts over recent decades. Some fought in the Kurdish rebellion of the 1980s, many died in the Kurdish Revolution of the early 1990s, and some were killed in the fighting against Islamic State. Many of them were older men who were no strangers to war and had spent their lives defending the Kurdish people and seeking an independent Kurdistan. Some were young men who felt the call of duty and likely would have spent their lives serving had they not met an early end on the battlefield. On the shelves around the photos, the café had memorabilia from these martyrs, including uniforms, medals, and weapons they had carried in defence of Kurdistan, most of it on loan from the families who wanted their loved one's sacrifice remembered. It was a solemn place to eat breakfast, I thought, but it was an essential stop in understanding the Kurdish fight for independence and their general right to live in a region where many of their neighbours wanted them gone.

The second day of the tour was dedicated to Kurdistan's non-religious history. As I said before, this region measured time in centuries, not decades, and many of those centuries were besieged by war or the threat of war. It was fitting, then, that our first stop was one of Saddam Hussein's former mountain palaces. It was located on the road to Amedi, and protected by a concrete wall which was covered in murals of past wars. Knowing Saddam Hussein, it didn't surprise me that he wanted his palace security walls portraying the successes of his military forces. One of the murals depicted a soldier with a shoulder-fired missile taking down a fighter jet. Curious which battle this depicted, I asked Govand who the soldier was shooting down. That was when he corrected my assumption. "Those are Peshmerga shooting down Saddam's planes," he told me, "This is a Peshmerga headquarters now." Well, then. To the victor goes the spoils. He tried to get us inside to see the palace, but the Peshmerga guards wouldn't let us in. Govand had encouraged me to try to take surreptitious photos while he talked to the guard, but discretion was the better part of valour. Besides, somethings were for my eyes only; not everyone back home needed to see pictures of everything.

From there, we made our way to Amedi, a town on top of a mesa with distant views in all directions and one road leading into the city. There was evidence of the location's occupation as far back as the 3000s BC, and it changed hands many times as empires came and went over the next 5,000 years. While the Kurds had lived in Amedi since sometime in the 1100s, the first indication of a level of self-rule over Amedi was in the late 1300s and lasted until the late 1800s. While not quite a kingdom, as many Kurds claimed, it was still an impressive run of semi-autonomy in a region of constant conflict.

The city was self-contained and self-sufficient, as many localities in Iraqi Kurdistan were. It had long since lost its strategic military importance despite its ability to serve as a stronghold should the need arise. The impressive part of the visit to Amedi were the views from the mountains just to the west. There was a large sign bearing Kurdistan's orange, white, and green flag and a viewing area to take in the breathtaking landscape with the mesa city in the foreground. There was a firepit near where we parked; it was easy to see why someone might want to build a fire and spend an evening enjoying time with friends with this scenery.

Govand recorded videos while I took pictures. He was building the Iraqi Kurdistan Guide Instagram page, and advertising these views did wonders. In the months and years following my visit, I would smile whenever I saw him post a new video, knowing that I had been exactly where he made the recording in his beautiful country.

With plenty of pictures in hand, we made our way to Akre. This wasn't on our original itinerary, but we had plenty of time, and Govand wanted to introduce me to some Kurdish traditions and unique food in the city. Who was I to say no to unique food?

Like Dohuk, Akre had undergone a large expansion after the 2003 invasion. Pulling into town, we drove on major highways, passing modern stores, banks, and even a technical college which would have fit right in back home. Also, like Dohuk, the old city was tucked away into the hillside with narrow streets which had clearly been around far longer than the cars that drove them, houses built on footpaths, and a scenic overlook on top of Sare Gri, an adjacent hill with historic cemeteries on either side.

For lunch, Govand took me to Xanedan Café & Restaurant, where we had some of the best food I had ever eaten. Govand asked which local dish I would prefer: Kufta or Qaliyah? Both sounded great, so we ordered both and shared. Qaliyah was a sort of meat stew which tasted as good as it looked, and I knew I would have to try to make it back home. While the Qaliyah was delicious, Kufta in Akre was the specialty dish. Kufta wasn't unique to Kurdistan. It was all over Egypt, as it was essentially meat wrapped in a pastry casing and boiled in tomato sauce. In Akre, however, they boiled it in yogurt, something not even the rest of Kurdistan did. I was sceptical about how plain yogurt could enhance a meal, but after trying it, I was hooked. If only I had the culinary expertise to make this stuff for my family!

To cap off our second day, Govand led me up Serê Kelê, the hill into which the old city was built. Govand explained that during the Kurdish New Year (called Newroz), Kurds from all over the world came to Akre to partake in the celebrations, which included climbing Serê Kelê with lighted torches as a symbol of the passing of the "dark season," i.e., winter, to the "light season," i.e., spring. Newroz, which was tied to the spring Equinox, was just around the corner, and I would only miss it by a couple of months.

I fell asleep on our way back to Erbil. It wasn't that I had done a lot of walking during these two days, but I the self-induced stress of my first few days had caught up with me after these stress-free days with Govand. I kept my hotel room in Erbil for the week, so I didn't have to bother checking in again or unpacking my entire backpack. After a fried chicken dinner from a local Kurdish restaurant (again, at the concierge's recommendation), I showered and collapsed into bed.

The final day of the tour was dedicated to the Hamilton Road, a feat of civil engineering from the late 1920s that connected Erbil in Iraqi Kurdistan with Iran. Archibold Hamilton was specially selected as the lead engineer based on his expertise and experience with the Admiralty during the First World War. He chronicled his journey in his book *Road Through Kurdistan: Travels in Iraq*, and Govand used the book as a reference for several stops along the way.

Admittedly, the Hamilton Road was not very interesting from a historical or cultural perspective. As the book's title suggested, it was a road through Kurdistan. Its importance notwithstanding, a road was a road, and me not being an engineer or Kurdish historian, I couldn't fully appreciate the gravity of Hamilton's accomplishments.

Even so, it was a wonderfully scenic drive once we got out of Erbil. Driving up the Masif Way (a series of switchbacks along the road to Rwanduz), I was treated to spectacular views of the plains which led towards Nineveh. Granted, Govand was driving like a bat out of Hell up the switchbacks (which, in Kurdistan, really just meant he was driving), so it was hard to get good photos, but, as with Saddam's palace, some things were just for me.

Our first scenic stop was the Geli Ali Bag waterfall. It was the cold season, so no one was there, and I could get close for pictures. In the summer months, the Geli Ali Bag waterfall was a vacation spot for Iraqis across the country. According to Govand, they dammed it up to create a pool-like area for people to cool off in the oppressive Middle Eastern sun. As a testament to its reputation and popularity in Iraq, it was featured on the back of the 5,000 IQD note, and I took a picture with one in front of the waterfall.

Not much farther from the waterfall was the last remaining portion of the original Hamilton Road. It wound around the right side of the Rwanduz river (when traveling toward Rwanduz), whereas the new highway, which was only several years old, ran along the left side. The old section of the road was carved into and out of the rocky mountainside. Because the water had cut a deep ravine, there wasn't a bank to fortify, so Hamilton and his tribal workers had to carve a road out of the mountain. In some spots, this was by flattening parts of the cliff, but in others, it was by blasting away the mountain and taking the road under the new overhangs. Even though I wasn't an engineer, I was impressed with the determination it must have required to take on the mountain like that. I figured this must have been the most challenging part of building the road, but Govand told me it wasn't and that we would see the most challenging part at our next stop.

The next stop was Rwanduz. Like Amedi, Rwanduz was built on a strategically defensible rock formation. Instead of a mesa, it was built between two gorges, created by the fork where the Rwanduz river met the Akoyan river and backstopped by Korek Mountain. At the bridge across the first gorge stood a bust dedicated to Hamilton. Even though the Kurds weren't particularly proud of their rule by the British, it was undeniable that his achievement provided economic opportunities that otherwise would never have been attainable.

The views of the gorge were the most amazing I had seen yet on my travels. It was winter, so the grass was green, and the recent rains made the canyon glisten in the sunlight. It looked like it would be great hiking; Govand confirmed it was, but not at this time of year as it would be too slippery to traverse safely.

It was this part of the Hamilton Road that Hamilton described as his most challenging. Crossing the gorges at Rwanduz caused innumerable problems and required innovative engineering to cross successfully. I found this hard to believe, as the bridge across the first gorge was no more than ten metres, but, again, I wasn't an engineer, and Hamilton didn't have the technology available to him that we have today. Indeed, the original bridge had since been replaced with a more modern one; there was no need to risk the safety of modern vehicles with an old bridge.

If I thought the views from inside the gorge were beautiful, they had nothing on the views from the cliffs on the outskirts of the city. I felt like I was in an IMAX film set on the cliffs of Victoria Falls! I didn't know it then, but this was the deepest gorge in the Middle East, with parts extending down 300 metres. It was a sheer rock drop-off from the city to the halfway point where the rock met grass. Even then, it was a steep slope down to the magnificent river, which had carved this gorge over timescales I couldn't possibly fathom. When I saw the photo Govand took of me standing on the precipice, I instantly knew that it would be the cover for this book.

We drove through Rwanduz out the back road, which rose to the ridge that looked down upon Hamilton Road and the surrounding areas to the Bekhal Water-falls. These were much bigger than the Geli Ali Bag, and cafés and shops traced the falls up the hill from which they came. The area around the pool at the bottom was built up, and I could best describe it as the Kurdish answer to the Riverwalk in San Antonio. It was the low season, so it wasn't crowded like it would be in the spring and summer, but there were still many people about. It was easy to picture the scene in the peak season, with the roaring falls, kids playing in the overflow areas, and Kurds, Arabs, Yazidis, and more from across Iraq enjoying tea and dinner on a week-end getaway from the dirt deserts of Federal Iraq. The number of resort-style hotels we had seen on the way over indicated this place became busy with regional travel-lers.

It was time to start making our way back to Erbil, so we continued down the road that took us along the ridgeline, stopping at a scenic outlook to enjoy the breath-taking views. With the sun behind the mountain, it was shady and cool as I surveyed the Road Through Kurdistan down below. These were the views I was used to when I lived in Colorado. I told Govand that while I would never get my dad to visit Iraq, if he did, we could have given him a lawn chair and the phonetic spellings of things to order at the small food cart, dropped him off in the morning, gone about our busi-ness, and he would still be marvelling at the beautiful Kurdish mountains when we came back through that evening.

Back in Erbil, Govand and I said our goodbyes. He was off on another tour the next day, but we traded contact info and social media handles to stay in touch. Over the next several months, I watched his Instagram presence grow, and travellers from all over the world flowed through the same sites I visited these past three days. Like me, I hoped they became comfortable in Iraqi Kurdistan and took their stories home to dispel many myths and overexaggerations about Iraq we heard in the West.

The next day was an easy one. I walked around town a bit, but mostly, I stayed at the hotel to rest up for my time in Turkey. I had an ambitious, fast-paced archae-ological expedition planned and would need plenty of energy.

✳   ✳   ✳

The Attack (in Syria)

Two in the morning came early the day of my departure. It was New Year's Eve, the halfway point in my year around the world, and I was headed to Istanbul. The concierge arranged for a taxi to take me to the airport at 02h30 for my 06h30 flight. Even though Erbil International Airport was small, the standard for international flights was to arrive three hours early, and Iraqi Kurdistan was no exception. Given there was a Coalition airbase sprawling out from the civilian airport, we needed to leave early so I could pass through all of the requisite joint Iraqi-Coalition security procedures (which I will not describe here for what I would hope are obvious reasons). By 03h30, I was checked in for my flight and offered an aisle seat in an exit row. It wasn't a long flight, but it was still a great way to kick off my time in Turkey.

Then, the day went south. From the time it took me to walk from the check-in desk, through customs and the American-style security checkpoint, and arrive at my gate, my flight was cancelled. The plane wasn't even in the country. The gate agents directed everyone back through the customs checkpoint to have our exit stamps invalidated, collect our luggage, and await further instructions. Fortunately, the security forces of the Middle East were bloated, and there were always a bunch of guys sitting around doing nothing, so they were conscripted into processing our visa invalidations. Within another ten minutes, I was back where I started the week: the cashpoint at the exit to the taxi rank.

To talk with the Turkish Airlines customer service desk, I had to re-enter the airport through the security checkpoint at the main entrance (a common feature of airports all across the region), which, while smooth, ended with me somehow breaking my watch. On the other side, the Turkish Airlines desk had no real information. They told us we could come back to try to get on the 14h30 flight and that they would pay for a taxi to take us back to our original hotels, for which they would also pay for the day. I wasn't one to take my chances with flying standby, and I had already gone through all those security procedures to get to the airport, so I decided to stay there. I had one hour of free Wi-Fi, my Kindle, a travel pillow, and the airport had a coffee shop. I would be fine, and it would ensure that I was the first one in the queue to get on that next flight.

While all this was going on, someone I knew texted me about an ongoing attack in Syria. It was unknown who was conducting the attack, but it was pretty substantial, and there were initial reports of casualties. My friend told me just for my awareness, as sometimes attacks in one area generated attacks in another. This entire week in Kurdistan, this wouldn't have bothered me, as I wasn't near the Coalition, but at this exact moment, the Coalition wasn't that far away. I still wasn't worried, but it was something to be aware of should rockets or missiles head our way.

While deciding where to park myself for the next few hours, I met a dual-Iraqi-Iranian citizen and his wife who were moving to Turkey. He had a friend on the flight from Istanbul to Erbil that was supposed to provide our plane. According to his friend, the flight had been turned around shortly after take-off and was returning to Istanbul. At that moment, I got the text telling me Coalition aircraft had been called in. This was more substantial of an attack than I had anticipated, but it explained why the flight had been turned around: the airspace was closed. I knew this was common during airstrikes, and the military worked closely with the air traffic controllers and airlines regarding these sorts of things. As annoyed as I was, I was perfectly content not to be in the same airspace as an airstrike raining holy Hell down upon the enemy. They say "big sky, little bullet," but better safe than sorry.

It was nighttime back home, so while I waited at the airport, I called my dad to give him an update. He was initially concerned, but the attack was hundreds of kilometres away, and I was on the same airbase as the Coalition, so his concern quickly dissipated. Then it was naptime at the airport, something I was no stranger to over the years.

Ultimately, we all ended up in Turkey late that evening without issue. The attack was defeated, the airspace was reopened, and I was exhausted. I was ready to be at the hostel and fall into a deep sleep without an alarm.

Reflecting on Iraq

Security precautions. I wanted to visit Iraq for a long time, especially Kurdistan, as a tourist, but I knew that such an excursion could be dangerous. I had been in far worse situations in the military, but at least then I had my unit around me. As a tourist in Iraq, it was just me, alone, without a local SIM card, no knowledge of the language, and in a land where the struggle for Iraq's future between Islamic State, Iraqi nationalists, and Iran was heating up (to say nothing of the Kurdish independence movement or the tribal forces down south which militantly defended their autonomy from federal interference from Baghdad). I needed to take some general security precautions to be on the safe side of things. Even if they ultimately would end up being unnecessary, as a first-time, solo, American traveller who once deployed there for the military, I needed to be careful.

I already mentioned being a "grey man," a term used for someone who dresses and acts in a manner to not draw attention to themselves. I didn't disguise myself as a Kurd; that would never have passed and only would have drawn suspicion. Instead, I tried to look normal. Some Coalition contractors lived in town, so no one would think anything of me as long as I looked normal. This meant wearing pants, hiking boots (versus my usual high-top boots), a solid-coloured shirt, and no hat. When it was windy, I donned my rain jacket. It was as normal as I could look without buying new clothes or going overboard.

I also let key people know where I was. These people knew who to call and what to tell them should I get in trouble. My old colleague serving as a first sergeant was one of those people. I texted him a few times a day to give him an update, and I later found out he talked to his superiors about his wild former boss who was traipsing around the region in case I got into a tight spot. Jo was another person I told, because she could deal with my family and the State Department. I also knew a liaison at the embassy in Baghdad, whom I had served with in the Coalition several years before. He knew I was there, and he wanted me to keep him posted, as there was a Diplomatic Security Service contingent in Erbil he could contact if necessary. All of this was highly unlikely to be necessary, but, again, discretion was the better part of valour.

If I were to return to Kurdistan again, I wouldn't bother too much with most of this as long as the security situation remained stable. I would still let people know where I was when I could, but contacting the Coalition and embassy, obfuscating things to my friends and family back home, and dressing down weren't necessary. That said, if I had to do it all over again, I wouldn't have changed my actions because I had no idea what I was getting into.

Money. Despite its twenty-year long struggle with transnational terrorism and decades-longer rule by a ruthless dictator, Iraq had not been locked out of the United States' banking system. Getting money from the cashpoints was easy as long as the bank knew it was me.

That said, the exchange rate in Iraq was a hot political and economic issue. The Central Bank of Iraq set the exchange rate at around 1312 IQD to 1 USD. At the cashpoints, that was the rate I received, and on the one occasion I paid with a credit card (at the hotel), that was the rate my credit card company charged. However, the business rates varied day-to-day, hovering around 1550 IQD to 1 USD. This meant any money I spent with a card, whether it be from pulling money out at the cashpoint or swiping my card at the hotel, was worth less than had I exchanged it at a money exchange. Indeed, the hotel manager explained this to me when I handed him my credit card, and he encouraged me to bring American dollars on my next visit to get the correct exchange rate.

Why the difference? In the public's estimation, the Central Bank of Iraq's rate was a political tool that wasn't grounded in reality. The public rate was based on the Kurdish and Iraqi businessmen that dealt in American dollars. Whatever rate they set for their business transactions was what the public used. This may seem exploitative to the average American, but it made logical sense. In Iraq, the federal government's unfavourable rating was seventy-seven percent during my visit, and it had generally not dipped below seventy percent (with rare, occasional exceptions) since 1990, while businesses kept the economy going, goods and services flowing, and people employed. It made sense, then, that whatever they claimed the exchange rate to be was what it was. Many blamed the Central Bank of Iraq's insistence on keeping the rate artificially low for the steady inflation of the IQD against the USD in the business world.

Homelessness. There was a distinct lack of homelessness in Kurdistan, and I do mean distinct. I didn't see beggars or people sleeping on cardboard boxes. What I did see were people of all ages hustling to bring in enough money to make ends meet. In Kurdistan, everyone in the family played a role, including the children, which was on full display at the markets. The old women were shopping for produce while young boys with orange wheelbarrows offered to carry their loads. I knew from my prior time in the region that if you could afford such a service, you used it. It wasn't considered charity or a luxury but a public duty to help others. These old women and children were no exception.

I made it a point to ask Govand about this. His response was, "We don't have any." Sure, there was the occasional bum who had given up on work and whose family had failed him, but by and large, everyone took care of everyone, and

215

everyone (especially men) worked. The only reason not to work was because you were either too old or disabled. In those cases, the family took them in and provided for them. In their culture, it was how things were.

Similarly, theft, robbery, and burglary were rare in Kurdistan. It simply wasn't their culture, and Govand told me that he could leave his car on the side of the road with the key in the cup holder all day, and no one would touch it. Of course, some opportunists bucked the system, and the police and Asayish aggressively pursued these offenders. "Better the police find you than the Asayish," Govand told me. I guess that was a deterrent all in itself.

"It doesn't matter; I am Kurdish." The Kurds have lived in the mountains for centuries, and they have fought and died for their freedom for almost as long, including resisting initial Christian evangelical incursions into their lands. As time went by, though, religion faded as a substantial dividing factor. The Kurdish people practised all faiths, from Yazidism to the Abrahamic faiths to Baha'i, but they long ago recognised that their enemies were not their fellow Kurds who practiced a different religion. To be sure, there were Christian communities and Jewish communities, but these were secondary identities to being Kurdish. Govand told me that he had friends and people he had known his entire life whose religious affiliation he never knew. One time, at a shop, he asked the owner what he was simply out of curiosity. The owner's response remained with me: "It doesn't matter; I am Kurdish." The message was loud and clear. There were plenty of things to divide us, especially religion, but, at least for the Kurdish people, there were concerns and desires that transcended religious differences. If they fought amongst or divided themselves over religion, they would never attain social and political unity, and the dream of having a free and independent Kurdish nation would never be achieved.

"What is next for Iraq?" Govand asked me this towards the end of our second day. During our time together, we had deep discussions about Iraq's history. Govand was interested in the perspective of someone who had served in the American military in Iraq, and I was interested in the perspective of someone who lived through the invasion. My response was that, for the first time in three decades, Iraq was relatively stable. The country was one of the most historically important countries in the world, the cradle of civilisation, and home to many important scenes from the Bible. Ancient Mesopotamia ran straight down the centre of the country, through the Fertile Crescent, and the Tigris and Euphrates were two of the four rivers that flowed from the Garden of Eden. I hoped this stability would last and Iraq's tourism industry would begin to flourish. I didn't want foreign travellers coming in and changing the country, but I wanted people to be able to see the places which were so fundamental in understanding the Abrahamic faiths and the history of the world.

Govand liked my answer and hoped I was right. I asked what he thought was next for Iraq. He stared out the windshield as he thought. Without taking his eyes off the road, he told me, "Since I was born, there have been five wars in Iraq: the Kurdish rebellion, the 1990s civil war, the American invasion, the 2000s civil war, and the war against ISIS. I am not sure what is next for Iraq, but I am sure it will involve war." It was a sobering moment between two people on opposite sides of the conflict. I served in one of those wars, but he lived through all five. Unfortunately, I had to agree with him. Unless something fundamental changed in the region, Iraq's relative peace would likely be short-lived.

Chapter Sixteen

Turkey: A Historical Paradise

I knew I wanted to go to Istanbul from the beginning. It was one of the few places on my list of "must-sees" when Jo and I initially mapped out our trip. When looking at Jordan and Iraq, flights to Turkey made logical sense at a great price, so it fit into my plans nicely. After talking with Tahli, I turned my adventure through Turkey into an archaeological tour. Turkey was one of those countries whose individual history was deeply intertwined with all of humanity. Some people tried to warn me off going because of the ongoing anti-Israel protests popping up across the world, but Turkey was a big country. My experience thus far had proved that as much as these countries and their citizens didn't like Israel, they hated losing Western tourism dollars more, so I threw everyone else's cautions to the wind and spent the first three weeks of the new year traveling from one place in history to the next. Besides, I had to leave Iraq anyway, and there were only so many options out of Erbil.

Istanbul

By the time my flight landed, I cleared customs, and collected my bags, it was coming up on 18h30, and I was exhausted. My nap at the Erbil airport wasn't great, and the two Iraqi men sitting next to me drank mini-bottles of whiskey (which they illegally brought on the plane themselves), keeping me from sleeping on the plane. I was also hungry. Options for lunch at the airport in Erbil weren't exactly plentiful, so I caved and ate some fast food at the airport before heading to my hostel in the city centre.

The taxi from the Sabiha Gökçen International Airport wasn't expensive, which was nice, but the drive took an hour and a half. There were two commercial airports for Istanbul. tThe main airport, called Istanbul Airport, was on the northwest side of town, about a forty-minute drive from the hostel; it was also connected via the city's metro system. The other airport, Sabiha Gökçen International Airport, was outside the city to the east. This was the "budget" airport, where regional flights and budget airlines primarily operated. That would explain the non-refundable 100 EUR ticket with a cancellation fee from Erbil rather than the several hundred Euro tickets directly into the main airport. Such was the life of a budget traveller.

My driver could tell I was exhausted; I could barely keep my eyes open as we wound ourselves out of the airport roads and towards the highway. Through a translation app, he told me it would be over an hour until we arrived at the hostel, so I could sleep if I wanted to, and he would wake me once we arrived. Under normal circumstances, there was no way I would sleep in a taxi, both because some drivers couldn't be trusted not to steal your stuff and because I was excited to see my new destination. On this occasion, I made an exception. The driver seemed trustworthy enough, and I passed out against the window. Two hours later, I was showered and collapsing into my bed at Lola Backpackers Hostel.

In Egypt, Tahli, Peta, and Gav told me I would need at least a week to explore Istanbul, which would likely not be enough to get the full experience. Istanbul was considered Europe's largest city (Turkey was considered part of Europe when it was convenient for the Turks and the Europeans), divided in half between the European side to the west of the old Byzantine city walls and the Middle Eastern side to the east. Some people mistakenly referred to the two sides as the Christian and Muslim sides, but Istanbul was predominantly Muslim (as was most of Turkey), and this misnomer inaccurately reflected the people who lived there. While tens of thousands of Christians lived in Istanbul, that was a small fraction of the more than 15,000,000 people who called the city home.

I did some sightseeing on my first day in Istanbul. I needed to get used to being back in a Westernised city. Even though Erbil had modern additions, it was still a standard city in MENA, especially in the city centre. Add that to the tour where we purposely went to centuries-old sites, and it had been just over two months since Jo and I left London (and Europe) behind. Despite its long history, Istanbul was relatively modern, especially in the city centre, and it took most of the day to adjust mentally to wandering the streets amongst tourists, locals, and businessmen alike. Admittedly, I struggled with the adjustment, just like when I returned to the United States after my deployments to Africa and Iraq. Fortunately, I had time to acclimatise this time around.

I toured around town, taking photos of the great mosques in the city, perusing Turkish delight shops, and generally enjoying a long walk on a cloudy day. In my wanderings, I stumbled upon an art exhibition called "Gazan Child." It was dedicated to the children whose lives had come to a tragic end during the ongoing conflict in Gaza. Despite my agreement with Israel that Hamas must go, it was heartbreaking to know the many innocent child deaths that goal entailed. While I didn't believe Israel was deliberately targeting children, the densely-packed nature of Gaza meant their deaths as collateral damage were almost unavoidable, maybe even inevitable. While these artists didn't take the wider conflict, strategic positioning, or military tactical details into account, their focus on the children certainly was cause for reflection on the significant impact of war. Hamas didn't care about the bicycles that lay in the rubble any more than the Israelis cared about the backpacks with their straps torn off.

A particularly stirring and illuminating exhibition was the enlarged scans of drawings from Gazan children depicting their reality. I took only a few photos, because I wanted to respect the artists' and the exhibitions' emotional impact on others. One of these photos depicted a Palestinian flag flying from a barren tree with the sea and mountains in the background and Israeli fighter jets overhead. Another de-picted Israeli tanks firing on Palestinian civilians and ambulances. While I knew this in my head to be a common propaganda point for Hamas, it clearly showed the child's perception of the world around them, something that could not be discounted as lifelong traumas born in their infancy. Of course, some of the drawings depicted the aspiration of Palestinian victory over and conquering of Israel, something they were taught in schools as the only solution to the question of Palestinian sovereignty in their Hamas-sponsored/-controlled education. I was sure the activists intended the totality of the display to be an anti-Israel message, but the combination of the heart-breaking childhood experiences with what I knew to be Hamas propaganda dimin-ished how seriously I took their message. That may sound cruel or inhumane, but I worked in the counterterrorism world for far too long to overlook the artists' inten-tions and political biases.

I left the exhibit contemplating the conflict in Gaza and continued to think about it as I strolled through a nearby park. The conflict was a dominant social factor in my travels in MENA, and the news was inundated with mass protests in Western capitals (indeed, there would be a 10,000-person protest in Istanbul during my time there). Part of my leaving my security firm and old life behind was to get away from all of this terrorism-related stuff; my life had for too long been dominated by the threat and politics of terrorists across the world, and it had taken its toll on me men-tally, emotionally, and spiritually. Until October 7th, I managed to avoid nearly all influence from and interaction with the news. I lived in ignorant bliss for months, finally gaining solid control over myself and my future away from the world of ter-rorism, but now it was everywhere I went. I wished it would all go back from whence it came; I wanted to be far away from all of that, not wandering into politically-motivated art exhibitions, seeing "Terorist Israil" spraypainted everywhere, and large Palestinian flags flown between buildings by people who had little-to-no grasp on the minutia of what was going on.

I continued contemplating these thoughts through lunch and ultimately wan-dered into a local mosque. This was the first time I would ever enter a mosque as a solo traveller (apart from the tours in Morocco and with Govand in Iraq), and I didn't quite know what to expect. I removed my shoes, silenced my phone, and walked onto the carpet in the large, open worship hall. I made it a point to stand to the side, as I didn't want to interrupt anyone who may be praying, studying, or worshipping, and it was bad form (and in some cultures disrespectful) to stand in front of those who directed their prayers towards Mecca.

There was a spiritual aura about the mosque, something I noticed in some of the cathedrals of Europe as well. A scene from the Christian film *War Room* came to mind; someone had been praying in that room. The room had a reverence, respect, and spirituality to it as men came and went (women had a separate entrance and prayer area, per Islamic tradition dating back to the Prophet Muhammed). While I would not dream of praying to God as a Christian in a mosque, both out of respect for my own religion and theirs, that didn't mean I couldn't reflect on the religion's role in the world and my life. Some men sat in corners studying the Qur'an, some lay prostrated deep in contemplation and prayer, while others came and went, com-pleting their obligatory prayers before moving on with their day. After a long while of self-reflection and observations, it was time for midday prayers, so I returned to the city.

I immediately walked to the Hagia Triada Greek Orthodox Church, which was built in the late 1870s. Inside were beautiful, polished stone floors and columns, and the altar at the front of the church looked much like the one I had seen in Trieste, Italy, several months before. While the architecture was neo-Baroque, I couldn't help but feel there were heavy Mudejar influences due to the proximity to the Islamic influence of the Middle East. I wasn't familiar with Greek Orthodox practices or traditions, so the symbolism contained in the art which adorned the space between windows and the bannisters around the upper galleries was lost on me, but that didn't mean I couldn't appreciate it for its apparent importance to the Greek Orthodox community (except for the Christmas tree and Nativity out front from the recent holiday; those I knew).

After a bit more sightseeing, I headed back to the hostel. I had walked a lot that day and looked forward to some Turkish street food. I teamed up with a guy named Jules, an American studying and working remotely in Europe, who was well-travelled for his age. Jules had a rule that he only ate local foods while travelling and had a list of dishes he wanted to try before returning to his studies. I, on the other hand, knew nothing of local cuisine, so I followed his lead as he searched the streets for a local kebab place. Jules' logic was to find a place that looked good in person, then check Google for reviews. To him, the fewer reviews, the better; that meant it wasn't a touristy place. I could see the logic, even if it wasn't logic I would abide by myself, as we ate cheap kebabs on the side of a busy street. The kebabs came with Aryan, a yogurt drink found across Turkey. I liked yogurt, but it didn't look appetising, so I passed mine off to Jules. The combination of yogurt and meat didn't sound logical to me.

I decided on my second day in Istanbul to visit the famous mosques. They cost money to enter, were high-traffic tourist destinations, and long queues formed throughout the day. I had seen them the day before, and, not being someone with the patience or desire to wait in large crowds, I opted to arrive at the mosques early. One of the great pieces of travel advice was to show up early or late, not at convenient hours, for popular attractions, as most tourists liked to have a leisurely morning, late breakfast, and timely dinners.

I visited the Hagia Sophia Grand Mosque first. It was indeed grand, with tall spires and a massive, domed structure that dominated the skyline. Under this dome, I was sure, was the main worship sanctuary, with the other windows and rooms leading to prayer rooms, the women's gallery, and offices. The grounds contained remnants of times gone by, including columns, tombs, and stone Christian relics. Hagia Sophia was originally a Christian church built in the late 340s by the Romans, with expansions and renovations leading to its current form occurring in subsequent centuries. In the 1400s, when the Ottomans conquered Constantinople, the church became a mosque, a role it served for nearly 500 years before being converted to a museum in the 20th Century. It wasn't until 2018 that it reverted to service as a mosque again. I learned none of this on-site. Maybe I would have had I hired a guide, but I found that doubtful. I was no stranger to selective histories in this part of the world, especially when it came to religious differences. Had I known this history at the time, I probably wouldn't have appreciated the architecture and grandiosity of this place of worship in the moment, as I would have been too focused on the narrative rather than the aura of the moment.

Inside, the mosque was more beautiful than I could have imagined. The Hassan II Mosque in Casablanca was grandiose and intricate, but it was intended to be that way from its inception. Hagia Sophia was a converted church, and its architectural elements integrated the Roman and Byzantine construction with Islamic decor. Naturally, any paintings or depictions of the Bible had been plastered or painted over; Muslims did not believe in depicting religious scenes in art. The domes were painted using the Mudejar style of Islamic art with arches, geometric shapes, and Arabic writing bringing a sophisticated simplicity to the interior. The entirety of the worship area was covered in a green carpet (green being the colour of Paradise, nature, and supposedly Muhammed's favourite colour). Everyone was barefoot or wearing socks, as shoes were considered unclean, and I wondered how long it had been since shoes had touched the carpet. Maybe some unknowing tourist got past security with their shoes on the day before, or maybe it had been 500 years since Constantinople fell to the Ottomans.

I sat in a corner and people-watched for a few minutes as I took in the atmosphere. Groups gathered around English-speaking tour guides, local men partook in their daily prayers and reflection, and cameras and phones pointed towards the ceiling. I took a few snapshots when I arrived, but I mainly wanted to bask in the experience of visiting an active holy site where people had been worshipping in some way or another for two millennia. I didn't want to be the guy that came, took pictures, and went home to talk about how great it was without truly experiencing what I saw.

After a while, I departed for the Blue Mosque, directly across the park from Hagia Sophia. The Blue Mosque was built in the early 1600s, over 1,000 years after its partner across the park. Like Hagia Sophia, its minarets dominated the skyline, and its dome was centred between them. Officially, the mosque was called the Sultan Ahmed Mosque, but its blue dome and predominantly blue interior gave rise to its more popular nickname. I wasn't able to visit the inside of the Blue Mosque. Because I had spent the early morning at Hagia Sophia, the queue to enter the Blue Mosque was long, wrapping around the corner of the adjacent courtyard. I didn't want to waste my time in Istanbul waiting in queues. Besides, the midday prayer time was approaching, and there was little chance I would be able to enter the mosque for more than a few minutes before all tourists were made to leave, so I explored the beautiful courtyard which contained the original ablution fountain before heading off for lunch (which consisted of tavuk shish, or chicken kebabs, pita bread, rice, and a delicious, spicy sauce whose name I never learned).

I intended to visit the Tokapi palace after lunch, but it cost 55 USD to enter, which was far more than my daily budget allowed and, frankly, far more than I was willing to pay. Despite the palace's historic and artistic value, I wasn't willing to pay that much for a few hours in a place where I didn't have a special connection or interest. Nonetheless, I visited the grounds and the adjacent park just outside its walls, both of which were open to the public, where I discovered the Istanbul Museum of the History of Science and Technology of Islam.

As its name suggested, this museum was dedicated to Islam's intersection with science and technology. It was well-established in the scientific community that Islamic scholars had an enormous understanding of the universe, physics, mathematics, and more, but much of the knowledge, manuscripts, and writings were lost to time, in no small part due to religious conflicts and beliefs. I had recently finished a book titled *The Bad-Ass Librarians of Timbuktu,* which told the riveting tale of evacuating centuries- and millennia-old manuscripts out of Islamic State's and al-Qa'ida's territory after they conquered much of Mali, and I was interested to see what this museum had to offer.

It was an interesting museum, with astrolabes, surprisingly-accurate globes from before the age of exploration, wartime technology, including weapons and seafaring vessels, and reproductions of tools using the methods and materials described in the manuscripts. While it could get repetitive (I could only look at so many astrolabes before getting the point), it was well worth the 300 Turkish Lira (TRY) (about 10 EUR) for the entrance ticket. Or it would have been, had an American guy not been filming his elementary school daughter exploring the museum using a high-dollar camera setup and staged scenes for YouTube. I didn't begrudge YouTubers (as someone who posted videos for my family back home), but I took issue when they interfered with the general public or used their young children to make money. I had to breeze through parts of the museum to stay ahead of them, as the father had zero concern for anyone else (i.e., me) or their museum experience.

After a few days of exploring the main part of the city centre, it was time to strike out in search of Istanbul's Byzantine history. The Walls of Constantinople still stood around the city, and exploring them was a good way to spend a day outside the busy tourist areas. The main parts of the preserved walls were far from my hostel, about ninety minutes by foot, so I grabbed breakfast at a shop around the corner, stopped for some coffee, and put it in two-foot drive around 09h30. I could have taken public transport, but I wanted to see what the city was like between the major attractions.

Along the way, I came across the Fatih Social Complex. This complex, built just after the Ottoman conquering of Constantinople, included a mosque, a library, a medical clinic, a bath, and more. The Fatih Mosque was built in 1767 in a more modern style than the rest of the complex. While I didn't explore the rest of the complex (it was closed to visitors, as parts of it were still in use), the mosque was beautiful. It had green gardens and fountains for locals to gather and children to play. Unlike Hagia Sophia and the Blue Mosque, there weren't hordes of tourists queued for 100 metres to enter. I simply walked up, took off my shoes, and entered.

The Fatih Mosque was more typical of your neighbourhood mosque. The sanctuary was a large, open, carpeted area which was occupied by children playing football when prayers were not underway. An attendant was present to preserve the traditions and sanctity of the mosque against sacrilege (namely by ensuring women wore headscarves, people took off their shoes, and no blasphemous activity was occurring), but this was a community centre in the off-time. Families trusted their children to play at the mosque, and I couldn't help but think of how things were back in the United States, where churches were increasingly becoming fortresses with automatic locking doors, bullet-resistant windows, and state-of-the-art security systems.

I couldn't name the last time I walked into a sanctuary unannounced and found it unlocked back home. And I was supposedly in the land where terrorism was more likely! I respected the Turks for keeping their mosques open to the public and the trust and confidence the public had in mosque officials to safeguard their children.

Like most churches and cathedrals, most mosques had a stand for reading and conversion materials, and the Fatish Mosque was no different. They had Islam 101 books in many different languages, including English, Spanish, French, Russian, and German. I picked one up that discussed how we knew Islam to be the one true faith from a historical and scientific perspective. I wasn't interested in converting. I was confident enough in my own faith not to be swayed by a single booklet, especially after my professional experiences with the Muslim faith. Still, I was interested in learning about and understanding Islam at a deeper level for my own edification. I read the booklet over the next week or so, and I found it wholly unconvincing, with logical leaps, debunked scientific claims, and quotes from world leaders I knew to be untrustworthy as their evidence. I couldn't use this booklet to condemn another faith; they just didn't win me over.

After a long while at the Fatih Social Complex, I stopped for some tavuk shish before continuing on my way to discover Byzantine Constantinople. My next stop was the Palace of the Porphyrogenitus, a museum dedicated to the anthropological history of the area built into the remaining façade of a Byzantine palace from the 1200s. The museum portion, while a nice facility, wasn't the most impressive, probably because I wasn't an anthropology guy. On the ground floor, though, was a model of the Walls of Constantinople and the important Roman and Byzantine sites around them. While most of the walls had been removed as a part of the city's expansion over the years, the eastern-most wall was still relatively intact and served as the "official" dividing line between the European and Middle Eastern sides of the city (although I took the view that the Bosphorus Strait was a better, natural, sensical dividing line, geographically speaking, as it physically divided the European continent from the Middle East).

I decided to walk the walls. Why not? I had nothing else on the schedule for the day. Some of the ruins I could climb and survey the surrounding area as a palace guard might have done 1,000 years ago, while others I had to marvel at from the ground. Some of the gates, like the Gate of Charisius, were still intact and passable for pedestrians on a stroll along the dirt walkways. The Aqueduct of Valens, installed in the 300s, also still largely stood, with 921 metres of the original 971 metres of stone engineering spanning the city with roads passing alongside and under its arches. While no longer in use given modern technology, it was amazing to see the famed Roman engineering we were taught in school up close. The Aqueduct of Valens dropped one metre for every kilometre of aqueduct, which meant over the entire span of what I was looking at only had a drop of ninety-two centimetres from one end to the other. I couldn't see it with the naked eye, but that was enough to keep water flowing to the city's cisterns.

It was time to head back towards the hostel, but right next to the Aqueduct of Valens was the Shehzade Complex, which included a mosque and tombs I decided to explore. It was on the way, after all. This mosque was built in the 1500s as a memorial to Shehzade Mehmed, governor of Manisa and son of the then-Sultan of the Ottoman Empire, who fell ill and died during public celebrations of recent miliary campaigns. While the official cause of his death was unknown (aside from sickness), historians assessed that he likely died of smallpox. Prince Mehmed was buried in a mausoleum at the mosque, a mausoleum which I was allowed to visit along with several others on the grounds.

On the inside, like the Fatih Mosque, the Shehzade Mosque boasted an open room with red carpet and chandeliers that hung from the ceiling to provide light as the sun began to set. Unlike the Fatih Mosque, visitors were not permitted into the main portion of the sanctuary; this area was reserved exclusively for Muslims. I wondered what would happen if the cathedrals of Europe prohibited anyone who wasn't Christian from entering the sanctuary while sermons and masses were not actively underway. I didn't have to wonder long; I knew the same public understanding and tolerance afforded to mosques didn't extend to Christians in modern times, something I found regrettable seeing as earlier that day I wished churches back home would keep their doors open to the community around the clock like the mosques in Turkey did.

My journey back to the hostel took me back towards Hagia Sophia and the Blue Mosque, so I took a small detour to see the Little Hagia Sophia Mosque at ChatGPT's recommendation (I didn't like to use ChatGPT for planning, but it provided a great starting point). This was a small mosque near the water on the southern border of Istanbul and the Sea of Marmara. Like many other mosques in Istanbul, it was originally a Christian church built during Byzantine times in the 500s; the Ottomans converted it in the early 1500s after they conquered Constantinople.

A Western woman at this mosque wanted to enter, but the guard wouldn't let her as she didn't have a headscarf. On the one hand, I shook my head at her because I thought it was common knowledge that women were not permitted to enter mosques with their heads uncovered. On the other, we were on the European side of the Bosphorus Strait, and she was a tourist and not a Muslim, so I found it a bit exclusionary. I let her borrow my shemagh, which I wore almost everywhere in MENA, and helped her wrap it around her hair so it wouldn't fall off. The guard gave me a thankful nod and a smile; I guess his not rolling his eyes at an ignorant tourist was a plus. Like the Shehzade Mosque, a wooden barrier prohibited visitors from entering the main part of the empty sanctuary.

I had a bus to catch the next day with laundry to do before then, so I forced myself to return to the hostel to wrap things up in Istanbul. My next stop was Selçuk, home to the Roman city of Ephesus, the addressees of the Apostle Paul's letter "Ephesians" and where Paul started a riot for his evangelicalism. I couldn't wait.

Selçuk

It was a long eight hours on the bus from Istanbul to Selçuk. The bus didn't have a toilet, but the driver stopped every two hours. I took note because this was likely to be the case on every bus ride through Turkey, and I didn't want to be caught drinking too much water or coffee before a long ride to the next city. I figured the reason for the stops, besides changing passengers, wasn't for a bathroom break, but a smoke break. Turks couldn't scramble off the bus fast enough to light a cigarette. I knew everyone in Turkey smoked, but this was a next-level nicotine addiction.

We rolled into Selçuk late in the evening, around 21h00. I was the only passenger getting off, so the bus didn't bother pulling into the parking lot which served as the bus station. The driver pulled to the side of the road in the heart of town, offloaded my bags and me, and took off. I was alone on a dark street in what looked to be a sleepy town. Fortunately, the hostel was within eyeshot, and within thirty minutes, I was falling asleep in my two-person dorm room (which I had to myself for the time being).

I got a late start on my first day, and it was raining, so Ephesus would have to wait. Instead, I visited the Ephesus Archaeology Museum in the afternoon. It wasn't a large museum, but it was densely packed and provided an excellent refuge from the downpour outside. Besides the descriptions of life in Ephesus (in both English and Turkish), the most interesting part of the museum to me was its exhibit covering the Temple of Artemis, one of the Seven Wonders of the Ancient World. I didn't know this temple was in Ephesus, although had I paid more attention to the Book of Acts, I might have caught on a bit sooner. While the Temple of Artemis was almost completely destroyed (with only one reconstructed column remaining), the fact that I was this close to yet another of the original Seven Wonders excited me. While I knew I wouldn't see the magnificent structure the museum's model depicted, that I could see any of it was something I hadn't even considered when I first began my travels.

The rain cleared up overnight, and after breakfast at the hostel, I was headed off to Ephesus. I could have gotten a taxi, but it was only a forty-five-minute walk. Besides, I could enjoy the Turkish countryside, fresh air, and packs of dogs roaming the roads and fields along the way. One pack tagged along with me for a long time until they got distracted by something in a field and took off under the fences to chase it down.

There were two entrances to Ephesus. The south entrance, which was on the uphill side, could be accessed by taxi. That was a long walk, so I entered at the north entrance, where all of the tour busses parked, which meant I would have to walk uphill to see the city, but the way back to town was downhill. If the first law of travel was what goes down must come up, then I decided to take advantage of the laws of gravity for a change. The tickets were expensive, 700 TRY (just over 23 USD), but breakfast was included in the hostel price, food wasn't too expensive for lunch and dinner, and I would be spending the entire day at the site, so it was a cost I was willing to tolerate (some time after my visit, the price went up to 40 EUR, which would have pushed my budgetary limits).

Initially, I took my time walking the grounds, taking photos, and comparing what I saw with what I learned in Pompeii and other sites about Greek and Roman architecture, engineering, and city design. I opted not to pay the 300 TRY for the audio guide, which I almost came to regret. On a whim, I opened the Rick Steves Audio Europe app to see if he had anything to offer. To my surprise, he did! It was about ninety minutes long, but I knew it would take longer with my pausing, rewinding, and taking side trips to look at something.

The top of the hill, next to the south entrance, held the Agora, which was once a shopping area with a statue of Isis at its centre. It was now little more than an open green field surrounded by stone walkways. It seemed small to me, but much of the city was still lost to history, reclaimed by nature after it was abandoned in the 1400s after the Ottoman invasion. The Ottomans, however, were only the final salvo in the city's long decline. Between military conflict with the Persians, Arabs, Seljuk Turks, and Crusaders, and the port silting up and cutting off access to the Aegean Sea, the city's unceremonious end was a long time coming for almost 1,000 years. What remained was left to crumble until serious archaeological efforts commenced in the late 1800s.

On the north side of the Agora was a small amphitheatre (about 1,500 seats), which served as a sort of town hall where the city's leaders debated and decided municipal business. It was well-preserved, especially compared to some other sites in the region. It was buried up to its top rows in dirt before its excavation. Nature literally buried the theatre under tons of earth after its abandonment over 500 years ago. It was incredible to consider that even great stone structures like this one could be completely subsumed by the earth in such a short amount of time. This theatre, and the basilica next to it, weren't cannon balls or pottery fragments; they were feats of human engineering and craftsmanship, centres of political and social activities, yet they didn't stand a chance once nature decided to take over.

I moved down to the top of the main street, the entrance to which was marked by the Hercules Gate. From the Hercules Gate, I could see most of the major sites in town. Most of the city was a pedestrian-only zone, so the trademark ruts in the brick I had seen before were absent. Down this road, I found the remnants of Roman baths, public toilets, the Temple of Hadrian (so named for one of the Roman emperors), and terrace houses (which I would come back to). Whereas large swaths of Pompeii and Rome were either destroyed or off limits to tourists because of ongoing archaeological studies, I could freely explore Ephesus. Of all of the "old things" (as Jo would say) I had seen so far, this site gave the most comprehensive and preserved view of Greek and Roman life.

At the bottom of the street stood the Library of Celsus, an impressive building built by the Romans in the early 2nd Century. Its façade reminded me of the Monastery and Treasury in Petra; unlike at Petra, though, I could actually enter the library. It wasn't very deep, but it was also not a library in the modern sense. Bookshelves wouldn't have lined the walls; instead, shelves stocked with scrolls would have been the order of the day. The Library of Celsus was the third-largest library in the Roman Empire, only behind Pergamum and Alexandria, neither of which remained. Of course, the surviving portion was only a fraction of the size of the original library, which suffered tragedy after tragedy, such as invasion, fire, and earthquakes, and it was believed that the library originally measured around 180 square metres in size, bigger than the house where I was raised. The façade had to be restored in the 1970s, as it was destroyed in an earthquake in the late 900s (or maybe early 1000s; scientists weren't precisely sure). Based on the façade, the library looked two or three stories tall, which explained the impressive size combined with the short width.

According to legend, the Egyptians became jealous of the Library of Celsus and worried that it might become more notable and extensive than the Library of Alexandria, so they stopped sending papyrus to Rome to subvert their scroll and, consequently, knowledge production. Thus, parchment was born, ultimately leading to the invention of books. It was ironic that the Egyptians' jealousy was what made them obsolete. I wondered what it must have been like to study the papyrus scrolls and animal-skin books in the Library of Celsus in its prime. Granted, the Greeks and Romans would probably swoon at the libraries we have today, with multiple, exact copies of almost every book ever published, large study halls, and an infinite amount of knowledge.

Further down the road was Ephesus's great Roman theatre. It was massive, though not quite as large as the one in Amman. While not as large as Amman, it was of infinitely greater importance, at least to Christians like me. This theatre was the site of Paul's near-execution. According to Luke's Biblical account in Acts, Paul was preaching the Gospel at Ephesus, part of which called for the Ephesians to abandon their pagan gods, specifically Artemis. The Romans' primary concern, according to Luke, was not the religious belief but the impact on trade, as those whom Paul "led astray" from Artemis and towards Jesus were no longer frequenting the Temple of Artemis or the tradesmen who made their living creating the silver shrines dedicated to Artemis. That Artemis and their beliefs would be discredited was a consequence of the impact on their trade (which, to me, should have been an indicator of what their beliefs truly were). The Ephesians then dragged Paul and his associates to the theatre to answer for their crimes, which, to that point, they had committed none. After hours of shouting and jeering, the city clerk finally quieted the crowd, assured them of Artemis's reputation in the world, and reminded the citizens that there were laws in their city and the Roman Empire which they must abide by, including avoiding the charge of rioting. Paul and his associates were ultimately released, but it was a close call for them (though they all would have gladly been martyred for their faith, which Paul ultimately was).

I was awestruck to stand in the same place as the Apostle Paul, especially knowing he almost met his end on the stage where I now stood. Ephesus's Christian importance did not stop with Paul's near-martyrdom. His letter to the Ephesians continued to implore them to abandon their pagan gods and gave his instructions for how families should treat each other, including that wives should treat their husbands as the head of the household and husbands should love their wives as Jesus loved the Church.

According to some Christian traditions, but which was new to me as it wasn't a Biblical account, John brought Mary to live in Ephesus when he came to preach the Gospel, although the exact timeline of when this would have happened and whether or not Mary was with him were still debated within the Christian community. While I couldn't be sure Mary had actually lived at the House of the Virgin Mary (which I didn't visit), it was still something to be in the same place where two of the most influential Apostles, authors of the Bible, and Catholic saints once lived and preached. Being there somehow made it all real to me in a way that thirty years of church, sermons, and belief never could.

As I exited the theatre, I faced the Harbour Road. Today, it led towards a closed excavation site and the far-off Aegean Sea, about seven kilometres away. When Ephesus was a sprawling metropolis, the harbour road led to the harbour, as Ephesus was a port city on the Aegean. Over hundreds of years, the port filled with silt, ultimately pushing the city farther and farther inland. The loss of sea trade accelerated Ephesus's decline. Nature always won. One might wonder if this was some divine intervention against the city for its treatment of Christians, but Ephesus eventually became a predominantly Christian city, just like the rest of the Roman Empire, despite maintaining symbols and temples dedicated to Greek and Roman gods, so it was a more fitting description that nature simply took its course, burying the port and the city, and moving civilisation in other directions.

With my tour finished, I backtracked to the terrace houses, which required a separate entry ticket. Unlike most of Ephesus, these houses were under active archaeological excavation, and the site was housed under a roof to protect it from the elements. The houses currently under excavation were only a few of the many that were built into the surrounding hillside. Not everyone could live in the bustling city, and those who could afford the luxury and expense of a hillside home lived away from the commercial and social activities.

The most impressive pieces of the terrace houses were the mosaics that decorated the floors and walls. Yes, the architecture and structural design were impressive, especially given the tools and economies of the day, but the mosaics looked like paintings. Despite being grids of individual small stones, the images popped as though they were painted by Picasso. As much as I may want to, I could never even sketch, let alone paint, sculpt, or create from pebbles, the lions, flowers, angels, and people, which were still clear in the stone 2,000 years later. And all without the help of computers or design programmes. I wondered if we would be able to create such masterpieces in modern times if we lost all of our technology. Some people would, but society writ-large would be learning from scratch, and places like these 2,000-year-old houses would become sources of intense architectural and interior design study, not just archaeological or historical research.

After more than five hours at Ephesus, I was hungry, so I started the long walk to the lower entrance. Along the way, a dog started following me. I wondered if he wanted something from me, but he just hung around. I had seen him earlier, and the other dogs treated him as an outcast for some reason. I could see his ear was tagged, which meant he was vaccinated, so I didn't mind his company.

On my way towards the exit, I took a detour to explore the ruins of the Church of Mary. It was largely destroyed, much worse than most of the excavated city, which I attributed to being separated from the main thoroughfares and nearer the silted-up port. Once upon a time, it served as the seat of the Bishop of Ephesus, a position it held for several hundred years before, like the rest of the city, it was abandoned. The site wasn't roped off, so the dog and I explored its many offshoots, baptistries, and once-prominent chapels. At one point, the dog turned a corner away as I climbed a hill to overlook the church. When the dog turned around and saw I was missing, he searched for me as though I were his owner. When he finally spied me on the hill, I watched as he looked for a way to join me, ultimately jumping up the stones to take his place at my side. I didn't know why this dog decided he was mine, as I hadn't paid him any special attention, but he had made up his mind, and he followed me out of the church, down the Harbour Road, through the exit, and to the on-site café. He wasn't allowed in the café, and I hoped that he would get bored and move on while I was inside eating, but that hope was dashed when I came outside and found him waiting patiently to continue at my side.

On the walk back to Selçuk, I stopped at the location of the Temple of Artemis. As I said, there was only a single column remaining (and even this one was a reconstruction from 1973), but that didn't take away from the fact that it was a column from one of the original Seven Wonders. Scattered around the field where the temple once stood were stones which were probably part of the temple complex, and according to the information boards, some of the artifacts discovered at the site date back to the 1300s BC. It was hard to picture the large, Parthenon-like temple (or Pantheon-like, depending on whether you were comparing it to the Greeks or Romans) sitting in what looked to be a pretty small field, but centuries of domestication and transformation of Selçuk under the Ottomans and Turks made it hard to remember that there were probably many buildings and merchants which occupied the surrounding areas. Of course, conquest, disaster, and religious conversions also played their part in the temple's destruction. In the 300s BC, it was largely destroyed by a fire after only 200 years of existence. After Ephesus became Christian, it was believed that the temple was converted to a church, and as one empire conquered another, it eventually became just another relic of the past.

The dog stayed close as we continued to Selçuk. He stopped to sniff an old man eating a chocolate bar on one of the park benches, and I hoped he would find himself more enthralled with the possibility of a sweet treat than me, but he kept glancing my way and eventually abandoned his quest to run to my side. I felt bad for the dog. He was tagged, vaccinated, neutered, and not malnourished. If I weren't going to continue travelling the world, I would have taken him home with me (although, I'm not sure the hostel would have liked me bringing in a stray). I wasn't looking forward to leaving him outside the hostel's floor-to-ceiling glass doors and windows when I headed to my room. Fortunately, he became distracted by a street vendor just before the turn onto the street to the hostel, so I disappeared without him seeing where I went. It was a shame he had to live on the street; he really was a sweet dog.

The rest of the day, I explored the rest of Selçuk, but to be frank, there wasn't much to see. It was like my hometown in that way; most of its businesses were to support the people who lived there or the tourists who came to visit Ephesus, with the latter being far less plentiful than the former. I managed to get the full-service treatment for a much-needed haircut, though, at the cost of 500 TRY. A bit expensive for a haircut, especially in Turkey, but it was the works, including a beard trim (if you could call what little facial hair I had a beard) and a wash. There was something to be said about Turkish barbers; they were masters of their craft.

On my final day in Selçuk, I explored some ruins near my hostel. I didn't know what exactly they were, but they seemed interesting enough. I was shocked to learn that these ruins were the Basilica of Saint John. *The* Saint John, the one whom Jesus entrusted with Mary's care as he died on the cross. The site was in ruins, like most of Ephesus, and it had disappeared from the historical record by the 800s, just a few hundred years after its construction. Like other churches in Ephesus, the Basilica of

Saint John wasn't constructed all at once but was built upon the ruins of the church which came before it.

Even the first church established on the site was built on another structure: the tomb of Saint John himself. The tomb was dug into the ground, and some Christian traditions held that it was a cave under the original church where John preached. According to one tradition, when he reached an old age (over 100 years old), John climbed into this cave and closed the opening, at which point he ascended into heaven in what was called the Assumption of John. When the tomb was opened by Constantine the Great, an occurrence which was clear in the historical record, it was found empty, devoid of clothes or other relics, giving rise to the claim that John, like Jesus and Mary, was assumed into heaven rather than joining them after a natural death.

This was the only section on the entire site that was kept clean, preserved, and clear of debris. The cover was made of polished stones, which in all likelihood had been reconstructed, renovated, or restored, given the state of the basilica. Even so, it was respected as the tomb of the only Apostle who stayed with Jesus as he hung from the cross. A rope surrounded the tomb to keep tourists away from the tempting photo opportunities with the stone cover on the ground and the columns on either side. I was glad of this because some tourists were more interested in pictures than reverence. I understood to an extent, being someone who had visited so many places and taken thousands of photos over the past six months. Even so, I still respected religious sites, such as the Yazidi tombs in Lalish, the Muslim tombs in Istanbul, and the representations of Catholic saints all across Spain. I wished others understood the importance of sites like this tomb to people of the respective faith.

I spent a long time at the Basilica of Saint John, far more than I would have under any other usual circumstance. I was fascinated with understanding the church's layout compared to the still-active cathedrals in Europe. I envisioned what this basilica must have looked like when it was an active church, especially knowing (or at least believing) that John the Apostle was buried under the altar.

Of course, that was all anyone could do: envision. Despite the sizeable ruinous site, there were no actual records of what the basilica looked like in its prime. There were oral and written descriptions by emperors and travellers, but archaeologists have only been able to approximate the basilica's original design. Fortunately, there was a reference to the Church of the Holy Apostles as the model; this allowed archaeologists to give a hypothetical depiction of the basilica before its abandonment. This hypothetical model was displayed in a glass case up the hill from the basilica.

The Basilica of Saint John was still under archaeological study and excavation, so on the north side of the basilica, up the hill, and just past the hypothetical model, was a sort of open-air museum where the archaeologists organised and documented their finds. While the dirt walkway was open to the public, the organised rows of artifacts were technically off limits, as indicated by the bright red signs in both Turkish and English. Since this was the first time in a long time I saw actual signs advising tourists to stay off the ruins, I went ahead and abided and continued up the hill.

On the hill above the basilica and Selçuk stood the Ayasuluk Castle, a Byzantine fortress which overlooked the entire landscape. It made sense with the seaport of Ephesus just down the road that the Byzantines would want a fortress that could defend both the sea and surrounding countryside. Like Ephesus, the castle changed hands as empires rose and fell, a phenomenon on clear display as the castle had both a basilica and a mosque. While most of the castle's interior had withered away with time, some structures, like the cisterns (some of which were more like bunkers that water repositories), mosque, basilica, and surrounding walls and towers were still standing, though wrecked by the passage of time. I hoped I could climb the castle walls and survey the land as a military commander might have done 2,000 years ago, but they were closed to the public. Granted, no one was there watching me, but a person standing on top of the castle would probably have drawn attention, and I didn't fancy a night in a Turkish jail.

Having had my fill of the castle, I returned to town for dinner before packing my bags. I had two buses ahead of me the next day. Even though there was a nice enough train station in Selçuk, the train wouldn't take me to Bodrum. Nor would any direct-transfer buses, it turned out, so either way, I had to go to Aydin. I opted for the minibus, mainly because it was cheaper and had more departure times. It was also a fifty-minute drive versus an hour and a half via train. After an afternoon lay-over and a three-hour bus ride from Aydin, I finally rolled into Bodrum.

Bodrum

My arrival in Bodrum was not the most endearing experience. I arrived at the hostel late, again, around 20h00 or 21h00, to find it closed. I rang the doorbell, and no one answered. I called. No answer. I knocked. Same. I was stranded on a dark street on the southern coast of Turkey, and my hostel wasn't open, which perturbed me because they had explicitly asked me when I would be arriving so they could ensure someone was there. I stood in the dark, empty street of a town which, during the peak season, would have been busy with local and international tourists, but now was a ghost town as the local shops had boarded up for the night. A few metres down the road were a hostel and hotel, so I decided to get a room for the night there and sort the hostel business out in the morning. The hotel room pushed me over budget for the day, but at least I had a double bed and shower to myself.

The hostel attendant was highly apologetic the next day; the owners hadn't told her I would be arriving. Maybe she was saying that to cover herself, but my communications with the owners made me think she was telling the truth. Regardless, she wanted to make it right, so she refunded me the night I missed (which I hadn't figured as a guarantee), upgraded me to a private room, and gave me a discounted rate. As perturbed as I was from the night before, she went the extra mile to overcome my inconvenience, so all was forgiven.

Of course, all this meant getting a late start in the morning, and I only had two full days to see Bodrum. I was there, solely at Tahli's recommendation, for the Bodrum Museum of Underwater Archaeology. I was looking for a career change away from the security field, and underwater archaeology seemed like an interesting combination of my undergraduate degree in history and future experience as a divemaster. Besides, I loved the sea and learning about those who lived life on the deep blue water, chasing the never-ending horizon.

Naturally, the museum was closed on my first day there.

After consulting the internet, I embarked on a walk of the city's Greek and Roman history. Like most cities in modern-day Turkey, Bodrum changed hands as empires came and went, from the Persians to the Greeks to the Romans and Byzantines to the Ottomans, and each left its mark. And, like most cities in modern-day Turkey, the most visible of these empires were the Greeks and Romans. Even though the city had long since modernised and transformed itself into a summertime tourism hotspot, it was an important port in ancient times that connected Turkey directly to the Mediterranean, unlike Istanbul and Ephesus, which connected Turkey to the Sea of Marmara and Aegean Sea, respectively. And, continuing in the historical footsteps of my Turkish tour, Bodrum ultimately lost its strategic military importance after it was ruined by earthquakes. Although it would occasionally be fought over by conquering empires, it became a sleepy fishing town for several centuries until its revival as a tourism destination.

I started with the Roman theatre on a hillside overlooking the town. It was a smaller theatre than the grandiose ones in Ephesus, Amman, and even Carthage, but it was still a substantial structure with 4,000 seats. That was about three times the size of Ephesus's smaller Odeon, but less than half of its original capacity. According to the information boards, the Bodrum theatre's original capacity was 10,000 people. That was an easy comparison, as the Sevilla bullring held 12,000 spectators. The performance area was small and circular, meaning the theatre's seats extended more up than out. Having stood in Sevilla's bullring, it wasn't difficult to imagine what it must have looked like with spectators all around. There was no room for stage fright in a place like this.

The theatre overlooked the city below, and the views of the Mediterranean and outlying islands were beautiful in the winter sun reflecting off the sea. Not even the highway, which ran directly in front of the theatre, could diminish the view (although I was sure the performers wouldn't have appreciated cars flying by them in front of 10,000 people).

It was a short-ish walk from the theatre to the Mausoleum at Halicarnassus. I wasn't expecting too much from it after passing the Temple of Mars on my walk to the theatre (the Temple of Mars was long-since gone, and it now was just an open field littered with trash). I didn't realise that the Mausoleum at Halicarnassus was one of the Seven Wonders of the Ancient World. This would mark my third Ancient Wonder, with seeing the rest being impossible as their remains were all destroyed in some manner or another (except for the Lighthouse of Alexandria, which would require me to return to Alexandria during the dive season to see its remains littering the seafloor in the eastern harbour).

The Mausoleum site was smaller than one might expect for one of the Seven Wonders, but after 700 years of the city growing around the site destroyed by earthquakes, the small size was unsurprising. Time, and society, moved on. Back in its prominence, though, the Mausoleum stood forty-five metres tall by thirty-eight metres wide by thirty-two metres deep. Despite the expected size, the site would have been categorised as a "mega mansion" if it were a modern house, so maybe it was bigger than my eyes and photos perceived. The foundations were sunk several metres into the ground, and the eponymous tomb of Mausolus was deeper still. It was difficult to envision what the Mausoleum would have looked like in its prime standing in the courtyard with columns on their sides and grass growing over the stones. Fortunately, the information boards nearby gave a clear picture of what the Mausoleum looked like before its destruction, as it stood well into periods of documented history before meeting its destruction by earthquake.

The Mausoleum was dedicated to Mausolus, a governor in the First Persian Empire and a man who, despite his non-Greek origins, was enamoured with the Greek way of living. Mausolus established the city of Halicarnassus, where the modern-day town of Bodrum now stood and where the Mausoleum took its name. According to the information boards, Mousolus's tomb was a full fifteen metres tall, a third of the overall height, and he designed the tomb himself with Greek artists and artisans finishing the designs after his death. The result, which stood for 1,000 years before being destroyed by earthquakes, was so impressive and grandiose that languages around the world took Mausolus's name to describe above-ground tombs: the mausoleum.

With my walk of Bodrum's Greek and Roman history more-or-less complete, I turned towards the sea, stopping for a pizza on the way. While I loved Turkish food, Ruby's Pizzeria had rave reviews and was a short walk from the Mausoleum. It was a ten out of ten experience, especially considering it was the off-season. I pulled out my Kindle and enjoyed one of the best pizzas I had ever eaten on the front patio while reading about the history of the Christian faith in the region. It wasn't very Turkish of me, but that was traveling for you.

The Bodrum Marina was what I would call a sea walk district. Yes, there were sailboats of all sizes in the actual marina, but the real draw were the shops and restaurants where tourists could enjoy their time and, more importantly, spend their money on summer getaways. I didn't eat too many of my meals here, having learned the lesson of eating local food for tourist prices before, but I did enjoy strolling along the water and through the cobblestone streets in the midday sun. I was glad there weren't a lot of tourists; the streets were quiet, and the shop owners didn't hassle me as I walked by. I made regular stops during my mornings and afternoons at the Mahfel Café, a seaside self-service café. It would have been impossible to get a seat during the tourist season, but in the off-season, old men played dominos and read the paper, and women gathered to share in the day's gossip. It was a great place to relax in the sea breeze while enjoying a hot glass of Turkish tea and a good book, especially considering it wasn't too cold, yet (although it would be by the time I left; I was racing a cold front east across Turkey, and it would occasionally catch up to me before I raced off to the next city).

On my second and final full day in Bodrum, after a peaceful morning drinking coffee and reading at a coffee shop in the marina, I set off for the Bodrum Museum of Underwater Archaeology. The museum was set in the remains of the Bodrum Castle or the Castle of Saint Peter, depending on whose language you chose to use. Like most seaside fortifications, the castle was a strategic military outpost designed by the Knights Hospitaller to defend against the Ottomans. While not directly commissioned by the Catholic Church, the Pope welcomed its establishment to defend Christians against their hostile neighbours. Over thirty years in the early 1400s, the Knights Hospitallier built this structure, only for it to fall in 1523 to the Ottoman Empire. Such was the fate of religious buildings of the time.

Touring the castle was essentially broken into two parts: the castle and the archaeology museum. Touring the castle was easy and interesting, given the Knights Hospitallier's international composition. Each of the four towers was designed by a different nationality, English, French, German, and Italian, depending on which knights designed and participated in its construction. It was a fascinating display of unity amongst countries who would later end up fighting against each other in two World Wars and who were currently (at the time of the castle's construction) fighting each other in the Hundred Years War. Of course, the Knights Hospitallier were dedicated to the Pope and the Catholic Church, not their respective countries, so the fighting in Europe was a foreign conflict to them. Naturally, each left their individual, non-Christian marks on the castle, as coats of arms above doorways were plentiful, and the chapel had long since been converted to a mosque.

The underwater archaeology museum portion was a testament to Bodrum's importance as a trade port between the Mediterranean and Aegean Seas. All of the artifacts and shipwrecks in the museum came from the local area and dated from the 1500s BC to the 1500s AD, spanning nearly every empire which conquered or traded with modern-day Turkey. There were entire ships reconstructed from their remains, exhibitions of Islamic-designed glassware, Sevillian silver from Spain (which was once under Muslim rule), and even Egyptian seals, including one from Nefertiti (whose bust Jo and I had sought out in Berlin a few months before). All these impressive finds notwithstanding, my favourite part of the museum was the video presentations about the ins and outs of underwater archaeology. I was enthralled by how archaeologists and historians applied their trade in the underwater environment, especially considering that many of the shipwrecks were far from the coast. These presentations showcased how seemingly-unrelated fields and expertise came together to understand our history. It made me wonder if it was better to be an archaeologist trained as a diver or a diver trained as an archaeologist. I hoped for the latter, as I became intrigued with such diving as a future career opportunity.

I spent hours and hours at the Bodrum Castle and Museum of Underwater Archaeology. It was simply a fascinating place, at least to me, and I let Tahli know I was grateful for her insistence that I visit. Admittedly, I thought, it would have been boring to most people I knew, but that was why I was solo. I only wished I could have been around during the dive season to see some of the archaeological sites myself!

With the only thing I wanted to see in Bodrum in the rear view, I went in search of Iskender for dinner (a combination of lamb döner kebab, tomato sauce, pita bread, and plain yogurt) before heading back to pack my bags. I was on a whirlwind tour through Turkey, and the cold front was starting to creep up on Bodrum. It was time to make my way further east.

Pamukkale

After a second stop in Aydin (this time for dinner), I off-loaded the bus in Denizli, about fifteen minutes south of Pamukkale. The bus didn't get me to Pamukkale, but because Pamukkale was an international tourism destination, there were ample taxis to get me the rest of the way. Pamukkale was home to Hierapolis, an ancient

Greek city whose hot springs made it a healing destination for over 2,000 years. I was there, again, at Tahli's recommendation, as the site was extremely well-preserved and, apparently, well worth a day or two visit. I, again, had a private room, this time at the Green Garden Allgau hotel, which was about an hour's walk from the Hierapolis archaeological site.

I wasn't sure what to expect at Hierapolis. On the one hand, I wanted to see more of the Greek, Roman, and Christian influence and history in Turkey. On the other hand, I had seen more than a normal person's share of Greek and Roman history in the past several weeks, so I didn't expect to be blown away. This wasn't a knock on Hierapolis or those who studied the finer differences of civilisations gone by as found in the rock, but as a traveller, eventually you start to want to move on. I was only in Pamukkale for two full days, so I decided to give one day to Hierapolis and the other to exploring the city. It seemed like a good compromise.

The walk to Hierapolis was almost entirely uphill. There were several entrances to the site; the main tourist entrance on the west side was way too far for me to walk to first thing in the morning, and the entrance which took you up the hot springs required visitors to remove their shoes so as not to damage the travertine pools, so the east entrance it was. I hadn't entirely managed to outpace the cold front this time, so I was in my long-sleeve Henley, Columbia jacket, and reliable military fleece beanie despite there not being a cloud in the sky. Needless to say, I was sufficiently warmed up to explore the expansive site by the time I arrived at the ticket counter. I was not sufficiently ready for the steep price to enter. At 700 TRY, it was a budget-pusher for sure. Fortunately, breakfast was included at the hotel, and there were cheap places for dinner on the walk back.

Within minutes of being on-site, I knew my plan needed an overhaul. Aimless wandering wouldn't get me anywhere on a site that big. There were two museums outside the central tourism point, hot springs to enjoy, remnants of castles and churches, important tombs, and anything else I could think of that would be in an ancient Greek city. This was Turkey's version of Petra, and I needed to plan like it. Fortunately, I was not too proud to admit I needed two days to explore (which was unfortunate for my daily budget, but such was travel life sometimes). I decided to focus on the outlying areas on this first day and the in-lying areas, including a dip in the hot springs and the museums, on the second. With a rough plan taking the pressure off, I was off to see some incredible archaeological finds.

I started at the theatre. This was one of the few instances of Romanisation in Hierapolis after it was incorporated into the Roman kingdom from Greece. It was an impressive structure, just as all large Greek and Roman theatres were. It had seats for 15,000 spectators, including an imperial box for important government representatives. Unlike most other theatres I had seen, the stage was large and rectangular with a façade reminiscent of the Library of Celsus or the Petra Monastery, which provided the space and backdrop for more elaborate productions, and there were pathways under and behind the stage that allowed the performers to move about out of the audience's sight. In the semi-circular area which usually served as the stage in such theatres was the orchestra pit. It was sunk two metres into the ground and surrounded by a stone wall that eventually gave way to the stadium seating. It was no wonder French historian Baptistin Poujoulat described the theatre in this manner: "In the whole Orient, there is no theatre in a better state than that of Hierapolis."

As I sat in awe of the architectural marvel surrounding me, I wondered not about what sort of tragedies and comedies must have been performed in this place but what it would have been like to have witnessed a bullfight in the orchestra pit. At 15,000 seats, it would have tied for the ninth-largest bullring in the world. It wasn't a far stretch to imagine such a possibility, as one of the roots of modern-day bullfights was Rome's gladiatorial performances. Granted, such a thing probably didn't happen in Hierapolis; with a few exceptions, Hierapolis retained its non-Roman culture even after it was incorporated into the Roman Empire.

I pulled myself away from these musings to walk to the Martyrion of Saint Philip. *The* Saint Philip, the Apostle who was tested by Jesus in John chapter six when He fed the five thousand. I didn't know much about the Apostle Philip, primarily because there was not much mention of him in the Bible outside of John chapter six. I knew of *a* Philip who brought Christianity to Ethiopia, but that was Philip the Evangelist. I later learned that not much was known of the Apostle Philip outside of his appearance in the Gospel of John and that nearly all modern-day traditions related to him stemmed from second-hand accounts and extra-biblical scrolls. To me, that didn't make those stories any less true. After all, we knew from various texts that many biblical figures were, in fact, real people outside of their roles in the Bible, so why shouldn't we believe such things when we came across them in regions where they were known to live? Clearly, the evidence suggested Philip lived, preached, and died in Hierapolis.

The Martyrion of Saint Philip was, essentially, a church which was reportedly built atop Philip's tomb. Despite being in ruins due to a fire in the 400s or 500s, its layout was discernibly octagonal and centred around a large, open room where there was once a large altar. Rooms and hallways would have radiated out from the octagonal walls back when a domed roof was overhead. Despite tradition, however, there was little-to-no proof Philip was buried under the church, as excavations of the central areas turned up nothing.

As someone with a history degree who worked in the security field and who was a former police officer, I knew most stories were grounded in some level of truth. Many things in life could not be proven beyond a shadow of a doubt, but we could make substantial assessments and inferences based upon the evidence available to us. How else would we even dare to interpret the meanings of ancient temples, cultish religious symbols, or even the supposed writings of ancient leaders? Egyptology, for example, was an interpretive science based largely upon our interpretations of the Rosetta Stone, hieroglyphs, and the architectural organisation of various temples and shrines. History and archaeology weren't exact sciences, but they were as close as we could get to the real thing. As such, I found it hard to believe that, given the biblical and extra-biblical tellings, Philip wasn't buried beneath the church, or at least in the general area.

Nearly 2,000 years later, in 2011, that suspicion was confirmed, as archaeologists found what they believed to be the tomb of the Apostle Philip. It wasn't under the church but in a 1st Century mausoleum, which was later incorporated into the 4th Century Church of the Sepulchre. The name "Church of the Sepulchre" literally means "Church of the Tomb," which in and of itself wouldn't mean much in terms of the Apostle Philip (churches across the world were replete with tombs). Inside the tomb, however, Greek prayers inscribed in the walls talked of the Apostle Philip, and one of the engravings portrayed a man holding a loaf of bread, a clear connection to the story of John chapter six. Unfortunately, there was unlikely to be a future, conclusive connection, as the tomb was devoid of remains and relics which may have given more credibility to this being the actual tomb of the Apostle Philip; however, some accounts indicated the remains and relics were moved from the tomb to Rome into what is now the Church of the Holy Apostles.

Given the facts and inferences before me, I was convinced I was standing before the Apostle's final resting place. Sure, I probably couldn't convince a jury at a criminal trial beyond a reasonable doubt, but I could undoubtedly believe any case made in the history books, journals, and theological circles. This was a significant moment for me. Just days before, I had been at the tomb of the Apostle John, months before I had been near Peter and Paul in Rome, and now I was standing before Philip. I had joined the thousands, maybe even millions, of pilgrims who had come to this spot to pay their respects and tribute to one of the Twelve at the nearby fountain which, according to tradition, sprung forth on the spot where Philips' blood was spilled during his martyrdom. I wondered how many other apostles' tombs I could see as I travelled the globe. Probably none in the immediate future, but that didn't mean there wasn't a distinct possibility that I could see them all in my lifetime. Of course, not all of their locations were known, but that was neither here nor there in the moment.

Re-invigorated after this unexpected discovery, I set off for the rest of Hierapolis. I was excited to discover what sort of a place brought one of the Twelve to preach and die nearly 2,000 years before. In this spirit, I headed towards the temples dedicated to the Greek and Roman gods Apollo, Neptune, and Mercury. These were located down the hill to the south of the theatre. While each of these temples were separate, they were all congregated around the Plutonion, or Pluto's Gate. While Pluto himself was venerated there, the Plutonion was an allusion to his role as god of the underworld, so named because of the cave which led to a chamber filled with toxic carbon dioxide gas. While it was easy to see why people held the belief that this cave was an entrance to the underworld considering entering it could indeed spell certain death, it was really just a product of geologic activity which forced the gas up from the Earth. To me, there were indications that the priests knew something of this, as they would crawl along the floor seeking oxygen pockets before returning outside to "prove" that they were divinely protected. My scepticism's potential hypocrisy did not escape me; I believed similar things in the Christian realm, such as the resurrection of Jesus, which very well could have a yet-undiscovered scientific explanation. Even in the United States, the snake-handling preachers of Appalachia used tricks such as milking rattlesnakes before a sermon to "prove" their dedication to God and deliverance from Hell. Where my potential hypocrisy ended, however, was that I knew these tricks and didn't believe in them, much as I wouldn't have believed in the divine protection of the priests entering the Plutonion.

Unfortunately for regular tourists like myself, each of the three temples was off-limits for excavation, except for a small, elevated walkway that took you through the middle of the site. It was disappointing that I couldn't visit these religious sites of old, but after wondering where I should and shouldn't be walking at so many other sites in the region, I appreciated the conservation effort. Not all tourists respected the importance such places and beliefs played in history and our understanding of the world, and the temples surely would have been eroded by photo-seeking tourists trying to get just the right angle to post on social media.

It was pushing lunchtime, and I had been walking for hours by this point, so I caved and ate lunch at the over-priced tourist café at the visitor centre. As expected, the food was mediocre, but I didn't have much choice, seeing as I would be at the site all day. I didn't have the time nor the desire to walk forty-five minutes downhill to eat in town just to walk forty-five minutes back to see more of the site, especially considering re-entry on the same ticket wasn't allowed. Lunch was expensive, but it wasn't an hour and a half plus 700 TRY expensive. Besides, it gave me the opportunity to scope out the hot springs for my visit the next day.

I wrapped up my first day taking the long walk north towards Hierapolis's main commercial thoroughfare. This thoroughfare was similar to Ephesus's in that it was bound by a gate on each side which divided it between pedestrian-only and chariot zones. Looking closely, I could make out the 2,000-year-old ruts in the excavated ground where the chariots and carts once rolled through the city. It was a two-lane road, as indicated by the occasional raised line of stones which bisected it (these stones were used as crossing points so pedestrians could avoid walking in the water after a rain and as guidelines for where wheeled carts and chariots should move). Because I was walking from the centre of Hierapolis outward, I was doing the typical tour of this area in reverse; thus, I was able to form my assessments of what I saw, such as with the road situation, and then confirm or correct them as I came upon information boards. I was impressed with how much I had learned as I confirmed one assessment after the next.

I finally reached the northern Byzantine Gate, which served as the main (and ceremonial) entrance to the city and part of the fortification wall that once surrounded it. I was at a decision point. I could continue north and explore the large northern necropolis or turn around and see the travertine pools. Seeing as I had already decided to return the next day, I continued my long walk into the necropolis. The northern necropolis was impressive not because of its size or architecture but because of the number of mausoleums and sarcophagi it contained. For a town of 100,000 people, I was amazed at the more than 1,200 above-ground tombs scattered across this graveyard. To be sure, these tombs primarily belonged to influential and well-off families, but to see so many was captivating. The tombs were scattered about on either side of the main path. At one point in time, they were probably arranged in a grid, but two millennia's worth of erosion, neglect, earthquakes, and excavation betrayed their original organisation. While some of the tombs had stories connected with them, most were nameless after 2,000 years. It was a pointed reflection on life and death; despite their prominence, influence, and wealth during their lifetime, their names and notoriety were ultimately erased by the sands of time.

When I reached the far end of the necropolis, it was time to start towards the hotel. The sun was setting, the site was closing soon, and I wanted to be able to leave the same way I arrived rather than be forced out the farther main entrance. As exhausted as I was, I was glad I used my first day to explore the outer regions of

Hierapolis. This gave me time to relax and slow-roll the museums, pools, hot springs, and other inner areas the next day before my long bus ride further east. I stopped for some Adana kebab (a sort of spiced lamb), then fell into bed reflecting on the spiritual aspects of my day.

About ten hours and forty-five minutes later, I was paying my 700 TRY to re-enter Hierapolis, this time with a towel, change of clothes, and swim shorts in my bag. This would be an easier day than I had been having as far as walking was concerned, at least I hoped so. It was cooler this day; the cold front had caught up with me despite my best efforts. That made it the perfect weather to jump in the hot springs surrounding the visitor centre as I waited for the sun to warm the air to a tolerable temperature.

The pool, called Cleopatra's Pool, was the last of the site's still-functioning baths that used natural thermal vents to provide heated water (the larger, public baths now housed parts of the Hierapolis Museum). Unlike the nearby travertine pools, Cleopatra's pool was not a natural formation. Instead, it was created as a gift to Cleopatra of Egypt by Marc Antony of Rome, and it once sat beneath what must have been the imposing Temple of Apollo. The placement was surely no coincidence, as many believed the natural hot springs possessed healing properties, and one of Apollo's domains in Roman mythology was healing and disease. Despite the temple's destruction in an earthquake during the 6th Century, many still believed in the water's healing properties. Maybe this was because of tradition, maybe it was because of the natural ease and feelings of wellness that instinctively come from hot water, or maybe it was because some of the temple's columns fell into the pool, where they still remained, and carried with them some of Apollo's healing powers. None of this mattered to me. It was cold out, there was warm natural spring water, and I had an entire morning to bask in their warm, crystal-clear embrace. I stayed in Cleopatra's Pool for what seemed like only a few minutes, but it was several of hours, because all of a sudden it was time for lunch before I heading for the museum.

The Hierapolis Museum, which was included in the 700 TRY ticket, was actually a series of disconnected rooms with different exhibits. The museum was built in the original public baths, a large building built directly on top of the central point for the thermal vents. It was a shame these baths were no longer active as hot springs, but between tourism and earthquakes, I wasn't surprised they had been usurped for other purposes, especially considering half of them were closed to the public for archaeological study.

The first room, the museum's main display, contained the most well-preserved sarcophagi, statues, and reliefs. Most of them were white marble, although some had been restored with the original pieces adhered to plaster interiors (I had learned this was a common restorative practice when I was in the Valley of the Kings in Egypt). The names, professions, and stories of those buried in the sarcophagi accompanied most of them, unlike the tombs in the northern necropolis the day before. One of the statues belonged to a "health official." I commented out loud and in texts that I hoped we didn't memorialise our public health officials this way after the botched handling of the COVID-19 pandemic. Another statue depicted a priestess dedicated to Isis (the Egyptian goddess of motherhood and protection), which was probably sculpted after Rome conquered Egypt rather than imported from Egypt itself. Still other reliefs depicted scenes of gladiators facing off against each other or wild animals. It was not lost on me that we still celebrated such events nearly 2,000 years after these reliefs were sculpted, be it in the form of bullfights in Spain or mixed martial arts in the United States, maybe even more so when factoring in the spectatorship television and the internet brought.

The second room was the Small Artifacts Gallery. As the name suggested, it was full of small artifacts, including vases, cups, bowls, figurines, and other items the size of my hand. Tahli probably loved this room, seeing at was her field of study, but I was more interested in the stories of people than the composition of pottery.

The most interesting room contained findings from the theatre. If I wanted stories, this was the room to visit. It mainly contained sculpted reliefs, each telling its own story of a different performance, in whole or in part. The first relief I encountered portrayed the scene where Hades kidnapped Persephone with a chariot pulled by four horses. Another showed the birth of Apollo, depicting him leaping from his mother's womb as she clung to a tree. And so went the reliefs around the entire circumference of the room. Fortunately, the reliefs had descriptions and overviews of the myths from which they came.

I was disappointed that the area surrounding the antique baths was closed to the public. These places were often closed "for excavation" while no excavation was underway. My disappointment abated slightly when I saw the long tables and organised rows of artifacts being sorted and catalogued. Evidently, I wasn't the only one with such sentiments over the years, as security guards were posted to prevent people from entering. In atypical Turkish security guard fashion, they were alert and paying attention, so I didn't push the envelope.

In any event, it was time for the travertines. These were "Insta-famous" for their cascading white pools that flowed from the top of the 200-metre-tall hill. In the summer, they were full of crystal blue, warm water with tourists from around the world soaking themselves in the sun. In the winter, when I was there, there were still locals in the pools, but the water levels weren't what they would be in six months' time. With the lower water levels, the pools were much cooler in the winter air. They weren't uncomfortably cold to stand in, but I wasn't about to get much further than calf-deep. With clouds from the incoming cold front overhead, the pools didn't shine their brilliant blue and white as seen on social media but reflected a dull off-white and grey. At this time of year, sitting on the stone benches and terraces overlooking the travertines and Pamukkale was more pleasant than doing the same soaked in lukewarm water.

When it came time to leave, I decided to take the "easy" route back to Pamukkale. The travertines led straight down to Pamukkale by way of a semi-worn path through them as they headed south. I would have to walk them barefoot, but the water in them was lukewarm, not cold to the touch, so made my way downward. That was a mistake. The travertine rock was freezing cold against my wet, bare feet, just as the stone was in the Yazidi temple at Lalish, and some of the pools were so shallow that the cool, winter air turned the standing water from lukewarm to downright cold. My feet quickly turned red and painful from the walk, and any chance I could, I stood in the warm, moving water as it made its way steadily downhill (and cooled along the way, I would add). What I hoped would be a pleasant travel story rapidly turned into an experience I couldn't wait to end. By the time I reached the bottom, I was ready to soak my feet in a warm bath back at the hotel, which was still a ten-minute walk away; fifteen with me gingerly limping on my freezing feet.

It was a long bus ride to Göreme in Cappadocia the next day, and the morning came quickly. Fortunately, the hotel arranged a taxi to take me to the Denizli bus station, seeing as the rideshare apps hadn't made it to Pamukkale yet. I arrived at the bus station several hours early for the bus. The bus company's website sometimes didn't work, and this was one of those times, so I had to book a ticket directly at the company office. I had seen online how fast the routes filled up, and I didn't want to take any chances. Besides, with an eleven-hour bus ride ahead of me, it wasn't like I would be doing anything else that day. Fortunately, they had plenty of tickets, although my bus wasn't for a few more hours, so I settled in for coffee and a croissant at the station's café.

My morning would not be entirely peaceful, however, as I noticed two men come out of the back part of the bus station where I assumed the offices were. They walked straight to me from the other side of the reasonably large bus station. The one that spoke the most English (which wasn't much) flashed a badge and Turkish General Directorate of Security identification card and said, "We are undercover police. I need your passport." Not being one to argue with the police in this part of the world, I complied, and he thumbed through the pages. I wasn't particularly worried about being carted off to jail, but I was curious why they made a beeline straight for me from beyond public view. He thumbed the pages and asked me which country I was from. I told him, "America," knowing that the word was the same in Turkish, to which he replied, "Which country?" This was an annoying question, as many younger people in Europe were pushing to stop calling the United States "America" because they thought it was insulting to everyone else on the two continents. I was perturbed that a Turkish undercover police officer would make this distinction. When I told him, "United States," he replied, "No, what country?" So, I said, "America," to which he, again, replied, "No, what country?" He was getting irritated with the back and forth as I again told him, "United States." I wasn't trying to give him the run-around, especially with a language barrier, but I didn't know what else to tell him.

That was when he clarified, "No, what country? Montana, Texas, New York...?" "Oh!" I said, "Texas," laughing at the miscommunication (not that it didn't say it in my passport in the first place...). It was then that the other man, who didn't speak English, stopped him thumbing through my passport and pointed to the pages. I didn't even have to look to see which pages he was looking at; it was my Iraqi Kurdistan visas, with the red "Invalid" stamp jumping off the page. I knew the Turks were no friends of the Kurds, and I didn't want to somehow get caught up in this ethnic dispute because of some Shi'a terrorists in Syria a couple of weeks before. Lucky for me, after a few more questions about where I was going, why I was in the country, and, more importantly, when I was leaving, they returned my passport and went on their way back to their surreptitious office.

Some people I knew would have been annoyed, caused a scene, or freaked out at such an interaction, but after six months of continuous travel and more than a few sketchy situations over the years, I had learned the best course of action was to remain calm, comply with requests, and, if things got too sketchy, ask for the embassy. While they never told me their reasons for questioning me, I quickly put together the most likely scenario once they were out of sight and I was safely sipping my coffee. I arrived at the bus station several hours before my bus was scheduled to depart and bought the ticket in person instead of online. From an internal security perspective, I could understand why they were interested. I looked like someone from a particular line of work with a particular American agency who was trying to arrange a meeting and get out of town without giving the government details of my travels in advance. Did I know this to be the case for sure? Of course not, but it seemed like the only plausible explanation then and now. Besides, it gave me a good laugh to think about it all. Almost every time my passport was checked in any country, a police officer or security guard saw the blue cover of the American passport, and they handed it back or waved it aside. They weren't interested in Americans; they had more significant concerns, like Islamic State terrorists trying to smuggle themselves into Europe, human traffickers smuggling refugees for outrageous prices, and criminal gangs corrupting society, politicians, and the government.

After I satisfied myself with this explanation, I pulled out my Kindle, read more about Christian history and the politics of Rome, and, eventually, boarded the bus for Cappadocia.

Göreme

As was the pattern in Turkey, I rolled into Göreme late in the evening. Fortunately, my hostel wasn't very far, and I had eaten dinner at one of the stops on the way. I wasn't sure exactly what I was doing in Göreme; I knew Cappadocia was a popular tourism destination for the views, hiking, and hot air balloon rides, but that was the extent of my knowledge. I wasn't willing to acknowledge it yet, but I was wearing out after moving so quickly through Turkey, so day-to-day planning had started to fall by the wayside.

I only had two days in Göreme, so I needed to be judicious with my time. I decided to focus on hiking. If the scenes were as great as they appeared on Instagram and YouTube, two days of hiking was a great use of limited time. At least, that was what I thought until I got lost on my first hike. I had decided to hike the Love Valley Trail for the promising views over Göreme. Just on the west side of Love Valley was the famous hot air balloons' landing zone, so there had to be some great landscape views. Unfortunately, the trail was unmarked for hikers, so you had to find your own way via trails carved into nature by earlier travellers. We called these "cadet trails" in the military because cadets in training would always follow the identifiable trails to their next objective rather than going off the beaten path.

Well, I fell into the cadet-trail trap and rapidly found myself at the bottom of the valley instead of the ridge above. It was an interesting conundrum. On the one hand, I was about 60 to 100 metres below the cliffs where I hoped to be. On the other, I was where all of the pictures of the valley online were taken. You win some, you lose some, and sometimes it all cancels out, and all you can do is make the best of where you end up. In that moment, I stood beneath the forty-metre-tall rock formations that gave Love Valley its name, at least according to one legend.

Love Valley's name depended on the source you were reading. According to one legend, two soldiers (one male, one female) from feuding villages fell in love at first sight when they were sent to settle the feud. Their subsequent marriage and family, so the legend went, were not enough to reconcile the feud between the two sides, and the wife's village killed the husband, after which the wife committed suicide. As punishment, God rained stones upon the valley as a warning to anyone who may stand in the way of youthful love in the future. It was a nice legend, but it was legend nonetheless.

A second, more believable story was that the name stemmed from the sort of capstone rocks which adorned the forty-metre-tall rock formations. The capstone supposedly looked like a heart, but I didn't see it. The third story was even more believable, in that the name came from the phallic shape of these same formations. That I believed. Of course, the second story was probably the most accurate, seeing as the valley had been around far longer than our obsession with all things sex (not that ancient peoples weren't; they just didn't tend to name things after it).

In any case, I stood at the base of these imposing tower-like formations, just like the ones I saw on my phone while trying to figure out where I had taken a wrong turn. I really wasn't sure I had taken a wrong turn based on the pictures, but the fact that I was in the valley instead of on the cliffs was what detectives called a "clue." Not one turn back on a trail until it became abundantly clear there was no more trail to follow, I continued on my way. I followed the paths in the tuft rock, which I wasn't entirely sure weren't just the paths rain flowing into the valley had made as opposed to people, as they continued up parts of the cliff side to turn back down towards the valley. At one point, I had to slide down a steep bit of loose rock to keep following the path, and I was reminded of the video game *Uncharted 4: A Thief's End* that I loved to play back home. There was plenty of sliding in jeans and cargo pants in the video game, but their pants were made of special material which wouldn't rip, snag, or tear no matter how bad the terrain was. My Wrangler travel pants weren't as durable, and sliding down the rock left a permanent, faded, white streak down the rear seam.

I finally came upon what I was sure was a hiking path, as it was well-trodden, wide, and traversed by a group of high-school-age teenagers and what looked to be a teacher. Another clue! I must have been a sight to see coming out of the brush alone with my tan Wranglers, olive-drab messenger bag, and Goorin Bros Henry Jones fedora. Some smiled and said hello in English, others stared, and some started singing "The Raiders March." I politely smiled back, used to and embracing such characterisations by this point in life, and finally found my way out of the other side of the valley. While I hadn't made it atop the cliffs overlooking the valley, it was an eventful day, even though my roundabout path put me halfway to the next town on the main road.

The long walk back to Göreme was worth it, though, as the city was situated in the middle of a valley whose ridges marred the landscape in nearly all directions. As I walked, I was treated to terrific views of the tuft-rock-laden landscape. The topography was intriguing. Rather than seeing mountains rising up as one might expect to see based on the topographical map, it looked like the towns, caves, and rock formations were dug out from the ground. The scene looked like one long, flat plateau stretching out in all directions with roads, trails, and everything else cut into it as though carved into a block of clay where the point was to waste as little as possible. It almost looked like an ant farm, except with delicious food and a richer history.

After lunch at a scenic overlook, I finally returned to the hostel for a siesta. I had my fill of hiking and walking for the day. While uploading some photos and watching a bullfight from Mexico in the common area, I fell into conversation with a guy named Sonny. Sonny hailed from Europe and had been travelling the world for a while. He wasn't a professional YouTuber or anything, just a regular guy curious about the world. He was in Göreme to cross taking a hot air balloon ride over Cappadocia off his bucket-list. We fell into deep conversation about things we had learned in our travels, our favourite places, unique experience, and, ultimately, the state of world affairs. Sonny was genuinely interested in my (an American's) thoughts on the strategic situation in Ukraine and Israel and how a potential second presidential term for Donald Trump might affect those conflicts. We talked for hours and hours until I finally had to go to bed before I fell asleep right there at the table. Even though we wouldn't see each other after leaving Göreme in a couple of days, we periodically kept up with each other on social media, continuing to exchange travel stories, country tips, and thoughts about major events in the world.

On my second full day in Göreme, I headed east to hike Sword and Red Valleys. As it was the farthest away, I started in Red Valley and intended to work my way back to Sword Valley and Göreme. The weather had other plans, as about twenty minutes into my time at Red Valley, rain started falling. It wasn't hard, at least for the time being, but I was far too far away from town to get caught in a downpour, so I abandoned Red Valley for the closer Sword Valley. At least then I would be close to a warm shower and a dryer for my clothes. I planned to do laundry that night anyway.

As luck would have it, the road back took me by the Aynalı Kilise, called the Mirrored Church in English. Like most of the original dwellings in the region, this church was carved into and out of the tuft-rock cliffside in the mid-900s (although there were indicators that the church may have dated to the 500s). The church faced north, which was odd as someone who once lived in Colorado. South-facing façades, buildings, and driveways ensured the sun melted the snow, while north-facing ones provided shadows which kept the snow from melting and the air from warming. The north-facing windows probably kept the church cool in the summer, but I could only figure that they also kept it cold in the winter, colder with the wind whipping through.

The inside of the Mirrored Church was simple, with unpainted walls except for the exclusively red adornments. The hand-painted crosses on the walls and ceilings and the decorations on the support beams looked to have been done in the same style as the Bayeux Tapestry in Bayeux, France, despite the two being separated by 200 years and the entire European continent. The church got its name from these hand-painted adornments, as the rooms were symmetrically painted. Even the crosses on the walls and ceilings were perfectly centred (or as nearly as could be seeing as they were hand-painted). It was an impressive display of artistry, considering the crudeness of the tools available.

This church also served as a monastery for a time, and the upper floors were dedicated to monastic living. There was a kitchen with a flat, stone cooking area, water cistern, wine press, and even a beehive. Some rooms were only accessible via small corridors barely big enough to squat through. These were the Cappadocian version of Europe's priest holes, where priests, monks, and their valuables sought refuge when the church was under siege. These rooms were dark with no natural sunlight able to reach them. Fortunately, the man who sold the tickets provided a torch for everyone to use. As an American, whose freedom of religion and practice thereof was enshrined in our constitution and a driving factor in the original settlements, it was difficult to imagine what it must have been like to know that a man of the cloth was being persecuted by the government or other religions to the point of having to climb into dark, damp holes for long periods of time. While modern-day Turkey had freedom of religion codified in its constitution, there was still substantial societal mistrust of non-Muslims (specifically, non-Sunni Muslims), and some government officials considered missionaries of non-Muslim faiths as a threat to Turkish society. It wasn't beyond the realm of possibility that the priest holes in places like the Mirrored Church may once again find themselves in use should religious fundamentalism retake the country, either via the government or terrorist groups.

The rain had let up by the time I left the Mirrored Church, so I continued my way to town. After my time at the 1,000-year-old church and monastery, I was reinvigorated to explore some of the region's religious, specifically Christian, history. I abandoned my plan to hike Sword Valley in favour of visiting the Göreme Open Air Museum, a monastic village-like area whose caves, dwellings, and churches were open to the public. These monastic villages were all over Cappadocia, as Saint Basil (the region's bishop for many years) was a proponent of the monastic lifestyle. Many of these caves were either off limits by government regulation or inaccessible because of the terrain, but the Open Air Museum was part of Turkey's national museum network. It was carefully maintained, with security guards in key areas to enforce rules on tourists and ensure the site's continued preservation. I appreciated this enforcement, as it was the first serious attempt I had seen of the deliberate balancing of tourism and archaeological conservation in a long time.

Most of the Göreme Open Air Museum was composed of simple cave dwellings. That description wasn't an insult, nor did it diminish the site's religious importance; it was simply an apt description of the life in Cappadocia for hundreds of years before modern times. Tables, beds, altars, storage vats, everything was carved out of the rock face in a simple, unassuming manner. After all, monasticism included rejecting the modern niceties of life in favour of austere contemplation devoid of distractions.

The most impressive and, in my opinion, important caves at the Open Air Museum was the Dark Church, so named because of its lack of natural sunlight. The Dark Church's entry was through a cave opening, then right through a short hallway before turning left into the sanctuary. This design prevented distraction, and light, from the outside world during worship. During my visit, it was dimly and carefully lit so as not to diminish the paintings inside. The sign outside and security guard in the sanctuary made it crystal clear that photos were not allowed, so it could remain preserved for generations and centuries to come. It occurred to me that they could have simply banned flash photography, but I knew tourists couldn't be trusted to abide by that rule. Which was a shame, because it was one of the most vibrant and beautifully-painted religious sites I had ever seen.

The Dark Church's frescos told stories from Jesus's life. Depending on the wall you were facing, you could see the story of the Annunciation, Assumption, Crucifixion, Resurrection, miracles, and more. If you knew your Bible, there was little need for interpretive hoops to understand what you were seeing; the frescos were so well-preserved that their meanings came across as clear as if they had been painted that morning. The domes depicted Biblical figures which figured prominently in Christ's story. The Four Evangelists were painted on the domes' support arches, drawn full-length and holding scrolls as the authors of the Gospel. Surrounding Jesus inside the dome were the Old Testament prophets, a detail I appreciated as they were commonly omitted from Catholic cathedrals. The four archangels were also present, depicted in the four corners of one of the domes as though they were guarding their Saviour. I only knew of the three Catholic archangels, Michael, Gabriel, and Raphael (and, personally, only recognised Michael as such, as he was the only one specifically designated an archangel in the Protestant Bible). The fourth was Uriel, who was venerated in the Byzantine Catholic, Eastern Orthodox, and Anglican churches. Naturally, the Apostles were also depicted beneath Jesus, as they were the ones who carried His message to the world.

I was astounded at the frescos' vibrancy, clarity, and religiosity. I took my time viewing them as tourists and groups came and went, annoyed they couldn't take photos of the beautiful church. I put them out of mind as I carefully examined the millennia-old depiction of Jesus's life. The guard noticed me studying them as someone who was more than the typical tourist on a picture-taking tour. As I turned to leave the sanctuary, he caught my attention and asked, in the little English he knew, "You understand?" while pointing at the frescos. When I told him I did, he quickly glanced around, nodded to me, and said, "You take photo. It's okay." I was shocked! This guard was stringently enforcing the rules, which I appreciated, and now, with the church empty, he was willing to let me take a few. Not wanting to disrespect the church or the site, I hesitated at first, but he assured me it was alright. I didn't take many, just two from the entrance, but I was beyond grateful for the mementos. My travel-long mission of learning about Christian history and depictions in art was paying off in ways I couldn't have imagined.

After exploring the other churches at the Open Air Museum, which were impressive and well-maintained but not as vibrant as the Dark Church, I left for Göreme. I had foregone lunch and was hungry. As I walked along the downhill stretch to food, I reflected on the Dark Church and its frescos. It must have been a surreal experience for monks to reflect and pray in such a place. I wanted to believe it was these same monks that painted these scenes, with the painstaking detail and vibrant colours being a testament to their dedication to their faith, but it was more likely that these paintings were commissioned by the Church or government (though that didn't take away from their religiosity).

With the rain passed and the cold front catching up to me once again, I settled in for the night. I turned in my laundry to the hostel to wash overnight, searched for some tavuk shish, and booked my bus ticket for the next day. It was crazy how quickly a day in the life of a traveller could change so drastically from wake-up to lie-down. I had been hiking, taken a religious turn, and then busied myself with administrative tasks, all in the course of about ten or twelve hours. One thing was certain: going home, whenever that happened, would be a major adjustment.

Ankara, Istanbul, and Crossing the Continent

The bus to Ankara was relatively short, only about five hours, so my day wasn't totally wasted on travel. Even so, I was wiped. I was trying to push it off, but my last three weeks had flown by so fast as I covered half of Turkey that I hadn't had time to have a proper rest. There were museums to see, mosques to visit, and political influences to observe, but I didn't have it in me. When I awoke on my first morning, it was hard to pull myself out of bed. Not even my morning espresso got me going as I struggled to keep my mind focused and eyes open. It was a losing battle, and I ultimately surrendered. I resigned myself to spending my time in Ankara resting, reading, planning, and writing while giving myself a break before I flew to Oceania in a few days.

I was disappointed, initially. These moments always felt like failures on the road, especially when they cratered my plans for entire cities. But you can't outrun your mind or body no matter how hard you try; eventually, the fatigue, unfelt stress, and need for a break will take you down. I still had another four months of continuous travel to go, and they were going to fly by with my planned route of ten days in Bali, three weeks in Australia, two weeks, each, in New Zealand, Vietnam, and Cambodia, and three weeks in Thailand, before landing in Mexico for two months of diving. If I kept pushing myself, I would never make it, and I risked becoming sick from exhaustion (something I had seen in the military; it wasn't a pretty sight). So, I gave myself permission to slow down and blow off Ankara. Before I knew it, three lazy days passed and I was back at Lola Backpackers Hostel in Istanbul preparing for my flight to Bali.

Fortunately, many of the friends I had made in Istanbul before were still there, so I didn't feel like I was wasting my time. Between takeout, beer, cards, and playing with the hostel cats, we caught up, swapped stories, and enjoyed the company of our fellow nomads. Like all good things, this, too, came to an end, and just before the end of January, I boarded my transcontinental flight to Bangkok with onward travel to Bali.

Reflecting on Turkey

Converting churches. Empires and religions changed often in Turkey's long history. I was struck by how many mosques were built on top of or converted from Christian churches, which were themselves built on top of or converted from Greek or Roman temples. I saw this same phenomenon at the Philae Temple in Egypt, where the Christians took over, defaced, and converted the Egyptian temple to a Christian place of worship. This was something I didn't like seeing. I felt my own religion was disrespected. Christianity wasn't a thing of the past; it was the largest religion in the world, and the denigration of our sanctuaries and places of worship was offensive. Just because empires changed hands didn't mean the local faith auto-matically disappeared. After all, we condemned such forced conversions in our his-tory, be they the Native Americans during colonial times or the Jews before their 1452 expulsion from Spain. More recently, the world was outraged at Islamic State's forced conversion, persecution, and execution of those whose territories it con-quered. While I was wholly opposed to judging the past by the standards of the present, it was still something that offended me. I couldn't imagine that if the situa-tion were reversed, the world would not be outraged at Christian churches and ca-thedrals sitting atop the remains of a converted mosque.

Security in Turkey. Westerners, especially Americans, would recoil in shock if we applied the security measures in the United States that were standard day-to-day realities in Turkey. For example, there were checkpoints along the roads where police stopped vehicles, especially public transport busses, and checked everyone's passport to ensure they were present legally. These checkpoints weren't just on the border. I encountered them on every bus ride through Turkey's interior, sometimes a couple of times a trip. If you were found to be present illegally, have an outstanding warrant for arrest, or any other issue with the police, they would arrest you on the spot. No civil rights, no lawyer, nothing. Just you in the back of a police car until they made their way to the station to process you. The same was true of my encoun-ter with the undercover police. Americans were notorious for pulling out their phones at the first slight from police in an attempt to win a lawsuit. There was no such right in Turkey, and compliance wasn't just expected, it was compulsory.

As a result, I didn't feel unsafe in Turkey, just as I hadn't in Iraqi Kurdistan. These checkpoints weren't intended to enforce compliance with the regime but to secure the country against threats. The passport checks weren't looking to harass travellers or extort money but to catch criminals, terrorists, and traffickers. While this may offend people from my country, this was the common style of security and policing in the world. Our Western style, based on the principles of Sir Robert Peel, was just that, Western, where we were secure in our persons, property, and commu-nities. From a global perspective, we lived in a luxurious security situation that peo-ple worldwide would literally die for.

Chapter Seventeen

Bali: An Indonesian Vacation

My boss from my security firm went to Bali for his wedding anniversary while Jo and I were following a matador around Spain. He found a fantastic ten-day itinerary, stayed in nice resorts, and ate carefully curated food. His response to my asking about his trip: "Bali was amazing...If I didn't have kids I would take my retirement and move there next week." Coming from him, that was a ringing endorsement because he was someone who wanted to live in a cabin in the woods in Montana. Being sold, I made a stopover on my way to Australia to do some diving and enjoy the tropical weather. It was cheaper than flying directly to Australia, too, making the decision that much easier.

Sanur

My flight from Istanbul to Bali was a long journey with a stopover in Thailand. I flew across five time zones, which was fewer than I expected. Even so, it was a nine-hour flight to Bangkok and another four hours to the Denpasar International Airport on Bali; I was fortunate to have a row to myself on both flights. When I left Turkey, I was in the middle of the cold front I had been racing eastward, as I had crossed back west to Istanbul. Almost fifteen hours on an airplane, five time zones, and an equatorial crossing later, I was deplaning in the hot, humid air of Oceania. People looked at me like I was crazy for wearing pants, a sweatshirt, and my shemagh when I came off the jet bridge. Most of them were there for a tropical vacation and dressed like it. I had flown from the Turkish winter to the Oceanic summer and was dressed like it, too.

Bali was an island of Indonesia, which required visas for American travellers. I could have applied in advance, but I wanted a visa in my passport instead of some printed piece of paper like I got for Egypt, Jordan, Iraq, and Turkey. It wasn't a difficult process, and Bali's reputation as a tropical getaway incentivised the government to streamline the visa process. The longest part of getting my visa was the queue, which itself didn't take too long, and after a few minutes I cleared customs and was standing outside in the wonderful hot and humid air.

My hostel had arranged for an airport pickup. It was on the expensive side (relative to Bali prices, anyway), but after fifteen hours on airplanes, I didn't care. While still on a budget, I allowed myself to turn this ten-day stopover into a vacation. A real vacation, where I relaxed, didn't go all out on travel experiences, enjoyed drinks on the beach, went diving, and took in the warm, tropical sun. The clock was ticking fast now, with my countdown to divemaster training in Mexico accelerating with each passing day. It would start to feel like a runaway train sooner than later. What better place to prepare for that than the beaches where the Indian and Pacific oceans met?

After about thirty minutes of driving, we arrived at the hostel in Sanur. Sanur was a tourist town and felt a little like Cancun, Mexico. The main road was lined with Western restaurants, Starbucks, and Balinese restaurants offering tourists the "authentic" experience for inflated prices. Set inland off the main road were hotels with security guards, chauffeurs, and luxury suites. Behind that part of the city was where the locals lived and where my hostel (which Southeast Asian countries called homestays) was located. We were on a nondescript, one-lane-but-two-way street behind the busyness of the tourist drags, but close enough to walk anywhere I wanted. For a vacation during long-term travel, it was a great compromise of budget and location.

The homestay had a few new rules which were unique to this part of the world. Firstly, shoes were not allowed inside the building past the entry way. That was perfectly understandable, given how muddy the roads could get in the rains that would inevitably come during my visit. Secondly, we could enter the temple on the terrace, but only if we wore long pants, covered our shoulders, and remained respectful. After Turkey, this was no problem for me, but the fact that there was a temple on the terrace was intriguing. Indonesia, a country which comprised over 17,000 islands, boasted the world's largest Muslim population. I knew this from prior jobs, and I was admittedly somewhat concerned to travel there, because I knew of Indonesia's problem with Islamic State and other Islamist extremists. Bali, however, was an exception, as it was overwhelmingly Hindu, a religion which I knew almost nothing about outside of their protestation against eating beef. The temple on the terrace, I learned, was a common household adornment. While not all home temples were large, gated areas, almost every home had some location for practising their faith, even if they were just small shrines on an altar. I appreciated their devotion to their faith, and I more than once mused about how Christians in the United States, where church attendance was in steady decline, could take note.

After a nap and a call back home, I wandered into Sanur. I wasn't going to explore much after a very long travel day, but I wanted to try some of the delicious food my former boss raved about. I made my way north along the main road, where I could stop at the bank of cashpoints not far away, in search of some budget-friendly, delicious food. As I walked, it was impossible not to notice how much Western tourism had taken over the city. Almost every sign was in English, and the food prices were cheaper than at home, probably to give tourists a perception of it being cheaper while still ranking in substantial profits, but it still seemed pretty expensive. Of course, all these restaurants targeted tourists, and it reminded me of walking down through the Hotel Zone in Cancun.

That is, until I walked past a narrow restaurant where the lone waiter was wearing cut-off jeans (literally), no shoes, and was sweating in the lack of air conditioning. He had the look of a man who was hustling to provide for his family in an area where he was up against big money. He was too busy to shove a menu into the face of every passerby, whereas the other restaurants were eagerly trying to usher you in. I picked up one of the menus (which were in Indonesian and English) to check the prices. Seasoned chicken with rice and vegetables for 40,000 Indonesian Rupees (IDR). That came out to about 2.50 USD. A large water was another 15,000 IDR (about 1 USD). This was the place I was looking for! Sure, it took a little while to get the food out, seeing as there was one waiter and one cook, but it was well worth the wait to have a more authentic experience than all the top-rated restaurants with expansive menus I passed on the way. To be fair, this restaurant offered high-priced meals of pork ribs and snapper if you wanted them, but the prices still were nothing compared to his surrounding competitors (who, just a few metres away, were offering the same 70,000 IDR pork ribs for a substantial 125,000 IDR!).

Being completely satisfied with my evening meal, I steadily made my way back to the homestay. I was still jetlagged from the flight and was ready for some rest. I missed the days where I didn't get jetlagged from jaunts across the world. Before this trip, I had only experienced it once when I flew from Texas to Kuwait for the military. On my numerous flights to and from Europe and Africa in my late twenties, I never experienced jetlag, but I guess a lot of things changed after you turned thirty. I was too fatigued to stay out, but too alert to go straight to bed, so I hung out on the pavilion-like terrace with a German guy who had just checked in. We regaled each other with travel stories, each of us shocked with some of the other's. He couldn't believe I travelled through parts of Iraq, and I couldn't believe he travelled the United States via Greyhound bus. It was a hilarious situation to find myself in, justifying travelling to Iraq while decrying travelling my own country via bus. As a European, it was a totally foreign idea to travel to Iraq, but seemed entirely natural to travel a Western country via their low-cost bus system. It was amazing how travelling shifted our perspectives and how we carried our own ethnocentric ways of thinking on the road.

As luck would have it, my first and only full day in Sanur started with a torrential downpour. It was the rainy season in Indonesia, something I knew before coming but couldn't appreciate before seeing it for myself. The rain came down hard, not in sheets, but as if a shower faucet above the island was completely opened up. From the terrace, it was a surprisingly peaceful sight. Of course, I wasn't out working in it like many of the locals were, and I wasn't here for my once-in-a-lifetime family vacation, either, so I could (literally) afford to take it in a lighter mood. After a couple of hours, as I heard it would from my former boss, the rain stopped, and the sun shone once again upon the island, increasing the humidity to about a million percent as the rain evaporated around me.

Once the rain let up, I took a stroll to the beach. I wasn't getting in the water seeing as I had to pack my bag that night, but I wanted to see this side of the global ocean for the first time. When I finally made it down the public access walkway to the beach, I couldn't help but smile. I could now say I had gazed across the ocean from both sides. It was January; the March before, I had sat on the beach outside Todos Santos on the Baja Peninsula, staring west across the largest ocean in the world, wondering what life would look like in a year. Whatever I imagined then, it was nothing like the life I was living now. I never dreamed I would be on Bali on vacation, not with my income, savings, and budget, but there I was, almost a wholly different person than the last time I laid eyes upon the Pacific.

Still being a little jetlagged, I looked for a local coffee shop, which I found along one of the beach access roads; although, it stretched the meaning of the word "shop." It was more of a roadside bar, behind which the family who operated it lived. Places like this served the best of everything, and the gathering of family friends laughing and cutting up at the counter was a good sign. They invited me into their conversations with open arms; they even switched to English for my benefit. I learned this coffee shop was started by the owner's father, and he took it over not too long before. Not that his father had passed away or anything; he just wanted his son to take it over so he could stop working. Over the next couple of hours, we talked about everything, from travel experiences to our different cultures to what our original homes were like (they were from a different part of the island) to light-hearted politics. A family of Australians, which were plentiful on the island, joined in at one point, and after the owners' friends left, the Australians gave me some pointers for travelling through Australia. Was it how I intended on spending my morning? Not at all. Was it a waste of a day? Zero percent. Mornings like this were the exact reason I was on the road in the first place, to engage with new people and cultures in a meaningful way.

As I prepared to leave, a large group of locals came down the road singing, dancing, and carrying a coffin. The owner encouraged me to follow them. This was a Ngaben, a funeral, he told me, and they were going to burn the coffin (and the body) on the beach and scatter the ashes into the ocean. The Ngaben were not a mourning of loss like those so prevalent in the West but a celebration of the deceased's life and the soul's onward journey to the afterlife. While the Ngaben was technically a Hindu practice, it was unique to Bali, combining Hindu beliefs with local traditions. For example, the burning of the body was viewed as the best way to ensure the soul ended up in the upper realm of the afterlife (i.e., Heaven, in Christian terms) instead of the lower realm (i.e., Hell or Purgatory) (these are rough, not exact, comparisons). And burn it they did. I don't know what I was expecting, but it wasn't setting the coffin on fire in the middle of a singing and dancing crowd on a beach. I at least expected a formal cremation area, but the only thing formal about it was where they placed the wood for the fire. It was quite the sight to see, especially as a Westerner. I didn't stay until the end, when they would collect the ashes to later scatter into the ocean. I knew how long it would take a body to burn in a standard bonfire.

After more wandering on the beach and over-priced seaside meals, it was time to pack up for my next destination on Bali. Time had started to race by, but I hoped it would slow down over the next few days. I had a four-day, ten-dive package booked in Amed, on the northeast side of the island, that I was looking forward to for 4,800,000 IDR (about 300 USD). Between the fantastic dive experience in Aqaba and my upcoming divemaster training, I was ready to get back in the water.

✳ ✳ ✳

Amed

The public transport system between cities on Bali was... interesting. There were legitimate bus companies that moved people around the country, and they were in ample supply to meet the demand from tourists and locals alike. That said, coming from Turkey, where the buses were air conditioned, modern, and had a bus attendant who provided snacks, drinks, and made sure you were prepared for your stop, it was an adjustment. On Bali, the buses were really twenty-passenger vans (at most) which may or may not have had air conditioning, depending on which van you were in. On top of that, some roads across the rural parts of Bali were not exactly well-maintained. I would describe them as passable on a good day. The bus stops, too, were not stations, but Google Maps pins on the side of the road. In Sanur, it was outside of a convenience store. When I arrived to Amed, it was the parking lot of a café. I wasn't concerned about safety or security; it was just an experiential adjustment.

The drop-off point was in Amed proper, but the pin for the dive shop's hostel was another ten-minute drive away on a winding, hilly road. I tried to use the Grab app (Southeast Asia's version of Uber) to get a ride, but there weren't any drivers in the more remote regions. A local man, clearly trying to make money off tourists who didn't know this, offered a ride for 50,000 IDR. This was more expensive than a Grab would have been, but I didn't have much of a choice. It was funny how easily it had become to get into the car with random strangers over the last seven months. He gave me his number for my return trip. Usually, I wouldn't take it, but I had seen my options.

I was at the Bali Reef Diver's dive shop dressed like I was ready for a long hike, not a dive trip. Unfortunately for me, there was a miscommunication regarding my booking. I was booked at the hostel, but they had given me their resort address. The dorm was a thirty-minute drive in the opposite direction. More than a little exasperated on a hot morning, I asked if there was any room at the resort. Any room would do; I just didn't want to mess with another thirty minutes of travel. There were some, but it would increase the price from 4,800,000 IDR to 7,200,000 IDR (a difference of about 160 USD). That was fine with me. While I didn't want to go any more over budget than I already was for these few days, I rationalised that I was on vacation and could afford to act like it. As a consolation for my troubles, the resort upgraded my room without extra charge and offered me an additional night after our diving was over. It was their slower season, so they had the space, and they were already making more money from me than they had originally planned.

That's how I found myself settling into an ocean-view bungalow with a king- and queen-sized bed, a beautiful bathroom, air conditioning, lounge chairs from which I could read to the sounds of the ocean, and the resort restaurant just outside my door. Even better, the dive shop was at the resort entrance at the top of the hill. I wouldn't have to get up early to catch transport to the dive sites. I could enjoy leisurely mornings with the included breakfast, coffee, a book, and the ocean breeze. My Balinese vacation was shaping up nicely.

I dropped my bags, had a quick lunch, and prepared for my first set of dives. The dive shop and I agreed to a schedule of two, three, three, two for each of my dive days, which included the day I arrived. Fortunately for me, because of the mix-up, we weren't in a rush, as my guide was at the other location. While I waited, I talked with the owner about his dive operation. All of their guides were locals, per Indonesian law, and most of them were brought up within Bali Reef Divers, so they were trained in the company way of doing things from the outset. Having once been a skydiving coach, I knew the value this brought to the company; it was always tricky hiring someone who was trained elsewhere. Even if they had the same exact certifications as everyone else, there were bound to be differences that could cause issues.

Because this was the low season, I more-or-less had a private guide. On our first day, we went to Jemuluk Bay and the Pyramids. Jemuluk Bay was a coral garden accessible via the shore, and the Pyramids were an artificial reef that looked like, well, pyramids. Even though most shops listed the second site as a boat dive, we entered both via the shore, something I was used to doing from Aqaba. They were beautiful dives where we saw all manner of creatures, including a six-legged starfish and moray eels. It was the refreshing afternoon I needed after the morning of bumpy van travel across the island.

Jemuluk Bay was setup for divers. There was a large, covered, concrete plat-form for divers to set up their gear and reminders everywhere to conduct the five-step buddy check. There were also snack carts. The locals knew divers well; we could put away our bodyweight in snacks between dives. Of course, with opportun-ism like this came risk, and my guide warned me not to leave anything attached to my gear, not even in the pockets, as it was likely to come up missing. In a place where an outrageously-priced meal cost 125,000 IDR (about 8 USD), a 300 USD (about 4,500,000 IDR) GoPro could go a long way in supporting a family.

I committed to eating my meals at the resort restaurant. Breakfast was included, and, quite frankly, it was the easiest option, seeing as there weren't many others within a sensible walking distance. The meals weren't obscenely overpriced, cer-tainly not to the levels I had seen in Sanur, and I could have done worse than to eat good food with my Kindle within walking distance of a shower. Plus, the sun setting behind me meant I could stare into the horizon and get lost in my thoughts. And get lost I did. A lot had changed in the last year, and I was happy to be in a secluded tropical paradise with nothing but the sounds of the ocean to keep me company as the water faded to black in the night.

On our second day, I paired up with Dijana, a beautiful girl from the Balkans who now lived in Germany. Well, was living in Germany. When I met her, she was working remote from Bali. Sort of. She had been downsized out of her company two different times in recent months, but, because of generous German labour laws, she received six months' severance each time, and she was using that time to travel. She arrived the night before from elsewhere on the island, having driven her motorbike in the pouring rain with her pack sitting between her legs.

Dijana and I first visited the United States Army Transport Liberty wreck. The USAT Liberty was torpedoed during World War II by a Japanese submarine after twenty-four years of service, including service in France during World War I. It was a great dive for multi-level diving, as the ship's depth ran from five metres down to thirty metres. It was a relatively open wreck, making it an easy dive for new dive partners. We followed the wreck with a visit to the Tulamben drop-off, a wall which dropped seventy metres to the ocean floor. This was my first experience with a wall, and I loved it. I got a feel for the different levels of marine life, as certain fish and coral tended to live at different depths along the same wall. Again, we went down to thirty metres, but didn't stay there nearly as long to stay within safety limits, and steadily made our way back up, seeing long, cylindrical schools of fish on the swim back to shore.

Dijana didn't do the third dive with us. She, instead, elected to lay by the pool at the hostel location and soak up the sun. No complaints here. We had hit it off straight away, and we spent lunchtime talking before I headed off for the third dive of the day at another coral garden. For months to come, we exchanged reels and memes on social media about diving, and I wanted to team up with her again for another travel experience.

I learned a serious lesson on my third day of diving. Three, actually. We were doing a drift dive, or what the dive shop called a drift dive. As I knew it, a drift dive was where you started at the top end of a current, let it carry you down with minimal swimming, and exited either to a known point on the shore or a boat. What my guide called a drift dive was swimming into the current. He warned me that how far we got would depend on the current, but the goal was to surface right in front of the resort. That was not the case. The current was strong, really strong, and I struggled to keep up. I sucked down air quickly, and I felt like I wasn't getting enough oxygen with every breath. I seriously considered ending the dive and heading to the surface, even though I knew that was problematic from a safety standpoint. I couldn't even make it to the rock my guide was trying to rest behind, and I struggled just to remain stationary without flying back in the direction we came. Enter lesson one: know your limits when diving against the current.

I also had trouble communicating with my guide. In diving, you were supposed to dive as a pair, but it was not uncommon for guides, when they only had one customer, to lead a bit ahead and the customer to follow. Was it the correct answer? No. Was it common practice across the world? Yes, and for hypothetically good reason. The guide could lead the dive while the customer enjoyed it while following. Unfortunately, the hypothetically good reasons didn't outweigh the correct reasons to dive together: if there was an issue of any kind, immediate communication was essential. As I struggled against the current, I watched as my guide swam further and further ahead. I had no way of signalling him, as I didn't have a tank banger, a shaker, or even a piece of metal to use as a makeshift noise maker. I decided that my dive watch wasn't worth the rapidly-approaching problem of being alone in the water and forced to conduct an emergency descent, so I took it off and used the metal surface ring to bang against my tank. I was careful-ish not to break it, but I needed the noise. Fortunately, my guide heard it immediately and turned around. Enter lesson number two: always, always, always carry a communication device.

While we held our position as I caught my breath, I felt a major stinging sensation on my left leg. I didn't know what it was, nor did I pay too much attention to it in the moment. The feeling came and went as we went along the dive, but my guide noticed me looking at my leg and immediately saw what had happened. He pointed at a piece of coral and shook his finger at me. It was fire coral. Technically, fire coral wasn't coral, but it lived up to its name. I had dragged my entire leg down the side of some, and I had the welts to prove it. Enter lesson number three: don't touch the fire coral, not even on accident!

The current ultimately took us back to the Pyramids site, so we swam on the surface back to the resort. The current was easier going on the surface, but getting to the resort was still a struggle, especially with the burning on my leg. Fortunately, the dive shop was prepared for it, and they hosed my uncovered extremities with vinegar to stop the stinging. The vinegar hurt worse than the fire coral, but at least it would counteract the venom. And it was venom, although it was nonlethal to humans. Of course, I later learned that movement could cause the venom to spread, and I had just done half a dive and an entire surface swim kicking through the water, so that probably didn't help matters.

Despite these three crucial lessons, I still had a fun day of diving, with us returning to Jemuluk Bay to dive another wall and section of the bay, which was populated with thousands upon thousands of garden eels. These small eels buried themselves in the sand and, from a distance, looked like a bed of seaweed. As we moved closer, the eels sank into their holes, and it looked like a wave emanating around us as the eels closest to us sank all the way in and the eels farthest stayed all the way out. I wished I could have gotten an up-close look at them, but their natural instincts outranked my tourist curiosity.

My final dive day was an easy one, as we dived the Boga Wreck and Monkey Reef. The wreck was intentionally sunk to create a dive site and included a car in its hold. The reef was, well, a reef. A nice, easy reef dive to cap off my Balinese vacation was just when I needed. I forgot to take my sunglasses off when we went into the water, so I stuffed them in the pocket of my dive jacket. My guide and I laughed when we came up, because I was able to put them on right away. I was the only person he had ever taken that came out of the water with his sunglasses on.

Thus, my dive trip came to an end. Just like that, it was time to head back to Sanur and board a plane out of the country. While I enjoyed my ocean-view bungalow to the fullest extent, I was ready to be back amongst other travellers. After another day on the beaches of Sanur, I took a Grab taxi to the airport.

While at the airport, I texted with Jo. We had been apart for about two months, and she had spent most of that time in Australia. She asked me where I was flying to next, and when I told her Cairns, she replied, "When do you get here?" I was confused, but apparently, she was in Cairns and flying back to the United States the next day. Talk about luck! We agreed to meet that night for dinner and hang out with some of the friends she had made as she travelled up Australia's eastern coast.

Reflecting on Bali

The heat and the humidity. I missed the heat and humidity. Jo and I purposely planned our trip to avoid the winter, but I hadn't quite made it in Turkey and Iraq. The winters weren't bad yet, but I still missed the heat. Even though we had spent a fair amount of time in the heat in North Africa, we hadn't been anywhere humid since Spain. I was from East Texas, where the humidity was always high, so it was what I was used to. Many people complained about it, and I was one of them until I moved to dry Colorado a few years before. Whenever I landed somewhere humid, be it Maui, the Yucatan, Texas, or Bali, I was always overcome with happiness. I would always say, "Man, I've missed the humidity," and even text that to friends. It was an odd thing to miss, considering how much more it made you sweat and raised the "feels like" temperature, but maybe it made me feel like I was back home. I wasn't looking forward to going back by any means, but the humidity always made me nostalgic and reflective. Good thing, I guess, because I had another five months of it ahead of me.

Westernisation. Bali was a major tourism destination, and the main parts of the city were increasingly Western. It was something I always struggled with as a traveller, because I wanted to experience the cultures as they were, not as Westerners wanted them to be. On the flip side, tourism brought major money and provided desperately-needed jobs to the country. Starbucks brought good pay and benefits where an independent coffee shop couldn't, large restaurants bought more product than mom-and-pop eateries, and variety brought with it more tourism as people moved around.

That said, I had to applaud Bali's attempts to balance mass tourism and preserving Bali for the Balinese. The law requiring dive shops to employ local dive guides, for example, prevented Westerners from moving to the island and taking local jobs while providing new opportunities to locals to support the tourism industry. Their property laws, too, were, to me, admirable. Foreigners couldn't outright own property in Bali. Foreigners could rent, lease, or acquire right to use titles, but that was as far as ownership went. This prevented Westerners from moving in and driving up prices on the locals more than tourism already did. Of course, there were some loopholes. For example, a right to use title authorised the holder to develop the land, and these leases often lasted thirty or more years, so it was de facto ownership. It wasn't a perfect balance, but it was better than I would experience in Mexico, where developers intentionally sought Western (specifically, American) buyers who could afford the foreign investment taxes and price tag.

Chapter Eighteen

Australia: Foreign and Familiar

The "Land Down Under" was a place which captivated travellers, explorers, and anthropologists for decades. To many, it was the last true frontier remaining, where everything could kill you, people were crude, informal, and lacked Western sophistication, and where you could connect with nature in ways not possible anywhere else on the planet. That was why I wanted to go. Australia, like Europe, was a rite of passage for travellers; whereas Australians backpacked Europe, Europeans backpacked Australia. I wasn't sure what to expect when I arrived after months in MENA, but I looked forward to the change in scenery, culture, and language before heading into the foreign, final, Southeast-Asian leg of my trip.

Cairns

I was flying to Cairns to dive the Great Barrier Reef. I wanted to dive the reef before I turned thirty, but didn't quite make it. Cairns also made logical sense for the next stage of my trip. I would travel south down Australia's east Coast before hopping over to New Zealand. This was the opposite direction most people went, but I had never been one to go with the flow. It worked out, as I could link up with Jo for a night on the town. She was the master of Australia travel now, somewhere I had never been, and the travel roles were now reversed. It was her turn to steer me in the right direction in a new country.

It felt foreign to be in an English-speaking country after travelling so long. The only places I travelled where English was the primary language were Ireland and the United Kingdom, and I left them behind over three months before. Clearing customs and the bio-security checkpoint were easy enough, and the man I sat next to on the plane gave me a ride to the hostel, which he called "The Jack." He jokingly gave me the tour of the town on the ride in. "And on the left we have the hospital, over there is a hotel, and just over there is the ocean." Cairns, he said, was a place you came to leave for nature. There were all sorts of beautiful hikes and dive sites to see, but the city itself wasn't much to speak of to him.

Jo and I arranged to meet at a burger place a block from my hostel. I was starving, and I didn't even try to change out of my travel clothes before heading for food. I looked every bit the adventurer in this city of college-age travellers and partiers in my tan pants, boots, shemagh, and Goorin Bros fedora. I would have been lying if I said that wasn't the image I wanted to project to Jo and her friends after three months solo in MENA.

When Jo finally arrived, she was in clothes I had never seen her in before. I joked, "I see you went shopping!" I wasn't making fun of her for it. We learned a lot about ourselves, both as individuals and as a duo, in our travels together, and one thing about her was she liked cute clothes on the road as opposed to the versatile, dull travel clothes so many professional backpackers advocated. While we were travelling together, this had become a headache for me when it came time to pack for airplanes, but now that we had separated, it didn't bother me. Besides, she was clearly happy. Two months in the Australian summer, clothes she was comfortable in, and a ton of new friends had turned her almost into an entirely different person from when we had decided to split up in Tunis. Compared to her, I must have looked ragged and worn out.

After our so-so burgers (a constant complaint of mine across the world), she invited me out with her friend for his birthday. I didn't have plans, as it was a travel day, so I acquiesced. It had been a while since I had been out for a drink (except for two Guinness during my stopover in Bangkok), and it was a little early to turn in. Besides, I couldn't deny myself to see what kind of company she was keeping these days. So, we headed off to Gilligans.

Gilligans was a large complex, with the hostel upstairs and the large, boisterous bar on the ground floor. Boisterous was an understatement. This was the place to be in town for a night out. Sometime after we got there, the bouncers started checking ID cards, and the queue wrapped around the block. It had been a long time since I last visited such a loud, crowded place, at least since Jo and I were in Belfast. It was an adjustment, and I was clearly out of my element. But then I met Emma, a girl from Northern Ireland just outside of Belfast, and we hit it off straight away. Jo knew I was a sucker for the Northern Irish accent, and I loved the attitude of the Northern Irish girls we had met. I always said I like the Northern Irish girls, "because they are always up for a good fight. Hell, they've been fighting one for centuries!" Emma laughed at the line as I told stories from Belfast. She was astounded that I would go anywhere near the Shankill or Falls Road area and thought I was the bravest guy ever for walking across Belfast without regard for which type of neighbourhood I was in (i.e., Catholic or Protestant).

She and her friend were on working holiday visas in Australia, staying upstairs at the Gilligan until they changed hostels the next day. They picked Gilligan's because it was cheaper and had a reputation for a lively atmosphere. They were changing hostels because "lively" meant "raucous partying," and her friend said there was not a single night she hadn't awoke to find couples, sometimes more than one, having sex on the floor or in the adjacent bunks. Such was the life of the party hostel in a sleepy town, and I hoped this wouldn't be the case over at the Jack (fortunately, my room was a much more mellowed crowd).

As Emma and I talked over a beer, I felt something I had never felt before: my hat came off my head. I whipped around fast to see a guy in a button-down Hawaiian shirt and shorts putting my hat on his head. Where I was from, back in Texas, there were only two reasons to take a man's hat off his head: to f*** or fight (as they saying went). Well, I wasn't gay, so that only left one option as I grabbed a hold of his collar and pulled him right back into me. I felt his shirt rip as I did, but I didn't care. My Goorin Bros Henry Jones had been with me to five continents, two military deployments, an intense breakup, several career changes, and everything in between. I had it so long that it was no longer in production. This idiot had no idea what he had stepped into as I stared him straight in the face with a balled fist at my side and said, "Give it back." I wasn't looking to get thrown in Australian jail on the first night, but I wasn't opposed to the idea, either. He fired back, "You ripped my shirt!" Tough luck. "Give. It. Back." He finally acquiesced and came in for a bro hug. He was on a dare from his friends at a nearby table to take it, and he rapidly came to regret taking them up on it.

As I turned back to the table, I made eye contact with Jo. She was shocked not so much that the guy took my hat but that I didn't give him the beatdown such stupidity deserved. She told me, "I saw it in your eyes. You were out for blood." I certainly was! Having watched the whole thing, Emma asked if I knew that guy, and I told her what he told me. He was on a drunken dare from his friends to take my hat, but where I was from, that was cause for a fight. You didn't touch a man's hat!

Emma took a sip and said, "I thought you were going to hit him!" to Jo chimed in, "Oh, I *knew* he was going to hit him!" I guess people like me, dressed like Indiana Jones or Nathan Drake, were just nerds to dumb twenty-somethings on their party trip through Australia, but I was a far cry from "just" a nerd. Part of me wished he hadn't given it back when I told him to just so I could have driven the point home to him, his friends, and anyone else who might have been watching. I was fairly confident I could count on Jo to back me up if I needed her to, although she probably didn't fancy spending her last night in Australia in jail for my antics.

Once the excitement calmed down, Emma and her friend went to a room with a DJ, but I wasn't feeling that. Too many people and too loud of music, and I was ready for bed. Jo felt the same. We didn't even have to talk about it. We just looked at each other and agreed, "Too many people..." So, we said our goodbyes and went our separate ways. She was starting her journey back to Texas the next day. She had some family stuff going on, and I knew she was homesick and had been for a while. But, and I told her as much several times in the coming months, I couldn't help but be proud of her for taking this journey. Sure, she didn't make it the whole year she had intended, but she travelled places, saw things, and made friends that no one back home would experience. After these last few months of flying solo, she had a renewed confidence and happiness about her that I hadn't seen in a while. In the coming years, we would travel together several more times on shorter trips and always have a blast.

Now that I was back on my own, I made a tentative plan for Cairns. I had three full days, so I mapped them out: explore the town (and do laundry), dive the reef, and go for some waterfall hikes. That seemed like a great way to spend my limited time in Cairns and get a healthy mix of what this town near the frontier had to offer.

My first day was alright. I did laundry, visited an outdoor store (my water bottle, Jo's Nalgene she bought in Austria, had broken in Turkey), and called my parents. It was a hot, humid day, something I missed but wasn't quite prepared for. I was sweating like crazy as I walked under the cloudless sky. In many ways, Cairns was like my hometown. Outside of the few streets near the coastal promenade, it was spread out, and having a car was a must if you lived there; the two-story mall was a refuge for teenagers who weren't in school and wanted a public place to hang out in the air conditioning; and there were more chain restaurants than I had seen in months, which I hadn't been used to since leaving the United States. It was strange being in this English-speaking country with all the commonalities of home.

I both liked it and didn't at the same time. It wasn't like being in Dublin or London, where English was the primary language but which were more akin to Madrid or Berlin than towns in East Texas. I was starting to understand what the man from the plane had told me; this was a place you came to leave, a good place to raise a family, but somewhere that didn't offer an incredible number of things "to do" for travellers and recreationists in the city itself. It felt strange yet normal to visit a Country and Western apparel store that sold long-sleeved pearl snaps and cowboy boots; this was something I did home just to have a look around. The abundance of country music, specifically Texas country music, was a shock to the system as well. I had stopped listening to country music almost a decade before as a consequence of an intense breakup. Since then, I avoided it with an almost militant zeal, but now, in Australia of all places, I heard it everywhere. It didn't sit well with me as I quickly moved on from any place playing songs from the past.

All of the foreign familiarity aside, I eventually wandered into the Reef Hotel Casino. I often said, "If I was a gambling man, and I am, I would bet..." I loved roulette and spent a substantial amount of time learning winning strategies in my early twenties. Granted, they hadn't paid off so well back in Venice, but this was a new house, and I was eager to give their wheels a spin. I gave myself 200 Australian Dollars (AUD), about 125 USD, to lose (it was always important to give yourself a limit on what you were willing to lose). I was wary of losing it quickly, as I enjoyed the casino atmosphere just as much as I did playing the game, and I didn't have anywhere else to be until the next day. Fortunately, that became a non-issue as my strategies paid off, and I quickly doubled my money. I sat at the table for a bit longer, winning some, losing some, but ultimately netting a few hundred AUD over the course of a couple of hours. Not a bad haul, and I resolved to use my winnings to pay for a trip to the Australia Zoo in Brisbane (which cost a whopping 90 AUD for a one-day ticket when you factored in the train to get there).

My second day in Cairns was the day I was looking forward to. It was time to dive the Great Barrier Reef! My motivations for doing so were twofold. First, it was the Great Barrier Reef. Enough said. Second, it was the only part of Gary Allan's song "A Feelin' Like That" that I hadn't checked off the list. I hoped it would live up to the hype in my head and I would finally find the feeling described in the song.

I dove with Divers Den on their large dive ship, the *AquaQuest*. I didn't know what to expect, as I was used to small groups, small boats, and shore dives, but the *AquaQuest* and its crew surpassed any potential expectations. Their spacious dive deck allowed divers to prepare their gear and get in the water efficiently, and their onboard air compressors meant we didn't have to change tanks (something which could get interesting on smaller boats). The safety procedures were top-notch, especially their double confirmation that everyone was on board. It wasn't that I had been concerned about safety in the past, but you didn't know a great operation until you saw one, and Divers Den was a great operation. There were ample instructors, an on-board medic, and a large galley for snacks, lunch, and hanging out (out of your wetsuit, of course).

I booked a three-dive excursion, which meant I was able to do two forty-minute dives and a fifty-minute one, the last two of which were just me and a dive buddy. Most of the divers were doing Discover Scuba Diving (DSD), which meant they were holding on to instructors the entire time and only doing one dive. Like most people that skydive, they only wanted to do it for the experience, not as a hobby or profession; and, like most people that skydive, they were all a combination of enthusiastic and nervous. I fell in with a group of girls travelling together in the galley and put on my skydiving coach hat to help put them at ease.

On the first guided dive, I paired up with a girl who had her Advanced Open Water certification. Our guide told us that as long as we stayed within visual range of the group, we could stray a bit down the wall to look at some of the other marine life. As cool as that was, I almost wished she hadn't said that; my dive partner had "piece of candy syndrome", where she chased every extraordinary creature she could find (at a respectful distance). It would be an interesting next two dives, that was for sure.

On our way back, we passed the DSD crowd. They took longer to get going as they had to practise a few safety skills underwater and get comfortable breathing through their mouth with the regulator. They looked like octopuses or starfish floating through the water; the instructor was in the middle with four DSD divers holding on tight. It was slow, but safe, going for the once-in-a-lifetime experience of diving the Great Barrier Reef.

After about an hour on the surface, my partner and I were back in the water. One instructor gave us their recommended route around the reef, which we tried to follow, but our unfamiliarity with the area led us astray. Not that we were lost; we were just geographically mislocated. Like good divers, we headed towards the deepest point first, where the reef gave way to the sandy bottom that led into still-deeper waters. We hadn't talked about it, but we both wanted to see a shark. We were new divers, and all new divers wanted to see sharks (well, the non-aggressive kind, anyways; I had no interest in coming face-to-face with a bull or tiger shark). We got our wish. A reef shark was settled just on the other side of the reef. It rested on the bottom, and we hovered (as best as two newer divers could) and watched for a few minutes. Eventually, it tired of our presence and swam into the deep blue beyond, and we couldn't hide our excitement. We threw our arms up, celebrating twenty metres deep like a NASCAR driver who had just won the Daytona 500.

Our first unguided adventure didn't stop there, however, as we headed back into shallower waters to see the more colourful coral. We were warned about the titan triggerfish in our pre-dive brief, and we kept a sharp lookout for them as we swam along. It was their mating season, and they were known to divers around the world as highly territorial. That they were. We unknowingly swam over a mating pair's nest under a large piece of coral. The triggerfish weren't on guard outside, but in the nest, which was why didn't see them. As a part of our routine dive, I looked over to check my buddy's air, which was when I saw her fighting against the water. Bubbles were everywhere as she punched and kicked at something. I didn't need to ask what it was; I knew. When I turned to face ahead, one of the triggerfish was right in front of my face, within arm's reach. We stared each other down as I quickly turned to my right and it kept pace with me. I never thought I would be in a position to punch a fish before, but there I was about to have the opportunity. The encounter seemed to last minutes, but I knew it was only a few seconds, and we finally swam out of their territory. We happened to be passing the guide from our last dive, and she asked if we were okay. We were, but we decided to head back to the boat. We were coming up on time, anyways. That was when I learned my buddy had been bitten on the leg, and she had a triggerfish-teeth-shaped bite mark just above her ankle. It hadn't drawn blood, fortunately, so she was no worse for wear with a story to tell.

Our third dive was more-or-less uneventful, although we did see another shark. This one wanted no part of us and bolted the second we got too close. Back on the boat, we returned to the group in the galley to catch up on everyone's day. Most loved their experience, while some said they were a one-and-done diver. Fair enough; at least they had given it a try. Most people lived in two dimensions, their feet never leaving the ground on which they walked, so I always gave credit to those who gave diving, skydiving, and other three-dimensional sports a try. One of the girls was going skydiving the next day. She had only done one dive, so she was technically in the clear to jump the next day, but the industry standard was to wait at least twenty-four hours before flying to avoid decompression sickness. She was leaving the day after her jump, though, so she would abide by the letter of the rule rather than the spirit. Not a big deal, but not an example I was likely to follow.

Being one to press my luck, I returned to the casino after the dives. I set aside my 90 AUD for the Australia Zoo, but played with my original 200 AUD and what-ever winnings I had left. After another couple of hours at the table, I was up again. I made a mental note to return and press my luck again. If I would never gamble in Venice again, the same superstition held that I would undeniably gamble in Cairns if I were ever there. Even when I returned the next day, as I was down to my last few AUD on my final bet before breaking even, I hit a 17-to-1 bet and walked out several hundred AUD in the black. Not even the dealer could believe it. He looked back and forth between the wheel and my bet, trying to understand what had just happened. All he could come up with was an impressed, "Wow..."

My final day in Cairns, I intended to hike one of the trails to a waterfall. Unfor-tunately, it was the wet season, and while there had only been a little bit of rain during my stay, the storms from the week before had completely washed out the roads. There were signs closing off the access roads and government notices online about on-going recovery efforts. Luckily, these were just washouts and not the deadly mudslides of California. So, I hung about town, hit up the casino that one last time, and read my Kindle. I also went scouting for a new hat (which I discuss more in the "Reflecting on Australia" section below). Tahli and her mom recom-mended I look into an Akubra, the iconic Australian brand, so I visited some of their authorised dealers to get an idea of what I might want in a new hat.

My next stop was Brisbane to see Tahli and a bit more of Queensland than I could see on my own. To get there, I flew from Cairns to Gold Coast and then took the local train to Brisbane. The train from Cairns to Brisbane took more than twenty-five hours, the bus took more than thirty, and both cost hundreds of AUD. Flying with Bonza Airlines, an ultra-budget Australian airline, only cost 75 AUD, including a checked bag, and only took two hours. That was a no-brainer. Hats off to the Australian family in Bali for tipping me off to them. (Unfortunately for anyone reading, the airline ceased operations two months later in April; the company leasing the entire fleet to Bonza suddenly and unexpectedly terminated the leases overnight with no warning, forcing Bonza Airlines to shut down amid the ensuing debt crisis).

Brisbane

Landing in Gold Coast was the easy part; getting to Brisbane was the tricky bit. For the uninitiated, the public bus system in Queensland wasn't intuitive. You couldn't buy a ticket on board, and there were no ticket terminals or desks at the airport. When I asked one of the bus drivers what I could do, she told me it was on me if I wanted to be arrested by the transport authorities and ride without a ticket. Talk about unhelpful information. Fortunately, a help desk in the middle of the airline counters pointed me in the right direction. I had to buy a transport card, add money, then swipe it on the bus. The only place to buy such a card at the airport was the WHSmith convenience store at the other end of the domestic arrivals hall. As frustrating as the whole process was, at least this card (called the Go Card) worked on all public transport buses and trains, so I didn't have to manage multiple tickets during my time in Brisbane.

The trip to my hostel in Brisbane took about two and a half hours, including a bus to the train station, a train from southern Gold Coast to Brisbane, and the walk from the train station to the hostel. It wasn't a particularly difficult journey; I was just irritated with the bus system and the particularly unhelpful driver that told me my best option was to risk arrest. I noticed on my walk to the hostel that there was a Queensland Police Museum and resolved to visit (an ill-fated endeavour, as it was closed during my time in the city).

On my very first day in Brisbane, I headed north to the Australia Zoo, the home of the Irwin Family. Besides diving the Great Barrier Reef, this was the only other thing I wanted to do in Australia. I grew up with Steve Irwin, and it was a sad day when he died doing what he loved. His son, Robert, had taken up his mantle and become the new face of the Irwins' conservation efforts. I hoped to see Robert perform at the daily Crocoseum show, but, if not, I still loved zoos. Like, loved, loved zoos, so much so that a group of friends once took me to a zoo to cheer me up after my first long-term girlfriend and I split up in college.

There were some amazing exhibits at the Australia Zoo that I hadn't encountered anywhere else (not that I had gone to zoos across the globe to be an authoritative expert). Chief among them were the regular, free shows in the different parts of the park where wildlife volunteers showcased animals and their stories to small audiences. I didn't have to pre-register; I just showed up at the exhibit at the pre-determined time. The zoo showed off the tigers' majestic agility using an obstacle course of meat to demonstrate how they think, move, and learn. I had never seen tigers up close before, only from afar, and they were not as fearsome as their eerie roar suggested. Of course, I was separated from them by a large, glass wall, and I probably would have found them deathly fearsome had I been in the enclosure.

Another exhibit near the Crocoseum was the Steve Irwin exhibit, which was dedicated to the life and times of Steve Irwin. Being there was a little emotional; even when I was in trouble as a kid, my dad still allowed me to watch *The Crocodile Hunter* for the education. It was a testament to how many lives Steve touched during his all-too-short life and just how dedicated his team was to animal conservation. It reminded me of the special episode he did where he stayed awake during knee surgery to show his fans what it meant to be an advocate for wildlife and the Earth's conservation. He also named his daughter, Bindi, after a crocodile, as if we needed further proof of how much he loved animals.

When the time for the daily crocodile show came, I made my way to the Crocoseum. It was open seating, so I picked a spot where I could see the entire show. I had no indication whether or not Robert would be there (he was a wildlife photographer and dating a woman who lived elsewhere in Australia at the time), and I hoped that the show would live up to the standard Steve had set during my childhood. *The Crocodile Hunter* episodes playing on a loop on the jumbotron were an encouraging sign.

I was in luck. Robert was there! Watching him felt just like watching his dad, mannerisms and all. Despite only being twenty years old, he handled the performance like a master. He expertly controlled over his team, both with hand signals and commands, remained engaged with the audience, and kept the crocodile in check the entire time. As he held a piece of meat out for the crocodile to jump for, he said, "If it sounds like I'm scared, it's because I am!" With that phrase, Steve's legacy lived on, and I knew he would be proud of the direction his son had taken. Robert was proud, too, and dedicated every show to Steve. It was an emotionally-moving display for someone who had grown up with Steve as a major part of their childhood entertainment. I hoped I would be able to say hello to Robert, shake his hand, get a picture, anything, but it was not to be. Some tourists were irritated with this, but I bought the security guard's explanation. Robert was an Australian celebrity in high demand with a busy schedule. As much as he wanted to spend his entire day at the zoo meeting people, his life just didn't allow for it (although, he probably wished he could slow it down from time to time to enjoy the people his family had touched over the years).

The rest of the exhibits were equally exhilarating, from the kangaroo enclosure to the African savannah to the hyperactive meerkats. Describing them could take an entire book unto itself. I stayed until closing time, taking in as much of it as possible, before boarding the train back to Brisbane. It was a day well spent.

I spent the next couple of days with Tahli and her family. After visiting another casino (where I won even more), a couple of free, mediocre museum visits, and some more hat hunting, Tahli picked me up outside the hostel, and we drove off to meet her mother, Peta, in Sunshine Coast. Tahli wasn't wearing shoes (she never did at home), but she was wearing her trademark overalls and bucket hat. I don't think I had ever seen her, in person or pictures, not wearing her trademark outfit. It was quirky, but it didn't bother her, and I respected that. She was a traveller and archaeologist-in-training; she didn't have time to care what anyone else thought about her clothes.

Tahli and Peta wanted to show me some of lesser-known Queensland. They were both of a more liberal persuasion than I was, so they wanted to show me some things I might not otherwise know to see. The first of these were the Little Rockey Creek Grinding Grooves. These were deep grooves in the river rock where the Gubbi Gubbi people once sharpened their tools. Essentially, they were natural whetstones. The grooves ran deep into the rock, showing how much they had been used over the years. Well, 30,000 years, to be exact. The Gubbi Gubbi were the original inhabitants of the area, and just four months after my visit, the Australian government granted them a "native title" over more than 900,000 acres of land in the Sunshine Coast area, including the creek where we were standing.

After a visit to the nearby creek (where we all became covered in tiny leeches), we headed off for lunch and in search of some of Australia's "Big Things." I wasn't one who liked to call other cultures weird, but this was a weird one. Australia was home to a number of "Big Things" which were, in essence, large depictions of various objects, be they animals, fruits, instruments, whatever. They were originally novelty tourist traps, but they took on a life of their own and now had a cult-like following. Every Australian had their favourite "big thing," and they were willing to argue the virtues of their chosen thing to the death. They took me by the big macadamia nut (the office of an adventure park) and the big pineapple (it was just a pineapple), and I had to admit... I didn't see the point in them at all. Maybe it was because I wasn't Australian or because they were obviously tourist traps, but I had to maintain that this was one of the weirdest cultural things I experienced in my travels.

After ending the day at the beach, we drove to Peta's father's house for the night. I don't think they even told him we were coming; they just showed up with me as their plus one, and he took it in stride. I had an air mattress in the converted garage, which was more than enough after the crowded hostel in Brisbane, and my own shower, so I had no complaints. I even tried Vegemite on toast at their coaxing. They lathered it on thick, but I took a light layer. Good thing, too, because it was not pleasant. It was an acquired taste, and I wasn't going to acquire it any time soon.

Before I knew it, I had to move on to Byron Bay. Tahli and I said our goodbyes, and she dropped me off at the bus station. It had been an enjoyable but packed several days in Brisbane. Hopefully, Byron Bay would slow things down.

Byron Bay

Byron Bay was a tourist beach destination in New South Wales, although it hadn't always been that way. It was a small town by almost any measure, and it was organised around a city centre with all the infrastructure of a decent-sized city. The bus stop was only a few minutes from the hostel, which belonged to the Youth Hostel Association. The name was a misnomer, as anyone could stay at their locations, but their target audience was young travellers, and that was who was there for the most part. There was no air conditioning in the hostel, so it could get hot during the day in the rooms; that was just incentive to stay out and about, although it messed with my siesta time.

I didn't have a plan in Byron Bay, so I committed to a dive trip. The first day, it was cancelled due to wind; the waves were too rough to get the boat into the water safely. The morning dives were cancelled the next day as well, but we managed to set sail in the afternoon. Unfortunately, the re-arranging meant that some people got cut from the second dive so that the boat could accommodate some DSD divers. That meant I would only get one dive in in Byron Bay, but that was better than none.

The dive site was the Julian Rocks Reserve, known for its leopard sharks. Every shark had a different personality. Reef sharks were skittish, bull sharks got their name for their size and temperament, and leopard sharks were named for their leopard-like spots. One dive instructor described them as "sea puppies" because they were unafraid of divers at popular dive sites despite their natural disposition to avoid humans. They would even bump into them as they swam around. Unlike most sharks, leopard sharks formed schools. Although they were naturally nomadic, the Julian Rocks Reserve was a hotspot for them in the Australian summer. Fortunately, that's when I was there (at least the back end of it), so I would be able to see plenty of them in the leopard shark capital of the world.

The dive site was beautiful, and the leopard sharks lived up to their reputation. One bumped into me almost immediately upon descending to the bottom; it was totally unbothered. They were smaller than I anticipated, but then again, so were most sharks, especially to those whose only real experience with them was in *Jaws* films and megalodon documentaries. At depth, their spots didn't shine brilliantly like in pictures online, but that was to be expected. I was viewing them as a fun diver, not a photographer.

The rest of the dive was a struggle. There was a moderate current and a moderate surf that made movement difficult. The current in Amed was fresh on my mind, and I was more than a little concerned with my ability to keep up with the guide. My dive buddy struggled more than me, but at least we were together. Lesson learned. I tried to time my kicks to take advantage of the swell against the current and was mostly successful. The trade-off was missing out on the scenery. I didn't miss the big things, like the large turtles, but enjoying the general view came in at a distant second to keeping up in the current. Upon surfacing, I learned I wasn't the only one struggling in the current. People with far more dives under their belt told me they struggled as well.

I spent almost the entire last day at the beach, either at a café, a bar, an ice cream shop, or on the beach itself. It was a peaceful day sitting next to the water and the first time I could relax to the crashing waves in Australia. Even though I had a free day in Cairns, there wasn't a good beach to sit beside and pass the day. Sure, there was the esplanade, but that just wasn't the same. The sounds of the ocean had a calming effect on my race to Mexico, and I sat and stared off to the horizon much like I had done eating dinner in Bali. I could do that for hours, with thoughts and emotions swirling around in my mind, undefined, mixed together, as though a decade's worth of my subconscious was competing for my attention. It was peaceful, and I hardly noticed the growing crowd around me as the sun set behind us. They faded into the background as my mind focused on the ocean, horizon, and infinite possibilities in life after travel.

My disappointment in Australia bothered me. I didn't feel like I was experiencing it the way Jo or fellow travellers had. I was more or less stuck in the cities with my ambitious travel plans. I didn't have the time to rent or buy a camper van and head off into the bush, and that's what I really wanted. I also didn't have the money. Australia wasn't a budget-friendly destination, and some days, it was a struggle to manage spending, especially with the high demand for hostels driving the price to 50 USD per night.

I tried to keep an open mind and give Australia the benefit of the doubt. After all, I was the one rushing through. I thought I might return on a working holiday visa, but I had aged out of that programme as an American. Visiting was still an option, but I would be limited to three-month stints and not allowed to work. Australia was expensive, and I was unemployed and entirely reliant on my savings to continue travelling unless I dipped into my retirement investments, which I didn't want to do. Ultimately, as I sat there staring out over the Coral Sea, I decided that I was the one not giving Australia its due. While I may never be able to do so, there was a reason so many people moved there on working holiday visas. Even Summer and Rick, the two New Zealanders Jo and I met in Pamplona, were living, working, loving Australia in Perth, and at that very moment enjoying an off-season trip through Western Australia.

Sydney

The journey from Byron Bay to Sydney was not the one I had planned, nor was it enjoyable. I had intended to take the bus from Byron Bay to Grafton and the train from Grafton to Sydney. It would have been a fourteen-hour trip, but most of it would have been on a train where I could get up, walk around, get snacks, read a book, and take a nap. Because of the storms between Brisbane and Byron Bay, however, the tracks were flooded, and the train couldn't pass through. This wasn't a matter of delay but a matter of possibility. The train couldn't get to the station from Brisbane, so the train company laid on a series of buses to run the train's route. Admittedly, the bus drivers were extremely professional, courteous, and really knew their routes. They had done this many times before and assured us we would stop for lunch along the way.

I was not looking forward to twelve hours on a bus. I was dressed for the train, which, to the non-traveller, may sound ridiculous, but I wore different clothes on the bus to be comfortable in the cramped space. There was a French woman in the seat next to me, also on a long-term backpacking trip, who said the same thing. Neither of us were upset at the situation; we didn't control the weather. But neither of us were particularly thrilled with it, either. C'est la vie.

As we cruised towards Sydney, I heard a familiar band on the driver's radio. It was Josh Abbott Band singing "Galway Girl." In all the places I expected to hear Josh Abbott Band, a replacement bus to Sydney was not one of them. Josh Abbott Band was followed by Chris Stapleton and Pat Green. I wasn't thrilled at hearing country music from home, but after texting with an old commander from my military days, I was less opposed. A lot had changed in ten years, even more in the last one, and I couldn't keep avoiding something I once enjoyed because of a relationship that was consigned to a different decade in the history books. Besides, I was wearing a new hat now, an Akubra, and I looked every bit the Australian vaquero. Maybe it was time I started to act like it, and myself.

271

I will preface my experience in Sydney by saying that I thoroughly enjoyed the city! There was a rivalry between Melbourne and Sydney, and I experienced them back-to-back. I came down squarely on the Sydney side of the debate. Whatever disappointments I may have had in Australia so far due to my rush through the country were substantially alleviated during my brief three days in Sydney. Like Cairns, I made a tentative plan: explore the parks and outdoor scene on my first day, visit the Sunday markets and museums on my third (I made sure they were open this time), and head to the famed Bondi Beach on the third day. I was sure to have a healthy mix of Sydney's culture by the time I left for Melbourne.

After a morning mochaccino, my first order of business was to head to the Tumbalong area, which included a nice park, an aquarium, the Australia National Maritime Museum, and a sea walk along the bay. It was a nice walk through a few parks, although most had large sections roped off with caution tape. The primary mulch distributor for Sydney had delivered the last shipment (or few) contaminated with asbestos. Talk about a problem! I couldn't help but be amused that after seven months abroad, I was back in a country similar to mine where multi-million-dollar errors could wreck the scenery of otherwise beautiful parks. As it was the end of the week and time to call home anyway, I called my dad to tell him about the asbestos. One thing he and I could do was talk about the government for hours on end, and the fact that it was the Australian government suffering the screw-up was no exception.

By the time we got off the phone, I found myself at Tumbalong, also called Darling Harbour, a bay and ferry stop next to Sydney's central business district (which Australians referred to by the acronym CBD). Far from being a peaceful sea walk, it was packed with people. It looked like one of my brother's sports competitions from when he was a kid, complete with soccer moms, ice chests, and matching team jerseys. I had stumbled into the Lunar New Year Dragon Boats Festival. Dragon boat racing was a rowing competition in which teams of between sixteen and twenty-six rowers paddled dragon boats (traditional Chinese river boats akin to long canoes) along a pre-defined distance. It was a competition for time, not a direct one-on-one race, to avoid accidents. These particular races were to celebrate the lunar new year and the Chinese Year of the Dragon. Other festivities, such as the lantern festival and parades, I would miss as they were the week before or after my visit. Even so, I decided to find a piece of concrete to call my own and watch the races. I had no idea dragon boat racing, or rowing in general, was such a big deal in Australia. In hindsight, this was the east coast of Australia, where there was no shortage of water sports on the ocean and rivers which wound through the cities, so it shouldn't have surprised me any more than high school American football being so popular in Texas.

I was impressed with the stamina it took to compete in these races. Rowing was no joke, especially when it was to the tune of someone else's drum, and some of these teams were competing several times in the day as they made their way to the championship rounds. It was also a hot, sunny, cloudless day, and I was sure they were roasting in the holding areas and their boats. I knew what waiting around in the sun was like from riding my motorcycle and diving. It was exhausting in its own right, but these teams didn't show any indication they were wearing down. One group after the next paddled the 500-metre stretch to get to the next round. Some miscalculated and paddled in arcs or circles while others sailed straight and true. It was an impressive display of sportsmanship to reign in the lunar new year, and I wished I could watch them again the next day. I could, but then I would miss out on the other things I wanted to see. And with that thought, I broke my gaze on the water and headed deeper into the CBD. I had a massage appointment (it had been a while, and I was starting to get tight and sore after my whirlwind tour through Turkey and dive trip to Bali) before I set off for the Sydney Opera House.

The Sydney Opera House was as iconic in person as it was in pictures. It stood at the point of the CBD, jutting out into the bay. From the ground, it was magnificent as its brown and tan exterior balanced well with the blue water. It was difficult to get a full-size picture of the building up close between the tourists and the relatively narrow walkway (when compared to the water around it). There was a reason most of the exterior shots in films came from the nearby bridge or a helicopter. Nonetheless, I was in awe of a building not once did I think I would ever see. I wouldn't be able to attend a performance there (the price was far beyond my budget), but that didn't bother me. The Opera House was a beautiful work of art in its own right. It was no wonder there were several groups taking wedding and engagement photos on the steps with the Opera House as a backdrop. Some people may have found it cliche, but it was quintessential Sydney; for locals an expatriates alike, it was a symbol of the life they lived in this wonderful city.

Continuing around the Sydney Opera House, I came to the Royal Botanic Garden. This garden had been in place since 1816 and solidified Australia's prominent role in the science of botany. For over 200 years, this site provided studies on how to make plant life more resilient and plentiful in Australia's relatively infertile soil (the country was mostly desert, after all). Nearly every modern botanical marvel in Australia could trace its roots to this garden, from fruits to vineyards. Not all of the experiments and studies were successful, of course, as man could only conquer so much of nature, but in the land of a penal colony, self-sufficiency was crucial; in the land of the now-independent and free Australia, national pride was as well.

I spent a fair amount of time in the gardens. I had nowhere pressing to be, and my hostel wasn't the best place to relax, so I took my time perusing its various sections. I wasn't the only one, as older couples strolled the paths, students studied their textbooks on the well-manicured lawns, and young couples laid on blankets together in the shade. Looking east across Finger Wharf, I saw a few of Australia's warships docked at His Majesty's Australian Ship (HMAS) Kuttabul naval base on Garden Island. One was the HMAS Brisbane, an air warfare destroyer which would later become the first Royal Australian Navy ship to fire a Tomahawk missile. The other was the HMAS Adelaide, a landing helicopter dock (one of only two in service at the time). The landing helicopter dock was Australia's compromise answer to the aircraft carrier. Australia didn't particularly need aircraft carriers, but it required sea-landing capabilities for search and rescue, humanitarian relief, and force projection. It made sense, in the moment, to be standing in a royal garden looking at these two particular ships; their presence so close to such an important place of scientific study projected their role as the defence of the realm, not the projection for force, which was a far cry from the military in which I served.

With those parting reflections, I headed back to the hostel. A Northern Irish guy from Belfast named Brian was providing beers to anyone willing to join him on the roof. Technically speaking, our hostel didn't allow outside alcohol, because there was a club on the ground floor with a liquor license. Honestly, none of us cared, not because we were obstinate travellers, but because the building owners didn't care about the hostel. We were just another way to make money to them. They didn't even have an in-person receptionist to talk to when issues arose; the only person any of us had contact with was the cleaning lady, who was a South American immigrant who didn't speak much English. Those of us who spoke Spanish talked with her when we crossed paths; she was a very nice, sweet older lady who loved her job and did everything she could to make our stay as pleasant as possible when it came to cleaning the place every day. Brian figured no one from the building would notice nor care if he brought beer to the rooftop considering we had to use a side entrance in an alleyway just to get to our rooms. He figured right, for the most part.

Brian provided beer to about twelve of us but wouldn't let us pay him back. "Beers have a way of coming back to you," he told us. How right he was. Brian's real goal was to get people to hang out together, as the hostel was wholly uninterested in the guest experience. He and I were the only ones up there for a bit, so we talked about Northern Ireland (a lot was happening politically at the time) and our travels. He had some wild stories from Amsterdam, and not even having a plane delayed by a terrorist attack or being questioned by undercover Turkish police could top them. As day turned to night, more people showed, and before too long, we had a motley crew of travellers gathered around the table. There were Norwegian fitness girls, British budget travellers (and self-described "cheese thieves," given the outrageous price of cheese in Australia), a Texan in an Australian hat, and a Northern Irish free spirit. Somehow, a game of King's Cup got started, followed by Never Have I Ever, and it just went downhill from there. It was a great night with new friends, and we were even treated to the weekly fireworks show in Darling Harbour from the rooftop. Eventually, though, the security guards from downstairs shut us down. We weren't being rowdy or loud; they didn't want us interfering with their business. Our motley crew had some choice words for them.

I couldn't tell you who suggested it, but it was made abundantly clear to me that I should visit the Sunday markets in The Rocks neighbourhood. These wouldn't be in full swing until midday, so I spent the morning at the nearby Barangaroo Reserve. The Barangaroo Reserve was a project designed to restore the land to a semblance of what it looked like almost 200 years before. While it wasn't entirely possible, given the adjacent neighbourhood's continued growth, the small, fifteen-acre reserve provided haven to over 75,000 trees and plants. Cars were kept away, and the running track circumnavigated the park along the sea, thus preventing erosion from runner after runner exercising in the park. Like the Royal Botanical Gardens, it was a quiet place to relax in nature.

But I had just woken up, and wasn't looking to relax in nature on this particular day, so around 11h00, I made my way to The Rocks Market. The market wasn't in full swing quite yet. I guess it was a Sunday, and between the bars on Saturday nights and churches and/or hangovers on Sunday mornings, people were slow to get up and moving. I was also a morning person, and I found myself constantly frustrated in my travels at how many things weren't open at 09h00 or 10h00. The best I could do at this hour was find some outdoor seating and hope for an early lunch. For some reason, I elected to try chicken parmesan, a dish I knew well and ate in Cairns. I had to hand it to the Australians; they really knew how to make a delicious parmesan-crusted chicken in American-sized portions. While I was eating, an older group, probably in their fifties or early sixties, sat at the same table as me, and we fell into a two-hour long conversation about everything from travel to food to politics (American politics fascinated everyone). They told me of the housing crisis in Australia, the best foods to try (apparently chicken parmesan was the most-ordered dish in Australia), places to visit, and were impressed by the new Akubra I was wearing. It was fantastic lunchtime conversation, and showed that a moderate conservative like me and people who were, in their own words, "so far left, [they] would probably fall off the edge of this table" could have a civilised, enjoyable conversation despite our differences. Not everything was a fight, and every topic had a lot of laughter stashed away in there somewhere.

When it came time to part ways, they wished me luck on my travels and wanted me to enjoy Melbourne. "It's a real groovy city," one of the ladies told me. Groovy wasn't a description I would have applied to anything in my travels thus far; that just made it something more to look forward to as my last stop before flying to New Zealand.

By now, the market was popping as locals and tourists alike browsed the boutique and artisanal stalls. There was something for everyone, everything, and every occasion. From homemade bags to homemade gelato and homemade whiskey (legally? I assumed...), you could find it at these shops. I was sure some of it, like the jewellery, was just gimmicky stuff, but the food stalls all looked pretty amazing. In some ways, I felt like I was walking through the market behind Shar Park in Erbil, with throngs of people moving in both directions. In Sydney, though, they weren't shopping for everyday necessities with children hustling wheelbarrows to provide for the family. After three months in MENA, this scene was familiar, yet foreign, an odd sensation for an English speaker in a Westernised country.

The market stretched all the way to the Dawes Point Battery under the Sydney Harbour Bridge. This battery was once the coastal defence battery that defended the inland bays, harbours, and wharfs against seaborne threats. These weren't hypothetical threats, either, as the possibility of war in 1790 threatened attack from the Spanish Navy. To see the battery today, which was now a park with a few guns as historical markers, you would never guess it served as a sprawling military fortification for 130 years. Time, the technology of war, and centuries-old feuds all ultimately moved on, and the fort was demolished to make way for the highway which now passed above it. Like the Rabat in Sousse, the Citadel of Qaitbay in Alexandria, and the Ciudadela in Pamplona, the time had come for the public to enjoy them in ways which preserved their history to the greatest extent possible. For me, it was a place to admire the Sydney Opera House from across the quay while enjoying artisanal gelato on my way to some museums. Naturally, I snapped some photos of the Opera House from the opposite side of the water; they were even better with the ocean in the foreground.

The Museum of Sydney was worth a visit, but at the end of the day, it was, well, a museum of Sydney. Like so many other city museums, it told the city's history. It was an interesting place with documentaries in the theatre about the Sydney Opera House's history and construction, but I moved through it pretty quickly. I was looking forward more to the Justice and Police Museum down the street, which was only open on the weekend. I had already missed the Queensland Police Museum and didn't want to miss this one, too.

My dad had been a police officer for almost forty years, and all I ever wanted to be growing up was a police officer, too (and, for a short time, I attained that dream). I loved learning about other countries' police services and systems, especially in the Commonwealth nations, as those systems were the origins of policing in the United States (contrary to growing popular opinion which believed our system started after our Civil War). This museum was set in a former police station, courthouse, and jail, the combination being common in the early days of modern policing.

Over the next two hours, I learned about policing in New South Wales. In the main courtroom, there stood a cage that housed those who were to be arraigned or tried, which would be considered cruel, oppressive, or humiliating today. I imagined the sneers and jeers ringing forth from onlookers as menaces to society pleaded their case. Adjacent to the courts was the police station, which looked exactly like it did in some of my favourite Victorian-era police dramas. A desk sergeant handling public queries, seats for subjects awaiting processing, and a list of police regulations and city ordinances on the wall. Back in its day, this police station probably wasn't a busy place, but if it were still operating today, it would be a madhouse in the tiny space.

The museum complex was bigger than just the courts, jail, and police station, which, to me, was curious. Surely something filled the exhibition halls before the museum. A museum staffer answered this question for me: police and their families used to actually live at the police station. The upper floors (off limits to tourists) and other areas were housing units until the officers were moved into new accommodations to make room for the expanded court system offices, which themselves were ultimately moved to accommodate more police offices. Ultimately, the entire police force would vacate the premises in 1986 after over 100 years of service and the building would re-open as a museum a few years later.

My favourite exhibit in the museum, by far, discussed the Aboriginal Trackers. In early Australian history, bushrangers would commit crimes against travellers before seeking refuge in the wilderness to avoid capture. These attempts were successful against the standard police officer who didn't have the skills or knowledge to pursue an adversary who was versed in navigating the harsh terrain of Australia's frontier. Enter the Aboriginal Trackers, indigenous people employed by the police to track criminals in the bush. They proved an invaluable service not just in tracking criminals but in locating missing livestock and rescuing stranded or injured travellers. Without the Aboriginal Trackers, many people would have died from exposure or worse, and the bush would have remained a haven for criminals. Unfortunately, as the exhibit made clear, the Aboriginal Trackers were not paid a fair wage when compared to their police counterparts; for the dangers they took, one might have thought racism and moral superiority could take a back seat, but that just was not how things were back then. It was a sad truth of colonial times, some of which still persisted.

Rain started to roll in, so I high-tailed it to the metro station to try to beat it back to the hostel. I had a laundry day coming up, but that didn't mean I wanted to hang my soaking wet clothes off the side of the bed and drip water everywhere. That, and the recommendations for drying my new Akubra was to wear it until it dried, which could take a while. I wasn't opposed to wearing a cowboy hat to bed, but this wasn't one of those occasions.

On my last day in Sydney, I headed for the famed Bondi Beach. Jo hadn't said much about it to me, although I knew she went from her Instagram stories, but I couldn't be this close to one of the world's most famous beaches and not go. Close being a relative term, as it took a solid hour to get there from the hostel via public transport. Every other tourist had the same idea, and we all swarmed the buses early that morning to make the most of the day. At least it was a Monday, so the local weekend crowd wouldn't be there.

Bondi Beach was unimpressive. It wasn't as much of a letdown as the Liberty Bell in Philadelphia or the Mona Lisa in Paris, but it was up there. It was a beach. Nothing more, nothing less. Well, actually, something less. Jo had warned me about swimming at the beaches in Australia; most required a stinger suit because of jelly-fish, and those that didn't only had narrow, marked areas you could swim because of rip tides. Bondi Beach was one of those places where the swimming areas were so narrow that wasn't worth it to get in the water if there were little kids around (which there were). Sure, the surfers had free reign on the water, but they wore wet-suits and were specifically trained in how to handle rip tides. To add insult to injury, there was yet another storm rolling in, and the clouds blocked out the sun and the pressure system kept the cool wind blowing. Not exactly sit on the beach, read a book, and listen to the waves weather.

Determined to make the most of my time at Bondi Beach, I opted to walk a path around the coast called the Bondi to Bronte Coastal Walk. This coastal walk wound through a few beaches to connect to the two main ones (as the name suggested). Despite the weather, it was a nice walk on the ocean. There were few people, so I could stop and look to the horizon for long periods and let my thoughts swirl around. It occurred to me that just a few days before, I was contemplating my disappoint-ment with Australia, had that disappointment alleviated over the past couple of days in Sydney, only to be met with poor weather on my only day at Bondi Beach. Such was life. At least I would miss the wet season once I got to Vietnam, Cambodia, and Thailand, and I could spend a lot of time outside hiking in New Zealand. That alone was worth looking forward to as I again made for the hostel to avoid the rain.

The rain came and stayed, and I was drenched during my journey to the airport the next day. I was soaked, as was my Akubra, but fortunately I had invested in high-tech, heavy-duty rain covers for my pack. People huddling under overhangs looked at me as though I was crazy for walking in the rain like I was, but it was amazing what one could do when they didn't have a choice (or had to be at the airport by a specific time). But that would not be the end of my rain-induced woes. The storms had delayed the flights from Melbourne to Sydney, which meant my plane from Sydney to Melbourne hadn't yet arrived. In fact, the preceding flight from Sydney to Melbourne hadn't arrived yet, so our flight was more than an entire flight time behind. Ordinarily, delays weren't a big deal; I just found a spot on the floor to claim as my bed until the time came to board. Sydney, however, had laws governing how many planes could take off and land every hour and restrictions on those hours. The staff informed us that if the plane didn't arrive by a specific time, we would be stuck until the morning and that if it arrived just in time for us to get off the ground, we would all have to cooperate, hurry up, and take our seats. Having flown on airlines across the world, I knew the "cooperate, hurry up, and take our seats" part of the plan was the most problematic; non-frequent flyers, families, and tourists were terrible at all of those things.

Fortunately, the plane landed before the hurry-up time, and we were wheels up before the legally mandated curfew. It was an interesting punctuation mark to an enjoyable time in Sydney.

Melbourne

Because of the delay, I arrived in Melbourne late, and it was still a thirty-minute bus ride from the airport to the city centre and a fifteen-minute walk steadily uphill to the hostel. Needless to say, I was sufficiently wiped when I walked through the sliding glass doors only to be confronted with the nightlife at the hostel bar and pool hall just getting started. I hoped it would remain on the ground floor and not make its way to the room.

Which room was anybody's guess, as there was an issue with the booking system and I couldn't check into my requested sixteen-bed dorm. No one knew the problem, but the receptionist assured me they had a bed for me if I would give them a few minutes. As long as I had a room for the night, I didn't care. I just wanted to sit down. She eventually came to me with the issue and the solution. The problem was that they had overbooked the sixteen-bed rooms, and I had been dropped, seeing as I was the last one to check in. The solution: they would put me in a six-bed room on my first night and an eight-bed room for the subsequent nights. Fine by me. While the twenty-four-bed room in Prague hadn't been bad, I got the feeling that the Melbourne backpacker crowd in the large rooms was rowdier and much less considerate regarding their late-night antics.

The six-bed room only had three occupants: a Northern Irish girl from Belfast named Indie, a girl who I would only see when she woke me up coming in later in the night, and me. Indie was in the shower when I arrived, so I surprised her a little when she came out. She was finishing her night and getting ready for bed (I later learned this was an early bedtime for her, as she could put pints away with the best of them), and we hit it off straight away. It started with me asking where in Northern Ireland she was from (I guessed from the accent), and it went from there. We talked until almost three in the morning about Ireland, travel, family and friends back home, everything. Indie was on a working holiday visa in Melbourne, trying to get an interim bartending job before she moved to Sydney for her permanent management gig. She was in her late twenties and decided to travel after living in Barcelona, leaving everything behind, including her now ex-boyfriend. I could empathise, having locked all my belongings in storage the year before. Somehow, we both ended up in the same eight-bed room again later in our stay and became fast friends.

I planned for four total days in Melbourne, more a function of cheap flights to New Zealand than anything else. Four expensive days. Jo, Tahli, Luka, and many others had warned me about how expensive Sydney was. In my experience, it had nothing on Melbourne. Everything in Melbourne was expensive; the hostel, food, coffee, everything. It was no wonder there was no room in any of the hostel's massive refrigerators. Even on my generous travel budget, I had a hard time keeping costs down; the true budget travellers in their late teens didn't stand a chance if they didn't cook all of their meals. I elected to cook two meals every day, and it was still a struggle to stay below my 135 AUD per day budget.

As luck would have it, it poured rain on my first day. The extra day there was a turn of fortune, as I could get a cheaper flight and afford to spend nearly all day at the hostel updating the blog, reading, and trying to meet people. I met a girl named Emily from Canada over welcome beers, and we hit it off, too. She was really into discussing political and social issues with people she disagreed with, so that's where the conversation went. I was a moderate conservative, while she was a self-described liberal. We agreed on almost nothing, but that didn't mean the conversation was terrible. We enjoyed it, and I was shocked when she came to my defence with someone else. We were discussing a specific hot-button issue, and a guy chimed in to tell me I shouldn't say what I was saying because others might be offended and have a different opinion. She jumped in immediately. She vehemently disagreed with me, but she defended my ability to have and express an opinion in a private conversation because that was how we learned about each other and eventually reached a consensus. She even questioned his security as a man if he was so fragile that he couldn't be around someone with a different opinion. She was a pretty sharp tack for a nineteen-year-old without her Canadian driver's license!

The weather finally cleared the following day, so I explored Melbourne. I didn't have a plan; I would wander about and see what I could find. I decided the Yarra River that cut through town to the bay was as good a destination as any. I could make my way to the river before steadily working back into the CBD, visiting the National Gallery of Victoria, enjoying the scenery along the blue water, and touring Fed Square on my way. That was the goal, anyway. The National Gallery of Victoria was closed, and the river was farther away than I had anticipated. I got there to find the gallery closed, so I walked the south side of the river and enjoyed an expensive lunch (but not by Australian standards) at Arbory Afloat, which served Mexican food and Mexico-inspired cocktails at the time. The food wasn't bad, but it was expensive considering I was closing in on much tastier, 1 USD tacos in Quintana Roo.

My visit to Fed Square was much more impressive, specifically the ACMI Museum, a celebration of Australian film. For film and theatre fanatics, this was a first-rate experience. The museum walked visitors through Australian cinematic art from the earliest days of Zoetropes (spinning displays of static pictures which, when in motion, gave the illusion of a moving picture) to mirror tricks to advanced modern technology. There was a Claymation set of *The Crocodile Hunter*, Canadian tuxedos from Technicolor Westerns, and cameras of all shapes, sizes, and eras. My personal favourite display was the Zoetrope of the Cuphead video game. I had never played the game, and the Zoetrope was made with a modern 3-D printer, but it was a marvel that such a thing could have existed, made by hand, back in the Old West days. Things like this were staples of the Hell on Wheels and frontier towns in my country. It was amazing how much Australia had in common with the perception of the Old West, and how familiar some things were to back home.

After having my fill of cinematic history, I began my journey back to the hostel. It was coming up on siesta time, and I wanted to make a few more stops before my nap. Chief among those stops was Saint Paul's Cathedral, just a short walk from Fed Square. Saint Paul's was an Anglican cathedral, a holdover from British colonial times. Anglicans made up about ten percent of Victoria's Christian population and ten percent of Australia's overall, second in both only behind Catholicism. The two weren't incredibly different, and their split in 1534 over Henry VIII's demand for an annulment was really the main difference. In most, but not all, practices, they were all but the same. The differences between the Baptists and Methodists back home were more substantial, and they were so similar that most people didn't know the difference.

Nonetheless, Saint Paul's Cathedral was a beautiful structure in the Gothic style, though it was clearly not hundreds of years old, nor did it try to give that impression, unlike the Almudena Cathedral in Madrid or Saint Paul's in London. Saint Paul's in Melbourne was built in the 1890s (with additions coming later) on the site of Melbourne's first Christian service. I loved the symbolism, although I could see how the indigenous people might take offense to its presence given their beliefs had been around tens of thousands of years as opposed to just 190 years for the Christians.

Despite the name and Anglican affiliation, the cathedral's sanctuary looked like it belonged more to Islamic art than the Gothic style in which it was built. The stained-glass windows featuring scenes from the Bible and prophets, of course, never would be in a mosque, but the black-and-tan-striped stone and pointed arches were more akin to the minaret at the Hassan II Mosque in Casablanca than Notre Dame in Paris or the Duomo in Milan. But what did I know? I wasn't an engineer or architect, just a lowly traveller and casual observer. I wasn't going to question the architect, the diocese, or one of the city's most important landmarks.

With that, it was siesta time, although I later ventured back out in search of some performance undershirts before leaving for Southeast Asia. These were surprisingly difficult to find in the brand and colour I wanted, so the search took up the entirety of my afternoon. By this point in my trip, I had already made the decision to head back to Spain long-term, and I was looking to change out some of my clothes. After a year of travel wearing the same five undershirts, it was time for an update. The search in Melbourne turned out to be in vain, and I returned to the hostel empty handed.

In a completely uncharacteristic turn of events, I went out drinking that night. Indie was off and meeting with friends, and she invited me along. I wasn't a night owl or a big drinker, but I could stand to get out for the night. Indie took me to a few places, most of which I would describe as grunge bars. Granted, that description was based on most of my drinking taking place in Irish pubs and Texas dance halls. In any case, we had a great time. I wasn't going pint-for-pint with her or her friends, mainly because I was drinking Guinness and they were drinking... whatever they were drinking. I knew how to drink Guinness, and I was putting them away three sups at a time. Indie and her friends were impressed, but I cut myself off after only a few. Alcohol kept me awake, and I wanted to sleep through the night. Indie, on the other hand, who had somehow ended up in the same room as me, stayed out all night long. It became a running joke that we would say hi and bye as we crossed paths at the threshold to the hostel, me on my way to coffee and her on her way to bed. This wouldn't be the last time I went out drinking with her and her various friends, and it certainly wouldn't be the last time she put me to shame with her Northern Irish drinking stamina.

Emily and I spent the next day hanging out together. We had hit it off, she was heading to a new hostel later in the day, and there were a few things we both wanted to see and do. Brian, from Sydney, turned me on to a festival elsewhere in Melbourne. The Johnston Street Festival was an annual Hispanic/Latin-American Festival that took over a street to celebrate Hispanic and Latin-American heritage. It was a long walk away, but Emily and I had boots made for walking and a limited budget, so that was nothing to us. Besides, we would spend the whole time talking anyway, so the walk would fly by. At least, it did until we showed up at Johnston Street, and there was no festival. Odd, because the festival's Instagram page was posting stories in real time. It turned out that there were two Johnston Streets. The other one was closer to Melbourne than the street we had walked to. Oh well, at least we got our exercise in under the hot Australian sun.

The festival was more like a Mexican block party. The street was shut down, food vendors selling carne asada and other mostly-Mexican foods were everywhere (at Australian prices), and there were a few music venues for Spanish-speaking artists to perform. Some of them were old men playing traditional music on their guitars while the largest of them had a rapper performing in Spanish. Neither of us knew the rapper nor could understand the lyrics (my Spanish had deteriorated quite a bit since leaving Spain many months before), so we opted to leave after only about thirty minutes or so at the festival. It wasn't a waste; it just wasn't for us. Brian would probably have loved it, as he used to live in Sevilla, Spain, and spoke more Spanish than I did at the time.

Undeterred by our lacklustre experience, we went to the weekend Queen Victoria Market we had heard so much about. Unfortunately, this was Friday, and the market didn't kick into full swing until Saturday. Emily was heading off to meet friends at another hostel that afternoon, so that was one I would have to take solo the next day. With that, we went our separate ways, her to her next hostel with friends and me in search of food. I settled on a Spanish restaurant which served paella. This was my second time having Spanish food in Melbourne. While it was expensive compared to Spain (5 AUD per croquetta!), I was surprised at how many delicious Spanish restaurants were in Melbourne. There were less than 3,000 people of Spanish heritage in a city of over 5,000,000, but the Spanish food never disappointed. I probably could have made my Valencian paella last for two meals, but after walking all over northeast Melbourne, I packed it away. The paella was delicious, but it was served with a fork. The Valencian abuelitas would not have stood for such blasphemy.

After breakfast and coffee at the hostel the next morning, I returned to the Queen Victoria Market. It was a night-and-day difference from the empty pavilions and parking lot from the day before. Merchants, fruit stands, artisans, clothing and book vendors, and visitors were everywhere. This market put The Rocks Market in Sydney to shame. I spent hours perusing the stalls. Although I already had my Aku-bra, I still checked out the hat vendors to see what they offered; I was already car-rying around my Goorin Bros Henry Jones until I got home, so what was another hat if I liked it? I was also on the lookout for small souvenirs to take back to my family. Even though I was still several months out from being able to send stuff home, I only had four countries left on my itinerary before settling in Mexico, so I decided I could afford to stow away some small trinkets.

As much as I enjoyed the Queen Victoria Market, and I did enjoy it, it was just a weekend market at the end of the day. Extensive and comprehensive, sure, but I could only spend so much time wandering the stalls. It didn't have the same feel as the souks I loved in North Africa. It felt too organised and boutique for me to spend hours upon hours simply enjoying the environment.

Right about the time I was considering leaving the market, I had a thought that caused my heart to sink, and I rushed back to the hostel. I had a flight the next evening to New Zealand, and I had forgotten to apply for my electronic travel au-thority! At the time, they recommended providing two to three days lead time for the travel authority, and I was less than that away from boarding a plane. This could be a costly mistake between the missed flight, new flight, and last-minute hostel expenses. I booked another night at the hostel just in case, and resigned myself to taking it one day at a time. oOne costly day at a time.

Just as the point came to book another flight, the travel authority came through! Lucky for me, in a strange way, the hostel had to put me in a different room, so my bags were already packed. When I saw the email, I jumped up from the table, yelled, "It came through!" and bolted for the door. Forty-five minutes of walking and buses later, I was checking in for my flight amongst the absolute chaos and meltdown Jetstar was experiencing. I didn't know what caused it, nor did I care as long as I was checked in to make the flight to Christchurch. I had the Kiwi mountains on my mind.

Reflecting on Australia

Island nation security. Before flying to Australia from Bali, I had to go through a second layer of airport security just for our flight. Indonesia was considered an elevated security risk for Australia, and the Denpasar International Airport didn't meet Australia's security requirements, so additional checks at makeshift check-points were required for every Australia-bound flight. As a traveller, I was annoyed, as I was at Indonesia's border, not Australia's, and I didn't think Australia should have a role in security there. I knew how the United States handled these things, and it was not like this. On the other hand, Indonesia was a hotspot for Islamic State, and the group would take advantage of every security gap it could to strike out at the West. Jetstar was an Australian-flagged carrier, so the Australian government understandably didn't want to take that risk. Public opinion wouldn't care where the flight originated or who was responsible for the security; all it would care about were the Australians that were killed due to perceived government incompetence.

Landing in Australia, I had to go through a substantial biosecurity checkpoint. This wasn't a vaccine check but a check on everything else. Everyone deplaning had to walk over a special walkway that scrubbed and disinfected their shoes, and there were special biosecurity officers whose job was to screen travellers for biosecurity threats. Everything from hiking to medication to being near livestock in the past week was cause for additional inspection. Dirty shoes in checked baggage were cleaned even more, and I had to answer the biosecurity officer's questions about why I was travelling with so many antidepressants in my bag. Nothing was off limits, as the biosecurity officers had sweeping authority to deny you entry into the country for non-compliance.

As an island nation, Australia had a unique ability to totally cut itself off from the rest of the world, and it could prevent the introduction of foreign hazards simply by telling someone they couldn't land in the country. The same was true of New Zealand. Both wielded this power liberally during the COVID-19 pandemic, and while I acknowledged the government's sentiment that they should protect their citizens from biosecurity threats at all costs, I couldn't help but think of the hypocrisy of that position when it came to my own country. Popular opinion in Australia was widely against President Trump's immigration policies while they refused to accept asylum seekers from outlying islands. It was "security for me, but not for thee," and not a single Australian I discussed this with over subsequent months could see the hypocrisy.

Acknowledgement of Country. In Australia, it was customary for every flight and event to start with a "Welcome to Country" or "Acknowledgement of Country." These "recognised" the indigenous tribes' claims to land which colonial settlers took from them. In the United States, there was a raging, almost unhinged, debate over "stolen lands," and there was no consensus over who "traditionally" owned land in the country. American Indian (the legal term in the United States for indigenous peoples) tribes fought over land for centuries, various swaths of territory constantly changed tribal hands, and no two maps of American Indian territorial claims were the same. In Australia, that was not the case. There were thousands of years of traceable history of just a few "traditional owners," and the map was more clearly defined. As such, it was easy to acknowledge the Aboriginal peoples' roles and rights in the lands in which they lived.

While it was intended as a genuine recognition, and many people still considered it as much, to me, it came across as a token concession to social justice activists. The Jetstar and Bonza Airlines flight attendants clearly read off a script and rarely acknowledged a specific group when landing in a new city; they simply "acknowledge[d] the Traditional Owners of the land" where we took off and landed. I felt the same tokenism at museums and other public buildings, as the Acknowledgement of Country was posted on a sign at entrances with little fanfare or meaningful effort. It was cold, unfeeling, and disingenuous to me, more a function of political demagoguery than legitimate social concern. I wasn't opposed to the Acknowledgement of Country; I simply had no use for token apologies for past transgressions from people who were not there, knew little of why they were giving such tokens, and had no personal interest or emotional investment in them. I found the token, scripted, impersonal sayings more offensive to the Aboriginal peoples than respectful.

"The Indigenous." My issues with the Acknowledgement of Country aside, I also saw blatant racism towards the Aboriginal people. Over the years, I had become increasingly intolerant of ethnocentricity. There were legitimate critiques between cultures to discuss, and some cultures simply weren't compatible with others, but acknowledging and discussing those critiques and incompatibilities was fine as long as it was done in a respectful manner.

Being from Texas, we had a front-row seat to tensions arising from the differences in cultures. Some were legitimate, such as fifteen-year-old Mexican boys refusing to listen to their female teachers because in Mexico, at fifteen, the boy was now a man. That incompatibility was clearly an issue, as there were different cultural norms and laws in the United States. Other issues were not legitimate, like when I watched a judge tell a mother that they didn't believe that her kids usually ate dinner around 22h00 and that the mother had better stop lying. Except, the mother wasn't lying. In Mexico, that was normal, and the family in question was Mexican. It was ridiculous for that judge to say that the mother was lying based on the time of day her family ate dinner.

In Australia, there were similar issues with the Aboriginal peoples. Many lived in segregated communities and according to their own values. Some brought those different values to the cities, which could cause some friction, as the Aboriginal peoples would refuse to abide by the norms and laws which governed all of Australia. That was a legitimate critique, and one which caused a lot of social safety net pressures. At the same time, I met several Australians who looked down upon "the Indigenous," as they called them. When I asked why cold medicine was behind the counter at the pharmacy, I was told, "Because the Indigenous steal it to get drunk." I highly doubted it was only those of Aboriginal heritage stealing cold medicine to get drunk; homeless people and alcoholics the world over did that. I was also told, "the Indigenous think the laws don't apply to them." In some cases, I was sure that was true, but I was also sure that wasn't a substantial part of the population. As best I could tell, the Aboriginal tribes writ-large valued law and order, even if they disagreed with it, and worked through the political process to maintain their rights and achieve their objectives (something they had been successful doing since the 1990s). Saying "the Indigenous think the laws don't apply to them" was no different than those back home who said, "black people are criminals" or "Mexicans are dangerous." Was it true to an extent? Sure, and there were legitimate discussions on that subject, but it certainly wasn't true across the board. I eventually got to the point where if I heard someone refer to "the Indigenous," I just assumed whatever came next was going to be a racist remark, not because the word "Indigenous" itself was a slur but because that was how everyone I met used it.

Housing crisis. In my travels across the world, the number one issue on the minds of young people was the worldwide housing crisis. Home prices and rents were rising everywhere, and younger Millennials and Gen Z-ers were concerned about their ability to own their own place someday. This wasn't the same as the financial crisis fifteen years before, where banks gave out unsecured loans and created a housing bubble that eventually popped. There was no indication of such a bubble. Instead, the cost of lumber, worldwide inflation not seen since the Carter administration, high demand in high-population areas, and individuals and corporations buying single-family homes to turn them into rental properties or short-term vacation homes were driving prices skyward. For a young twenty-something with a regular twenty-something job, individual housing was a pipe dream.

Australia felt this as badly as New York, London, Barcelona, and elsewhere. Byron Bay, once a small, industrial town of all trades, was now dominated by tourist rentals and vacation homes. One of the shop owners I talked to lamented, "There are no locals left here, anymore. They've all been priced out." While I was in Australia, a heartbreaking story of a woman who was living in her car with her dogs hit the news. She had been forced out of her home as her pension couldn't keep up with rent hikes. She struggled to buy petrol, her only source of electricity, heating, and air conditioning, and she was racking up road fines as she navigated the life she had been forced to live.

These stories were told around the world, with Barcelona and New York passing ordinances which restricted short-term rentals to keep the price down for locals. University students in London often lived two or more hours away by train, forcing them to buy expensive round-trip tickets multiple times a week to attend classes just so they could have remotely reasonable housing costs. When a single bed in a sixteen-bed hostel room cost 51 AUD a night, it was no wonder it was a concern for young people. I didn't know what the solution was, but the emotions surrounding the concern ranged from despair to simmering anger to near-revolt. I knew that, sooner or later, something would have to give; the world couldn't tolerate an entire generation or few unable to afford a place to live. I desperately hoped it wasn't in the same way the last time the housing market crashed.

The end of an era. In Egypt, I noticed something that saddens me to this day. After seven years of loyal service, my Goorin Bros Henry Jones fedora was starting wear a hole in the crown. You couldn't see it from the outside, but the light starting to poke through was unmistakeable on the inside. That hat had been with me everywhere since I bought it. It was a staple of my wardrobe, an instantly-recognisable accessory that announced my presence and, in the professional world, brought a bit of old-school, professional style with it. I hoped that I would be able to repair it, but it was crushable wool, which was not known for its durability or repairability. Worse, it was now out of production with no replacement.

Tahli and Peta recommended I look into an Akubra. The Australian brand was just eleven years younger than the iconic American Stetson; whereas a Stetson wasn't instantly recognisable the world over, an Akubra was. I told them I would look into it, but I wasn't sold. I wanted something crushable in a similar style so it could take a good bashing as it travelled the world, but also something that could stand the test of time as my Henry Jones had. Akubra didn't offer many crushable options, and the ones they did offer looked cheap, like something I would get from Wal-Mart.

For the money they cost, I wanted something distinguished, in a similar style, durable, and, preferably, crushable. It was a tough bill.

In Cairns, I went on the hunt. There were two Akubra dealers, one in the mall and one in the weekend market. After researching online, I was interested in the Adventurer. It was the one which looked most like my Henry Jones, at least online. It wasn't crushable, but the rabbit pelt Akubra was known for made up for that in durability. I found it at the store in the mall and was instantly turned off. For my head shape and height, the proportions were all off. The crown was too tall, the brim too short, and I looked like a cartoon character. Dejected, I hoped the night market had better options.

It did.

It had most of the Akubra hats, including the classic Cattleman, but I was still looking for something similar to my Henry Jones. And there it was. On the top shelf, out of reach, was the collection of Akubra Anglers. That was the hat; I knew it at first sight. I eagerly tried them on, only to learn that they didn't have my size. My search would continue, but at least now I knew exactly what I was looking for when I walked into Brisbane Hatters in Brisbane. I walked in and told them, "I'm looking for an Akubra Angler in Loden, size sixty." The attendant simply said, "Follow me." A few hundred AUD and a quick reshaping session later, I had found my new hat.

It was the end of an era. Of course, I kept my Henry Jones, and it remains at my home to this day, but changing hats was more than just changing hats to me. I bought my Henry Jones at a time when I was seriously overhauling my personal and public image, a result of personal baggage, heartbreak, and a desire to take some control of my out-of-control life. Changing to the Akubra Angler meant leaving all of that behind. I wasn't that guy anymore. I was similar, but not the same, with an entirely new direction and outlook in life. The Angler was similar, but not the same, and an entirely new look in my wardrobe.

Indie. Indie was a beautiful girl from Belfast, one who could hold her alcohol, have deep conversations, and, I was sure, hold her own in a fight. Of all the friends I made travelling across the world, she was the one I would keep in contact with the most. She was building a life in Australia, though, and wasn't looking to move back to Northern Ireland if she didn't have to. She had long, brown hair which sometimes looked black if the lighting was right. She mainly wore black clothes, although jeans were a staple, but not quite like a Goth kid from high school. Her sense of humour was great, and she had a penchant for bathroom graffiti.

We hit it off straight away and continued to hit it off long after I left Australia. We would reunite again, in Belfast of all places, for a dinner and a night out with her friends. The conversation then was deep, covering lost loves, hopes for the future, and some hilarious roasts around the table. When her friends took off, we went to another bar, where the laughter gave way to more introspective conversation.

We were both looking for someone and were pretty candid with each other about that. Me? I could see that someone in Indie. Not that it was love at first sight; it certainly wasn't. But it was a great connection from the get-go. My mom told me several times she was expecting me to come home with a Spanish or Irish girl, and the thought occurred to me when meeting Indie that it wasn't entirely out of the realm of something I would want (experience with Jenny in Galway notwithstanding). I told her as much once, although not in a gushy, high-schooly, "I have a crush on you" way. It was more of an "if we were in the same place long-term, I could see us going somewhere" way. I was never quite sure how she took that outside of in-stride, but the fact that we remained friends (even as she dated other people in Australia) told me she probably took it just fine. Besides, we both agreed long ago that "travel relationships should remain just that," and neither of us was looking to jump into something just to go distance again.

The good thing in all of it was I finally could admit to myself, after all the women I developed mini-crushes on before, that I was legitimately ready for a relationship again. It had been ten long years since I dated anyone seriously, but all of the baggage that held me down was in the past. Even if Indie and I never saw each other again (which, I was sure, we would), I knew I was no longer afraid to put myself out there with women. Granted, I was out of practice, as I so aptly demonstrated time and again, but at least I was finally ready to cowboy up and get back on the dating horse again.

Chapter Nineteen

Cowboy Up: Coming to Terms and a Blown Knee in New Zealand

New Zealand was the adventure capital of the world. I had met several Kiwis, as New Zealanders were called. Summer, Caitlyn, and Rick were all dive professionals, and I worked with a New Zealand Defence Forces officer in the military. After city life in Australia, I was ready for some outdoor adventures in New Zealand. The Kiwi summer was fading away, but autumn hadn't quite arrived, so hopefully, I could enjoy two weeks in the great outdoors before heading to Vietnam for the beginning of the end of my year of travel.

Christchurch

As was typical for me in this part of the world, my flight into Christchurch landed late. My hostel was a 50 New Zealand Dollar (NZD) taxi ride away. I wanted to use Uber, but the late flight made it a "high demand" time, so prices skyrocketed as I and everyone else tried to get to our homes and hotels. I was only staying at the hostel that night; an entire stay was far too expensive. If I thought Australia was expensive, New Zealand was worse. The Kiwi Dollar was slightly weaker than the Aussie Dollar, but the conversion was oppressive when combined with New Zealand prices.

Christchurch was a small, quiet city compared to Melbourne. Literally quiet, not figuratively. There were plenty of people about, but there wasn't that bustling sensation I would have expected from the largest city on the South Island and the second-largest city in the country. For a population of almost 400,000 people, I expected a more city-like experience. I found the quiet disconcerting at first, but after a stroll along the Avon River, I was glad for the peaceful aura it projected. For the first time in a while, I felt a comforting calm wash over me.

I was only in Christchurch and on the South Island because that was where the plane landed; had the cheapest flight been to Aukland, New Zealand's capital, I would have been on the North Island. Summer, Caitlin, and Rick from Pamplona told me to avoid Auckland, so I was glad to be on the more beautiful island. Because that was the only reason I was there, however, I didn't have much by way of a plan. I knew I wanted to go hiking and/or diving, but that was it. As I walked along the Avon River, I pondered what I should get up to (with the assistance of ChatGPT, of course).

The stroll took me to the Christchurch Botanic Gardens, uncrowded on a Monday morning, and eventually to the Arts Centre Te Matatiki Toi Ora (the Christchurch Arts Centre, for short). The Arts Centre was the South Island's hub for music and art, co-located with part of the University of Canterbury. The university originally owned the Gothic buildings, constructed in 1873, but had since moved as the student population grew. Some of its departments, like health, education, music, and arts, remained, while others were at the main campus. I thought about visiting the main campus but decided against it. I wanted to enjoy the old, Gothic architecture more than I wanted to see a modern university.

The Art Centre offered a concert during the lunch hour in what they called The Great Hall Lunchtime Concert Series, something they put on every Monday while the university term was underway. Having nothing substantial on my agenda, I decided to attend. It only cost 20 NZD (about 12 USD) for a forty-minute concert, which was great for an afternoon of entertainment before making the long walk with my bags to my next hostel. The performer was Fiona Pears, a Christchurch local and violinist who composed her own songs, toured the world as part of various musical groups, and produced her own CDs (one of which was with the City of Prague Philharmonic). Everything about her, from her mannerisms to her word choice, screamed tortured artist to me, but that didn't detract from her talent. Her compositions were beautiful as she effortlessly moved from ballad to waltz to tango. It wasn't easy to make a living as a musician, but she was doing a marvellous job at bringing emotions to life through her music.

With a sufficiently satisfying, peaceful morning of solitude and music calming my mind, I gathered my bags for the thirty-minute walk to my new hostel, called Jailhouse Accommodation. It was a literal jailhouse converted to a hostel, and their advertising proclaimed "Accommodating people for over 140 years!" This was the old city jail, the last one to actually lay within the city limits, which closed in 1999. It was certainly a 19th Century jail, based on its cell-block organisation, Draconian bathroom setup, and sixty-centimetre-thick walls. I had been in plenty of jails before, but never spent the night in one, so this was a first. The hostel played to its jailhouse history, referring to guests as inmates, providing white and black striped bedding, and featuring exhibitions on the ground floor regarding the jailhouse's history. As far as gimmicks go, this was one I could get behind, as it literally brought travellers into the jail to experience one of Christchurch's important historical city buildings. The only downside to the hostel was its location outside the city centre, but that was a trade I could make for a few days.

On my second day, I spent most of my time in the Riverside Market area. As nice as it was, it was just a market. The main area was mainly food vendors, and the surrounding area was a shopping district. It didn't take long for me to walk the whole thing, but I didn't have anything better to do, so I decided to continue my hunt for new undershirts and peruse the tourist shops. I was meeting Caitlin and her friend for ice cream later (she was at university in Christchurch), so I killed time with my computer at a coffee shop researching some post-travel life paths. I wasn't freaking out about whatever came next, but every so often it bothered me, so I would satisfy myself that I had options by going down internet rabbit holes looking into doctoral programmes, non-governmental organisation jobs, and how to become a career travel writer. After a bit of research, the uncertain feelings usually passed, and I could go back to living in the moment.

My time with Caitlin and her friend was great, and we had fantastic conversations. Caitlin travelled Europe for several months on a break from university before we met, and now I was carrying her torch forward by exploring her country. Her friend hadn't travelled to that level, and she was fascinated by stories from places like Spain, Turkey, and Iraq. Her friend was also interested in learning about life back in Texas. Things like owning a firearm were totally foreign to her, especially with how easy it was in Texas to own multiple like I did. Caitlin, on the other hand, was no stranger to firearms, as she was a hunter (something that was hard to picture without looking at her Instagram posts). I didn't know there was as much hunting as there was on the South Island, but I would soon learn just how liberal the laws were concerning controlling the deer population.

I mapped out my plan for my two weeks on the South Island for them to evaluate. Their judgement: it sucked. I had planned to make my way north, where most of the good diving was, but they told me the season had passed. The best direction to go was south, towards Queenstown. Down there were the best hikes, the best views, and, crucially, the best ice cream in all of New Zealand. Luckily, I hadn't booked bus tickets yet, so I adjusted my plans accordingly to head to the southern half of the South Island of the southernmost country in the world (by some measures, although by others it wasn't even in the top five). My new plan took me to Queensland, Wanaka, and Te Anau, a plan they readily agreed with.

After what seemed like a minute, our time together expired; they had to return to their studies. I had another day in Christchurch ahead of me, but not much to do with it, and soon I was at the bus station making my way to Queenstown.

Queenstown

The bus ride from Christchurch to Queenstown took every bit of eight hours. The views made the difference between this long bus ride and the one from Byron Bay to Sydney. The first couple of hours from Christchurch to Burkes Pass were cloudy and rainy, but once we came out on the other side of the pass, I saw the most beautiful scenery I had ever seen. Iraqi Kurdistan was beautiful, but the South Island was on a different level. To describe the vibrant blue skies, turquoise lakes, and mountain backdrops as picturesque would be a gross understatement. For six hours, from Burkes Pass to Lake Tekapo to Queenstown, my phone was glued to the window, taking pictures of the magnificent Kiwi countryside.

The bus drivers added to the drive. I wasn't on a tour bus; it was just a regular public transport bus, like Greyhound or FlixBus, but the drivers treated us like we were on a tour. They recalled the history of places we passed, interesting facts about different farms and animals, and told stories of their many years driving a bus. The first driver we had was driving the same bus route his father had driven for fifty years, a legacy he was proud to continue. Through this driver, I learned about hunting deer in New Zealand. Deer were invasive, introduced by Europeans for hunting in the 1800s, and the population was out of control. As such, as long as you had hunting and rifle permits, it was legal to hunt wild deer without limits all year long.

The only off-limits populations were the ones maintained and tagged by ranchers. I immediately texted my stepdad about this; as an avid hunter, he would love a year-round deer season.

The drivers were fans of country music, like the driver from Byron Bay to Sydney, and I had no choice but to resign myself to the fact that I was going to have to listen to it for hours at a time while moving between cities. Given my cowboy-esque look with my new Akubra, I should have been more welcoming of the throwback to home. After all, my mental block against country music was almost a decade old, and a lot had changed in that time. Somewhere on the road, a Cody Johnson song played, and I halfway committed to myself to look up some of his music when I had some free time. He was a Texas Country artist, former bull rider, and Texas to the core. Maybe I could start my journey back to country music with some of his hits.

I arrived in Queenstown without much fanfare, and the city itself was small. Only 28,000 people lived in the entire Queenstown urban area, and only 1,000 of those resided in Queenstown Central. Almost its entire economy revolved around tourism, with hiking and water sports in the summer and skiing and snowboarding in the winter. With activities available year-round, it was no wonder this was the adventure capital of the world. I looked forward to hiking; it was too cold for diving or doing anything on the water (for me, anyways), as the water was never warmer than sixteen degrees Celsius, even in the middle of the summer.

In planning my two weeks in New Zealand, I resolved to use Queenstown as my jumping off point to other parts of the South Island. The bus system used a hub-and-spoke setup, where going to smaller, outlying towns meant transiting through and changing buses in Queenstown. Unfortunately for my plans, the buses left Queenstown before the outlying buses arrived, which meant I would spend random nights in the small, scenic town as I moved between cities. This was no bother, outside of staying in random hostels of varying quality here and there, as I found an Irish pub there that served decent Guinness and worthwhile food (a rarity in New Zealand, I found). Plus, I could enjoy the Patagonia Chocolates ice cream shop Caitlin raved about (and I indulged many times, as it was some of the best ice cream I had ever tasted!).

Being in Queenstown for the views, I opted to hike Queenstown Hill as my first outdoor adventure. The summit was less than 1,000 metres above the city, and the path was well-trodden and defined, making it an easy first trek. Even walking uphill to the start of the trek provided breathtaking views of roads leading off to Lake Wakatipu and the mountains beyond. I sent a few pictures back home, and no one believed I wasn't using a filter. The sky was just that clear, and the views were just that scenic. Even as I sucked wind on the way up (travel backpacking not being the same as hiking backpacking), I kept saying to myself, "Wow...that's incredible..." (reminding myself of my dad in doing so; that was the way he always described amazing views at first sight). The summit was no disappointment, either, even though it lay far beneath the surrounding mountaintops. As any skydiver will tell you, the best views of amazing landscapes usually were not from the top looking down, but from the ground looking up or the middle looking around. Queenstown Hill was a testament to that idea.

Excited from my hike up Queenstown Hill, I resolved to do the longer, more difficult hike to Ben Lomond Peak. A guy in my hostel room had done it that day, and he warned me that the reviews online were true: this was a difficult hike. I had a tendency to take online hiking reviews as exaggerated for the benefit of newer hikers, especially after living in Colorado where people on their week-long mountain vacation overestimated their abilities, but he had just completed the hike and told me it was "an a** kicker." It was a 1,500-metre summit from the city to the top, and it would take me all of eight hours. I should have taken his information more seriously.

I set off at 09h00, starting on the Tiki Trail, which eventually connected with the Ben Lomond trail. This first stretch was brutal, and I wasn't the only one who thought so. Despite the defined path, it was a steep uphill walk for the first several hundred metres of elevation. A third of the elevation change to the peak happened in this stretch. Most people weren't into hiking and opted to take the gondola up to the viewpoint and restaurant. At 64 NZD per one-way trip, hiking was just fine by me.

From the viewpoint and restaurant, the Tiki Trail gave way to the Ben Lomond trail. The next couple hours along the trail took me through a Douglas Fir forest (which was great for the shade), a dirt path that took the long way up the hill, and eventually the Ben Lomond Saddle. A sign just outside the forest portion gave the distances and estimated times to the next waypoints. The saddle was three kilometres and one to two hours away; the summit was four and a half kilometres and two to three hours away. I could have continued to Arthur's Point fourteen kilometres away, but I didn't have camping gear, and I wasn't sure I would be in any shape to get that far after seeing the time and distance estimates. I knew from my military days that a five-kilometre walk took the average person forty-five minutes to an hour, so seeing it would take upwards of three hours to make it three kilometres was a serious reality check.

The journey to the saddle provided some incredible scenic outlooks of Lake Wakatipu and the mountains behind it. Off to the east, I watched flights from Australia and elsewhere in New Zealand sink below me on their final approach to the Queenstown Airport. The last time I was above the flights around me, I was under a parachute as a skydiving coach; now, I was a hiker in New Zealand. As times changed, the thirst for adventure remained.

Despite the views, the hike to the Ben Lomond Saddle was abusive. It never quite flattened out, and it rose at steep intervals from time to time. I considered myself to be in decent shape, but after so many months of not working out except for humping my bags from city to city and hostel to hostel, my fitness was shot. Just when I thought I was getting close, I came across the next sign saying it would take another two hours to hike the final three kilometres to the summit. I was still an hour away from the saddle...

The last kilometre and a half had a warning: "track not maintained past this point." I would traverse a rocky ridge from the saddle to the summit. It was daunting as I could see hikers on the ridge steadily making their way upward. Several people were stopped on the saddle, with some opting to remain and enjoy the views from there rather than continuing to the summit with their group. It was a tempting proposition. I was gassed, and a dull ache was setting in in my bad knee. It was time to cowboy up, put my head down, and go. If I quit then, I would quit again, and I wasn't one for quitting. I hadn't come all that way not to make it to the summit, so I started the trek upward. Sometimes, I took it just ten steps at a time, sometimes I shot for the next part of a switchback, and many times I stopped for several minutes for a break, but I slowly found my way up the rocky ridge until it again turned into a better-maintained path. The worst was behind me, and I finally arrived at the summit.

The views were breathtaking. To the south and west, I could see straight down the narrow Lake Wakatipu as it wound its way around the mountains. It shown turquoise from the glaciers that ground the mountain rock into a fine powder that settled on the surface. In the distance, I could see some peaks starting to accumulate snow; the winter was fast approaching. To the north were the jagged ridges that lie between the mountains. I imagined what it must have been like for the first people to navigate those steep ridges, be they Aboriginal tribes or colonial settlers.

Before heading down, I called my mom from the summit. Of all the places to have cell service, this was not one I expected, but I knew she would enjoy seeing the views. She was with some of her friends when I called, and I heard her tell them, "It's my son. He's calling me from the top of a mountain in New Zealand." The fact that she said it so casually made us both laugh. My brothers, their wives and girlfriends, and my mom were teachers, and I was halfway around the world, unemployed, and video calling from the most beautiful place any of us had ever seen after leaving my six-figure job with a master's degree. It wasn't ironic; it was freeing. I was living a new life, one I enjoyed and one my parents fully supported (even if they wished I would find a way to make money).

The trek down was almost as difficult as the trek up, as the rocky ridge before the saddle tested the limits of my knee and quad strength. Stopping myself from gaining too much momentum downhill was a physical challenge in itself, one which put a lot of pressure on my now aching bad knee. After the saddle, the going got a little easier, but my knees continued to take a beating on the random steep downhill sections. I was relieved to finally reach the Douglas Fir forest; it was shaded and had a shallower incline where I could recover before heading down the Tiki Trail. By the time I reached the hostel at the bottom of the hill, I was drenched in sweat, my legs were burning from the day-long workout, and I was ravenously hungry for some ribs at the pub.

After almost nine hours on the trail, all I wanted to do was sleep before catching the bus to Wanaka in the morning. Unfortunately, I had one of my random bouts of insomnia that night. There was never any reason for it, at least not that I knew, but I was wide awake in my bed all night, which meant I had a front-row seat to the guy and girl trying to hook up in an adjacent bunk. They started by making out on the balcony but quickly moved to his bed across from mine. Unfortunately for them, they were afraid of getting caught, so every time I moved, coughed, rolled over, or otherwise disturbed the squeaky bed, they stopped what they were doing. They never got far, and they were as frustrated at their inability to hook up without getting caught as I was at my inability to sleep. Eventually, I said out loud, "Y'all do whatever you want; it ain't gonna bother me." That killed their mood, and they went straight to sleep. They were probably glad when they woke up and I was gone.

Wanaka

Wanaka wasn't far away, less than two hours by Intercity bus, so I was there by lunch. The hostel wasn't close to the drop-off point, but it wasn't a far walk, either. It was just uphill (which meant walking downhill into town to walk back uphill to the hostel every day). Because of the way the buses worked, I only had two full days in Wanaka. There were several hiking trails to explore, but with my limited time, I settled on two: the Glendhu Bay Track, which wound around Lake Wanaka on a relatively flat path, and the Roys Peak Track, the most popular hike to Roys Peak. I would do one each day, in that order, and spend the rest of my time relaxing in the lakeside cafés.

The Glendhu Bay Track was an easy walk with beautiful, ground-level views. There were more short trees and colourful bushes along this path than I saw in Queenstown, which provided a great foreground to the snow-capped mountains in the distance. It reminded me of my hiking trip to Hawaii, except the low-lying mountains didn't get covered in snow during Hawaiian winters. Once I got past the main beaches, I saw hardly anyone; it was just me, my thoughts, and the wind ripping across the lake. I wasn't sure how far I had hiked along the trail when I decided to turn back. If I had gone the entire distance, I would have found myself in Glendhu Bay, the next town over on the other side of Roys Peak. I was just out for a leisurely hike, not the full round-trip experience on this track, so I turned around at a nice round spot and made for Wanaka and the Patagonia Chocolates ice cream that awaited me.

I was almost there when my good knee started to have a dull but shooting pain. It wasn't my knee, really, more below it. I chalked it up to overuse, but I was close to town, so I would be able to rest it in just a few minutes. With every step, though, the pain got worse and worse. By the time I reached the Wanaka Tree, I was limping hard; by the time I made it to Rotary Park, I was dragging my leg behind me. This was some of the worst pain I had experienced in years. Not since my skydiving accident more than three years before had I experienced such pain. I set a direct course for the ice cream shop, not because I wanted ice cream that badly, but because it was the nearest place I could sit down for an extended period of time (but I still got ice cream).

I was in pain, and not the good kind. They say to listen to your body, and I believed in that maxim, but I had no indication that I was on my way to a leg injury during my hiking trip through the South Island. It came out of nowhere, and it crippled me. I was concerned I might have torn my ACL or Patellar tendon. I wasn't concerned; I was worried. My brother had popped enough tendons playing sports that I knew how debilitating the surgery and recovery could be at home, let alone halfway around the world. I had travel medical insurance, so the money wasn't my concern. The basics, like going for food and returning to the hostel, were. After a long time at the ice cream shop, I limped uphill to the hostel to suffer in bed with my Kindle. I was lucky that a physiotherapist just happened to have checked into my room and was kind enough to give my knee a look free of charge.

The physio told me he didn't see indications of a tear, which was great news, but with the level of pain I was describing, I probably had a bad sprain. The only way to deal with a sprain like that was to put a brace on it and rest. An excellent prognosis for my health, but a terrible one for my time in New Zealand. My hiking plans were summarily cancelled, and I would spend the rest of my time taking it easy in the small towns.

So much for seeing the sunset from Roys Peak the next morning.

I was frustrated that it was my good knee that gave out. I knew how to handle when my bad knee hurt, but my good knee was major cause for concern. I had no idea how I would have sprained one of the ligaments on a flat path, and my next eight weeks of travel were more-or-less already booked, and it was a lot of moving around with my twenty-kilogram travel bag plus my messenger bag of electronics. This had the potential to totally derail my entire trip until I got to Mexico, and I was concerned about diving for months on end there, too. These injuries could take weeks and weeks to heal under the best of circumstances, which I certainly didn't have, so I needed to be extremely careful.

I had a hard decision to make, but it was the only one available. I would continue on my planned itinerary, even if it meant sitting around at a hostel or café for the entire time in a city. At least I could catch up on my reading, films, and music. Looking back, if it weren't for this injury, I would never have gotten back into country music. I would have been hiking and focusing on the adventure, not reconciling with the past. On the one hand, I wished I could keep up the adventure. I wanted to bungee jump in Queenstown and hike several more tracks. On the other, this was a forcing function to sit with myself and work through some things.

So, over the next few days, I listened to country music radio online while sitting at cafés, scrolling social media, and organising my thoughts for my future book project. The radio station pushed a lot of Cody Johnson, Justin Moore, and Luke Combs, three great artists, along with the Chris Ledoux song "Cowboy Up," which was the exact situation I found myself in. How many times had I told my brother to cowboy up when he was in a rut? I may not have been able to get wholly back in the saddle, but at least I could keep myself from staying down. After all, bullfighters took horns through the leg and got right back in the ring the next week. I was no bullfighter, but the bullfighting season was days away, and I found some inspiration in their resilience as I looked forward to watching the fairs as I healed up.

Of course, that didn't alleviate the boredom over the next few days, especially with the overnights in Queenstown as I moved about, but at least I was listening to music I enjoyed again, reading a good book, and had my favourite Spanish tradition to get through it all.

Te Anau

Te Anau was the last stop before the Fjordland National Park, home to great hiking and scuba diving. For me, it was a boring one-horse town on a lake. I was stuck taking it easy while everyone around me headed out to the wild outdoors every day. I spent two days there eating mediocre food, drinking coffee, keeping myself entertained with music and books, and watching past bullfights to psyche myself up for the Feria de Fallas in Valencia, Spain, in a few days. I was limping heavily, careful not to overdo my movements, as I prepared to take on Southeast Asia at breakneck speed. It probably would have been a great time otherwise, but I just wasn't lucky enough to experience it this time around.

Ultimately, I found myself on the road back to Christchurch. A week after blowing out my knee, it was starting to feel better, though I was still extremely cautious. I paid for an Uber to get me to and from places to be on the safe side. Emergency medical care in New Zealand may be expensive, but quality emergency medical care in Southeast Asia was going to harder come by. It was better not to risk it.

On my last day before leaving New Zealand, I had a terrible realisation... again. I forgot to apply for my Vietnam visa. I had a stopover in Australia, so I had a couple of days' buffer, but that wasn't much when dealing with one of the five remaining communist governments in the world. This was an expensive mistake. I had to cancel my cheap red-eye flight to Hanoi and spend two days in Melbourne, which was painful on the budget. I had hoped to recoup some costs in Vietnam and saw those savings trickle away in Melbourne. I was concerned the Vietnamese government would take the entire two weeks to approve my visa, but it came back a few days later. Longer than New Zealand, but not long enough to totally destroy my plans for Vietnam.

Better late than never, I finally was on a nine-hour, overnight flight from Melbourne to Hanoi with an entire row to myself. There was a silver lining in everything.

Reflecting on New Zealand

Fitness. I worked out at least three, preferably five, times a week before I left home. I wasn't self-motivated to work out but took fitness classes to keep me active. My fitness level had seriously deteriorated since leaving the United States. I could see it in my pictures on Ben Lomond Summit and feel it as I gassed myself on the trails. I could still hump a ruck with the best of them, but that was out of necessity for hauling my pack around, not fitness.

I wasn't paying the least bit attention to the types of food or how much I was eating, something I did back home, which, when combined with my generous travel budget, meant I was eating too much and too much garbage, especially in Australia and New Zealand where sugar was plentiful in everyday foods. I was used to "cleaner" foods in MENA (i.e., not pumped full of hormones or sugar water), so the sugar influx over the past month had thrown my sugar cravings into high gear. It didn't help that I loved ice cream. Even with "cleaner" foods, though, their portions were still fairly large at the restaurants where Westerners (and even locals) ate, and a lot of those diets included high levels of carbohydrates, which I knew my body didn't process very fast. My injury in New Zealand, I knew, wasn't just due to overuse; it was also because of a poor diet, carrying around some extra weight, and failing to keep my fitness up while travelling. I wouldn't solve this problem before landing in Mexico, but it was something I would have to get control of if I wanted to keep going.

Accepting some things. Country music was growing on me again, and I started to build a playlist of songs that spoke to me in my current situation. They were mostly upbeat songs along the theme of cowboying up and becoming who we are today because of what happened in the past. "How I Got to Be this Way" by Justin Moore, "Fever" by Garth Brooks (especially the Chris Ledoux version), and "Lot of Leavin' Left to Do" by Dierks Bentley were immediately added, with more coming as I heard them or encountered situations that reminded me of them from years before. Brad Paisley's "Southern Comfort Zone" and Justin Moore's "Stray Dogs" felt like the summary of my life, as I had become a bit of a drifter and found myself cutting loose from the path I had set myself on, personally and professionally, when I decided to join the military almost fifteen years before.

The truth was, I was the family outcast. I told my mom I felt this way several times over the years, and it felt like a burden more than anything else. As I built my playlist, I realised it only felt like a burden because I was still trying to fit in back home and meet familial expectations. It was high time I let go of all that. I was an Akubra-wearing, bullfight-loving, world-travelling, proud Texan who didn't care for American football, hunting, or the fake niceties of the small town where I grew up. I was different, part of the out-crowd, and how I had changed, saw the world, and viewed myself were proof of that.

Chapter Twenty

Twelve Days in Vietnam's Northern Beauty

I had no real reason to visit Vietnam. I wasn't pulled there by a sense of adventure or history. It was just on the list when Jo and I arbitrarily made our tentative plans to travel the world. Eight months later, I was continuing with that arbitrary plan. Vietnam would be the first and only communist country that I would visit in my travels, and I was a little nervous to see the cultural differences that would bring. However, the United States and Vietnam were on good diplomatic terms, and the country was a part of the traveller's circuit in Southeast Asia, so that was where I began the final leg of my fast-paced travel journey to Mexico.

Hanoi

I landed in Hanoi well-rested and ready to take on Vietnam. My Vietnam Airlines flight was only about half full, so I had an entire row to myself, and the seats reclined far back. Those who were "never recliners" in the airplane seat debate would have hated it, but people like me who used the seats they paid for loved it. It was the only time I could point to when I arrived in a new city after a nine-hour flight rearing to go. After coffee at the airport coffee shop, of course. It amused me that in one of only five remaining communist countries, the airport in the country's capital catered to Western tourists. It was a truth I witnessed the world over: national morals and values were one thing, but Western tourism dollars reigned supreme above all else.

The public transport bus into Hanoi was cheap. Really cheap. It cost 5,000 Vietnamese Dong (VND), which was around 0.20 USD. There were other, faster options, like taxis, private shuttles, and nicer buses, but I was on a budget like everyone else, and 5,000 VND for a bus sounded way better than 45,000 VND for a private shuttle (granted, that was an argument of just a couple of USD difference). It was hot and humid, just as I expected it to be, and I texted my mom from the bus that, with the price, I could understand why authors throughout time travelled to such places to write their books. Maybe I should go to Southeast Asia to write my first book?

My hotel was in the heart of Hanoi, in the middle of the touristy nightlife district. I didn't know that when I booked it; I just saw the price and distance to the city centre. As I only had twelve total days in the country (courtesy of forgetting to apply for my visa far enough in advance), I was perfectly content to be in the thick of the touristy area for convenience's sake. It was a nice place, too, called the Queen Café Hotel & Pub, and the manager, Bella, was fantastic. Bella talked me through my time in Vietnam and helped me organise my itinerary and book excursions (being on limited time, I was willing to go on guided tours to experience what I could). She even agreed to let me use the hotel as my base in Vietnam, which meant I only had to take my day pack with enough clothes to last the duration of an excursion rather than all of my bags. Not bad for the grand total of 570,000 VND (less than 23 USD) for all three nights!

It was still morning when I arrived, so I wandered the city centre before formally checking into the hotel. Once I got past the tourist-centric restaurants, I was exposed to the crazy shopping district. Shops advertising "Made in Vietnam" apparel, bags, and gear lined the streets and were crammed with merchandise. It had never occurred to me, but almost all of my performance clothes were made in Vietnam or Cambodia, so it wasn't outside the realm of possibility that these were the real deal. Maybe they were defective items given for local resale or something? After checking in, I resolved to do some digging, as I was still looking for new undershirts. Ultimately, I learned these items were, in fact, not the real deal, as the authentic items were all legally required to be shipped out of the country, and the hefty re-import tariffs made it unaffordable for these Vietnamese shopkeepers to have such an ample supply. That said, the popular opinion online was split between those who decried the "scam" and those who purchased and reviewed the items. The consensus from the latter group was, sure, they were fake, but they were high-quality fakes that were more or less as good at a much cheaper price. I would have to agree with that sentiment after buying two "Under Armour" shirts myself (and, almost a year later, I'm wearing one of them as I write this chapter!) for 400,000 VND total (about 8 USD each).

Motorbikes zipping everywhere were easily the most stressful part of Hanoi. Well, the traffic in general, but the motorbikes specifically. Motorbikes were the way of getting around for the Vietnamese who lived in the city, and it wasn't uncommon to see an entire family of four or five loaded onto one heading down the street. The rules of the road, for what little value they provided, were, in practice, non-applicable to motorbikes as they bolted around corners, the wrong way on one-way streets, and totally ignored stop signs. The police definitely didn't care (unless they were parked in a no-parking zone, at which point they were towed without remorse), and crossing the street in Hanoi was almost the same difficulty as Cairo, just with the added trick of no one stopping for anyone.

Not far along the crazy streets, I walked into Hoàn Kiếm Lake. A low-lying fog covered the lake in the humid morning, and I could feel the humidity increasing as I got closer. There were many such lakes around Hanoi, and there was a temple on an island where tourists were moving in and out via the bridge. This was the Ngọc Sơn Temple, built in the 1800s and dedicated to three Chinese mythological figures and Trần Hưng Đạo, a Vietnamese hero who defended Vietnam valiantly through all three Mongol invasions in the 1200s. I made a mental note to visit the temple more thoroughly during my stay.

Hoàn Kiếm Lake was also the site of one of my favourite legends. I once had a passing interest in the overlap of mythical creatures and reality, as almost all myths and legends had some grounding in reality (even if the reality was that the legend was demonstrably made up). The legend of Kim Quy fascinated me. As one version of the legend went, during a campaign against the Chinese, Kim Quy, a mythical golden turtle, appeared to the Vietnamese Emperor out of the lake to deliver him a magical sword to aid in his battles. When the battle was over, Kim Quy appeared out of the lake again to return the sword to the Dragon King. For decades in the 1900s, Vietnamese and international researchers searched for evidence of a large turtle in the lake, whose murky waters were only two metres deep at the deepest point, only to find no such evidence. Only once, in the 1960s, was one found (and killed) by a fisherman, and the species was thought to be extinct (if it existed at all). Imaging, sonar, dredging, nothing could confirm the turtles existed until one was caught on video in the 1990s, and the species was cemented as the likely inspiration for the legend of Kim Quy. Unfortunately, the species was so rare and elusive that the last known turtle was found dead in 2016. I held out hope, however, that the legendary reptile still lived on in the murky lake waters just out of reach of all of mankind's technology, just as it had for hundreds of years. I couldn't wait to visit the temple and see the taxidermised specimens inside.

I continued to wander the city throughout the afternoon, finding many of its streets outside of the tourist centre to be just as busy, crazy, and filled with cramped shops, albeit without the English-language advertising. My tentative plan started to take shape. I had two full days (excluding my first travel day) to see the city, which was bigger than New York City but held the same number of residents. I was still concerned about my knee, which was why I eventually cut my aimless wanderings short, but it was starting to feel better as long as I wore my knee brace and high-top boots instead of my hiking boots (which didn't have good padding, and I couldn't wait to change them out in Mexico). I set an ambitious course for the next day, opting to visit most of the historic temples in one, long, circular course around the city. This would leave me free to have an easier next day resting my knees (both the injured good one and my usual bad one would surely be hurting by then). Plus, the Feria de Fallas was beginning in Valencia, Spain, and I wanted to watch the bullfights with OneToro TV.

With that plan in mind, I set off the following day after a mochaccino at the coffee shop across the street on my tour of the city. I intended to start at the Ngọc Sơn Temple but found myself walking straight into Vietnam's version of National Police Week on the streets surrounding Hoàn Kiếm Lake. It was more like "First Responder's Week," but the concept was the same as back home. The various emergency services elements set up booths for kids of all ages to engage with those who protected their community. Of course, the firefighters had the cool video screens to simulate fighting an actual fire with their extinguishers; never underestimate a fire department's ability to get good exposure. Similarly, the ambulances and medical personnel had mock situations where participants could practise treating a casualty (although I had more than my fair share of practice with this from my military days, so I passed). From a traveller's perspective, I found the presence of the Vietnam People's Public Security (PPS) forces the most interesting. These were a quasi-military organisation which served as Vietnam's version of the national police. Unlike Western national police forces, the PPS was a part of the armed forces and under the political control of the Communist Party of Vietnam. While there were municipal police forces in major cities and the provinces, these, too, ultimately came under the control of the PPS and, consequently, the Communist Party. Maybe that was why there were so many police-looking uniforms around the city; nothing exerted control like the looming spectre of "public security."

It was a short walk from the first responder exhibitions to the Ngọc Sơn Temple, so I began my temple tour of the city. It cost 30,000 VND (just over 1 USD), which was probably why it was such a popular spot for tourists. I was willing to bet most of the foreign tourists coming and going across the bridge were utterly clueless about the temple's significance in Vietnam's history; it was just a good spot for photos. The temple was in the pagoda style, which was common for both Buddhist and folk-religious temples alike. Photos were forbidden inside, something I adamantly respected, except at the exhibitions of the Hoàn Kiếm Lake turtles. Given these were the source of one of my favourite legendary creatures, I was ecstatic upon entering the display. The turtles were surprisingly flat, and looked nothing like turtles I was used to seeing while snorkelling or diving in the Americas. The shell was almost pancake-like, and the necks and claws extended far outside its protective barrier. Could they even retreat to hide inside their shells? Granted, they didn't have any natural predators in the lake, so evolutionary processes probably deemed that ability unnecessary. It wasn't hard to see, though, how these turtles could elude detection for decades and centuries at a time. They were so flat that even the best of nets could easily pass over them if they buried themselves in the bottom, despite their large overall size. Combine that with their ability to remain under water for seven hours or more in cold water (and the water was rarely warmer than four degrees Celsius), and my hope that there were more somewhere in the lake burned just a bit brighter.

Several blocks away, I moved to visit Văn Miếu – Quốc Tử Giám, in English called the Temple of Literature, a Confucian temple built in 1070 which also housed Vietnam's first national university for over 700 years. The temple was a series of five courtyards, each different from the last. The first two contained well-manicured lawns, Koi ponds, and brick walkways. They were serene escapes from the crazy city just outside the walls. Wedding parties seemed to think so, too, as several took photos in central walkways as individual tourists and guided groups made their way through the site. I rolled my eyes as I saw the culture which frustrated me so much in Europe take no one else into account as they snapped their photos. At least I was in their country, so I couldn't complain too much, but I would remember that the next time someone complained about my country and culture. I wasn't the only one; the local guides would get frustrated and charge their groups through the parties.

The third courtyard contained the Thiên Quang well, a large, square pond whose name in Vietnamese literally translated as "well reflecting the light of the sky." It symbolised receiving the knowledge of the universe, as represented by the rolls of those who successfully passed their doctoral exams engraved on the 116 stones erected alongside with stone turtles serving as their foundation. The turtles' heads were rubbed white on the darkened stones from hundreds of years of visitors rubbing their heads, probably for luck on their doctoral examinations, and they were now behind a decorative fence to prevent tourists like me from further contributing to their deterioration. That was fine; I was trying to get a good picture of the well along with everyone else. It was a good thing I had long since given up on trying to get photos without other people in the background; that would have been a losing battle.

The final courtyards contained trinket stalls, the Confucian temple, and houses dedicated to the teachers and professors who once taught at the university. Photos were allowed in this temple, so I could capture the ornate, gold statues of Confucius and his parents. They were all new. In 1946, the French Army, during its colonial conquests in Vietnam, destroyed the entire temple with artillery fire. I could only assume that was why pictures were allowed; this wasn't a centuries-old, active temple anymore. It should have been, but human nature and imperial desires ended almost 900 years of religious practice on the site.

It was now lunchtime, or close to it anyways, but I couldn't read Vietnamese and had no idea what food was what in the area. I ultimately decided to grab something from a guy with a food cart outside the Temple of Literature's back exit. Best as I can describe, he was selling was a thin, Vietnamese version of a taco whose contents I didn't even want to guess. For 20,000 VND, I grabbed two, and a Vietnamese family offered for me to sit with them as I ate. They spoke zero English, but through primitive sign language, I told them I was a traveller on a mission to one day write a book. They smiled at my attempts to communicate, which, fortunately, they understood to an extent, and peeled off a ball of rice for me from their bag. No spoon, chopsticks, or forks, just a guy handing me a loose ball of rice in his hands. Some people might have worried about getting sick, but I was more worried about offending them. Besides, I needed more to eat after my two small Vietnamese taco things.

From there, I made my way to the Mausoleum of Ho Chi Minh, the North Vietnamese leader the United States "advised" against during our controversial undeclared war more than fifty years before. The mausoleum was the centre of political activity in Hanoi, with the Presidential Palace located to its northwest, the Vietnamese National Assembly, Ministry of Foreign Affairs, and Ministry of Planning and Investment lying to the east, and several embassies forming a sort of diplomatic quarter to the southeast (of course, the United States Embassy was located in its own complex several blocks away; security being the greater concern than proximity for the most powerful country in the free world).

The mausoleum itself was huge, massive, a testament to its namesake in Bodrum, Turkey. It's dark, grey, square, concrete structure was at the same time an impressive piece of architecture and a deification of Ho Chi Minh, such was common for leaders of communist revolutions. I wonder how many workers and labourers could have been helped with the 25,000,000 USD it cost to build in the 1970s (almost 138,000,000 USD in today's economy)? That was the nature of communism, though, to protect and venerate the leaders while oppressing and controlling the laypeople, all in the name of a utopian state that would never come. I opted not to pay the 40,000 VND to visit the tomb; the grounds were free, and I valued it from a cultural and historical perspective, but I wasn't going to contribute my capitalist dollars to a communist cause. The irony was not lost on me as I explored the beautifully-manicured grounds and took in the beautiful garden which surrounded the mausoleum on all sides. I was careful not to step too close, though, lest I incur the whistle and wrath of the police officers and armed military personnel guarding the mausoleum on all sides. Their exotic dress uniforms didn't mean they would hesitate to shoot someone who didn't heed their warnings.

I sat and rested on a concrete ledge on one of the outlying lawns that occupied the space between the mausoleum and the National Assembly. Even in death, Ho Chi Minh kept the National Assembly under close eye. The ceremonial changing of the guard was occurring (at least, I assumed it was ceremonial), just as it happened at Buckingham Palace in London, the Palacio Real in Madrid, the Prague Castle in Prague, and the Tomb of the Unknown Soldier in the United States. Some things were the same for militaries across the world. One of the police officers overseeing a work detail kept giving me sideways glances, but I was pretty sure he was judging the tourist sitting on a short ledge and not about to yell at me for some violation. I hoped so, anyways; my knees needed the break.

The final stretch of my walking tour took me north of the mausoleum to Chùa Trấn Quốc, the Tran Quoc Pagoda in English, a famous Buddhist temple with a tall lotus that stretched fifteen metres above the surrounding lake. Getting there entailed walking across a very busy bridge, as the pagoda was on an islet jutting off of it. The walk was fine enough; crossing the four lanes of traffic was the tricky part, but after putting on my best Cairo impression, I made it to the front gate. It was free to enter, which, along with the tall lotus, was probably why it was full of people.

The lotus was the star attraction. While the temple was built in the 500s, the lotus only dated to 1998. Buddha sculptures on each of the eleven hexagonal levels looked out of each face's window. Everyone wanted a picture of and with the lotus, which was understandable. I didn't have an issue with that; my issue came, once again, with those who gave no consideration to others and took their time milling about in front reviewing every photo for its Insta-worthiness. It was no less irritating than it had been at the Prague Castle several months before. It was beyond me how people could be so oblivious and inconsiderate, especially with today's technology where you could snap a crystal-clear picture on the go. Today's generation could never survive with the disposable cameras of yesteryear.

The temple was, to me, much more impressive. No one was allowed in because it was still active, and a Buddhist liturgy was underway. Worshippers sat barefoot on the floor, covering every available piece of ground. It was crowded, and tourists leaned in the doorways to take photos and videos of the chants and recitations (which I found outrageously disrespectful). All around the entrance, and filling the altars and walls, were flowers, boxes of food, shoes, you name it. I had seen this at other temples and asked a nearby English-speaking guide what these were for. They were religious offerings as diverse as the people who brought them. They offered what they had, and it was the responsibility of the monks who maintained the temple to disperse them as necessary. Sometimes, these offerings went to the monks them-selves, sometimes to visitors, and sometimes to charity. It depended on the specific temple, but an offering received by the temple was considered blessed by Buddha. As long as its subsequent purpose was one of compassion, it was generally accepta-ble. In the end, what mattered was not what happened to the offering after it was given to Buddha, but that it was given in the first place.

As someone who wanted to learn more about world religions, I was glad to have the opportunity to witness the liturgy, even if I didn't understand the words or specific practices. On the other, I despised that tourists could wander about while it was underway. How would my congregation back home feel if Vietnamese tourists walked around the sanctuary taking pictures while the praise band was singing or the pastor was preaching, whispering amongst themselves and interrupting our weekly worship? How would the Catholics of Spain feel if the same happened in their cathedrals during Sunday mass, or the Muslims during the Friday sermons?

Putting these thoughts aside, I started the forty-minute walk back to the hotel. It was a long forty minutes after seven hours on my feet. I saw more temples and historic sites as I stumbled into them along the way, and I was well on my way to exhaustion. Even so, it was a fantastic first day in busy, chaotic Hanoi. Even though the look was different, Hanoi had a similar feel to Marrakech or Cairo, and I felt right at home. Grey instead of golden brown, overcast instead of sunny, humid instead of dry, but it still gave me that sense of belonging these sorts of places provided. But I was a tourist, not a resident, and I knew that life was very different as an expatriate or local, especially in a communist country.

I took it easy the next day. I watched a bullfight from the Feria de Fallas the night before with my morning coffee, something I didn't realise just how much I missed. I also wandered around the local area and visited a few shops for fun before packing my day bag to head to Ha Giang. I had a long bus ride ahead on one of the nicest sleeper buses I had ever taken to get to Ha Giang before heading off on the Ha Giang Loop.

Ha Giang Loop

I received only two pieces of advice from fellow travellers about my travels in Vietnam: spend my limited time in the north and don't skip the Ha Giang Loop. Indie (the Northern Irish girl from Melbourne) was adamant that it was one of the most beautiful sights in the world, and I was sold. I could have taken a bus to Ha Giang and driven it on my own (I had a motorcycle license), but I was wholly unfamiliar with the landscape and Vietnamese language, so I opted for the excursion Bella offered at the hotel in Hanoi. It was all-inclusive (except for tips), and the marginally more expensive price was worth not wasting valuable time with the hassle of figuring everything out on my own.

I arrived in Ha Giang expecting a sprawling provincial capital but found a small, dispersed city. The roads were just well-kept enough to keep traffic flowing, and in place of sidewalks were muddy paths, probably because of rain in the area. The city was farther north than I realised from my limited knowledge of Vietnam (which stemmed almost exclusively from stories from the Vietnam War). I was almost to China and would find myself staring across the border (and even technically crossing it) more than once over the next few days.

I was what the tour company called an "easy rider," someone who rode on the back of a motorbike while a local guide drove on the front. I was disappointed; I missed riding my motorcycle and looked forward to taking one around the winding mountains. My guide, Luan, assured me this was the better option. I could focus on the views, taking photos and videos, and not being harassed or arbitrarily fined by the local police. I was literally just along for the ride.

The first day was a long ride out of the city and into the mountains. I had to hand it to Luan; he was candid about the flow of things, and getting away from the jurisdiction of the local police was pretty much priority number one at the outset. It wasn't that they were corrupt, necessarily, but that the Ha Giang Loop had exploded in popularity, and foreign motorbike riders were often unlicensed and ignorant of the rules of the road. In the provincial capital, the police needed those sorts of issues under control. They didn't bother the easy riders, just the self-riders. Discriminatory? Yes, but that was just how things were in this part of the world. I wasn't about to decry a widely-accepted governmental (and cultural) practice as an American; I just took it as another reminder of how great things were in my country, where we didn't have to legitimately worry about such things.

Over the next four days, my jaw stayed open as we passed one breathtaking view after another. The mountains of north Vietnam were covered in lush, green forests, and the winding roads moved with the landscape instead of coarsely cutting through it. Sometimes, the roads took us on long, sweeping paths up or down a mountain, and sometimes, we climbed out of a valley on short, tight switchbacks, making the Masif Way or Spilk Pass in Kurdistan look easy. There was something beautiful in the way these switchbacks snaked through the saddles, and we almost always stopped at the top for a few minutes to stretch our legs and take in the seamless pairing of the natural landscape and manmade roads.

We skirted the mountainside in several valleys while large, towering rock formations sprung straight up from the earth in the valley. These steep formations weren't impossible to scale, but they weren't something I would want to climb. One wrong step could send you tumbling down the steep rockface to a painful hospital stay, at best, or an untimely death, at worst. Looking across these valleys as we drove by, I thought about the Vietnam War. American troops hadn't made it this far north, and I considered them lucky for having not done so. I wouldn't have wanted to fight through this terrain, not with the North Vietnamese forces having infinitely more discipline than our troops, intimate knowledge of the terrain, and nothing but time on their hands to defeat the South and its American supporters. These tall rock formations would have been perfect forward observer and mortar emplacements to wreak absolute havoc on American troops, and close air support would have had a tough time penetrating these valleys, especially with the support the Chinese and Soviets were providing. The Battle of Ia Drang Valley would have paled in comparison to battles here.

In the morning of our second day, Luan took us to a viewpoint where, unknown to us, there was a People's Army of Vietnam (PAVN) outpost. We didn't know it, but we were just 100 metres away from the border with China, probably less. Luan left us with the other guides to ask the PAVN outpost if we could cross behind their building to see a geographic marker that the Vietnamese and Chinese governments established in 2001 showing where the two borders met. The PAVN agreed, provided we kept our voices down and didn't draw attention to ourselves. We had five minutes. To get to the marker, we walked past a rolled back mesh-wire fence where farmers were tending to their crops. When we got to the marker, a simple, concrete structure, we saw the tall, steel, barbed-wire topped fence which served as the border between the two countries. There were cameras, too, with the Chinese People's Liberation Army (PLA) on the other side monitoring the border. Luan explained to us that this wall was fairly new; Vietnam and China used to be on good terms, but China's competition with the United States since the border marker was emplaced had soured relations between the two countries. In fact, Luan told us, the real, official border with China was the mesh-wire fence was walked by on our way to the marker; we were technically standing on Chinese soil, which was why it was imperative we keep our voices down and keep our cameras pointed away from the border fence. That explained why he needed the PAVN's permission for us to walk back there.

A few minutes later, we were again staring across the Vietnam-China border, this time across the Nho Quế River. The border fence was there, too, cutting down the mountain to the river and back up the other side. Again, there was a PAVN outpost. Farmers tended to their crops, the border not seeming to mean much to them. Luan explained that to go down to the fields and the river, everyone needed permission from the PAVN, as there was an understanding between the two sides that each would safeguard their side of the border while still allowing farmers to cultivate their fields. Luan told us we would not be allowed down there, so there was no point in asking. Out of curiosity, I asked him what would happen if someone went down the path without the PAVN's permission. His answer was succinct: "They will shoot you."

On our third day, before the group split between those heading back to Ha Giang and those continuing to the fourth day of the drive, we took a break from riding with a river cruise down the Nho Quế River (on the Vietnam side). The water was a resilient turquoise colour, resulting from the minerals and specific type of algae that lived there, and cut deep into the surrounding mountains. This was an Insta-famous spot, something I didn't realise until we sailed between the two tall rock faces on either side of the narrow strait. The tour guides knew their customers; everyone took turns taking pictures off the bow with the mountains in the background. It was hard to capture the vibrant colours and natural beauty through a camera lens, but we did our best.

Our tour group was a great combination of people, from the guides to the easy riders to the two self-riders. Jorge and Carlota were a couple from outside of Barcelona, Spain, and were travelling Southeast Asia for a few weeks together. They were absolutely in love, and had been for years; I really enjoyed talking about Spain with them. Carlota didn't speak much English, so I could practise some Spanish while in Vietnam of all places. Lars and Jan, the two self-riders, were Dutch guys motorbiking through Southeast Asia. They had some wild stories from their trip through Laos, and they were definitely the party instigators in the group. Camila was a Brazilian girl studying in Germany. She was a self-avowed communist, something I found ironic given where she was from and where she lived. She didn't try to shove her beliefs down our throats like most self-identified communists, but we did have a clash of ideas a couple of times about Vietnam's communist government and capitalism's influences.

Camila and I were the only two that continued into the fourth day. Initially, it was only me, but the prospect of a three-to-four-hour, non-stop ride back to Ha Giang after lunch was all the incentive she needed to take another day through the mountains. We leisurely made our way back, making frequent, long stops to take in the views and waterfalls.

That third night in our homestay, Camila wanted to talk to me about travelling, not to share stories but to get advice. By then, I had been on the road non-stop for more than eight months, and she was four weeks into her first ever long-term trip. The truth was that long-term travel was demanding, something you couldn't truly appreciate until you did it yourself. After four weeks, she was starting to wear out, having been constantly on the move on her own in a foreign country. She was beginning to realise just how many decisions people made in a day, from what to wear to what to eat, which, back home, didn't usually take much thought, but travelling added up to take a significant mental toll. I assured her she was not crazy nor alone; every traveller felt the way at some point or another. I skipped Ankara because it all caught up to me there. I told her it was all a learning experience and to listen to her body. If she wasn't there mentally, spending an entire day at a coffee shop binge-watching a TV show to skip the day's decisions was perfectly fine. If she was worn out, there was nothing wrong with taking a rest day; after several months of travelling, I had learned to schedule them when I guessed my body would put me down. Camila was also frustrated with the fact that she hadn't worked out, had sex, or read a book in a month. Travelling was all about priorities, I told her, and those things we prioritised back home often fell to the wayside on the road. We talked for about an hour, after which she felt much better about the emotions she was experiencing on her first big solo trip. She decided to spend a few days in Hanoi after Ha Giang relaxing before flying to meet friends in Thailand. She clearly hadn't been to Hanoi; it wasn't the most relaxing place.

Unfortunately for me, our leisurely fourth day brought something I had thus far avoided in my travels: food poisoning. At least, I thought it was food poisoning. All I knew was that I was sick to my stomach. At every stop, for lunch, a view, a waterfall, I had to walk off into the trees to throw up. It wasn't easy going, either, as my body fought the urge even though it really needed it. I hadn't eaten or drank anything anyone else hadn't, but I was heading downhill fast. Even keeping water down was difficult, and I was reminded of my time in the Sahara with the military forcing my unit to keep drinking water as dysentery swept through the base. As much as I didn't want to put anything in my stomach, I needed to keep the water coming, especially in a place as hot and humid as Vietnam.

Food poisoning aside, the waterfalls were beautiful, and Camila and I enjoyed about thirty minutes in a pool of frigid water popular amongst tourists. After spending some time acclimatising on the rocks, I jumped off the waterfall into the pool. This far north, the rivers were cold from the winter, and those who jumped from the waterfall before dipping a toe in felt the shock as it took their breath away upon impact. Luan made me jump twice because he didn't get a video of me doing it the first time.

The four-day tour flew by, and it was time to head back to Ha Giang. I still felt sick, and there were still several hours until the night bus back to Hanoi. I spent those hours outstretched on one of the benches at the hostel; for some reason, it made my stomach feel better, and I continued throwing up every so often. Luan was worried, but I assured him it was just a bug or food poisoning. I knew what actual sickness felt like, and this was not that. Even so, I didn't look forward to my top bunk on the night bus to Hanoi. Once along the way, the driver came to what my dad would call a "four-wheel stop" for me to puke on the side of the road. It was better to stop for me to throw up than it was for the smell to spread through the bus and cause everyone to puke with me. The driver and the attendant were both irritated with me, but there wasn't much I could do about it except try to get the next round of heaving my guts out of the way at each rest stop. Luckily, that four-wheel stop was the last of my major incidents, and I started feeling better with each dry heaving session. I was happy that whatever it was passed so quickly; I didn't want to spend my last few weeks on the road sick.

Sa Pa

I only had the daytime at Queen Café Hotel & Pub in Hanoi before taking off for Sa Pa in northwest Vietnam. It would have been faster to head from Ha Giang to Sa Pa, but I needed to refit my gear in Hanoi. I was taking another night bus (this time with a bottom bunk) on a three-day hiking excursion through Sa Pa's rice fields. I was a little concerned about my good knee holding up, seeing as I had just spent four days on the back of a motorbike, and it wasn't completely healed, but that worry didn't overpower my desire to cram everything I could into twelve days.

We pulled into Sa Pa early in the morning, and the tour coordinator wasted no time dividing everyone into groups. I opted for the "budget" tour, so I would sleep in homestays rather than be shuttled back and forth to the hotel. After the homestays on the Ha Giang Loop, I wasn't concerned about the accommodations. The homestays were all very nice, comparable to a large family cabin in the woods back home that cost a few hundred USD a night to rent, and the families who owned the homestays were great people who wanted to give their guests a first-class experience. Despite being the "budget" option, we still lived in luxury compared to the local population.

Our first day was less of a hike and more of a leisurely stroll to the villages in the valley. After breakfast at the hotel, our group set off with an English-speaking local guide. She was Hmong, a regional ethnic group who migrated from China in the 1600s and 1700s. The Hmong people were relatively well-integrated with Vietnamese society, although they still had practices which were in direct conflict with Vietnamese law (specifically, polygamy). Under her traditional clothes, she wore black leggings. Like our guides in Morocco, the image was important, but comfort was paramount. I didn't begrudge her; modern technology, especially if she could afford it, significantly improved performance clothing, and she hiked this valley every day during the tourist season.

Accompanying our stroll was an entourage of Hmong women from the local villages selling handmade products, including bandanas, bags, coin purses, and more, out of packs on their backs. Our guide explained that this was how these women made their money for the year; once the rice season arrived, they would be wholly consumed with tending to their family fields to harvest food for the following year. In this part of the world, it was common for women to get an off-season job, as the rice they cultivated was rarely, if ever, sold for profit. It was just enough for their family to survive, and some families still had to buy more when their fields couldn't provide enough. Our guide was once one of these women, but she learned English from tourists and eventually became a guide. She preferred it, mainly for the money, but also because it was an easy off-season job she could enjoy before the physically demanding harvest season.

The walk to the villages in the valley was almost entirely downhill, and the Hmong ladies kept up the entire way. Unlike many of the tourists, they weren't winded in the slightest on the occasional uphill. These women did this every day, hiking uphill to meet the tourists in the morning and downhill with them in the afternoon. Our guide, too, walked for hours on end up and down hills, both with tourists and to go her home at night. These women were fit. Not a gym in sight, but they had the endurance of an amateur athlete. It was amazing what one could do when they didn't have a choice, and there was no choice in these valleys. They needed to make money.

The valleys near Sa Pa were different than those in Ha Giang. Whereas Ha Giang was mountainous and rocky, Sa Pa was lush with wide valleys between the mountains. These valleys were perfect for growing rice, and looked just like the stereotypical picture of cascading rice fields as far as the eye could see. The fields weren't the vibrant green seen in curated photos online; they were full of brownish-green water, held in each level by short, mud ledges around the perimeter. The few crops planted for the spring harvest hadn't ripened yet, and most of the fields were either resting or being prepared for the coming wet season. The main harvest was in September. Despite the colour difference in expectation vs reality, I still found the valleys a beautiful display of the interaction between man and nature. There weren't industrial farms here, no large tractors, no exploitation of the land on a mass scale. Instead, the valleys were filled with everyday people taking care of the land that took care of them. Most used oxen to till their fields, some used petrol-powered tillers, and several still tilled the land by hand with axes, machetes, and garden hoes.

Our first two days of hiking were more or less on level ground around the valley. There were some climbs, like to the Nhà hát CatCat, a waterfall and an outlook where we drank coffee, but for the most part, the hikes were easy. I was glad to enjoy the views without destroying my knee. A group of us on the tour bonded together on the hikes, and we talked about everything. There was a Bangladeshi psychologist involved in cutting-edge research on post-traumatic stress in London, a former Mexican soldier named Addiel who loved running long distances on the dirt roads every morning, and an Indian man named Saurabh travelling the region on holiday from work in the West. Addiel and I talked about bullfights. He was a supporter, not because of the performances, but because of the longstanding culture surrounding them, and he was glad someone like me could talk intelligently not just about the performances but the laws, the cattle ranches, and the political issues surrounding them. Addiel, Saurabh, and I talked about politics, the rise of then-former President Trump, and the many immigration crises across the world. The Bangladeshi psychologist and I discussed Islam. I gained a lot of perspective and insight into the religion and its politics from someone who described herself as "the wrong kind" of Muslim (because, as she put it, the world only cared about Muslims if it was politically expedient to care, like the Palestinians in their conflict with Israel, but not like the Bangladeshis being attacked by their own police). In those two days hiking Sa Pa, I had more informed, diverse, respectful conversations on hot-button social and political issues than I had in many years in the United States.

The third day, everyone left back to the city of Sa Pa except for Addiel and me. We were the only two of the more than twenty people who booked for a third day. It seemed like a long way for people to travel just for a two-day hike, but that was just my opinion. Addiel ran his customary route from the homestay to Sa Pa and back, which was no joke of an uphill climb, before breakfast, and then we set out with our guide, carrying our bags on our backs. This day, we climbed the mountains for the views. The initial ascent was anything but easy going, and Addiel and I both were hurting by the time we got to the top. Of course, he had already gone for a long run in the hot, humid morning, so he had an excuse; I was just out of hiking shape. Our guide fared better than both of us. She did this for a living, and the climb was nothing to her. Addiel and I commented on her fitness and the size of her calf muscles. I guess if we had to work this hard for our money, we would be fit like that, too.

There were few tourists along the route, only three going the opposite direction, so we had all the time in the world to take it in. Along this route, we saw "behind the scenes" preparations of the rice fields. It wasn't that everything before had been for show; the cottage tourism industry had just surrounded it. On the mountain, we saw it mostly free from the money injected below. Families with small fields with pantlegs rolled up were knee-deep in the muddy water, covered with the splatter from their tools impacting the flooded fields. These families didn't have large plots of cascading fields; they had one or two, just enough to feed their family for the year, and many still would have to buy more rice at the market. Some had oxen or goats to help maintain the field. These animals were unbothered by our presence, more concerned with their grazing than being territorial.

We eventually started downhill. It was steep, though not quite as steep as the walk up, and I moved a lot slower than Addiel and our guide. I didn't want to hurt my good knee anymore, and my bad knee was tricky enough on downhills. It gave them an excuse to take a break as I caught up with them at my slower pace. Before too long, we were back at the bottom, eating lunch and fresh fruit before taking a couple of motorbikes back to the hotel in Sa Pa. Another three-day adventure in Vietnam was over, but the night bus wouldn't arrive for several hours. Addiel and I elected to wander the town of Sa Pa a bit. We weren't going anywhere in particular, just getting a sense of the surroundings.

We were shocked when we came to the first major square after leaving the hotel. It looked like a scene straight out of a 1960s spy film. There were red flags flying high from flag posts, alternating the red banner with a yellow star, the Vietnamese flag, and the red banner with a hammer and sickle, the communist flag. The Vietnamese were a proud people, especially those from the north, so seeing so many national flags wasn't particularly surprising. The hammer and sickle, though, caught us off guard. It shouldn't have; Vietnam was one of the last few communist regimes

in the world. We would continue to see the communist flag throughout our wanderings. I wondered if I would see the same flag if I ever made it down to southern
Vietnam?

After a shower and changing clothes at the hotel (they had a shower just for
travellers), I boarded the night bus for Hanoi. The clock on Vietnam was approaching zero, and it was time to fly to Cambodia.

Reflecting on Vietnam

Sex tourism. Across the world, sex tourism was a controversial topic. In some
countries, like Austria and Australia, brothels were legal, licensed, and regulated. In
others, like Spain and the Czech Republic, erotic massages were legal while prosti-
tution was not. And in others, still, like most of the Middle East and the United
States, all forms of sexual-contact business were illegal. Vietnam was in the latter
category, but the sex tourism industry continued to flourish. Every night walking
down the street, I was accosted by pimps showing me pictures of naked women
offering me a "happy ending." There was even a large erotic massage parlour in the
city, with high-end security, Western-style screenings and tests for employees, and
fancy facilities. I knew about a thing called "sex tourism," where foreigners travelled
to places where procuring sexual favours was easy and legal. Apparently, one out of
two wasn't bad, because the industry was in full-swing (no pun intended) and out in
the open.

The laws weren't enforced in Vietnam; otherwise, I wouldn't be accosted with
pictures of naked women every night in Hanoi. I wondered how many of these girls
were in it because they wanted to be, had to be, had no other option, or were forced
to be. In countries where the industry was legal, there were legitimate concerns
about human trafficking, and the regulatory agencies were diligent in investigating
and busting illegal businesses. But in Vietnam, where it was outright against the law,
it seemed to operate with impunity. The apparently first-class massage parlour even
had exhaustive reviews online, with the owners replying to almost every single one.
It was a crusade I couldn't start while I was in country, but I wondered what all the
authorities would find if they peeled back the layers of the rampant, illegal industry
that was openly violating the Communist Party's law and doctrine. I didn't have to
wonder too much. The answer was probably the same as being an anti-Zionist in
Amman: morals were one thing, but Western tourism dollars were another.

Border security. During my first year of travel around the world, the United
States suffered from a crisis at the southwest border. Illegal border crossings climbed
into the millions per year after hitting record lows pre-pandemic, reports of people
on the terrorist watchlist crossing the border became more frequent, and the debate
over the border wall and asylum became heated to the point of poisonous.

It amazed me, then, that Vietnam had locked down its border situation. That
wasn't to say that there wasn't illegal immigration between Vietnam and its neighbours, but its immigration laws were clear and enforced. If you didn't have a visa to
enter, you were deported when caught. If you tried to climb the border wall, you
were arrested, if not shot. Talk about deterrence. Granted, Vietnam was a communist

country, so I didn't want to be too quick to point to the Vietnamese as a shining example of how the United States should handle its borders (or any government policy), but the stark contrast between those advocating for free and open borders back home waving the hammer and sickle while openly supporting communism or socialism and the actually communist country was impossible to ignore. It was a paradox that no one has been able to rectify to me, not even the self-avowed communist on the Ha Giang Loop.

National pride. The Vietnamese were proud people, especially the northern Vietnamese. They won the war, held off the giant war machine that was the United States' military-industrial complex, and the people's party claimed defeat of the capitalists. It was refreshing to be around people like Luan, who were legitimately proud of their country. Ho Chi Minh was a national hero, especially in the north, and there was little tolerance of anyone saying otherwise.

One of Luan's chief complaints about Vietnamese-Americans was they weren't truly Vietnamese. To him, and the majority of others I encountered and likely in the country, the Vietnamese who fled to the United States after the Vietnam War were cowards, traitors, and abandoned Vietnam. "They are not really Vietnamese," he told me, because they didn't speak Vietnamese. They didn't try to learn the language in the United States despite claiming the heritage. Luan told me he could always tell when someone's family had abandoned Vietnam after the United States pulled out, because they knew nothing of Vietnam since. More offensive was that the flag of the Republic of Vietnam (i.e., South Vietnam) was commonly displayed in Vietnamese communities in the United States. The Socialist Republic of Vietnam was the only Vietnam in the world once the war ended, yet the traitor's flag was still flown proudly by those who no longer lived there. Even worse, Ho Chi Minh City was colloquially called Saigon in the south, and the Tân Sơn Nhất International Airport's designator was still "SGN." I understood how this was offensive and insulting. It was comparable to the over a century old debate in the United States about the Confederacy. The Confederate flag symbolised something the country as a whole flatly rejected, fought a war over, and settled long ago in law. Those who flew the flag considered it their heritage, and often invoked rhetoric like, "the South will rise again!" even though the Confederacy was far in the past.

Did I support the communist regime? No, absolutely not, nor did I venerate Ho Chi Minh as the Vietnamese did, but it was easy for me to recognise that popular opinion and history were on Luan's side. I had to agree with him.

Poverty. I thought I had seen poverty before, but I was wrong. In Hanoi, it was hard to imagine how little money families had. It was the nation's capital, which, naturally, was wealthier than the outlying provinces, but there were still signs, like families of five on the back of a single motorbike, including toddlers and infants. On the Ha Giang Loop, it still wasn't easy to see. The roads were mostly well-paved, tourists were spending their money at the makeshift stalls, and the homestays where we slept were generally nice, multi-room houses. The same was true of Sa Pa.

But the signs were still there. For example, on the fourth day on the Ha Giang Loop, we rode down a road which the three-day tours (the most common ones) skipped. It was in severe disrepair, to the point of being undrivable. Luan told us the communist government controlled when and how roads got fixed, and even those with the material and tools to fix them weren't allowed to do so at their own cost. Moreover, several of our guides had families in remote villages they wouldn't see for months as they worked the off-season as tourist guides to provide for their families. Luan told us that it was just him, his wife, his mother, and his child back home, and he hadn't seen them in weeks because he was working as a guide to provide for them.

The story that stayed with me the most was a man who told us of the debt his family owed the bank. His family had taken out a 1,000,000 VND loan from a bank to pay for a sudden, unexpected expense. That was about 40 USD. It was a soul-crushing debt that he paid off 5,000 VND a month. That math came out to less than 0.20 USD a month that he gave the bank, which weighed on him. He told us the financial laws in Vietnam required him to pay the agreed amount per month or pay in full. Paying extra wasn't an option, so every month he tried to put away just a few hundred VND extra so one day he could pay the remaining debt in full. For that, he paid the price of not seeing his family for weeks or months at a time.

To hear him tell the tale, it was heartbreaking that less than half of my daily budget would literally change his life. That was true poverty. It was humbling, enlightening, and shaming, all at once, to think about any time where I had even joked that I was broke, strapped for money, or otherwise in a financial strait. I did not, nor could I ever, know what poverty truly felt like. I could only witness it and try to bring the experience back home for others to learn.

A traveller's realisation. On one sweeping curve around the mountainside in Ha Giang, as I leaned with my GoPro extended to capture the scene, I had a sobering thought that was a long time coming: It would be hard to return to real life. My life the last several months was one discovery after the next, from scenery I never knew existed to religions I knew nothing about to food combinations I never would have put together. I was on the back of a motorbike zipping around near the Chinese border in the mountains of Vietnam with my ten best friends whom I had just met a few days before. No one back home could possibly understand what I was experiencing just by looking at the photos and videos. The only people who could genuinely understand were travellers, people like me who decided to ignore real life for a while and seek more than what a job back in our hometowns had to offer. Degrees and money were important, but not at the expense of truly living, and for the first time, I seriously wondered if I would ever find myself settling down again back home.

Chapter Twenty-One

Cambodia: A Confrontation with Poverty in the Jungle Heat

Cambodia was a place I knew next to nothing about. Like Vietnam, it was on the list simply because Jo and I added it during our cursory planning a year before. I didn't know what to expect in Cambodia. I was told it was expensive and had beautiful beaches, but I hadn't heard of it being on the typical Southeast Asian traveller's circuit. I was utterly unprepared for my experiences there, but Cambodia would soon be one of my favourite experiences in a year of gallivanting across the globe.

Siem Reap

I boarded the flight to Cambodia with my visa in hand. I could have applied for a visa on arrival, but I didn't want to risk getting denied, nor did I want to deal with the inevitable queue of tourists I shared the plane with. On the plane, I sat next to Diva, from the Balkans, and Immy, from the United Kingdom, neither of whom had their visas yet. They were travelling long-term, too, though not for the full year I had planned. Neither of them worried about getting their visas on arrival, nor, it turned out, did they need to. The Siem Reap–Angkor International Airport had the most efficient visa-on-arrival system I had ever seen, with an assembly line of paperwork, payment, passport processing, and visa issuance. I breezed through customs with my visa in hand, but Diva and Immy had their visas-on-arrival processed and cleared before our bags arrived at baggage claim.

It was the evening, about 19h30, when we went in search of a taxi. They were ridiculously expensive, especially for Cambodia, at almost 100,000 Cambodian Riel (KHR) (which was 25 USD, as the KHR was pegged to the USD at 4,000 KHR to 1 USD). This was marginally outside of my budget and way outside of Diva's and Immy's. Diva had the idea to book a tuk-tuk using Grab for all three of us and our bags. Tuk-tuks weren't designed for that load, especially around corners, but that didn't occur to us until we were taking sweeping curves on the way to the city centre. I could actually turn the tuk-tuk just by sticking my hand out of the window (a trick I learned in skydiving planes), and the cars on the road blew past our slow-moving, three-wheeled adventure on the shoulder. The three of us laughed incredibly hard the entire hour-long drive to their hostel, and we agreed to hire the driver to take us to the temples of Angor in two days. After all, that was the main reason people came to Siem Reap.

During the intervening day, I explored Siem Reap. My hostel was a ten-minute walk from the city centre, which in Europe wasn't bad, but the Cambodian humidity caused me to sweat as soon as I stepped into the street. By 14h00, it was forty degrees Celsius, and that wasn't taking into account the heat index. Being from East Texas, I was used to this sort of humidity, and I was naturally built for it, something I knew but had never been so thankful for in my life, not even when I was deployed to the Sahara or Iraq.

Siem Reap's city centre was a tourist district if I ever saw one, full of Western-style restaurants, bars with live music, and a healthy mix of local "cultural" customs mixed in, namely in the form of Garra rufa fish pedicures and massage parlours openly offering "happy endings" (like Vietnam, they were illegal, but openly provided). If the street pimps in Hanoi were annoying, then the massage parlours in Siem Reap were irritating as they yelled for you to come in offering you a "special price," and I had to walk by them multiple times a day on the road to and from the hostel.

Looking back, that first day in Siem Reap seemed like a waste; all I did was wander around, going to fish markets, trying the Garra rufa fish treatment, and seeking a pair of linen pants to visit Angor the next day. At the same time, this was a tourist city, and more than half of the local economy was in the tourism sector. Despite being Cambodia's second-largest city, the tourist areas were pretty small. The outlying areas were either local neighbourhoods supporting the tourism industry or resorts. To that end, I was surprised prices weren't more Western. It was a delicate balance of making money and not inflating prices for everyone, but a 1500 KHR iced mocha (0.38 USD) in the mornings still seemed insanely cheap when Western tourism dollars were everywhere. I appreciated it, though, as even 1500 KHR was more expensive than Cambodians would pay, and I hated it when places inflated local prices to make an additional dollar off tourists.

It was an early pickup on the second day to head to Angor. Our driver had the itinerary arranged for us to arrive at the ticket office just after it opened. The Angkor Wat Archaeological Park cost 37 USD per person for a one-day visit, which was steep, but necessary for the site's upkeep with the more than 2,000,000 visitors trampling around them every year. The early wake-up was a good idea; we and everyone else planned to visit the Angkor Wat (main temple) for sunrise, and not long after we finished our paperwork the tours showed up and filled the counters and hallways. Fortunately, we had our breakfast from the on-site coffee shop and bakery long before those large groups mobbed the place.

Angkor was the capital city of the Khmer Empire, which reigned over most of Southeast Asia from 802 to 1431. Even though the empire fell 600 years before, the Khmer people lived on; they were the largest ethnic group in Cambodia, and their language, Khmer, was the national language of Cambodia. Because of this, the temples of the Angkor Empire were still considered holy sites for Hindus and Buddhists, so we had to dress in a respectful manner. That meant covering my knees with a pair of linen pants (which I promptly ripped somehow) and a short-sleeved shirt I bought in Vietnam; for Immy and Diva, that meant covering their shoulders (with long-sleeve overshirts) and their legs. I considered this normal after visiting mosques in Istanbul, but that was in the Turkish winter. In the Cambodian spring, it was still normal, just significantly hotter and more humid.

Angkor Wat, the main temple, was an artificial island temple unlike anything I had ever seen. The site had effectively been abandoned for a century and a half after the fall of the Khmer Empire, and Angkor's fall as its capital left the ruins to sit unmolested by man before European explorers "rediscovered" them in the 1500s. Even then, they were left alone until the 1800s, and restorations didn't start until the 1900s. The result was a beautiful, dark, stone complex whose temples silhouetted the sky above the surrounding trees. The temple was in the centre of the island, with outlying stone houses dotting the grounds on the walk in from the parking area. I wondered if the reason for the darkened stones was humidity caused by the lake where the island was situated, something I knew could happen from monuments in Madrid, Egypt, Turkey, and Hanoi. For reasons unknown to archaeologists, this temple faced west, whereas most faced to the east, making it popular for tourism. The sun rose directly behind the central atrium, and the tower looked like a beacon of light for observers and believers once the sun reached the top.

The walkways along the exterior of the main temple were lined with reliefs telling folk tales, accounts of military battles, and local history. These reliefs were in great condition, but their meanings were indecipherable without the information boards. They were carved in a style that I simply did not understand, even with the explanation. The walkways were also a common throughfare for the resident troops of wild macaques monkeys which called the area and temple home. These troops included nursing mothers, aggressive males, infants, and juveniles, and were unbothered by the tourists. I wasn't surprised that they were unbothered, given the millions of tourists which visited the area every year, but I still wanted to maintain a respectful distance. Interacting with tourists was one of the worst things for wild animals, especially those with the social intelligence of monkeys. In a world dominated by social media, the respect I was trying to exhibit was increasingly uncommon as people prioritised clicks and views over conservation and the environment.

Immy, Diva, and I explored Angkor Wat for a while, climbing the steps of the tallest atrium, observing the still-active Buddhist temples (which were fenced off to visitors), and taking in the beautiful, though unfamiliar, architecture of a time gone by. I didn't see any Buddhist monks visiting the site, but I learned it wasn't uncommon for them to visit, given its cultural and religious significance. Every year, on Visakha Buja Day, Buddhist monks organised ceremonies to commemorate the birth, death, and enlightenment of Buddha. It was hard to imagine what this ceremony would look like in person in the throes of all the tourists traipsing over the stones.

Throughout the rest of the day, we visited many other temples and Khmer buildings in the park. The Bayon Temple, known to tourists as the Temple of Smiling Faces, was another of the main temples in the Khmer city and served as its geographic centre. While not nearly as well-preserved as Angkor Wat, the dozens of stone towers, once numbering more than fifty, still clearly portrayed the smiling faces of Lokesvara for which it was known. Some estimates put the number of faces at over 200, but the exact number was debated. Lokesvara was a Buddhist figure

associated with compassion, but archaeologists believed these carvings were mod-
elled off King Jayavarman VII, who built the temple. Like Angkor Wat, the reliefs
surrounding the temple portrayed folk tales, myths, and historical events. Once
again, I had to take the information boards' word for it.

The most famous of the temples, maybe even more than Angkor Wat, was the
Ta Prohm Temple. This temple was featured in the Angelina Jolie film *Lara Croft:
Tomb Raider*, where it was presented as holding the key to a lost treasure which
enabled the beholder to control time. I hadn't seen the film yet (despite it being more
than twenty years old), but I thought it would be interesting to see a temple so majestic it could be used as a mythical place setting. In actuality, it was less exciting
than the others, even the smaller ones where we only spent a few minutes, mostly
because it wasn't in the best repair. In the years since Angkor's abandonment, this
temple was overtaken by trees which grew through and over the stones, and now
were part of the protected site. Because of this, and what made the it less enjoyable
for me, there was an elevated tourist walkway through the temple. I admired the
conservation effort, and the crowd of selfie-stick-wielding tourists was proof that it
was necessary. Even so, it took away from the overall, personal impact. Then again,
maybe I was just becoming judgemental towards tourists after nine months on the
road.

Throughout our day, Diva, Immy, and I chatted with our guide about his life in
Siem Reap. He loved driving tourists, not just because of the pay, but because he got
to share in foreign cultures while practising his English. It was a point of pride for
him that he was the one who got to show us around. He was divorced with two
children, a son and a daughter, but he only had any real interaction with his daughter.
Over the next two weeks, I came to understand that divorce, while uncommon in
Cambodia, had some customs that came with it, either legally or as a matter of culture. One of those customs was divided custody of children, where children over
seven chose who to live with, except where a court decided as a matter of the child's
best interest or fairness to the parents. As such, it wasn't uncommon for children to
be divided between the parents, each receiving full custody of an equal number of
children. Our guide received custody of his daughter, while his ex-wife received
custody of the son (with whom he had little interaction). He lived for his daughter
and told us he put every spare amount of money into her education. He wanted her
to attend private schools, which were far superior to public schools, and to attend
university to become a doctor. As long as she succeeded, he would work to ensure
she had the very best. It was an equally sad and heartwarming tale from someone I
had met only two days before.

Once we completed the entire Angkor loop (although there was no way for us
to visit all seventy-two major temples), our guide dropped us at Immy's and Diva's
hostel. I was going back into the city centre to lunch, which wasn't too far. We tipped
him well and parted ways. I would see Diva around some in Siem Reap, but I was
back on my own.

On my last day in Siem Reap, I took a sunset tour of Kampong Phluk. "Sunset
tour" was a strongly misleading statement of what the tour would be like. Most of
the tour was through the Kampong Phluk fishing village, southeast of Siem Reap
just off the Tonlé Sap, the largest freshwater lake in Southeast Asia. My tour group

consisted of Westerners dressed for a scenic sunset experience, me included, and we all looked the part in our sandals or tennis shoes, shorts, and nice summer shirts (well, I didn't have a nice shirt, but most everyone else did). What we got was so much more impactful, at least for me.

Kampong Phluk wasn't just a fishing village; it was a poor fishing village of about 900 families. It was called a "floating" village, because all of the houses were on stilts so they could survive the wet season. Houses were a loose term, especially by Western standards. These stilted homes could best be described as elevated lean-tos, shoddily supported on thin, wooden beams and held together with amateur engineering. The families in Kampong Phluk built the houses themselves in the dry season. Our guide, a local man named Bon, told us that, on the cheap side, the materials for these homes cost about 10,000 USD, the equivalent of 40,000,000 KHR, an oppressive amount for a community where the average annual income was 6,400,000 KHR. Those who could afford builders hired them, but most couldn't, so every able-bodied male in the family, from young children to great-grandparents, helped build their homes when the river receded. When I asked about maintenance cost on these homes (I didn't think the wooden support beams could last long being submerged underwater half of the year), Bon told me it was best for every house to be completely rebuilt every five years or so, but many couldn't afford it, so they reinforced the support beams with new wood whenever they started to deteriorate. He pointed to a nearby house that was leaning pretty severely as the original support beams were giving way, "That house will need to be rebuilt, but the family can't afford it..."

It was the dry season, so we walked through the village on the riverbed, which was graded over every year to make a driveable dirt road. Under the houses, women were hard at work smoking fish and chicken to save for the family to eat or sell at the market. It didn't smell great, to put it lightly, but it was what had to be done to afford to live. The schools were also on stilts, and we learned there were two school times during the day. Half of the children attended in the morning and the other half in the afternoon. Families needed their children in the fields or on the fishing boats, and spending an entire day at school just wasn't an option. Education was important, but surviving was a necessity.

Bon took us to one of the homes to see how the local villagers lived. The home was spacious, about the size of a two-bedroom apartment, but without the niceties of back home when you considered generations of families living under one roof. There was little electricity, often just one generator or solar panel enough to run one outlet to charge phones, maybe an appliance, and there was only one bedroom where the parents slept. Bon told us that on a wedding night, the parents would sleep in the living room with the rest of the family while the newlyweds slept in the bedroom, separated by a simple bedsheet as a door. The kids who lived in this house sold water and soft drinks from an ice chest for 1 USD a piece. It wasn't much, but it added up over time. I opted for a bottle of water; 4,000 KHR was obscenely expensive for a bottle of water in Cambodia, but it could be life-changing in this village.

Under another home, I saw a group of friends drinking beer in the shade after a long day at work. Bon seemed to know them, and they all were in good spirits. I asked him if it was common for them to drink there, and he said yes, but not to get drunk, just to enjoy each other's company. "Don't have much, but we happy while we here," he told me. That was something, and it made a lasting impression as I started scribbling in my notebook. This was an experience I had to take home. I was staring truly abject poverty in the face, and it smiled back at me over a beer. It was hard work being poor, rebuilding your house every few years, making hard choices about your children's education, and sharing everything you own with your extended family. This was the first time in all of my travels, in my life, that I truly understood how lucky I was to be born in the United States, and why it was people from all over the world went through fifty miles of Hell called the Darian Gap just for the chance of crossing our borders. It was hard to comprehend, even more difficult to explain. Even our poorest of poor had more opportunities, programmes, and assistance than this entire village, but we lost sight of that in the interconnected geopolitical world we lived in with the world's strongest economy, most influential leaders, and captains of industry. Only one thought kept recurring as I struggled to process what I saw: "Holy s***..."

As promised, we ended the tour with a sunset cruise down the Tahas River to drink at a floating restaurant on the lake. The couples took it as a romantic evening, but I got lost in conversation with Bon. I couldn't comprehend it. We were tourists on a sunset tour, taking our photos and enjoying our drinks, through a town which had never anticipated being a tourist spot. In the wet season, it wasn't possible to walk the paths, see the old women smoking fish, or see the stilts almost ready to give way as the boat wakes battered them for five months. In the wet season, it was a sunset cruise through and through, but we were in the dry season and afforded what I viewed as the rare opportunity to see what life was like during the hard time of year in the village.

As if to put an exclamation point at the end of my feelings, Bon asked us all for a review on Trip Advisor. These reviews dictated which guides were kept on during the low tourist season (i.e., the wet season) and which were laid off. The guides made substantially more money from tourists than they did fishing, and to be kept on made a substantial difference in their quality of life. His request was impossible to ignore.

I hadn't quite decided where I was heading to the next day, but this tour solidified it for me. I didn't want to take the typical tourism circuit through Cambodia and explore the beaches and carefully-curated experiences. I wanted to see Cambodia through the eyes of locals. According to my internet searches, the best way to do that was to go on hiking excursions in the national parks out east, so that was where I headed. I booked my ticket to Banlung in Ratanakiri Province on the border with Vietnam. It was an eight-hour van ride along mostly unpaved roads to get there, a sign of just how little infrastructure there was outside of the major cities. It was a rocking, bouncing, jolting ride to get there, but I knew that was the direction I needed to go. It was time to do what I had wanted to do my entire trip around the world: take a good, hard look at what life was really like in other countries.

* * *

Ratanakiri

The van dropped me on the side of the road in Banlung, Ratanakiri Province. My homestay was supposed to pick me up, but there was a miscommunication, so I was on the side of a dirt road with my bags, waiting for a tuk-tuk to find me. I sent a picture of it to my mom and commented that my life had taken a hard left turn somewhere along the line. I went from making six figures at a security firm in Colorado to sitting on the dirty sidewalk with my backpack waiting for a tuk-tuk in Cambodia.

The homestay, called FamilyHouse & Trekking, was a fine place, all things considered. It wasn't Ha Giang Loop nice, but this also wasn't the Ha Giang Loop. It was a modest place, built by hand from logs procured from the jungle. Pu Thea, the owner, was a man not much older than me, laid back, and did everything he could to make his guests' experience the best they could be. Even though we were far out east, he had a full house, with most of his private cabins occupied and my shared room full (granted, it was only three people). Every bed had mosquito nets, and every room had its own bathroom and shower. We shared the shower drains with the frogs; that's just how things were in that part of the world.

Pu set me up with two French couples going on a three-day "all-inclusive" trek through the Virachay National Park. I use quotes for "all-inclusive" because it was, but not in the way Westerners thought of all-inclusive. The homestay provided hammocks, mosquito nets, transportation, water, and food, but we would be humping it all on our backs for three days. There were no roads where we were headed. Pu told us he usually had porters, but it was the harvest season, so they were all out in the jungle hunting for malva nuts. I didn't mind. The French couples did; they weren't expecting to have to ruck on their three-day hike through the jungle. Pu also recommended we wear long pants to avoid insect bites and getting stuck, poked, and cut in the bush. It was good advice.

We loaded up the next day with our guide, JC (as he called himself, jokingly referring to it meaning "Jesus Christ" or "Jimmy Carter"), and made for the Tonle San River. The homestay's tuk-tuk could only hold four people, so I was on the back of JC's motorbike for the hour-long ride. We started out on paved roads, but those turned to orange dirt once we exited the city. My baseball cap would be permanently stained a rust colour from the ride. Once at the river, we loaded a canoe and sailed east for our three days in the jungle. The boat was serviceable, but that was about as good of a description as I could give; the driver steadily bailed water out of the back as the motor sucked it in. I had been in a similar situation in Africa years before, and I laughed to myself wondering how I could possibly be there again.

On the other side of the river, we met up with a ranger whom the French girls named Tchi Tchi (because they couldn't pronounce his full name). JC thought this was funny because that was the name they used for dogs. The ranger didn't like it at first, but he eventually accepted it. The word "ranger" was a loose term as well. Tchi Tchi wasn't a government official, nor did he have any formal training in navigating the forest, search and rescue, survivalist tactics, or anything else Westerners would expect of someone calling themselves a ranger. Tchi Tchi was a "jungle man" (JC's words, not mine). He grew up and lived there, and he knew it better than I knew my hometown. He didn't need government certifications or training to survive; his people had been doing it for hundreds of years.

With that, we set off. The opening walk was on a dirt road in the hot midday sun. It would easily top more than forty degrees Celsius without the humidity in the shade as we hiked in open country. The French girls wore tank tops, and their shoulders burned before we reached the jungle. I could feel the back of my calves burning, too, but at least that was easier to handle. The ranger led the way at a brisk pace in flip flops, wearing a boonie hat, black shirt, and black cargo pants cut into capris, and he carried the steel cookware on his backpack. He whittled a stick as he walked, paying no mind to the Europeans falling behind in his wake. He never left us behind, but he did get far enough out to pause and wait for some of the group to catch up more than once over the next few days.

When we made it to the jungle, I realised quickly that the tree canopy came with a major trade-off. It was cooler in the shade, which was welcome, but the trees blocked the wind while increasing the humidity. The only reprieve from the heat (and the gnats that swarmed our faces when we stopped) was to keep moving. That was the only wind we would get in the jungle. I understood the French couples weren't used to rucking all of their food and water on their backs for three days, but they wanted to stop a lot more than I or Tchi Tchi did. I wasn't against taking a break, but as soon as we stopped the sweat poured down my face like a waterfall. I was from the Piney Woods of East Texas, had deployed to both the Sahara and Baghdad in the summer, and had trained outdoors for months at a time with the military in Kentucky, but this was the hottest and sweatiest I had ever been. Over the next three days, I heard the choruses to Rodney Atkins "Farmer's Daughter" in my head on repeat. It was the only song I could think of that came remotely close to describing how hot it was, and it made me crave a tall glass of sweet iced tea like never before.

Along the way, Tchi Tchi stopped to show us some valuable plants in jungle life. He had an eye for these things and would stop suddenly when he saw something we should see. Redwood, for example, was rare in this jungle, and it was illegal to cut it down. If we found it on the jungle floor, though, it was supposedly free game. The illicit redwood trade was strong in Cambodia, especially amongst those who made their livelihood off the jungle itself, as there was high demand for the lumber in China for furniture. That the people who lived there needed to make a living somehow didn't excuse the illicit trade and environmental damage, but it made it understandable.

Tchi Tchi also showed us the malva nuts the locals were harvesting. Malva nuts were expensive, only found in three of Cambodia's northern provinces, and they were a key fruit in traditional medicine. They were only harvestable one month out of the year, between March and April, and the harvest was dangerous work. The nuts grew in the tops of trees, which easily ran to a height of thirty metres and had no branches to climb. Everyone, JC told us, knew somebody who had died falling from the tree. At 40,000 to 60,000 KHR per kilogram (about 10 to 15 USD), they were worth the danger; just 100 kilograms in the month-long harvest could provide enough income for an entire year. JC negotiated with some passing farmers for a handful of nuts for us to use for tea over the next few days. Malva nut tea was good for the immune system, and we needed as much help as possible as we ventured farther and farther from the nearest hospital.

After about eight hours of hiking, we finally arrived at our campsite. We weren't exactly exhausted, as the hike hadn't been through rugged terrain, but we all had sweat through our clothes. My tan travel pants were a few shades darker from all the sweat. The campsite was along a river, so while JC and Tchi Tchi prepared dinner, the five of us tourists went for a swim. My bad knee ached, and a cool thirty minutes in the water flowing over the rocks did wonders to soothe the muscles. My good knee, fortunately, was healed and not giving me any trouble.

Dinner that night consisted of frogs from the river, homemade beef jerky, rice, and bamboo soup. I passed on the frogs; something about them just wasn't appetising, but the French devoured them readily, proving the stereotype. The bamboo soup was a mix of vegetables in water roasted over a fire in a bamboo shoot for hours until they were liquified. Which vegetables, I wasn't sure, but the soup was delicious, especially over the bowl of rice and combined with the jerky. It wasn't a lot of food (though we certainly weren't undernourished), and it really made me think about what it was like to live in the jungle. This was what they ate, and we were probably eating it in larger quantities than were available to those who lived on their small farms throughout the area. Frog gigging wasn't just a redneck hobby like it was back home; it was a crucial activity to find food, as was spearfishing with the stick Tchi Tchi whittled earlier. Throughout the night, hunters and fishermen passed by the campsite looking for frogs, fish, and snakes to turn into food for their families.

Our second day in the jungle was another eight hours of hiking. We paused for lunch near a freshwater source to replenish our water bottles. I was grateful for this, as I was burning through water faster than I wanted to. When I was in the military, I trained to ration limited water, but that was many years before, and I hadn't sweated like this in as long as I could remember. As we were in the heat of the day, we took a longer rest stop at lunch, and both JC and I took naps while the French couples talked with each other in French. I was glad to be on the move again, though, to have the wind finally moving past my face.

Our campsite that night was, again, along the river, but this time it was next to a trickling waterfall. In the wet season, this waterfall would have been thunderous with all the water rushing from the mountains upstream, but in the dry season, it was hardly a trickle, and the pool below it was almost brackish. I was fascinated by a fish guarding and teaching its newly hatched fry in one of the shallow outcrops. There weren't a lot of natural predators there, but millions of years of evolution still dictated that the fish teach and protect their offspring.

At this campsite, everyone stripped down to their underwear. We all washed our shirts and pants we'd worn over the last two days in the river, and we covered the rocks with our Western clothes to dry in the sun. Tchi Tchi, too, washed his, but that was because those were the only clothes he had. JC kept his jeans on. They were his only pair of jeans and looked worse than the one year he had owned them. He cut them off at the knees halfway through the day with Tchi Tchi's machete; he was going to buy a new pair for the year when we got back to Banlung.

Tchi Tchi's brother joined us that night, and he brought with him bottles of happy water for us to drink with our jerky, rice, and bamboo soup. I knew happy water from Vietnam. It was basically distilled rice wine, but it smelled, tasted, and felt awful, and it only got worse with every sip. Happy water originated when alcohol was illegal in Southeast Asia, and it continued to gain popularity as legal alcohol was introduced at prices which local nationals couldn't afford. Having had my fill of it in Vietnam, I avoided drinking with them, something Tchi Tchi and his brother respected more than everyone else. Eventually, the seven of them drank all they had, so Tchi's Tchi's brother went to get some more. I wasn't sure how long they stayed up drinking. My hammock called my name early.

We had a late morning the following day. Our hike wasn't too far, only six hours, and about two of those were out in the open. On the way, we stopped at Tchi Tchi's house. Like the homes in Kampong Phluk, it was on stilts, though not quite as tall. Tchi Tchi and his wife built the house themselves, just as they had cleared the surrounding land for rice and cashew fields. His wife was out in the field, and his youngest son (only about three years old) was in the house. The French girls wanted to meet his other son, but he was nowhere to be found. He was in the jungle climbing the trees for malva nuts. He was twelve years old.

On our walk back to the boat, JC told us about himself. "I'm just a farmer," he told us, and he had a daughter at home. Like the driver in Siam Reap, he was divorced, and his ex-wife had custody of his other child. JC worked to keep his daughter in private school, and he hoped one day she would go to university, meet a good man, and get married. That would be a good life. When we asked how he got into being a guide, JC told us it was a matter of luck. He was a receptionist at a hotel, and a friend asked him if he would be a porter for his tour company. That turned into him learning English and getting officially certified through the government to lead tours, and now that was his full-time off-season job. Like Luan in Vietnam, he missed being home, but he loved meeting people from all over the world, and being a guide was a better off-season job than many could afford. For example, he wasn't risking his life climbing thirty-metre trees for fruit.

Before returning to Banlung, JC took us to a Bunong village. These villages were all over east Cambodia, especially along the rivers. The Bunong fled the cities by the tens of thousands under the Khmer Rouge and Pol Pot. They were targeted for their religious belief in animism, which, in Pol Pot's view, had no place in Cambodia's future. After the Khmer Rouge fell and Cambodia restored the monarchy, the Bunong people remained in eastern Cambodia, as they were effectively exiled after decades of persecution. They were isolated in poor communities that were almost entirely dependent on NGOs to provide healthcare and education. JC took us to one of the schools. It was nice, with a classroom for each group of grades and a small library. It was also empty. It was the harvest season for malva nuts, so school took a back seat.

On the ride back to Ratanakiri, I reflected on my time in the jungle, Tchi Tchi, and the stories which JC had told us of life in rural Cambodia. JC and Tchi Tchi clearly enjoyed their lives, and their skills afforded them opportunities the Bunong people didn't have. Even so, they lived hard lives. JC was turning around the next morning to guide another group on another three-day hike through the national park.

It was hard work being poor.

Mondulkiri

I continued my eye-opening tour of Cambodia by traveling three hours south to Monourom in Mondulkiri Province. I was visiting the Mondulkiri Project, an organisation which rescued elephants from cruel conditions, from tourist attractions to logging operations. I stayed at Tree Lodge, the Mondulkiri Project's partner accommodations, where I had a bungalow to myself for the first time in a while. Well, mostly to myself. I still shared the shower drain with the frogs. I only had two full days in Mondulkiri. I was less than a month from being in Mexico, and I still had a jaunt through Thailand coming up, so I spent my entire two days with the Mondulkiri Project.

The Mondulkiri project was an NGO founded in 2013 when it signed an agreement which ceased logging operations in the local area. The project bought a large swath of land to use as an elephant sanctuary and began their work saving Asian elephants. As of my visit, there were five elephants, each with their preferred area in the jungle. The project wanted to save more, but elephants needed a lot of space to live, and the options were financially limited. That was where people like me came in. Our tours helped fund the acquisition of more land to save more elephants, which would, in turn, attract more tourists and perpetuate the cycle. That was the goal, anyway. At the same time, the project provided jobs to a local Bunong village. Caring for the elephants was an around-the-clock task, so there were plenty of opportunities. Of course, there could always be more if the project expanded.

I was in a group of about fifteen people visiting the elephant sanctuary over two days. The first day was wholly dedicated to learning about the elephants and the Mondulkiri Project. After a brief introduction, a guide led us into the jungle with a backpack full of bananas, the elephants' favourite treats. Our first encounter was not far down the trail with Sophie. Sophie was rescued from an illegal logging operation, where she hauled logs uphill for hours upon hours each day. Seeing her then, we couldn't tell, as she was full of life and her trunk snuck bananas from unsuspecting tourists. She was gentle and let people touch her while feeding her bananas. She was also smart, as elephants were, and she sneakily made for the backpack full of bananas which were out of sight up a hill. The guide told us that during the COVID-19 pandemic, all of the elephants, but especially Sophie, got depressed at the lack of tourists (and bananas). They were social animals, despite living in their own parts of the park, and the Mondulkiri Project wasn't sure how they were going to react when people finally returned. "They are happy now," the guide told us. "They have bananas!"

The next elephant, not too far away, was Happy. Happy was a lazy elephant, according to the guide. Whereas the others took the bananas from us with their trunks, Happy just held her mouth open for us to deposit them. This turned off some people; they found something about an elephant's vertical slit for a mouth unnerving, especially if it licked their hands retrieving the banana. Like Sophie, Happy was rescued from a logging company.

The next two elephants were Princess and Comvine. Princess was blind in one eye, either due to an axe injury inflicted upon her by a former owner or due to a branch sticking into her eye after slipping (depending on the source), and skittish around people on that side. Elephants had monocular vision, which meant she was blind to half of the world. The guide cautioned us against approaching her too quickly and recommended that we approach Comvine first. Comvine was Princess's friend, guide, and protector. At more than seventy years old, Princess was old, and Comvine's thirty-year-old presence calmed her amongst the tourists. Both were rescued from the tourism industry, and both loved bananas.

The fifth elephant we only saw from afar. It was a male, a bull, and the guide advised us to keep our distance. The word "bull" was enough convincing for me. He was across the river, behind some trees. Far enough not to be a threat, but close enough to keep a watchful eye on us. The Mondulkiri Project hoped that introducing the bull would result in one of the females having a calf. There were only about 600 Asian elephants left in Cambodia, and sanctuaries like this one could prove crucial in saving the species from extinction.

After a communal lunch, the group headed to the river to play with the elephants in the water. It was the heat of the day, and the elephants knew the routine. The water meant cooling off, and the tourists meant bananas, and Princess and Comvine instinctively met us at the river. The guide encouraged us to splash water on them. If we didn't, they would just do it themselves. This was how they regulated their body temperature and cleaned off the dirt they scattered on themselves throughout the day to deter insects. Playing with elephants in the river wasn't on my bucket list, but it wasn't something I was going to balk at, either. We stayed there for about two hours before Comvine and Princess had their fill and ambled back into the jungle. We all stayed a bit longer. The water was cool, and the Cambodian jungle was hot and humid. Some of the group was heading to their air-conditioned hotel at the end of the day; some of us were staying in hammocks. For us in the latter category, the water was a much-needed reprieve.

As we waited for dinner, I got to know Patrick, a Spanish-Irish man who lived in Albacete, Spain, and went to university in Valladolid. Naturally, we talked about all things Spain, from the bullfights to the festivals to its similarities with where I was from. We also talked about Ireland, another of my favourite countries. I could hear the Spanish and Irish accents come out, depending on what Patrick was talking about. Even he found humour in the combination. Patrick offered me a place to stay and a tour guide if I ever made it out his way again. I was sure I would and told him I would take him up on the offer.

The second day at the Mondulkiri Project sanctuary was a six-to-eight-hour hike through the jungle. It wasn't a hard trek by any means, and we passed through farms, waterfalls, and open fields of recently-destroyed vegetation (from a fire). Passing through the first farm, I got a hard lesson in the science of botany. Cashews were a staple crop in this part of Cambodia. Tchi Tchi in Ratanakiri actually had cashew trees on his farm. Cashews were a fruit which also produced the nut I was accustomed to. The fruits were safe to eat straight off the vine if they were ripe, which we did both in Ratanakiri and on the jungle trek with the Mondulkiri Project. The nuts, however, were not, and they had a natural urushiol coating beneath the skin to ward off predators. The urushiol was roasted out of the cashews before they were sold on the market (so anytime you saw a bag of "raw" cashew nuts, they were actually roasted), but they were wholly inedible in the wild. It turned out that if a cashew fruit became overly ripe, the urushiol would seep into the fruit and mix with its plentiful juices. I learned this the hard way when I bit into a cashew fruit and immediately felt a burning, sticky sensation in my mouth. I didn't know what was going on, but I tossed the fruit and immediately broke out my toothbrush and toothpaste. I learned some years before that washing your mouth out with water, milk, or any other liquid was near-useless when it came to things that irritated your mouth; you needed to scrub any oils off your tongue, gums, and lips to stop the burn. As I was brushing and scrubbing, I could feel my hand starting to itch. The juices ran down my hand and caused a rash. I doused my hands in water and scrubbed them with my towel (I was doing laundry soon anyways), and I hoped the damage would be contained. I didn't know what exactly was happening in the moment, but urushiol was the same poison contained in poison ivy and poison oak, and I was extremely allergic. Over the years, I had taken great pains to avoid the abundant plants back home, but eating a fruit off the vine in Cambodia, which had been fine for days and everyone else, finally did me in. It was a grave mistake that would plague me for weeks.

Urushiol poisoning notwithstanding, the hike was fun, and I got to know several other members of the group while enjoying the incredible views. We also stopped at waterfalls along the way. While we couldn't stay long at many of them, I got a great video of me standing in front of one with my bamboo walking stick and Akubra. I looked like a true adventurer, the fuchsia and blue backpack not taking away from the aesthetic.

We ended our trek at the Putang Village, a Bunong village where houses (which were large, circular buildings with thatched roofs) smaller than the one I grew up in housed upwards of nine families. These homes had no windows, no electricity, and no amenities whatsoever. Cooking was done at a separate facility, and materialism didn't exist in the remote villages. The homes were for sleeping and not much else. That same thought came to me again: it was hard work being poor.

With my time in Mondulkiri ending, I enjoyed some rice, chicken, and vegetables for dinner with Patrick and others before retreating to my bungalow to pack my bags. With the urushiol juices, I had to be careful to pack it so I wouldn't cross-contaminate my clothing and gear. I didn't want to wash my clothes to go through all of that again because my backpack held trace amounts of urushiol oil.

As I packed, I listened to country music on internet radio and decided to build a playlist of the songs I enjoyed the most on YouTube. I made playlists in Africa and Iraq that I still maintained and decided to pick up that old tradition on The Great Gallivanting. I would have it on repeat in my ears on travel days over the next few weeks, and I felt myself coming even closer to re-embracing my favourite style of music. I would need it on my jarring seven-hour van ride to Phnom Penh the next day.

Phnom Penh

I was in Phnom Penh primarily because the flight to Chiang Mai, Thailand, was cheapest from there. I knew little about the city outside of the fact that it was Cambodia's Capital, but my dad told me the city was a household name when he was growing up during the Vietnam War. The war next door, the Nixon Administration lying about carpet bombings in Cambodia, and the Khmer Rouge genocide were all things I learned about in history class, but knowing my dad had lived during those times made me want to learn what I could in my short time in the city. I was only there for two full days, with one dedicated to laundry, a haircut, and other administrative tasks, so I only had one day to experience what I could.

Phnom Penh was hot, and I mean really, really hot. I texted my dad, "supposed to get up to 102 feels like Hell's basement later today," when the sun was halfway into the sky. Between the humidity and concrete everywhere, I was sweating like I was still in the jungle. Fortunately, there was a slight breeze, and I could stay in the buildings' shadows when walking through the city. I was built for the heat; I would even venture to say I liked it, but this was next-level stuff. Not even in the Saharan summer did I sweat this much. Usually, I preferred to wear pants when visiting cities, but it was too hot and humid for that. Besides, mine were all trashed from the jungle treks.

As I only had one day to do as I pleased, I opted to learn about the Khmer Rouge and the genocide it perpetrated against its own people. JC from Ratanakiri talked about the Khmer Rouge as though it were an event in Cambodia's history, but it was a four-year tyrannical period followed by twenty years of political influence and guerilla warfare across Indochina. Its ruler, Pol Pot, was held up by opponents of communism as one of the most genocidal dictators of the Cold War, with between 1,500,000 and 3,000,000 deaths, and placed him in the ranks of Stalin (who killed almost 2,000,000 people in the gulags alone). Pol Pot's victims were executed and buried in what were known as killing fields; these were literal fields where over 1,000,000 Cambodians deemed a threat to the regime and the communist revolution were unceremoniously wiped from the earth. I wished I had time to visit the killing fields of Phnom Penh, but I knew that was stretching it on limited time without an organised tour. Instead, I found the Tuol Sleng Genocide Museum, where I could learn everything I needed in one place.

I must admit, as I write about the Tuol Sleng Genocide Museum, my eyes tear up, and my heart sinks into my chest. It was categorically the most emotional, heartbreaking, breath-taking tragedy museum I had ever visited. It was not a museum for the faint of heart, as the Cambodian government was committed to keeping the stories of the horrors the Khmer Rouge's victims endured alive. They considered it a duty to their memories and families, and the audio guide warned listeners what they were going to see and hear was disturbing. The guide was not wrong. I saw many Western tourists in tears after some of the exhibitions, and I had to take a break from the exhibit halls to process what I saw. I had witnessed Islamic State mass executions, dissected terrorist attacks from around the world, and read every magazine al-Qa'ida and Islamic State published, but that was all professional, almost academic. The Tuol Sleng Genocide Museum was a personal experience, one which I could not have prepared myself for no matter how much I read about it online. There was no censorship, no pulled punches, and no apologies for telling the entire truth of the barbaric atrocities committed in the name of Khmer Rouge's communist revolution.

The museum was housed in a former high school, the Tuol Svay Prey High School. It looked like a miniature university campus or military barracks, with five buildings arranged on a city block. It once served the local neighbourhood, but in

1976, the Khmer Rouge turned the high school into Security Prison 21 (S-21). The regime converted the classrooms to prison, interrogation, and torture cells, electrified the perimeter fences, and covered the windows with iron bars. In the courtyards, which were now green with a beautiful memorial and a fountain, they added torture devices. It was a small prison only able to hold about 1,000 people, but over its four-year existence, 20,000 people would be held, tortured, and executed there. That number wasn't staggering enough on its own, but when I did the mental math, I realised that meant turning every bed in the prison over every two and a half months or less. That rivalled the Nazis' Dachau, where more than 40,000 people were killed over twelve years. And these camps were everywhere. Had Pol Pot's regime continued as long as the Nazis, the Khmer Rouge's genocide could easily have surpassed the Holocaust.

The first building, Building A, was primarily the prison and torture cells, preserved as they were found. Prisoners were shackled to beds for interrogation and tortured in these rooms. Not just any beds; *these exact beds*. When the Vietnamese Army liberated Phnom Penh, they left these rooms exactly as they were found. They were evidence of war crimes not just against Cambodian dissidents but against ethnic Vietnamese who lived in Cambodia. On the walls hung pictures of the last individuals tortured in the very room in which the photos were taken. The prisoners were killed and left to rot as the prison guards fled the approaching Vietnamese Army. Much like the Nazis, they fled rather than stand up for the ideals they professed.

The courtyard held the gallows, once a climbing rope for school students in the playground, where torture was carried out in plain view of all prisoners and guards. Some prisoners were suspended from the gallows by a rope bound to their hands and wrists behind their back, similar to Roman crucifixion without the cross. Lashings were a common form of punishment, and one of the posted rules prohibited crying while obtaining lashes; doing so would incur more lashes with electric wire. Others were hung upside down and nearly drowned in nearby vats of water in an extreme version of waterboarding to extract confessions. Whether or not those confessions were true were immaterial; they were executed either way. Only twelve people survived execution at S-21. Four of them were children. These children were lucky to survive S-21. A standard intake procedure was to simply execute children. Sometimes, babies were used for aerial target practice.

Building B contained exhibitions describing the Khmer Rouge regime, its ideology motivating the genocide, and photos of prisoners (both mugshots and executions). This building demonstrated how much control the Khmer Rouge exerted over the country. Simply picking a mango off a vine instead of purchasing it through the regulated processes was considered theft and a crime against society worthy of execution. Starvation was less important than your commitment to the Party. Other stories included "arrest by kinship," where families were arrested for being affiliated with a prisoner. It was guilt by extension, not even association, as the web of prisoners' families grew with each additional arrest. Under Pol Pot, an arrest equalled guilt. After all, the Party would not make an unlawful, extrajudicial, or outright false arrest. With all the frivolous arrests, one prisoner asked, "If Angkor arrests everyone, who will be left for the revolution?"

The Khmer Rouge exterminated everyone. Like all genocidal regimes, it started with political dissidents but quickly moved to ethnic minorities, academics, religious practitioners (especially Buddhist monks), and its own party via purges. These groups were loosely defined. The "academics" category included more than university professors and those with degrees; it included those with "intellectual qualities," which included wearing glasses and speaking multiple languages. In Cambodia, where Khmer, Vietnamese, Chinese, Thai, French, and English were common due to trans-peninsular migration and Western intervention, speaking multiple languages wasn't uncommon. Some would call it a necessity. It was also a death sentence.

Building C contained more prison cells. The outside walkways were covered by a mesh fence anchored into the ground. The Khmer Rouge put up this fence to prevent prisoner suicides. After all, there were valuable counterrevolutionary confessions to be obtained before they were executed, and suicide prevented those confessions. The prison cells were small, only a metre wide and about two metres deep. They contained an anchor point in the corner where prisoners were shackled to the building. On the walls next to the main entrance was the key depository. The key depository was just a piece of wood with hooks attached and numbers written or etched into the wall below it. No need to turn the prison into a fancy holding facility when most of the prisoners were on their way to the killing fields.

Prison S-21 wasn't just a torture and interrogation centre. Like the Nazi death camps, it was also used for "scientific research." Khmer Rouge doctors conducted scientific experiments on live prisoners, what normal people called torture by vivisection. These experiments started on animals, but with all the available human subjects, they transitioned to using prisoners. Prisoners were already marked for death; there was no reason to waste their scientific value.

I spent hours at the Tuol Sleng Genocide Museum. For such a small site, no more than a city block, it told the most detailed story of almost any museum I had ever visited, except maybe the Topography of Terror museum in Berlin. It was almost too much, not in terms of information, but in terms of horrors. The human mind could only take in so much. It was one of the few times since leaving the military that I was grateful for being exposed to such things in the counterterrorism world. I could handle the atrocities mentally and emotionally. Many people I saw could not, and they elected to listen to the audio guides outside the buildings where they didn't have to see the vivisected bodies, torture chambers, and pictures of the victims. The organised tour groups moved through the site in less than an hour, just long enough to get the point across without completely immersing unready tourists in the terrible things that went on there forty-five years ago. Those of us who were on our own took longer, and many took time in the courtyard between buildings to process what we saw and prepare ourselves for what was next. As a traveller, I felt I owed it to the survivors who insisted the site remain intact and serve as a museum to tell the stories of the thousands who passed through S-21. They survived unimaginable terrors, and their story needed to be told.

I was dazed as I left the Tuol Sleng Genocide Museum. I had too many thoughts swirling around my head, despite the notes I had taken to get them out. That wasn't an experience I could just move on from and head to the next cool thing, so I took my time through the city that afternoon and slowly wound my way to my hostel. I stopped at a mall for a late lunch, ready for the air conditioning to cool down after being outside or in non-air-conditioned buildings all day. The mall was new, so it was still about half empty and didn't have local food. I didn't care. I had fried chicken from a regional chain, knowing full well that fried chicken in places like this would be fresh and delicious. In a shocking but welcome development, the place had sweet tea, something I had longed for since the jungles of Ratanakiri. I must have been quite a sight for the mall's patrons in my shorts, ankle-high boots (they were comfortable on my aching bad knee), Akubra, fried chicken, sweet tea, and messenger bag.

After stopping at a few more monuments along the way, I was back at the hostel for an afternoon nap. The Tuol Sleng Genocide Museum had taken it out of me, both from the heat and the mental energy it took to process it, and I needed to rest before heading to Thailand, anyways. I didn't want to get halfway through the country just to get taken out by exhaustion like I had in Ankara a few months earlier. To that same end, I took it easy the next day as well. I got a much-needed haircut, handed my laundry off to the hostel to clean, and enjoyed time reading my Kindle and listening to music at some terrace restaurants during lunch and dinner. I also called home, anticipating that I wouldn't be doing so as much over the next three weeks traversing the entire length of Thailand.

I had an early morning to get to the airport. I could have hired a taxi, but the hostel offered its own service. I opted for their budget option, which was a tuk-tuk. It didn't move fast, taking almost an hour to get to the airport, but for the price, it was worth it. Besides, I came into Cambodia on a tuk-tuk; I might as well leave on one, too.

Reflecting on Cambodia

Poverty. After Vietnam, I thought I had seen poverty, where 40 USD was a life-changing sum. In Cambodia, however, I was immersed in it. While most travellers headed for the beaches and party towns, I was in the jungle with people who lived every day working in the Cambodian heat just to survive. I would never know what it was like to ask where my son was and learn he was climbing thirty-metre-tall trees for fruit; I would never know what it was like for that to be an everyday occurrence. JC had one pair of pants, and he made them last a year before he bought a new pair as a farmer and guide. Plenty of impoverished people in the United States only had the clothes they were wearing; few of them harvested their own food in the forty-plus-degree heat and high humidity in the sun all day wearing those clothes. Building a house was considered a luxury in the United States; it was a necessity in Cambodia, while things like running water, electricity, and a foundation capable of withstanding floods were foregoable options.

After seeing the abject poverty in Cambodia, I became hardened to much of the plight and political rhetoric surrounding poverty in the United States. My country was a land of opportunity, even for the homeless and poor. We had vast social programmes, both private and government-funded, which provided meals and shelter to the downtrodden. In the city where my dad worked for more than thirty years, there was an out-of-work man who spent every night outside of a work programme office hoping to be first in the queue for any random jobs that came in that day. How did he spend his money? On two beers every single day. One of the private programme administrators once told us that there was no reason any person in the city should ever go without a roof over their heads or a meal; there was that much money in place to support our struggling citizens. There were even news reports and documentaries of people living on the streets in California that had iPhones and Amazon Prime accounts as they took benefits intended to get them a job and a place to live.

In Cambodia, being poor was hard work. Sleeping on the streets and begging for money weren't options. In the wet season, entire streets disappeared, making stilted shelter a necessity that had to be built by hand. There were only two ways to get food: grow it or buy it. Chances were, if you couldn't grow it, you couldn't afford to buy it. JC and Tchi Tchi walked the jungles for days and weeks at a time to earn money for their families to survive. JC had buffalo to help till his fields, something he could afford with the money he made from guiding tourists. Tchi Tchi did not; his wife and two kids tended to their fields and crops by hand every day of the year. Americans, not even in the direst of financial circumstances, couldn't imagine what this level of poverty was like.

"You can't compare atrocities." At the Tuol Sleng Genocide Museum, I was infuriated to find graffiti on the walls of one of the prison blocks: "end Israeli Genocide." I understood there were inflamed passions on the anti-Israel/pro-Palestine side of politics as a result of Israel's response to Hamas's October 7th attacks from Gaza, but to see this graffiti in a memorial to the victims of the Khmer Rouge was a level of insensitivity and disrespect reserved only for the most ignorant of social justice warriors. I stared at the graffiti for what must have been thirty seconds as I stifled my outrage that someone would defile a place designed to remember the victims, families, and atrocities perpetrated by a murderous communist regime. It was not lost on me that the person who drew that graffiti probably supported socialist or communist policies; that was how the battle lines were drawn in the political sphere.

A man behind me, named Uri, said, "This is infuriating," and he left the room so fast it could almost be said he stormed out. I met with Uri outside the building, and we talked about the graffiti and how disrespectful it was. Uri was a former Israeli special operations soldier who fought in Gaza. He was a firsthand witness to the ideology Hamas had poisoned Gazans with, and he was a firsthand witness to Gazans who, on a large scale, supported that ideology. Uri told me Western media went far too easy on Hamas and Gazans, and that there was a fundamental, intentional refusal to acknowledge the realities on the ground. At the same time, Uri was heavily critical of Israel's resettlement polices in the West Bank. "Israel holds a lot of responsibility" for the plight of Palestinians in the West Bank, he said, and he was an advocate for changing those policies.

All of that notwithstanding, Uri said, "You can't compare atrocities." The retaliation against Gaza was in no way comparable to Pol Pot's genocide in Cambodia, not in scale, in ideology, or brutality. Pol Pot's genocide was also in no way comparable to the conflict between the Palestinians writ-large and Israel. One was driven by a political party and inflicted upon its own people; the other was a quasi-religious conflict where there were belligerents and political objectives on both sides, regardless of how incompatible they were. The Palestinian people could not fathom the horrors which the Khmer Rouge inflicted upon its millions of victims; the Cambodians could not fathom what it was like to be fighting a foreign power for your ancestral homeland. To Uri, and I would have to agree with him, the two were wholly incomparable. Neither the statistics nor the motivations mattered to the victims and those affected, and to compare the two in any way served only to minimise one side, the other, or both. To graffiti a memorial site like this one didn't advance the Palestinians' cause; it defiled and disrespected the Cambodians who suffered. The Palestinians, especially Hamas, would not stand for someone graffitiing "Long Live Khmer Rouge" on a memorial to the martyrs in the fight against Israel. There was no justifying this graffiti or its message. It was, simply, wrong.

Chapter Twenty-Two

Thailand: The Final Stretch

Thailand was *the* place for world travellers. It was cheap, had a robust tourism industry, and possessed a healthy mix of outdoor adventures, beaches, party scenes, and cityscapes. Of all the places Jo wanted to go on The Great Gallivanting, Thailand was always on her list. While disappointed she didn't make it, I decided to check it out. Maybe one day we could come back there for a few weeks together? I had no expectations for Thailand. By the time I made it there, I was along for the ride.

Chiang Mai

I landed in Thailand with little fanfare. I had a long stopover in Bangkok before flying to Chiang Mai for the Thai New Year. Jo and I wanted to celebrate Songkran, the Water Festival, when we visited Thailand and built our regional travel plans around the festival. On a trip to Hawaii the year before, I met a couple who told me we should celebrate it in Chiang Mai instead of Bangkok because it was a smaller town with a more festive atmosphere. Now that I was flying solo, I didn't have reason to doubt them, and, shockingly, the cheapest way to get there from Phnom Penh was to fly.

Unfortunately, I had another run in with urushiol, the cashew nut poison that seeped into my cashew fruit a week before. When I landed in Bangkok, my right hand started to itch like I hadn't felt in years, followed shortly by my left hand and my forearms. I chalked it up to stupid tax, just like the scam in Jordan, and bought some antihistamines and calamine lotion from the airport pharmacy. I knew scratching it would only make it worse, so I gritted through the itching sensation all the way to Chiang Mai. By the time I arrived, the rash had appeared all over my body, from my neck to my arms, torso, back, rear-end, and thighs. I counted myself lucky that it somehow missed my groin. The itching was insane, and it was going to put a severe damper on my time in Thailand. I knew how allergic I was to poison ivy, and my mom was, for the first time in all of my travels, worried about me, because she knew, too.

Sweating only made the rash worse, which was terrible news in Thailand in April because sweating was what I would be doing the entire time. As much as I wanted to explore Chiang Mai when I got there (I had plenty of time left in the day), I couldn't handle it and holed up in the hostel. I was a walking calamine lotion commercial for five days, and I burned through at least two bottles of it as I lathered myself up twice a day. It was insufferable, and I scoured the internet for home remedies to find some relief between doses of antihistamines. After hours and hours of searching, I found a random comment on a Reddit thread that recommended taking the hottest shower I could stand for as long as I could stand it. It would feel like Hell on Earth in the moment, but the hot water would inflame the itching and cause the body to dump all of its histamines to combat the inflammation. These histamines caused the itching, and it would take several hours for my body to produce more (about eight hours), so it should provide long-lasting relief when combined with the calamine lotion. Thank God, it did, and I developed a daily routine of a long, scalding hot shower in the morning, afternoon, and evening, which enabled me to enjoy Chiang Mai as much as possible while also getting a decent amount of sleep. I might have looked funny covered in dried-out, pink lotion, but at least I was out and about.

Home remedy notwithstanding, I still couldn't venture into the Thai heat and humidity for long, as the itching would drive me insane. I discovered I could go walkabout for about two, maybe three, hours at a time before needing to return to the air conditioning. This meant taking it down a peg in Chiang Mai during Songkran. It was disappointing, but c'est la vie. To make the most of my downtime, I alternated watching the bullfights in Spain (it was the Feria de Abril in Sevilla) and getting started on my book project. I had never written anything outside of a professional setting in the military or with my security firm, so I needed to map out my goals, structure, voice, everything, and figure out what story I wanted to tell in my debut travel memoir. I spent half of each day working on the book project, a few hours on the bullfights, and the rest of the time out in town. It was a good thing I was an early riser; I could make the most of my time to accomplish all three.

Songkran was the Thai New Year, celebrated as a Water Festival. The water stemmed from the Buddhist tradition of washing away one's sins for the new year by pouring water over a Buddha statue. This practice was still conducted in the temples during Songkran, but the Water Festival was the popular part of the holiday. For three days, the city centre, bound on all sides by the moat which once protected the city from invaders, turned into a giant water fight. Kids, families, tourists, and locals patrolled the streets with their water guns, cannons, and buckets to engage in the water fight to end all water fights. No one was off limits, and families who lived in the city centre stood buy with giant trash cans full of water for people to refill when they ran dry. On the roads surrounding the moat, there was no need for these trash cans; people simply refilled in the nasty, stagnant moat water.

Songkran didn't start until my second day in Chiang Mai, and it did so suddenly. I was at lunch at a café when I saw the first sign: a pickup truck with a group of people in the back spraying passersby with water guns. I had my computer, so I high-tailed it to the hostel. It wasn't far away, but Chiang Mai wasn't a big place either, and the threat of water guns and buckets increased with each passing second. As I hurried, several Thai kids took aim at me, and I shouted, "Computer! Computer! Computer!" as I passed. Luckily, their parents understood and stood them down. I wouldn't write at cafés any more in Chiang Mai, that was for sure.

After safely stowing my computer for the day, I bought a couple of water guns from a nearby shop. I came all this way to enjoy Songkran, and I wasn't going to let the unbearable itch of an urushiol rash prevent me from doing so. I bought a giant super soaker as a primary weapon and a small water pistol as a backup in case I ran dry. This was all fun and games, but I was still a military man at heart, and I wasn't about to be caught unawares and out of ammo by some neighbourhood kids!

The neighbourhood kids were the most fun out of everyone. They lived for Songkran, and who could blame them? If we had a three-day, city-wide, free-for-all water fight when I was growing up, I would have loved it, too. They watched un-suspecting targets walk down the street and squared off with us on the sidewalk with everything from small water pistols to impressive backpack systems that operated more like flamethrowers (or, rather, water throwers) than water guns. Sometimes, they would try to sneak around cars to get to you, and you had to launch a spoiling attack to fend them off. Of course, they were near their parents and, crucially, trash cans full of water for a quick refill, so they never ran out of water. I, on the other hand, did, and on multiple occasions was swarmed by four or five little children hosing me down when they realised I ran dry. It was all in good fun, and we all laughed together when they finally emptied their reservoirs into me. Their families always offered a refill for me to continue down the road, where I would relive the scene time and again. It was a cool feeling to be bonding with people I didn't know across cultural and language barriers to celebrate the new year.

Of course, there were also the tourists, like me, in town to celebrate, and we often got into gun battles across the street from each other. It was an unspoken com-petition to see who could ambush and soak the other first. Sometimes, it was a one-on-one fight; more often than not, I found myself in a one-on-four confrontation. Oh, the plights of a solo traveller. Inevitably, we would all lose when one of the pickup trucks of goggle-wearing assailants drove by and soaked us all with their huge buckets. When it came to battle, it didn't matter if it was in the army or a water fight; artillery always beat small arms, and I was on the wrong end.

This water fight lasted for three days. In parts of the city, it went on day and night, but for the most part, it lasted from mid-morning to the evening. It legitimately went all day and night in Bangkok, but I was glad not to be there. In Chiang Mai, I could eat lunch and dinner without the threat of becoming a casualty in my dry clothes. It also meant the Sunday night markets continued without interruption. Cit-ies across Thailand hosted these markets every week. Everything was available, from clothes to cooking competitions to art to discount massages (legitimate ones, not illicit, erotic ones). The market spanned several blocks and multiple side streets, and I enjoyed wandering around to see what was available. I was in my last country before heading to Mexico, so I could afford to buy a bulkier souvenir if I wanted to. Ultimately, I opted for an hour-long foot and leg massage for 200 Thai Baht (THB), the equivalent of just a bit more than 5 USD. The massage was long overdue, and the Thai massage ladies dug deep into my calf muscles, shins, and the soles of my feet. The massages I had gotten elsewhere in my travels were good, but these ladies knew how to get deep into the knots and elicit some relief. I made a mental note to enjoy these whenever I could.

Four days in Chiang Mai both dragged on and flew by. The days flew by, but each day seemed to go on forever. The urushiol rash, scalding hot showers, hista-mine dumps, writing, and the bullfights made each day seem longer than it should have been. Being early to rise and alternating between wet and dry clothes all the time didn't help, either. When I left Chiang Mai, I was bored when I shouldn't have been. There was plenty to see and enjoy in the city, especially the festival, but I had difficulty enjoying it after the first day. Maybe I was just tired or had too much on my mind. In any case, I left Chiang Mai with the festival still underway, and my Grab driver carefully navigated the party and flying buckets of water on our way to the bus station.

I was headed for Pai, which was described to me in Cambodia as a "quiet little town up in the mountains." I certainly hoped so. I could use some hiking...as long as the rash cooperated.

Pai

The road from Chiang Mai to Pai was so curvy that the bus ticket came with a motion-sickness warning. The drive was a solid two hours, uphill, full of switch-backs and hairpin curves. The bus was a van, air conditioned, sure, but cramped, with everyone's luggage tied onto the roof, elevating the van's centre of gravity. The drivers were aggressive to brake, accelerate, and turn, and any notions of sleeping through the abusive ride were quickly erased. Jo would never have made it, and I heard a story of a girl who threw up four times on the way up a few days before. The rest stop halfway up was less of a bathroom break and more of a recovery stop so you could prepare for the second leg of the drive.

We pulled into Pai after dark, and I had a fifteen-minute walk towards the river that ran through the east side of town to my hostel. Despite the night, it was hot and humid, and I itched like crazy with my pack on my back. The histamine-dump show-ers had worked their magic, but the rash was still several days from clearing up. I couldn't wait to take a scalding-hot shower to relieve the itching and call it an early night. The shower wouldn't be scalding hot, though. It was lukewarm at best, so I just had to deal with it for a few days.

Pai was anything but a quiet little town up in the mountains. It was a tourism town, and everything there catered to adventure tourism, from hiking tours to ATV rentals to drunken river floating. It was not the centre of natural Thailand I hoped for, and I was quickly burned on the destination. Weed and mushroom dispensaries were everywhere, even at my hostel, and there seemed to be little local culture left.

Disappointed in what I found in Pai, I made it as relaxing a trip as I could. I developed a morning ritual of having breakfast and coffee at a café on the river about ten minutes away from the hostel before wandering to a massage parlour for an hour-long foot and leg massage. I spent some time mapping out the book project, reading, and watching the bullfights in Spain. I thought it might have been a waste of a trip, but I wanted to do those things regardless of where I was, so at least I was in a tourist town whose hippie culture I didn't want to partake. My mind remained pre-occupied with these things, and I wasn't enjoying Thailand as much as I should have been as a result. Songkran was fun, but my mind was elsewhere, so I decided to change my plans after Pai. That is, I decided to make plans after Pai, as I didn't know where I was going between leaving Pai and heading to Bangkok a week or so later. I re-searched the best beaches in Thailand. I settled on Kanom Beach in south Thailand.

It wasn't developed like Phuket, and the reviews online described it as being more-or-less untouched by Western tourism. Getting there wasn't straightforward, but that just made it even more appealing. I decided to head there for a writing retreat. Ian Fleming took writing retreats to Jamaica, and Levison Wood, my favourite modern travel writer, isolated himself on writing retreats in various parts of the world to finish out his projects. This was my first, so I wanted to spend my opening salvo without the distraction of feeling like I was missing out.

With buses, flights, hostels, cabins, and train tickets booked, I made the long walk to see the White Buddha at sunset. It was located on the grounds of the Temple on the Hill, a Buddhist temple in the hills above Pai. It was only a thirty-minute walk uphill from the hostel, and I hoped it would be an amazing sunset view.

It was.

There were only a few people at the White Buddha. The young travellers were probably all napping and readying themselves for another night on the town. From his perch atop the 353 steps above the temple, the White Buddha gazed over the countryside into the far-off mountains. It faced the east, overlooking Pai, welcoming the rising sun (as was the norm for Buddhist temples). I wasn't far from Pai, but it was peaceful at the temple. It was easy to see why Buddhist monks settled here to seek enlightenment; I could let my thoughts flow freely and focus on one topic at a time in the still, quiet sunset. I hoped tourism's influence on the town below wouldn't creep up the hill and someday cause the monks to close the temple to visitors.

I left Pai on the first bus of the morning. It was a two-hour drive down the winding road to Chiang Mai, an hour and a half flight to Bangkok (plus pre-take-off/arrival time), a metro ride, and a fifteen-minute walk to get to my hostel for the night. It was a long travel day of short trips on the way to a day-long train journey the next morning.

Kanom Beach

The train to Kanom Beach took me on a nine-hour journey skirting the country's east coast. The train was nice enough and not too rickety (it was nothing like the train through Tunisia), and there was an attendant that came through and took lunch orders at the midway point. There wasn't Wi-Fi or electrical connections, but for 524 THB, I got my money's worth. I was glad to travel by train. Trains didn't take it out of me as much, and they were substantially more comfortable than even the nicest of buses. The train wasn't my only travel mode, though, and once we reached Phunphin, I got an hour-and-a-half "taxi" (which was really just a guy with a car offering rides) to my cabin across the street from Kanom Beach.

The reviews of Kanom Beach were right. It was nearly untouched by Western Tourism. There were a few small resorts on the road running the length of the beach, but for the most part, it was an isolated hotel community. It was a forty-five-minute walk to the city of Kanom in the sweltering heat and oppressive sun, which I made once, and I was the only Western tourist I saw during my entire week-long stay. At Happy Resort, my cabin was a one-bedroom with a refrigerator, air conditioning, Wi-Fi, and an enclosed bathroom (which I still shared with a pair of frogs in the shower drain) across the street from a beach access point. I couldn't have picked a better place for a peaceful, quiet writing retreat.

I had the same routine every day: coffee and breakfast at a café about a ten-to-fifteen-minute walk down the road combined with several hours of writing, lunch at one of the beachside restaurants on the way back, a siesta and a bullfight on OneToro TV, dinner, a beer, and more writing at another beachside restaurant (there were only a few, so I repeated them several times), then back to bed to rinse and repeat. To some, that may sound monotonous, but the routine was key in keeping my mind focused on the book project. Besides, sitting by the ocean's rolling waves as the sun set behind me provided the perfect atmosphere for deep reflection as I wrapped up for the day. Often, I was the only person at the restaurant; it was like I had the whole wide-open sea to myself.

As the peaceful days slowly passed and I immersed myself in my afternoon bullfights, I longed to return to Spain. I was loving Southeast Asia, exhaustion and urushiol aside, but I felt the strong call of something that had endeared itself to my heart. I started to read books on bullfighting, and I watched a three-hour documentary that delved deep into the world of tauromaquia. I didn't just want to watch the bullfights in person, I wanted to experience everything they had to offer, from the ferias to the culture to the protests. I was already going back to San Fermín in Pamplona to run with the bulls in July; the plan was to attend the entire festival, hopefully as a season-ticket holder to Feria del Toro. The impressive performances I watched from afar during the Feria de Abril in Sevilla, not just from the matadors, but also the picadors and peones, solidified in my mind that I was going to go back to Spain for as much as the bullfighting season as I could with my visa-free travel in the Schengen Area. There in my bed on an isolated beach in Thailand, I resolved to extend my year around the world for another six months. I would travel Spain to attend ferias across the country, culminating in the Feria de Otoño in October, before heading to the Moroccan coast to finish out my book project. I would still be home for Christmas, but I wanted, almost needed, to immerse myself in the world of capes, swords, and bulls. After a few days of reflection, I told Jo and my parents about my plan. All of a sudden, I was no longer staring down the barrel of the end of a gap year, but a whole new life of travel, experiences, and emotion that I could hopefully turn into a new career. There on the seashores of Thailand, I closed the book on my old life for good.

Kanom beach was the rest stop I needed. Time was flying by faster than I could have imagined when I made plans to go to Mexico at the beginning of May. For the first time in weeks, no, months, I finally felt like I had some semblance of control over my days. But, as though the universe decided I had lingered too long, the week came to an unceremonious end as I loaded my bags into a Grab taxi for the journey back to Bangkok. I was meeting Emily, from Melbourne, there. It was her first city in Thailand and my last. Two ships passing in the night.

Bangkok

I arrived at the train station in Bangkok a little after 18h00 that evening. The hostel Emily and I were staying in wasn't too far away, especially given Bangkok's extensive public subway system, something I hadn't experienced since Sydney. Riding in an air-conditioned subway car was a pleasant change of pace as I traversed the city. It was still a ten-minute walk to the hostel, but that wasn't bad. Emily was already there, having arrived earlier in the day, so I dropped my bags, and we headed out to dinner. She told me some wild stories about the hostels she had stayed in since Melbourne. I had a policy of staying only in hostels with at least an eight out of ten rating on Hostelworld; I would drop to seven out of ten if it were a particularly expensive city, but that was my floor. After that, I splurged for a hotel room or Airbnb. Emily, being the adventurous, inexperienced, and broke traveller she was, stayed in the cheapest place she could find on Google Maps. She searched "Hostel" over a city and picked the cheapest place without digging into the reviews. She had some nasty experiences involving cockroaches, rats, mold, you name it. It made me appreciate my amphibious roommates in the shower drains across the peninsula.

I only had three days in Bangkok. Emily had a few more, but she was changing hostels after I left to meet up with some people she met along the way. I had to admit, it was nice to be paired up with someone for a few days. Jo and I may have overdone it with our more than five months together, but there was something about having a travel partner that made the days more pleasant. Emily and I could talk about life, our travels, what we were seeing, goals, you name it, as we walked Bangkok's busy and deserted streets. One of our most-common jokes was about how many 7-Elevens there were in Thailand. They were literally across the street from each other or on opposite street corners, and they were all always busy. Immy (from Cambodia) had told me 7-Eleven sandwiches were a staple of her diet when she was there, and it was easy to see why. The air conditioning wasn't a bad thing, either.

Emily and I spent our first day in Bangkok wandering and talking. We didn't need a plan in a city like this; one would come to us. Somehow, our aimless wanderings landed us at the ICONSIAM mall across the river. It was a long walk away, but we hardly noticed. I was still looking for some undershirts (having left one in Cambodia by accident), and the mall was an air-conditioned reprieve from the fifty-degree Celsius heat and humidity. Even so, we were wholly unprepared for the ICONSIAM mall. It was a massive cultural collision of East meets West. On the ground floor, a large local market sold tourism trinkets, clothing, and traditional food. It was crowded with tourists like us, but it all looked fantastic, and we agreed to eat lunch there after we finished exploring. The upper floors contained Western shops like Under Armour, Uniqlo, and car dealerships. Car dealerships? Yes, car dealerships. High-end ones, too. They used the service elevator to get their cars to the upper floors, and Emily and I laughed about this for days to come. You wouldn't find car dealerships on the third floor back in Texas, that was for sure!

Right as we decided to eat lunch, I got an email from the Plaza de Toros in Pamplona, Spain. I had made the cut for new season tickets, and they needed to know what section I wanted. I stared at my phone with my eyes as wide as they could go before rapidly firing back that I wanted three seats in one of the shaded upper decks. My heart raced with excitement as I explained to Emily what these season passes meant. They were hard to come by, and many were passed from generation to generation. Some pass holders had ancestors who had watched the bullfights there at the same time as Ernest Hemingway, and I had the opportunity to join those ranks. I tried to call Jo to make sure she was still on board, but she was asleep because of the time difference, so I made the judgment call that she was and placed the order. The back and forth took a bit, and Emily and I sat at the market until the reservation was confirmed and paid for. Emily didn't mind; she had never seen a bullfight, but seeing how much I loved them, even from Thailand, interested her in learning. Maybe she would attend one herself, someday.

Once the season ticket business was settled, we continued our aimless wanderings, taking a ferry across the river and slowly snaking our way back to the hostel. It was a long day of walking, and while I wouldn't quite say we were exhausted, we were ready to call it an evening. I opted for an hour-long foot and leg massage down the street from the hostel while Emily showered, and we spent the rest of the evening talking in the common area at the hostel. I even picked up a guitar and played a few of my staple cover tunes. I might have tried to woo Emily with my singing, but that would have been a relationship destined to fail. As Indie once told me, "Travel relationships should remain just that.".

We spent our second day in the area surrounding the Royal Palace. Thailand, like Cambodia, was a monarchy that lasted more than 700 years (except for a brief break during a civil war in the 1700s). The Thai people were proud of their king and way of life, which we learned about at the Museum Siam, our first stop on our tour of the country's history. The Museum Siam was dedicated to exploring, in their words, "what it means to be Thai." Despite being a kingdom just 200 years younger than the British monarchy, there was substantial disagreement over what it meant to be Thai or Siamese (Thailand's historical name until 1939). Songkran, for example, was one of Thailand's most loved celebrations, one known across the world, but the older generations didn't view the water fights as a legitimate part of Thai tradition. Some criticised Pad Thai, the national dish, as an import from China in the 20th Century, while others saw it as a vital part of Thailand's national identity. Even religion divided parts of the country, with Buddhism being the most practised but Hinduism influencing, and in some minds corrupting, Buddhist practices in the country upon its arrival. Despite these widely practised religions, animism had been in Thailand for far longer, and some considered it the true Thai religion. It was a fascinating place to discover the true essence of what it meant to be Thai from different points of view. For only 100 THB, it was a morning well spent, especially with the iced coffee we had at the coffee truck on the museum's grounds. The nearby tapas bar, which served a combination of Spanish, Tex-Mex, and Thai fusion foods, certainly didn't hurt either, and I got to introduce Emily to one of the many reasons I loved Spain.

Emily wanted to visit Wat Phra Chetuphon Wimon Mangkhalaram Rajwarama-hawihan, called Wat Pho for short, and known as the Temple of the Reclining Buddha in English. I had no objection; my plans were non-existent, and it would be interesting to see the inner workings of a Buddhist temple. I was wearing shorts and a t-shirt, and I hoped they would let me in. My shorts went below the knee, but you never could tell if that was good enough. Emily was in a shirt and sarong, and we knew she would be fine. It was a funny twist of fate where my, the man's, clothes could be the issue and hers, the woman's, would be fine. Seeing as this was one of

Thailand's most famous temples, they let me through without issue for just the 300 THB entry fee.

The Temple of the Reclining Buddha was a masterpiece of Thai architecture. It looked exactly as one would expect a first-class royal temple to look like if the only reference they had were films. The buildings were vibrant, with white walls, orange and green tiled roofs, and towering spires that adorned temples and dotted the grounds. The temple spires shone a bright gold under the cloudless sky, and those that dotted the grounds provided a beautiful landscape as we explored the site. Some of the temple complex was off limits; it still served as a public university focusing on health, and one of the Thai massage schools provided the required 800 hours of training for practitioners to be officially licensed. Most of the tourists remained inside the temples, whereas Emily and I wanted to see as much as possible, so we were by ourselves most of the time. That made for spectacular photos of the grounds most tourists wouldn't see.

Of course, the namesake temple was the one everyone was there to see, so we eventually wandered over, took off our shoes, and entered the massive building. The Reclining Buddha was a massive forty-six metres long and fifteen metres tall. It was as described: Buddha reclining, resting his head on his hands, propped up by his elbow. While the statue had a golden exterior, it was made of brick and plaster; the gold was plating, probably a function of cost as the Golden Buddha, located in a separate temple in Bangkok, was only three metres tall, but contained more than 5,000 kilograms of gold worth almost half a billion USD. The brick and plaster interior notwithstanding, it was still a magnificent feature of the temple, and it was intriguing that the Reclining Buddha wasn't a pilgrimage destination for Buddhists. Even so, many Buddhists visited the temple to pay respects and give offerings as part of their religious practices. Emily and I were careful not to interrupt these people or walk in front of them, a habit from my days in the Sahara.

As beautiful as the temple complex was, we could only stay there for so long. It wasn't massive, and there were few exhibitions dedicated to the temple's history. Such was the case with active religious sites the world over, and if I wanted to learn more about Buddhism or the Temple of the Reclining Buddha, I would simply have to do my research. We intended to visit the nearby Royal Palace, but, alas, they wouldn't let me in with my shorts that barely covered my knees. It was bound to happen sometime, and we slowly meandered our way back towards the hostel in the fifty-four-degree Celsius heat. We stayed close that night, venturing to a night market near the hostel after a shower and siesta (clearly my idea). We didn't know what we were going to do the next day, but it probably involved a lot of walking, so we rested up.

All we did was walk the next day, through a marked historic path through the Bang Rak Silom district. This district was once a significant port in Bangkok, and goods from all over the world flowed through the now non-existent harbour. As the port gained popularity and importance in the 1700s, temples, cathedrals, and even a mosque were constructed to serve the growing community. Like Ephesus in Turkey, eventually, the district grew increasingly inland, and the riverside neighbourhood declined in importance.

Our walk through the district took us to these temples and cathedrals, none of which we were allowed to enter, and the mosque was closed outside of prayer times, which I found odd given my experiences in MENA. We struck out time after time as we wandered the empty streets. Our only reprieve was the general post office, which contained a Starbucks where we could take a break and cool off. It would be a story for the books if the most interesting part of our walk were a post office.

Undeterred, we continued the walk after cooling off, and somehow, somewhere, stumbled into a Michelin Star restaurant! As we walked down the sidewalk, I noticed a small, red, square plaque on a restaurant on the opposite side of the street. "Is that... a Micheline star?" I asked Emily. Upon further inspection, it was, and the menu was more than reasonably priced, especially for a Michelin Star, so we elected to eat lunch a little early. I couldn't believe our luck; this was the second time on The Great Gallivanting that I had accidentally discovered a Michelin Star restaurant where there shouldn't have been one, the other being in Cazalla de la Sierra, Spain, eight months before. Like the restaurant in Cazalla de la Sierra, it did not disappoint, and my lemon and herb chicken with spicy sauce was just what I needed to brighten the day. Otherwise, I would have considered it a complete wash.

That said, as was the case with every last day in a country, a wash was in store, so we made our way back to the hostel so I could clean my clothes and pack for the long flight ahead. I was headed for Los Angeles, California, for a medical examination before my divemaster training started less than a week later, so, after coffee at Tim Horton's (Emily's idea, as it was a Canadian icon), we went our separate ways. She went to another hostel, and I went to Los Angeles by way of the Philippines.

In a matter of days, I would completely circumnavigate the globe.

Reflecting on Thailand

Contentment. It was an odd feeling leaving Thailand because, for once, I didn't have any major breakthroughs, realisations, or encounters that made me reflect on different parts of life. Finally, as I was preparing to settle in Mexico for a couple of months, I was leaving a country with nothing on the table. I wasn't yearning to stay, nor dying to leave. I could have slow-trailed my way across the south, dove the reefs, and partied it up in Phuket, or I could put the whole country in the rearview. I might have thought this discouraging, but I was at peace with it. Thailand was a great country to go backpacking in, and it offered something for everyone, but I didn't have to race to see anything, nor did I feel like I was missing out. I could always return to see more temples and explore Buddhism if I wanted to, and that was probably in the cards, but if I didn't, I was content with my experience.

I sought that contentment, something I had missed out on over the last ten years. There was always a next goal, career milestone, personal achievement, or thing to see or do, but I had never left something behind, said, "I'm happy with that," and let it go. Thailand wasn't Amman, where I was militantly against returning, nor was it Spain, where I couldn't wait to return. Something about that sat perfectly with me.

Chapter Twenty-Three

Mexico: Relaxing, Diving, and a Family Vacation

I was always nervous about visiting Mexico before I began my year around the world. I had taken trips to Los Barriles, on the Baja Peninsula, Cancun, and Tulum before, but I never could overcome the jittery feeling that came with being too alert in an unfamiliar place. That feeling came from my military and security firm days, which were far in the past by the time I arrived in Mexico this time around. This time, I looked forward to Mexico. After places like Tunisia, Iraq, and Turkey, especially after October 7th, I wasn't jittery or nervous anymore. I had two months of diving ahead of me, and I couldn't wait to be in the land of tacos al pastor, quesadillas de pollo, and cochinita pibil.

Tulum - Hostel Life

I landed in Cancun, Mexico, on the first of May, my last flight for two months. I had been through this airport before but was more comfortable this time. I was unbothered by people yelling for me to get into their taxis, not concerned about being pickpocketed or scammed. I was a professional traveller now, nonchalant about such trivialities as I bought a ticket for the next bus to Tulum, two hours away. I had just missed the last bus, so I sat against a pole and passed the two hours before the next one with some calls home. It was official: By landing in Cancun, I circumnavigated the globe. It was only ten months since I left home, but it seemed like forever, and my family and friends congratulated me on literally travelling around the world.

Tulum was a city I fell in love with the year before. I went there for a week-long vacation, which included getting my open-water diving certification. The Mexican government wanted to turn Tulum into a smaller version of Cancun, but the locals and the infrastructure couldn't support such a lofty goal, so the pueblo settled into purgatory between the two. There were tourist shops and restaurants where you could speak English and pay twice the price, and there were local places where you had to speak Spanish to get a delicious meal for just a few USD. The cenotes, sinkholes that connected with the underground river system, were plentiful, there was a free public beach, and, for the history-inclined, plenty of ruins on the Yucatan Peninsula to explore.

I stayed at Hostal Lum, the same hostel I stayed in the year before. It easily ranked as one of my favourite hostels in the world, right up there with TOCHostel in Sevilla and Sunset Surf Hostel in Morocco. The managers, Laura and Mo, ran a smooth operation, and the atmosphere was great for those who liked to relax during the day and party at night. They had hostel-wide activities every day, from visiting the cenotes to the beach to salsa dancing to taco tours in some of the outlying barrios. It helped that the hostel was barely off the main road, Avenida Tulum, so I could walk anywhere I needed during my two-month stay.

I met a lot of cool people at Hostal Lum. Besides Laura and Mo, who I continued to talk with long after I left, I met Irene, a Spanish girl with the perfect accent, Charlie, a British rugby player and volunteer-turned-vagabond in South America, and Lillian, a Spanish teacher turned TikToker who lived elsewhere in Mexico and used her platform to promote hotels and restaurants (and, later, to teach Spanish lessons). Of course, I met people I preferred not to see again, but that was the nature of living in a hostel for two straight months.

On any given day, Laura had a game of Skyjo, a card game whose rules and goals are too complicated to explain on paper, going in the common area, and we would have anywhere from just the two of us to upwards of ten people gathered around the table, competing for bragging rights. The game was a fixture of my time there, and Charlie developed a habit of doing everything possible to ruin Laura's chances at winning, often self-sabotaging himself in the process. He didn't care, but Laura did, and her frustrations only egged him on. Being one to learn from the masters, I picked up his strategy, which almost got a beer can thrown at me more than once.

The hostel had a bar, too, open only in the evenings, where the volunteers took turns serving as the bartender. I wasn't a big drinker, so I never had more than one or two drinks a night, but whether it was one or two depended on who was playing bartender. Charlie was a natural-born salesman and the second-best bartender at the hostel, so he almost always managed to pull me into his orbit and get me to drink more (the best bartender in the hostel was Sogand, but she didn't have Charlie's natural salesmanship). Irene, on the other hand, was a terrible bartender. She was energetic and engaged, but her drinks never turned out for some reason. It became a running joke with the volunteers and long-term guests like me that the bar would operate at a loss any time she was on it, because we wouldn't drink her drinks even to generate buzz to draw in the other guests. She could get me to drink beer, though, mainly because she was a cute Spanish girl and she couldn't really mess up handing me an unopened can (unless she dropped it...). A volunteer that came later, Noeme, a French girl that looked like she came straight out of *The Sound of Music*, rivalled Irene for her last-place bartending skills.

Of course, there was the fair share of hostel drama, too, as volunteers and long-term guests alike violated Indie's rule against travel relationships. It never failed that a one-night stand turned into a potential relationship doomed to fail, which crashed and burned in spectacular fashion. Unlike back home, everyone at the hostel lived together, so the ups and down, on-again off-agains affected everyone who wasn't personally involved. Charlie commented once that one couple had three moods, "f******, fighting, or happy, and I've seen all three of them today" (it wasn't even lunch time). As the primary manager, Laura hated dealing with it, but that was the price of leadership (and a paycheck).

We all respected Laura as the manager. There were plenty of hostels where the volunteers ran the show with little-to-no oversight. Others didn't even have volunteers, like the hostel I stayed at in Sydney. Routine things fell through the cracks in those places, like replenishing toilet paper and mopping wet floors. Not at Hostal Lum under Laura. She wasn't an owner who lived elsewhere; she lived on site and was involved in everything that happened within the hostel's walls. We all knew the place would come crumbling down around us if it wasn't for her, and we told her as much.

Granted, that didn't mean everything was sunshine and roses. People were still people; no amount of leadership could change that, nor could it fix stupid. For example, Laura couldn't teach everyone how to use a gas stove. It wasn't a difficult concept, and it was one that anybody who had gone camping or lived with gas in their house could easily handle. Unfortunately, in many places in the world, specifically Europe, gas appliances were legally phased out of production, so the younger generations didn't know how to use them. This was how a girl named Gina came to burn all of the hair off her arms while Charlie, Laura, and I were downstairs playing a game of Skyjo. We heard a loud "bang" that was obviously an explosion. I was facing the desk with the security cameras and saw the light flash across the screen. The three of us charged upstairs, but I was the only one who saw what had happened. Gina was freaked out, and I only went upstairs to check on her. Having dealt with all of this before, Laura jumped into action to fix the problem.

The problem? Gina didn't know how to use a gas oven. She turned on the gas, lit the pilot light, and prepared her food while the oven warmed up. When she went to use the oven, she saw the pilot light was out and relit it. What she didn't know, and apparently didn't smell, was the gas continued flowing even with the pilot light out. So, when she pulled the trigger on the lighter, she ignited the gas, which sent a fireball out into the kitchen. She said she had almost died, but I saw the flash on the security camera. She didn't almost die, but I told her she was lucky to have her eyebrows. She scolded me for making fun of her, but Charlie told her I wasn't. She really was lucky to have her eyebrows. She did lose the hair on her arms, but that wasn't a big deal. Laura and I, being the only two older than thirty, talked downstairs; for being so tech-savvy, these Gen Z-ers were utterly clueless.

The Gen Z-ers were also highly opinionated on things they didn't fully understand, just like all young people from the dawn of time. As an American and a "cis-white male", I was the "bad guy" in every conversation, whether it was about the immigration problem in my country, the American-European security alliance, or the myriad conflicts in the Middle East. It didn't matter that I had a Masters of International Policy with concentrations in intelligence, European security, and transnational security, a graduate certificate in Advanced International Affairs with concentrations in diplomacy and intelligence, a career in the security sphere, or five years and two deployments with the military. I was a straight, white, American male, so I could not possibly understand the world to the level of young, twenty-something, Europeans (especially women, as at least the men would hear me out). During one hostel conversation, two German girls, in trying to convince me they were right instead of having a dialogue, told me, "The way you think, you sound like a dumb redneck." They expected me to be taken aback, but I replied, "Where I'm from, that's not an insult." Of all the political and social conversations I had in ten months of travel, I found these young European women in Tulum to be the most closed-minded and incapable of having a two-way dialogue. It was an important lesson; there was no sense in trying to have a conversation with people who were unwilling to consider an alternative viewpoint. This lesson would serve me well (and save time and oxygen) in future travels.

My days at the hostel were not all social all the time, though, despite the friends I met and good times we had there. I was the boring old guy, up at 05h45 in the morning, out the door by 07h00, siesta around 14h00, dinner at 19h00, and in bed by 21h30. I was training as a divemaster at a local dive centre six days a week for the next two months, the Tulum equivalent of an office job. At least my office was beneath the waves.

Tulum - Divemaster Training

After a week in Tulum, I started my two-month divemaster training with Tulum Diving Center. I had looked forward to his training for months, and I frequently talked diving careers with Summer, who was now working as a dive instructor in Western Australia. I was only certified as an Advanced Open-Water Diver (AOW) with the Professional Association of Diving Instructors (PADI), the second level of dive certifications, with only thirty-seven dives under my belt, so I had a long way to go before being able to call myself a true professional. While it only took forty dives to be certified as a divemaster, that was very little experience, and I learned in my skydiving days that the bare minimum qualification was indeed the bare minimum. I also needed two other courses, the rescue diver course and the emergency first-responder course, before I could start the divemaster programme, so that was where my training began.

My instructors were Craig and Cathy, an American couple who had lived all over the world working as dive instructors, guides, and dive shop owners. They were both Course Directors with PADI, which meant they had the highest possible certification in the diving world and could provide virtually any training PADI offered. Craig didn't look nor act his age, as he had been diving and living life for more than fifty years. He knew how to communicate across cultures and build a rapport with almost anybody he met. From live-aboards off the Baja Peninsula to owning a dive shop in Japan to organising international dive trips for friends and customers alike, Craig had all the experience a world-travelling dive instructor could ask for. Cathy, who hadn't been diving quite as long, was the most efficient dive instructor I had ever seen. She once worked in a dive shop in Seattle where she would be the only instructor for ten new open-water students, and it showed in how she conducted her courses. She was a proper "train to standard, not to time" type and knew the PADI courses and manuals inside and out.

Craig took me through the rescue diver course, mainly at Cenote Ponderosa and Casa Cenote, which were large, open cenotes perfect for dive training. Like training I received in the military, the skills weren't the hard part. Towing, lifting, resuscitating, all of that was the easy part of the rescue course (which was not to diminish their importance, as they were the course's foundation). Handling, communicating with, and controlling panicked divers was the hard part, and Craig put me through the ringer. With each successive scenario under the water, he became increasingly panicked, showing me many different scenarios he had dealt with in his half a century of diving. On one memorable dive, I took his metal oxygen tank straight to the face as he thrashed about (not on purpose, though, just the way the scenario played out), knocking my mask clean off, forcing me to continue the rescue mask-less. While some people may have viewed this as extreme (again, it wasn't on purpose), I actually loved it. This was realistic training, "battle-focused" we called it in the military, and after three days in the water with Craig, I felt thoroughly prepared for the various rescue scenarios.

As part of the two-month-long training, I received specialty diver certifications as well, with Cathy taking me through most of those. These specialty diver certifications provided extra skills to recreational divers to better enjoy the broad spectrum of diving available across the globe. One of the most important (and fun) courses for me was the Deep Diver course. This course allowed me to dive to a depth of forty metres, a full ten metres further than the AOW certification allowed me. That may not sound like much, but it was a substantial difference considering standard open-water divers could only travel to eighteen metres. This training focused mainly on the physiological effects of diving at these depths. Narcosis, which was when the gasses in your body affected your judgment and decision-making at depth, was a real threat, just as hypoxia was a concern at high elevations. To train for this, Cathy took me to a cenote called the Pit, a deep, conical cenote that went far deeper than recreational limits allowed. Once at forty metres, I had to do a simple crossword puzzle on a graphite slate, which would give both Cathy and me an indicator of how susceptible to narcosis I was. Fortunately, I wasn't affected at all, but she had stories of people who couldn't pick out the simple words no matter how much time they were given, let alone use the underwater pencil to circle them. As a divemaster, it was essential to recognise that my natural limits were further than some people I might be taking, and being cognisant of others' decisions at that depth could prove to be lifesaving. Indeed, one of their staff members, Juan Carlos, later told me a story of a customer he took to the Pit who suffered narcosis at just fifteen metres, and Juan Carlos had to end the dive and jump into rescue diver mode to get him back to the surface.

Ultimately, I completed six specialty courses with Craig and Cathy: Deep Diver, Underwater Navigator, Search and Rescue Diver, Emergency Oxygen Provider, Enriched Air Diver, and Equipment Specialist. When combined with the dives I would do for my divemaster certification, I would be eligible for the Master Scuba Diver rating at the end of my training. According to PADI, fewer than two percent of divers become eligible for and received the rating. This made sense, as most people were vacation divers and only went beneath the surface a few times a year. The real benefit, though, was informal advice from Craig. As a divemaster, I would likely be paired with the less-experienced divers on the boat, even on personal dive trips. It was under the guise of safety (which had some merit), but, really, it was to make the hired guide's life easier. Instead of dealing with that, I could show my Master Scuba Diver card, which demonstrated I was proficient in several disciplines and certified as a Rescue Diver, but didn't betray that I was a dive professional. I might still get paired with the less-experienced divers, but the guide would be far less likely to pass on their responsibilities to me. I had experienced that as a skydiving coach, too, where I would often end up on jumps with newer skydivers to help them build their skills while non-coaches with far more jumps and experience than me would do their own thing. I didn't mind, as teaching was something I enjoyed and was good at, but it was still a nugget to stash away in my mind.

And, thus, began my divemaster training. The divemaster course itself was only ten days from start to finish and included everything from basic teaching skills to advanced dive planning to increasing my swimming skills. Given I was in Tulum for training for two months, we stretched those ten days to fill in when there weren't customers. Gaining experience in the dive industry was invaluable and harder to come by than a simple two-week course. Interacting with customers, hauling tanks, cleaning equipment, and guiding dives under my instructors' supervision built my confidence over the two months.

Some of the customers were fantastic, like a British woman in her forties who was seeking new experiences across the world. She was extremely nervous when she arrived at the shop for her initial swim test (which included a 200-metre swim and treading water for eight minutes), but not even an accidental bloody nose damp-ened her spirits by the time we surfaced from her last open-water dive. Other stu-dents were not as fantastic, like an American man who could barely swim 100 me-tres, let alone tread water for eight minutes. He tested me in everything I had learned from Craig and Cathy. He would bolt to the surface from a depth of less than five metres in a panic, which could easily kill him if he held his breath. Several times, he tried to use me as a floatation device because he couldn't think through his fear enough to inflate his buoyancy control device (the dive jacket that filled with air to keep you afloat or at a constant depth in the water). As much as I wanted everyone to succeed and excel in diving, some people just weren't meant to live their lives in three dimensions, and I was grateful when the instructor gave me the signal indicat-ing we were terminating training for his safety.

Other dives provided interesting experiences with certified divers. We took one girl who only spoke French. She communicated with us through her mother at the shop, but her mother wasn't going with us on the ocean. Fortunately, courtesy of my time in the Sahara, I had a decent knowledge of basic French, so I was able to serve as a limited translator. Things like getting ready, counting down, and commands such as "come" and "wait" were simple enough when combined with industry-stand-ard hand signals, and she ended up seeing some cool stuff on her dives, including a manatee, which was rare in that part of Mexico.

Other divers we took on their first cavern tours, which required a cave-diving instructor at the front and, preferably, a divemaster at the rear. The Yucatan Penin-sula was known for its cenote diving, especially the cave and cavern systems which connected all of the cenotes via an underground river system created when the me-teor that killed the dinosaurs impacted the Earth millions of years before. Cavern dives took us through areas that still had natural light and direct access to the surface but were in an overhead environment. This niche diving style showcased underwater rock formations and drew thousands of divers a year to Tulum. Of course, cavern diving wasn't for everyone, and some people only did the first one before deciding to stay at the surface. That was a smart call, and one which we supported. It was better to be on the surface wishing you were under the water than under the water wishing you were on the surface. For her part, Cathy and Craig loved cave and cavern diving, and the cenote river system was the entire reason they moved to Tulum in the first place.

As with all outdoor sports, the weather took its toll on us. Sometimes, we couldn't get out on the boats for a scheduled reef dive because the wind was too strong and causing hazardous waves. Our worst weather impact was a stretch of ten straight days of rain. It effectively shut down everything in Tulum, from diving to ruin tours to lazy days on the beach. It was an uncharacteristically long rain outside of the hurricane season, and it continued to wreak havoc on diving long after the rain had passed. It rained so much and so hard that the water liquified dead leaves, turning the cenotes a gross, brown colour with little visibility. It also caused the underground river current to run dangerously fast, even causing maelstroms at the ends of cenotes where the open water met the next cave in the system. The ten-day storm had a cascading economic impact; we couldn't dive, which meant the cenotes couldn't open or operated at a loss, meaning local workers weren't paid. Out of near desperation, some dive shops took customers into the questionable conditions, but for the most part, the cenote operators refused to allow entry until it became safe again.

After a week or so, Craig and I coordinated with Casa Cenote, where we trained during our second day of the Open Water Diver Course, to check out the situation beneath the surface. The maelstrom at the front end of the cenote had vanished, but the cenote was still a greenish-brown, far from its usual crystal-clear. Once under the surface, Craig and I were immediately swimming against a strong current, far stronger than the current in Bali, and I was concerned about a repeat performance. Unlike in Bali, the cenote had a sandy bottom, and Craig and I crawled along the entire length of the cenote's first stretch to the cave where the underwater river system entered the cenote. We could see the current as we crawled, as sand particles were suspended in the water, just like out of a film. Once at the cave, we felt the water rushing in as it made its way to the ocean just a few hundred metres away.

Once around the bend in the cenote, however, everything calmed down. We were out of the force of the underwater current, and the water was substantially clearer. The fish, however, were all in the wrong place. Most species had certain places they stayed based on their needs. For example, the tarpon tended to be under the mangroves at bends in the cenote, freshwater crabs usually were found on large boulders, and the saltwater reed fish were usually at the cenote entrance, where the salty ocean water mixed with the cenote's fresh water at the last cave in the system. This time, the reed fish were far away from the cave, the crabs flitted through the water all over, and the tarpon were at the surface across the calm part of the cenote, eating the copious amount of algae which had accumulated.

As we passed under the tarpon, I thought, "Man, Panchito will have a field day with this!" Panchito was the resident crocodile, about two-and-a-half metres long, that lived in the mangroves surrounding the cenote. He was a gentle giant, long used to people swimming in his tropical domain. Part of my job with customers in Casa Cenote was to look for Panchito, and he had a few spots he liked to hang out during the day. One of those was on the rocks beside where the tarpon were enjoying their feeding frenzy, and I saw his tail hanging in the water. I found that odd with all of the fish right there, but when we surfaced, it was obvious why he wasn't enjoying this opportunistic meal: he didn't have any energy. Crocodiles were cold-blooded reptiles and relied on the sun to regulate their body temperature, kickstart their metabolism, and have energy. We hadn't seen the sun in two weeks, and Panchito was taking in what he could while sleeping on the rocks. As Craig and I floated by on the surface, he opened one eye to look at us before drifting back off to sleep. Never in my life did I think I would be just two metres away from a sleeping crocodile and not be the least bit concerned.

Craig and Cathy were not the only instructors I worked with in Tulum. Hector was their other instructor with whom I worked the most day-to-day. He was from Cozumel and had been a dive instructor for twenty years. Over the course of two months, Hector and I became close friends, and I learned a lot about diving from him. When it was just Hector and me at the beginning and end of a day, we would talk about all sorts of topics, from funny stories to family to history to current affairs. Hector was a smart man and well-read. He knew his Mexican and American history to a degree most people didn't. From the Battle of Chapultepec during the Mexican-American War to the geopolitics influencing mass migration through Southern America, this Mexican dive instructor from Cozumel put my graduate degree compatriots to shame. "Nobody reads anymore," Hector once told me. He was right, and his knowledge and insight proved that even in a country without the high formal education standards of the United States and Europe, the written word still reigned supreme.

Hector was also close to his family, who all lived in Cozumel. He talked about his mother and daughter all the time. He never talked down on them, and to see how proud he was to have the family he had was something you didn't see in the United States anymore outside of grandparents. His mother loved the corridas de toros, the bullfights, just as I did, and while Hector did not like nor approve of them at all, he loved that his mom and I had something in common. It was another bonding point for us, especially when I was able to send him pictures of Roca Rey, the young Peruvian matador, to show his mom a few months later. She was in love with him (as were all of the women, and some of the men, who watched him perform or followed him on Instagram). Hector more than once joked that I should come with him to Cozumel to meet his family. He could drop me off with his mom to watch the bullfights on television while he went diving with his friends. I didn't get around to taking him up on that offer while I was in Tulum, but I figured I would have the opportunity again one day.

In hindsight, my divemaster training in Tulum was a long process, but in the moment the days flew by. In no time, my two months of training were over, and I was a certified divemaster with more than double the number of dives I started with, six specialty certifications, my Master Scuba Diver rating, and an internship to put on my resume. In my final days with Tulum Diving Center, Craig sat me down to talk about what it meant to be a divemaster and, one day, an instructor. He didn't give me the book answers; this was a heart-to-heart from a man who had literally dedicated his life to the dive profession. He talked to me about what it was like to seek out jobs as a newly-certified divemaster, how to be a steward of ocean conservation, and the realities of running a diving operation. I shouldn't expect to get wealthy by any means, he explained, as divemasters made good money relative to the local economy, not necessarily by American standards. What I lacked in money, though, I would more than compensate for in memories, friends, and valuable life experience. Hopefully, I would never suffer from a diving-related injury, but, eventually, something happened to everyone, and Craig walked me through the different insurance offerings that would offset the major costs associated with things like decompression chambers and seaborne life flights. It felt like a "passing the torch" series of conversations, from a man with fifty years of experience to someone with just two months, and I would never forget my time with him, Cathy, or Hector.

It was bittersweet to end my training. I had my certifications and was officially a dive professional, but it meant leaving behind the only semblance of a real life I had had in a year. In characteristic fashion, life moved on to the next stage.

Family Vacation

When I made the decision to travel to Tulum for two months of dive training, my mom asked if she could visit for vacation. By the time she arrived, it had been a whole year since I left home, and that was a long time. Even when I was in the military or working in Colorado, we would see each other in person every few months. Even though I video called every week, it wasn't the same, and she was ready to see her baby boy. My only condition was that we wouldn't stay at an all-inclusive resort. That was the only way she ever vacationed in Mexico, but this time, she would have a travel experience and live my life for a few days. I acquiesced to getting an Airbnb; I wasn't about to subject her to the craziness (and weirdness) of hostel life.

About a month out from her arrival, my younger brother asked if he and his then-girlfriend (now wife) could come as well. I didn't mind; it would cheapen the cost of the rental car to split it four ways instead of two. But I told him Mom and I had a plan, and that plan wasn't a Hotel Zone vacation. At first, he was cool with that, but by the time they arrived, they just wanted a Mexican beach getaway. That was probably for the best. Mom and I travelled well together; my brother and I, not so much, and we needed separate spaces throughout the trip.

My brother and his girlfriend arrived first, flying into the newly-opened Aeropuerto Internacional de Tulum Felipe Carrillo Puerto, about forty minutes outside Tulum via bus. I met them at the bus station and introduced them to La Chiapaneca, a cheap taco place that was a staple of my diet in Tulum. He couldn't believe the food was that cheap (my standard order cost 50 MXN, about 3 USD) and that good.

My mom arrived the next day to Cancun, and I met her at the airport. After an hour of our phones not working for some reason, she finally found me and we were on our way to Tulum. It was strange to her to be driving down the highway in Mexico. I remembered when it was strange for me, too, the first time I did it in Baja California Sur over a year before when visiting a friend. In the United States, all anyone heard about were the cartels, violence against tourists, and dangers Mexico travel presented. All of that was founded in certain parts of the country, like the northern border states, but Mexico was just like any other country. There were safe parts, dangerous parts, and parts where the safe and dangerous areas overlapped. Tulum was one of the safe parts; most of the Yucatan Peninsula was. Western tourism dollars were just too valuable for the Mexican government to allow otherwise.

The first order of business for my mom and me was to get into the water. I managed to talk her into trying Discover Scuba Diving, the introductory dive class where she was accompanied by an instructor (Craig) and a divemaster (me) at all times. She loved skydiving with me before, but going beneath the surface was a completely different experience. She was nervous, but she gave it a shot.

To put it lightly, scuba diving was not her thing, not in the least. It wasn't that being under the water scared her. She loved the idea of being down there with the turtles and the fish, but she couldn't get past water getting into her mask and her eyes. That was a big thing for most people, but after several tries, we couldn't get past the mental block. That was no problem. I dove next to her a few feet below the surface to ensure she didn't hurt herself by bolting to the surface. Whenever I saw her start to panic, I grabbed a hold of her and levelled her out so the water in her mask would be laid flat against the glass and away from her eyes. That worked until it became too much, at which point we surfaced, dumped her mask, and went down again. At the turnaround point, I inflated her dive jacked enough to keep her at the surface, and she snorkelled the rest of the way back. Honestly, though, that was more than most people would have done. She was at least willing to admit to herself and me that this wasn't for her after trying it. That was more than the one student I had dealt with who tried to use me as a flotation device rather than admit he couldn't do it. More than anything, she got to see what a day in my life was like these last two months, which she enjoyed more than anything else.

The next day, we went to Valladolid. Our goal: see Chichén Itzá, one of the modern Seven Wonders of the World. This would be my third modern wonder in my year around the world and her first ever. It was a two-hour drive away, which she was perfectly comfortable with by now. She was less comfortable with the parking situation at Chichén Itzá. On the drive in, men in official-looking yellow safety vests with red flags tried to flag us down to park in their "parking lots," which were dirt fields where they charged tourists to park their cars. I was a wary at first, having had some bad experiences with this setup in the United States for concerts and sporting events. Ultimately, we parked in one of these dirt fields not too far from Chichén Itzá. It cost 50 MXN (plus a tip for the attendant), and we avoided the long, single-file queue of cars and tour buses trying to cram into the official parking lot.

We didn't have an official tour guide. Maybe we would have enjoyed the history more had we had one, but we were really there to enjoy time together in a new place. We were lucky that we committed to getting there early. Even though the parking lot was beyond full, the park was still pretty empty, and we didn't have to deal with large groups of people to get good pictures. The sun also wasn't directly overhead, so there was plenty of shade around the outskirts. While my mom found Chichén Itzá's history interesting (it was one of the largest Mayan cities, which once governed the entire Yucatan Peninsula and was the site of one of the most important battles during the Spanish conquest of Mexico), we didn't pay too much attention to it. Maybe that made me a bad amateur historian, but family time was family time.

We spent the next two days at various cenotes. Several of them were around Tankah Pueblo, one of the Mayan villages around Tulum, where we went snorkelling and ziplining as part of their park experience, which helped to fund the pueblo and provide jobs to the Mayans that lived there. The first time my mom stuck her head in the water with the snorkel, everyone heard her yell, "Oh my God!" through the snorkel. Snorkelling from the surface was much more her speed than diving. The other cenote we visited was my favourite place to spend a relaxing day, Cenote Cristal, just a few minutes south of Tulum. It was a small cenote, but it was never full of people, and the tables and hammocks were always shaded. Plus, there were a lot of pond turtles that lived in the perfectly clear water, which made snorkelling there a fantastic experience.

For their part, my brother and his girlfriend stayed mainly in the Hotel Zone. They were there for a Mexican beach getaway, not the travel experience my mom had signed up for, so we generally only saw them at breakfast and dinner. Ironically, they both got sick during their trip, while my mom and I did not. So much for "safe" tourist restaurants in the Hotel Zone (where they had most of their meals) and "unsafe" street food in the pueblo (where my mom and I had most of ours). They did come with us to Cenote Cristal, though, and enjoyed the day in the jungle water.

After five days, it was time for everyone to head home. My mom and I said goodbye to my brother and his girlfriend and drove two hours to Cancun. She was heading back to Texas, and I was flying to Spain. My year around the world may have been over, but The Great Gallivanting still had a long way to go.

Reflecting on Mexico

Security theatre. Tulum, like Cancun and Cabo San Lucas, was far too important for tourism to allow the cartels, criminal street gangs, human smuggling organisations, or anyone else to threaten tourists. While Tulum was a safe place, the local, state, and federal governments dumped an obscene amount of money into Tulum's security. At any given moment, the main road through town had at least two, if not more, pickup trucks with soldiers, national guard, or police officers in the bed, locked and loaded with carbines and mounted machine guns, while the barrios had national guard and police patrols circulating among them constantly. While there certainly was crime to be deterred and investigated, this was all just security theatre. The threat didn't justify the expense or resources. Sending a message to Western tourists, though, did. As long as Tulum was perceived as safe, the tourists would continue to spend their money there, providing vital jobs and income to local businesses.

To the outside observer, like my family, this was off-putting. Where we were from, police resources were allocated by call-for-service volume, which meant that if there were a lot of police in an area, it was because those areas needed more police. Moreso, using the military for domestic policing in the United States was outright illegal, a holdover from Reconstruction after the Civil War. So, it was understandable that first-time visitors were wary of the aggressive posture, but that was all it was: posture. I had been in countries around the world where this was normal. In France, the Gendarmerie openly carried Uzis and soldiers patrolled Paris in squad formations; in Iraqi Kurdistan, the Asayish's primary purpose outside of the cities was to provide an armed deterrent against terrorist groups and criminals; in Vietnam, the police were one of the largest arms of the government and were simply not to be crossed. Outside of our American bubble, security theatre was the norm, not the exception. On the one hand, I was thankful that we didn't have the heavy-handed government hanging over us all the time. On the other, I wished Americans could understand how great we had it that security theatre wasn't even considered as a normal course of action.

Friends like family. In Tulum, I met a lot of great people, many of whom I discussed in this chapter. What I loved about Hostal Lum during my stay this time around was how everyone acted like family. We looked out for each other, getting each other food while we were out and about, talking about things that needed talking about in the personal world, and enjoying each other's company. In too many hostels across the world, visitors tended to stay to themselves or their groups. They were there to travel on their schedule, not make friends or waste time playing cards around the coffee table in the middle of the day. But we weren't just travellers; we were in Tulum for long periods of time. There was plenty of time for going, seeing, and doing, and we did plenty of that, but there was also something to be said for spending time in binging a TV series together (like Laura turning me on to *Yellowstone* or Charlie watching a few faenas from the bullfights I was watching in Madrid). I would stay in constant contact with several people from the hostel, especially Laura, Mo, and Charlie, long after leaving. The same was true of Hector, who I talked to off and on until I returned to Tulum again, not necessarily about diving, but just about personal and family stuff (plus, I had to send him pictures of Roca Rey for his mom whenever I saw him at a bullfight).

For the first time in a long time, I felt like I was living in a family environment. It had been fourteen years since I moved out of the house to leave for college, where I lived in dorms with the same people (as part of the military training programme) for four years until we graduated. Since then, though, I had lived on my own, save for the stint in Africa with the military, where everyone lived, ate, and worked together. While I made great friends in the military, I always went home to an empty apartment at the end of the day. Not so in Tulum. Whenever I came back from diving, dinner, or coffee, there were always people to crack a beer with and enjoy the evening. That was a feeling I longed for when I left the Sahara, and one which I found again on the Caribbean coast.

Hometown? When I first visited Tulum the year before I started travelling long-term, I fell in love with the city. I was still on edge about visiting such places back then, a consequence of confronting the worst the world had to offer in my chosen career, so wandering the streets made me uncomfortable, and there was no way I was taking a bus instead of renting a car. Even so, after a week of learning to dive and making new friends, I texted an old commander from the military to tell her that, for the first time, I found some place I honestly thought I might settle down. It was a small town most people I knew had never heard of, but large enough to sustain an income if I decided to make that decision. It was also far away from any of the emotional baggage I needed to leave back home.

Fast forward a year, and I was calling it home, at least for a little while. The streets no longer set my teeth on edge, and I wasn't afraid to try the taco truck off some side street for fear of food poisoning. I became a regular customer at some restaurants, and even developed a traveller's crush on one of the baristas at the coffee shop around the corner. By the time my family came down, I was on a first name basis with several people around town, and they were all happy to meet my family. I would even get into jabbing conversations with Many (who owned Taco Many's) about the United States, food, and films whenever I ate at his truck.

Would I settle down in Tulum in the long run? I had no idea. What I did know was that for the first time in a decade, I finally felt like I had found somewhere I really belonged and could call home.

Part Two

Reflections

A Note on Reflections

Throughout this book, I have given thoughts on different social and political issues that affected my travels in specific countries. I have also discussed various emotions, frustrations, and epiphanies I experienced as I walked across the Earth. With the following reflections, I aim to discuss topical issues pertaining to experiences across multiple countries. Some of them will be simple musings, while others will be controversial discussions on sensitive topics. Some readers may agree with my thoughts while others may not. My goal in this section is not to preach or provide my own opinions on world affairs as though I was a member of a politician's campaign staff. Instead, my endeavour is to portray my experiences as a traveller. While it is unavoidable to completely separate my personal opinions and biases, as that would be to go against human nature, I hope the reader can appreciate my primary goal is discussing these issues from the perspective of a traveller who spent an entire year living out of a backpack, having discussions with both locals and fellow travellers, and experiencing a life-changing journey of realisation and discovery.

Reflection #1

War and Conflict: Reflections from Northern Ireland, Palestine, and Kurdistan

War. A constant in human history, the dominant force by which empires rise and fall, and a force which has freed, enslaved, saved, and decimated ethnic, religious, and racial groups throughout time. As I travelled the world, I came face to face with war. The Vietnam War, the Iraq War, the Spanish Inquisition, the Invitation of William and Mary, World War II, the conflict in Gaza, and the list goes on. I was no stranger to war, having served in it myself, but as a traveller, it took on an entirely new face. War wasn't simply politics by other means but an ugly, destructive, indiscriminate force through which nations were born and innocent bystanders were killed.

This wasn't a hypothetical or detached observation. I met people who fought, suffered, and were invested in modern-day conflicts. From convicted paramilitary terrorists in Northern Ireland to Palestinians who hated Israel to Kurds who mourned the martyrdom of their family members and friends, it was impossible to ignore the role war and conflict played in today's world.

United Ireland: Armed Conflict for an Inevitable Result

In Belfast, I took a tour through West Belfast, a district home to both Irish Republicans and British Unionists separated by a five-kilometre-long, fourteen-metre-tall wall. These so-called "peace walls" were once a fixture across Northern Ireland, preventing sectarian violence between neighbouring Catholic and Protestant communities. The wall in West Belfast was just one of many that divided Belfast during The Troubles, and its continued presence served as a reminder that despite the Good Friday Agreement between the paramilitaries and the government, the political struggle continued.

But why? The Troubles ended thirty years ago, Ireland gained its independence 100 years ago, and the partition which separated Ireland and Northern Ireland was a democratic process. Catholics were no longer systematically oppressed as they once were, 10 Downing Street had long acquiesced to Home Rule in the form of a devolved Northern-Irish parliament, and the people were represented in the British Parliament by duly elected Members of Parliament. By all legitimate measures of democracy, Northern Ireland had achieved everything it could want via the democratic process. Sure, the Catholics didn't get to rejoin the Republic of Ireland, and the Protestants had to live with a devolved government that would, at times, be dominated by the Catholics, but that was democracy in action.

Unfortunately, neither side saw it that way. The Catholics believed that any British rule over Ireland was intolerable, and there was some legitimacy to that argument. After all, the Normans invaded Ireland after taking control of Britain, which wasn't a democratic process. Then, centuries later, the Invitation of William and Mary of Orange to take the British throne specifically occurred because the Protestants didn't want a Catholic, who was next in succession for the throne, to become the monarch, and, as a result, it became illegal for a Catholic to become the King or Queen of the United Kingdom of Great Britain and Northern Ireland. The entire British presence on the Emerald Isle was predicated on oppressive policies from across the Irish Sea. The Protestants, on the other hand, saw this as a long-settled conflict. As was the case with all human history, Ireland was conquered, and war after war shaped political power and land reclamation. Now, the primarily Protestant, Unionist people of Northern Ireland wanted to remain a part of the United Kingdom. Any separatist actions, militant or political, were seditious, anti-democratic, and violated the basics of the political process in which the Catholics were included.

These two opposing views meant open, armed conflict was inevitable. The amnesty for Catholic paramilitaries who killed hundreds of innocent people during The Troubles (which they called "casualties of war" despite being the deliberate targets) returned convicted, violent militants to the streets of Belfast, with some becoming high-ranking government officials despite their murder and terrorism convictions. While they advocated for the political process, their paramilitary knowledge and connections could quickly return to being a threat to the tenuous peace and Protestant neighbourhoods. By the same token, the increase in right-wing nationalism in the United Kingdom had given rise to a new generation of aggressive Protestant political activists, with the newest company of the Ulster Volunteer Force, S-Company, forming in 2022, which in turn only fuelled, and in some minds justified, Catholic concerns about continued political discrimination and oppression. While both sides wanted peace, neither seemed willing to seek it.

The so-called peace wall was evidence of this unwillingness. Both sides wanted the wall to come down, but it had only been expanded in the years since the Good Friday Agreement. As technology advanced and sectarian sentiments simmered, the original concrete wall couldn't keep Molotov cocktails, rocks, grenades, and other projectiles from making it over the wall between neighbourhoods. After almost 1,000 years of war, the conflict was nowhere near over. As an outsider, I couldn't see any other inevitable outcome than a united Ireland, but to get there would almost certainly entail at least one more bloody conflict. After all, the Easter Rising galvanised the Irish into seeking independence, the Irish War of Independence gained that independence, and The Troubles forced the British government to the negotiating table to end the political oppression against the Catholics, so why wouldn't another war, or two, or three, finally see the withdrawal of British government, politics, police, and military forces from the Emerald Isle entirely? It was a conflict as inevitable as it was regrettable in my view. Maybe the inevitable united Ireland could be achieved via a peaceful, political process, but innocent people were bound to be caught in the literal crossfire.

The Kurdish Independence Movement: Is it Even Possible?

The Kurds were one of the most important American allies in the Middle East. Despite being a non-self-governing ethnic group, they were reliable, disciplined, and tenacious when combatting Saddam's armies, al-Qa'ida terrorists, and Islamic State's takeover. They were also separatists in every country in which they lived. They actively fought against the Assad regime in Syria, conducted bombings against Turkish diplomatic outposts in Europe, and instigated multiple rebellions in Iraq and Iran. In only one of the four Kurdish regions had the Kurds obtained semi-autonomy in the form of a devolved government, Iraq. Even so, the four Kurdish regions of Iraq, Iran, Turkey, and Syria united to form Kurdistan, a region of predominantly Kurdish people with a shared identity that dated far before any of the modern-day countries existed. As a regional ethnic group, the Kurds were younger than the Arabs and Persians but older than the Turks.

So, what was Kurdistan, given this complicated ethnic and regional history? Kurdistan had never been a truly independent state, despite Kurdish claims to the contrary. At most, it had achieved semi-independent kingdom status under the over-all control of a larger empire, such as the Persians or Byzantines. Despite centuries of conflict, the Kurds were a nation without a country.

The lack of country status and their reliability as Western allies only fuelled Kurdish separatism in the four Kurdish regions. The Peshmerga defended Iraqi Kurdistan against Islamic State, the Iraqi Army, and Turkish incursion, and maintained bases high in the mountains; the Kurdistan Workers Party (PKK) conducted a guerilla warfare in Turkey; the Syrian Democratic Forces (SDF) (which were largely, but not exclusively, Kurdish) fought to bring down the oppressive Assad Regime and fend off Turkish military invasions in Syrian Kurdistan; and several different militant groups, including the Kurdish Free Life Party (PJAK) and Democratic Party of Iranian Kurdistan (KDPI), were in engaged in a decades-long, on-again off-again insurgency against the Iranian government. Unfortunately, these movements were not united under a single political party or banner. While they all sought a free, independent Kurdistan, that was about as far as the political cooperation extended. Internal disputes, tribal feuds, money, and tactics divided the four regions, and unifying their efforts was a constant struggle.

There was, once, an offer of an independent Kurdistan after World War I. The Treaty of Sèvres would have ceded what would become the Kurdish region of Turkey as an independent Kurdish nation. The treaty, however, never came to fruition. The new Turkish government, born out of the ashes of the Ottoman Empire, abandoned the treaty after securing its own independence, opting instead for the Treaty of Lausanne, which definitively ended any notion of an independent Kurdistan. The Turks were not alone in this decision against Kurdish nationalism, as the British mandate in Iraq and the League of Nations also opposed an independent Kurdistan. Unlike the Partition of Ireland, which was decided between two competing belligerents, the division of Kurdistan was decided for the Kurds by third parties, forcing them out of the political process altogether and leaving them one alternative: armed conflict.

Unlike a united Ireland, I did not see an independent Kurdistan as an inevitable end state. Middle Eastern countries were fierce in defending their territorial claims, an understandable position after the fall of the Ottoman Empire, the Iranian Qajar government, and the West carving up the region under the Sykes-Picot Agreement. If the four countries governing the Kurdish regions conceded Kurdish independence, which group was next? Would the Yazidis be given an independent state? Would the tribals forces of al-Anbar province be allowed to secede? Would the Shi'a Crescent cut the Middle East in half? And what of PKK terrorists in Turkey? It was unfathomable that Turkey would grant them amnesty, and it wasn't apparent to me that an independent Kurdistan would end the PKK's guerilla warfare and terrorist attacks against their northern neighbour. Nor was it apparent that Turkey would cease its incursions into Syrian Kurdistan, as Turkey and Syria were not on the best of diplomatic terms, despite both being allies in some form with Russia. Further complicating the discussion were the founded accusations of war crimes by Kurdish militants, as allowing Kurdish independence would be seen as a de facto endorsement of torturing prisoners, mass internment, and summary executions as a legitimate means to a political end that would be echoed in Afghanistan, Palestine, China, Chechnya, the Sahel, and many other places where such ethnic conflicts existed.

But what was the alternative, never-ending fighting? It was a complicated situation, but the only real solution I could envision was Iraq's: a semi-autonomous, regional government. To reach that agreement, though, the Kurds would have to agree to shutter their militant elements (leaving the Asayish as the internal security force), hand over terrorists who committed crimes outside of Kurdistan, and agree not to enter into unilateral treaties with countries like the United States. They wouldn't control their currency or monetary policy nor be allowed to independently decide crucial government policies like tax and immigration regimens. Those were a lot of concessions for a watered-down version of independence which could be dissolved at the whim of a new government in Ankara, Baghdad, Damascus, or Tehran. Maybe never-ending fighting was the only way...

Palestine: Two Sides that will Never Agree?

The modern conflict between Israel and the Palestinians has raged for more than seventy-five years. The establishment of the State of Israel after the Holocaust was seen not just as righting a historical wrong, but a necessary concession to the world's most persecuted ethnic and religious group, the Jews. Unfortunately, that state came on the backs of Arabs who lived in the British Mandate for Palestine, whose families had lived there for generations under Ottoman rule. These Arabs, who would later self-identify as Palestinians, had their land usurped from them by foreign, Western powers for the purpose of righting centuries' worth of wrongs perpetrated against the Jewish people. As if on cue, in 1948, the Arab armies of Lebanon, Syria, Iraq, Egypt, and Transjordan (the predecessor to modern-day Jordan) invaded the British Mandate for Palestine to prevent the creation of a Jewish state. It was the exact attitude and hatred for the Jewish people that instigated the need for Israel in the first place. Over the next seventy-five years, one conflict after the next raged between the Arabs and Israel, with Israel emerging victorious at almost every turn.

For the Jewish people, the animosity towards Israel and the constant warfare and terrorism waged against them were proof that they needed a country to protect themselves against inherent international hatred for their race and religion. The Arab nations didn't even try to establish diplomatic relations with the Jews in 1948; they used warfare, usually a weapon of last resort, to forcibly prevent the Jews from gaining political power and national sovereignty. Any fears that the world was poised to wipe the Jewish people from the face of the Earth were justified after the events of the 1940s. In the following years, the Arab nations expelled the Jews, much as the Europeans had done long before, forcing them to migrate to the only refuge they had in the world: Israel. And why shouldn't they settle there? The land where Israel now sat was undoubtedly and undisputedly the Jews' ancestral homelands.

The Arab invasions and creation of the State of Israel both failed to take into serious account the one people who would be most affected: the Palestinians. While the Palestinians, contrary to popular claims, had no ethnic ties to the ancient Philistines, that did not change the fact that, as an Arab subgroup, they had lived in the region known as the British Mandate for Palestine for centuries. Just as the Kurdish people changed hands as empires rose and fell, so did the Palestinians. While the creation of the State of Israel was a necessary step in world affairs, the partition plan which divided the British Mandate for Palestine between an Arab nation and a Jewish one failed to bring the Palestinian Arabs' issues and concerns to the table. It also failed to definitively define the Palestinians' country, ultimately tying them to Transjordan instead of giving them independence or control over the territory in which they lived.

So, conflict ensued, and Israel expanded its influence and territorial claims over the entirety of the former British Mandate for Palestine. The original partition plan ceded the West Bank (in larger form than it is now), Gaza (also in larger form), and the area known as the Golan Heights to the Arabs, but as the Arab nations and Palestinian militant groups waged war against Israel, the Arabs and Palestinians lost more and more land. The regions of Gaza and the West Bank were de facto governed by Egypt and Jordan until after the Six-Day War, at which point Israel forced the Arab militaries out and conquered the land. The Israelis claimed these lands were rightfully theirs under the long-standing human tradition of warfare and conquest. The Arabs and much of the international community declared them occupied territories that should be procedurally handed over to an undefined government which had the best interest of the people who lived there in mind. That debate raged throughout (and long after) my first year of travel across the world.

The fighting would never end so long as each side claimed the rights of territory from the other. Unfortunately, the Jordanian people would not accept the State of Israel on their border, regardless of the position their government may take, something I witnessed and had impressed upon me by Jordanians time and again during my travels there. Egypt, for its part, was willing to accept a two-state solution and wash its hands of the entire situation. Egypt needed to move on to more pressing matters in its diplomatic relations with Israel and the United States, like Iranian and Shi'a political influence and terrorism affecting trade in the region. Lebanon, too, as an Iranian puppet state, would never recognise Israel on Arab lands. Israel was in the same camp, as it would not cede biblically-important lands and the historical Israelite kingdoms of Judea and Samaria (in the modern-day West Bank) to an Arab, Muslim nation. The two sides were at an impasse that could only result in prolonged conflict.

To me, there was only one legitimate solution: the two-state solution. Both sides had to abandon territorial pipe dreams to stop the fighting. Israel wouldn't control the former Judea and Samaria, and the Palestinians ejected from their homes during the Nakba would never return. The only way to stop the fighting was to sign a peace accord recognising two, equal, completely-sovereign countries, each outlawing and punishing terrorism, being allowed to foment their own trade agreements, and each maintaining its own military and security services. Neither nation would rule "from the river to the sea," and to think that would ever be the case was to live in an unattainable alternate reality.

Who are the Real Casualties?

No armed conflict is without its casualties, but those involving dreams of independence or secession have far more innocent bystanders than state-on-state conflict. State-on-state conflicts typically entailed a grievance, exhausted political options to resolve that grievance, and used force as a weapon of last resort to achieve a desired goal; the laws of armed conflict, international treaties, and resolutions from various international and supranational institutions governed military operations in warfare. Non-state actors abided by none of those criteria, which yielded far more innocent bystander casualties than actual participant casualties.

During The Troubles, the Irish Republican Army wasn't an organised army that combatted the government institutions that held the power of partition. Instead, it routinely targeted civilian institutions, like libraries, pubs, and hotels. The IRA killed far more Catholics than it did Protestants, and far more civilians than it did paramilitaries or British soldiers. The Protestants, under the guise of defending their countrymen and the monarch, focused more on the IRA but still conducted reprisal attacks and summary executions of non-combatant Catholics.

Palestinian terrorist groups, like Hamas and the Popular Front for the Liberation of Palestine, almost exclusively attacked civilian targets in Israel. The very day that I wrote this chapter, they bombed three civilian buses across Israel. Their rocketing campaigns intended to kill as many Israelis and damage as much public infrastructure as possible, forcing Israel to deploy the Iron Dome to protect its citizens. Why weren't they specifically targeting the government entities which oppressed them? Easy, they were too hard of targets. It was much easier to kill the random Jew than it was to wage a legitimate war of independence. These groups famously had no regard for Israel's retaliation, either, and in the wake of October 7th, evidence arose that they actually counted on Palestinian deaths in the attack's aftermath to bolster support from the international community.

The Israelis, too, stood accused of deliberately targeting civilians, which continued to be a hotly debated subject long after my year around the world ended. What was evident to practitioners of war, however, was that extreme collateral

damage in Gaza was almost impossible to avoid. It was simply too densely populated, too congested, and to launch even the smallest of warheads on a targeted strike
against a Hamas terrorist was likely, almost certain, to kill civilians, bring down an
entire building, or damage critical infrastructure.

The Kurds, for their part, had not inflicted the number of Turkish civilian casualties as their Irish and Palestinian counterparts. Still, their attacks against Turkish
diplomatic outposts in Europe threatened to bring foreign countries into the conflict,
whose people had no interest in the Kurdish independence issue one way or another.
The Turks were not so deliberate, and estimates for Kurdish civilian casualties
ranged from a few hundred to the tens of thousands.

Regardless of the rightness or wrongness of an independence or secessionist
movement, civilian non-combatants bore the weight of the conflict the most. Civilian casualties created political pressure to bring an end to the conflict and were often
exploited by belligerents to achieve their goals. Tens of thousands of innocent bystanders would disagree with that tactic… if they were here to do so.

Is Armed Conflict the Answer?

Who results to terrorism, insurgency, and guerilla warfare? Security studies
scholars pointed to all other options being exhausted, but counterterrorism and military professionals knew otherwise. War was the "easy button" for political movements. Change via the political process could take years, decades, or even centuries.
The Civil Rights Movement in the United States was proof of that, where even a
century after the Civil War, the abolition of slavery, and the passage of the Reconstruction amendments, black people were still forced into second-class citizenship,
and it quite literally took sending in the Army to forcibly integrate schools. Catholics
in Ireland tried their Civil Rights Association to better their situation only to be fired
upon by Protestants who refused to participate in a government with former IRA
members thirty years after the signing of the Good Friday Agreement. The Palestinians have never been able to negotiate a deal to their liking, nor have they ever had
the true power to bend the negotiating parties to their will. The Kurds, too, tried the
political process, only to be undermined and stabbed in the back by Turkey, the
United Kingdom, Iraq, and even the United States at times.

Could the political process eventually lead to a peaceful change for these movements? Maybe, but no one can know for sure. For the people seeking that change,
they wanted it now (in the past, really), and they were willing to do whatever it took
to achieve that end. With no real political power nor international support (despite
the politicians' rhetoric and demonstrations we see on the news), there really were
no options other than armed conflict.

War Solves a Lot of Problems…

I do not support terrorism, guerilla warfare, or seditious movements. In a perfect
world, the political process and democratic participation would resolve these long-
standing conflicts in ways every party could accept. They may not like every part of

every treaty, but at least they could put the spectre of war, car bombs, and indiscriminate rocket attacks behind them.

If history told us anything, though, it was that war solved a lot of problems. War stopped the Holocaust. War achieved African independence from France. War forced Mexico to accept the modern border with Texas. In the Global War on Terrorism, Western de-radicalisation programmes failed spectacularly at a massive expense to the taxpayer, while drone strikes picked terrorists off the map one by one, preventing an incalculable number of attacks and saving innumerable lives. War converted the Greek outposts in Turkey to Christianity and, later, Islam. War prevented a Catholic from ascending to the British throne. In human history, war was often the answer.

It was an undeniable, unsettling fact that war solved many of the world's problems, to the point where we used "war" as the term of choice for any serious plan of action. The "War on Drugs," "War on Police," even the "War on Belly Fat" (as one of my subordinates once termed his physical fitness plan). To deny war as an answer was to deny reality, a reality that people like Northern Irish Catholics, the Kurds, and the Palestinians lived every day, and one which Westerners had a hard time understanding in the 21st Century.

Reflection #2
Religion and Belief: Unifying and Destructive Forces

While travelling the world, I encountered a variety of religions, societies, and practices. I came from Small-Town, Texas, where everything was done the same way all the time, and the stereotypes of small towns rang true. Those stereotypes weren't universal in my country, or even my state, and the political and social strife the different values and practices caused when they clashed were not just unhealthy, they were socially destructive. New Yorkers didn't hold the same values and beliefs as Kentuckians, the slogan "Don't California My Texas!" had become a mantra for those where I lived opposing the values of those who moved there, and our socio-political discourse had become toxic as groups that were pro-this or anti-that came to blows, literally and metaphorically, in battles which drug everyone else along with them. Yet, at the same time, my small town was buoyed by the cultural forces which influenced it for decades, insulated from Austin and Washington, DC, politics, just a dot on the map along the interstate that connected Atlanta to Dallas. While the politics would ultimately affect us via the legislature, our day-to-day living situation, where church attendance was on the rise, the community looked after each other, and, for better and worse, everyone knew everyone else's business, would largely remain unaffected.

After a year of travel which took me to twenty-six countries, I gained an appreciation for which countries had strong, cohesive societies and those which didn't. Some of these observations came through interacting with local people, while others came through conversations with travellers. After about my tenth month of travel, I noticed a pattern: the strongest, most-cohesive societies were communities and countries which had strong, near-universal religious and cultural beliefs, and the most fractured and divided were the ones where multiculturalism was prioritised over a common set of beliefs or identity. It was the West that was socially crumbling, not the Middle East, North Africa, or Southeast Asia, despite having the most robust economies, lowest poverty rates, and unlimited possibilities available to its people. At the same time, the West was also the least wrought with war, armed sectarian conflict, and religiously-, ethnically-, or culturally-motivated persecution. It was an interesting paradox, one which surely meant there had to be a balance in there somewhere where strong social cohesion resulted neither in division nor warfare, but a true melting pot of all the positive things people had to offer.

✳   ✳   ✳

Cohesive Societies and Forces for Good

The United States has become an incredibly divided place. The different sides of the political spectrum all blamed different things for this division, from radical gender theory to fundamentalist religion to racism and socialism. In the years leading up to The Great Gallivanting, I watched as a post-9/11, cohesive society ripped itself apart, with any legitimate effort to reach across the centre line clawed back by activists and fear of social, financial, and political retribution. Americans increasingly had less and less in common with each other, especially across state lines, and even within religious denominations, as both the Catholic and the Methodist churches had divided themselves over political and social issues. The same was true of Germany, France, Ireland, and the United Kingdom. The ubiquitous West was crumbling from the inside out, so much so that it was impossible not to notice as I travelled the world.

Where did I not see this crumbling? Spain, Italy, Morocco, Kurdistan, and Cambodia, to name a few. It was clear that these countries were substantially more united than the major international power players. I could feel it just walking around, and it was clear on dating apps when I was in genuinely cohesive countries. Not everyone agreed on everything, obviously, but there was some greater, unifying power that kept the differences from dividing their societies into smaller and smaller sects that became more and more adversarial with one another.

What was that power? Shared religious and cultural values. Most of Spain identified as Catholic, and the annual festivals celebrating the patron saints were city- and country-wide celebrations, not simply organised by one church or association of churches, but a combination of religious, governmental, and social organisations. A similar homogeny was evident in Italy as well, where being Italian and holding generally conservative religious values held the country together when the mass immigration policies orchestrated by Germany in the European Union threatened to tear the country apart. Neither Spain nor Italy was anti-immigration, charity, or helping those fleeing oppression, but they ardently defended their countries' cultural and religious values and refused to give in to external pressures to change.

The same was true in Morocco and much of the rest of MENA. Sunni Islam and its values generally united the Arab world, and Shi'a Islam did the same where the former Persian Empire's influence continued. Like Christians, not every Muslim adhered to every aspect of their faith (indeed, many drank, scammed, and engaged in extra-marital sex), but the basic tenets served as a moral and societal compass. In Turkey, mosques were used as a sort of public square, where children were left to play (outside of prayer times) under the protective roof of Allah. While not every person practised Islam, the values which stemmed from the most popular religions governed the social contract and influenced these countries' laws. In countries where religion was held in high regard, I saw the most stable, cohesive societies.

Kurdistan was a similar story, although not with religion. The shared Kurdish identity, which had been persecuted for centuries, fought for its very existence in the mountains, and survived invading empires and armies, held Kurdistan together as though it were bound by glue. It didn't matter if someone was Shi'a, Sunni, Christian, Jewish, Yazidi, or atheist; they were all Kurdish. They valued family, had little regard for Western "progressive" relationship practices, and were committed to one day seeing their people free and self-governing. Sure, there were Western influences, especially with clothing and food, but those influences didn't divide the Kurdish people into sectarian groups like social issues had divided the Methodist Church in the United States. Instead, these influences delineated generational groups from one another, just as generational groups were divided everywhere else.

Communal beliefs and religious practices were also pivotal forces driving lower crime rates, stronger family bonds which fended off homelessness, and more resilient communities in the face of adversity or disaster. The earthquake in the Atlas Mountains, for example, would have utterly crushed most cities in the United States, between selfish interests, criminals exploiting the disaster, and governmental regulations. That isn't to downplay the human toll the earthquake took, as almost 3,000 people were killed and tens of thousands more had their homes and livelihoods affected or destroyed. Even so, in Marrakech, where most of the deaths occurred, the community bound together to take in those who lost their homes, clear the roads, rescue belongings, and restart life to the point where Jo and I could hardly tell there had been an earthquake at all. That was a far cry from the annual fires, hurricanes, and floods back home where bureaucratic infighting and political finger-pointing caused aid and services to be delayed no matter how much a community may want to help their neighbours (in some cases, it was even illegal to provide assistance in a disaster area!).

As I traipsed through villages, spoke with locals and guides, and interacted with travellers, I found that widespread, collective religious and cultural beliefs were driving factors of cohesion, not division, and it was the West's obsession with the new quasi-religion of social justice that was turning us against each other. When social issues beat out religion and our communal values as the foundation of our social contract, not even religion could keep us together.

Source of Division

Religion and belief were not always a source of good and cohesion, though, and I saw their dark side several times throughout my travels. This dark side usually appeared when different religions and beliefs competed for dominance in a given society. This was on full display in my country, where something as simple as building a mosque in the financial district of New York City was enough to cause a nationwide uproar. I could remember when teaching evolution in high school was controversial because it clashed with the fundamentalist, Creationist view of the world. In the 2020s, that controversy seemed trivial, with the federal government targeting religious groups and even the Catholic Church as a whole for "extremist" activities. Legal battles raged as Satanists wanted to erect monuments on government grounds where Christian monuments (specifically, the Ten Commandments) once stood. Criticising Islam was a social taboo, and talking negatively about Israel, even when not discussing Judaism, immediately got you labelled an antisemite.

In Northern Ireland, the religious differences led to literal armed conflict. While it was true the modern conflict was less about religion and more about politics, the source of the conflict, the systemic oppression of Catholics over centuries, and control over the monarchy were all rooted in in the Protestant-Catholic religious divide, which itself stemmed from one Pope's refusal to give one King an annulment for his divorce. I was a rare crossover personality, where I identified politically with the conservative Protestants but nationalistically with the liberal Catholics. It was unfortunate, to me, that this divide was causing young people to abandon religion altogether. Most of the Northern Irish Millennials and Gen Z-ers I met resented the division and, in their words, "have no use for religion."

In the Middle East, it was impossible to ignore the animosity Jews and Christians held towards their Muslim countrymen in certain places; that animosity was usually mutual. Where great synagogues and cathedrals once stood, mosques had been built. "To the victor go the spoils" was true enough in imperial conquest, but places like Jerusalem, the Temple Mount, Babylon, Ephesus, and mountain monasteries, were a living testament to the centuries-long religious persecutions which continued to this day. The Yazidis were basically isolated in communities all to themselves in Iraq after Islamic State's genocidal rampage against them, and even in the culturally-cohesive Kurdistan, Jewish and Christian towns, villages, and communities formed to safeguard their own.

London and Paris (and the United Kingdom and France writ-large) were the most visible sources of religion as a divisive force. These countries were under severe strain from illegal immigration from North Africa and the Middle East, a product of European Union policies driven by Angela Merkel when Germany held the presidency. These once-religiously cohesive cities had been infused with Muslim migrants, which was in and of itself not a problem, but the migrants largely refused to assimilate into their new cities and countries. When combined with the secularisation of society in general, the latest infusion of Islamic religious beliefs into historically Christian and increasingly atheist or agnostic communities caused political and social strife these countries were unprepared to handle. The conflict between these different groups' values increasingly divided these countries to the point where Jo and I couldn't experience London's historical district without being confronted with anti-British graffiti and flags of foreign nations strewn about.

Forceful Disruption

Religious and cultural homogeneity and the resulting stability were not always a peaceful venture. Throughout the ages, evangelism and crusades forcibly, either through social pressures or at the point of a sword, converted one group of people from religion to religion. Judaism was once the only Abrahamic religion, of which there were now three, and the scars of social and national conversions from Judaism to Christianity to Islam were all over the Middle East. The Romans and Greeks, each with their own theologies, weren't excepted, as Paul caused a riot (according to the Book of Acts) in Ephesus while preaching against Artemis, whose great temple wasn't far away. Even these great empires were eventually converted from their long-standing religious practices to Christianity. That was hard to fathom, given that many of these empires were now predominantly Muslim countries.

As much as I loved Spain's culture and adherence to Christian-based values which aligned closely with my own, Spain was not always such a homogenous,

Christian-values-based country. In 1492, the same year Colombus sailed for the New World, Spain ejected any Jew who refused to convert to Christianity. Jews who refused to convert or leave were killed. That was a far cry from Paul's preachings at Ephesus or John's evangelism from a Roman prison. This ejection disrupted not just Spanish society, but North Africa's as hundreds of thousands of Jewish people sought refuge elsewhere more than 400 years before the re-establishment of Israel. In fact, the Jews had been ejected from more than 100 countries. Despite once being a large diaspora across the Middle East, the Muslim-majority countries also forced their Jewish neighbours, many of which were Arabs, out of their countries once Israel was established. These events fundamentally reshaped societies as religious homogeneity consolidated influence over cultures and social values. In some of them, including American allies like Morocco and Saudi Arabia, distributing or even possessing a Bible was illegal. For three religions purportedly based around the same frameworks, they sure didn't overlap well, and the convergence of two or more resulted in social upheaval and persecution.

Modern history was also replete with instances of religious-based warfare, from the Crusades attempting to retake Israel from the Muslims to the Umayyad Caliphate conquering the Visigoth Iberian Peninsula and establishing Islamic rule there. Even within religions, wars were fought over the influence and values of one denomination over another, like the Catholics and Protestants in Ireland and the Sunnis and Shi'a in Iraq. Some of the most impactful violence and social-political upheavals across the world happened not when one religion opposed another but when two sects of the same religion clashed over the particulars. In my hometown growing up, there was a massive debate between the Methodists and the Baptists on whether you had to be fully immersed in water to be baptised or if pouring or sprinkling water over one's head was enough. This slight, ultimately inconsequential difference caused a huge rift between friends, and people even voted in school board elections based on whether someone was of the same denomination as them. One would think that the big banner of Islam, Christianity, or any other major religion would unify the sects and denominations more than the small particulars would divide them, but one would be wrong. Sometimes, these small particulars were more divisive than disagreeing with an entire, different religion.

Atrocities

The world was no stranger to religiously motivated crimes against humanity. The 1992 genocide in Bosnia sought to eradicate Bosnian Muslims, the Armenian genocide in 1915 sought to annihilate Christians in Armenia, and, of course, the Holocaust decimated the Jewish population of Europe. Such atrocities were a stain on the history of Europe, but they weren't contained to the continent, nor were they wholly motivated by the belief in one religion over another. Religiously-motivated persecution and anti-religious sentiment were sources for abhorrent actions across the world.

The clearest example of modern-day atrocities perpetrated in the name of religion was the Islamic State genocide of the Yazidis, where the world watched as 5,000 Yazidis were killed by the Sunni extremist group. Even though Islamic State was "defeated" in Iraq (in 2017) and Syria (in 2019), Yazidis remained missing. Some of them were likely dead, especially the men, while many women and children were probably still held as sex slaves. Even if they were freed and returned home, they were now considered unclean in their culture. They would likely never marry and would forever be consigned to second-class citizen status through no fault nor action of their own.

The Cambodian genocide under Khmer Rouge was a perfect example of anti-religious atrocities. The Khmer Rouge were not a religious group by any measure, and religion threatened their rule, especially religious minorities. Hundreds of thousands of religious minorities, including Muslims and Christians, were executed in Cambodia's killing fields. The animists who managed to escape fled to the countryside and remained there decades after the restoration of the monarchy. It was simply too painful, and they too isolated after decades in hiding, to willingly return to the fold of a society which not too long ago sought their eradication. China, where I technically spent all of five minutes, was well known for its current persecution of the Uyghur minority. Why? Because the Uyghurs clashed with the Han, the Chinese majority, during a series of protests, and the Chinese deemed them a threat to civil order. Rather than stick to interning and "re-educating" the Uyghurs within its own borders, China took the extra step of chasing Uyghurs across the world. Through its alliances, influence, and international organisations, China was rendering Uyghurs from abroad to face internment, "re-education," and likely, torture in China. Some crucial, regional American allies were involved in these renditions, including Egypt, Saudi Arabia, Morocco, and the United Arab Emirates.

The pursuit of a cohesive, unified society around shared cultural values and religious practices almost inevitably brought discrimination, oppression, and mass executions. Was this worth it? Cambodia was now a peaceful country of Buddhists and Hindus where the minority animists were constitutionally free to practise their religion openly. Bosnia now guaranteed freedom of religion in its constitution, with the Muslims and Christians roughly dividing the country in half, although the tensions between the two tended to isolate them from each other. Spain enshrined freedom of religion in its constitution, despite being a Catholic country that once expelled all of Jews from the peninsula. It was difficult to tackle, knowing that one's social stability and cultural values came on the backs of religions which had been the targets of genocide by those whose values I also held.

Homogeny vs Multiculturalism - Finding the Balance

The juxtaposition and seeming-incompatibility of the two notions that religious and cultural homogeneity were forces for cohesion, division, national success, and atrocities was something which I wrestled with throughout my travels. My favourite countries were the ones that were generally united in their beliefs, where their social contract was governed by shared values, and where common religious practices provided a solid foundation for their country's success. I loved Spain, even though I wasn't Catholic, because its society was governed by conservative, Christian-based principles. I loved Turkey, even though I wasn't Muslim, because of the clear positive impact Muslim beliefs and practices had on their everyday society. I loved

Kurdistan, even though I wasn't Kurdish, because of their view that being Kurdish, something they all shared, was worth more than anything else that could divide the Kurdish people.

And I had disliked Germany, where the country suffered from political strife that seemed to infect every aspect of their lives. Ireland, especially Northern Ireland, was a place I loved. Still, I found I couldn't openly give an opinion on politics or religion because the tenuous peace between the Catholics and Protestants still simmered beneath the surface. My home country, the United States, was ripping itself apart as anti-religious activists and faith-based groups clashed over social and political policies, tearing apart even the best of friendships in the process. The idea of a cultural melting pot, where the best of cultures from around the world melded together in a flourishing society, had changed to a tossed salad, where all of the separate ingredients contributed to an overall whole but were still independent from each other. We could pick out the ones we didn't like.

For my part, I loved the idea of a cultural melting pot and wasn't a fan of the tossed salad. I was a proud Texan, but that didn't mean I couldn't appreciate and incorporate aspects of other cultures I enjoyed. Assimilation didn't necessarily entail abandoning one's home culture; it just meant someone had to integrate themselves into the overall whole. Where a home culture was incompatible with the new country, the new country won out. That was my view, and one which solidified during my travels.

This required a delicate balance and evaluation of what cultural practices really were fundamental and which ones would upset social cohesion. In conversations about this topic, travellers often posed this question: What would happen if a Muslim family moved into my hometown in Texas? People were shocked when I told them no one would care. Wasn't small-town Texas a close-minded, Christian place? Maybe to an extent, but we didn't care if someone was Muslim, Jewish, Catholic, or Protestant. Sure, if someone wore a headscarf at the local grocery store, people may side-eye them, because it was out of the ordinary, but they would move on after a minute or two. Most people wouldn't care if a mosque was built in our town. We would draw the line, though, at having the call to prayer on loudspeakers five times a day, as was the custom in Muslim-majority countries (and even Dearborn, Michigan, the largest Muslim community in the United States). Believing in Islam, practising your beliefs, wearing traditional clothing, those weren't things that would cause social upheaval, but subjecting the Christian majority to endure calls of "Allah is the Greatest," "I bear witness that there is none worthy of worship except Allah," "I bear witness that Muhammad is the Messenger of Allah," and "There is no one worthy of worship except Allah," five times a day would not be tolerated, especially if it was in Arabic instead of English. At that point, the social contract governing freedom to practise religion would be violated, as the majority non-Muslim population would be forced into accepting Muslim practices in a place where that was not the culture.

The balance between creating a cultural melting pot and maintaining a strong, cohesive, culturally-united population was difficult, and articulating how it could or should happen was harder still. Personally, when those two came into conflict, I would opt for the latter, having seen the destruction and division multiculturalism could bring when it supplanted homogenous values, religious or otherwise. The United States used to be united around the American dream and American exceptionalism. We put a man on the moon, stood up for the persecuted, and even spearheaded the collapse of Apartheid. Yes, we were once a slave-holding country, but we were the first Western nation whose population voted against slavery, even fighting a war on behalf of the enslaved to end it. While we were of different religions and racial/ethnic backgrounds, we were all Americans at the end of the day. That had changed somewhere along the way. The rallying notions of American exceptionalism and leadership in the world somehow became things to be ashamed of rather than celebrated, and anyone who still believed in the American dream was considered an oppressor who was out of touch with reality in mainstream social discourse. Christians and Jews were made out to be extremists while abortion rights activists and anti-theism became mainstream. The United States, after losing its cohesive cultural identity, was ripping itself apart and dividing itself into smaller and smaller groups, groups which attacked each other rhetorically and literally in the fashion of fascists, communists, and socialists the world over.

Was any specific religion the answer to this division? That I couldn't say, but a culturally uniting identity that trumped all other divisions and provided the base for our cultural melting pot was sorely needed. That wasn't just my opinion; it was a fact born out throughout humanity. It raised a question from Will, from the United Kingdom, that was cause for reflection and contemplation: "When are we multicultural enough?"

Reflection #3

Narratives from the Middle East: My Experience with the Never-Ending Conflict

Jo and I were sitting on the couch at her cousin's house in the United Kingdom when the news broke. Another war in the Middle East had erupted, threatening our travel and Christmas plans. Over the next three months, I travelled MENA, coming face to face with people who were directly or indirectly affected by the conflict between Hamas and Israel. I made it a point to listen more than I spoke, as I was a foreigner in a land where the conflict was real, raw, and placed sides against each other on first principles. I travelled to Morocco, Tunisia, Egypt, Jordan, Iraq, and Turkey, taking in the view of locals and travellers, trying to keep an open mind on what I was hearing. Unfortunately, what I witnessed did not reflect well on the region or its people when it came to the Palestinian-Israeli conflict. Rationality, verifiable facts, and legitimate discourse were out the window, and dogmatism, religious fervour, and racist sentiments reigned supreme while innocent bystanders, opinionated as they may have been, were caught in the crossfire.

The Outbreak of the Conflict

On 7 October 2023, in an event that would come to be known as October 7th, Hamas, the Iranian-backed terrorist group which ruled the Gaza Strip, launched an unprovoked attack of more than 5,000 rockets against Israel, attacked a youth festival, and initiated a ground and air offensive along the Gazan-Israeli border. The result: 1,139 dead, 254 kidnapped, and the highest casualty count of Jews since the Holocaust. As the days passed, videos from the attacks made it to traditional and social media, and the world was exposed to Hamas' crimes of rape, torture, summary executions, and abuses of Jewish corpses.

Israel retaliated, launching an aerial campaign, ground offensives, and targeted drone strikes against Hamas targets in Gaza. The death toll mounted quickly, as Hamas intentionally moved amongst the population, stashed their weapons caches, communications equipment, and headquarters elements in hospitals, schools, and underground tunnels, and hid in refugee camps. Millions of Palestinian civilians were caught in the crossfire, losing loved ones, homes, businesses, and all of their worldly possessions in Israel's retaliatory campaign.

The entire world was caught off guard. Israel's intelligence agencies completely missed the build-up for the attack, as had the American Central Intelligence Agency, British Secret Intelligence Service, and Jordanian General Intelligence Department. As news and intelligence agencies alike scrambled for accurate, real-time information, the fifteenth war in Gaza commenced. During the fifteen months of fighting (as of this writing), peace deal after peace deal collapsed as both sides accused the other of acting against the terms of each agreement. After just three weeks since Hamas' attack, the war moved to Gazan soil; it would be the deadliest war for Palestinians in more than seventy years.

Sitting in her cousin's apartment, Jo and I figured the war would fizzle out in a matter of weeks. What we watched from Hamas was abhorrent, but these armed conflicts between Palestinian terrorist groups and Israel flared up from time to time. It was an unfortunate but normal course of life in the region. Once the war passed the two-week mark, however, we realised it wouldn't end any time soon. Western governments clambered to provide support, the Arab nations struggled to remain vocal without giving tangible support to Gaza on their own, and cities across the world wrestled with chaos stemming from anti-Israel, antisemitic, pro-Palestine, and/or pro-Hamas protests.

Conflicting Narratives

Reality quickly fell into the background as pro-Palestinian/anti-Israeli and pro-Israeli/anti-Palestinian interest groups, supporters, and politicians swarmed the internet and television screens to make their voices heard. In the digital age, reporters no longer needed direct access to the conflict zone to bring stories to the rest of the world; social media and live streaming provided unprecedented views of the casualties and destruction from inside Gaza. Israel was caught unable to compete with the narratives coming from inside the Gaza Strip, as it didn't have a social media presence there to leverage. All Israel could do was report its findings, what little intelligence it possessed, and fight on the airwaves to give their version of events. Not even the American Intelligence Community could accurately report what was happening. It was a total information blackout for one side of the conflict.

Palestinian narratives revolved around Israel's alleged indiscriminate use of force. Videos of drone strikes inside refugee camps, the levelling of apartment buildings, and families digging their children out from beneath the rubble conveyed to the world the horrors of the conflict. It was impossible not to be moved by what we saw. I knew what seeing a dead child, especially one obliterated in war, could do to the most hardened of soldier or police officer; the average person was rightfully brought to tears over the tragedy. These images drove college students across the world to stage massive protests demanding that their universities boycott, divest from, and sanction the Israeli government and companies. "From the river to the sea, Palestine will be free," was the common refrain. "We are all Hamas" was right there with it as Hamas painted itself as the defender of Palestinians against an aggressive Israel that didn't care if it killed women and children, destroyed schools or hospitals, or limited aid shipments and caused mass starvation amongst Gaza's more than 2,000,000 inhabitants.

Israeli initial narratives focused almost exclusively on lumping Hamas in with Islamic State. Israeli defence officials were on every major news network invoking an unrelated terrorist group's actions to make the comparison with the terrorists they were facing in Gaza. Israel released videos from its investigations showing the shootings and rapes at the music festival, photos of massacred babies with American intelligence officials, and broadcasted the faces of the kidnapped and missing as far and wide as possible. From inside Gaza, its embedded reporters showed weapons caches found in hospitals and tunnels that connected Hamas terrorists to sites across cities. Israel was fighting a war of survival in a region where Arab countries either expelled or made life intolerable for their Jewish populations, and Iran-backed, -trained, and -funded terrorist groups attacked Israel on multiple fronts. After fifteen wars in Gaza and the death toll from October 7th, Israel made it clear: they had had enough. Hamas had to go, and anyone who stood in the way of that objective would be considered to be aiding an internationally-designated terrorist organisation.

For my part, I believed Israel more than Hamas for the main reason that Hamas was a terrorist group that ruled Gaza with an iron fist. Many of Hamas' claims were provably false, like when they claimed Israel shut off Gaza's water supply (Israel did cut off what they provided, but that was only ten percent of the total Gazan water supply). I also understood the physical terrain in Gaza. It was so densely populated that any military action would inevitably cause collateral damage, both human and infrastructure. When taking that into consideration, the images after the targeted strikes made far more sense than they did when claiming that Israel was intentionally killing civilians. Hamas' leader was also camping out in a hotel room in Qatar, himself a multi-billionaire, while he dragged innocent Palestinians into another war that they could not possibly win against their will. I wasn't excusing all of Israel's policies towards Palestinians, but in this war, I believed Israel's version of events far more than Hamas' curated social media concoctions.

Travel, Tourism, and Innocent Bystanders

Jo and I were initially concerned about travelling in MENA after October 7th. Once it became clear the conflict would not end in the near future, we debated our planned trip east. We ultimately decided to take it one country at a time, as things could shift rapidly in asymmetric warfare. What I ultimately learned, as I said many times in Part One, was that Western tourism dollars mattered more than supporting Palestine. The United States backed Israel, for better and worse, and doing anything beyond writing a strongly worded letter about Israel's prosecution of the conflict risked incurring a travel advisory or financial investigations into businesses with access to the American banking system. Morocco needed to keep the United States happy if it wanted its continued recognition of sovereignty over Western Sahara, Egypt needed to keep the United States happy to keep tourists flowing and joint counterterrorism operations in the North Sinai Governate running, and Jordan and Iraq both were active Coalition partners in the fight against Islamic State. Only

Tunisia could risk inflaming tensions with the United States; Tunisia didn't have much to gain, lose, or offer, given it wasn't a strategic partner in any real capacity.

Nonetheless, tourism across MENA suffered. The Houthis, an Iranian-back terrorist group in Yemen, were firing missiles at passing ships and even into Israel territory from across Saudi Arabia; cruise ships flying American, Canadian, or European flags simply couldn't risk taking a hit traversing the Gulf of Aden as they headed for Hurghada, Aqaba, Eliat, or open sea. Despite travel advisories assuring travellers that popular tourism destinations were safe and isolated away from the conflict in Gaza, tourism plummeted as travellers rescheduled or outright cancelled their plans. It didn't help that the major budget airlines based in Europe cancelled any flight path over Gaza (despite Hamas not having anti-aircraft weapons capable of firing up to 10,000 metres). Places like Aqaba, Wadi Rum, and Petra became ghost towns, and Morocco's tourism industry took a second hit after the earthquake in the Atlas Mountains. Local businesses suffered, and national economies took major hits when expected high-season income failed to materialise. The conflict in Gaza affected Arabs across the region as innocent bystanders suffered the consequences of a war they neither started nor wanted.

Anger, Fear, and Hatred

Seeing so much death and destruction live on social media invoked emotions not felt in the West arguably since 9/11. The world's hearts broke for Israel, the victims, and the hostages in the days following the war; they continued to break as Palestinian non-combatants were killed, maimed, and uprooted across the Gaza Strip.

That heartbreak quickly turned to anger in the West. It became nearly impossible to hold a civil conversation about current events without being called a terrorist, Zionist, baby-killer, genocide-supporter, or other slur for your opinions. In the cities, massive protests lasted for days and weeks on end. Many of those protests turned violent and targeted Jewish synagogues and students who were wholly unaffiliated with the conflict outside of their religious or ethnic backgrounds. College students called to "globalise the intifada" and the liberation of all of Palestine, plainly stating that Israel was a fake country created on land which should be Palestine. "We don't want no two state, we want forty-eight" harkened to a time before the Israeli state, and "there is only one solution: intifada revolution" in no uncertain terms called for an armed uprising against Israel and its supporters. American Jews, especially students, avoided wearing clothing that affiliated them with their faith, and many (in some communities most) were concerned for their personal safety.

Jordan was a starkly different situation. The emotions ran the spectrum of negative, from fear to anger to hatred. I wasn't sure what to expect there, but I was confronted with beliefs, alternative realities, and emotions I couldn't identify with as an outside observer.

In Aqaba, fear was the dominant emotion. As there were few tourists, I didn't confront the issue of Gaza during my typical day. There was no need to protest as there was no one to convince. Jordanian businesses also needed to be inviting to the few of us who came despite the conflict. Aqaba wasn't a hub of political and social activity; it was a tourism destination, and it was suffering enough without adding emotional fervour into the mix. My hosts, however, were not above such things. One night, they held a dinner on the back porch and invited Louise (a French girl at the hostel) and me to join them. While the conversation started fun enough with stories of years gone by, somewhere along the line, the conversation turned to Israel, Gaza, and American foreign policy. Louise was, luckily for her, not knowledgeable in this region's long history, so she could stay quiet, listen, and avoid being baited into the conversation. I, on the other hand, was and could not, and the group knew it as they tried to pull me into their rantings about the Zionists, Israel, and the global Jewish conspiracy.

I was appalled at what I heard, and I hoped my face didn't show it. According to my hosts, Israel wanted to establish a Jewish state "from the Nile to the Euphrates." Worse, they said, Americans and our government supported such an endeavour, and we were intimately involved in fuelling Israel's expansion across the Middle East and fully supported the complete genocide of the Palestinian people. When I finally told them they would be hard-pressed to find an American that actually supported what they were saying, they told me, "That is what you believe, even if you do not know that you believe it, because that's what the Zionists believe, and the Zionists control your education, your businesses, and your government!" I was shocked, and I knew my face couldn't hide it in the face of such a bigoted conspiracy. It was the sort of thing I had only ever heard from skinheads, neo-Nazis, and white supremacists. It was a total break from reality.

Did they not know that Qatar, who once funded al-Qa'ida, was one of the largest overseas donors to American universities? Did they not know that many intellectuals in the United States trusted Al-Jazeera reporting more than any American, European, or Israeli source? And did they really think that the United States, NATO, or the Arab nations would really stand for a war of aggression against not just the Palestinian territories, which was a reasonable concern on its own, but against Jordan, Syria, Lebanon, Saudi Arabia, Kuwait, Iraq, and Egypt? Did Israel even have the population, let alone the army, to prosecute such a war? And, if all of that happened, could it sustain the war financially as the United States, Europe, the Arab nations, and even Russia locked Israel out of the global economy, expelled its diplomats, and seized its assets?

Not only had they not thought that through, but those realities didn't matter to them. They were so inundated with fear of the Zionist bogeyman that they couldn't think rationally when it came to anything related to Israel. Every Israeli, Jew, and American was a Zionist that sought Palestinian extermination, even if we weren't. There was no way I was going to attempt to change their minds. They lived in a completely alternate reality than the rest of us.

In Amman, I didn't see fear. I saw anger. A lot of it. Everywhere. While I was in Aqaba, the entire country took one day to boycott so-called Zionist businesses, such as Starbucks and McDonald's, to protest Israel's retaliation against Gaza and the United States' support for it. Fair enough; that was a legitimate socio-political act. In Amman, though, they took it a step further and boycotted these businesses outright. In my hostel, there was a sign stating, "This place does not welcome Zionists of anyone who supports the 'Israeli' Apartheid Regime," coupled with a list of businesses whose products we were prohibited for travellers to bring inside. It wasn't just food, either. L'Oreal, Carrefour, Tide, Hewlett Packard, Simens, Motorola, The North Face, Verizon, Patagonia, REI Co-op, and more composed the ever-expanding list of businesses accused of supporting the "genocide" in Gaza. I never tested their willingness to throw me out for my Verizon phone, Patagonia jacket, REI sandals, or Carrefour groceries, but it seemed bad business sense to kick travellers out for using standard travel gear.

There was anti-Israel graffiti and propaganda all over Amman. Israel was a "fake" country; only "Philistine" existed in their minds. From the river to the sea, Palestine would be free. Which river and which sea were questions I didn't want to ask because the natural follow-up question would have been, "So, then, what would happen to all of the Jews and non-Jewish Israelis that live there?" I knew the answer would have been that they were welcome to live in a Palestinian country, but I also knew that the neo-Nazi rhetoric I had heard would prevail instead of cooler heads. Retribution upon Jews would have resulted in a second Holocaust, and the "Zionist" regimes of the world would have no choice but to step in, just as they had in Bosnia, Kosovo, and Iraq and failed to do in Rwanda. The war the Jordanians and Palestinians feared, the one that would establish an Israel from the Nile to the Euphrates, would come to them not by Israel's actions but their own. They were just so blinded by anger and hatred that they couldn't see the long-term effects of their calls to end Israel's existence.

An Off-Ramp?

Was an off-ramp in this conflict even possible? I liked to believe that people and countries acted in their own best interest, but I knew that was not the case in this part of the world. That wasn't to disparage the region, but decades- or centuries-long national tensions, tribal feuds, and religious practices won out more often than legitimate, sustainable solutions to ideological conflict. Propaganda was more important than truth, power more important than political legitimacy, and winning was worth any hardship brought upon the people by their rulers.

As far as Israel was concerned, the country reached its "I've had it!" moment with the attack on October 7th. Hamas had ruled Gaza for almost twenty years. Instead of turning the Gaza Strip into a land of economic opportunity or investment, the regime dug up the water pipes to turn them into rockets to shoot into Israel. Israel demonstrated in its retaliation that Hamas was no longer going to be tolerated as it indiscriminately slaughtered Israeli citizens using illegitimate means of force to achieve its political ends. Israel had evacuated every Israeli from the Gaza Strip when Hamas took over governance in 2006, but Hamas continued its attacks while refusing to hold elections, feuding with the Palestinian Authority in the West Bank, and accepting terrorist finance and assistance from Iran and Hizballah in Lebanon. The de-facto Palestinian state of Gaza was actively demonstrating that the only outcome it would tolerate was the total obliteration of Israel, and Israel was no longer standing for it. Hamas had to be exterminated, just as Islamic State, al-Qa'ida, and Boko Haram had to be exterminated in other countries.

On the opposite side, Hamas was unyielding in its pursuit of a united Palestine. Their lands were "stolen" by the West to create Israel in the post-World War Two world, a condition imposed upon the United Kingdom in the Sykes-Picot Agreement when it was assigned the Mandate for Palestine in 1916. In the coming years, Israel instituted a settlement policy across the partition's boundaries which was largely seen as illegal, often using police and military force to oust Palestinians who lived there. Israel controlled trade, aid, and security for all of the Palestinian territories against the wishes and consent of the Palestinian people and, worse, the doctrine of Islam, where consenting to a Jewish state was to legitimise a religion which had heard the words of the prophet Muhammed and flatly rejected them. Further, Hamas would not consent to granting land or legitimacy to a government who interred children as terrorists and dropped entire apartment buildings in the pursuit of individual alleged terrorists.

Much to the detriment of the Palestinians, the surrounding Arab nations with any ability to shape the situation effectively washed their hands of the entire situation. Jordan had relinquished its claim to the West Bank, which Israel annexed in the wake of the Arab nations' spectacular failure in the Six-Day War. Egypt had built a wall along its border to Gaza and sent in the army to secure it because they were more concerned about terrorists slipping into northern Sinai than they were supporting the Palestinians against Israel. Hizballah in Lebanon hadn't given up its attacks against Israel, but it lacked the resources and firepower to cause any significant damage in Israel's underpopulated northern region, especially with the Coalition in Iraq and Syria targeting Hizballah's network as part of its overall security strategy. Worse for the Palestinians, the Arab countries, many of whom forcibly expelled Jews or set conditions so horrible that Jews were forced to flee for their lives, refused to accept Palestinians who wanted to escape the conflict in Gaza. Jordan and Egypt, where many ethnic Palestinians lived, denied Palestinians citizenship, effectively making them stateless persons.

Given all this and more, I found it difficult to believe that an off-ramp was possible. Each side saw its cause as the only righteous course of history, and no one was genuinely interested in finding a mutually acceptable end to the conflict. The Palestinian people in Gaza wouldn't rise against the terrorist regime, Hamas wouldn't hold elections it might lose, Israel wouldn't tolerate a terrorist state next door, and the surrounding countries wanted nothing to do with the conflict outside of lip service. In their retaliation (which after fifteen months may even have been called retribution), Israel steadily eroded international support for their war in Gaza, while no country with diplomatic ties and economic interests with the West would support Hamas.

Without a significant shift in the political and religious views on one or both sides of the conflict, the war would continue. Those Palestinians, Israelis, Jordanians, and businessmen who hadn't asked for the war would stay in the crossfire.

Reflection #4

"The Smartest American I Know" and Why We Need to Do Better

In Brisbane, I met a British guy named Will. When he heard I was American, he asked about the situation at the southwest border with Mexico. He thought there had been a sudden, massive change in migration, and the United States was suddenly under pressure from hundreds of thousands of illegal migrants. He was shocked to hear this wasn't new and that our border crisis, in its current form, was decades old. "We don't hear about that in the UK," he told me. "We only know what CNN tells us."

Over the next hour, Will and I discussed a host of political and social issues. I was no stranger to this conversation, having had it on hostel couches throughout my travels. What made this conversation different was Will's habit of asking questions rather than making points. "What about [insert government policy or social issue here]?" What should my response have been? To me, my obligation was to explain the totality of the issue before offering my opinion; that explanation included criticisms, sometimes harsh ones, of both sides of the issue. I thought I was having a regular political discussion with someone from another country, but Will saw it as something much more. This was the most honest, thorough, informative conversation he had with an American on issues which weren't discussed in the United Kingdom.

"You're the smartest American I know," he said at the end of our conversation. He intended it as a compliment, and I certainly took it as such, but I also found his compliment dismaying. I didn't have any special knowledge or insight on any given topic (except for security issues). I was just a normal guy who learned about the world, explored political and social issues, and made informed decisions and assessments. It hadn't occurred to me as a traveller how rare that type off discussion was. It sat with me as a grave indicator of just how much influence the United States had lost in recent years, and why Americans needed to do better when it came to discussing our policies and opinions, both at home at abroad.

America's Place in the World

The United States was the most influential, most powerful country in the world. It stood as a pillar of democracy, a beacon of light for oppressed peoples around the globe, and a defender of the weak. Our number one export wasn't oil, cars, or any other tangible good but physical, financial, and political security. Without the United States, even the most powerful of Western democracies would be forced to bend to Russia, China's, or even Iran's will, to say nothing of terrorists, human smuggling organisations, corrupt financial institutions, and corporate espionage. The United States may have been a reluctant participant in World War I and forced into World War II, but it emerged as the world's leader in the aftermath. The Soviet Union tried to provide an alternative to democracy and capitalism, but it ultimately collapsed under the weight of its citizens' demands for human rights, representative governments, and financial freedom.

Even with our domestic political turmoil, the world continued to look to the United States for leadership and strength. How we handled mass migration translated to Europe, access to American financial markets and banking systems drove international business decisions, and the tone and timbre of our political discourse influenced political parties worldwide. What we did, the world emulated, or at least tried to.

"Without the United States, we have to turn to China, and nobody wants that," an Australian told me in Pamplona, "and your country needs to figure its s*** out." He was referring to the Biden administration's perceived crackdown on free speech, political opponents, the values the United States purported to uphold, and the extreme focus on identity politics that was separating our "melting pot" of a country into its individual ingredients. Whether or not these perceptions were real didn't matter; the fact that these issues were even a mainstream political discussion was causing substantial upheaval in the developed world and eroding confidence in America's ability to defend itself and ensure its own political future, let alone anyone else's. We were cracking the door open for the likes of China, Russia, and Iran to provide alternatives to the current order in countries far beyond our borders. Right, wrong, or indifferent, that was the role the United States played on the international stage, and how we played that role could determine the future of governments worldwide for years and decades to come.

The Unipolar Moment Has Passed

The world was once divided between democracy and communism, capitalists and socialists, and that division united Americans and rallied democratic countries around us to defeat the Red Giant. There were plenty of missteps, like Iran-Contra, the Bay of Pigs, and the Vietnam War, but we never strayed from the path of protecting the world from the worker's revolution that cost hundreds of millions of lives. We made quantum leaps in technology, spearheading space exploration, inventing computers, synthesising vaccines, and bringing the internet into existence; we started international aid programmes to combat food shortages and disease; and we intervened in genocides and conflicts to protect the marginalised and persecuted. Those endeavours ultimately caused the Iron Curtain to fall, freedom to sweep across the world, and communism to recede to just five countries. The United States became the only force in the world whose voice, power, and influence could raise and cripple social movements and governments, a place of prestige we occupied for nearly thirty years.

That unipolar moment has passed. The United States, through its actions and the actions of others, lost its dominance in the world. True, no other country could compete with the United States on the entire international stage, but the world was no longer one international stage divided between democracy and communism; it was now a regionalised world, where Muslim values dominated the Middle East, China increasingly controlled the Indo-Pacific, impoverished African migrants disrupted European societal norms, and Mexican drug cartels effectively controlled Central American borders and governments. That is not to say that American influence had been erased, but it was no longer the monolithic behemoth it once was. Instead, we were fighting a multi-front diplomatic conflict where each front differed entirely from the others. We were in a situation where, for example, the transgender issue had Europe criticising us for not being progressive and accepting enough as a matter of societal compassion and, simultaneously, the Indo-Pacific laughing at us for even considering that men and women weren't inherently, intrinsically, undisputably different. Within three months, a French woman told me, "Europe is laughing at you for having this problem, because who cares? It's just a toilet!" and a Malaysian man told me, "We are laughing at you over here! Your country actually thinks these things? We need you to get back to reality so we can focus on the real issues!"

The unipolar moment had passed, and America no longer possessed the independent, internationally accepted ability to set a single policy for the world. We would have to compete in regional affairs using regional values if we ever wanted to keep our place as the dominant political force in the world.

Americans Increasingly Don't Understand the World

It is an unfortunate statement, but Americans, both individual citizens and our government entities, now increasingly fail to grasp the realities of the world in which we live. It was entirely foreign to us that Ukrainian citizens in Crimea and the Donbas region welcomed Russian intervention, protection, and annexation. In our view, that was undemocratic and a crime of aggression on Russia's part, but it wasn't that simple. You would be hard-pressed to find an everyday American who knew why Crimea was a part of Ukraine in the first place or that the Russian empire traced its roots back to Kyiv, which was in modern-day Ukraine. It was also foreign that countries like Sweden and Denmark had highly-restrictive immigration policies. If they were true democracies, why wouldn't they welcome the downtrodden and poor into their societies? The world had changed a lot in thirty years. Germany, as a unified country, had only existed since the fall of the Soviet Union; the European Union, a supranational source of regulation and economic control across twenty-six countries, was younger than me; and the centre of gravity for transnational terrorism shifted from Libya to Afghanistan to Iraq. Islamic leaders both ruled over countries with an iron fist and ushered in the Arab Spring. With all of these changes, it was incumbent upon Americans, if we hoped to hold our place in the world, to learn about such events, what caused them, what their friction points were, and why some people, even a majority of people in some countries, were opposed to the very idea of democracy, freedom of religion, open immigration, or Western intervention.

In my travels, finding an American who could talk intelligently about issues on which they held staunch opinions was difficult. They wanted open borders, but failed to recognise the strain those border policies had on social institutions and public order; they wanted the United States to pull its military out of places like Poland, Germany, Iraq, and Japan without regard for the instability that would cause; the vast majority didn't even know that the United States invaded Mexico in the 1800s because the Mexican government nullified the Texian treaty with Santa Anna establishing Texas's borders. It was unfathomable that Muslim women *wanted* to wear a headscarf as a part of their religious practice, that the most successful periods in Russia's history were when they were led by a single strongman-type leader, or that Southeast and Central Asian nations weren't overly concerned about climate change. The "gender apartheid" in the Middle Eastern and African world was a legitimate issue where women were systematically oppressed, silenced, and forced to do as their men commanded, but, as big of a problem as this was, where the next meal, water, medicine, or war was coming from was bigger still. There were more pressing matters to address, and vast cultural differences made almost impossible for an outsider to understand, let alone accept.

But did we even try? Were Americans known as people who wanted to seek, learn, and understand foreign cultures without judgement? Were we even capable of passive participation in cultural practices that violated our own values? My observation was that we were not. As a society, we had become narrow-minded idealogues which turned other nations off, and sometimes caused them to actively seek alternative voices and influences. In hostels across the globe, I encountered more Americans that wanted to change the world to our narrow view rather than accept that the American way of thinking and behaving was no longer the only way.

Inform, Not Debate

As a country, the United States was accustomed to being "right." Our defence policy was the "right" policy, our War on Terror was "right," and our views on the LGBTQ community were the "right" views. The consequence? We didn't take into account the other side of the argument. Why was the War on Terror good *and* bad? Why were LGBTQ discussions necessary *and* widely opposed? Why were American security exports a force for good *and* instability? Americans no longer learned both sides of an issue; we were demagogues willing to die on our political hills. Mass migration was either good or bad; instituting religious laws either violated or safeguarded human rights; there was no in-between. This wasn't a question of nuance; it was a question of understanding.

My favourite conversation to illustrate this point was about the wall President Trump wanted to build across the southern border. To the political left, the wall was racist. To the political right, it was an indisputably necessary security precaution. I was neutral on the issue, which inflamed passions on both sides. I was a racist bigot who didn't care about American security. But why? There were plenty of instances where walls worked, in Turkey, China, Iraq, and Israel, to name a few, and the southern border needed something to stem the flow of illegal border crossings. At the same time, a wall was a triage solution which could cut the natural flow of goods and services across border communities, and a wall didn't fix the undeniably broken American immigration system. Most Americans couldn't articulate both sides of this argument, nor any other political or social issue.

That inability eroded America's influence in the world. If we were truly pillars of democracy and beacons of light, shouldn't travellers be unofficial ambassadors for our country? Our military, Peace Corps, and aid organisations didn't have a substantial, regular presence in Vietnam, Cambodia, Morocco, Spain, Indonesia, or Australia, but our travelling public did. Our youth encountered people from across the world and were often the only interactions with Americans other cultures would have. Should we waste that valuable influence spreading one-sided values and talking points, or should we use that influence to inform the world of our countries' differing views on a subject? Should we spend our time debating the legitimacy of another person's culture and beliefs, or should we explain how those cultures and beliefs both integrated or clashed with our own? I found my best course of action in any political conversation was to take the neutral stance, despite my moderately-conservative values, not to be wishy-washy or people-pleasing, but because that was the best way to open a critical dialogue. I spent more time discussing the different facets of an issue than I did arguing for my own personal beliefs, and I found that opened more doors, made stronger connections, and did more for American influence than the idealogues who pushed their own political and social views on others.

Our Division Has Cascading Effects

Americans do not understand the position we hold in the world. During the Clinton administration, European North Atlantic Treaty Organisation (NATO) members wanted greater separation from the United States and to seek their own, independent path. Then-Secretary of the State Madeline Albright declared that there would be "no decoupling of European defence structures from NATO, no duplication of NATO capabilities, and no discrimination against non-EU NATO members." In essence, the United States and Europe were bound together by an unbreakable vow. For twenty years, that speech put an end to any notion of independent European security initiatives and intimately intertwined the American and European political and social landscapes. If Europe tried to shed its American partner, the consequences could be dire and may even have cracked the very foundations of European democracies and independence.

That was no longer the case. America's division fractured our country's foundation. The courts, our law enforcement agencies, the White House, our legislature, every institution designed to protect Americans' God-given and inalienable rights codified in our constitution were under attack and highly distrusted. You were either for or against the police, for or against the Supreme Court, for or against the LGBTQ community, for or against the military, for or against our alliance with Europe, for or against multiculturalism or homogeny. There was no in-between, and there was no debate. We cracked our own foundation, and there was now legitimate concern that the United States may not be a reliable, lasting partner. In ten years, we joined, left, joined again, and left again the Paris Climate Accords. In those same ten years, we reduced our military to the smallest it had been in decades only to increase it again a few years later, then announce a series of cuts that would see a net defence budget decrease of thirty-five percent over five years. Were those the actions of a reliable political partner? Were the congressmen, presidents, and voters who mandated these policy swings people our partners could rely on?

The United States' social and political divisions caused turmoil in the world. If Europe couldn't rely on our agreements with them to last longer than a single presidential term, they would have to decouple their security and political interests to be capable of withstanding the threat from Russia and China. If Europe couldn't rely on our energy exports, there were few alternatives to importing oil and gas from Russia, regardless of how the Europeans felt about Putin's war in Ukraine. If Australia couldn't rely on consistent trade with the United States, the Chinese would muscle into their industrial base, and Australia wouldn't have much choice but to accept them. If our obsession with identity politics isolated our Middle Eastern partners, who could they turn to for trade and security guarantees where they wouldn't have to sacrifice their religious beliefs and cultural practices?

Americans must do better. We must recognise that our waning influence in the world is not a source of good or democracy but a source of erosion and conflict. We must understand that our way is not the only way; our beliefs are not the only beliefs, nor are they accepted by billions of people worldwide. Our rhetoric, policies, and alliances must be built on mutual respect and understanding. We don't have to agree with everyone we meet, but we must keep an open dialogue going. That dialogue may yield eventual, natural change in other countries and cultures, or it may not, but we have to recognise that our mutual interests far outweigh our particular differences. Sure, that is ultimately a governmental function, but we, as a collective of individuals, control the direction our country takes, and we desperately need to get back on track, not for our own sake, but for the world's.

Reflection #5

Talking Politics with Fellow Travelers

Many things unite people across the world, but that thing is politics more than anything else in today's time. Over the past several decades, global value chains, trade agreements, joint-immigration enforcement, military operations, supranational institutions, and more have increasingly governed our lives. For travellers, cultural differences, visa and immigration enforcement, and security policies were issues that affected everyday life as we moved about the world. Some of us had easier travel than others, while others had a harder time accepting common cultural practices codified in law.

Being affected by politics at every turn, it was no surprise that hostel conversations inevitably turned to political and social issues in our interconnected world. In a time when society was inundated with political pundits and there were exactly two things you didn't bring up at family dinner (religion and politics), young people on the road were starved for legitimate civil discourse about the issues they cared about. When I first started travelling, conversations with other travellers revolved primarily around my plans and goals for my year around the world. As I progressed in my journey, those conversations shifted to my observations, things I had learned, and my opinions on certain parts of the world now that I had been there. Travellers were genuinely curious, and talking politics with a diverse group of people became as much a skill as it was a forbidden topic around the table.

Everything is Political

A friend once told me that all religion was political. At first, I disagreed with him, and we had it out a few times over that notion. I surely didn't believe that my own faith was a political force, but he made a lot of good points when he turned the conversation away from the personal issue of Christianity and the professional issue of Islam. There were theologies across the Middle East who based their laws on the Quran. Islamist extremists hated man-made laws and democracy, because the only laws and the only authority that mattered were those of Allah. In our own country, the justice system was colliding with certain Islamic religious beliefs, like the subservience of women and honour killings. Was that not a political force? Then he turned the attention to Christianity. Who were the main proponents for anti-abortion policies and what was their justification? Who were the main supporters of Israel and why? Was it not a common refrain that our country was founded on Judeo-Christian values, and did we not declare that our civil rights were given by our Creator? I had to admit, he had a point. As much as I didn't see it that way or want to believe it, religion was a political force.

It was not just religion, though. It was everything. In Northern Ireland, asking someone about their Catholic faith and family heritage was a political conversation. In Barcelona, inquiring about the severe pickpocketing problem inevitably turned into a debate about trans-Saharan migration. Buying Starbucks in Jordan was an overt statement of your support for a Zionist regime in Israel and Palestine. The anti-bullfighting movement took to the courts and the legislatures in Spain, Mexico, and Colombia in seeking to end a centuries-long cultural practice, while in France, members of parliament refused to take up the issue because they would be voted out of office either way. In London, praying silently in your head outside of an abortion clinic was a political issue governed by Parliament and the courts, not the leaders of the Anglican or Catholic churches. Funnily, my home town once had a run-off school board election where the issue wasn't Republican versus Democrat, but Baptist versus Methodist. My friend was right, but only partially so. It wasn't just that all religion was political; everything in today's world was political.

For this reason, hostel couches often turned to deep, philosophical debates about the viability of one political issue or another. That wasn't to say that travellers sought political discord - far from it, I would think - but young men and women, especially in Generation Z, maintained strong opinions on anything and everything. In their travels, they wanted to hear from others about their views on a given topic and would become an evangelist for their beliefs. Sometimes, those conversations remained respectful and courteous; sometimes, they turned adversarial. Such was the nature of having a meaningful conversation with people of differing views. I loved these conversations (mostly), as how strongly one advocated their beliefs and, more importantly, how adept they were at responding to counterarguments and different, equally-valid opinions on the subject, revealed someone's true nature.

Just my being American turned into a political conversation more often than not. A simple, "Where are you from?" turned into debates over the validity of the Trump or Biden presidencies once I said I was American. In a casual conversation with a German girl of Moroccan descent, I mentioned that I used to be a police officer. She immediately fired back with, "Did you shoot any black people?" Just my personal history started a political debate about American policing that she, as a European, simply couldn't understand, which ultimately resulted in my being called "a dumb redneck," which, itself, was a political identity in the United States these days as us rednecks were "clinging to our gods and our guns" (in the words of Hilary Clinton).

In the travel world, where people from all over the globe gathered together willingly in hostels, pubs, cenotes, and tours, everything was political.

✳   ✳   ✳

Reading the Room

Just because everything was political didn't mean that everything needed to be discussed with everyone. During my military career, I coined a phrase to describe my conversations with people who argued fervently without having foundational knowledge of a subject: "They know far too much for knowing far too little." We all fell into that trap; I certainly did more than once in life. That was a sort of rite of passage for young people in today's world. Unfortunately, young people who knew far too much for knowing far too little were also the most vocal in their opinions, and I was not someone who could let someone with an air of superiority or a loud voice spout off their false claims.

Over the course of twelve months in hostels on five continents, I had to learn a valuable skill when it came to those people: reading the room. Despite my relatively successful professional career in the security world, I never developed that skill. In a world of terrorists, cartels, and criminals, politely telling someone that they were wrong, gently guiding them to the correct information, or letting them believe in falsehoods was not something I could abide. We had a mission; we needed accurate information and valid assessments, and anyone who was flat-out wrong on the facts of the situation needed to be corrected immediately. The last thing we needed was for commanders, policymakers, and corporate executives to make high-impact, often political security decisions based on inaccurate information because we were too soft or polite to correct someone with a microphone.

Common area conversations over cards and tequila weren't going to yield high-impact decisions of any kind. Life didn't literally hang in the balance, nor did the fate of millions of taxpayer or shareholder dollars. Many people, like Tahli (from Brisbane), Jack (from the United Kingdom), Louise (from France), and Emily (from Canada), held different opinions than I did on a number of topics. Despite our differences though, we were able to have respectful, mutually-beneficial conversations on things that inflamed primal passions, like abortion, the conflict in Gaza, transgender issues, and American intervention in the Middle East. Within minutes of the conversation beginning, it was clear that they were willing to have a legitimate discussion.

Others, like the aforementioned German girl, Many (from Mexico), and my Jordanian hosts in Aqaba, were not so willing. They often made that clear from the beginning with intentionally insulting statements. Many told me, "Don't tell people you're American. Tell them you're from Canada or something. Nobody likes Americans anymore." He was a staunch anti-Trump Mexican, which was understandable, but he wasn't willing to discuss the specifics while respecting my opinion. Rather than debate him, I moved these conversations into neutral political territory before trying to move him to a different subject. Many was never going to understand an alternative viewpoint, because he didn't *want* to understand an alternative viewpoint. The same was true of the Jordanians who told me that the United States supported an Israel from the Nile to the Euphrates. There was no way to rationally explain how ridiculous that sentiment was and have them listen. Instead, I had to let them rant about their beliefs. Even people back home said things like, "They don't like our freedom," when talking not about the terrorists in the Middle East but the French people. Twenty years of anti-French sentiment in certain circles blinded them to the realities of the world, and no amount of experience or respect they had for me would convince them otherwise.

It was best just to let them talk. Some people didn't want to change their minds. The Turks would always hate the Kurds, the Jordanians would always be in ideological conflict with Israelis, and those who were opposed to American interventionism and security influence always would be. The trick was to read the room early to avoid getting drawn into long conversations that would go nowhere.

Culture Matters

When discussing political issues with fellow travellers or locals, it was essential to understand that our cultures differed. It wasn't just the attitude towards women, our non-belief in Islam, or our attitude towards Spain in Morocco that separated Jo and me from Moroccans ideologically; their entire worldview was shaped by a culture that was entirely foreign to us. The Kurds, having endured centuries of fighting for their very survival, welcomed Western influence, military support, and money (importantly, money) into their cities, but that didn't mean they agreed with the growing bourgeois view of polyamorous marriages, standards of police behaviour, or federalism over tribalism. The Vietnamese, who revered Ho Chi Minh and had Draconian border policies, would never agree with prevailing Western views of communism, economic priorities, or migration.

These were the facts of life in the world. Despite the West's dominance on the international stage, we weren't the only players. At the United Nations, Morocco, Iraq, and Vietnam had little pull over the United States, United Kingdom, or France (all permanent members of the Security Council), but inside their borders, they were free to do, believe, and behave as their cultures and values saw fit. Their people, in choosing to travel or immigrate to other countries, carried those values and beliefs with them wherever they went. That was difficult for Westerners to understand. For example, when Jo was trying solid perfume in Morocco, and the vendor asked my permission to touch her. He wasn't trying to be oppressive towards *her*; he was trying to be respectful towards *us* in his cultural way. He wasn't going to touch another man's woman without asking that man first, just as he wouldn't touch another woman out of respect for his wife. Western women, however, were often aghast that Jo would subserviate herself to me in this manner. To us, men and women were equal and independent, and *any* practice that placed men above women was wrong. Jo and I didn't take it that way, nor should we have, but most Westerners, especially young women, would not accept that it was a respectful cultural practice, not necessarily an oppressive one.

Understanding these cultural differences was crucial when discussing politics with travellers and locals. Otherwise, you would end up in a meaningless debate where both sides talked past each other. Ashamedly, the "civilised" Western world was the worst at understanding this, whereas the Third World was far more understanding of Western practices when explaining why they weren't socially acceptable in their countries. Us "tolerant," "inclusive" Westerners could learn something from the "oppressive," "backwards" Third World.

Jack Rogers

Dialogue, not Debate

In my country, it was almost impossible to have civilised conversations about political and social issues. The battle lines were drawn on every issue; you were a baby killer or a sexual enslaver of women, a communist or a fascist, a conspiracy nut or a government shill. In the news media, the phrases "what the [insert name of the other side here] don't understand is..." and "what they want is..." were two of the most overused phrases in our political discourse as each side sought not just to communicate their ideas and positions but to also define their opponents' without their presence or input. Rational dialogue on socio-political issues, which included everything from faith to family to fiscal responsibility, had become impossible as people sought to be right more than they sought to understand.

As a traveller, and especially as an American, inducing dialogue was far more important that starting a debate. By no means was every side of an issue valid, even under the guise of cultural differences, but those clear moral issues were fewer in number than many would like to believe. Most of them revolved around murder, sexual exploitation, slavery, torture, genocide, and other true crimes against humanity. Despite what social media activists and television pundits would have us believe, however, most issues in the world didn't rise to that level, and we needed to stop acting like every different perspective was an aberration unworthy of public discussion. Most issues, like socialised healthcare, immigration and border security policy, the militarisation of the police, military interventionism, and the role of government and parents in education, while important, were simply not worth the heartache, anger, and soiled friendships they brought. I wasn't a "dumb redneck" for saying I didn't think renaming Americans as Estados Unidense, Yankees, or US-Americans was ridiculous any more than someone who thought Basque independence from Spain and France was a complete and total afront to Spanish and French identity. If we spent more time listening to understand and communicate rather than listening to respond or label, our political discourse would improve 100 times over, and social tensions would calm to levels that didn't threaten to disrupt friendships, governments, and alliances.

As a traveller, that was an important lesson I tried to bring into every political conversation, and one which I had to learn myself. I first started learning the difference between dialogue and debate in Dublin, where a man who worked with American companies wanted to discuss the 2020 election without allowing me to finish a sentence. His friends of twenty years later told me that was how every conversation with him went. He didn't care about my views; he only wanted to tell the world his. From then on, I sought to listen to understand and speak to communicate. Nobody would be convinced by my emotions or passionate defence of my ideas, but they would be convinced by my respect for their position (or at least their right to communicate it) and calm explanations of what I believed in and why. Once I learned that lesson, I found myself engaged in long conversations about abortion issues, the conflicts in Gaza and Northern Ireland, the southern border and mass migration, and even bullfighting, where at the end of the discussion, we would part ways saying how great of a talk it was and how we wished we could have these sorts of civil discussions back home.

Starved for Civil Discourse

Young people were starved for civil discourse, especially in the West. Everything in their lives was political, and they were some of the most politically active people in democratic countries. That didn't mean they voted en masse; in fact, the youngest voter demographics turned out to vote less than their older counterparts. What that did mean was they marched, protested, and attended rallies in large numbers over issues which they held in high regard. Hundreds of thousands, maybe even millions, of young people marched in support of Palestinians across the world after October 7th, university students across the West protested college administrations' policies during the 2020 George Floyd protests, and the Occupy Wall Street movement relied on young people to take to the streets. During the 2024 presidential election (which happened just after my year of travel ended), Turning Point USA, an "organization whose mission is to identify, educate, train, and organize students to promote freedom" (according to its website), was primarily responsible for driving voter turnout in favour of the Republican candidate. Anyone who thought young people were apolitical was sorely mistaken.

But they were starved for civil discourse. Everything about their lives was political, but between the legacy media, social media, and poor examples in their legislatures, young people lacked the ability and opportunity to have intellectual, civil discourse about political issues. They were entrenched in the battle lines that were drawn for them, but they didn't necessarily like it. Sonny, a European I met in Turkey, routinely messaged me after our first meeting to ask about political events in the United States and my opinion on various current affairs. Germans had a hard time understanding why the conservative parties gained ground in every election, and civil conversations with an outside observer about German politics gave them insight they didn't get at home. I even discussed my opposition to transgender people serving in the military *with a transgender person* and brought them over to my view simply by having a civil conversation not fuelled by emotion, religious zealotry, or inflammatory rhetoric. That person asked, "Why can't your president explain it like that?" Great question.

Young people lived in a world where politics infected every part of their lives. While this wasn't their doing, it was how they grew up, and the lack of good examples of how to handle that reality manifested itself in impassioned pleas, dramatic political activism, and little opportunity to learn and discuss the issues which they cared about in a civil, productive manner. They were starved for civil discourse, and it shouldn't take conversations on hostel couches in foreign countries for them to finally experience a positive, productive, respectful conversation about the state of the world.

Reflection #6

Limiting Factors: Dealing with Barriers to Travel

Travelling the world was not without its friction points. As fun and life-changing as long-term travel was, it came with a host of barriers most people never concerned themselves with in their everyday lives. A plane ticket was expensive, but it was a standard cost of planning an annual vacation, and most vacations for people I knew were to places that were friendly to the United States. Mexico, Australia, Bali, the Dominican Republic, and Europe were all common vacation hotspots where American passports were welcomed without much of a bureaucratic two-step. We were all friends (or, at least, our money was all friendly), and we would have an entire year to save up for the next two-week vacation.

Long-term travel was different. Jo and I didn't save our money for a year for a two-week vacation; we saved for ten months for a trip of an undetermined length of time to unspecified places that would cost an unknown amount of money. During our travels, we charged headfirst into countries and situations and occasionally slammed hard into rock-solid barriers to whatever we were trying to do. We were free agents in life, able to go anywhere and do anything, or so we thought until we confronted barriers we had never encountered before. These barriers weren't always insurmountable, but we had a lot to learn when it came to navigating our way through constantly changing legal, cultural, and financial situations as we traversed the globe.

Citizenship

At my security firm, one of the things I worked on was transnational travel issues. There, I learned one of the most vital aspects of a traveller, regardless of whether it was for business, leisure, or nefarious purposes, was their citizenship. A person's citizenship determined which doors were open and which doors were closed, and some citizenships were worth more than others, sometimes with a specific dollar amount attached. As an American, I didn't have to concern myself with these citizenship issues. The blue American passport basically guaranteed entry to every country. Sometimes I had to get a visa in advance, but that was more of a formality than it was a restriction. Had I wanted to, as an American, I could have gotten a visa on arrival at Baghdad International Airport. If I wanted to travel to Iran, a country on the United States' diplomatic blacklist, I could have with a government-approved, guided tour. I was fortunate to have such access across the world, and often times internal security checkpoints would see my blue passport and simply move on without checking it.

Sasha, a friend I met along the way, was not so fortunate. He was an American citizen, so that passport afforded him the same access as me; however, he was also a Belarusian citizen. With the War in Ukraine in full swing and Belarus being staunch allies with Russia, Sasha had very real concerns about travelling places on favourable diplomatic terms with Russia and Belarus. He didn't want to be detained and sent to Eastern Europe to fight on the side of a war he didn't believe in. Israeli citizens, too, were barred from entry into many countries because those countries didn't recognise Israel as a sovereign country. Palestinians were in a bind, as their passports were considered only as identity documents in many countries, not passports or citizenship documents, so they were subject not just to an inability to travel but to harassment from government officials.

Most people never realised how fortunate we were as Americans on a number of levels. Having nearly unrestricted access to the entire world was one of those levels. I would never have to go to a Spanish consulate or embassy to apply for a visa to run with the bulls in Pamplona. I could just go. Meanwhile, someone from Egypt, Belize, or India needed to demonstrate they had financial means, provide an itinerary and the address where they were staying, and more. I had never been one to assert any sort of privilege, but being an American was the greatest privilege one could have as a traveller.

Past Travel

As Americans, it was hard to imagine discriminating against people based on their papers. After all, that was something Nazi Germany or Communist Russia did. In other parts of the world, though, that was the norm. One of the most significant discriminators was your travel history, which was contained in the stamps and electronic chip in your passport. Bi-lateral diplomatic ties certainly extended beyond the bi-lateral participants.

For example, Vietnam refused to stamp a passport where a Chinese visa existed, and outright refused to stamp Chinese passports altogether. Why? Because of a territorial dispute in the South China Sea. Both China and Vietnam claimed a certain island chain, and China included a map where the chain belonged to China in their passports and on their visas. For Vietnam to place a permanent visa in a book which placed those islands under Chinese control amounted to a tacit concession in a decades-long diplomatic dispute. Vietnam wasn't obstinate about this; they simply provided a non-attachable visa rather than attach one to a passport permanently.

Israel was a country where travel had to be carefully planned. Over a dozen countries, including Bangladesh, Kuwait, and Iraq, all places travellers may visit, refused entry to anyone with an Israeli stamp in their passport. Lebanon's laws subjected anyone with an Israeli stamp in their passport to arrest. Israel instituted a policy of issuing unattached visas to travellers to alleviate these countries' laws. Still, that system wasn't foolproof, so much so that American government officials were issued two passports: one for an Israeli stamp and one to keep "sterile." When planning The Great Gallivanting, Jo and I knew we wanted to be in Israel for Christmas, but that meant making serious decisions about our itinerary to be sure we wouldn't run into problems in Iraq (although, after October 7th, that issue was moot).

Health

During the COVID-19 pandemic, the world was introduced to health-related travel restrictions. As Americans, we were legally required to be vaccinated against a host of communicable diseases as children, so most countries didn't concern themselves with our vaccine cards. However, with COVID-19, everyone had to show proof of vaccination or a negative infection test to cross borders and board planes. Many in the United States viewed this as a violation of our constitutional rights, but that was not how the international community viewed things. Countries had a vested interest in prioritising the health of their citizens above all else.

Some countries required additional vaccines. When I was in the Sahara, I had to provide proof of a yellow fever vaccine, a disease that was extremely common across Africa and South America. A polio meningitis vaccine was required to travel to Saudi Arabia during the Hajj. While these weren't extreme barriers to travel, they were important ones because you would be refused entry upon arrival and returned to whence you came. At best, it was an expensive plane ticket. At worst, they could mark you as a deported person, at which point visa applications to places like Egypt, Turkey, and Australia could get complicated.

Medicines mattered, too. In the West, we didn't concern ourselves much with non-narcotic medicines. Antidepressants were prescribed by doctors, but were mostly uncontrolled/unscheduled, as were things like sleeping pills, anti-diarrheal tablets, and allergy medication. However, in places like the United Arab Emirates, you could be arrested on drug trafficking charges for a list off more than 300 medicines, including melatonin, a naturally-occurring chemical in our bodies. Saudi Arabia, too, was strict about prescribed drugs. While the Saudis mostly didn't restrict travellers from entering the country if they had medicines prescribed in the West that couldn't be legally obtained in Saudi Arabia, they did restrict the quantities you could have to thirty days or the duration of your stay, whichever was less. For a trip around the world, that meant crossing Saudi Arabia off the list, as I had a year's worth of everything. Even in Australia and New Zealand, I had to undergo additional questioning about my medication and why it was prescribed. Intrusive? Maybe. Necessary for their own security? Possibly. Did I have a choice in the matter? Absolutely not.

Money

The single, most significant barrier to travel has always been money. For almost ten years before leaving on The Great Gallivanting, I watched YouTubers and travel vloggers talk about their travels, read blogs and newsletters from famous world travellers, and got hooked on real-life adventurers' stories. Money never seemed to be an issue for them as they jetted around the world. Of course, they had a source of income: their travels. The vloggers had sponsorship deals and enough views to monetise their channels, newsletters from authors had advertisers and subscription revenue, and the world's greatest adventurers all had some sort of financial backing, be it a government-funded expedition in centuries gone by or pre-negotiated book deals in today's world. I, like most people, had none of those.

My only saving grace when it came to travelling the world was my security firm job, where I was afforded the opportunity to make six figures in USD a year. While in the military, I set my retirement and emergency funds in the direction I wanted them, so while at my security firm, I aimed at a new goal: a long-term travel fund. The six figures weren't enough in and of themselves, and I carefully tailored my lifestyle to save money to support leaving everything behind.

While travelling, though, I learned a new lesson: money dictated everything. Some costs were hefty, like airline tickets and Eurail passes, but necessary, while others were outright extortionate, like taxis in North Africa, Jordan, and Mexico. It didn't matter that Jo and I had a relatively large daily budget (especially for travellers); some of the extortionate costs could really kill our finances. Even everyday costs, like food in Germany and accommodations in Australia, challenged our finances to a breaking point. In some places, we just gave up on the budget. We didn't go crazy, but in Dublin, Rome, and Melbourne, it was just too crushing to live on our allotted funds. It really made me wonder how travellers on smaller budgets than ours (which was most of them) could make it.

On top of that, must-see experiences like the Basilica de la Sagrada Familia in Barcelona, the Colosseum in Rome, and the Australia Zoo in Queensland only compounded the financial situation. Could we really travel across the world just to forego these world-renowned sites because of money? Jo's position was that we shouldn't, and I reluctantly had to agree with her. Who knew when the next time we could afford the time, flights, and budget to travel to Australia would be? Those costs were already paid, and not going to places we had always dreamed of seeing because of the daily budget didn't seem right.

Dealing With Barriers

Jo and I were fortunate that these barriers to travel were surmountable for us. That was not the case for many travellers. Luka, from Sevilla, would never have been able to go to a bullfight in Spain had Jo and I not already had the rental car, and even then, he was making serious financial decisions in paying for the ticket and the Michelin-Star meal we stumbled into. The rental car was a heftier expense for Jo and me than we would have liked. Still, we could make it pencil out over the coming weeks. Sasha had concerns about being deported for military service in a foreign conflict, which wasn't unheard of in the international travel world. In contrast, my biggest concern was being recalled back to active duty in the United States. At least I would have been fighting for my own country's interest and not some third party's.

As far as money was concerned, it came down to discipline, and Jo and I not-so-occasionally had days where we only did free things (outside of meals) to recoup some costs on major, unexpected expenses. Others we met along the way, like

Michaela in Galway, took time off to volunteer at a hostel to prolong their travels with a free bed. That was one reason the volunteers in Tulum were there for so long. Two-foot drive became the default in many places to avoid taxi fares; I could have taken a taxi from my hostel to central Aqaba, but walking was free.

Unfortunately, I was the limiting factor when it came to health. I was taking medicine for issues from my military days that simply wasn't allowed in large swaths of the Muslim world. As much as I wanted to visit Oman, the United Aram Emirates, Saudi Arabia, and Qatar, that wasn't an option for me and, as an extension, Jo. It sucked knowing that I was the reason she had to cross these countries off her list, but I had to have my medication and preferred to stay out of Emirate jail. It wasn't just the Arabian Peninsula, either, as the Egyptians almost confiscated my medication and pill splitter on my way out of the country. It was a real downer to know that, for reasons far outside of my control (some of them not even based in medicine, but in regional religious practices), I couldn't travel my favourite part of the world, but, as I have said many times in these pages, c'est la vie.

Really, though, these limiting factors weren't a major problem for us American passport holders. Having the privilege of being born in the world's most influential, most powerful country meant that we could overcome most barriers without substantial headache. Our American passports would keep us out of most arbitrary trouble, and we could get to most countries without much hassle. Govand, in Iraq, even told me that I could easily travel the region by myself as an American, as the Asayish knew the American passport and wouldn't bother me. The Iranian-aligned militia groups would probably leave me alone, too, to avoid a multi-polar diplomatic conflict and retribution from the United States military. The Europeans paid ransoms for their citizens; the United States launched raids with Navy SEALs, Delta Force, and AC-130 gunships raining artillery from the sky.

Talk about privilege.

Reflection #7

Exhaustion: Wearing on the Mind and Body

Exhaustion was a real problem on the road, especially if you weren't prepared for it. Travel vloggers and YouTubers rarely discussed travel burnout and how to handle loneliness, stress, and fatigue on their once-in-a-lifetime world tours. Confronting exhaustion felt, more often than not, like failure, not a natural part of life, especially if it hit at the exact moment I was heading for a city I wanted to explore. In my first year of travel, I learned a lot about mental fatigue and exhaustion. The pressure to make every day count with my limited time on the road (relative to the rest of my professional life) was real and mounted increasingly as I travelled through cities people back home didn't even know were worth visiting or saw sights I never imagined still existed. More than once, I confronted exhaustion head-on as I tried to fight through it. More than once, I failed, but every time, I learned something new about handling the natural wear, tear, and toll full-time gallivanting across the world took on me physically, mentally, and emotionally.

Exhaustion Will Take You Down

My first true experience with exhaustion during Jo's and my travels was in Malaga, Spain, a few days before we flew to Germany. We had been running hard the past two months, and it finally caught up to me in the form of a massive migraine. I was no stranger to migraines due to a concussion I got in the military, but this one was different, and a type I had experienced in some high-stress jobs before and after my military days. My eyes hurt, my forehead felt like it was going to crush itself in, and I couldn't think straight. Every thought came back to how much my head was pounding just behind my eyes. All I could do to alleviate the migraine was put on an eye mask and go to sleep. Even then, I couldn't sleep like normal; I had to sleep on my back, which was uncomfortable, but the only way to keep the pain from migrating down once side of my face.

This scene would play out a few times in my travels, in England, Tunisia, Egypt, and Ankara. There was usually, but not always, a migraine, and I couldn't focus on anything but how exhausted I was. I wasn't physically exhausted, I didn't think, but travelling took a mental toll most people didn't understand. Every day, decisions had to be made. They weren't matters of life and death, but the little ones like where to eat, what to see, and which combination of clothes to wear all added up to a substantial amount of mental energy. Several times through my year circumnavigating the globe, this mental exhaustion took me down. It wasn't until Thailand, just a week before leaving for my extended stay in Mexico, that I learned the early signs of a coming takedown and could head it off with a break. Travelling was exhausting, especially moving as fast as I was from city to city, country to country, and burnout eventually catches up with everyone, even if it has to put you down by force.

Joyless Experiences

I could tell exhaustion was coming for me when I stopped enjoying things I should have enjoyed. Hiking in Cappadocia, for example, was one of those things. While it was projected to rain on my second day there, I felt like I was looking for a reason to return to the hostel rather than continue to Sword Valley. It was highly likely that had I not come across the churches and monasteries, I would have spent the rest of the day doing nothing. It was only a matter of will that I stopped in the first place; I told myself I wouldn't be back here again and needed to check them out. Fortunately, I did, because they were great experiences, but I was forcing myself to take an interest. The fact that I didn't spend longer reading the boards and taking notes at the Göreme Open Air Museum was proof of that.

The same was true at the Luxor and Karnack Temples in Egypt, where Jo and I, during our free time, basically wandered the site rather than took in the history and mythology. Even watching the bullfights in Spain from Thailand proved to be more an academic exercise than a hobby and performance art I enjoyed. It was like my mind knew I was supposed to take pleasure in these things, but my body couldn't muster it. My body wanted me to rest, and after days of pushing it off, it decided to steal away my ability to enjoy things to prove a point. When that wasn't enough, as in Ankara, it put me down.

Impaired Judgement

One of the most dangerous and expensive side effects of travel exhaustion came in the form of impaired judgment. Health experts and military commanders alike warned about the impacts of going too long under stress, without sleep, or mental down time. It wasn't just physical fatigue or sapped happiness that got to you; your ability to make sound decisions took a nosedive. That happened to me, too, while travelling, and I was fortunate that I didn't end up in bad situations.

In Tunis, for example, when Jo and I first landed, we had been up since 02h00 that morning, and we were wiped as we tried to figure out the best way to get to Sousse, two hours away. Jo agreed to the first "taxi" driver who offered his services, who wasn't a taxi driver at all, but a guy with a yellow car and a non-functioning meter that he put up to make it look like a taxi. I liked to chalk this up to our willingness to take chances with local people, even if it was an expensive chance, but, in reality, it was because we were tired, frustrated, and didn't want to deal with the brain power it would take to find the best, cheapest option. I made the same mistake in Amman and Alexandria, too, where my desire to get to where I was going and sleep far outweighed my rational decision-making ability.

Depression and Stress

The real threats to travel came when exhaustion was combined with loneliness, homesickness, and severe stress. Travelling full-time was hard work and a lifestyle unlike any I had lived before. In the military, we had objectives, defined roles, and a battle rhythm that governed our days and weeks; as a police officer, I had a clear mission forty hours a week; and at my security firm, we had client and organisational needs that needed to be met. Travelling, though, was one long, experiential journey. There was no mission, end state, or defined schedule. To paraphrase the cliche, the journey itself was the goal. That was all well and good, but it certainly wasn't the whole story.

Part of travel exhaustion was the constant stress of not knowing what came next. It wasn't just the next leg of the trip that was unknown and nebulous but the next meal, the next hour of each day. It took a lot of resilience to make decisions that made you happy, kept you within budget, and allowed you to meet new people. When Jo started solo travelling, I watched from my bed as her stress levels skyrocketed while she researched flights, hotels, and visas. It was a lot to do and learn, especially if you had never travelled before. It could quickly become overwhelming. For some people, that only made it worse, as not knowing or having a plan was more stressful than all the work and brainpower it took to create one.

In the worst of circumstances, loneliness and depression set it. Most people, when living once-in-a-lifetime experiences like a gap year of travel, found it hard to imagine that you could get depressed on the road. It was very easy, especially when exhaustion came into play. When your mind and body struggled to keep up with everyday tasks, it could get difficult to stay positive. When I was flying through Turkey, I remembered an episode of *Departures*, an adventure travel series about two friends travelling the world, where one of the guys said he went days without talking to people sometimes. I certainly felt that from Ephesus through Bodrum and Pamukkale to Göreme. It seemed like the only people I talked to were taxi drivers, hotel receptionists, and waiters at restaurants. I was alone with just my thoughts and my phone, and it was hard to be in a place where all of my friends wished they could be while living their very successful lives with careers, spouses, and kids. It became harder and harder as time went by to relate to people back home, and when it was just me, exhausted, at a deserted restaurant eating another slab of Adana kebabs, that could quickly turn into a downward spiral.

Recovery

Exhaustion, depression, loneliness, and stress were all temporary mental states that would eventually move on if I could take the time to physically and mentally recover. It wasn't a matter of "gritting through," as I had done for so many years before, but taking deliberate steps to come out on the other side. For me, the best remedy was to park myself in one place for an extended period, preferably at least a week. That wasn't always possible, like in Ankara, but in Morocco, Thailand, and Mexico, a week or more in one place allowed my mind and body to relax, naturally heal, and detox from the stress hormones. Additionally, I used that downtime to update the blog I was keeping, edit social media posts, and stare off into the horizon while my thoughts swirled and sorted themselves like my mind was a defragmenting computer.

Staying in one place helped me to make friends, even temporary ones, and to share a drink, meal, and game of cards with them at the end of each day helped to relieve the stress long-term, solo travel entailed. Back home, I lived alone, but I had regular, human contact with people I worked or went to school with, even during the COVID-19 pandemic. That wasn't always the case on the road, and these longer periods in one place helped build those human connections that we all desperately needed. I could always call home, too, and it seemed like during my loneliest times on the road, I spent the most time texting with my mom, dad, and certain friends back in the United States. I would even venture to say that, if it weren't for those times, I wouldn't be as close with them as I am now, even though I spent over a year away from home.

Part of these break periods included setting the expectation of zero expectations. It was important as a full-time traveller to not let your travels dictate your life; I needed to be in control of my agendas, taking deliberate advantage of opportunities, remaining flexible, when necessary, but always being sure that life didn't just happen to me. It was too often that a "we don't have a plan" adventure turned into one which was hardly memorable or enjoyable. Instead, when I was exhausted or down, I told myself, "There are zero expectations right now. Don't set an alarm, watch a film, read a book, but don't worry about seeing or doing anything this week." Giving permission to myself to do nothing was different than doing nothing out of circumstance, and it was amazing how much better I felt after a week of deliberately taking a break.

Reflection #8

A Poverty-Stricken World

I had never witnessed true poverty before. I had seen the poor, the homeless, the oppressed, but true poverty had always eluded me. Not that I knew it, nor was it something I sought out, but that hard reality slammed into me like a freight train when I finally came face-to-face with it across the world. From the Berber tribes in Morocco making their money with carpets to the Cambodians climbing trees in the jungle for fruit, seeing this poverty-stricken world as a traveller was an eye-opening, gut-wrenching, soul-churning experience that changed my view of the world in fundamental ways. Suddenly, I saw my suits, personal library, German car, British motorcycle, and 300 USD backpack for what they were: a sign of just how fortunate I was in life that I was born and raised in a country where I was practically immune from the meaning of true poverty. Most in the rest of the world were not so fortunate.

The Top One Percent

Since the 2008 financial crisis, the Western world has been rocked by calls for the "top one percent" to "pay their fair share." That was a good tagline in an economy that saw the automotive industry, housing market, and energy prices crash, sending the worldwide economy into the worst recession since the Great Depression while corporate executives and bankers paid themselves huge bonuses with government bailout money. But who exactly were the "one percent" and what was "their fair share?" In the United States, the top one percent of taxpayers paid forty-five percent of government taxes, while the top one percent of worldwide income earners held just under twenty percent of global wealth. The first of those statistics seemed unfair to the top one percent, while the second greedy.

The truth was, the global one percent contained a large swath of the Western world. For a single income earner, earning just 63,000 USD per year put you in the top one percent for global income. That came out to half of American earners in the top one percent globally, something those who called for the top one percent to pay their fair share didn't understand. Even our poverty line, which, as of this writing, was just under 15,000 USD per year, was seated in the top fifteen percent of worldwide income earners. Compared to places like Cambodia and Turkey, where the average annual income was less than 2,000 and 11,000 USD, respectively, even our impoverished lived on substantially more money than most of the world.

Less than twelve percent of Americans lived below our poverty line, and only a few thousand lived below the world's median income. That is not to make light of our poverty issues, as they are relative to national economies; however, it puts into perspective just how lucky Americans were on the global scale to live in a country where even our poverty line placed us in the top fifteen percent of global wealth. That was life-changing money to Cambodians, Turks, Balinese, Vietnamese, and countless other nationalities and ethnic groups worldwide. We Americans were privileged beyond measure just to be born and live in such a wealthy country.

Systemic Poverty

Poverty, true poverty, was a systemic issue on the international stage. There weren't rich forces at play controlling the world economy like some conspiracy theorists may have believed, but there were real problems out of an individual's control that caused them to live in poverty. It wasn't simply a matter of moving or pulling yourself up by your bootstraps; when the average income for your country was 4,000 USD, getting out of a poverty-stricken world took more than sheer gumption.

Some communities were wrecked by oppressive regimes of decades gone by. The Bunong people, who fled to the jungle during the Khmer Rouge, still lived there, forgotten and left behind by an advancing society. They lived dangerously in the jungle, climbing thirty-metre trees for fruit that only became harvestable once a year, building their own houses on stilts, and tilling massive fields by hand. In the Sahara, the Tuaregs were similarly affected, as they fought rebellions for their rights as the governments controlling their lands increasingly sought Western investment over propping up their people. The Aboriginal tribes of Australia lived on their traditional lands in the same ways they had long before the United Kingdom arrived as modern Australia moved on to become the world's thirteenth-largest economy, leaving the Aboriginal tribes behind as the colonised areas developed in an era where the Aboriginals were seen as lesser people.

Others were subjected to modern poverty stressors which they couldn't dream of addressing on their own. The Chinese Belt and Road Initiative subjected nations across the world, but especially in Africa, to a form of national debt slavery, which caused inflation and drove up costs. In an uncertain trade situation with the United States, the Mexican Peso dropped twenty-five percent against the dollar in less than six months, forcing local bakeries and restaurants to increase prices to remain open. Egypt's currency black market, which, during my time there, offered 50 EGP to 1 USD instead of the official 30 EGP to 1 USD rate, caused the Egyptian Pound to see fifty percent inflation in just three months, from December to March. As inflation and costs rose, so did the poverty rates.

Socialist economies, like Venezuela, Vietnam, and Argentina (before the 2023 election), caused poverty with government policies as they regulated goods and services out of the hands of the workers and into the cities and business class. In Vietnam, for example, it didn't matter how much rock you had on your land; you had to sell it to the government at a low price so they could turn around and sell it to contractors (i.e., corrupt business friends) for a fair price. Argentina tried and failed to control poverty, as so many socialist economies did, by offering government jobs to bolster employment, thus creating more inflation for the entire country and driving continued poverty.

These stories and more could be found in every corner of the globe, from the wealthiest city in the United Arab Emirates to the poorest village in Yemen. Poverty was an issue that couldn't be tackled by infusing millions of dollars of cash into an economy or electing new officials. It required wholesale governmental, economic, and sociological changes that were too unrealistic to reproduce on a worldwide scale.

Hard Work Being Poor

"Man, being poor is hard work." I said this to myself countless times as I travelled Southeast Asia. I was fortunate in that I had never truly experienced poverty. Even in my time away from my professional life, I had enough money saved to put me far above any poverty line. While I felt the budget tighten in places like Germany, Ireland, and New Zealand, I was by no means hurting for money. I could afford to buy new shirts if mine ripped, a new daypack for just a few months, and plane tickets home if there was some emergency. I didn't have to make my own food, let alone harvest it, distil my own liquor, or go without a shower for days because I had no running water. Even as an unemployed world traveller, I lived better than most of the world's population.

That was not so across most of the globe. Being poor was hard work. Social safety nets and government programmes may have been the norm in Europe, the United States, and Canada, but in the jungles of Southeast Asia, the streets of Mexico, and the deserts of MENA, there were no such saving graces. To survive meant to work and work hard. No one was exempt, not men, women, or kids attending school. Everyone had to chip in to keep the family fed, clothed, and housed.

In Iraq, little kids scurried around markets with orange wheelbarrows, offering to carry groceries for shoppers. This wasn't for money for toys or ice cream like the small service jobs American kids did for their parents and neighbours. These wheelbarrows provided food and water to the family in an economy where the national government couldn't even be trusted to set a fair exchange rate with the USD, let alone provide for its people. Children barely old enough to walk and talk moved down the streets in Mexico, offering beaded bracelets, plants, and homemade honey and jams, trying to make money while their parents did the same. The average Mexican in Tulum made just 500 MXN per day (about 25 USD), and these odd goods provided vital income to families who otherwise would have nothing to eat.

In the jungles of Southeast Asia, that hard work intensified, as families worked farms year-round to bring in crops. Those fortunate enough to have learned English could get jobs as guides, but even that was hard work as they walked the jungles with new tour groups every few days. After a week of hiking the Cambodian jungles and three days of walking the rice fields of Vietnam, I was beat, but our guides simply rested overnight and started anew the next morning. Luan, my motorbike driver in Vietnam, told me how bad his knees hurt at the end of every tourist season,

411

but he had to keep driving his motorbike to provide for his mother, wife, and son, who were back home preparing the fields for harvest.

Happiness as a Choice

I would never forget Bon's words in Kampong Phluk: "Don't have much, but we happy while we here." In a village where the men spent their days in the dry season repairing houses, the women caught and preserved fish, and children worked the fields, they found a reason to be happy. At the end of a long day, they could sit in the shade and enjoy a cheap beer or happy water with their friends. That was a gut punch to someone like me who, when I made six figures at my security firm, could always come home with something to gripe about and ruin my off time. In the most impoverished parts of the world, there was always a reason for happiness. My dad told me many years ago that happiness was a choice. Back then, I was struggling with depression, which he didn't understand and undercut his point. Nowadays, though, I literally saw his point under shaded trees after a hard day's work.

JC was among the happiest, most upbeat people I met while travelling. He spent half the year tending to his farm and half guiding tourists through the jungle so he could afford to put his daughter through private school and, one day, university. He was lean and fit as a matter of circumstance rather than choice, and he only had the one pair of jeans, but he genuinely loved life. JC couldn't afford to buy fancy Bluetooth speakers, so he created sound amplifiers out of bamboo stalks using his machete, proudly proclaiming, "UBL!" when he was done. He made cups and utensils out of bamboo and sticks, as did Tchi Tchi, the ranger, because that was what they had back home. Whenever JC made something from bamboo or showed us some trick of the jungle, he proudly proclaimed, "I'm just a farmer!" By "just a farmer," he was implying that other professions seemed to outrank him in society's eyes, but he loved where he came from and how he lived. I couldn't imagine most Americans I knew proudly proclaiming they were just a farmer when they spent half their year marching through the oppressive heat in the Cambodian jungle without a breeze as gnats buzzed around their heads.

Luan, too, was one of the most upbeat people I met. He struggled to provide for his family with a newborn, but he always had a smile to wear, practical jokes to play, and a game of pool to hustle. Everything he did was for his son, and he wasn't shy about the financial strain having a young child put on his family. Even so, he loved his life. He told me, "I have friends from all around the world!" True enough, I was one of them. Luan also learned from people he met on the Ha Giang Loop, making him one of the more informed people I met in my travels, even more so than Westerners with university degrees and professional credentials. While there was plenty to get him down and that he would change about life if he could, Luan put those things on the back burner. Instead, he chose to live in the happiness of the moment.

People could always choose to be happy, even in the throes of extreme poverty. It was a lesson I needed to see and learn in what I realised was my far-more-than-comfortable life. While I would never disparage my own country's poverty-stricken citizens, my experiences with Luan, JC, and others made me re-evaluate my views on the poverty situation back home, where we had all sorts of government programmes, church outreach centres, and social safety nets to help people in need. Some of the happiest people I met were in places that had no such help.

Can't Solve it All

I heavily considered handing the man in Vietnam 1,000,000 VND to pay his bank debt, just as I frequently debated saying "no cambio" in Mexico or hesitating to negotiate with merchants in Tunisia. I could easily afford it and would hardly feel the impact of such an expense in the long run. It was, after all, a matter of 40 USD, less than half of my daily budget. Ultimately, I decided against it, just as I decided against large tips and accepting posted prices in souks. It wasn't a matter of money or principle, either. It was a matter of culture and long-term viability.

In many cultures, especially in the Middle East and North Africa, accepting charity was frowned upon. Instead, every gift of charity needed to be met with some service or good. The service didn't have to be of equal value to the gift; there only had to be an exchange. It was shameful for a man to accept free money from another man in many cultures, especially a foreign tourist. In some cultures, it was considered an insult even to offer. I wasn't culturally adept enough to know when and where such a gift could be offensive.

I also recognised, with some reservation, that if everyone thought like me, we would only compound the poverty problem. Infusing unregulated, outside money into the local economy only increased inflation. That was the problem Egypt faced, and one which long-term expatriates complained about in their chosen homes. For example, Bali was a cheap vacation destination, where you could get beautiful ocean-view villas for just 50 USD a night. Most people would happily pay more, and most businesses would love to charge more, but market forces were the same everywhere, and this would only inflate prices for locals. Eventually, they would be priced out of the area entirely. It was a law of economics that applied from giving financial assistance to the poor to subsidising farming to price-fixing petrol. If every well-meaning Western tourist gave money to poor farmers and labourers in impoverished countries outside of the government's monetary and fiscal policies and regulations, we would never solve the root causes of that poverty. We would only make it more expensive to be poor.

It was also true that paying or gifting more simply because we had the means could cause a dependence problem. It was a harsh thing to say, but too many places in the world had been disrupted by travellers, tourists, and philanthropists thinking they were doing a good thing by paying too much for something and helping out a family in need. As someone who had travelled to locations both on and off the tourism circuit, it became easy to tell where locals became dependent on unregulated foreign cash. Mexico was one of those places, something many Mexicans resented. Tipping in Mexico wasn't always a normal practice; it was something Americans did in high-tourism areas, because it was our culture to do so. That was understandable, to a degree, in the fancy resorts, but that culture steadily made its way out of the resorts and into the cities and pueblos. Tulum, a place I love, had only recently developed a tipping culture, and I knew several local Mexicans that hated it. It affected them as much as it did the tourists, as meals started to cost just a little bit more as tips became expected. Some restaurants didn't care about tips for their servers; they were usually the extremely grateful ones. Others expected it, and even put recommended tips on their receipts. Worse, petrol station attendants didn't expect a tip; they would instead scam you out of a 500 MXN note and pocket the difference. The result? I watched as prices on basic goods like bread increased twenty percent over two years. The dependency problem led directly to the inflation problem.

It was a hard reality to swallow. I could afford a 60 EGP tip to a baggage handler, a 1,000,000 VND donation to a new friend, or 82,000 IQD for a nice room in Iraq, but what I could afford or wanted wasn't the point. At some point, other travellers and I needed to realise that we couldn't solve the world's poverty problem on our own, no matter how hard we tried. It was too complex and grandiose a task for us to have any substantial positive impact, and it was far too easy to accidentally cause disastrous consequences for those we were trying to help.

We Are Truly Lucky

In no other area of life did I realise that Americans were truly lucky than when it came to poverty. Being born in the United States, being eligible for an American passport, and having the social safety net available to us put our citizens light-years ahead of the overwhelming majority of the world. We lived in a country where help was available in almost every city, where we didn't have to walk in forty-degree Celsius heat for eight hours a day and months on end to make enough money to provide for our children's education. Our economy wasn't wrecked with most of our population (indeed, hardly any of it) living beneath the world poverty line, and unregulated infusions of charity dollars didn't threaten the stability of regional and national economies. We weren't sending our pre-teen children up thirty-metre trees to pick fruit for a month to make enough money for the year, and we didn't have to leave our families for six months at a time to provide for their future. Sure, we had our problems, but we also had our fortune that most of the world's population couldn't even dream of having.

Just being born in the United States made us some of the luckiest, most fortunate people on the planet. I wished we would act like it.

Reflection #9

The Horizon and its Spiritual Alure

I was in love with the horizon. For as long as I could remember, I found myself staring off into the distance as I contemplated life, sorted my thoughts, and allowed myself to feel deep-seated emotions. The horizon was famous in pirate films for providing a life chasing the sun, full of extraordinary, unknown adventures and experiences. The rising sun that turned the night into day rose from the eastern horizon, and religions across the globe used this symbolism in their practices, beliefs, and architecture. Symmetrically, the horizon also took as the sun set behind it and the Earth rolled westbound ships beyond its border.

As a traveller, I got lost in the serenity and symbolism the horizon played in my life. It had an almost spiritual allure. It represented unlimited opportunities to come and missed opportunities taken into the past. It represented the freshness of the new day and took with it all the light and events that day had brought. I developed an almost spiritual relationship with the horizon as I sat along the ocean shores and the desert dunes, staring off into the far beyond, wondering what came next in life and what lay beyond my sight.

Serenity

In the world of travel, chaos was the norm. Life was a series of packing, unpacking, making buses, interpreting new languages, finding new restaurants, trying new foods, catching flights, meeting new friends, saying goodbye to new friends, and wearing out the soles of my shoes. Every traveller had to get accustomed to it, and not everyone could thrive in the constantly-changing day-to-day environment. I was. I thrived in it, even, as I had before I left off on my grand adventure.

But, as the saying went, the body kept the score. Every stressful event, trying day, and missed opportunity stored itself in your mind until it eventually manifested in a physical ailment. It was hard to see it coming, as in the moment everything seemed to be going exactly as it should. On the ocean's shores, however, it was as though the floodgates of my mind opened up, and all of those built-up stressors and feelings burst forth at the sound of waves rolling over themselves, washing ashore, and slamming into the sea walls. Had those floodgates burst in a hostel bed or on the phone with family, I would have collapsed into a wild depression; some things were hard to handle on your own, especially when in the presence of others who couldn't understand. But staring out into the horizon over the waves calmed me as I grappled with whatever was bothering me at the time. The longer I sat and stared, the harder it became to concentrate on any one thing. Any notions of reading a book on the beach were quickly dashed the second I sat down.

It was an odd calm that was itself chaotic. Thoughts and emotions swirled around in my head, indiscernible from each other, as they sorted themselves out. It felt like my brain was processing all the mental and emotional data it had stored up over however long I had been on the road, and this was the first time it had paused long enough to sort everything into its proper box. After bringing myself back to reality after however long I sat there, I always felt a sense of peace, not because I had achieved some grand epiphany, but because staring off into the horizon gave me something I desperately needed from time to time - a chance to sit, be still, and let my mind do its thing.

Clarity

Despite the chaos of swirling emotions and indiscernible feelings, there was always some trigger or theme to these serene moments. Maybe I had just been rejected by a girl, was worried about the future, or longed for something I didn't quite know what it was. In all the chaos of travel, it was sometimes hard to have a sense of clarity about life. The more I travelled, the less I knew I had seen; the more I experienced, the more stories I knew there were to find. Life was too short to spend time wringing hands over where to go or what to do next. Still, my mind, a product of military habit and American culture, was always trying to figure out what I should be doing with my life, either in the future or during my travels in a given country.

Staring out into the horizon brought a sense of clarity to those thoughts. As the wave of calm washed over me and my mind sorted my emotions from one another, whatever was bothering me would slowly take shape. On the beach in Malaga, I realised that I wasn't returning to my old life; this resume-bolstering trip, in an instant, transformed into a journey of realisation and self-discovery. Looking over the sands of the desert, watching the camel trains come over the far-off dunes against the Saharan sun rise, it occurred to me that it wasn't enough to simply be a world traveller; I needed to be an adventurer of some kind. Aimless wanderings weren't for me. In Thailand, sitting alone at an oceanside restaurant on my writer's retreat as the horizon turned from blue to pink to black with the setting sun, I discovered just how much I longed to return to Spain and immerse myself in the art of bullfighting. I didn't just want to watch them; I wanted to understand them at a deeper level and discover why it was they captivated my soul.

I never expected to gain clarity from the horizon, nor did I seek out the beach or the desert for that purpose. I knew it would surely come, but that wasn't something I could control. When my mind needed to sort some things out, it would find the right place and time to do its thing. It only needed the beautiful horizon line to allow me to feel what I needed to come to some necessary realisation.

What Lies Beyond?

The horizon was infinite. Not even the universe could be contained by our ability to perceive it, as it extended far beyond the distance light could travel. How far? No one truly knew. Here on Earth, the horizon wasn't genuinely infinite, but it represented endless possibilities on the other side of the unknown.

We could guess what lay beyond the horizon, just as we could guess what came next in life. We may even be able to make informed assessments based on navigational charts, weather data, reports from other ships, and our past experiences, but what lay just beyond visual range could never truly be known. In the Sahara, the dunes moved, something the Berber tribes and smugglers knew well, and no matter how many times you crossed that vast expanse of sand and rock, it was never the same trip twice. The ocean didn't move, but the weather shifted, and pirates were a real threat. With every kilometre of water you put behind you, another kilometre appeared ahead, bringing with it new, unknown conditions even the most seasoned captains had to work through to survive.

But what lay truly beyond? A destination? A goal? A person? If you walked north from the southern edge of Mali, surely you would eventually meet the Mediterranean Sea, and if you sailed south from Botany Bay, you would undoubtedly cross the roaring forties and find Antarctica. Those were certainties, but what about the in-between? Would you encounter a terrorist encampment, a Japanese whaling fleet, an army, a navy, a challenge so unsurmountable that you met your own death? The Earthly horizon may not be truly infinite, but its possibilities were. That was one reason I loved it, and as I felt myself drawn in by its alluring gaze, all of the possibilities in life seemed to present themselves all at once. If I chose to charge off into the horizon, who knew what I might find.

The Eastern Journey

Charge I did. For thousands of years, people across continents buried their dead with their feet facing east so they could greet the sun every morning. Catholic cathedrals, Buddhist and Hindu Temples, and Islamic mosques traditionally faced east, each for their own spiritual reasons, but the sun rose over the righteous and set behind the wicked. It was only natural, then, that I chased the sun. East. It didn't matter how far or fast I travelled towards the horizon; I would always find the sun rising on me and my travels. I could have travelled west, which may have made logistical sense, but I would only find the setting sun behind the darkened horizon there. I would never catch it; I could find myself suffering in eternal daylight or eternal darkness. On the eastern horizon, I was always promised a new day and night.

None of this mattered in the lead up to my travels, but as I sat beneath the rising sun time and again, I couldn't help but think there was some deeper meaning in my eastward journey. To the east, the horizon never concealed the sun but brought it forth for a new day and a fresh start. To the east, the horizon never took; it only gave as the Earth spun around, bringing new sights and adventures with each revolution. Writing these words, it seems metaphysical, but chasing the eastern horizon appeared to be an essential part of my journey of realisation and discovery across the world. Like the wind, I was propelled by forces beyond my control in my search for serenity, clarity, and whatever lay beyond this stage of life.

Reflection #10

The Modern Lost Generation

I was a veteran of the Global War on Terrorism, the "GWOT" as we called it. The terrorist attack of 11 September 2001 changed the entire socio-political landscape, as my generation grew up under the constant threat and spectre of terrorism. Like so many, I joined the military when I was old enough to fight in that war, deployed twice in service thereto, and found my way out of national service more than five years later, having seen some of the worst things humanity could throw at itself. I made my way through life with a plan afterwards, but the plan was hard to push through, as I never felt like things made much sense after coming home. The world had long moved on from the terror attacks of 2001, and those of us who had deployed in support of the ensuing conflicts were becoming fewer and fewer in the military and in increasingly less demand as the world's security situation shifted.

I felt lost, and with that feeling, I set out to see the world. I longed for the Middle East and North Africa, as they felt more like home than the Piney Woods of East Texas, and I couldn't wait to be back where I had once served. Before I got there, though, Jo, my travel companion for more than five months, convinced me to follow a bullfighter around Spain, and I became enamoured with everything about the centuries-old performance. Together, Jo and I read *The Sun Also Rises*, Ernest Hemingway's tribute to the bullfighting tradition and The Lost Generation, those World War I veterans who lived in excess after escaping the brutal conflict. A hundred years before my time, they were lost in disillusionment after the War to End All Wars scarred the battlefields of France, the bodies of the survivors, and the minds of those who somehow pulled through.

In reading Hemingway, I found myself identifying with the characters, from the main Jake Barnes, who was wounded in the war, to the stunning Brett Ashley, an army nurse turned promiscuous socialite, to Robert Cohn, the man who desperately wanted a change, but couldn't seem to find the right way to find it. I felt like they were all me, and I was them, and I found similarities between the Lost Generation and modern GWOT veterans as I travelled the world. We were at once different and the same, separated by 100 years' worth of technology and ideology, but bound together by the brutality we witnessed and disillusionment we felt.

The Global War on Terrorism – A Different Kind of War

The GWOT was a war unlike any the world had faced before. This was wasn't like the War of Drugs, which invoked the moniker of war for its own purpose, nor was it the World Wars, Korea, Vietnam, Desert Storm, or Bosnia, where there was a defined enemy and political objective. The GWOT posed the forces of governments against ideologies, diffuse guerillas, insurgents, and terrorist cells against organised military units and hard-stand forward operating bases, and entire people groups against one another (and sometimes themselves). The GWOT started on 11 September 2001, a day now known simply as "9/11," when al-Qa'ida terrorists turned civilian airliners into missiles to attack the economic, security, and political pillars of American influence. It was an attack that the world's security services could hardly fathom, and one which our entire security and defence posturing was unprepared to stop.

The 9/11 attacks kicked off twenty years of fighting Islamist terrorist groups on every continent. No one was exempt from its influence. Indonesia, the world's most densely populated Muslim country, a country known for beautiful beaches and not its worldwide political or social influence, became infected with Islamist extremists which both fought against the Indonesian government locally and provided a staging ground for fighters and propaganda to launch across the world. The ungoverned spaces of Africa, especially the Sahel region and the Sahara in general, fell to unions of local opportunistic groups and transnational Islamist terrorists, like the separatist Tuaregs and al-Qa'ida in Mali and Boko Haram and Islamic State in Nigeria, which themselves later dissolved as the transnational groups' influence subsumed the regional conflicts. Europe was rocked by one devastating attack after the next where the attackers ranged from lone actors inspired by Islamist extremism (2004 Madrid train bombings), attacks in the name of, but not directed by, transnational Islamist groups (2005 London bombings), to attacks directly perpetrated by transnational Islamist groups (2015 Paris Attacks). Not even Russia, who would surely issue swift retribution, was safe from Islamist terrorist influence (2010 Moscow Metro bombings). Nowhere was safe from Islamist terrorism, not even the United States. Even though al-Qa'ida and Islamic State only managed to conduct one actual attack in the United States between the two of them after 9/11, homegrown violent extremism, aka homegrown terrorists, grew and was responsible for attacks in the names of al-Qa'ida, Islamic State, and Islam in general which forced the American government to fundamentally shift how it handled its national security.

For twenty years, the Millennial generation's formative years were shaped by the GWOT. Taking off our shoes at airports became a routine practice to combat terrorist threats; our local police departments had to arm and armour themselves to handle a terrorist attack (in the United States, the military was legally prohibited from conducting policing operations inside the country); and everyone knew someone who deployed to safeguard our country against another 9/11. The idea that the fight against terrorism had to be "an away game" where "We fight the terrorists overseas so that we don't have to fight them here at home" (an exact quote from President George W. Bush) became second nature as we sent our troops to Iraq,

Afghanistan, Syria, Cameroon, Niger, and Somalia to fight for freedom against the terrorists.

But who were we fighting? Ten years into the GWOT, the United States killed Usama bin Laden, the al-Qa'ida leader who directed the 9/11 attacks. Less than two years into the GWOT, a joint American-Pakistani task force captured Khalid Sheikh Mohammed, the mastermind of the 9/11 attacks. Abu Bakr al-Baghdadi, the first leader of Islamic State in 2014, was killed in 2019 in Syria. The Iraqis declared victory over Islamic State in 2017, the Syrians followed suit in 2019, and al-Qa'ida had long fallen into irrelevance after the United States' invasion and occupation of Afghanistan. The truth was we were fighting terrorism around every corner, both at the strategic level and on the ground in Iraq, Afghanistan, and other theatres. We never knew when one of our own citizens would launch into an attack at a bank, a church, a school, an art exhibition, when a coordinated attack directed and conducted by Islamist terrorists from Syria would rock our peaceful Friday nights, or when terrorists would overtake social media hashtags to flood our feeds with their propaganda. Our troops, too, never knew who the real enemy on the ground was. Informants on one day supported the Taliban the next, meetings with tribal elders turned into ambushes, and anti-government or anti-American protests turned into overrunning an embassy, consulate, or operating base walls on multiple occasions. A friend of mine, a pilot for a contracting company, found himself unarmed on his first night on a "safe" operating base in Afghanistan when the Taliban suddenly attacked, scaling the walls to continue the attack inside the base amidst the chaos.

It was a war unlike any other. It was a war we were doomed to lose from the beginning, but one we had to fight nonetheless.

Post-9/11 Veterans – A Different Kind of Veteran

I was drawn into the GWOT as a military officer and deployed to the Sahara and Iraq. During my first deployment to the Sahara, we had little support compared to Afghanistan after twenty years. Training for this mission meant getting eighteen-to twenty-year-old warfighters into the mindset that we were in what I called the Sargasso Sea of terrorism (where our direct area of operation was stable, but we were surrounded by different groups with their own agendas, ideologies, and methods). We trained in austere conditions, carrying everything we owned in our packs, conducting ruck marches and long runs as I reminded them that our embassy (and nearest base of support) was hundreds of kilometres away, and several times ran out of drinkable water as we learned to ration our supplies. It may seem extreme to some, but we actually did run out of drinkable water in country; Boko Haram terrorists attacked and stole our shipments regularly.

We also had to learn from operations that had gone bad in the past. Restraint was key, as not every situation needed to be solved with gunfire. Talking, negotiating, and assessing threats from locals and armed militants was a tricky business, but one we had to learn. We watched films and documentaries about situations gone bad to learn lessons for our upcoming mission. We trained young men and women to recognise the differences in an Islamic State and al-Qa'ida attack, right down to the way they taught their followers to make bombs or conduct ambushes, because we weren't facing just one adversary; we were facing several.

For a group of people mostly in their young twenties, it was a total mind shift in thinking from how Americans behaved in wars of the past. There were no battle lines, clearly defined bad guys, or clear way to prosecute the GWOT. Even in the same country, tactics would change from region to region, city to city. In Iraq, Sadr City was a hotbed of Iranian-aligned and -supported activity, al-Anbar province was composed of individual tribal forces which may or may not have fought against al-Qa'ida and Islamic State, and the Southern Provinces were largely isolated from the war. Little kids would walk up to a military vehicle with a mortar round in their hand intent on slamming it against the truck, women, who previously were not combatants, would pick up their dead [terrorist] husbands' rifles to shoot at Coalition forces, and Coalition soldiers would be told they couldn't do anything about it until they could articulate a definitive threat. Many had to watch the entire decision-making process play out with their finger resting on the trigger as a child or woman turned from non-combatant to combatant; the moment to fire would come, but firing too soon would result in imprisonment, which meant thinking about what was about to happen and solidifying it in our memories.

It should have been no surprise, then, that the post-9/11 veteran hardly resembled the traditional view of an American warfighter. The rotating deployments, where we only did six to twelve months (or fifteen to eighteen, in the early days) in country, came home, changed units, and left again tore down our ideas of what life looked like. Every new unit assignment meant leaving friends with whom you had experienced horrible things and getting new ones with whom you would experience even more. Hypervigilance, anxiety, and a suspicious nature became our personalities we faced an undefined adversary, and many became angry at people, cultures, and a corrupted religion which cost them their limbs, friends, and any semblance of a normal life. To compound it all, less than one percent of the American population served in the military, creating a sort of warrior caste that couldn't easily fit back into polite society. We turned inward to support ourselves, often turning to dark humour and a twisted world view to cope with it all.

I was one of these veterans. We weren't the professional warfighters like Patton, MacArthur, or Moore. We were people who, as kids, had our world upended by terrorists and, as adults, found ourselves thrust into more political quagmires and moral dilemmas than almost any other warfighting generation in history. Those quagmires and dilemmas fundamentally changed an entire generation of warfighters in ways the world would find hard to accept.

A Country, and World, That Moved On

On 30 December 2022, the United States military stopped issuing its National Defense Service Medal (NDSM) to all service members. This medal was awarded to service members who served during wartime, and military regulations identified the periods of wartime service and the conflict with which those periods were affiliated. The NDSM was issued for veterans of the Korean War, Vietnam Conflict, Persian Gulf operations, and the GWOT. The period for the GWOT: 11 September

422

2001 to 30 December 2022. While warfighters were still engaged in counterterrorism operations across the globe, the United States military made the deliberate decision to conclude its ubiquitous War on Terrorism and to, instead, expressly authorise and delineate which units and service members were involved in combatting worldwide terrorism; no longer was every service man and woman fighting the war. While the Authorization for the Use of Military Force (known by its acronym AUMF) for both Iraq and Afghanistan were still in effect, the political forces were moving to officially repeal those, too. The Senate passed a bill to repeal the Iraq AUMF, and efforts to repeal the Afghanistan (and the greater GWOT) AUMF were gaining momentum.

The world's security landscape had changed. Mass migration, economics, and peer and near-peer competition replaced the GWOT as the main security issues for voters. Western nations were tired of nation building in the Middle East; it became abundantly clear that the root causes of Islamist terrorism stemmed from more than just a failure to appreciate democracy, Western values, and the need for economic development. There were substantial cultural differences that the West just couldn't understand, and, having finally learned that lesson, the West moved on, leaving just enough counterterrorism operations in play to keep a lid on now-contained threat. It was an understandable shift. The United States could only serve as a bulwark against terrorism in countries across the world for so long, and the rise of Chinese and Russian aggression simply took priority.

But what about those of us who fought in the GWOT? Jo and I deployed during the GWOT, and both of us had been face-to-face with terrorists. We knew about terrorist groups, tactics, and operations, but that knowledge suddenly wasn't a significant factor in policy or hiring decisions. Our knowledge was valuable, but jobs and agencies who needed our expertise were shrinking. We were put in the same position as farmers, truckers, and other careers which had outlived their usefulness over the centuries: learn a new skill or get left behind.

It wasn't just a new skill, though. Counterterrorism had shaped our lives, much as the Cold War and World War II shaped the lives of our parents and grandparents before us. We grew up in a world where security concerns weren't based on economics, Russia, or China. To us, threats were around every corner, and American society was unified around protecting our citizens from terrorists. We weren't unified anymore, as half the country didn't want to contribute to Ukraine's fight against Russia, Americans became disillusioned with interventionist policies in the name of democracy, and the young professional generation, Generation Z, learned about 9/11 in the history books. To them, the impetus for the GWOT was as foreign and distant as Pearl Harbor or North Korea crossing the thirty-eighth parallel. The country for which we fought, which had shaped our lives with policies focused on counterterrorism, and which rallied around the flag to defend our freedom from terrorists who sought to overthrow them, had moved on. We had been left behind.

The Modern Lost Generation

The Lost Generation were those World War I veterans, mostly young men and women who managed survive the war physically, whose lives were transformed by the war, and not in a positive way. They had seen death on a scale not witnessed in Western history. In just four years, between 15,000,000 and 22,000,000 (depending on the source) died, a number more than the maximum estimates from the Thirty Years' War and the Crusades *combined*, and more than 20,000,000 were wounded. Entire towns were levelled and the land scarred by trenches as each side raced to the English Channel as they attempted to out-flank each other. Not only did they witness death and destruction on the largest scale, but they also saw it occur in the most efficient manner of any war. The Lost Generation witnessed the first massive war with machine guns, tanks, and chemical weapons. When the war was over, how could they possibly return to lives they once lived, the people they once were? They were left disillusioned with life, prone to excesses, and rebellious towards the social and political norms which both sent them to war and tried to reintegrate them afterwards.

That was where I found myself, as did many other veterans of the Global War on Terrorism. Society wanted us back as though nothing had happened, as though we hadn't seen the brutality of improvised explosive devices, the genocidal rampage against the Yazidis, the sexual enslavement of women to provide children for the caliphate, the beheadings of journalists, and the summary executions via drone strikes with neither trial nor judge. In some ways, the GWOT generation was worse off than the Lost Generation because we were instantly transported home after our tours via high-speed aircraft with no time to decompress or process what had happened overseas. We arrived home just days after our final operations, expecting to pick up where we left off with our families, vacations, career timelines, and everything else, often switching units to be separated from anyone we might be able to talk to about what we experienced together.

Many of us became disillusioned with American society as it left us behind. I did. We were labelled "break glass in case of emergency," someone they would call when they needed us, but not someone they wanted around to remind them of what happened during our twenty-year fight against terrorism. Some of us moved on fine enough, reintegrating into society with corporate jobs after leaving the military, while others sought employment with security contractors or private military companies. Some, like Donny O'Malley, Drew Hernandez, and Richard Hy, founded media companies and social media channels to turn their horrible experiences into comedy and provide a place for veterans to process and laugh at their experiences. Some of us tried to reintegrate but, really, never came home. "Part of you never comes back," one of the non-commissioned officers that worked for me once said. He was right.

That was a big reason why I started travelling. I couldn't hack it with the office life, even when working in the counterterrorism field. While necessary, the cubicles and computer screens weren't authentic experiences, and writing briefs, analyses, and impact statements for clients felt like I was running in circles as an advisor instead of a doer. I had hoped that being a police officer would help give me a sense of purpose and belonging, but I quickly found that procedure, policy, politics, and paperwork were mattered more than good police work and serving the community (something my dad, a forty-year police officer, lamented at the end of his career as well).

Where did I find I could hack it? On the road. I could empathise with poverty, make calculated risk decisions when getting into strangers' cars, have meaningful conversations with strangers about the world, and experience a way of life no one back home could imagine. I embraced my outcast status, leaving behind all of my stuff to live out of a backpack, which felt more natural than the six-figure income, luxury car, and mountain-view apartment in Colorado. The bullfights, the fleeting love interests, the repressed wartime memories, and the complex emotions I read in Ernest Hemingway's books came to life as I made my way across the world, especially in Spain, Africa, and the Cambodian jungle. Like Hemingway, I saw a cruel masculinity in the man-versus-bull performance where honour, more than life, was on the line, a sense of honour which I both identified with and, secretly, wanted to test myself in a world where I felt I no longer belonged. Jo, for her part, felt similar, and it was something that we discussed more than once along the way.

But how could we describe it to those back home? We couldn't. They hadn't experienced terrorism first-hand, nor faced the difficulties of integration or rejection from the government we once served. We were lost in the world, like millions of our predecessors 100 years before. We were today's Lost Generation.

Reflection #11

Travelling with Post-Traumatic Stress Disorder

Just a few months before leaving on The Great Gallivanting, I reached a breaking point in my personal life, which culminated in a mental and emotional breakdown in an airport lobby while waiting for a flight back to Colorado. I had too many things in my mind that I hadn't been able to resolve or handle, and I was coming off of a security conference where all of those things converged in a single week. This was more than general life stress; it was a deep-rooted psychological problem that I had been dealing with for years. I just hadn't gotten help. This breakdown galvanised me into getting help, but it also put my life into limbo as I was eventually diagnosed with Post-Traumatic Stress Disorder (PTSD) from my time in the military, as a police officer, and at my security firm.

The help I received included various therapies to help reprocess memories; techniques to deal with triggers, symptoms, and habits I had developed as coping mechanisms; and a low dosage of medication. While grateful for all of the help from my fabulous care team, I was also nervous about my upcoming travels. In just a few months, I would be leaving for a year or more of non-stop gallivanting across the globe, which was pushing it as far as my care regimen was concerned. Would the therapy I received before leaving be enough to help me get through on my own? Were the coping techniques going to be effective in a foreign environment? Was my medication even allowed in other countries? I wasn't incredibly concerned with my physical ability to travel, but these questions were at the forefront of my mind as my one-way ticket to Paris quickly approached.

Dreams, Jitters, and Habits

I had never been in street-to-street combat, fortunately. Still, I had been surrounded by open, ungoverned desert where terrorists operated with little support beyond what we could provide ourselves. In Iraq, the Iraqi government made deals with illicit groups to fight the mutual enemy in Islamic State. We were now partners with Muqtada al-Sadr, the elected majority leader and former head of the Mahdi Army who was personally responsible for the deaths of hundreds of Americans. Worse, when I joined the military, Islamic State was targeting the United States in ways we couldn't combat fast enough, and there were Islamic State sympathisers everywhere. Threats abounded, and we in the security apparatus had to work over-time to keep them at bay.

Recurring dreams were a nightmare, literally. I could remember when they started after my return from Africa, and I was either running from something at full speed or being attacked by something I couldn't fend off. I would wake up ex-hausted, drenched in a cold sweat from the adrenaline rush I experienced in my sleep from these dreams. Those dreams could also be physically violent in the real world. It was not uncommon for me to wake myself up from punching a wall, kicking so hard I rolled off the bed, or yelling at whatever spectre haunted me that particular night. My British roommate in Iraq told me I once woke him up from yelling in my sleep, which was something considering he could sleep through an artillery barrage, so I knew that these night terrors could be loud and affect others. I was, then, rightly worried about sleeping in shared hostel rooms with people I hadn't met or, worse, new friends. I was also concerned about those times Jo and I would have to share a bed; she would not take kindly to me kicking her in the middle of the night or yelling in her ear. My medication and therapies significantly cut down the recurring dreams and subconscious violence. Still, they weren't gone completely, and I wasn't sure young travellers would understand, or even care for, my apologies.

I had also become jumpy. I scanned building roofs, refused to sit with my back to a wall, and took in every detail of every goings-on around me. It was hard for me to be in large, open spaces, like concerts and churches, and I never went to those unarmed. As a traveller, I was worried about that, as Jo and I would be unarmed in wide-open spaces and churches time and time again. After my experiences in Africa and Iraq, where the sounds of rockets replaced the call to prayer at times, I was wary of not hearing it whenever we found ourselves in MENA. I actually enjoyed the call to prayer; it was a soothing background noise that reminded me of a time when things, somehow, made sense. But several times Jo and I would look at each other across a lunch or dinner table and say to each other, "It's late...," or, "Where's the call to prayer?" We were in MENA after October 7th, too, where protests had filled the streets, targeted Western embassies, forced increased security measures, and caused non-Muslim worship centres to close. An absent call to prayer was probably innocent enough, but experience told me otherwise. Right or wrong, that was just how it was.

I had other habits stemming from PTSD as well. I was obsessed with my home phone's security to the point of carrying two phones, deleting non-travel email ac-counts from my devices, and installing security software to prevent any bad actor from accessing my personal information. I carried three wallets with different iden-tification cards, stashes of money, and credit cards in case one was stolen or I had to "bug out" and could only grab one as I hurried to safety. None of these included anything that connected me to the United States military or my former security firm, as I didn't want to end up a target of local security services. Was that likely? Abso-lutely not, especially where I planned to travel, but it was a habit born from my military days that eased my anxiety in foreign lands.

✳   ✳   ✳

Medication

My biggest concern, logistically, was my medication. I was carrying a year's worth of PTSD medication, which included an anti-depressant, beta blockers for panic attacks, and melatonin and diphenhydramine hydrochloride to help with insomnia episodes. I took two overseas trips between being prescribed these medicines and leaving for my year around the world, so I knew they generally weren't a significant concern, but two countries' laws were by no means indicative of the entire world's, nor was carrying a week's worth of medication the same as carrying a year's.

Europe would likely be a non-issue, and that turned out to be the case. Anti-depressants required a prescription, but they weren't regulated like narcotics. As long as I had my prescription on me, I wouldn't have an issue. The same was true of the sleep aids, though diphenhydramine hydrochloride wasn't available over the counter like in the United States, so I needed to make it last. Some countries restricted medications to a thirty-day supply, but given the Schengen Area's borderless travel arrangement, that didn't concern me as I would only go through customs inspection upon entering.

Travelling to MENA was another story. Muslim countries were generally more restrictive on medication. Culturally, they turned to religion, traditional medicine, and practices that didn't include giving out medication for every issue. On the one hand, I could accept and appreciate that attitude; on the other, it was a limiting factor for my travels. I couldn't go to the United Arab Emirates at all with my medication, and I could only transport enough into Saudi Arabia for the duration of my stay in that country. Those were two countries I wanted to visit, but I crossed them off my list for the foreseeable future. Egypt wanted to confiscate my pill cutter as a weapon, despite being explicitly allowed in both carry-on and checked luggage.

There were other issues, too, in my travels. New Zealand and Australia had strict biosecurity regulations, and I had to explain what I was carrying, why I had so much, and what it was for to biosecurity officers at every customs checkpoint. While this wasn't a major hassle, it felt invasive. I hadn't even told most of my friends or family about my diagnosis, let alone my medication, and now I had to explain it all in the presence of strangers during the customs inspection. Diving was problematic, too, as any prescription medication required a medical waiver. That wasn't an issue, as I kept one on me, but some companies didn't even want to accept that once they heard I had a PTSD diagnosis. They either didn't want to take me or insisted I hire a guide in case I had an emergency. I won most of those battles with more than a fair bit of cajoling. I wondered if these dive professionals knew how therapeutic and positive diving was to someone like me.

Genuine Curiosity

Travellers were, by nature, curious people. They wanted to learn about things they would never experience, and serving in the military was one of those things for most of them. "What was it like?" was the most common question, and I usually responded with, "I loved being in the military and being in the military police." I would explain how having a defined mission, especially as part of the Global War on Terror, gave me a purpose, how I knew I was making a difference in my country's security and that I knew I had saved lives. The military had also given me access and insights to cultures outside my own that gave me a different outlook in life. Those answers were rarely the ones that travellers were expecting.

Unable to contain their curiosity, their first follow-up question was whether I had ever deployed to a combat zone. I had. Twice. Again, I put the positive spin on it, telling them deployments were fun in their own way, especially for personalities naturally attracted to military service. I made lifelong friends in the smoke pits, got up to shenanigans only service members would understand, and met amazing people from other militaries. That was all true, especially in Africa, when none of us wanted to return home because we were having such a great time.

Then the conversation always turned to the darker things of military service. "Have you ever shot anyone?" was the question they all wanted to ask. Some of them did. "No, but I could have," was my standard response. I could have; there were plenty of situations where I would have been justified in using force, but opted not to. Sometimes, travellers asked if I had issues from my service. I never lied to them. I did, but I was working on them with a combination of therapy, coping techniques, and medication. I wasn't a violent pressure cooker waiting to explode, but beheadings, abuses of corpses, and executing Christian children with rusty knives were things you simply couldn't unsee; rockets and bullets fired in anger, even if you weren't in any real jeopardy, were still sobering life events. Despite all of this, I told them, there was only one moral dilemma that stuck with me.

By and large, this curiosity wasn't morbid or ill-intended. It was genuine. Sure, some people wanted to use my service as evidence in their arguments against American security policies (interestingly, those people were universally young, German women), but most wanted to understand why people like me wanted to fight for our country in a conflict far removed from our borders. They also wanted to understand me and those like me who continued with life after the military. They were, in their way, trying to be respectful and understanding of a culture that was foreign to them.

Healing

Travelling the world was by far the best therapy I could have asked for as someone with PTSD. I needed to be reminded that the world was generally good and that not everyone or everything was out to get me. Yes, everything was political these days, and those political disagreements could easily lead to armed conflict, but not every issue yielded an actual, physical threat or moral dilemma. Meeting young people who would carry the torch into the next wave of international affairs reassured me that everything was, in fact, okay. Even when some of them knew far too much for knowing far too little, their isolation from and opposition to terrorism and warfare as an "easy button" was refreshing. Explaining the way of warfare and terrorism from the perspective of someone who was there without the ensuing political fight (which was common in my graduate programme) helped me to talk through and process years and years of internal turmoil that I hadn't been able to talk through before. The travellers I met, even for just a few days, became the support system I lacked back home.

The complete break from my professional life, where I had focused on security issues for almost a decade, also severed the mental link between threats and everyday life. At my old job, I would go from analysing security threats, writing briefs, and giving presentations during the day to home alone at night. There was no clean break in my mind as it continued to work through the topics of the day. It didn't help that my boss and I were friends who had both served as supervisors in some form or another, and we would have off-line, after-hours discussions over text about some of the higher-level issues in the office. Once I was boots on the ground in Paris, I was no longer subjected to the constant onslaught and reminder of the threats that were out there. I was blissfully ignorant after deleting all of the news applications from my phone and unsubscribed from security newsletters. If a bomb went off in New York City, I wouldn't have heard about it. I would eventually be forcefully dragged back into my old life after October 7th, with the attack dominating social media, comedy, and my travel plans, but that, too, would fade away.

After a year of travelling, I was more lost in the world than I had been since I left for university. I no longer had a life plan or ambitions to climb the corporate ladder or join government security departments. I didn't know what my future career looked like, how I would make money long-term, or where I would settle down. I was, however, healing from the mental and emotional carnage my past life had brought upon me. I still took more considerable risks than most people, but I was coming to terms with the negative aspects of life and becoming more positive in my view of humanity. I was no longer waking up from nightmares, and any time I kicked a wall in my sleep, it was from a dream about martial arts or another benign topic. I could talk objectively about the darker side of military service with travellers who were genuinely curious about my experience without ruminating on some of the things I had seen. I hadn't set out on my journey across the world to heal myself, but that was the effect my grand adventure had, and I was a better, more relaxed, and understanding person for it.

Reflection #12

How I've Changed from My Year Around the World

Travel for travel's sake was great and all, but taking a year off to travel the world had to have a deeper meaning. I had a family member who "travelled" on cruises, but he talked about his experiences as a romanticised, pre-packaged novelty that anyone could have if they could afford the time off from work and the expense of a long voyage on luxury cruise liners. That wasn't enough for me. When we started out, Jo and I zipped around Europe, seeing the "must-see" sights and hitting museums that held artifacts we couldn't see back home. As time passed, we grew tired of these generic experiences and longed for something more. We were on the trip of a lifetime. There was so much to learn and enjoy that we needed to embrace something other than just going, seeing, and doing. By the time we went our separate ways in Egypt, we both started to change and head down different paths of self-discovery. When we finally reunited again in Cairns, Australia, and, after my year of travel, in Spain, I could confidently say we both found a level of happiness and contentment that we never expected. Our gap year had changed our lives.

Things I've Learned

The world is simultaneously a much safer and more dangerous place than most people realise. The news, our politicians, and social media have the West in a stranglehold when it comes to our conceptions of foreign countries. Mexico was a dangerous cartel-laden country, London was a safe place just like my home town, Indonesia was a haven for terrorists, and Italy was the scenic, romantic getaway spot. It was all nonsense. I felt safest in countries like Mexico, Jordan, Iraq, and Turkey, where the news only broadcasts the bad things that happen, like kidnappings, ethnic conflicts, and terrorism. The truth was, yes, those things happened, but they were fairly isolated in specific parts of the countries where even the locals knew not to go. At the same time, the United Kingdom's violent crime rate was actually higher that the United States', but no one batted an eye when Jo and I travelled there. After my year was up, my friend Sonny, a European, travelled to Iran and had an amazing time. People thought he was crazy, but those same people had no problem visiting New York City or Chicago. The reality was the world was a far safer place than most people realised. At the same time, it was more dangerous. Basque terrorism at major festivals in the region was an issue the Spanish government actively concerned itself with, but most tourists had no idea that the region had only been peaceful for a short time. The same was true of Italy, where unchecked immigration and crime clearly scarred romanticised cities like Naples and Rome. I was never worried about a rocket exploding near me when visiting the Vatican, but I was extremely concerned about someone slashing my bag and stealing its contents, something which never once entered my mind in Iraq.

People are largely the same. The world over, people are mostly the same. We differed in our cultural practices and religions but wanted the same thing: Peace, safety for our loved ones, and the ability to provide a comfortable life. As an American, I would never understand what the Bunong people went through during the Khmer Rouge, but it was obvious what they worked for: their families' prosperity and happiness. Religious extremists would have us believe that one particular group of people, be they infidels, the unclean, or the lost, were fundamentally opposed to everything other religions or people stand for, when the reality was, they all wanted the same thing in life regardless to whom they did or didn't pray. Political demagogues were the same as they turned us all against each other, forgetting that our common goals and desires far outweighed our differences in opinion.

Common identities last. I discussed this one at length in an earlier reflection, but it is worth repeating. Societies with strong communal beliefs and identities lasted; those that didn't, fell. The Muslim armies conquered the world in a series of caliphates, sultanates, and empires that lasted almost 1,300 years. The Persians, who fought in battles only told in mythological tales, still survived in Iran, their ancestral home. The Aboriginal tribes in Australia and New Zealand traced their ancestry back over 10,000 years. The Christian empires in Rome lasted over 1,000 years, and those in Ethiopia lasted more than 700 years. Meanwhile, multicultural nations like my own tore themselves apart and broke themselves down into smaller and smaller factions, even fighting wars of secession less than 100 years after their formation.

Ideological zealotry brings down countries. Fervent ideological zealotry destroyed nations, especially when the supermajority of citizens didn't support it. Communist revolutions in places like Angola and Chile, fascist dictatorships in Portugal and Spain, and extreme political polarisation in the United States, United Kingdom, and European Union were proof. When people were so committed to their ideology that they couldn't hold a rational discussion, consider an opposing viewpoint, or tolerate dissent, the country and its constituents ultimately fell, either by crumbling from the inside or by foreign intervention.

Cash is king. In the West, we liked our credit cards and tap-to-pay with our phones. Most of the world lived on a cash system while we moved away from it at breakneck speed. Cash was the way of most of the world. When the internet went offline in Egypt, Europeans couldn't pay with their cards or phones, as their banking systems required an active connection. Iraq had a few cashpoints, but they were only located in major population centres; most of its financial business was conducted at money exchanges where you could change almost any currency. Mexico had plenty of cash points, and the tax regimen on credit card payments resulted in most businesses opting for cash-only payments. While Australia found itself in dire straits over access to cash and the United States moved towards contactless payments after the COVID-19 pandemic, carrying cash, even in large amounts, was the norm in most of the world.

My culture consumes far more than it produces. I don't mean that the United States doesn't produce goods or services; we do and have the gross domestic product to prove it. Culturally, though, we were a consumerist nation. We bought new clothes regularly, replaced broken possessions rather than repair them, and contributed to the global microplastics problem by not recycling or repurposing our goods and throwing them in the trash. In the Middle East, electronic gaming console repair was an entire industry. Entire hallways in malls were lined with repairmen fixing controllers, soldering new wires into place, and harvesting useable parts from truly broken systems, and these repairmen were all busy. When my sandals broke in Mexico, Hector, my dive instructor friend, jumped into action with elastic cords and a key ring to fix them. "Made in Taiwan, fixed in Mexico," he declared. Germans asked Jo and me if we were done with our plastic bottles so they could recycle them (for the payout, of course) rather than us throw them away. Southeast Asians were wizards at fixing broken motorbikes because they had no choice but to keep them running for as long as possible. My culture could learn a thing or few about repairing, repurposing, and recycling our stuff instead of simply trashing and replacing it.

Being poor is hard work. I touched on this in a few earlier reflections, but it is worth repeating. Being truly poor and poverty-stricken was some of the hardest work there was. Not to discount entrepreneurs', small business owners', or corporate and government executives' efforts and hard work, but there was a difference in fighting for your business and fighting for your next meal, sending your twelve-year-old child to climb thirty-metre trees without a harness to harvest fruit, or building your own house on stilts with your own two hands so you could withstand the wet season. Being poor took on an entirely new meaning when you could only afford to replace your only pair of jeans that you wore every day once a year.

People know too much for knowing too little. Especially young European women in their early twenties. The West was an opinionated place (case-in-point, this paragraph), and too many people had opinions on things they possessed no depth of knowledge or experience. I call out young-twenties European women, specifically, because they were the worst offenders when it came to preaching instead of discussing. We could all afford to listen a lot more and speak a lot less; when we speak, we should speak to inform rather than to condescend, preach, or convert.

There is a double standard for Americans when it comes to cultural acceptance. One of the most incredible things about long-term travel was experiencing new and foreign cultures. That said, Americans were the only group I encountered who were *expected* to set aside their cultural practices when abroad. The complaints about Americans were numerous; we were too loud, too patriotic, too casual in our dress, ate too much, and the list went on. We were expected to tone things down when abroad. Fair enough, except other cultures were not expected to do the same. When in Europe, criticising Asian tourists for slurping their food was considered bigoted towards their culture, even though it wasn't culturally or socially acceptable in places like the United Kingdom, Spain, or Italy. The Roma people adhered to Kris Roma (their cultural legal code) and marrying young, which Europeans and Americans were expected to accept even when those practices directly conflicted with our nations' laws and accepted social norms. Yet, when I ate fast food while walking in Europe as an American or, worse, Jo asked for ice in her drink, we were treated as cultural pariahs, Americans who couldn't leave our way of life behind when visiting other countries. I tired, and eventually became intolerant, of the double standard the world applied to Americans abroad versus every other culture.

My hearing is worse than I thought. I knew I had bad hearing from my military days. It wasn't gunfire that damaged it, but the never-ending, low hum of generators common on our forward operating bases. I did not, however, realise just how bad it was. It irritated Jo that I asked her to repeat things so many times. At first, she thought I just wasn't paying attention, but, in reality, I just couldn't hear her. It was worse during major festivals, like San Fermín, where the roar of the crowds was so loud that Jo and I had to yell to have a conversation and my ears would ring at night when I settled into bed. When speaking Spanish or French, the language barrier made hearing even harder. It was a real problem that I was going to have to deal with sooner than later. The fact that it was such an ordeal that I found it worthy of mentioning in this book was evidence of just how soon hearing aids were coming to my life.

Have a why. The most important part of travelling was to have a reason to travel. I started The Great Gallivanting to have a once-in-a-lifetime experience that would also give me an advantage in my professional life. A few months later, that changed, and I sought to find a new path in the world. Once I landed in Australia, after committing to the divemaster training in Mexico a few months later, I discovered that aimless wanderings didn't bring me a sense of purpose or joy. Travel for travel's sake wasn't enough. Having a reason, a purpose, was essential in maintaining happiness and sanity on the road. For that reason, I resolved to give every future long-term travel excursion a theme to guide my way.

How I've Changed

I have become independent to the extreme. I was independent before I left on my travels. I had lived alone for almost a decade, travelled alone for years, and generally had no personal support system back home. After a year abroad, though, that became extreme. I did *everything* on my own. I found my own transportation and food, sorted my own affairs, dealt with my own emotional exhaustion, built up my own faith, and provided for my own learning; everything was on me and me alone. Jo, too, learned this when she broke out on her own. Even as a divemaster, I found myself doing many things on my own simply because that was how I had done things for ten months. Joining a team for work in the future was going to be difficult, not because I was a loner, but because I had become used to living in a world where doing everything by myself wasn't something I wanted or liked to do, but something I *had* to do.

My tolerance for the American "oppression" narrative sank to an all-time low. The United States was actively ripping itself apart socially and politically. The airwaves were full of people calling out "systemic oppression" of various groups in my country, warning of "an economic bloodbath" should certain policies be enacted or people be elected, and a "crisis of conscience" for a country where being a Christian conservative was increasingly considered more extreme than being a blue-haired, gender-fluid, socialism-supporting, OnlyFans porn star. My countrymen had no idea what being oppressed was truly like. Women across the world were subjected to legally or culturally coerced female circumcision. Slavery and indentured servitude were still practised in large parts of the world, including Qatar, a strong American ally, which used slave labour to build the infrastructure for the World Cup in 2022. Accusing those who were opposed to teaching gender ideology in schools of committing "trans genocide" was an afront and insult to those people in the world who were *actively* being subjected to *actual* genocide. We waged political and cultural battles over "gay rights" because a Colorado bakery refused to bake a cake for a gay wedding while Hamas, Islamic State, Saudi Arabia, Chechnya, and Pakistan actively executed and tortured gay people, including beheadings, stonings, and throwing them off buildings. I became harsh, almost aggressively so, towards any American that wanted to tell me about how bad we had it when the truth was, we had no idea how amazingly lucky we were to live in the United States.

I started seeking dialogue more than trying to convert others to my way of thinking. People thought what they thought. As much as I would have liked to believe that people were open to other views and changing their minds, they weren't, especially if I, or anyone, tried to convert them to my way of thinking. Instead, I sought a dialogue where we exchanged ideas and perspectives rather than preached them. It was possible to challenge other ideas in a manner that wasn't insulting or condescending, an art lost in today's polarised world. It was also possible to understand an opposing view without agreeing with it or even endorsing it as valid. When talking with someone who wanted to preach or debate, I disengaged from the conversation or turned it towards a non-controversial topic. I had run out of energy to fight with people who weren't interested in a genuine conversation.

I became ready for a relationship. By the end of my year around the world, I had been single for ten years; an entire decade of my life had passed since my last real relationship. There were reasons for that, good and bad, but the truth was I was unwilling and unready to jump into an emotional connection with another person. After about two months of travel, I became open to the idea of a relationship. After meeting Jenny in Galway, I realised I was ready for one. After meeting Indie in

Australia, I knew it was time to leave all that emotional baggage behind and seek a life partner. It would be difficult as a full-time traveller, as moving from place to place every few days was hard on new relationships, but that didn't mean I shouldn't try, especially when I ultimately returned home.

I started to return to my East Texas upbringing. I loved being from Texas, but all that emotional baggage from my last relationship pushed me further and further away from reminders of the life I once lived. I stopped wearing my cowboy hats and boots and listening to country music; even my accent changed. Before travelling, I sought careers in the big city, like New York City, Washington, DC, or Miami; Small-Town, Texas, endeared itself to me less and less as the years went by. Starting in Australia, though, that changed. My new Akubra Angler was a hard-brimmed hat more akin to my cowboy hats than my Goorin Bros Henry Jones fedora. I started listening to country music again in New Zealand, learned about the ranching side of bulls while in Thailand, and began to reclaim my natural Texas twang after my family visited me in Mexico. My friend Laura, who managed the hostel in Mexico, turned me on to *Yellowstone*, which brought me back into the fold as far as horses and farming was concerned, something I had run from just a year before, and I even started watching rodeos after seeing them in the series. Now that I had unwound and taken a full year abroad to re-evaluate life, my affinity for the East Texas way of life slowly returned.

I calmed down and decided to walk away. When I had my breakdown at the airport a few months before I set off on my travels, I was wound up tight, high-strung, living my life with extreme highs and extreme lows. I didn't like chaos or adrenaline; I *needed* them to maintain a stable baseline. I was connected to everything going on in the world between work, news alerts, and online commentaries, and anxiety attacks were becoming more common. I was on a collision course with a mental hospital or worse. But after just a few months on the road and disconnected from my old life, I started to relax. I slept more peacefully, was less easily frustrated, and began to enjoy things like sipping a caña while reading a book on a busy street. I found a new passion in bullfighting and a new joy in learning about others' cultures and history. When it came time for Jo and I to leave Spain the second time, I realised that I was happier, more content, and less stressed than I had been since I graduated high school. Was I willing to return to my old ways and give up a peaceful life? No, I wasn't, and before we made it to the airport, I made the conscious decision to walk away. I had spent my entire professional life on a defined course which I loved, but it was going to kill me one day. Would I miss it? Absolutely, and many times during my travels, I wondered what it would be like to return to the security sphere after this life-changing excursion. Still, I could never overcome the feeling that going back would only set me back to square one. Ultimately, I decided that it wasn't worth it. Not for me.

I felt like I reclaimed myself. Over the prior fourteen years, I had given myself away. First, to my university, where I served in student leadership positions and dedicated myself to becoming a military officer and leader. Second, to the military, for which I sacrificed a two-year relationship and immersed myself in the world of transnational terrorism. Thirdly, to my last ex-girlfriend, who abruptly and unexpectedly ended things right as I set off for active duty. No matter how hard I tried, I could never reclaim myself. I sought out experiences as a skydiving coach, traveller, diver, security expert, and protector of those in need in hopes of restoring some part of me that was mine, but I failed at every turn. At best, I treaded water for more than a decade. After just a few months of travelling, though, I started discovering things that were truly mine. My love for bullfighting, my interest in religious beliefs and histories, and embracing the truly adventurous parts of travel (like the Cambodian jungle and helping others discover the underwater world) became things I embraced for myself and nobody else. I found my passion for writing and bringing stories and lessons from around the globe to people who otherwise would not experience them. Slowly, I became my own person again, and I was truly happy for the first time in as long as I could remember.

Epilogue: Now What?

Rounding the curve on the back of Luan's motorbike in Vietnam, I realised just how hard it was going to be to return home after such an incredible, crazy journey. How could I explain all I had seen, felt, learned, or experienced to those who rarely left the state? How could they possibly understand what it was like to sit with Palestinians on their back porch as they talked about their fear of and anger towards Israel, to have a commercial flight cancelled from Iraq to Turkey because of a terrorist attack in Syria, to shake hands with a matador before he took on six bulls, or to get cut off at an Irish pub in Dublin with six new Irish friends? How was I supposed to return to "normal" life after opening my eyes to the world? If deciding to leave everything behind in the first place was difficult, deciding to go home seemed impossible.

So, I didn't. I headed back to Spain to discover more about the world of bullfighting. I wasn't sure where that journey would take me, but I knew I was still searching for something that eluded me. My place in the world was no longer in the front seat of a patrol car or the cubicles of office life. I had given my formative professional years, my entire twenties, to helping secure my community and country. That wasn't a decision I regretted, but it deprived me of any sense of a normal life before it came time to settle down with a family and a serious career.

I decided to try my hand at travel writing. My granddaddy asked me to write a book about my travels, which was how this one came about, but in the course of remembering, narrating, and reflecting upon my travels, I realised that I enjoyed the process. Maybe I could bring stories from far off lands to life for those who, by circumstance or by choice, were unable to experience them themselves?

After three months in Spain immersing myself in the world of tauromaquia, I found my way home again, but I didn't stay long. After the holidays, a few interactions with friends, and some administrative life tasks (like taxes, doctors' visits, updating my will, things like that), I found myself back in Tulum, Mexico. It was cold in the United States, and there were too many distractions for me to successfully complete any major writing project. Besides, Tulum was a home away from Texas for me. I had friends there, some of them on a rotational basis as travellers came and went, and it was a secluded enough place that I could continue to escape from the hustle and monotonies of life in the United States.

What's next? I haven't a clue. Maybe I'll head down to South America. I still had four more Wonders of the World to cross off my list, and two were down there.

There was always the option of returning to Spain for the bullfighting season again. Or, maybe, I should head back to Africa to explore the continent that beckoned me to return for so many years. My options are limitless. I am not yet to the point of worrying about money; I could still travel on a budget for some time before reaching a point where I couldn't sustain myself for the rest of my life. One thing was sure: I wasn't heading back to the office.

I was a traveller, now. A restless vagabond, a wayward drifter, a lost soul searching for my place of rest in the far-off horizon.

Acknowledgements

Writing your first book is a project unlike any other. There are so many people who made this endeavour possible that it's impossible to list them all.

Naturally, I am eternally grateful to my traveling companion, Jo. Without her casual attitude toward my job interview, I never would have left the United States in the first place. While we certainly got on each other's nerves before we even made it halfway through our trip, our time together was undeniably memorable. It was Jo's idea to visit Pompeii, see La Sagrada Familia, take the tour through Egypt, and follow a matador around Spain for three weeks. Without her, I would have been too concerned about my daily budget to experience any of these adventures, and I would have missed out on some of the most memorable moments of the journey.

A special thanks to my granddaddy for encouraging me to write this book in the first place. It wasn't part of my plan, but knowing that he wanted to read it—between football games, Fox News, napping in his chair, dancing until two in the morning with his friends, and taking care of his horses—gave me ample motivation to share my stories. I definitely get some of my adventurous spirit from him.

Hostal Lum became my home away from home and part-time office as I worked on these pages. Laura, Mo, and Max, thank you for providing me with a place to stay, work, and escape the East Texas winter. I would offer to buy the next round, but we all know I'll be asleep before you head out on the town.

Similarly, the staff at La Fournée in Tulum deserves a special mention. They didn't have to let me sit and tap away at my keyboard for hours on end, six days a week, in the back corner of their bakery, but they did so with open arms. They kept the espresso (and the occasional mochaccino) coming, and were always up for a chat during my breaks from writing. Mariana, Lupe, and Hugo, thank you for the early morning coffees and empanadas de manzanas.

To all the friends along the way, thank you for being my support system as I wrestled with decade-old emotions in foreign lands. From sharing a Guinness with Irish friends to running with the bulls with Kiwis and discussing history, politics, and religion with Brits, each of you was an invaluable part of my world travels. A special thanks to (in no particular order) Tahli, Gav, Indie, Jason, Jack, Sonny, Andy, Will, Charlie, and Hector, my dive partner and mentor. Each of you played a role in shaping my journey in ways I'll never forget.

Of course, without my parents, none of this would have been possible. Despite giving them the occasional heart attack, they were always supportive and encouraging in my adventures. I couldn't have asked for better people to keep me grounded as I ventured out into the world.

About the Author

Jack Rogers is a former military man turned world traveller who has explored thirty-five countries across five continents. Driven by a thirst for adventure and self-discovery, he left behind a structured life to embrace the unknown. He codifies his experience in his debut travel memoir and his Instagram (@JRTVoyage), where he recounts the challenges, surprises, and transformations that come with long-term travel. From wandering the bustling streets of Marrakech to diving in the crystal waters of the Philippines, Jack's experiences have deepened his appreciation for world cultures, religions, and history. His reflections offer readers and intimate look at the power of travel to reshape one's understanding the world–and oneself.

When he's not exploring new destinations, Jack enjoys diving the world's oceans, watching the bullfights in Spain, and basking in the sun at a street-side café.